DEFORESTING THE EARTH

DEFORESTING THE EARTH

From Prehistory to Global Crisis
An Abridgment

MICHAEL WILLIAMS

The University of Chicago Press
Chicago and London

Michael Williams is emeritus professor of geography at the University of Oxford and a Fellow of Oriel College. He is the author, most recently, of *Americans and Their Forests: A Historical Geography* as well as the editor of *Wetlands: A Threatened Landscape* and coeditor of *A Century of British Geography*.

The University of Chicago Press, Chicago 60637
The University of Chicago Press, Ltd., London
© 2006 by The University of Chicago
All rights reserved. Published 2006
Printed in the United States of America
15 14 13 12 11 10 09 08 07 06   1 2 3 4 5
ISBN: 0-226-89947-0   (paper)

Library of Congress Cataloging-in-Publication Data

Williams, Michael, 1935 June 24–
    Deforesting the earth : from prehistory to global crisis : an abridgment / Michael Williams.
       p.   cm.
    Includes bibliographical references and index.
    ISBN: 0-226-89947-0 (pbk. : alk. paper)
       1. Forests and forestry—History.   2. Clearing of land—History.   3. Deforestation—History.   I. Title.

SD131. W53   2006
333.75'1309—dc22

                                                                                          2005034150

For Loré,
once again

CONTENTS

List of Illustrations   *ix*
Preface   *xv*

PART I   CLEARING IN THE DEEP PAST

1   The Return of the Forest   *3*
2   Fire and Foragers   *12*
3   The First Farmers   *35*
4   The Classical World   *62*
5   The Medieval World   *87*

PART II   REACHING OUT: EUROPE AND THE WIDER WORLD

6   Driving Forces and Cultural Climates, 1500–1750   *127*
7   Clearing in Europe, 1500–1750   *150*
8   The Wider World, 1500–1750   *191*
9   Driving Forces and Cultural Climates, 1750–1900   *226*
10   Clearing in the Temperate World, 1750–1920   *263*
11   Clearing in the Tropical World, 1750–1920   *318*

PART III   THE GLOBAL FOREST

12   Scares and Solutions, 1900–1944   *359*
13   The Great Onslaught, 1945–95: Dimensions of Change   *395*
14   The Great Onslaught, 1945–95: Patterns of Change   *431*

Epilogue: Backward and Forward Glances   *471*
Acknowledgments   *479*
List of Measures, Abbreviations, and Acronyms   *481*
Notes   *483*
Bibliographic Essay   *505*
Index   *511*

ILLUSTRATIONS

PLATES

2.1 Firing vegetation for cropping, Central African Republic   *16*

3.1 Regenerated tropical forest around the Mayan temples
at Tikal, Mexico   *51*

3.2 Town of Secota, Virginia, circa 1620   *57*

5.1 *Cutting Wood*, eleventh century   *93*

5.2 *Swine Feeding in the Forest*, eleventh century   *113*

5.3 *The Hunt in the Forest* by Paolo Uccello, circa 1470   *115*

5.4 European mine, sixteenth century   *118*

6.1 Frontispiece from Jan van de Straet's *Nova Reperta*, 1600   *130*

7.1 *Winter Landscape* by Lucas I. van Valckenborch, 1586   *161*

7.2 Charcoal making   *168–69*

7.3 Fuelwood cutters at work in a coppice, eighteenth century   *173*

7.4 An eighteenth-century shipyard   *175*

7.5 Timber owner, agent, and merchant, eighteenth century   *177*

7.6 Consequences of deforestation, 1601   *182–85*

7.7 Reforestation   *187*

7.8 The cult of trees: Blenheim Palace and its grounds   *189*

8.1 Water-powered *engenho*, Olinda, Brazil   *199*

8.2 *Backwoods Life in New England*, 1770   *206*

8.3 *The Beginning*, eighteenth century   *210*

9.1 Logjam in a river, Minnesota, circa 1920s   *246*

9.2 Boom being towed by steam tug, Rainy Lake, Ontario,
circa 1920s   *247*

9.3 Rafting yellow poplar logs, Big Sandy River, Ohio, circa 1920s   *248*

9.4 Logging railroad, Arkansas, circa 1904   *250*

10.1 *Land Improvement*, 1853   *265*

10.2 *"The Fighting Temeraire" Tugged to Her Last Berth to Be Broken
Up* by J. M. W. Turner, 1838   *280*

10.3   *The First Six Months,* circa 1849   *289*
10.4   *The Second Year,* circa 1849   *290*
10.5   *Ten Years Later,* circa 1849   *291*
10.6   *The Work of a Lifetime,* circa 1849   *291*
10.7   *Newly Cleared Land in America,* circa 1829   *293*
10.8   Selector's homestead, Victoria, Australia, nineteenth century   *312*
10.9   Pastures of the future: Gippsland region, Victoria, Australia, nineteenth century   *313*
11.1   *Clearing Mahogany down Rapids in Cuba,* nineteenth century   *327*
11.2   *Cutting and Trucking Mahogany in Honduras,* nineteenth century   *327*
11.3   *The New Clearing,* Ceylon (Sri Lanka), nineteenth century   *341*
12.1   Coffee plantation, Brazil   *374*
12.2   Deforestation for a coffee plantation, Brazil   *375*
13.1   Havoc wrought by chain saw, Parabara, Guyana, twentieth century   *399*
14.1   Migrant peasant family, Bolivian lowlands, twentieth century   *438*
14.2   Aspiring migrant family, Rondônia, Brazil, twentieth century   *447*
14.3   Improvised pastures and degraded scrubland, Rondônia, Brazil, twentieth century   *449*
14.4   Burning season, Rondônia and Mato Grosso, Brazil, August 1984   *453*
14.5   Herringbone pattern of clearing, Rondônia, Brazil, 1985   *454*
14.6   Clear-cut destruction of rain forest, Rondônia, Brazil, August 1992   *455*
E.1   Differing views on deforestation, 1989   *477*

FIGURES

1.1   Europe: reconstructed vegetation   *7*
1.2   Eastern North America: Paleovegetation   *9*
2.1   Possible uses of natural fire by early hominids   *15*
2.2   New Zealand vegetation, "Pre-Polynesian" and "Pre-Classical Maori"   *20*
2.3   New Zealand vegetation, "Pre-European" and "Present"   *20*
2.4   Zonation of Indian forest use   *27*
2.5   The creation of grasslands: pajonales in Peru and savannas in Colombia   *33*
3.1   Labor required to clear forest of varying age and density   *36*
3.2   Possible routes of development from hunting-collecting to other systems   *39*
3.3   Spread of agricultural settlement in Europe and western Asia during the Holocene   *41*

3.4   Distribution of axes of banded flint in Poland around the mining
      center of Krzemionki Opatowskie   44

3.5   Hypothetical Neolithic village settlement in the forest and its
      timber needs   46

3.6   Population density, deforestation, and soil erosion associated
      with long-term Maya settlement   52

4.1   Major timber- and grain-growing areas and trade routes
      in the Mediterranean basin   66

4.2   Landscape change due to siltation and fill in the West Macedonian
      Plain, Greece   83

4.3   Late Quaternary development of Mediterranean river valleys   85

5.1   Reconstruction of the major forest areas of Europe   88

5.2   Forest clearing and village foundation in the Odenwaldd   100

5.3   Landscapes of woodland clearing in Warwickshire, England   102

5.4   Forest clearing and settlement foundation, middle Yonne valley,
      France   103

5.5   Forest cover in central Europe, circa 900   107

5.6   Forest cover in central Europe, circa 1900   107

5.7   Hanbury, West Midlands, England: settlement zones,
      400–1318 and land use, circa 1300   108

5.8   Wood and timber in the medieval Muslim Mediterranean world   110

5.9   Woodland and settlement change around Hofgeismar   119

5.10 Iron industry of Sung China, circa 1100   123

6.1   European economy on a global scale, and other empires,
      circa 1500   132

6.2   European economy on a global scale, and the emergence
      of a core and periphery, circa 1775   133

7.1   Indices of firewood and general price rises in England and
      France, 1451–1702   153

7.2   Provinces, main vegetation zones, and fortified lines,
      south-central Russia   159

7.3   European towns whose populations exceeded 40,000   162

7.4   Coalfields and type of fuel used in the United Kingdom,
      circa 1680   165

7.5   Iron making in Europe, sixteenth century   171

7.6   Baltic and Scandinavian timber trade, seventeenth and
      eighteenth centuries   179

8.1   Circuits and stepping-stones across the Atlantic   193

8.2   Forests and plantations in Barbados, 1647   202

8.3   Spread of settlement, North America   205

8.4   Forest exploitation in Japan   223

9.1   Transformation of major global land covers, 900–2000   228
9.2   Energy sources in the United States as a percentage of total
        consumption   236
10.1   Furnaces and forges in France and competition for fuelwood
        supplies in the Paris basin   268
10.2   The percent of area of European Russia cleared, 1703–1914   273
10.3   Forest cover, Arzamas region, Russia   274
10.4   Geography of the European trade in Baltic "deals"
        (planks), 1784   281
10.5   Millions of acres cleared in the United States   287–88
10.6   Uses of timber in the United States, 1800–1975   296
10.7   Types of fuel used in the United States, circa 1880   298
10.8   Lumber cut and per capita consumption in the United States,
        1800–1960   302
10.9   Four stages of lumber production   304
10.10   Australia: percentage of vegetation severely modified since 1780   314
11.1   Percentage of land in forest in Uttar Pradesh,
        Bihar, and Orissa, India   332
11.2   Percentage of forest decrease in Uttar Pradesh, Bihar,
        and Orissa, India   333
11.3   Forests and wasteland under British control in India, 1899   345
11.4   Extent of coffee plantations, Brazil   354
11.5   Forest clearing in São Paulo State, Brazil   355
12.1   National forests of the United States, 1898, 1907, and 1980   365
12.2   Area of virgin forest, United States, 1620   367
12.3   Area of virgin forest, United States, 1850   368
12.4   Area of virgin forest, United States, 1920   368
12.5   Growth of forest "islands," Kissidougou area of Guinea   379
12.6   Annual net growth and use of timber in the United States,
        1800–2040   386
12.7   Conversion of forest to agricultural land and abandonment
        of agricultural land to forest, Carroll County, Georgia,
        1937–74   389
12.8   Swedish forest budget   393
13.1   Causes of deforestation   403
13.2   Annual releases of carbon from changes in land use and
        emissions from fossil fuel combustion, 1850–1980   410
13.3   Estimates of world forest extent, 1923–90   419
13.4   Tropical forest: annual pathways of conversion   426
13.5   Estimates of annual rate of deforestation, 1978–93   427

14.1   Deforestation in eastern Thailand, 1973–76   432
14.2   The Carretera Marginal de la Selva and areas of active
        colonization east of the Andes, 1950–70   436
14.3   The Generals' Plan: slicing up the Amazon basin   441
14.4   Deforestation in southeast Pará State, Brazil   443
14.5   Rondônia State, Brazil, and the herringbone pattern of
        clearing   448
14.6   Deforestation in the Brazilian Amazon, 1988   458
14.7   Forest clearing in peninsular Malaysia   460
14.8   Forest clearing in Central America   463
14.9   Global fuelwood deficits   464
14.10   Total roundwood, fuelwood, and charcoal production,
        1963–85   466

TABLES

4.1   Production and estimated area of timber used in four classical
        mining locations   79
9.1   Total industrial potential, 1750–1980   230
9.2   Increasing productivity of saws, seventeenth to nineteenth
        centuries   232
9.3   World population by major regions, 1700–1985, and projection
        to 2020   237
9.4   Length of railway line open by continent and major country,
        1840–1960   243
9.5   Crossties used and estimated hectares of forest cleared, world,
        1840–1960   244
10.1   Cropland and land cover change, temperate world, 1700, 1850,
        and 1920   264
10.2   Population, fuelwood used, and per capita consumption, Paris,
        1815–1900   269
10.3   Consumption of wood and timber products, Russia, 1890–91   276
10.4   Land cleared and man-years expended in forested and nonforested
        areas, United States, circa 1650–1909   286
10.5   Crossties used and acres of forest cleared, United States,
        1870–1910   300
10.6   Australia: minimum area of vegetation severely modified
        since 1780   315
11.1   Cropland and land cover change, tropical world, 1700, 1850,
        and 1920   319
11.2   Estimate of sleepers used and acres of forest cleared, India,
        1850–1940   339

12.1   World forest area, production, and deficits, circa 1923   370

12.2   Net forest change and annual rate of change, tropical and
       temperate worlds, 1700–1995   372

12.3   Cropland and land-cover change, tropical (developing) world   373

12.4   Estimated area of commercial and noncommercial U.S. forest
       and standing saw-timber volume   383

12.5   Estimated forest volume and annual growth and drain,
       United States, 1909–77   384

12.6   Cleared farmland, United States, 1910–79   387

12.7   Industrial and domestic timber removals, USSR,
       1913–83   390

13.1   Estimates of closed forest and open woodland in three
       continents, 1980–88   425

13.2   Estimates of forest area and deforestation, tropical areas,
       1980 and 1990   429

14.1   Extent of Amazonian tropical lowland and extent of land
       over 2,500 m, and % of population living over 2,500 m   435

14.2   Predeforestation area of forest, *cerrado*, and water, and
       deforested and isolated and edge-forest, Brazilian Amazon,
       1978 and 1988   457

14.3   Global export, import, and net trade of forest products, 1997   468

E.1   Current and forecast global production/consumption of wood
       and paper products   474

PREFACE

Probably the most important single factor that has changed the European
landscape (and many other landscapes also) is the clearing of the woodland.
—H. C. DARBY TO PAUL FEJOS, 19 July 1954

There are many gaps in the evidence—dark ages in time and dark areas
in space.
—E. E. EVANS, "The Ecology of Peasant Life in Western Europe" (1956)

THE THINNING, changing, and elimination of forests—deforestation, no
less—is not a recent phenomenon; it is as old as the human occupation of the
earth and one of the key processes in the history of our transformation of its
surface. More than 40 years ago H. Clifford Darby suggested that "probably
the most important single factor that has changed the European landscape
(and many other landscapes also) is the clearing of the woodland," and he
may well have been right.[1] Indeed, perhaps more of the earth's surface has
been affected by this process than by any other single human activity.

So this is a book about how, why, and when humans eliminated trees
and changed forests and wrought changes to the visible biotic landscape to
make new social and economic worlds around themselves and, in so doing,
transformed the face of the earth. For as long as I can remember, I have been
firmly hooked on what W. G. Hoskins called "the logic that lies behind the
beautiful whole."[2] So this is not a history of forests or forestry, less still one
about lumbering and land settlement, although all figure in this book; it is
not a history of industrial and domestic fuel use, although they enter into
the picture; nor is it a history of conservation and environmental concern,
although these loom large toward the end of this account. But it is an essay
in both landscape history and environmental change.

Because deforestation is a humanly activated and humanly induced process of environmental change, it is a part of the society that does the deforesting and is as much, if not more, about the people that do the clearing as about the number of trees cleared. The human impact on the forest has always followed from the prevailing way of life (or *genre de vie*) of human society in a given time and given place. This means that there is a need for each deforestation story to be firmly rooted in a context of its time and that the factors that have contributed to that way of life are sorted out. Many are of long standing, frequently very ordinary, and part of basic survival and have been present in most societies from time immemorial, constituting what Fernand Braudel calls "the structures of everyday life." [3] The need for wood for fuel to keep warm, to smelt metals, and to cook; the demand for wood for construction, utensils, tools, and ships; and the use of forests for "making" new land to grow food have not changed much since humans have been on earth, except inasmuch as the number of people utilizing them has grown inexorably. These processes might well be termed the "driving forces" or causes of change in the forest environment.

Nevertheless, such an explanation of change as being an outcome of driving forces often misses the point. Many contemporary deforestation studies isolate one or a couple of driving forces in order to explain, forecast, or prescribe action. But it is seldom that simple. Change is likely to mirror not one basic force but many, which are multilayered and interact in clusters. Moreover, nonmaterial forces like motivation, sentiment, symbolism (especially strong in forest environments), political, religious and social mores are largely ignored because they cannot be quantified or factored into explanations easily, especially if some sort of modeling is envisaged. Rather, I would favor Lynn White's idea of complex "cultural climates," which have promoted and encouraged change as a more realistic concept. [4] In the accounts of the classical and medieval worlds it is just possible to include these deeply buried streams of folk consciousness, belief, and memory into the narrative. But from the sixteenth century onward, the complexity and interaction of events and the sheer magnitude of change are more fundamental, extensive, and far-reaching. Consequently, separate chapters are needed for the early modern era after circa 1500 (chap. 6), the modern industrial era after 1800 (chap. 9), and to a certain extent the immediate post–World War II decades (chap. 13). Having said all that, however, it is one of my aims to calibrate, however crudely, the extent of deforestation in the past in order to give a concrete measure to the many vague generalizations about the process and to show that deforestation is not a new phenomenon. The area cleared since 1950 has only just about come near the amount cleared before that.

At all times, the evidence is fragmentary, and so one must infer much. There are great gaps that cannot be filled, there is widespread ignorance of what does exist, and there are very few statistics that are wholly reliable. Much evidence is also highly prejudiced or used for purposes quite different from those for which it was written. The evidence of deforestation is a little like Charles Darwin's metaphoric description of the evidence of the geological record for his theory of the origin and evolution of species: "I look at the geological record as a history of the world imperfectly kept, and written in a changing dialect; of this history we possess the last volume alone, relating to only two or three countries. Of this volume, only here and there a short chapter has been preserved; and of each page, only here and there a few lines."[5] *Deforesting the Earth* is also a history "imperfectly kept," and we too look at odd volumes, separated chapters, and isolated lines, written in strange dialects for only a few countries, in the hope that these fragments make some overall sense about the process. This goes a long way to explaining the structure of this book and the many examples used. I hope that the reader neither misses the detail of the wood for the trees nor, and more important, the bigger picture of the forest for the trees.

Consequently, this book is divided into three parts that reflect major stages in the relation of humans with the forest and our understanding of what went on. Part 1, "The Deep Past," deals with an epoch characterized by "dark ages in time and dark areas in space," "dark" because of our ignorance of how forests act as living ecosystems and of what human activity took place.[6] Deforestation may be about as old as the human occupation of the earth itself—controlled fire being perhaps coterminous with the emergence of Homo erectus some 500,000 years ago—but there are enormous gaps in our knowledge of the where and the when of the process, and there are equally large problems of interpretation of evidence. In part 2 we are on surer ground, and "Reaching Out" deals with the massive changes occurring in Europe and the territories it affected overseas after about 1500. Part 3, "The Global Forest," is concerned with the great onslaught on the world's forests in the twentieth century up to the present day. However, even today, a certain "murkiness" remains. For all the outpouring of literature on tropical deforestation, the process is surrounded by much debate, uncertainty, confusion, and even obscurity. If that is true about the present, then how much more so must it be about the past?

If this book is seen to have a Eurocentric focus it is for good reason. First it is a matter of the origins of innovation and change in the forest, and second, of the availability of evidence. China, Japan, Africa, India, and other parts of the world are treated fully where information exists.

Third, much of the history of the world during the last five centuries has been a history, in very large measure, of the things Europeans (and North Americans) did to themselves and to others, and how non-Europeans reacted to them and were frequently adversely affected. That, after all, is what the rest of the world thinks is wrong and criticizes.

However, one thing is certain: whichever lens one chooses to look through at the past, peoples of all cultures and at all times have seen the forest as a valuable resource to be used. This is the story of how they changed or destroyed that legacy of the incomparable green mantle that clothes the earth.

PART I

CLEARING IN
THE DEEP PAST

Chapter 1

The Return of the Forest

Ever since the dawn of Holocene time, when global conditions remotely
like those of the present-day first evolved from the ice ages, humans
have always impacted the natural environment.
—W. R. DICKINSON, "The Times are Always Changing: The Holocene Saga"
(1995)

PROLOGUE: THE END OF THE ICE AGE

IF EVER THERE was a beginning to the modern forest it was at the end of the
Ice Age just over 10,000 years ago when the great sheets of ice that covered
much of the Northern Hemisphere began to melt and retreat. Then the Holocene, or most recent age of the Quaternary, was born, and the modern forest began to emerge around the world. Almost immediately humans began
adapting and changing the evolving physical landscape. Before the thawing
began, a wintry blanket had held the world in its grip for over 10,000 years.
Ice over 4 km thick covered both North America and northern Europe, and
smaller ice caps existed in the Alps, the southern Andes, and even parts of
eastern Asia. Because of the water locked up in the ice, sea levels were up to
100 m lower than today. Land bridges were exposed between Britain and
Europe, Alaska and Asia, and the islands of Southeast Asia were joined to
mainland Asia, allowing humans to migrate between land masses.

Then, about 16,000 years before the present (hereafter BP), the great
sheets of ice began to melt slowly and retreat. A new world vegetation map
began to emerge. Europe had no forests except in isolated pockets or refugia
in Iberia and southeastern Europe. A wide tundra zone covered most of the
Continent, in which the predominant vegetation was shrubs and steppelike
grasses capable of surviving the harsh climate. Forests did occur, however,
in Japan, and in the pine and spruce woodland of eastern United States.

A tundra zone also existed in North America, but in contrast with Europe it was much narrower, being only 100 km–200 km broad.

If the temperate areas were colder then the tropical areas were drier; ancient sand seas (ergs) extended to places where there is tropical and subtropical forest today, for example, in western Africa and Florida, and great dust plumes swept out to sea to leave revealing depositional sequences on the ocean bed. Throughout Africa and Latin America, aridity reduced the extent of the rain forest and left it as a series of isolated refugia where, it is thought, they may have developed their amazing biodiversity. Most rain forest existed in Southeast Asia, and surprisingly, in the currently arid Southwest of the United States.

When the ice began to melt the change was not sudden, and during the next 8,000 years temperatures moved slowly upward by some 4°C or 5°C to become something like those of today. What caused the climate to change then, or at other geological times, is not known. There are a number of hypotheses, the most likely being the Milankovitch hypothesis based on the regular variations in the earth's orbital geometry, which fluctuates as it circles the sun. In addition, toward the end of the Ice Age, the sheer bulk of the ice would have created conditions that would have deflected the moisture-bearing winds fueling the fresh supply of snow away from the ice. Also, the large quantities of cold freshwater on the ocean surface would have acted like a lid over the denser seawater, thus reducing evaporation in summer and leading to thick layers of ice in winter.

The retreat was long and uneven; oscillating climatic conditions, particularly in northwest Europe, caused it to advance again many times, only to retreat even farther later, always accompanied by changes in sea level. The water that had been locked in the ice began to melt and form huge rivers that gouged river channels across the northern continents, which must have had to cope with volumes of water up to 20 times that of modern rivers. The result was sandy and gravelly outwash plains that spread over vast areas. These were subsequently eroded by wind, the dust being carried away many thousands of miles from the edge of the ice front to create the enormous, thick loess deposits stretching from northern Europe into Central Asia and China, in the pampas of Argentina and Uruguay, and in the Great Plains of the United States, with pockets in Washington and Idaho. In the tropics, greater humidity acting on unconsolidated and bare soils caused massive erosion to produce the greatest sediment yields of the age.

In short, the end of the Ice Age heralded a new era in the history of the world. Its physical, surface geography was largely made anew and the landscape began to take on something like its present day appearance, although its climate kept on fluctuating. Opportunistic species moved with bewildering speed and kaleidoscopic complexity to colonize the new land, and the forest mantle returned to something like its old, though now radically changed, habitats. And humans were not far behind.

WRITING THE BIOGRAPHY OF THE FOREST

It is a common notion that the world was a stable, pristine place before the industrial age. Deeply rooted in Western psyche and its culture is a myth that nature is a passive, harmonious, God-given backdrop against which the drama of human life is played out, the "sound and fury" of human existence contrasting strongly with the notion that "earth abides." But this is a myth. When George Perkins Marsh made the revolutionary and unfashionable statement in *Man and Nature* in 1864 that "man is everywhere a disturbing agent. Wherever he plants his foot, the harmonies of nature are turned to discords," it was rarely believed.[1] How could the humans of the past with such low levels of culture and technology radically alter the natural world around them?

The forest, in particular, has never been still. Not only is it a living, ever-changing entity that is affected directly by both short- and long-term environmental changes, particularly climate, but it is also severely affected by quite minor human disturbances. Agriculture, domestication, and the control of fire have all been roughly coincident with the formation of the modern forests during the last 10,000 years, and their interaction is inseparable.

Consequently, if we want to understand how humans have changed present forests, we need to travel back along the distant corridors of time to when the forests were being formed after the end of the Ice Age. Just as people have biographies, so forests have their own histories that can be unraveled and documented. But unlike human biographies, the writing of forest histories needs something more than words alone. Pollen analysis and radiocarbon dating are essential components of the language of those histories.

Pollen analysis, or palynology, entails the boring of cores in peat deposits or lake and riverine sediments and counting the grains of different tree-pollen types preserved at different levels of the deposit. The quantities are indicative of past vegetation communities and, by implication, of past human disturbances of the environment. These data are usually presented in the form of pollen diagrams showing the concentration of the percentage values of the various pollen and spore types, arranged stratigraphically.

Pollen emissions can be prolific; for example, in areas of temperate vegetation they can reach up to 10 metric tons annually per square kilometer of land. Some trees produce more than others; beech (*Fagus*) produces twice as much pollen as lime (*Tilia*); elm (*Ulmus*) and spruce (*Picea*) twice as much again as beech; and alder (*Alnus*), birch (*Betula*), pine (*Pinus*), oak (*Quercus*), and hazel (*Corylus*) twice as much again as elm or spruce; in other words, eight times that of lime.

While the samples usually show a clear relative sequence of different pollens, an absolute chronology is difficult unless the samples are interbedded with datable human artifacts. The advent of radiometric techniques gave palynology a new certainty. Most natural, living elements (e.g., wood, charcoal, peat, seeds, bone, shell, cloth, rope, or soil) absorb a mixture of isotopes, of which the most common is radiocarbon (^{14}C). But following the death of the plant or animal, ^{14}C decay occurs at a fixed and known rate. Hence the measurement of the ^{14}C remaining in the fossil will provide an age for the death of that organism. Results are usually expressed as an age in years before present (BP)—present being AD 1950—with a standard deviation appended. Thus a date of 5000 ± 50 indicates that there is a 68 percent probability that the date is in the range 4950–5050.[2]

THE RETURN OF THE FOREST

Armed with these techniques, sufficient data had been accumulated by the 1980s for the scattered information to be collated into continental histories of forest distribution and change in Europe and North America. Although the two continental analyses are not strictly comparable in terms of methods and detail, the overall conclusions stand close comparison. Vegetation belts migrated over several hundreds, if not thousands, of kilometers in response to fluctuating climate and followed a roughly similar sequence.

Europe

At 10,000 BP ice sheets still dominated Fennoscandia, Iceland, and a small ice sheet was present in Scotland. Europe's tundra, steppe, and birch-conifer boreal forest remained largely unchanged and dominated most of the lowlands of northern Europe, although some deciduous trees were beginning to move out of their southern refugia (fig. 1.1*A*). Around the Mediterranean, herb-dominated steppe was being colonized by the typical mediterranean plants, like olive, pistachio, and evergreen oak.

Then, with a rapid climate amelioration during the next 1,000 years, there were dramatic changes in vegetation everywhere, and by 9,000 BP the outlines of the modern forest were becoming evident (fig.1.1*B*). Certainly, by 8,000 BP the transition was complete; the mixed deciduous forest had

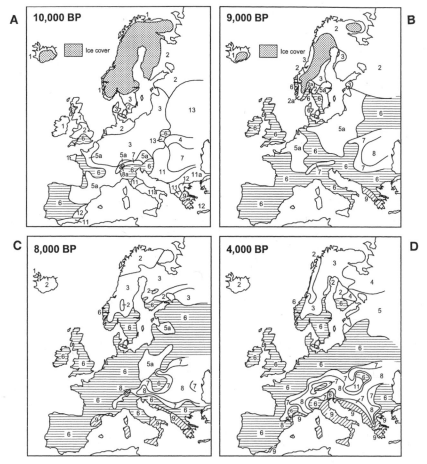

Figure 1.1 Europe: reconstructed vegetation, 10,000, 9,000, 8,000, and 4,000 BP (Source: after B. J. Huntley and J. B. Birks, *An Atlas of Past and Present Pollen Maps for Europe: 0–13,000 Years Ago* [Cambridge: Cambridge University Press, 1983]): *1*, Tundra; *2*, Birch forest; *3*, Birch-conifer forest; *4*, Spruce dominated forest; *5*, Northern mixed conifer-deciduous forest; *5A*, Northern mixed conifer-deciduous forest (*pinus* variety); *6*, Mixed deciduous forest (horizontal shading); *7*, Montane mixed conifer-deciduous forest; *8*, Montane mixed-conifer forest; *9*, Mediterranean forest (*diagonal shading*).

moved from Spain and southern France to dominate the land area of the British Isles, Spain, France, central north Europe, and southern Scandinavia. In extreme southern Europe the deciduous forest gave way to the first substantial manifestations of a typical mediterranean evergreen oak and pine forest. The boreal (birch-conifer) forest was pushed northward to northern Scandinavia and Russia, and tundra and steppe all but disappeared, as had all permanent ice (fig. 1.1C).

During the next 4,000 years the vegetation change slowed down as temperatures stabilized, with the exception of the development of a well-marked western alpine zone of montane forest and the expansion of the mediterranean vegetation mix over much of Italy and the coastal littoral of the Balkan Peninsula. Thus, by 4,000 BP the distribution of trees was looking remarkably like that of today as the climate took on a contemporary complexion (cf. figs 1.1C and 1.1D). But while the distribution of the main biomes was similar to that of today, their composition was not. New trees, such as oak (*Quercus*), lime (*Tilia*), alder (*Alnus glutinosa*), and ash (*Fraxinus excelsior*), invaded and dominated locally. Hazel (*Corylus avellana*) and elm (*Ulmus*) spread even more rapidly. Other trees, such as spruce (*Picea*), did not expand to their present distribution until a slight deterioration of climate, which was noticeable by 2,000 BP. Between 2,000 BP and the present, there has, if anything, been slightly more cooling and the further expansion of boreal forest.

North America

Although glacial conditions were more fully developed in North America than in Europe, the absence of any marked thermal oscillations during the Holocene meant that the return of the temperate forests began earlier. At its maximum extent in 18,000 BP the Laurentide ice spread as far south as about latitude 40°, and a narrow belt of tundra separated it from a quite broad band of boreal forest. The temperate mixed forest was confined to the warm Gulf and south Atlantic plains.

The distribution of the forest had not changed significantly by 14,000 BP (fig. 1.2A), but after that time the retreat accelerated and there was a marked northward shift of temperate deciduous forest and mixed coniferous/northern hardwood forest, which pushed boreal forest and tundra ahead of them, with a corresponding expansion of the southern evergreen (pine) forests on their southern margin. By 10,000 BP the distribution of the forest was getting a decidedly modern appearance, although the ice still sat firmly over what is now the Canadian Shield (fig. 1.2B). By 6,000 BP the ice was all but gone and the forest had extended to very nearly its modern limits (fig. 1.2C).

It is thought that the migration northward of American vegetation was slower than in Europe because the wide distribution of pollens and seeds was inhibited by the dominantly east–west trending rivers compared to Europe's generally north-flowing rivers. The general northward movement of vegetation assemblages was accompanied by another trend, which was the progressive eastward shift of the prairie/woodland ecotone (not shown), which reached its maximum eastward extent about 6,000 BP, only to retreat somewhat in more recent times (fig. 1.2D).

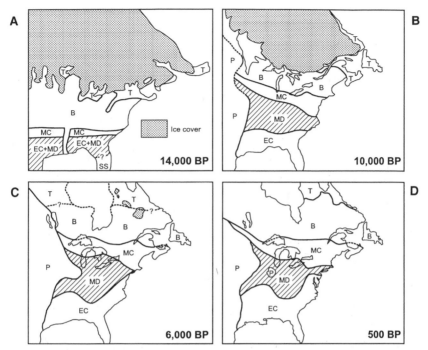

Figure 1.2 Eastern North America: Paleovegetation, 18,000, 10,000, 6,000, and 500 BP
(Source: adapted from P. A. Delcourt and H. R. Delcourt, "Vegetation Maps for Eastern
North America: 40,000 yrs BP to the Present," in *Geobotany,* ed. R. C. Romans [New York:
Plenum Press, 1981], 2:123–66): *T,* Tundra; *B,* Boreal forest; *MC,* Mixed conifer forest;
EC, Oak-hickory–Southern pine forest; *MD,* Mixed deciduous forest; *SS,* Southern
evergreen forest; and *P,* Prairie.

The Tropical World

The temperate world was not the only part of the globe where vegetation
was radically affected by climatic change during the last 10,000 years.
Probably equally dramatic changes occurred in the tropics, but we know
less about them. But the story is slowly being unraveled and is vastly more
complex than thought. Since the 1950s, evidence has been accumulating
for some tropical pollen sites, which, taken together with high lake levels,
sediments, and artifactual data from Africa in particular, show that aridity
was replaced by increasing moisture and that low temperatures were giving
way to higher temperatures. This climatic change allowed the tropical forest to expand—both laterally so as to reclaim areas of fossil sand dunes, as
in West Africa, and vertically so that montane vegetation climbed back up
the mountains by as much as 1,500 m–2,000 m—especially in East Africa,
New Guinea, and the Andes when glaciers melted and retreated. The long

isolation of species in the remnant ice-free refugia of Latin America which had encouraged marked differences in species and flora type now ended with the onset of warm, pluvial conditions, so that a vast reservoir of bio-diversity was created that still exists today.

THE HUMAN IMPACT

As the forest changed, so humans colonized the newly vegetated land with remarkable rapidity, doing all those things that humans do: foraging, firing, hunting, selecting species and rejecting others, turning the soil, fertilizing it, trampling it, and mixing it. Some trees moved, flourished, or were elimi-nated, just as surely as if they had been affected by changing climate. So, even as the forests were changing in the climatic seesaw of the millennia of the early Holocene era—slowly assuming their modern, historical distribu-tion and form—the people who witnessed and survived that Ice Age from the tundra to the tropics were in the active process of changing their compo-sition and density. It was a coevolution of humans and vegetation.

Thus, during the last 6,000 years, if not longer, many of the changes in vegetation reflect adjustments to human disturbances, brought about by the increasing density and spread of population, the use of fire, technolo-gical advances, the cultivation of exotic plant species, and the introduction of grazing animals. In Europe, forest clearing, cultivation, the cutting of tree sprouts and limbs for fodder, and the localization and intensification of grazing all had their effects on opening up the forest canopy and thus creating opportunities for invasion by early succession forest taxa, such as fir (*Abies*) and birch (*Betula*). The deliberate clearing of the forest accom-panied by cultivation of cereals by Neolithic and post-Neolithic peoples led to forest fragmentation and the introduction and inadvertent spread of disturbed-ground weeds and ruderals, like plantain (*Plantago*). Some trees, such as the walnut (*Juglans*) and the olive (*Olea europaea*), became naturalized well beyond their native ranges as cultivation and grazing elimi-nated native plant competitors, and they were even deliberately spread and planted for their food value.

Similarly, in North America humans played an important part in shaping the vegetational development, quite contrary to some ecological accounts that see change as a purely post-Columbian event. Bottomland forests in the central Mississippi, lower Illinois, and Tennessee river valleys were cleared extensively as cultivation expanded along floodplains and lower terraces. The cultivation of squash (*Cucurbita pepo*) began as early as 7,000 BP, to be followed by other exotics such as the sunflower (*Helianthus annus*) and bottle gourd (*Lagenaria siceraria*), and later still by maize (*Zea mays*) and beans (*Phaseolus vulgaris*). The story of weeds and ruderal invasions paralleled that of Europe. Other changes, far greater than are generally acknowledged, occurred in the forests at the oak-savanna transition, the forest generally being eliminated by fire to be replaced by more valuable grasses.

Less is known about the tropical world, but all the indications are that the impact was no less. The changes affected the forest in all continents and are explored in greater detail in the following two chapters.

In sum, then, in addition to the natural, climatically induced changes, the human impact was early, widespread, and significant, and the forests of the world changed accordingly. Across the globe, the first halting steps toward deforestation were under way. In the space of 10,000 years (a mere 500 generations) humans were going to have an effect on global vegetation only slightly less dramatic and widespread than that of the Ice Age in the 100,000 years before.

Chapter 2

Fire and Foragers

There are no virgin . . . forests today, nor were there in 1492.
—W. M. Denevan, "The Pristine Myth: The Landscape of the Americas in 1492" (1992)

It has long been thought that prehistoric peoples were a nonfactor in environmental change and degradation. Their numbers and densities were too low to bring about significant change; their technology was insufficient to cause alteration; and their livelihood was in perfect harmony with nature. However, even before the climate, vegetation, and landscape had achieved their modern character, humans were at odds with nature, changing it, manipulating it, and attempting to tame it. Vast areas of forest and grassland were burned, vegetation was altered irretrievably, soils were changed, and fauna were eliminated. Indeed, it is increasingly difficult to think that any forests, from the tundra margins to the tropics, were ever pristine and untouched; all were being changed in form and composition.

Some of the changes were probably natural as the forest adjusted to the climatic shifts associated with the retreating ice, progressing through a succession of stages and achieving, eventually, a theoretical climax state. Whatever the truth of that, there should be no doubt about the role of humans in bringing about change in the "deep" past. Each shift in the complexity and sophistication of technique and culture merely made the human impact more certain and pronounced. Even the mildest and slowest change could be cumulative, leading to dramatic long-term effects. At the very simplest level, hunter-foragers manipulated vegetation by fire in order to round up and slaughter game, causing irreversible change to forest extent and composition. The hunter-foragers gave way to agricultural, including irrigation, societies that deliberately manipulated the soil and water supply, thereby radically altering and replacing one vegetation cover by another. In turn

12

these gave way to urban/industrial societies that sent out shock waves of innovation, modernization, and change into their surrounding hinterlands in the form of fuel demands, crop productivity, and land use change.

In many ways the distinction used in this and the next chapter between foraging and farming in altering the forest is a difficult one to sustain. In many societies there was, and is, a seamless continuity between the two, the distinction decreasing the nearer one comes to the present. In reality, both used fire, the foragers almost certainly more than the farmers. Nevertheless, it is a convenient distinction which underlines a particular emphasis in the subsequent account.

FIRE: "THE FIRST GREAT FORCE"

Fire was, in the words of Omer Stewart, "the first great force employed by man," and it was crucial in the story of deforestation.[1] With fire humans accomplished the first great ecological transformation of the earth, to be followed much later by two others of the same order of magnitude: the development of agriculture and animal husbandry 10,000 years ago, and the rise of large-scale industrial production a little less than 200 years ago. Humans assimilated fire into their biological heritage, thereby gaining access to the world's biota, and the biota, in turn, acquired a new regimen of fire transformed by human society. Fire, suggests Stephen Pyne, was the first of "humanity's Faustian bargains."[2]

So much must be supposed, but imagination and logic suggest that before "natural" or wildfire was domesticated by developing tools to create new, controlled fire, much thought and energy must have gone into preserving fire rather than extinguishing it. There is no evidence in the ethnohistorical literature of past and contemporary aboriginal societies of a conscious effort to extinguish opportunistic fire or concern to protect vegetation. Fires were left to burn and smolder for weeks on end. In areas of seasonal drying and strong winds, the effect on the vegetation must have been dramatic.

Wildfire is a great modifier and has its own ecology, and if frequent and regular enough, vegetation adapts by shifting toward species (pyrophytes) that can regenerate after a fire or even withstand it. For example, many plants have a thick, fire-resistant bark or buds that tolerate high temperatures, or they reproduce below ground. Other trees and shrubs have seeds that are stimulated by the heat of fire. Without heat the trees cannot germinate and they die. While repeated burning discourages woody plants that cannot adapt or regenerate, it encourages a greater growth of annual and perennial herbs and grasses, through structural change and the fertilizing effect of the proteins and minerals left on the ground. The forage available in deciduous woodlands may increase many times over for a number of years.

To the early hominids, fire was complex, subtle, and dynamic; it was also destructive, irreversible, purposeless, and self-generating. But they also were to learn that the many negative qualities of this destructive force could be turned to positive and productive uses (fig. 2.1).

First and foremost, if humans could mimic nature's own fire drives caused by windstorm and lightning, the world was made more habitable and usable. Land was cleared and plant and animal resources were increased (see plate 2.1). Even the most primitive of aboriginal peoples seemed to grasp intuitively the idea that deliberate burning improved vegetation by promoting, maintaining, and increasing the growth of favored plants such as grasses, forbs, tubers, wild fruits, wild rice, hazelnuts, sunflowers, camas, bracken, cassava, and blueberries, which in turn encouraged greater numbers and densities of animals. Burning also helped to control the distribution of animals, making hunting more predictable and thus more efficient because less time and energy were expended on stalking individual animals into areas of dense forest. Additionally, fire opened up the tangle of woodland and jungle by removing the dense understory of brush and small trees, so that visibility was improved, travel facilitated, and surprise attack from animals and other humans minimized. Simply put, widely spaced trees and clear meadows offered greater mobility and more productive and safer hunting. The reduction of vegetation cover for rousing and driving game is one of the most frequently cited reasons for deliberate burning throughout the historical aboriginal world, and it would have been equally as true in the past. Anything to facilitate the hunt was desirable. Early hominids had only sharpened and fire-hardened wooden spears for hunting; not until later, when the more versatile and long-range bow and arrow were perfected, could the task have become more efficient and safer. One also can speculate as to whether more accessible herds allowed a selective culling of animals, which might ultimately have affected the age, sex, and species components of herds. Such deliberate manipulation might have been the first step in the herding/husbanding/domestication of animal populations and would have contributed to the emergence of concepts of ownership and territoriality.

Not only were large mammals "flushed out" by fire, so too were nutritious insects, lizards, and rodents from trunks, holes, caves, and burrows, and even honey could be safely collected from combs. Night fishing by torch was very productive. The opposite was also true of fire: it had a purgative effect, ridding the ground of poisonous snakes, scorpions, and spiders and a host of ticks and bugs, while many peoples in the Americas learned to live in perpetual smoke to ward off flies and mosquitoes.

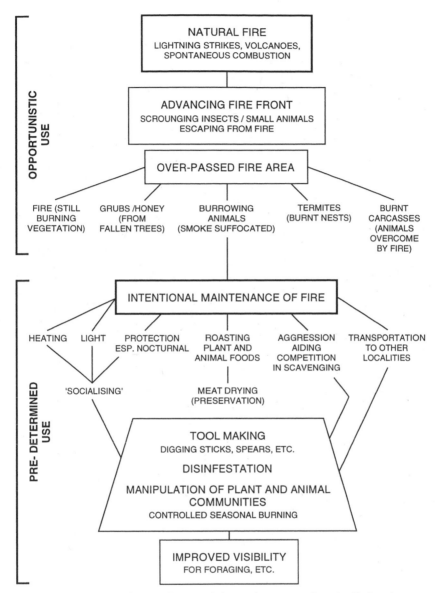

Figure 2.1 Possible uses of natural fire by early hominids. (Source: after J. D. Clark and J. W. K. Harris, "Fire and Its Roles in Early Hominid Lifeways," *African Archaeological Review* 3 [1985]: 3–27.)

Plate 2.1 Using fire to clear vegetation is a practice as old as humankind. Firing vegetation for cropping, Central African Republic. (Mathieu Labourer, Still Pictures.)

Finally, there are few foods that do not benefit from the application of heat. Therefore, the second great benefit of fire was in cooking and boiling, which leached out toxins, softened tough fibers, and reduced bacteria and fungi, extending the range of foods available and leading, presumably, to better health. In addition, the application of fire for cooking became the model for ceramics and metallurgy.

Thus, fire became embedded in human cognition and sociocultural be-havior. It is, says Pyne, "a maddening amalgam of human and ecological history."[3] Fire could be used for protection as well as aggression; it ac-companied ceremonies and entered belief systems as a purifier and atoner through sacrifice and ordeal; it entered into concepts of creation and dam-nation in many religions. At a more prosaic level, it certainly made life more comfortable and sociable and contributed to civilization. Fire was a source of heat and light, giving protection against cold and darkness and warning off predators, thus facilitating territorial expansion and population increase. Because of the comfort and security it offered, it became a focus for group and community life and enhanced communication and solidar-ity. Fire may have encouraged such practices as meat eating, food sharing, the division of labor, and new forms of sexual behavior, thereby helping to weld early groups into coherent units. It is most likely responsible for the formation of the characteristics of the family unit in society, the hearth being a potent image of (and in) family life and sedentariness and the focal point for gathering, discussion, and dissemination of group wisdom.

All these practical benefits and cultural mutations led to repeated and regular use of fire in most societies in the world, creating high concentrations of plants and animals that could provide humans with useful products, primarily food. The human monopoly of fire separated Homo sapiens from all other primates and beings and made them the dominant species on the earth and its ecological manipulators. The implications for deforestation were enormous.

BEFORE THE ICE: PREHISTORY "CAUGHT ALIVE"

The obvious advantages of fire as a facilitator of life and provider of food are well attested by examples of vegetation changes from around the world in the deep past of prehistory. Human fire use preceded the Ice Age. Australopithecines, remote ancestors of modern humans, go back at least 1.5 million years, and it is likely that they used sites such as Olduvai Gorge in the East African Rift Valley. However, it was only with the migration out of the African heartland and into Europe and Asia of the descendants, Homo erectus, about 1 million years ago that we get more definite evidence of the human control of fire. Evidence of burning in association with animal bones is found in sites from around the world from between 500,000 and 300,000 BP. There is also evidence of the use of fire to harden bone and wood for implements, particularly hunting spears. Undoubtedly, too, fire would have helped people to keep warm in the colder northern area into which they had moved, especially with the recurring advances of ice during the mid-Pleistocene.

The finds are at settlement sites, which suggests that the fires were not caused naturally by lightning strikes, which are universal and widespread. Nevertheless, to find unequivocal evidence of the deliberate use of fire to manipulate vegetation solely to facilitate hunting activities is difficult. Fire sticks (kindling sticks) leave little archeological evidence. But one clue to vegetation change exists—and that is the animals that were killed and their skeletal remains.

Sometime during the late Paleolithic/early Mesolithic, between 16,000 and 10,000 BP, there was a massive decline in large mammals, such as mammoths, mastodons, woolly rhinoceros, giant deer, and cave bears. The decline during this "Pleistocene overkill" was most noticeable in North America, where some 33 out of 45 genera of large mammals disappeared between 11,500 and 11,000 BP. South America lost 46 out of 58 genera, while Europe and north Asia lost seven out of 24, as cave bears, lions, hyenas, mammoths, and woolly rhinos disappeared abruptly by 12,000 BP. South Asia and sub-Saharan Africa were relatively immune: only two out of 44 genera disappeared, their large beasts stocking the zoos of the world today.

The cause of this dramatic decline is a mystery. Epidemic disease and cosmic accidents are ruled out, and the conventional explanation has been that climatic change caused a re-advance of the forests, which reduced the rich grass and herb vegetation of the northern plains, while rising sea levels hindered animal migration away from the areas of stress. More recently, others have noted the almost perfect coincidence of the decline of large mammals in North America with the emergence of "anatomically" modern humans, the Clovis people, a late Paleolithic hunting culture with a distinctive technology of flaked stone spears. These scientists have postulated that the large mammals, tame and unwary of humans, were butchered, leading to a massive overkill and eventual extinction. The most likely explanation is that a combination of two forces worked together, namely, human predation reduced animal populations already stressed by a climatically reduced geographical range.

But many questions remain. Even in such conditions, could Upper Paleolithic peoples have been capable of totally exterminating so many species? Why did so many of the species killed in North America not feature significantly in the human diet? Why did humans technically similar to the Clovis people, and present in Europe since circa 35,000 BP, not kill off the mammals well before the classic overkill phase? Also remarkable is the fact that during the subsequent 10,000 years of the Holocene very few species have become totally extinct until the relatively recent rise in population numbers, the extension of human land uses, the reduction of natural habitats, and the advent of firearms.

Another and more likely explanation for the loss of animal species is that as humans struggled to maintain open habitats for hunting in the face of forest advance they severely modified the structure and stability of the ecosystems by fire. Now the mammals were more vulnerable to the stresses of the physical and human environment around them. The likelihood of this scenario is bolstered by the striking historical analogy of the destruction of large fauna in the Pacific Islands (particularly of the moa, a large ostrich-like flightless bird, of New Zealand) by the seafaring, immigrant Polynesians during the first millennium AD. Here, in the words of archaeologist Jack Golson, prehistory has been "caught alive."[4]

The Polynesians reached Madagascar between about AD 100 and 500, Easter Island about AD 400, Hawaii about AD 800, and New Zealand between AD 900 and 950. In the 117 km² of Easter Island, clearing for agriculture, firewood, and large timbers for moving the *moai*, or massive stone face statues, together with frequent fire, resulted in "a deforestation which must surely be one of the most extreme examples of its kind anywhere in the world," leaving scarcely a single tree.[5] Dramatic as it was, however, this deforestation came nowhere near the destruction by fire of almost half of the forest in New Zealand by the Maoris. The Maoris brought no plants with them and came as hunter-gathers. The moa, a large, ostrich-like, flightless bird standing up to 16 ft high, was their principal source of protein, without equal in any of the Pacific Islands. Moas also provided material for clothing and for most implements and were known as *kuranui*, "the great treasure" or "primary source." In the absence of any large predators moas multiplied to vast numbers, tending to congregate on the forest edges and clearings. The Maori soon learned the value of fire in pushing back the forest edge and in driving the moas to places where they could be slaughtered more easily. Once started, the fires were fanned by the desiccating nor'westers that then, as now, sweep from the mountain across the foothills and the rain-shadow plains on the eastern side of the South Island during the hot, dry summers. The mixed broadleaf-conifer forests could not withstand fire, did not regenerate, and were replaced by bracken, fern, tussock, and scrub. The denudation initiated the first great cycle of humanly induced soil erosion that buried old forests near present-day Christchurch under 12 ft of detritus. About a hundred years later the interior beech forests went the same way. By 1250 there were barely any moa left to hunt, and by the time of European colonization they were extinct. Thus, by the mid-thirteenth century a mere 8,000–12,000 people in South Island had destroyed about 8 million acres of forest and driven the moa to the verge of extinction (fig. 2.2). By the time of the fairly precise European vegetation surveys of circa 1800, the forest, particularly in the North Island, had been reduced even further; subsequent clearing for agriculture and sheep grazing completed the task of denudation begun 1,500 years earlier by the Maoris (fig. 2.3).

With such evidence, one can well believe Captain James Cook's comment during the 1770s that throughout his voyages between the Pacific Islands "we saw either smoke by day and fires by night, in all parts of it." However, because of the prevailing myth of the harmony of preindustrial peoples with nature there has been a reluctance to accept what he saw and its consequences.[6]

Just as near-temperate New Zealand experienced acute deforestation with the influx of the hunter Maoris, so did near-tropical Madagascar during the early phase of the Polynesian immigration, circa AD 100–500. At least 14 species of large lemur, large avifauna, aardvark, and pygmy hippopotamus became extinct in the western forests. Charcoal layers in pollen remains show clearly that fire was used extensively both in natural

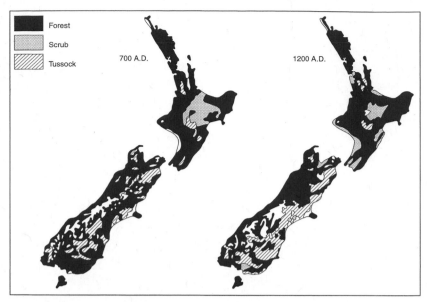

Figure 2.2 New Zealand vegetation: "Pre-Polynesian, AD 700" and "Pre-Classical Maori, AD 1200." (Source: R. G. Cochrane, "The Impact of Man on the Natural Biota," in *New Zealand in Maps,* ed. A. G. Anderson and D. Brunch [London: Hodder & Stoughton, 1977], 32–33.)

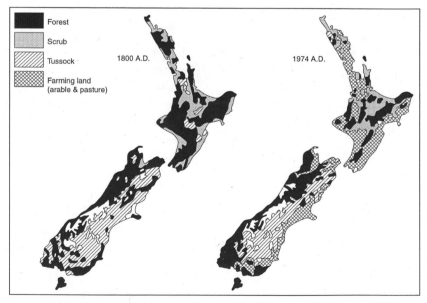

Figure 2.3 New Zealand vegetation: "Pre-European, AD 1800"; and "Present, AD 1974." (Source: R. G. Cochrane, "The Impact of Man on the Natural Biota," in *New Zealand in Maps,* ed. A. G. Anderson and D. Brunch [London: Hodder & Stoughton, 1977], 32–33.)

grasslands and in forested lands. The extinction spasm was over by circa AD 900, when hunting-gathering was replaced by cattle pastoralism and swidden farming, known as *tavy,* both maintained through the succeeding centuries by an endless cycle of fire. By the time of European contact in the late eighteenth century, over three-quarters of the central plateau was in grassland, and fire was common.

Whether before the Ice Age or after, the dramatic decline of large fauna is a direct result, and surrogate measure, of the ability of humans to alter their forest environment by fire. We have to concede that the Pleistocene "overkill" was more likely to have been a Pleistocene "overburn."

AFTER THE ICE: EUROPE

It is only from about 6,000 BP in Europe, about the same time in South America and elsewhere, and probably only from about 1,000 BP in eastern North America, that clear evidence comes to light that hunter-foragers were playing an active role in the transformation of the forest.

In Europe the evidence of vegetation manipulation is present but patchy until after 5,000 BP, except in Britain where Mesolithic foragers attempted to open up the thickening canopy of vegetation in order to encourage red deer and wild pig. They must have been aware of the effect of sunlight on the greater productivity in the openings and edges of the forest and of the cessation of the vernal efflorescence of the forest floor with the closing of the overhead canopy in late spring. Consequently, when the climate warmed after the glacial retreat and the deciduous high forest, especially lime, developed an almost totally closed canopy that shaded out the growth of grasses and herbs, they set about destroying it. Over 100 sites in the Pennines and North York Moors show repeated fires associated with layers of charcoal, lithic remains, and some animal bones. Frequent lightning strikes in one spot is unlikely; in any case, as Ian Simmons points out, the damp forest is "about as likely to burst into flames after a lightning strike as a sackful of wet socks."[7] Most of the fires were on the forest edge or openings, and areas as large as 5 km in diameter were affected. The shade-tolerant oak and ash cease to dominate the pollen count, and their place is taken by scrubby hazel, with lesser quantities of rowan and bramble, and substantial amounts of grasses and herbs. Even nettles (*Urtica*), a sure sign of disturbed ground, appear. The net ecological effect was to replace the high, mixed deciduous forest with a mosaic of open-canopy woodland with grassy clearings near water sources, the ideal hunting ground.

Iversen's 1941 notion that there was no clearing in the pre-Neolithic forest because people were forced to give way to dense forest advance and seek the "open" coastal fringes during the Atlantic period of climatic optimum has been influential and has colored generations of subsequent work. "Large parts of the country must have been almost empty of human beings," he wrote, and his co-worker, Jorgen Troels-Smith, went so far as to make the incredible suggestion that "scarcely 30 people divided among 5 or 6 families probably constituted the entire population of Denmark at that time." [8]

But the many years that separate Iversen's pioneering and necessarily cruder work from the finer spatial and temporal resolution palynological techniques capable of detecting episodes of burning used in Britain by, for example, Simmons and Innes, goes far to explain this apparent difference. Nonetheless, it is strange that the pollen diagrams of Scandinavia leave no record comparable to that for Britain, especially as Mesolithic foraging groups certainly inhabited northern, western, and parts of Mediterranean Europe in well-defined "social territories," their subsistence systems revolving around seasons of exploitation, which depended on the availability of game, fish, and forage. The degree to which the forest was a barrier to penetration and manipulation depended on the type of forest prevalent. The damp boulder clays and silts of the northern European plain would have been dominated by dense lime forest that would have provided little opportunity for burning except around its edges and in clearings; but the sandy and gravelly outwash soils to the south, and the extensive friable loess soils in particular, would have dried out enough in summer to provide ample opportunity for deliberate firing.

Perhaps the most persuasive evidence of the intensity of the Mesolithic impact is the widespread and sharp decline in elm (*Ulmus*) pollen across the Continent in the relatively short time between 6,400 and 6,300 BP in southern and southeastern Europe and culminating in Britain between approximately 5,000 and 5,200 BP. Hypotheses of natural causes such as a colder climate or fungal pathogens have serious shortcomings, and the only conclusion is that it must be anthropogenic. Yet here too are mysteries. It could not be agricultural clearing as tree pollen other then elm declined far less rapidly. The only plausible explanation is that in the absence of winter grass under the dense forest canopy the young elm leaves were fed to stall-held cattle and that excessive pollarding eventually led to the death of the elm. But this, too, is problematic. It would take vast herds of cattle to cause the pollen decline recorded, and the evidence of cattle in such numbers is not present. The most likely explanation is that selective trimming combined with widespread burning to thin out the forest led to the decline, as the elm does not regenerate easily after fire.

While the forest was destroyed it was also valued. Wood was the most valuable and versatile raw material available in the past. Not only did it furnish shelter and heat but also the material for a range of tools and weapons necessary for survival. Mesolithic societies had acquired considerable knowledge and appreciation of the qualities of different timbers and their suitability for different functions—the elm and yew for bow staves, pine for arrow shafts, hazel for spear shafts, and tough root wood for ax hafts. Bark quality was also understood: the resistance of birch bark to water and its usefulness for hut floor insulation and net-float construction; the use of its pitch for caulking artifacts and preparing leather, and the use of willow bark to provide the thread for making the nets. Even tree fungus (*Fomes fometarius*) was stripped of its outer skin and used for tinder.

An impressive array of over 600 different Mesolithic wooden artifacts have been identified at over 200 sites in Ireland and Britain: dugout canoes, kegs, bowls, boxes, and baskets, as well as the more usual weaponry and tools, such as ax hafts, bows, spear and arrow shafts, sheaths, scabbards, shields, clubs, hammers, forks, knives, looms, and wheels. Because of their organic nature, many are well preserved in wetland locations. This catalog excludes the palisades and structures in forts, and the worked rods, brushwood hurdles, pegs, and planks that went to make up the prehistoric trackways and platforms that straddled the low-lying wetlands in the Somerset Levels and the Fens—literally millions of pieces. Perhaps even more impressive is the evidence of the conscious management of the surrounding woodlands by coppicing to stimulate the growth of long, straight poles from the trees' stools.

All the evidence of clearing and wood use points to the fact that a greater continuity of technology existed between the Mesolithic and Neolithic than is usually supposed. The later Mesolithics were not, as the eminent archaeologist, Gordon Childe thought, the primitive fag end of the hunting and gathering Paleolithic age who became absorbed by the superior new Neolithic agriculturalists; rather, they were the sophisticated and innovative precursors who not only heralded the Neolithic agricultural age but hastened its establishment. Indeed, Mesolithic and Neolithic are "definitional nightmares" that are more likely to obscure than to clarify. As far as the clearing of the forest is concerned, these "ages" mask a continuity of ceaseless change and modification that began over 6,000 years ago.

AFTER THE ICE: NORTH AMERICA

The Forest or Eastern Woodland cultures of pre-Columbian North America may be separated by up to 5,000 years from the forest economies of

Mesolithic Europe, but there are many parallels. There were also differences. In Europe, evidence depends almost entirely on archeological techniques for retrieval and interpretation, whereas in North America, an inquisitive audience of literate and artistically inclined newcomers left a record for all to read and see. The New World they found filled them with curiosity and awe, and although they did not, by any means, understand or appreciate what they found, their accounts and sketches bring Indian forest use vividly alive.

Despite the eyewitness accounts and the rapidly accumulating botanical and archeological evidence, the impact of the Native American on the eastern forest—even of his existence—has been strenuously denied in the past, and still is by some. During the nineteenth century, writers such as Longfellow, Thoreau, Parkman, and Fenimore Cooper and painters of the Hudson River school and it descendants, such as Cole, Catlin, and Church, extolled the idea of an untouched, virgin, and virtually uninhabited forest wilderness. Such a Romantic vision served as a stark contrast to heighten the heroic struggle of the pioneer farmers, who were subduing the unending forest by clearing. These pioneers were replacing wilderness with a "made," humanized landscape, darkness with light, and fear and evil with hope, redemption, and civilization. This vision has become a part of the American heritage.

The idea of a nonhumanized "presettlement" landscape/ecology is equally attractive for many modern-day ecologists, anthropologists, biogeographers, and "wilderness" enthusiasts, for it acts as a benchmark against which to measure subsequent change, as well as a datum toward which conservation policy must aim and against which change can be measured. Thus they would prefer using the concept of "pre-European" landscapes as "natural analogues against which modern environmental impacts can be judged."[9] In their concept of conservation, the past (and even present) rural populations are missing. The celebrations—or commiserations, depending on one's point of view—to mark the quincentennial of the Columbian landfall have similarly, but for entirely different reasons, created a vision of a virtually untouched paradise in which the Native American was more readily admitted, but who lived benignly and in harmony with nature. Somehow, in this naive view, they were always "natural ecologists" whose mental constructs precluded cultural activities that would be destructive to the environment. Pre-Columbian America

> was still the First Eden, a pristine natural kingdom. The native people were transparent in the landscape, living as a natural element of the ecosphere. Their world, the New World of Columbus, was a world of barely perceptible human disturbance.[10]

It was the blundering European who transformed, destroyed, and devastated it all. Such views tend to be accepted uncritically by nonscientific audiences with a conservation agenda.

The unintentional alliance among mid-nineteenth-century romantics, contemporary ecologists/conservationists, and latter-day politically corrects has obscured the fact that, first, there was an impact, and second, as William Denevan has pointed out, it was "neither benign nor localized and ephemeral, nor were resources always used in a sound ecological way."[11] On the contrary, there is abundant evidence that by 1492 the Native Americans had modified the extent and composition of the forest by burning, clearing, and foraging, creating forests in many stages of ecological succession, making and expanding grasslands, and otherwise engaging in the first steps toward deforesting the landscape.

For the "deniers," ancient and modern alike, ignorance or willful omission of the magnitude and effect of Indian numbers has played a part in their views. Rather than the 8 million to 15 million native peoples present in all the Americas just prior to 1492 as was previously thought, modern biological and archival reconstruction has put the number at between 43 million and 65 million, some even suggesting double that figure. Such numbers must have meant extensive ecological transformations. Subsequent devastating pandemic diseases of common Old World pathogens like measles and influenza, as well as a host of more virulent diseases like smallpox, cholera, dysentery, and yellow fever to which native Americans had no immunity, led to a demographic collapse, so that perhaps only 5.6 million people remained by 1650—a mere million of which were in North America.

Because forest disturbance is largely an outcome of human numbers, and given the high total number and density of the original population, it would not be surprising that the first Europeans found a profoundly manipulated landscape. However, because of the rapid decline of native human numbers through disease, that humanized landscape physically receded before forest re-advance and, also, figuratively "receded" in the collective consciousness. Human transformation has been increasingly discounted to a point where it has been almost denied. Indeed, despite the in-migration of perhaps 2 million Europeans by the middle of the eighteenth century, it is probable that the forest landscape of 1750 was less humanized than that of 1492, when Indian numbers and their impact was at their peak. With such evidence, the terms presettlement and postsettlement should be consigned to the intellectual trash can. States of "natural" and "equilibrium" have probably not existed since the end of the Ice Age.

The truth is that in the Eastern Woodland cultures, fire use was an integral part of the economy, not only for hunting and foraging but also for cultivation. Many Indian tribes moved easily and smoothly between the two modes of production. The Penobscots of Maine, for example, had a two-part existence, being big-game hunters of moose inland during the winter and returning downstream to live in villages and plant maize on the river islands during the summer. Thus, the criteria by which we make distinctions and judge cultural achievement in the Old World Neolithic, such as domestication, agricultural control, sedentariness, pottery, and trade, simply do not apply to the American Indian.

The evidence of human modification of the forest is early, stark, and clear. In many settlements (such as those of the Huron, Iroquois, and Cherokee), there was a hierarchy of fire uses in the forest that had a broad locational expression. There was a core of fire-cleared ground for fields and cultivation. Beyond this was a zone of intensive fuel, berry, and nut gathering, which merged into a more extensive, distant zone that was periodically opened up by fire to extend open grassland, promote the growth of fresh grasses; and encourage small game and foraging. Beyond that was an area in which wild-fire burning was common for driving or encouraging large game. (See fig. 2.4.) Fire created a favorable environment, especially on the mixed forest-grassland edge, where returns of game and cultivated foods could be maximized.

The Native Americans were careful stewards of fire as a tool to manage the land and to promote their welfare. Cereal grasses were fired annually, basket grasses and nuts about every three years, brush and undergrowth in the forest about every 15 to 30 years or more; and annual broadcast fire in the fields got rid of vermin, disease, weeds, and regrowth. Fire for defense and hunting occurred as needed. As in most economically primitive societies, fire was a natural and integral—even sacred—part of the Indian landscape and livelihood. The contemporary record of the nature, purpose, and effect of Indian fire for foraging is rich, and only a fraction of the evidence can be selected. Fire alone, without any other activity, produced three major changes in the forest: opening up the forest, creating grasslands, and altering the composition and range of trees.

The Opening of the Forest

The repeated use of broadcast fire on the forest to free it of underbrush affected the density of trees. Many Europeans approaching the eastern coast had seen evidence of great conflagrations even before they landed. Mark Catesby said of the Carolinas in 1747:

> In *February* and *March* the inhabitants have the custom of burning the woods, which causes such a continual smoke, that not knowing the cause it might be imagined to proceed from fog, or a natural thickness of the air.[12]

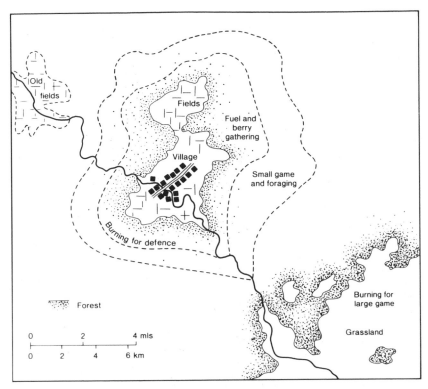

Figure 2.4 Zonation of Indian forest use. (Source: after M. Williams, *Americans and Their Forests* [New York: Cambridge University Press, 1989].)

Thomas Morton, who had lived in New England for several years by 1627, made the connection between vegetation type and fire:

> The Salvages are accustomed to set fire of the Country in all places where they come, and to burne it twize in the yeare, viz; as the Spring and the fall of the leaf. The reason that mooves them so to doe so, is because it would other wise be so overgrowne with underweedes that it would be all coppice wood, and the people would not be able in any wise to passe through the Country out of a beaten path.

This repeated broadcast firing of the undergrowth

> destroyes the underwoods and scorcheth the elder trees that it shrinkes them, and hinders their growth very much; so that hee that will looke to finde large trees and good tymber, must not depend upon the help of a woodden

prospect to finde them on the upland ground; but must seeke for them . . .
in the lower grounds, where the grounds are wett.

The result was to open out the forest and to create a sort of ecological secondary association: "The trees growe here and there as in our parks; and makes the Country very beautifull and commodious," Morton wrote.[13]

Elsewhere, similar landscapes were encountered. The area around Salem, Massachusetts, was described by Francis Higginson as being "open plains, in some places five hundred acres, some places more, some lesser, not much troublesome for to cleere for the plough to goe in," while the forest around the Roanoke River in Virginia had become so open and parklike that William Byrd could say, "There is scarce a shrub in view to intercept your prospect, but grass as high as a man on horseback." [14] Again, Andrew White, on an expedition along the Potomac in 1633, said that the forest was "not choked up with undergrowth of brambles and bushes, but as if laid out by hand in a manner so open, that you might freely drive a four horse chariot in the midst of the trees"; and a little earlier John Smith in Virginia had commented that "a man may gallop a horse amongst these woods any waie, but where the creekes and Rivers shall hinder." [15] The ability to ride a horse or drive a horse and carriage between and under the trees became a favorite literary trope to describe the open nature of the fire-burned forest, but it was, nonetheless, true. If the opening-out went far enough, then small meadows—or prairies, as they were called later—resulted, evoking another set of typical descriptive comments. As early as 1654 Edward Johnson had observed that the thinness of the timber in parts of New England made the forest "like our Parkes in England"; and Adam Hodgson, on a journey from Natchez through central Mississippi, found that the forest was "delightful, open and interspersed with occasional small prairies and had the appearance of an English Park." [16] While these were mainly aesthetic judgments about a familiar landscape the observers liked, nevertheless they were also comments on the type of fire-opened forest encountered, and which we know were far more common than the dense, impenetrable, dark woods beloved of the Romantic imagination.

The Creation of Grasslands

Wherever fire was more frequent and devastating, completely open ground was the result, even though rainfall was sufficient to support trees. The sparsely growing, parklike forest gave way to what were variously called plains, barrens, openings, deserts, prairies, or, particularly in the South, savannas—all individual patches of open grassland in the main body of the forest, varying from a few acres to many thousands of square miles. Their location and extent varied, but the farther west one moved the more frequent the clearings became, and they merged into the true treeless prairies. But one did not have to go that far west to find large "openings" in the forest. Some of the first major prairies encountered were on the Rappahannock River in Virginia and, particularly, along the Potomac to the Shenandoah Valley. Traveler after traveler through the valley commented on the "large level plains," "the large spots of meadows and savannas wherein are hundreds of acres without any trees at all," and the "firing of the woods by the Indians."[17] Similarly, the enormous and anomalous openings of the bluegrass country of western Kentucky, later invaded by the European grass *Poa pratensis*, excited much comment, as did other openings in eastern New York that the Iroquois kept open by repeated firing in order to promote grass growth for game. There were further examples in the "prairie belt" of Alabama and adjacent parts of Missouri. Over a century ago, Asa Gray, the noted botanist, was convinced that all the openings east of the Mississippi and of the Missouri up to Minnesota "have been either greatly extended or were even made treeless under Indian occupation and annual burnings."[18]

Burning promoted the browse for the three major animal food species: the bison, the elk, and the white-tailed deer, the latter being the major food source in the eastern forests from the beginning of human occupation. "The aborigines of New England," said Timothy Dwight in 1821, "customarily fired the forests that they might pursue their hunting with advantage." Dozens of other commentators and eyewitnesses from John Smith in the early seventeenth century onward described, in various ways and with various details, what Mark Catesby witnessed in 1747 in the coastal plains and "desserts" of Florida and Carolina every October, when "deers, bears and other animals are drove by the raging fire and smoak, and being hemm'd in are destroyed in great numbers by their guns."[19]

The creation of individual openings by fire did not approach in either impact or extent the destruction of the forest along its whole western edge. From Wisconsin south to Texas repeated firing by the nomadic hunting cultures of the Plains Indians sustained the grassland vegetation against forest encroachment and extended the grassland at the expense of the forest. The range of game was extended by continually burning the forest edge in order to prevent timber regeneration, as well as setting massive wildfires to drive the buffalo to convenient slaughtering places. Fire was of critical significance in altering faunal habitats, and as the forests were burned and opened out the buffalo, for example, spread throughout the continent, crossing the Mississippi via newly formed openings in about AD 1000, entering the South by the fifteenth century, and penetrating as far east as Pennsylvania and Massachusetts by the seventeenth century.

Climatic conditions alone cannot be evoked to explain the origin and peculiar purity of the prairie grassland, just as they cannot explain the expansion of the buffalo. When fire was suppressed with European settlement, the forest began to encroach on these openings. For example, the "oak openings" of southwestern Wisconsin were reckoned to have decreased by nearly 60 percent between 1829 and 1854 following the control of fire; and oak-hickory forest advanced into the Illinois grasslands at between 1 and 2 mi in 30 years after fire ceased. Not until there was complete occupation of the prairies for agriculture and the suppression of wildfires did the advance of the forest stop on its western edge. Most ecologists are now prepared to support the bold and unequivocal statement of Roger Anderson that the eastern prairies would have disappeared and have been replaced by forests "if it had not been for the nearly annual burning of these grasslands by the North American Indians" during the last 5,000 years.[20]

Altering the Forest Composition and Range

Frequent burning had one other permanent and far-reaching effect: it altered the composition and range of species in the forest by reducing their number and simplifying their biological components. For example, the extensive open loblolly (*Pinus taeda*), longleaf (*P. palustris*), and slash pine (*P. elliottii*) forests of the Southeast are a human-induced plant community maintained by fire within the general deciduous region of the eastern woodlands. Their needle-leaves and their cones only open with the heat of fire. Fire suppression has led to the invasion of the southern pine forest by hardwoods, such as oak and hickory, which are replacing them. In the West, sequoia, Douglas fir (*Pseudotsuga menziesii*), and ponderosa pine (*P. ponderosa*), and red and eastern white pine (*P. resinosa* and *P. strobus*) in the North, while not strictly fire types, require fire to ensure their reproduction.

At the same time, fire encouraged fire-tolerant and sun-loving species and promoted conditions favorable for the growth of edible, gatherable foods, such as strawberries, blackberries, and raspberries, all of which fostered human occupation and made further alteration of the forest composition more likely. Moreover, native plants like groundnuts and leeks were dispersed more widely.

Everywhere in the forests of North America, fire setting together with other modification activities represented a "long and steady pressure by human action on plant assemblages."[21]

AFTER THE ICE: THE TROPICS

The forests of the tropics, no less than those of the temperate world of Europe and North America, bear unmistakable signs of human manipulation and change. Yet even as late as the 1950s, their reputation for being untouched and pristine was as strong as it was in 1450. In 1958 the celebrated tropical botanist-ecologist Paul Richards thought that until recently humans had had "no more influence on the vegetation than any of the other animal inhabitants," which produced the counterargument by Carl Sauer that humans had "been around from the beginning" and that burning, swiddens, and the manipulation of species had modified the forest extensively everywhere to make it largely anthropogenic in form and composition. Similarly, a few years earlier, Gerardo Budowski had stuck his neck out and declared the adjacent and intermingled tropical savannas were the result of a "sequence of forest felling and repeated burnings." [22]

The palynological and historical record of the tropical forest is complicated by many factors, as well as by there simply being less information. No forest is uniform, and the tropical forest is strikingly not so. Broadly speaking, there are humid, moist forests where the fire record is quickly obliterated by rapid and luxuriant growth, and on their margins there are seasonally dry forests or savannas where seasonal droughts and frequent natural fires complicate the record of change. It is likely that these latter forests would have been much more extensive in the drier past, extending into areas that are now moist forest. Second, even more than in the temperate forests of the Northern Hemisphere, pure foraging without some sort of cultivation was rare, and consequently to attribute anthropogenic disturbance to hunter-gatherers alone while ignoring slash-and-burn activities is erroneous.

Despite all the complications, tropical forest pollen diagrams everywhere show a reduction of primary forest taxa and a rise in secondary (often ephemeral) forest taxa and other elements of seral vegetation such as tree ferns and grasses. There is no way of knowing conclusively whether the cause of the change is natural, by lightning strikes, for example, or tree falls, which are very common, or if it is humanly induced. Thus, fires in the northern Amazon basin at 6,000 BP and southeastern Venezuela at circa 3,500 BP that have thinned and altered the forest may be a result of either natural or human activities but are often associated with human settlement. On the other hand, there is abundant evidence of disturbance by burning in the Americas and in West and East Africa for 3,000 BP; Sumatra, 6,000 BP; Taiwan, 4,000 BP; Fiji, 3,000 BP; and New Guinea, 6,000–9,000 BP, all accompanied by agricultural activity.

In the south and central Amazon basin there is widespread evidence of charcoal, so much so that it is difficult to find soils that are not studded with charcoal. It is possible, of course, that some of this is a result of natural lightning fires, but it is more likely to be clearing for swiddens and the manipulation of the forest for useful plants (see chap. 3). Indeed, ethnobotanists like Darrell Posey, William Balée, Anna Roosevelt, and Laura Rival assert that much of the Amazonian forest is a "cultural artefact" or "anthropogenic," as native peoples have developed successive resource management strategies to cope with fluctuations in population dynamics and disturbances. It is a mosaic of different ages, compositions, and structures made all the more complex by the propagation of useful tree crops like nuts, palms, and bamboo, so that plant diversity has increased. Posey concludes that even in areas where Indians have disappeared, "the hand of human manipulation and management may still be evident."[23] Similar arguments can be made for the Maya lowlands and other parts of tropical Central America. It is estimated that up to 40 percent of the tropical forest is secondary forest resulting from periodic clearing, and almost all the remainder has suffered from some sort of modification.

Evidence of the modification of forest on the tropical savanna-forest interface by fire, and the probable extension of grassland at the expense of forest, is widespread. The best examples are in Central and South America where the record of changing forest composition, forest opening, and lack of forest "purity" parallels that of temperate North America. For example, the extensive pine forests of the cooler upland regions of Nicaragua, Guatemala, and Mexico are analogous to the pines of the U.S. South. If the seedlings escape destruction by fire during their first three to seven years, the trees grow and are fire resistant; but if fire is subsequently absent, as happened with the abandonment of land with the Indian decline, then the forest is invaded by mixed hardwoods that gradually replace the pines. The dominance of the pines, therefore, was a temporary result of the fire regime.

Similarly, many of the savannas and small openings of South America are humanly induced. Putting aside the extensive *campo cerrado* of Brazil, which are partially produced by reason of being on toxic oxisols soils, or the *llanos* of the Orinoco lowlands, which are periodically inundated floodplains or consist of soils of impeded drainage, there is evidence that the edges of many savannas are affected by anthropogenic action. J. G. Myers went so far as to say, "I have never seen in South America a savanna, however small and isolated or distant from settlement which did not show signs of more or less frequent burning," although that might include "natural" burns.[24]

However, it is in the smaller "openings" that there is clear documentation of human origin. The small, scattered grasslands, or *pajonales*, on

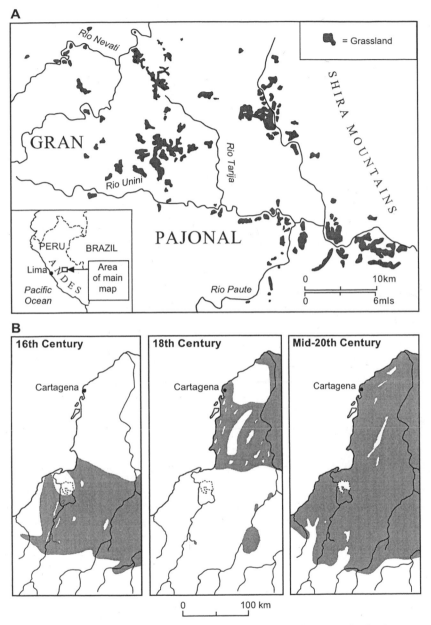

Figure 2.5 The creation of grasslands: *A, Pajonales* in Peru; and *B,* Savannas in Colombia.
(Source: based on G. A. J. Scott, "The Role of Fire in the Creation and Maintenance
of Savannas in the Montaña of Peru," *Journal of Biography* 4 [1977]: 143–67; and
L. R. Gordon, *The Human Geography and Ecology of the Sinú Country of Colombia,* Ibero-
Americana, no. 39 [Berkeley and Los Angeles: University of California Press, 1957].)

the Andean foothills of east-central Peru were created, maintained, and extended by the Campa Indians (fig. 2.5). They are probably abandoned dooryard swiddens but repeated burning is still practiced because the low grass cover is of more immediate use close to home (as well as for all the defensive, game, antipest, and foraging reasons noted before) than is the rank secondary forest growing on exhausted soils.

Further north in the Andean foothills of northwestern Colombia, there is clear documentary evidence that in the basins of the San Jorge, Cauca, and Sinu rivers, the open savanna that greeted the first Europeans in the early sixteenth century had reverted to forest by 1750 with Indian decline, except around a few surviving settlements (fig. 2.4). Then with European settlement and cattle ranching around the growing colonial settlement of Cartagena in the north new savannas were created. By the mid-twentieth century, both the Native American and European savannas became one large cleared area.

Nearly half a century ago Grahame Clark suggested fancifully that if one could have flown over northern Europe during Mesolithic times it would have been doubtful if

> more than an occasional wisp of smoke from a camp fire, or maybe a small
> cluster of huts, would have advertised the presence of humans: in all essentials
> the forest would have stretched unbroken, save only by mountain, swamp or
> water, to the margins of the sea.[25]

But the chances are that one would have seen something very different: massive smoke plumes, and clearings, and mosaics of different age planting and structures in a forest that was anything but unbroken and uninhabited. The same would have been even truer over the forested areas of the Americas at any time before 1492. Perhaps, then, one can agree with Denevan, who concludes that in Latin America "there are no virgin tropical forests today, nor were there in 1492."[26] Whether it was Europe, the Americas, Australia, New Zealand, or Asia, it was a far more altered world than we have ever thought.

Chapter 3

The First Farmers

It is almost incredible, in retrospect, how rapidly people seized the opportunities afforded by post glacial conditions.
—W. R. DICKINSON, "The Times Are Always Changing: The Holocene Saga" (1995)

CONTRARY TO popular opinion the life of the hunter-foragers was anything but a brutish nightmare of hand-to-mouth existence; in nearly all cases their supplies of food were secure and abundant, and their diet was varied. Fire had added a predictability to productivity, and waterside locations were particularly favorable, with an abundance of shellfish, fish, and fowl. So why did early humans start the time-consuming and heavy, laborious task of chopping down trees, as a prelude to yet further tasks of soil preparation, weeding, manuring and irrigating? There are many estimates of the labor required to clear the forest, which vary enormously with the density and age of the trees, the hardness of the wood, the degree to which fire can be incorporated in the process, and the type of agriculture performed. However, we get a clue from an example in western Africa (fig. 3.1), and the conclusion must be that clearing land took up most of the laboring year and was anything but an incidental and leisurely task. Rousseau's comment in 1755 that "vast forests had to be changed into smiling fields which had been watered by the sweat of men" held much truth.[1]

Nevertheless, agriculture had many advantages. Its yield was reasonably predictable, which freed people from perpetual hunting, foraging, and movement and released their energies to pursue other occupations—which is the basis of civilization. With the appearance of the plow in the late fourth millennium BC, of traction and the controlled manipulation of stock and their incorporation into the agricultural regime, agriculture began to make

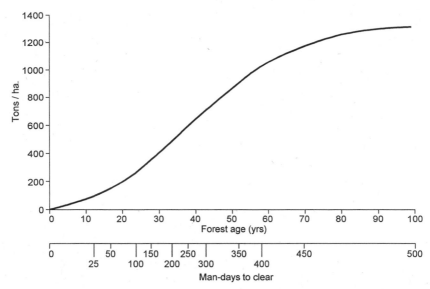

Figure 3.1 Approximate amount of labor required (in person-days) to clear forest of varying age and associated density (in tons moist weight/ha), West Africa. (Source: based on I. Wilks, "Land, Labour and the Forest Kingdom of Asante: A Model of Early Change," in *The Evolution of Social Systems*, ed. J. Friedmann and M. J. Rowlands [London: Duckworth, 1978], 504.)

massive inroads into the world's forests and change the vegetation cover of the land.

It is difficult to be precise about the true impact of the first farmers on the forest. Evidence of clearing is fragmentary because it has been regarded as the incidental accompaniment of agriculture. Few literary sources exist; and, as has been emphasized before, clearing leaves nothing in its place or remains from which to reconstruct events. In addition, it is difficult to summarize the multitude of individual events that took place over such a vast sweep of space and time. It is truly a case of what Estyn Evans called "dark ages in time and dark areas in space."[2] But, archeological, pollen, and macro-plant remains (plant remains larger than pollen grains and phytoliths) exist in sufficient abundance for one to build up a picture of considerable environmental impact and change.

DOMESTICATION AND CENTERS OF AGRICULTURE

The process of crop domestication that led to agriculture, a more sedentary existence, and, hence, clearing is a mystery. Little is known about how, when, where, and why it happened. There was no "big bang" or "revolution,"

Neolithic or otherwise, when the supposed meat-eating diet of "primitive" hunting humans was replaced by a more omnivorous diet of plant foods. Rather it was a gradual change.

Much early thinking revolved around the idea that there were centers of agriculture and domestication, spread widely throughout the world. The idea of multiple hearths was first suggested by Alphonse de Candolle in 1855, who thought that China, southwest Asia (with Egypt), and intertropical America were the main centers of diffusion. Later, in 1922, Nikolai Vavilov enlarged these three regions to eight independent "hearths of domestication" on the basis that these regions had the greatest varietal diversity of crop plants. Since then there have been many refinements of Vavilov's idea and suggestions for additional centers, including the eastern woodlands of North America, New Guinea, parts of West Africa, and parts of India.[3]

The concept of centers of origin of cultivated plants has been remarkably pervasive and long-lasting and has profoundly influenced thinking on the origins and spread of agriculture for well over half a century. However, the concept is now discredited. The pathways to agriculture have been several, and they were often followed independently in geographically separated populations.[4] Consequently, attention has shifted to attempts to understand the social and environmental circumstances that must have led to the transition from hunting, gathering, and collecting societies to those in which the independent adoption of plant cultivation and domestication dominated and then diffused, at different times in different parts of the world.[5]

From the beginning, hominid diet was a mixture of plant and animal sources and resembled that of the other primates. Certain plants were favored around camps, and natural vegetation was disturbed, enriched, and selected, which encouraged the coevolution of species. A symbiosis developed between the food requirements of humans and the ecological needs of plants so that food plants seemed to grow naturally and miraculously around human habitations.

Hybrids thrived in niches created by dump heaps (or middens) and on open cleared land, where the "natural" successional process was disturbed and competition reduced. Humans were attracted to plants that served their needs, and while gathering them, some individual plants that had poor dispersal mechanisms, such as pods that did not open at maturity and would not have survived in the wild, were also collected. Some of these were subsequently planted and gave rise to crops, such as pea and beans, whose seeds could be efficiently harvested. Gathering changed imperceptibly into planting, sowing, transplanting, weeding, and harvesting (although they probably were coexistent and not sequential), and the first stages in the development of agriculture occurred. These involved the colonization of plants that were useful—in other words, an ecological adaptation—even toleration—to "open" situations and to disturbed or unstable habitats of bare soil with few competitors.

An important factor in the domestication process was defecation. The seeds of sweet corn, tomatoes, lemons, cucumbers, and many more edible plants, as well as the fruits of shrubs and trees, can pass intact through human and animal guts (their reproductive vigor may even be enhanced), to be subsequently dispersed and reproduced. In the case of humans, the peripheral latrine areas common to virtually all societies would become new gardens in time.

In time, incidental domestication caused by the unconscious coevolutionary relationship between humans and plants gave way to a specialized domestication, in which humans directly interacted with useful food plants by either aiding dispersal or destroying unwanted plants (weeds), finally culminating in full agricultural domestication, in which conscious actions like plant selection, forest clearing, weeding, and irrigation favored food plants. The greater the size of the population, the greater its effectiveness as a modifying and dispersal agent.

Large-scale agricultural clearing not only altered and often degraded ecosystems but also led to a new system of land management. There was a typical sequence. Clearing, burning, and the break-up of the soil led in time to a simplified and unstable ecosystem that required more human energy to maintain fertility, check erosion, and combat disease. If the ground was then abandoned temporarily, a new successional cycle of regenerated vegetation would arise that would be subtly altered from their "natural" pattern. But if the ground was overexploited, the ecosystem would be degraded and changed irreversibly.

All this says nothing about the process and timing of domestication. Far from there being a single, simple path of progression from hunter-gather to sedentary agriculturalist, there were many pathways. One suggestion by MacNeish is of multiple, parallel and chronologically staggered paths of evolution (fig 3.2).[6] For example, starting from hunting-collecting bands (system A) in stage 1 at the top of the diagram, it is possible to reach the ultimate stage 3 of the agricultural villager (system E), through the transitional stage 2, via a variety of different and even crisscrossing routes (1–17) and their associated different intermediate systems. For example, horticultural villagers (system C2) and efficient foraging bands (system D) are just two possible intermediate systems along the routes of development. MacNeish's schema recognizes the possibility that a forest

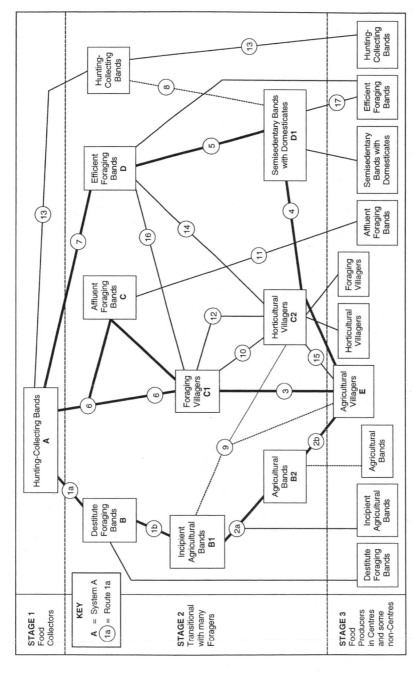

Figure 3.2 Possible routes of development from hunting-collecting to other systems. (Source: after R. S. MacNeish, *The Origins of Agriculture and Settled Life* [Norman: University of Oklahoma Press, 1992].)

foraging economy can exist in a number of different guises and can coexist with, or lead to, an agricultural economy. However, useful as this diagram is in illustrating the complexity of the process it is probably a gross simplification.

What we do know is that the process of plant domestication has taken a long time and has been gradual; there have been multiple origins and multiple paths of change; parallelism of farming innovation was not accompanied by simultaneous development; and cultural/economic change is not in synchrony with chronological change the world over. Domestication was the beginning of agriculture and settled life. Next to the control of fire it was the start of the second great cultural revolution in human affairs and the prelude to the first great attack on the forests. Accordingly, attention is now focused on the agricultural impacts on three major forest environments, Europe, Mesoamerica, and eastern North America.

THE NEOLITHICS AND FOREST CLEARING

While the Mesolithic foragers in Europe were successfully manipulating the thickening forest during the warm, moist Atlantic period, the agricultural innovations of the "Neolithic" farmers were emerging many thousands of miles away. From a core in the Middle East the agriculturalists spread gradually, at an average movement of 1 km/year, first into Anatolia and Greece, between 7000 and 6000 BC, and then in spurts and halts into forested central and western Europe after circa 5600–5500 BC.

The penetration of these first farmers westward is best understood by dividing it into two phases, the "primary" and "consequent," divided largely on the basis of distinctive pottery. The "primary Neolithic" ran from about 5500–4400 BC, the farmers being known as the Linear Pottery Culture (*Linearbandkeramik*) because of the distinctive simple, round ceramics decorated with incised and later punched linear, ribbon-like ornamentation. They were followed between circa 4400–3300 BC by the "consequent Neolithic," or Funnel Beaker Culture (*Trichterrandbecher*) farmers, so called because of their distinctive pottery, which featured a flared rim (fig. 3.3). Another route of western movement was via the Mediterranean fringe lands and is distinguished by Cardinal ware pottery.

Initially, the primary Neolithics were labeled "primitive agriculturalists" and therefore, it was thought, must have practiced "primitive agriculture," that is, slash-and-burn clearing, which periodically exhausted the soil. This encouraged them to keep moving on and provided the momentum for the overall movement. The general hypothesis was supported by the influential

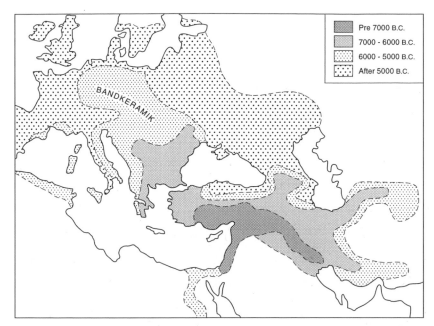

▨	Pre 7000 B.C.
▦	7000 - 6000 B.C.
⠿	6000 - 5000 B.C.
⠄⠄⠄	After 5000 B.C.

BANDKERAMIK

Figure 3.3 The spread of agriculture/settlement in Europe and western Asia during the early Holocene. (Source: after A. G. Sherratt, "The Beginnings of Agriculture in the Middle East and Europe," in *The Cambridge Encyclopeadia of Archaeology,* ed. A. G. Sherratt [Cambridge: Cambridge University Press, 1980], 102–11, esp. 108.)

archeologist Grahame Clark, who stated categorically that among the earliest farmers there could be

> no question of initiating systematic, permanent clearance and the formation
> of settled fields. Their approach was tentative and their agriculture extensive.
> Patches of forest would have been cleared, sown, cropped, and after a season
> or two allowed to revert to the wild, while the farmers took in a new tract.[7]

Pollen profiles of indicator species interbedded with charcoal from Denmark, part of the Iversen's classic *landnam* example—literally, "taking of land," or shifting cultivation—and the later vogue of the Boserupian thesis that intensification of agrarian systems came with population pressure, bolstered the hypothesis factually and intellectually. It was not until the late 1970s that the *landnam* theory was challenged by new discoveries in archaeology, so that what Jarman has called "prehistoric man as *Homo ignoramus* has . . . been gradually eroded."[8] The truth is that Neolithic agriculture/settlement was far more sedentary and stable than once thought, with lasting effects on the forests.

Primary Neolithic Settlement, circa 5500–4500 BC

First settled were the glacially derived, well-drained, windblown, fine soils—the loess—which spread in a broad but intermittent band across the northern and central parts of the continent, with a large outlier in the Hungarian Basin. This is contrary to the earlier idea that the loess was not open and steppelike but heavily wooded with a mixed deciduous forest of mainly oak mixed with lime and beech. The loessic soils were overwhelmingly favored because of their fertility (66–85 percent of all settlements), especially on gently shelving sites near floodplain edges where soils were mixed and water supply assured. The dense floodplain timber cover was chopped down with flint and polished stone axes, which modern experiments show were quite efficient. All but the most desirable timber, which would be reserved for the construction of buildings and palisades, would, presumably, have been burned in situ, the addition to the soil of ash and residual nutrients being a positive advantage to cultivation. Periodic slash-and-burn clearing in the surrounding forests would have provided browse, and even land for an occasional crop.

Typically, settlements consisted of substantial timber-framed and -clad longhouses, about 6 m wide and 8 m–50 m long, occupied by both humans and animals. The farmstead houses were clustered in groups of between 10 and 40 or 50, sometimes surrounded by a ditch, bank, and even palisade, surrounded in turn by intensively cultivated gardens or fields of wheat, with lesser amounts of barley, peas, lentils, and flax, and by meadows. It was not until the 1970s that the significance of these longhouses was appreciated; some had been occupied continuously for several hundred if not a thousand years, a stability and longevity that makes the ancient slash-and-burn hypothesis unlikely.

The evidence of mixed farming and sustained crop yields bolsters the idea of stability. The common assumption has been that the Neolithics could not clear enough forest to grow the grain they needed and that yields were only possible with constant movement to new ground (*landnam*). However, any shortfalls in diet and fertility were made up by a greater reliance on stock than has hitherto been thought possible. In particular, large numbers of cattle provided meat, milk, blood, cheese, and even yogurt, and sheep were also present, as well as some pigs. Meat is an obvious enough product, but dairy products are not, and they constituted what Andrew Sherratt has called the "secondary products revolution," milk being an advantageous way of enriching diet and rectifying vitamin deficiencies and of using the rich pasture grasses that colonized abandoned fields in this humid environment. Compared to cattle reared solely for meat, those reared for milk give four to five times the amount of protein and energy.[9] Cattle numbers were far greater than thought because the reproductive dynamics of domesticated herds show that in order to have sufficient breeding stock to make it economically feasible to extract milk and meat products, have some working beasts, and ensure reproduction, herds of between 30 and 50 cattle would have been necessary. The implications of such large herds for forest alteration through clearance, grazing, browsing, and trampling are enormous.

As for crop yields, experiments have shown that continuous cropping on loess and deep humus- and nutrient-rich soils was possible with only a slight reduction in yields over long periods. Additionally, if cereal crops were alternated with legumes and/or mingled with stock then permanent cropping was possible. The fertilizing effects of the nutrient-rich autumn river floods were also a bonus.

Consequent Neolithic Settlement, 4400–3300 BC

For at least another thousand years, the later Neolithic farmers and stockherders (the Funnel Beaker Pottery, or *Trichterrandbecher* culture) consolidated and intensified settlement on the loess, but now also spread farther west and north onto the glacially derived outwash of lighter silts and sands (giving heathland), and heavy, sticky, so-called boulder clays of the North European Plain, Scandinavia and the British Isles. The clays were covered by a far denser canopy of oak, lime, and beech forest than the loess to the south. Perhaps for the first time anywhere in the world, oxen and horses were used to aid traction by pulling primitive plows in these hard-to-cultivate soils. Plowing increased fertility by aiding soil aeration and allowing the incorporation of organic elements into the tilth (wool sheep were important in this), leading to greater intensification of production. More important, human labor was now augmented by a factor of up to four or five by animal power, and previously arduous tasks could be contemplated. Prime timbers could be selected and dragged or "skidded" out of the forest, but most significant, settlers could tackle the heavier, forested soils.

Clearing meant the development of axes. From about 4000 BC onward, the simple, wedgelike, stone "shoe-last adzes" of the primary Neolithic were being replaced by a true ax technology in flint and polished stone. The mining of ax flints became common across northern, forested Europe, with an output of over 400,000 ax heads annually. The flint of Grand Pressigny, France, is found throughout the previously wooded areas of that country. The mines at Krzemionki, the largest of the Polish mining centers, are even more instructive (fig. 3.4). Finds for the period between 4000 and 3400 BC spread over 100 km; those between 3400 and 2800 BC spread over 800 km.

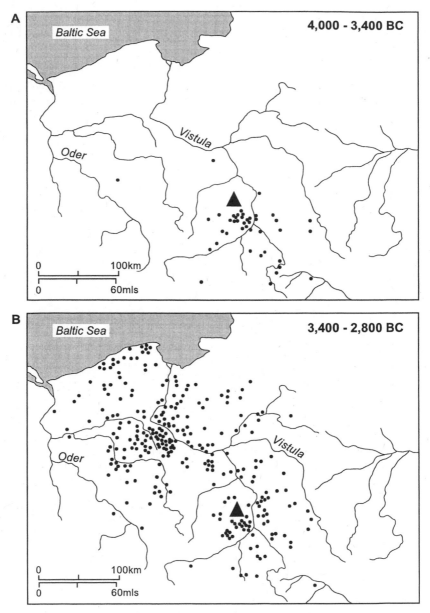

Figure 3.4 Distribution of axes of banded flint in Poland, around the mining center of Krzemionki Opatowskie. *A*, in the *Trichterrandbecher* period (4000–3400 BC); and *B*, in the Globular Amphora period (3400–2800 BC). (Source: after A. G. Sherratt, "Wool, Wheels and Ploughmarks: Local Developments or Outside Introductions in Neolithic Europe?" *Bulletin of London University Institute of Archaeology* 23 [1986]: 9.)

This expansion is a measure of the value and utility of the high-quality flints and gives evidence of the new scale of the attack on the forests from the mid-fourth millennium onward.

Put together, the evidence for Neolithic occupation over the space of some 2,500 years is of a more stable, sedentary society and diversified economy than thought up to now, a society that must have made intensive use of the predominant deciduous forest cover and its many resources. Susan Gregg has simulated the optimal farming strategies to arrive at the needs and management of risks in a hypothetical village settlement.[10] In her model, woodland is placed in a prime position. A typical six-household, 30-person village settlement would have needed to plant 13.2 ha of wheat and run a 40-head herd of cattle with 40 sheep or goats. The settlement would require 4.5 ha for houses, outbuildings, and garden plots, a wood-lot of 52.8 ha, with a further 4.8 ha for timber for construction purposes. The livestock would need 18.18 ha of pasture land (cleared forest?), 19.66 ha of natural meadows, and 2.56 km^2 for forest browse, which could be doubled to guard against overgrazing the forest in a fixed-location settlement (fig. 3.5). Thus, each group of 30 persons needed a little over 6 km^2 of woodland to survive, a staggering 20 ha per person. Even if this calculation is even only half correct, the impact on the early European forest must have been enormous. One must concur with P. I. Bogucki that the first farmers in Europe were "one of the most striking archaeological manifestations of later prehistory" because of the richness of their ceramic decoration, their technical achievements in building longhouses, their introduction of a new, mixed farming economy based on introduced plants and animals, and their destruction of their forested environment.[11]

"FROM PREDATION TO PRODUCTION": MESOAMERICA AND SOUTH AMERICA

The intertropical America was a rich source of unique plants, including maize, potatoes, manioc/cassava, a variety of beans, squash/pumpkins, chili peppers, vanilla, sunflower, sweet potato, avocado, coca, pineapple, tomato, cacao, tobacco, and cotton. In contrast with this wealth of edible plants, there were few domesticated animals; only dogs (for food), muscovy duck, the turkey, some guinea pigs, and, in the central high Andes, the camelids— the llama, the alpaca, and their wild relatives, the guanaco and vicuna. Thus, the complex interaction between livestock and crops that was the basis of mixed farming in the Old World was absent in the new. Everywhere, the ubiquitous starchy maize was the main food, diet being modified and balanced by high-protein beans.

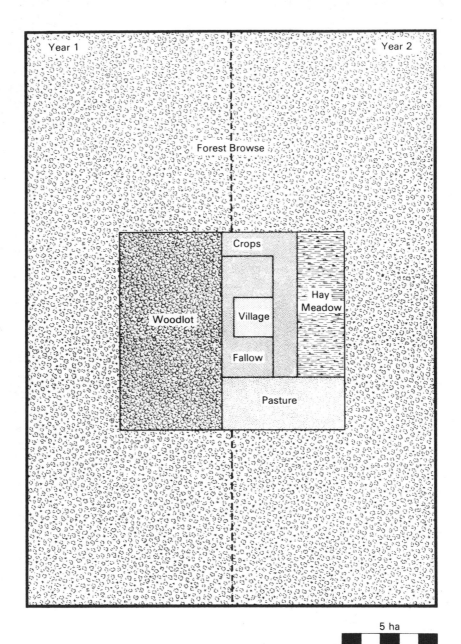

5 ha

Figure 3.5 A hypothetical Neolithic village settlement in the forest and its timber needs.
(Source: based on S. Gregg, *Foragers and Farmers: Population Interaction and Agricultural Expansion in Prehistoric Europe* [Chicago: University of Chicago Press, 1988], 165.)

Another clear difference from the Old World was the fact that the barriers of rugged mountains, deserts, and swamps created separated subcenters of domestication (and hence great biological and cultural diversity) in the Andes, in the semiarid intermontane valleys of central Mexico, and possibly the eastern woodlands of North America. It took thousands of years for foraging communities to become agricultural communities, the arbitrary figure of a 50 percent contribution from farming being used as a marker of what one writer called the shift from "predation to production." [12]

Foraging for cactus fruits, wild cereals, mice, lizards, snakes, and grasshoppers gave way to the selection of the larger and more productive cultigens, like chili, manioc, beans, and particularly maize, accompanied by sophisticated irrigation, terracing, and draining systems. In 3800 BC, cultivated maize produced no more calories than wild mesquite, but by 2000 BC a critical threshold of circa 200 km/ha was reached, and from then on it became possible for greater population densities to be supported, leading to village living, pottery making, and vegetation change. Cultivation gradually crept up the valley sides, and oak and pine forests were cleared. Chili, avocado, and runner beans appeared as subsidiary crops, and these were followed by lowland plants like squash, manioc, and sieva beans.

Of all the subcenters, two of the most outstanding were those of the Aztec and associated civilizations in Highland Mexico and the Maya in the Gulf lowlands of Yucatan and Guatemala.

Highland Mexico

The sophisticated Aztec and associated civilizations that the Europeans encountered circa 1520 were based on the gradual development of intensive agriculture during the Preclassic and Classic eras (circa 1000 BC–AD 300, and AD 300–900, respectively). The achievements of hieroglyphic writing, calendars, monumental architecture, and complex irrigation and draining systems made them among the world's highest civilizations. But they were also hierarchical societies in which priestly elites were supported by political structures that oppressed the masses and wrung the most out of the land. On the eve of the conquest, central Mexico was a network of agricultural systems that supported possibly 17 million people or more.

It was the increasing tendency to cultivate crops intensively on high-rainfall steep forested slopes, with resultant degradation, that gives us some of the clearest indications of the onset of deforestation, which is almost complete in the central valley of Mexico today. Agricultural deforestation was exacerbated by the prolific use of wood in everyday life.

One group that we know a lot about is the Tarascan or Purépecha culture, which had settled around the basin of Lake Pátzcuaro, some 200 mi west of Mexico City for about 3,000 years. The sixteenth-century chronicle *Relación de Michoacán* reveals that the Purépecha made prolific use of wood for constructing temples and houses, keeping warm, smelting metals, woodworking, and burning it in large fires for religious ceremonial occasions. Fire was interwoven into their cultural and religious lives, and they were made to gather firewood to keep alight "huge bonfires" in the houses of priests "until their backs were rubbed sore," on pain of death.[13] This was not unusual: the neighboring Tenochtitlan were much the same and kept ceremonial fires burning perpetually, often for human sacrifices. In a word, wood was an essential commodity that entered every aspect of the religious and practical everyday life of native Mesoamericans.

The environmental outcome of timber stripping was shortages and soil erosion. One example must stand for many. The already mentioned Lake Pátzcuaro basin lies about 2,036 m above sea level and is girdled by mountains. It is typical of the lake basins of intermontane Mexico. The average annual rate of sedimentation is about 3,700 t/yr–4,400 t/yr. But ^{14}C dating shows that this had been exceeded three times in the past. First, when maize began to be cultivated between 3640 and 2890 BP, it rose to 5,100 t/yr. With agricultural extension and intensification during the next millennium it rose to 10,300 t/yr, and then to a staggering 29,000 t/yr between circa 900 and 850 BP with the arrival of the Purépecha people, when agriculture and the cult of fire were reaching their peak.[14] Deforestation in the highlands was so severe that Montezuma II, the last Aztec monarch, prohibited woodcutting in a large area near San Bartolomé Coatepec. Some archaeologists think that the environmental equilibrium was so upset in Aztec society that it was already on the verge of collapse on the eve of the European encounter.

Erosion was widespread and can be traced today by the distribution of *tepetate,* an indurate, substrate, caliche-like formation exposed by sheet wash, which is the result of intensive cultivation and overuse in marginal land. In Teotlalpan, north of the valley of Mexico, *tepetate* was first exposed during periods of intensive hill slope cultivation between 800 and 200 BC, reaching a peak during the fifteenth and sixteenth centuries as population densities increased. Of course, the introduction of livestock during later Hispanic times accelerated erosion; but in some parts of the plateau the Spaniards found the land so depleted that grazing was the only form of land use possible. The implication is that the worst devastation had occurred before the arrival of the Europeans and grazing was a consequence rather than a cause of land denudation, but this is all a hotly disputed issue.

Whatever the true sequence of events, *La leyenda negra*—the Black Legend of the Spanish Conquest—is too readily evoked to explain environmental degradation in the continent and is often juxtaposed against what may be called *La leyenda verde*—the Green Legend—which mythologizes the environmental harmony of Amerindian cultures with their environment. Like agricultural societies everywhere they manipulated their land and it suffered as a consequence.

Lowland South American Forests

In lowland South America, especially Amazonia, it is unlikely that present-day food producing systems and strategies are of great antiquity and, therefore, are not representative of past conditions, which were simpler and less sophisticated. The present-day shifting agriculture that seems so ideally adapted to the environment with its minimal clearing, small plots, short cropping periods, long fallows, and intricate shade arrangements, together with low population densities and small temporary settlements, may well be no more than a modern innovation that reflects what the anthropologist, Alfred Métraux called "the revolution of the ax." [15]

It is probable that metal axes did not replace stone axes until well after the conquest. When they did, clearing efficiency may have been increased tenfold, or more, and a return to the Stone Age was impossible. Prior to that, clearing was probably too labor intensive to be common or frequent, and groups were more likely to have been foragers than farmers. Indeed, the prehistoric Indians of Amazonia were located predominantly in the resource-rich floodplains and adjacent uplands. Present-day Indians, in contrast, are located mainly in the *terre firme* high forests of the interfluves, where resources of soils, game, and fish are relatively poor.

The Gulf Lowlands

In the tropical forested environment of the warm, well-watered Gulf lowlands and swamps of Yucatan, Guatemala, and Belize, complex, agricultural societies of great antiquity flourished. The Olmec culture grew from about 1200 to 600 BC, to be superceded by the Classic Maya civilization, around centers such as Tikal, Bonampak, and Altar de Sacrificios. It covered over 75,000 km² and dwarfed the better-known upland cultures in the basin of Mexico, which were about only one-tenth its size. The Maya population rose steadily from approximately 161,000 in 1000 BC to 242,000 in 300 BC, then to just over 1 million in AD 300 to reach a peak of between 2.6 million and 3.4 million (density 117–151 persons per km²) by 800, which is comparable to those of prehistoric Old World tropical societies. Suddenly, in the early ninth century the population collapsed abruptly, dropping from its peak in AD 825 to 536,000 in AD 1000, to a mere 6,800 by 1900. The whole civilization was in disarray.

The striking image of the abandoned ceremonial buildings towering above the carpet of lush green tropical forest has tended to obscure the fact that at one time the entire forest had been removed to support this urban civilization (plate 3.1). Beneath the forest canopy a complex "farm-scape" has been discovered, with thousands of settlements ranging from small courtyard "farms," to grouped farms in hamlets, to large ceremonial sites like Tikal, with over 85 courtyards, ball-playing courts, and hundreds of other buildings. Up until about 300 BC the Maya practiced swidden agriculture, chopping down trees with stone axes or burning dead, girdled trees, setting fire to the refuse, and rotating the cultivation of maize. The remnants of "gardens" with concentrations of "useful" tree species in the middle of the present forest, often surrounded by low, dry stone walls, suggests that a variety of fruits were cultivated too. But because swiddening can rarely support more than 20 persons per km², food supply had to be augmented by the large-scale intensification of more "difficult" lands after AD 300. These consisted of well-drained limestone slopes with shallow soils, easily eroded by the torrential rains of the wet season once cleared; and lowland wooded *bajos* (low areas) and small savannas, which had subsurface clays and therefore were badly drained. The slopes required terraces to prevent erosion, and the lowlands, drainage ditches to be rid of surplus water. Consequently, tens of thousands of relic terraces covering over 10,000 km² have been discovered under the forest around the southeastern periphery of the lowlands. Together with these, over 120 km² of lattice-like patterns of ditches surrounding raised dirt platforms on which intensive cultivation and even double cropping could have been practiced have been detected under the forest on the eastern and northeastern periphery. These "raised fields" are similar to the more famous *chinampa* of the Basin of Mexico. To these sophisticated agro-engineering works can be added many more thousands of square kilometers of ditch patterns, particularly around Tikal, which have been detected by radar imagery. Both terraces and ditches were extremely labor intensive to make and to maintain, yet without them it is highly doubtful whether the population densities and complexities of Classic Maya culture could have been maintained.

As population increased from circa 1000 BC to AD 800, deforestation increased, soil erosion accelerated, and essential nutrients such as phosphorous were rapidly leached out of the soils of this potentially fragile environment. Productivity must have declined dramatically. Certainly, population

Plate 3.1 The ability of the forest to regenerate when human interference ceases is awesome. Here the tropical forest has completely recolonized the fields, streets, and squares around the Mayan temples at Tikal, abandoned sometime during the ninth century AD. (Tony Morrison, South American Pictures.)

numbers plummeted (fig. 3.6). In neighboring Honduras, the collapse of the Copán Mayan state between AD 850 and 1250 is attributed unequivocally to growing population, agricultural intensification, fuelwood demands, deforestation, soil erosion, and lowering agricultural productivity. But was complete environmental instability enough to explain the dramatic population collapse over most of Yucatan? They were certainly synchronous, but the causal linkages are tenuous. Anyhow, even if environmental overuse did lead to population decline it does not explain why the decline continued in a downward spiral for the next thousand years. Other hypotheses have been put forward, from "big-bang" disasters like warfare, disease, earthquakes, and drought, to more long-term reasons such as revolt and breakdown of the social system or an interactive combination of all these. Almost the complete opposite has even been suggested: that the abandonment of the very labor-intensive agriculture was a consequence of a prior population decline or, possibly, that disruptive sociopolitical forces led to the collapse of the infrastructure, leading to agricultural decay. Either way, however, humans did alter the forests, but in the case of the Maya, for some unknown reason, it was not as permanent as it has been elsewhere in the world.

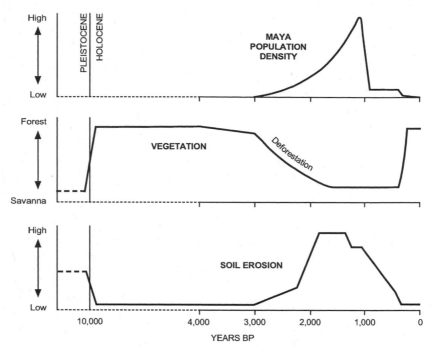

Figure 3.6 Population density, deforestation, and soil erosion associated with long-term Maya settlement on the terrestrial environment of the Peten lowlands, circa 10,000–0 BP. (Source: after E. S. Deevy, D. S. Rice, p. m. Rice, H. H. Vaughan, M. Brenner, and M. S. Flannery. "Mayan Urbanism: Impact on a Tropical Karst Environment," *Science* 206 [1979]: 298–306.)

THE INDIANS AND THE EASTERN NORTH AMERICAN FOREST

There are many physical similarities between the vast forests of eastern North America and Europe, but perhaps one of the greatest commonalities has been to underestimate—even to deny—the human impact of the past. Since the late 1980s the conventional wisdom about the origin and nature of agriculture in the eastern woodlands has undergone a complete revolution. From being the marginal, passive recipient (by some unknown diffusion process) of the three basic domestic crops of maize, beans, and squash from the "nuclear centers" of Meso- and South America after AD 900, the North American forests are now thought to have supported plant domestication for thousands of years.

Three broad settlement episodes can be identified. From at least 5000 BC or earlier, inhabitants of the river bottomlands of the watercourses that traverse the woodland (e.g., the central Mississippi, lower Illinois, Ohio, lower Missouri, Tennessee, and Kentucky and their tributaries) domesticated a series of species including sumpweed or marshelder (*Iva annua*), sunflower (*Helianthus annus*), ragweed (*Ambrosia* spp.), and chenopod (*Chenopodium berlandieri*) and may even have independently developed a species of squash (*Cucurbita pepo*). The river-bottom environments favored a coevolutionary process between humans and plants. The spring floods, constant channel changes, and annual soil enrichment created varied and changing habitats that encouraged adaptation, selection, and domestication. For example, a native American population existed for over 10,000 years in the Little Tennessee River Valley, the amount of vegetation disturbance growing in pace with the population. Pollens of domesticated crops are associated with evidence of clearing, together with lithic remains. The dominant closed structure of forest communities was changed, species were extended, old fields provided open areas for native ruderals to invade, and the amount of nonforest land increased, creating a culturally maintained landscape mosaic. The fields provided a dependable and storable supply of food for the late winter and early spring when fishing, fowling, hunting, and foraging were impossible, the Indians often moving residence with the seasonal shift in resources. Away from the rivers, the use of fire to facilitate hunting and promote the growth of desirable wild plants and herbage was widespread.

Then, between circa 250 BC and AD 200, Hopewellian farming societies emerged as fully fledged food production economies with recognizable village-type settlements. These societies possibly added erect knotweed (*Polygonum erectum*), maygrass (*Phalaris caroliniana*), and little barley (*Hordeum pusillum*) to the four existing domesticated crops. Finally, between circa AD 800 and 1000, corn (*Zea mays*) was imported from the tropical areas. Initially, it was a minor crop in a well-established food regime but suddenly diffused rapidly across the woodland from northern Florida to Ontario, playing a central role in the evolution of complex food-producing societies. The late adoption of maize in circa AD 200, and the six-century lag to the post–AD 800 "takeoff" is a mystery. Contrary to common perceptions, it is doubtful if even the settlements of the spectacular Hopewellian burial-mound cultures of the Middle Woodland times (0–AD 900) practiced extensive agriculture. It may initially have been a controlled ceremonial crop, but it is far more likely that the massive amount of forest clearing needed to grow it, and the maintenance of those clearings, stifled adoption until demographic pressures made the labor-cost-to-food-yield ratio more attractive. Then the forest suffered.

By the time Europeans landed in about 1600, fully fledged agriculture had only dominated as a way of life for perhaps 500 years or less on the eastern seaboard, and possibly a little longer farther inland. But the imprint of agriculture and settled life was unmistakable and locally intensive. Although enormous areas of "natural" forest remained, it was not the vast, silent, unbroken, impenetrable tangle of vegetation inhabited by savages that the romantic writers consistently churned out. Rather, it was a mosaic of fire-altered and humanly selected species in different stages of succession and of clearings and cultivated fields, earthworks, and ditches around villages and houses.

Clearing Methods

Clearing was hard work. Patches were hacked out of the forest and maintained by fire. Small bushes were uprooted and burned, and the bark of larger trees was either bruised or peeled away with stone axes, and the base burned when it had dried out. Occasionally, larger trees were felled with stone axes, but usually they and the bigger stumps were left in the cultivated area to rot. Smaller stumps were prized out with large crooked poles. The availability of fresh water and friable, fertile, well-drained soils were major factors in the location of the typical Indian village. Said one settler: "Wherever we met with an old Indian field, or place where they have lived, we are sure of the best ground." [16] Women broke the soil with digging sticks or light hoes, and a mixture of crops was planted, which always included maize. The plots varied in size from a few square yards to 200 yd^2, and the crops were grown in mounds or sometimes in rows.

Typical villages contained between 50 and 1,500 persons living in loose agglomerations of sturdy, defensible, weatherproof wooden houses, sometimes located roughly along a street, the whole covering between 150 and 600 acres and usually surrounded by a palisade. The Huron and Iroquois, in particular, built complex longhouses and palisades that needed vast supplies of conveniently sized timber. For example, a typical Huron village of about 1,000 people needed 6 acres of land for its 36 longhouses. The longhouses required 16,000 poles of 4 in.–5 in. in diameter and 10 ft–30 ft long, 250 interior posts of 10 in. in diameter and 10 ft–30 ft long, and 162,000 yd^2 of American elm or eastern red cedar bark for covering. The palisade needed 3,600 stakes that were 5 in. in diameter and 15 ft–30 ft long. If the density of settlement was great enough, then clearings merged into one another to make large open areas, but this was unusual unless along a riverfront.

But some settlements were much larger. Cahokia, in the Mississippi bottomland near present-day St. Louis covered 1,680 acres and held a minimum of 10,000 people, and possibly even 25,000. And it was not unique in size among later Mississippian settlements. It was the largest settlement in the United States until it was overtaken by Philadelphia in AD 1800. Approximately 800,000 wall posts were needed for Cahokia's house walls, to say nothing of roofing beams and other constructional timber. The 3-km palisade would have required at least 15,000 logs the size of telegraph poles, and it was rebuilt several times. The land was cultivated up to a radius of 10 km–15 km from the center, and fuel needs were enormous. It is thought that overexploitation of the timber resources of areas surrounding Cahokia led to its gradual collapse between AD 1050 and 1150.

The impact of the Indians on the forest went beyond the zone of cultivation; foraging in the forest continued for fibers, fruits, foods, medicines, and, above all, for firewood (fig. 2.4). Fallen or deadwood was collected mainly by the women, so that it was generally known as "squaw wood." In some groups fuel gathering was of such significance that it was an integral part of ritual activities, such as puberty rites. Consumption was enormous, and in time the search for wood covered an ever-increasing radius—even up to 3 mi—so that it became reasonable to fell trees in close proximity to the village. The older the settlement, the more likely it was that the forest edge had receded well away from the village.

The zone of fuel collection was also the area for foraging for wild fruits (persimmon, wild plums, papaws), berries, leaves, roots, and nuts—particularly acorns, which were consumed in vast quantities, along with chestnuts, pecans, hickory nuts—maple syrup, and medicinal berries like juniper and chokeberry. So important and crucial to dietary needs were these products that it is thought that the unusually high proportion of nut and fruit trees in some localities at present may denote the purposeful promotion of favored species in the past. Also, the natural propagation on nutrient-deficient soil of sun-loving, aggressive colonizing trees like sumac and sassafras, commonly called "old-field trees," is a good indicator of past disturbance in the forest. Beyond the collecting zone and well away from the village lay the area for fire hunting.

The Contemporary Record

The eastern woodlands were not homogeneous. The soils of the fertile river bottoms were far superior to those of the interfluves and uplands. Temperatures varied latitudinally, so that whereas one crop could barely be raised in the North, two could be taken in the South. Thus, the form of agriculture varied, too, and it is misleading to generalize.

There are dozens of contemporary descriptions of Indian villages and clearings from every state in the eastern half of the continent. For example, in Virginia, John Smith described the village of the Pawhatan:

> Their houses are in the midst of their fields or gardens, which are small plots of ground. Some 20 acres, some 40 acres, some 100, some 200, some more, some less. In some places from 20 to 50 of those houses together or but little separated by groves of trees. Near their habitations is little small wood or old trees on the ground by reason of them burning of them by fire.[17]

This description was accompanied by a sketch (plate 3.2) that, although perhaps somewhat diagrammatic in composition, depicts clearly the arrangements in the forest that other accounts substantiate. In 1620 William Strachey described the land around the present site of Hampton, Virginia, as

> ample and faire countrie indeed, an admirable pocion of land, comparatively high, wholesome, and fruietfull; the seat sometyme of a thowsand Indians and three hundred houses, as may well appeare better husbands [farmers] than in any part ells that we have observed which is the reason that so much ground is there cliered and opened, enough already prepared to receive corne and make viniards of two or three towsand acres.[18]

These examples refer only to the Tidewater area of Virginia during the early decades of the seventeenth century, but even in the back country in later years—in the Roanoke Valley and even farther inland—the land was described as "by the industry of these Indians . . . very open and clear of woods." Edward Winslow and Stephen Hopkins, who rode along the banks of the Taunton River in New England 1621, commented on the towns and fields deserted because of the effects of disease. The land "was very good on both sides, it being for the most part cleared. . . . As we passed we observed that there were few places by the river but has been inhabited; by reason whereof much ground was clear, some of the weeds which grew higher than our heads." And so it went on: in the Alleghenies, the valleys of Tennessee and Kentucky, the Ohio River Valley—even as far west as the Maumee River from Fort Wayne to Lake Erie in Indiana, the evidence is abundant. Some fields were mounded, while others had (and still show) ridge and furrow.[19]

Two regions were particularly noteworthy: the Iroquois country in upstate New York, and the Creek country of Alabama. In New York, the village of Genessee near present-day Rochester consisted of 128 houses and was said, in 1779, to be "almost encircled with a cleared flat which extended for

X X.

The Tovvne of Secota.

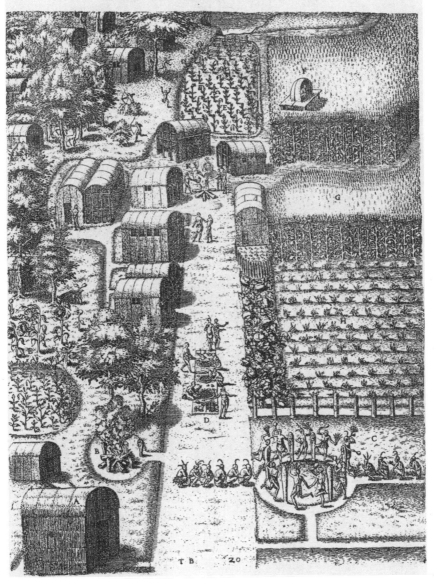

Plate 3.2 The town of Secota, Virginia. The sketch depicts various aspects of life in an actual Indian village. *H (far right center)* denotes corn in various stages of cultivation and maturity; *I (next to the corn)* depicts pumpkins, and in the *top left-hand corner* there is a hunting scene in the forest. (Source: John Smith, *Narrative of the First Plantation in Virginia* [1620], reproduced in Thomas Hariot, *Narrative of the First Plantation in Virginia* [1893]. [State Historical Society of Wisconsin].)

a number of miles covered by the most extensive fields of corn and every kind of vegetable that can be conceived," and there were other towns in the vicinity with fields of over 200 acres. In Georgia the descriptions contained in William Bartram's journal of 1791 and Benjamin Hawkins's *Sketch of the Creek Country* of 1798 are particularly vivid. Hawkins describes in detail the cultivation of 50 towns along the Coosa, Tallapoosa, and Chattahoochee rivers. One had fields extending "one mile and half," another "four miles down the river, from one hundred to two hundred yards wide," another "three thousand acres . . . and one third in cultivation," and so on.[20] The description confirms the claims by the De Soto expedition of 250 years earlier that it had passed through fields of maize, beans, and squash often in "great fields . . . spread out as far as the eye could see across two leagues of the plain." These scenes represented the culmination of a millennium of clearing.

Moving Fields and Settlements

Throughout North America, cultivation and settlement were accompanied by some mobility. Even the most sedentary tribes relied on foraging for a significant part of their diet, frequently causing the surrounding forest resources to be overused or worked out. In cultivated areas, yields declined; and the sheer accumulation of refuse, as well as infestation by weeds and vermin, also made a move desirable. Consequently, large portions of the forest were altered and in different stages of regrowth and succession.

Sometimes the whole settlement was uprooted. One authentic record is that of Onondaga, the capital of the Iroquois League, which was found in nine different locations between 1610 and 1780, or an average life span of close to 20 years at each site. Father Jean de Lamberville wrote in 1682 that the then-recent move had been made by the Iroquois "in order to have nearer to them the convenience of firewood and fields more fertile than those which they abandoned." Again, in the Creek country, Benjamin Hawkins described Tookabatchee on the Tallapoosa River as a town "on the decline. . . . The land is much exhausted with continued culture, and the wood for fuel is at a great and inconvenient distance, unless boats and land carriages were in use."[21]

These moves were not part of a system of shifting cultivation but were merely due to the fact that some settlements became unwieldy and unhealthy and that some fields were not in the most satisfactory location in relation to fuel supplies and continued fertility. Undoubtedly, the introduction and widespread diffusion of the metal ax by the end of the eighteenth century made clearing easier by a factor of possibly as much as 4.4:1 in light woodland, and many times that in dense woodland of large trees. Therefore it became more feasible for the Indians to move more frequently into unused and possibly more fertile areas of the forest.

A Changed and Changing Forest Landscape

Agriculture in eastern North America was widespread and intensive and, coupled with the foraging, firing, and hunting outlined in chapter 2, had a considerable impact on the forest. The aggregate extent of the accumulated modifications and deforestation is difficult to determine accurately, as the patches of clearing and burning were widely scattered and in various stages of regrowth. Also, there is no comprehensive record of the destruction of any considerable part of the pre-European forest to enable a calculation to be made, other than isolated eye-witness reports and the corroborative archeological and physical evidence in, for example, the extensive ridge and furrowed fields of Wisconsin.

On the basis of population numbers and field sizes, the anthropologist Alfred Kroeber suggested that 1 acre of cleared land on fertile soil, with mixed planting and a long growing season, might sustain one person per annum. More recently, Conrad Heidenreich has calculated that the Huron in Ontario needed 6,500 acres of cropland to support 21,000 people, about one-third of an acre per person—but when an extended fallowing cycle is taken into account, the amount of land needed might reach 2.3 acres per person. Thus, if William Denevan's estimate of a preconquest population of 3.8 million for North America is accepted, then about 8.7 million acres of forest would have been affected (and that would not have included abandoned clearings), which is about 3.2 percent of the total of 278.6 million acres of cropland in the easternmost states today. Some people, like Henry Dobyns, put the original population figure much higher, at double or even triple that of Denevan and, if correct, then the impact on the forest would increase proportionately. In his study of Virginia, Hu Maxwell calculated that if all the clearings that were cultivated and abandoned and all other burned areas were aggregated, a "conservative" estimate of treeless land would be between 30 and 40 acres per person, which compares with about 41 acres for Neolithics in forested Europe. Maxwell's speculation that another 500 years of Indian settlement would have reduced the eastern forests to negligible proportions is provocative, though probably exaggerated.[22] Undoubtedly, the greatest modification was in the area of the most frequent burning in the prairie, so that the grasslands together with the changed composition of the forests may have been the greatest and most enduring ecological, and even cultural, contribution of the Native Americans to the continent as a whole.

But speculation aside, the first farmers in North America were a potent, if not crucial, ecological factor in the distribution and composition of this major forest area; and by 1600 the eastern woodlands were a changed and changing forest landscape. The Indians' farming and associated foraging activities make the concept of "natural vegetation" a difficult one to uphold. This does not mean that there was no untouched forest, or even fluctuations of climate; but the idea of the forest as being in some pristine state of equilibrium with nature, awaiting the arrival of the transforming hand of the European settler, has been all too readily accepted as a comforting generalization and as a benchmark against which to measure all subsequent change. When the Europeans came to North America, the forest had already been changed radically. Their coming did not alter the processes at work; it was merely their superior numbers and advanced technology that accomplished that. Paradoxically, initially their arrival may have been instrumental in causing the forests to grow more rapidly and extensively than before. The waves of disease that accompanied and then preceded the Europeans wiped out the Indians, and subsequent fire control and suppression would have limited damage. The forest of 1750 was probably thicker and more extensive than the forest had been at any time for the previous thousand years.

THE REST OF THE WORLD

Space does not permit a detailed account of the impact of the first farmers in other parts of the world, and indeed, our understanding and knowledge of other regions is less well developed. For example, in the Far East the sequence of development leading to rice cultivation is not clear. In China, north of the big bend in the Yellow River, remains of domesticated pigs and dogs and wild plants have been found there that range from 6000 to 4000 BC. By 3000 BC slash-and-burn agriculture was present in central China, but the sequence whereby villages emerged and the way in which vegetation was affected is far from clear. The best evidence in the region comes from the peripheral area of Japan, where, like Europe and eastern North America, collecting and harvesting bands made great use of the extensive resources of the lush coastal lowlands that provided food in all seasons, the process being supplemented by the repeated introduction of cultivars and domesticates from China. Again, until the research is done in detail one can only suppose that the forest vegetation was first affected by fire, foraging, and slash-and-burn techniques until horticultural villages were established.

The story can be taken a little further. By the middle of the last millennium BC, southern and eastern Asia in particular displayed a flowering of civilizations in temperate and tropical forested areas. These defy easy summary but mention must be made of, for example, the growth of the Han Empire in China (which spread into Korea and Japan) and later empires in Cambodia (Angkor Wat), Thailand, Burma (Pagan), and Java. China flourished from about 600 BC into one of the most complex, innovative, and technologically proficient societies of the time; and although we know very little about its impact on the forest, it must have been great, if only through the demands for fuel for smelting and warmth, timber use in house construction, and agricultural clearing. It is a story yet to be told.

In contrast, the full flowering of civilization in the forested lands of Southeast Asia was neither early nor rapid. However, the region was well populated by 1000 BC and possessed advanced bronze and iron metal-working skills and developed agricultural systems. But its most spectacular achievements were in city building and monumental architecture, which in size and number equaled the splendors of Egypt and even Rome. These urban centers did not emerge until much later, after AD 500, and must have been based on efficient and intensive food production for rice surpluses in nearby locations. But no record has been revealed yet that allows us even to begin to unravel the impact of these civilizations on the forest. One thing we know is that in Angkor Wat, just as in Yucatan, once the maintenance of clearings for cultivation were abandoned, the forest reasserted itself and recolonized the urban areas, which were rediscovered only during the mid-nineteenth century.

In conclusion, then, two points can be made. First, for at least the last 7,000 years, and possibly twice that time in tropical areas, the forests of the world have been cleared, thinned, or altered by humans in their search for food, shelter, and warmth. Second, while the fact that the first farmers transformed the forest is incontrovertible, it is certainly almost totally unrecorded in detail, so the extent of clearing can only be guessed at. But without a doubt it was immense. It was the first great impact of humans on the face of the earth.

Chapter 4

The Classical World

Clever beyond all dreams . . .
—SOPHOCLES, Antigone

IT IS misleading to make a division between the prehistoric world of the first farmers in Europe and the "classical" world of Greece and Rome, as at an early point they were one and the same thing—the late Neolithic or Early Bronze Age, in cultural terms. In the lightly wooded lowlands around the Mediterranean, small-scale horticultural communities had been established since early Neolithic times (e.g., 6000 BC). Cereals and pulses were grown, crops were rotated and manured, and sheep, cattle, and pigs were integrated into the economy. Nut and fruit trees were selected, especially the fig, olive, and vine. Nevertheless, this has been canonized as the "classical" era and area, and it holds a special place in Western culture that is difficult to ignore. But it is more than a case of historical labels alone: the changes around the Mediterranean rim were extensive and distinctive enough to warrant separate consideration.

The 1,500 years of the Hellenistic and Roman periods, from about 1100 BC to the onset of the Byzantine age, circa AD 565, was an era of growing population, rapid urbanization, and burgeoning trade that moved large sections of the population up from a state of subsistence to one of exchange/consumption and brought a higher standard of technical civilization to all classes. Whereas the Mediterranean was effectively "prehistoric," in 1000 BC it was definitely "historic" by 500 BC. By then we can see not only the development of sophisticated technology (e.g. shipbuilding, irrigation, draining, aqueduct construction) but also the flowering of thought and action that affected attitudes to resources and nature. It was like a prologue to the modern age.

Iron replaced copper and bronze in agricultural implements, and the iron-tipped plow enabled the heavy and frequently densely timbered, but fertile, soils to be cultivated. The Greek polis, or city-state, emerged as a new unit of urban form and governance, and Greek and Phoenician shipbuilding reached new technical heights to enable extensive trade across the basin. After 300 BC, learning flourished—reason, logic, mathematics, and analysis of cause and effect ran side by side with more mundane but important things like capital accumulation, investment, and industry. Urban workshops, the division of labor, the use of silver as a medium of exchange, together with land improvement through manuring, irrigation, draining, special seeds, and animal husbandry, expanded the economy, and slavery, long a part of Greek society, flourished.

Greece expanded throughout the eastern Mediterranean and Asia Minor, as far east as the Ganges in India and the coast of East Africa, and later, Rome expanded westward into Spain, North Africa, the central and northern Balkan peninsula, and Gaul (France). Everywhere, investment in agriculture reached new heights, and colonization of new land and its subdivision by centuriation were widespread. Roads, docks, harbors, markets, aqueducts, and dwellings of all sorts abounded, while mills, olive presses, and irrigation works expanded agricultural production.

Land was the main source of wealth, prestige, and political power in the Roman world and farming was increasingly organized into large slave-operated estates, usually to the detriment of the small-scale, self-sufficient Italian peasant farmers. The forests were under siege. To safeguard this valuable and strategic resource, the state assumed ownership of them.

While expansion supported the pomp of imperial Rome, the seeds of decline were also evident by the turn of the Christian millennium. Urban dwelling declined, agriculture was neglected, and the supply of coinage could not keep pace with the expansion of new territories. The large slave-operated estates became inefficient with the gradual disintegration of slavery, and they tended to be replaced again by smaller, self-sufficient holdings, best described as peasant operated. These new operators absorbed and adopted the technical know-how, village craftsmanship, and use of a wide variety of agricultural tools, plants, and domesticated animals to create a revolution in village life and village production, thereby laying the agricultural foundations for the energetic medieval civilizations that were to come later in the Western, Russian, and Islamic worlds.

Besides its sheer modernity, the later classical world had a number of distinctive qualities that distinguished it from anything that had gone before. It was a literate world in which, for the first time, people recorded what they saw and what they did and linked that to a conscious, known past. Perhaps even more important, they recorded what they thought and conjectured about those scenes and actions. We do not have to rely on archeology or the inferences drawn from pollen diagrams, useful as these often are, in order to understand what was happening but can turn to the works of, for example, Homer, Strabo, Theophrastus, Cicero, Varro, Columella, Pliny, and others, which are full of clues about the forests, their habitats, and their utilization, though much is still left to conjecture.

A second distinctive feature of the classical world was people's consciousness of their power to control and even create nature, despite a strong belief that humans were a part of some larger, divine plan or purpose. Metallurgy, mining, building, trade, and, above all, agriculture and the domestication of animals changed the world. These changes were not an application of any theoretical science or profound wisdom but were the simple evidence of how the occupations, crafts, and skills of everyday life made changes possible, as well as ensuring a more orderly accessibility to the things humans needed.

The Greeks, in everyday action and in their mythology, began to think of humans as tidying-up nature and even, as it were, finishing creation. Above all, it was the busyness and incessant restlessness of practical people like the artisan, the farmer, and the trader that created order and stability by dominating the environment and changing nature. Through their inventiveness and energy, humans had become, as Sophocles said, "clever beyond all dreams." [1] The evidence of that cleverness and its consequences were perhaps displayed clearly in the intensely humanized and distinctive landscape of the Mediterranean basin. It was already an old and altered landscape by the time the Greeks were writing about what they saw.

THE MEDITERRANEAN ENVIRONMENT

The Mediterranean has a distinctive climate of marked wet winters and little rain during the summer months—even drought—which makes fire a constant natural hazard. As a result of this rainfall seasonality, the forest is sparse and open, and once cleared it shows less regenerative powers than do the forests to the north, except on wet, western-facing locations.

Undoubtedly, the broken topography of peninsula, island, lowland, and intervening upland has promoted variety: there are over 40 major tree species and at least 50 subvarieties, compared to 12 and 20, respectively, in the denser forests of central and western Europe. The lowland forests are evergreen pines and oaks, and northward they contain more deciduous oaks and beech, elm, and chestnut as these grade into the dense deciduous forests of central and western Europe. Southward vegetation becomes crooked, hard, and thorny, with spiny shrubs and steppe. Everywhere altitude has a marked effect on forest composition. In the Pyrenees, Apennines, and Balkan and Turkish mountains, trees grade vertically into denser stands, with evergreen, oak, beech, elm, and chestnut on the lower slopes (circa 2,000 ft), deciduous oak and sweet chestnut up to 4000 ft, and then fir and black pine on the upper slopes, culminating in prized timber like cedar on the crests of mountains in Cyprus, Lebanon, Syria, and North Africa.

Frequent violent storms caused soil erosion; exposed soils were leached and rapidly accompanied by gullying. Consequently, the heavy valley alluvium used for cultivation was not available until recently, and the lighter soils elsewhere must have once been better structured and more fertile in the past. Little is known about the distribution of the early forest, but figure 4.1 is probably a fair approximation of the dense stands. Suffice it to say that by the time of Homer in the eighth century BC, forest was still dense and abundant, especially on the upper slopes, which always caught the poetic and literary attention of the classical writers. It was not until Theophrastus (370–250 BC), a pupil of Plato and Aristotle, published his De historia plantarum, or The Enquiry into Plants (313 BC), that any systematic attempt was made to classify both wild and cultivated trees, their habitats, and characteristics. Theophrastus was struck by the importance of habitat on the type and quality of trees: "Some belong more to the mountains, some to the plains. And on the mountains themselves, in proportion to the height some grow fairer and more vigorous in the lower regions, some about the peaks." However, wherever they grew, provided they were on a northerly aspect, their wood was "closer, more compact, and better generally." Thus it seemed clear to him that "each tree seeks an appropriate position and climate," as particular districts "bear some trees but not others." In general, locality was more important than cultivation and care. For this consistent questioning of the relationship between a plant species and its total environment he used the word oikeios, the root of our modern word ecology. Armed with this generalization he then described the forests of the mountains of Lebanon and Taurus, the ranges of Asia Minor, the Macedonian highlands, many parts of Greece, western Crete, southern Italy, and finally of Corsica, which surpassed them all in terms of quality and thickness. De historia plantarum was probably the beginning of forest science and even of ecology.[2]

In contrast to this almost theoretical enquiry into the nature of the distribution of trees, stands were discussed only with reference to human use. This anthropomorphic view complemented the belief that humans could change and control nature; use and control went hand in hand. Thus, the focus on the mountain areas is explicable because they produced the best

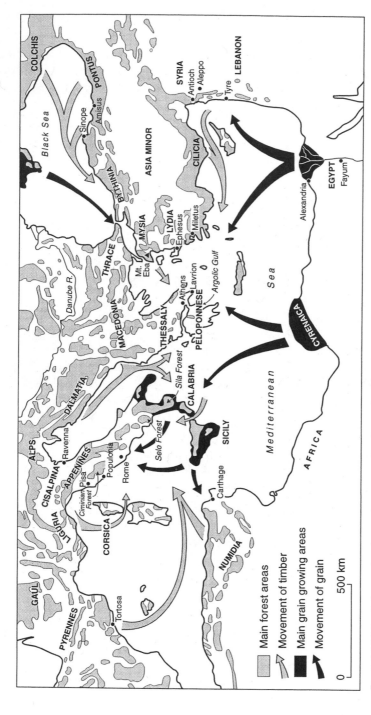

Figure 4.1 Major timber- and grain-growing areas and trade routes in the Mediterranean basin, fourth through first centuries BC. (Source: after M. M. Lombard, "Une carte du bois la Méditerranée musulmane [VIIe–XIe siècle]," *Annales, Economies, Sociétés, Civilisations* 14 [1959]: 23–54; and A. G. Sherratt and S. Sherratt, "The Growth of the Mediterranean Economy in the Early First Millennium BC," *World Archaeology* 24 [1993]: 361–78.)

timber for shipbuilding and construction. Starbo's second-century *Geography* provides further descriptions of the forests, but again, forests were of little interest unless they had economic value.

THE CAUSES OF DEFORESTATION

The forests were a prime resource as scores of expanding city-states of the Hellenistic world struggled to be self-sufficient, solvent, and powerful by gaining control over surrounding resources, expanding agriculture, and engaging in sea trade, which inevitably meant building ships. First Carthage and then Rome, capital of perhaps the greatest and most powerful empire seen up to that time, was doing on a grand scale what the small city-states had done centuries before. Given the central importance of trees in early human existence for warmth, shelter, construction, and agricultural land, it should be no surprise that each activity was a step on the road to forest clearing and in unison led to deforestation.

Cultivation and Grazing
The Mediterranean Basin

Clearing land to grow food was the primary cause of change in the forests. But, as ever, the clearing part of farming was ignored by contemporary commentators; it was a negative, destructive process, subsumed in the simple, obvious, everyday, essential process of getting food. Part of the silence may be due to the fact that on the large estates clearing was done by slaves, and there was nothing heroic in forced, slave labor. Contemporary commentators made observations on manuring, crop introductions, crop rotations, yields, and tree growing and grafting but rarely on getting rid of the trees. Consequently, we know little about it, to such an extent that one might think that shipbuilding, fuel gathering, house construction, or even forest fires were the main causes of forest denudation.

And yet, clearing for cultivation must have gone on everywhere. Homer likened tree-felling to the noise of battle, and in later centuries, the image of the industrious plowman, who "subdues his woodland with flames and plough" and who "carted off the timber he has felled," was common enough. When the chorus in Sophocles' Antigone wanted to exalt the power of Man they praised his success on the seas through navigation and on land through hunting, plant and animal domestication, and home building. But above all it was his success in transforming the earth by agriculture that was most striking:

> Oh, Earth is patient, and Earth is old,
> And a mother of Gods, but he breaketh her,

> To-ing, froing, with the plough-teams going,
> Tearing the soil of her, year by year.[3]

Much more explicit was the comment of the Roman writer Lucretius during the early part of the first century BC:

> day by day they [agriculturalists] would constrain the woods more and more to reside up the mountains, and to give up the land beneath to tilth, that on hills and plains they might have meadows, pools, streams, crops, and glad vineyards, and the grey belt of olives might run between with its clear line, spreading over hillocks and hollows and plains: even as now you see all the land clear marked by diverse beauties.[4]

In the end the mosaic of fields and groves on the lowlands and lower slopes appeared more wooded than perhaps they were. The large areas of tree crops, such as olive and later citrus, prompted Varro in the first century BC to ask, "is not Italy so covered with trees that the whole land seems to be an orchard?" Only the most inaccessible mountain areas remained totally forested.[5]

Given the growing appreciation of the power of humans to alter the earth it seems inconceivable that the paucity of direct references to agricultural clearing is a true reflection of what was happening. A hint is given by Strabo, quoting Eratosthenes (275–195 BC), about lowland Cyprus which was once "covered with forests, which prevented cultivation." But in time various activities altered that:

> The mines were of some service towards clearing the surface, for the trees were cut down to smelt copper and silver. Besides this timber was required for the construction of fleets, as the sea was now navigated with security and by a large naval force.[6]

But these nonagricultural inroads barely affected the forests. It was only when landless peasants were allowed to occupy "as their own property, free from all payments" that clearing accelerated. By 111 BC Roman law allowed anyone who occupied public land of up to 30 *jugera* (approximately 20 acres) to keep it, provided it was brought into cultivation. It was a kind of claim staking for freehold.

Later, Strabo commented on the clearing of the forests of Avernian in Campania that had been "brought by the toil of man into cultivation, though in former times they were thickly covered with a wild and untrodden forest of large trees"; and the vast Ciminian forest of southern Tuscany, which Livy described during the fourth century BC as "more impassable and appalling" than the forests of Germany, had all but disappeared two centuries later. It also seems likely that the forests of the Po plain were felled systematically during the second and first centuries BC as part of the "Romanization" of the Celtic Cisalpina and the creation of large estates within a framework of extensive centuriation.[7]

Felling was done by single- and double-headed bronze axes, saws, and wedges, which were later cast in tougher iron. Long saws, constructed of bronze sheets hammered into shape and cut regularly with pyramidal teeth, were also common, and the setting of saw teeth in alternate angles to aid cutting by raking out the sawdust was appreciated. However, the technique of notching a tree in order to ensure the direction of its fall was probably not understood, because guiding ropes were attached. The largest trees were girdled and left to die over a number of years, and the smallest trees were grubbed out. The best and largest timbers were taken out of the forest for constructional use, dragged out by human power, mules, or oxen, or even hoisted up on two wheels or floated out on accessible rivers. But a common practice was to burn all the timber on the spot and plow the ashes into the soil in order to fertilize it.

Soil fertility was a prime concern, and the type and size of tree were taken as an indication of the best soil, which was always best on new felled land, which put a premium on forested lands. If Theophrastus was the father of forest science, then Columella (circa 116–127 BC) could be called the father of soil science. He rejected superstitious ideas that fertility was related to the youth or age of the earth and was convinced that it was the accumulated debris of leaves and roots that produced the all-important humus layer. Clearing and plowing ultimately degraded that layer to create infertility. Thus human action was the culprit and could only be rectified by "frequent, timely, and moderate manuring." [8]

All types of stock were allowed to interrun with crops. Cows, pigs, goats, and horses were known from at least the seventh millennium BC in Crete and mainland Greece. In time, sheep came to dominate the stock inventory, not because of their wool (its use did not come until later) but because they were very efficient converters of plant matter into dung, which was essential to maintain soil fertility. If the well-watered pastures on the swampy coastal lands and deltaic flats—such as those of the Po, Adige, Arno, and Guadalquiver—were not enough during the long dry season stock were driven literally hundreds of miles to distant, upland pastures, especially on the wetter, western-facing slopes. Transhumance on a grand scale was particularly marked between the Apennines and their surrounding lowlands, with the broad *calles* or drove ways funneling the stock from upland to lowland. But sometimes even the alpine and upland pastures were still not enough to totally sustain the animals during the summer months, and then stock would be fed on supplementary fodder of young shoots and twigs from the lower branches of the deciduous trees, with a devastating effect on the forests everywhere. All stock inhibited forest regeneration and health by eating seedlings, roots, and shoots, as well as by trampling the ground and compacting the soil.

Pigs are essentially forest animals, thriving in the uncleared forest on the abundance of acorns, mast, and young shoots. They roamed in vast numbers on the southern slopes of the Pyrenees, which were "well-wooded with trees of every kind and with evergreens" and produced excellent hams that "rivaled those of the famed forests of Cantabria," said Strabo, while the ring of forests around the Po lowlands produced acorns in such quantities that "Rome is fed mainly on the herds of swine that come from there." [9]

The Other Classical World

While the label "classical" straddled a vast range of time, it also straddled a vast range of space, because as Greece and Rome expanded, new classical worlds developed outside the vicinity of the Mediterranean basin. The northern Balkans were conquered from 229 BC onward, Spain after 209 BC, Gaul from 125 BC onward, and the occupation of the British Isles lasted from 44 BC to at least AD 400. Of these the temperate forested lands from the Danube to the Rhine and Scotland are the most important. The usual view is that the British Isles, northern France, and Germany were forest-covered landscapes and largely devoid of people; Britain, said Strabo, was mostly "overgrown with forests," and "the vast expanse" of the Hercynian oak forest stood as a motif for all Germany—"untouched by the ages and coeval with the world," surpassing all wonders in its "almost immortal destiny." The German forest was wilderness, the place of strange beings and wild beasts, and the abode of hostile Germanic tribal groups who were a match for the legions. Fed on the descriptions of Tacitus, the Romans regarded the German forest with a mixture of "awesome admiration as well as repugnance"—admiration at its sylvan purity, which accorded with their own founding myths, but repugnance at its uncivilized "otherness" or "outsided-ness"—in other words, for being alien and "non-Rome." [10] But Romano-British and Romano-Gallic clearing, cultivation, and grazing in Britain and France was more widespread than thought, although Germanic lands still contained large tracts of untouched forest. It was a landscape already in the process of considerable transformation at the time of the Roman occupation.

Yet we know little about rural life in these territories, as what scraps of literary evidence exist are skewed toward urban life, and even then the preeminence of Rome dominates. Knowledge about the ancient world is largely identical to knowledge about living in the cities. Yet, there was a busy and active rural life. The accounts of the large slave-operated and tenanted estates in Italy; the affluent capitalist estates of Spain and particularly of Gaul; the rich farms of northern Gaul and on the left bank of the Rhine, particularly around Treves; and the active colonization of Roman emigrant colonists and veterans in Africa and on the Rhine and the Danube, together with the splendid cities supported, all add up to a picture of enormous rural activity and prosperity and, inevitably, clearing.

In northern Gaul, Germany, and Britain, conquest brought peace and hence greater cultivation, and the army provided an assured market. For example, over 106,000 acres would have been required to supply wheat to the army of occupation in Britain alone, and Britain even exported wheat to Rome. It was a land of farms and agricultural estates, villas and squires rather than of cities with surrounding peasants and small proprietors. The middle Danube region was the same. The remains of the large, luxurious villas are a testimony to the scale and complexity of this new capitalistic rural life, in which cultivation and stock rearing went hand in hand. Enormous inroads were made in the forest.

Shipbuilding

The building of ships, urbanization, and the smelting of metals loom large as destroyers of the forest in contemporary accounts, but it is doubtful whether their impact came anywhere near that of agriculture or domestic fuelwood use. Shipbuilding and smelting were extraneous, exotic activities that seemed alien and dramatic intrusions into the rhythms of everyday life compared to the timeless qualities of agriculture and pastoralism, or even the now-commonplace activity of building towns. Therefore, they attracted much attention, though in reality they accounted for only a small percentage of forest destruction. Nevertheless, the importance attached to the supply of timber for building ships cannot be denied; ships were crucial to the burgeoning economic life of the Mediterranean, and sea power was vital in the exercise of political control.

Trade had grown rapidly during the second half of the first millennium to bring the good things of life to a large section of the population. "Command of the seas," said one anonymous writer in the late fourth century BC,

> has enabled the Athenian to . . . discover refinements of luxury. . . . Every delicacy of Sicily, Italy, Cyprus, Egypt, Lydia, the Black Sea, the Peloponnese

or any other country has been accumulated in a single spot . . . [and they are in] a position to accumulate wealth.[11]

There was a core of capital- and labor-intensive manufacturing from the Levant to Greece, surrounded by a zone of higher-value agricultural products (wine, oil), and beyond that the specialized grain-growing areas of Cyrenaica, Sicily/southern Italy, and the Black Sea, with many separate and distant centers of manufacturing and supply, particularly in the Carthaginian and Phoenician western half of the basin. Farther away again, and up steep and near-inaccessible slopes, were the mountain forests and their timber (fig. 4.1). None of these regions of production could have existed without slaves for labor, silver for coinage, and ships for transport of bulky and precious goods. Despite some spectacular land conquests—the Persian and Roman empires being prime examples—it was sea power that was the decisive strategic factor in territorial aggrandizement of the competing city-states. Thucydides' account of the prolonged and bitter wars between Athens and the Peloponnesian League was basically an account of the growth of their navies, the search for men, and the command of timber supplies; the same could be said for the early wars of Rome against the Carthaginians. The possession of ships, for whatever purposes, was so important that Roman emperors offered privileges and tax incentives for their construction, and many a colonial enterprise was aimed at securing timber supplies.

Each conflict reinforced the need for ships, and each new colonization increased trade, which called for more merchant ships and warships to protect them. Some idea of the size of navies is gleaned from the fact that Athenian fleets may have reached 200–300 triremes during the Persian War of 480 BC. Moreover, Rome lost 700 quinqueremes during the 24 years of the First Punic War; and in response, crash programs of building were undertaken, as when Rome built 120 ships in 60 days during the first war against Carthage and, a year later, 220 ships in 45 days. And timber was available for their construction. The conventional trireme, in addition to the timber for the hull, needed 200 oars (170 for the three banks of rowers and 30 spares), two large steering oars, and a mast and yardarm. It might have been between 115 and 120 ft long.

Not only did the ships get more numerous, but they also got larger, especially when boats began to carry catapults for sinking their enemy instead of ramming them. Some ships needed 4,000 oarsmen and were large enough to carry 400 other crew and 2,850 marines. Later merchant ships even had a gymnasium, reading rooms, and baths on board. But these were extravagant exceptions intended for display and the more typical ship was approximately 130 tons, or less, which was maneuverable in the small harbors and jetties that had been constructed around the Mediterranean coast. One could go on, but the important point is that the strategic demand for special types of timber was very real; a lively trade for it sprang up in peacetime, and competition was intensified during wartime. The situation was more critical in the eastern Mediterranean because of the meager and irregular distribution of trees in the Levantine, Egyptian, and Aegean regions, whereas the abundant supplies and variety of species in the west meant that competition and conflict, while not absent, were not so intense.

Figure 4.1 gives a broad idea of where the major forests were and the likely routes of trade. Fir (*Abies alba*) was favored for shipbuilding. It was lighter than pine and did not decay. It grew best at or near the upper limit of tree growth on the highest mountains, over 3,000 m. Mountain pine (*Pinus nigra* in Greece and *Pinus laricio* in Italy), was stronger than fir and found on the intermediate mountain slopes. The parts of Mediterranean Europe that could supply these superior timbers were limited and included Sicily, the Sila forest of southern Italy, Macedonia, Mount Eba, the Taurus Mountains of Cilicia, and the areas of Asia Minor facing the shores of the Black Sea. Syria, on the other hand, used its cedar for ships, while Cyprus used Aleppo pine. The conflicts that arose from combatants jockeying to secure essential supplies confirm again and again that these were indeed the prime timber areas, and they remained so well into the nineteenth century.

Large timbers were floated down rivers to specialized ports developed at their mouths, such as Colchis on the eastern Black Sea and Ravenna and Luna on the Adriatic. Sometimes rafts were constructed and even floated across narrow seas, as in 400 BC, when Dionysus of Syracuse brought timber for shipbuilding from the Sila forest in southern Italy and towed it across the Straits of Messina by oar-powered boats to Syracuse. By about the second century BC, specially constructed ships for carrying long timbers were developed.

As Rome expanded new sources were sought continually. The mountains of southeastern Spain supplied prime ships' timbers, and Tortosa grew as a shipbuilding port, just as the Ligurian mountains fed the Genoese shipyards. By early AD there is some evidence that the timber of the Alps, Jura, and Vosges in northern Europe and the North African Atlas Mountains were either considered or used.

The strategic use of and need for timber in times of war and peace were first demonstrated in the classical world. They were going to be elaborated even more clearly by other maritime nations in the centuries to come—regionally, with the Muslims in the seventh to eleventh centuries and the Venetian Republic in the fifteenth and sixteenth centuries, and then globally, with the great sea powers of Spain, France, Holland, and England in the sixteenth to early nineteenth centuries. Naval demands on the forest were a major reason for concern about the abundance or dearth of trees.

Urbanization

The classical world was an urban world that allowed a sizable proportion of the population to indulge in the higher and finer side of life, and cultivate the mind. Civilization (from *civis,* Latin for "citizen" or "city dweller") is, etymologically speaking, "citification." The concentration of such large numbers of people meant a great consumption of wood for construction and fuel. Whereas country dwellers could either forage for or produce these materials as a by-product of agricultural operations with no visible short-term effect on the countryside, city dwellers could not. They were dependent on a complex set of trading relationships to sustain city life, from carpenters, builders, and wood haulers to charcoal burners and domestic wood carriers, some of whom might also have been farmers. The major classical cities also contained large, ceremonial public buildings, such as temples, circuses, theaters, palaces, baths, and assembly rooms, which required vast timber spans in order to straddle the open public spaces enclosed beneath. Consequently, just like shipbuilding, cities required carefully selected, large, straight timbers.

The population of cities is uncertain, but it is thought that Alexandria had reached at least 300,000 by the first century BC and that if slaves were included it might have even been double that. Below it was Pergamon, Miletus, Syrian Antioch, and Athens, which approached a quarter of a million, and there were about 30 or 40 cities between 30 and 100,000 inhabitants. Similar hierarchies of city size were evident in the Roman world.

Because of their sociopolitical importance and size, Athens and Rome provide the greatest detail about the use of timber. By the fifth century BC Plato complained that the demand for timber had denuded the hills and plains surrounding Athens and caused massive soil erosion.[12] This was probably exaggerated, a combination of myth and reality, as Plato builds up a picture of a past Athens when everything was much better—a Golden Age no less. Anyway, farmers were not so senseless as to cut down all their farm trees, which were always useful for building, making tools, and supplying urban demands for fuelwood and charcoal for cooking and heating, which was a profitable sideline for farmers for up to anything within 20 km of Athens.

The physical growth of Athens and its port, Pireaus, undoubtedly increased consumption. The grandiose public buildings needed big timbers, but it was the mass of smaller urban dwellings that consumed such huge amounts. Pitched, gabled roofs replaced flat ones; elaborate finishes like doors, lintels, windows, frames, and shutters became common, as did floor joists, staircases, balconies, and shingles. In addition, the need for domestic fuel, that almost invisible but essential commodity for cooking and warmth, would have grown in direct proportion to the growth of population. When the industrial demands for timber for smelting silver and iron and for fusing copper and tin to make bronze are considered, then fuelwood consumption might have exceeded all other uses.

During the second century BC, Athens and the other Hellenistic cities were eclipsed by Rome, which became the largest city in the world (until London reached a similar size in 1801). Its population was about 463,000 in 86 BC, 1 million by 5 BC, and possibly between 1.2 million and 1.6 million by the fourth century AD, with decreases from frequent epidemics being compensated for by massive rural in-migration. Building and rebuilding (owing to destruction by floods and frequent fires, as well as pure speculative construction and stylistic whim) went on unceasingly, and the city became filled with "many beautiful structures," as well as a mass of smaller ones, which required unrecorded amounts of timber from the forests.

In time, tiles and bricks replaced shingles and mud walls in order to limit fire hazards and provide structural stability for multistoried apartment blocks. But they too were great consumers of wood. They had to be baked in wood-fueled furnaces, as did clay and ceramic tiles used for floors and mosaics. It is calculated that every cubic meter (1.0 m^3) of burnt brick required nearly 150 m^3 of wood to make. Bricks also had to be fixed to one another, and intense heat was required ($900°C–1100°C$, depending on the type of stone used) to calcinate or reduce calcium carbonate (limestone or chalk) to lime, the basis of cement, plaster, and ultimately concrete. Each ton of lime required between 5 and 10 tonnes of wood to produce, depending on the quality of the wood. By the fourth century AD, 3,000 wagonloads of lime were required in Rome annually, half for aqueduct maintenance and the other half for the repair and general construction of buildings. When the development of glass manufacturing (and glassblowing) is added to that of bricks and tiles, then the energy requirement in building alone must have consumed a vast amount of wood. Even when concrete became more common—particularly for vaulting, which substituted for large beams— the demand for timber barely lessened because of its use in shuttering and scaffolding, though in such cases it could be reused a number of times and end up usefully as fuelwood.

The smaller constructional pieces were of oak, elm, and ash, as well as myrtle and beech, came from the Alban Hills in the immediate vicinity of

Rome. Larger timbers for beams and bridges, however, were transported from the fir forests high in the Apennines by river and sea, coming down west-flowing rivers to the coast, along the sea, and up the Tiber to Rome. The competition for timber for the city was such that lumbering for ship-building in the hinterland of Pisa had given way to the lumbering for building construction in Rome. But where transportation was difficult there was little exploitation, which explains the survival of quite dense forests throughout the Mediterranean until the nineteenth century.

Building construction was not the only user of wood. Heat was needed for cooking and for house warming in the bitterly cold winter months from late November to mid-April. More affluent households had charcoal braziers that produced a steady heat, warmer and less smoky than that of open fires. But poorer households must have had roaring, open, smoky fires that were inefficient heat-givers. North of the Alps there is evidence that some larger houses were centrally heated, either by single pipes led around the walls and even the ceilings or by hypocaust (literally, "fire beneath"), that is to say, the floor of the rooms being supported by short pillars and the space created filled with hot air from a furnace. Perhaps as much as 2 cords (approximately 7.2 m^3) or more were used daily to maintain an adequate heat, though in Britain there is evidence of the use of coal.

Two other peculiarly Roman customs or institutions consumed untold quantities of wood: cremation and hot baths. Cremation progressively supplanted burial in the later centuries BC, only to be reversed with the advent of Christianity. Its use of timber can only be surmised. However, we can be surer of the public baths and steam rooms, which held a high place in the culture of the city as social, medicinal, and hygiene centers and which ranged from the luxurious to the mean. We do not know how numerous they were until much later on, in the fourth century AD, when there were said to be 11 sets of large imperial baths and 856 smaller establishments in Rome. In time, public baths became common in towns throughout the empire, and private baths were attached to individual villas. One can make some reasonable calculations about the order of magnitude of fuel needed to warm a bath. Making a number of assumptions, the Welwyn baths in England brought to a constant requisite temperature of 70°C for the *Calarium* (hot bath) and 55°C for the *Tepidarium* (tepid bath) might have used 114 tons of wood a year, the equivalent of perhaps an acre of reasonably mature hardwood forest, or 23 acres of coppiced woodland. We cannot be more precise than that.

So how much timber might an average Roman town dweller have consumed? The answer, as always, will depend on an array of variables, such as status, affluence, and local climate. But if the consumption per capita of timber for fuel for heating and cooking alone in the less developed world today is on average 0.45 m³, and can rise to as much as 0.8 m³ in rural Africa where other energy sources are absent, then consumption in the more profligate Roman world, with its many more industrial uses for wood, must have been at least double that, to be between 1.0 and 1.5 m³. The likelihood is, however, that we are seriously underestimating the level of consumption. The only other reasonably reliable figure from a virile, inventive wood-based economy comes for North America in the late eighteenth century, for which an annual per capita consumption of 4.5 cords (576 ft³), or 17.3 m³, is suggested—a quantity 11.5 times greater than our calculation for Rome. But we are guessing; however, if the conservative estimate of consumption of Rome at the peak of its population is taken as 1.5 m³ × 1.5 million people, then 2.25 million m³ would have been consumed. If 300 m³ per acre is taken as an average density for hardwoods, then about 7,500 acres, or 11.7 mi² (30.34 km²), of woodland would have been destroyed per annum. If the consumption was greater, then the forest destruction would have been correspondingly larger. Overall it seems likely that fuelwood for all purposes may have constituted about 90 percent of all timber used in the Roman Empire.

Gathering must have spread farther and farther away as Rome grew and its urban influence penetrated into the surrounding countryside, aided by an ever-growing network of roads. The rise of the *lignari*, possibly traders concentrating on the production and transportation of *lignum*, or fuelwood, is indicative of the complexity of the urban trade.

In later centuries the very largest timbers were becoming more difficult to find, and the demand for fuel rose as smelting and brick and lime making increased. The big beams were now coming from the Black Sea coast and the Raetian Alps. The peculiar position of the baths in Roman society adds a few final clues. Sometime before AD 235, when the emperor Alexander Severus died, he had set aside local woodlands for stoking the Roman baths, but within a hundred years, logs were being shipped by salt contractors from points along the Italian coast and up the Tiber and, even, from North Africa.

The urban demands for construction, fuel, heating, and all other purposes have been considered in some detail to show that even at this early date they were very great. They serve as a measure and reminder of the constant drain on the forest in all societies, and with only few exceptions urban uses will not be dealt with in detail again in later chapters.

Metal Smelting

Throughout all ages there has been a tendency to exaggerate the contribution of metallurgy to deforestation. Metal smelting has always been regarded as an alien, commercial intrusion into the tranquility of the forest. But while the local devastation was always quite stark, the total effect was rarely as much as is commonly thought. Agricultural clearing was always a far greater culprit in the felling of trees but was rarely blamed because it was regarded as "natural" to clear and cultivate land.

While it is sometimes difficult to make a clear distinction between the domestic and commercial consumption of wood in urbanization, there is little doubt that mining and metal smelting were commercial pursuits. They were distributed widely throughout the Greek and Roman worlds. Bronze—a fusion of tin and copper—was commonplace from archaic times in Greece, and iron was becoming more so with every century. It was a manifestation of what has been called pyrotechnology and which required untold amounts of charcoal.

Calculations have been made of the impact on the forests of smelting at notable classical mining sites. But because of the many variables involved and the factors used in the statistical transformations there are many uncertainties. For example, the yield of timber per tree and the density of trees per unit area, all of which have to be average estimates; the number of years over which the exploitation occurred; the regrowth regime of different forests; the differing yields of metals for the same amounts of charcoal expended; and even the mixtures of other metals in ores, such as lead with silver. Some of the calculations are shown in table 4.1, and they refer to silver smelting at Rio Tinto, in southwest Spain; iron smelting at Populonia, on the Italian mainland opposite the Isle of Elba where the ore was extracted but could no longer be smelted due to the exhaustion of fuel; copper smelting in Cyprus; and silver smelting at Laurion (Lavrion) in southern Greece.

On the face of it, the figures are large, but not, perhaps, as startling as they appear at first glance, especially when one realizes that they are totals that stretch over centuries. Certainly there has been a tendency toward exaggeration: Wertime's "20–30 million acres of cut trees" as the total deforestation caused by the metallurgical industries of Egypto-Greco-Roman civilization inexplicably became "50–70 million acres of trees" in the next year; and Constantinou's calculation that 150,000 km^2 of forest was needed to serve the copper mines of Cyprus—which is 16 times the size of the island—is based on a misapprehension of the process of clearing over time and the possibility of forest regeneration.[13] Even in table 4.1 the 19,195 km^2 of forest cleared for Rio Tinto has to be averaged over at least 2,000 years or, if the classical impact is isolated from the total, only half the slags over 600 years; the 1,875 km^2 of Populonia over about 500 years; the 60,000 km^2 of Cyprus over 3,000 years; and the 631.5 km^2 in Lavrion over 550 years. If that is done, and some sort of rotational cutting is postulated, then

Table 4.1 Production and estimated area of timber used in four mining locations in the classical world

	Rio Tinto (Spain): Silver and Copper	Populonia (Italy): Iron and Some Bronze	Cyprus: Copper	Lavrion (Greece): Lead and Some Silver
Slag residues (tons)	30 million [1, 4]	?	4 million[3]	2.7 million[6]
Calculated metal production (tons)	?	500,000[1]	200,000[3]	1.4 million[6]
Charcoal needed per ton metal produced (kg)	450	4,520[5]	300,000[3]	450[2]
Total charcoal (tons)	13.5 million	2.2 million	60 million	631,350[3]
Wood needed to produce 1 ton charcoal (tons)	16[3, 5]	16[3, 5]	16[3, 5]	16[5]
Total wood needed (tons)	216 million	36.1 million	960 million	10.1 million
Yield of trees (kg)	Oak = 375	Pine = 800[1]	Pine = 800[1]	Pine = 800[1]
Trees needed	575.8 million	45.2 million	1,200 million	12.6 million
Density of trees/ha	300	240	240	240
ha of trees	1.9 million	187,500	6 million	63,135
km² of forest	19.195	1,875	60,000	631
Years of operation	2,000+	500?	3,000?	2,300?

Sources: (1) T. A. Wertime and S. F. Wertime, eds., *Early Pyrotechnology: The Evolution of the First Fire-Using Industries,* papers presented at a seminar on early pyrotechnology held at the Smithsonian Institution, Washington, D.C., and the National Bureau of Standards, Gaithersburg, Maryland, April 19–20, 1979 (Washington, D.C.: Smithsonian Institution Press, 1982), 135; (2) L. U. Salkield. "The Roman and Pre-Roman Slags of the Rio Tinto, Spain," in *Early Pyrotechnology,* ed. Wertime and Wertime, 137–47); (3) G. Constantinou, "Geological Features and Ancient Exploitation of Cupriferous Sulphide Ore Bodies in Cyprus," in *Early Metallurgy in Cyprus, 4000–500* BC, ed. James D. Muhly, R. Maddin, and Vassos Karageorghis (Nicosia: Pereides Foundation in collaboration with the Department of Antiquities, Nicosia, 1982), 13–24, esp. 22; (4) L. U. Salkield, "Ancient Slag in the South West of the Iberian Peninsula," *La Mineria Hispanica e Ibero-Americana* 1 (1970): 94; (5) R. J. Forbes. *Studies in Ancient Technology,* vol. 6, *Heat and Heating, Refrigeration and Light* (Leiden: E. J. Brill, 1964), 6; (6) T. A. Wertime, "Cypriot Metallurgy in the Backdrop of Mediterranean Pyrotechnology: Energy Considered," in *Early Metallurgy in Cyprus, 4000–500* BC, ed. J. Muhly, R. Maddin, and V. Karageorghis (Larnaca, Cyprus: Pierides Foundation, 1982).
Note: ? denotes information not available.

annual totals drop dramatically. They could be as little as 10 km²–15 km², or half that if a rotational cutting or coppicing was used. Locally it would have been devastating, but not the agent of massive change that is suggested; there were still ample reserves of timber on the mountains of Cyprus in the late Roman Empire.

But for all these calculations it is strange that if there was so much forest devastation there is no more positive evidence. The impact of smelting is probably exaggerated.

DEFORESTATION AND SOIL DEGRADATION

The rise and fall of great powers has fascinated observers in all ages; Edward Gibbon's *History of the Decline and Fall of the Roman Empire* and Edgar Allan Poe's beautiful lines on "the glory that was Greece / and the grandeur that was Rome" are two works that are embedded in the Western consciousness and conscience.[14] For contemporary writers about the environment the connection is clear: the link between "ruined cities and ruined land" is "inescapable," and more recently David Attenborough has seen deforestation as "the crucial blow" to settlement on the eastern and southern shores of the Mediterranean.[15] Like Henry David Thoreau, George Perkins Marsh, Paul Sears, Walter Lowdermilk, and Fairfield Osborn before them, they are convinced that deforestation and subsequent soil degradation were major contributors to the weakening of the classical world. While all note other, often unspecified, causes for decline, the one contributory cause— deforestation—slowly becomes the main cause. Repeated enough it assumes the character of truth. Arcadia becomes anarchy, ecological profligacy leads to ruin—a moral lesson that many in this environmentally conscious age would like to draw.

But it is far more complicated than that. While soil erosion most certainly occurred, and devastatingly so in places, it is more likely that constant war, ravaging epidemics, rebellion, invasion from outside, a declining population, and an excessive degree of urbanization, separately or in combination, operated on the land in an empire that had extended beyond its means. In particular, the slender margin of surplus agricultural production needed to sustain city life could have been a crucial factor, given that over 10 people were required to support one city dweller, even in a prosperous region. These pressures exposed the internal fragility, instability, and weakness of the sociopolitical system, all exacerbated by compulsory work stints, overtaxation, lack of capital investment in farming, a crumbling system of slavery, and intense class divisions, many of which were created by urbanization and which engendered a privileged bourgeoisie.

In any case, the very existence of widespread agricultural decline, land abandonment, and extension of large estate farms, or *latifundia*, to the impoverishment of the free peasantry needs to be questioned. An extensive survey of over 200 villas and their economy throughout Roman Europe revealed that there was actually a prolonged "boom period" in land occupation and farming, especially in south Gaul, southern Spain, Sicily, Pannonia, and the eastern empire during the third and fourth centuries AD, which turns the conventional interpretations on their head.

What is the evidence of the deforestation/erosion argument? The starting point is the fifth-century comment of Plato in the *Critias* that in the distant past, the soil of Attica was deep and the mountains "heavily afforested." But its trees had disappeared, some to provide rafters for Athenian buildings, and the mountains could now "keep nothing but bees." As he wrote, Attica was a naked upland: "What remains of her substance is like the skeleton of a body emaciated by disease. . . . All the rich, soft soil has moulted away, leaving a country of skin and bones. . . . The annual supply of rainfall was not lost, as it is at present, through being allowed to flow over the denuded surface into the sea."[16] The imagery is striking and has been quoted approvingly and frequently by geographers, conservationists, ecologists, and others concerned with environmental stability. But, as noted before, most commentators on the classical age are inclined to discount it as exaggerated, as Plato builds up a picture of a past Athens when everything was much better—an early example of nostalgia at work to evoke a Golden Age, which is such a perennial theme in the Western imagination. It is hard to decide whether what he writes is history, or mythology, or poetry, and it is probably no more reliable than his famous Atlantis myth. The naturally dry and sparsely timbered plain of Attica was certainly cultivated intensively for grain and planted with olive trees and, therefore, cleared; and while there was undoubtedly overcutting in the mountains nearest to Athens, there is little evidence of the same in more distant mountains, which were still heavily forested in the nineteenth century.

The idea that soil exhaustion was a cause for a general decay of the Roman world is not convincing, even if there were localized pockets of degradation around Rome and Athens, as seems likely. To extend the argument to all Italy is an unacceptable generalization. In the provinces, large new territories were taken into cultivation throughout the second and third centuries AD. Portions of the fertile fenland of Britain and lowlands of Holland were drained, North African olive and grain cultivation expanded brilliantly, and in Egypt flood control measures and irrigation made previously abandoned land more productive. The story was the same throughout the Levant and Mesopotamia, and the experience seems to run counter to the general degradation thesis. The fertility potential of the soil was rarely endangered in classical antiquity because the agricultural tools of the age were not big or strong enough to cause degradation; that was caused by overgrazing by large-scale cattle ranching during the Middle Ages. However, on the steep, deforested, terraced hillsides of Greece and other regions where slave raiding caused depopulation, it is possible that agricultural maintenance suffered, and the thin overlying mantle of soil was washed away.

That natural processes were accelerated with tree cutting and cultivation is obvious, but all in all, it is strange that in such a literate and observant world no evidence has arisen of concern about the excessive exploitation of the forests, no general alarm about depletion, no treatise on forest management, or examples of efforts to plant trees other than olive trees. Soil erosion is rarely mentioned, even as a minor problem. Of course, it is possible that the natural process was so slow and imperceptible that it was not noticed; natural processes are largely invisible because they are natural. And there are some hints of this. For example, Pliny was aware of the increased incidence of flash floods with clearing so that "devastating torrents unite when from hills has been cut away the wood that used to hold the rains and absorb them." Pausanias (circa 174 AD) compared the deposits from two river basins on the Greek Anatolian coast: the Achelous, from which the inhabitants had been driven out by the Romans and which presumably remained largely forested or with abandoned cultivated lands, and the Maeander, "which is ploughed up each year." The former did not "bring down as much mud on the Echinades [offshore islands] as it otherwise would do," but the latter "had turned to mainland in a short time the sea that once was between Priene and Miletus." [17] Similarly, Ephesus became landlocked with deposits from the Cyster by the third century BC, and other examples of delta formation and the herculean labors needed to dredge clogged harbors like Paestum and Ostia can be found around the eastern Mediterranean, as at the head of the Thermaic Gulf in western Macedonia (fig. 4.2). But alluviation is a natural phenomenon and may have happened despite deforestation.

In reviewing the paleobotanical, climatic, and archeological evidence for Greece, John Bintliff argues that given its harsh natural environment, one cannot expect "vast woods of lofty trees, nor well-developed soils." [18] In Crete, for example, steep limestone uplands cannot support woodland, but upland terraces and depressions can. Similarly, lowland soils can support forest in favorable places only. Thus, around the Minoan palace at Mallia are arable fields that have been cultivated intensively for almost uninterrupted millennia, and there is fine woodland in the surrounding hills. Pollen analysis in the Drama Plain, together with the corroborative evidence of

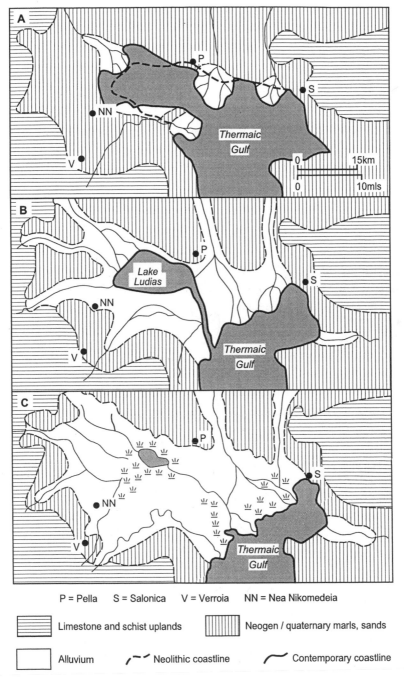

P = Pella   S = Salonica   V = Verroia   NN = Nea Nikomedeia

Limestone and schist uplands	Neogen / quaternary marls, sands
Alluvium	Neolithic coastline
	Contemporary coastline

Figure 4.2 Landscape change due to siltation and fill in the Western Macedonian plain, Greece. *A*, Greco-Roman; *B*, Late Roman; and *C*, AD 1900. (Source: after J. L. Bintliff, "New Approaches to Human Geography: Prehistoric Greece: A Case Study," in *An Historical Geography of the Balkans*, ed. F. W. Carter [London: Academic Press, 1977], 59–114, fig. 9*A–D*.)

travelers in the region during the last 500 years, suggests that the forests could, and did, regenerate successfully. If anything, the Roman and later medieval phase was a moist one in which woodland growth would have been encouraged. It is only during the last few centuries that there has been a return to a more "Mediterranean" climate, with natural forest recession in marginal locations. It was the massive clearances of the last couple of centuries with greater accessibility by road and rail that have created the present bare landscape, not the activities of the classical past.

The difficulty of disentangling the relationships among past climatic change, vegetational change, human settlement, and erosion and sedimentation phases has prompted much discussion. Claudio Vita-Finzi's original hypothesis of an Older (late glacial) and Younger (essentially medieval) Fill, both caused by natural fluctuations of climate and not human action, has gone through many revisions.[19] Early work suggested that a considerable amount of the deposition was not classical or preclassical in origin but post-Roman, with ^{14}C dating extending from AD 1150 to 1750, and that comparable deposition is not taking place today (fig. 4.3). Subsequently, others have suggested that the evidence of deltaic sediments represents an earlier phase of deposition and is not connected with the Younger Fill and that the confusion is due to a misunderstanding of the cycle of erosion and deposition in the Vita-Finzi model. Another conclusion is that the wetter the climate, the greater the erosion and hence deposition and that the period of maximum known deforestation during the last few centuries has been marked by minimum stream aggradation and incision into previously steeply graded sediments. Consequently, it is possible that the markedly wetter climate from AD 1000–1750 had caused the historical alluviation and that classical deforestation is not the culprit. The evidence of an increase in erosion rates in river basins around Rome of from 2 cm–3 cm/1,000 years in the second century BC to 20 cm–40 cm/1,000 years at present supports either early Roman clearing or the climatic change hypothesis.

In the classic case of the now abandoned lands of North Africa, it is likely that Roman settlement took place under climatic conditions that were more like those of the present than those of more humid medieval times. Many Roman wells and cisterns were still in use and any abandonment was due to neglect. Once the historical myths and proxy data are discarded the question could reasonably be put: "Did large-scale land use around the Mediterranean impede erosion rather than to encourage it?"[20] It is the very opposite of the received wisdom and suggests that deforestation was probably less severe than has been thought.

Nonetheless, everywhere the woodland was being thinned and removed as the population increased, cultivation was extended, and everyday life

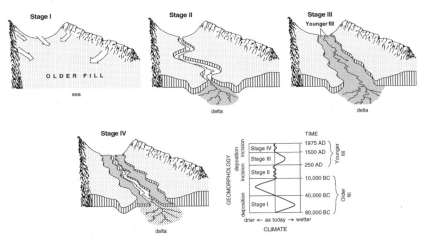

Figure 4.3 Late Quaternary development of Mediterranean river valleys, with climatic fluctuations and geomorphological phases, 80,000 BC to present. (Source: based on C. Vita-Finzi, *The Mediterranean Valleys: Geological Changes in Historical Times* [Cambridge: Cambridge University Press, 1969]; with additions by J. L. Bintliff, "New Approaches to Human Geography: Prehistoric Greece: A Case Study," in *An Historical Geography of the Balkans,* ed. F. W. Carter [London: Academic Press, 1977], 59–114, fig. 8.)

became more sophisticated. Locally, the effect was most marked in zones of intense utilization, as in the Apennines and around large cities or areas of mineral extraction, and elsewhere where strategic shipbuilding supplies were cut out. Soil erosion must have accelerated in places. The conclusion of Clifford Darby fifty years ago, that

> the Mediterranean lands were then more densely wooded than they are today but that already there had been considerable clearing and that the extensive forests which remained were for the most part in the mountainous areas

might seem bland and unsatisfactory to our more quantitative frame of mind in the present day, but it is essentially correct and is about as far as one can go in generalizing about the degree of change.[21]

CREATING A SECOND NATURE

As important as the amount of deforestation is our knowledge about the process and differing attitudes toward it. As in every age there is conflicting evidence. The Greeks, it is suggested, "generally tended to fear and revere wild nature more, while the Romans found the landscape both friendlier and more easily subjected to various human uses."[22] The Greeks certainly found meaning in the forest and thought of it as the original home of humankind where humans sprang from oaks. But this ended with forest clearing, the fallen trees being likened to warriors slain in battle. Because of this we can better understand the reverence for sacred groves as the abode of the gods and tree spirits, or dryads, and as a form of temple and hence holy sanctuary. Severe penalties for desecrating a grove acted as a deterrent to clearing and a motive for the preservation of portions of the original forest, though not always adhered to. But attitudes were ambivalent; cutting trees may have been the desecration of paradise, but it could also be the dawn of civilization.

Things were to change in time. Undoubtedly the classical age (particularly the Roman age) was the beginning of the modern world. There is evidence that nature was not being revered but being commodified, traded, and sold and that its possession was seen as a means to wealth and capital accumulation, as witnessed in the discussions on the profitability of farming. The development of private property (particularly by the latifundists); the dealing in land; the exploitation of slaves; the making of profits from trade, industry, and war; financial speculation; and the investment of surplus were all other examples of a new attitude. Avarice and an active willingness to exploit the material world and other humans for profit became common. Thus, "all the things in this world which men employ have been created and provided for the sake of men," said Cicero, and the forests were only as good as they were useful.[23]

Paralleling this view of nature was one that we have mentioned already, that of control and mastery, so that people no longer felt that they were of nature but above it. The very nature of nature was being changed by human ingenuity and industry. In his remarkably perceptive essay of 43 BC, *De natura deorum*, Cicero extolled the endowments of humans who had minds to invent, senses to perceive, and hands to execute and were consequently able to achieve "the entire command of the commodities produced on land." He continued:

> We enjoy the fruits of the plains and of the mountains, the rivers and the lakes are ours, we sow corn, we plant trees, we fertilize the soil by irrigation, we confine rivers and straighten or divert their courses. In fine, by means of our hands we essay to create as it were a second world within the world of nature.[24]

In other words, like all these other activities of humankind, the cutting of trees (and he instances that in some detail) had become second nature, but it had also helped to create a second nature in place of first nature.

Chapter 5

The Medieval World

That is what it was, a chain from theology to manuring.
—C. GLACKEN, *Traces on the Rhodian Shore* (1967)

IN THE ANNALS of deforestation, the experience of medieval Europe must be accorded a prominent place both for what happened in Europe itself and for what happened subsequently in the world. Whereas about four-fifths of the land surface of temperate western and central Europe had been covered with forests and swamps in about AD 500, possibly only half, or less, of that amount remained 800 years later.

Charles Higounet attempted to reconstruct the location of the major areas of "forest" on the eve of "*les grands défrichements*" of the eleventh to thirteenth centuries, and it is a useful basis or starting point for discussing the great medieval onslaught.[1] The map (fig. 5.1) is useful for another reason. At that time, forest was a technical term, not necessarily meaning "woodland" but, rather, land reserved for the use of the king, above all for his hunting. Thus, the shaded areas may not represent the only trees because there were certainly plenty of trees outside the forest, just as there were many clearings inside it. The "forest" represented areas of proprietary, political, and juridical power held by royalty and the nobility for hunting, and it is likely that the area was exaggerated. But when all was said and done, there were a lot of trees in the forest and some of it was very extensive and very dense.

Early documentary evidence of forest clearing is infrequent and incidental to other matters, such as rental returns, common rights, and lawsuits. But by the twelfth and thirteenth centuries, the story is unmistakable and documents "swarm" with allusions to clearing. In addition there is, for the first time, the evidence of place-names and field names as well as the tangible evidence of the fields and settlements that were created and that have survived in the landscape and are recorded on maps. The amount of clearing

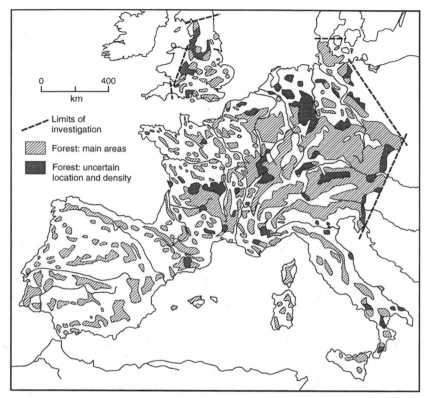

Figure 5.1 A reconstruction of the major forest areas of Europe on the eve of *les grands défrichements* of the eleventh to thirteenth centuries AD. (Source: based on·Charles Higounet. "Les forêts de L'Europe occidentale du Vᵉ au XIᵉ sièle," in *Agricultura e Mondo rurale in Occidente nel'alto medioevo,* Settimane di studio del centro italiano de studi sull'alto medioevo, 13 (Spoleto: Presso la sede del Centro, 1966), 343–98.

was underestimated because clearing took away something visual from the landscape and therefore often went unrecorded. Consequently, we are confronted with both conjecture and a great amount of detailed evidence that defies easy division and easy generalization.

AN ACTIVE AND ENERGETIC WORLD

The Middle Ages encapsulated an active and energetic world, which burst open after about 1100. "It was," said Kenneth Clark, "like a Russian spring. In every branch of life—action, philosophy, organization, technology—there was an extraordinary outpouring of energy and intensification of existence." [2] To take but one example, the hundreds of cathedrals and abbeys, and tens of thousands of parish churches, were monuments to the new self-confidence and wealth. In France alone, several million tons of stone were quarried, Amiens cathedral was large enough to accommodate the whole town of over 10,000 people, and the top of the spire of Strasbourg cathedral was 142 m, the equivalent of a forty-floor skyscraper—and none of these were that unusual. On the land, humans began to make conscious and purposeful decisions about its use and about population densities. The aim was a fuller and more intensive use of the land in order to increase productivity and promote closer settlement. Greater wealth was generated and, ultimately, greater power.

The same things could be said of China and Japan at this time, where vibrant and industrious civilizations also laid waste vast swathes of forest. But only a fraction of what happened there is known; clearing remains opaque and they are truly "dark ages and dark areas." [3]

A distinctive feature of the European story was the way in which the modification of the environment was linked with ideas, ideals, and practical needs. A belief in helping to create a divine, designed earth, in which nature was likened to a book revealing the magnificence of God, was shared with a need to understand and use nature for practical ends. The spread of Christianity and the cultivation of the land went hand in hand; it was, said Clarence Glacken, "a chain from theology to manuring." [4]

Thus, there emerged a "cultural climate" that favored and encouraged change. It consisted of an intangible mélange of belief, sentiment, superstition, motivation, symbolism, and even fashion, as well as empirical experiment and technological innovation. In practical terms, a novel system of agriculture was developed in Europe during the eighth and ninth centuries that suited its ecological and physical environment. The "agricultural revolution of the Middle Ages" that emerged shifted the focus of Europe from the south to the north, from the classical world of the Mediterranean to the great forested plains drained by the Loire, Seine, Rhine, Elbe, Danube, and Thames. It was on those plains that the distinctive features of the medieval world, and perhaps even of the modern world, developed.

In that "revolution," humans shifted from being a part of nature to being her exploiter; man and nature were now two things, and man was master. Nothing epitomized it more clearly than Charlemagne's renaming of months in terms of human activities—June was to be "Ploughing Month," July "Haying Month," August "Harvest Month," and so on. This change was reflected in illustrated Carolingian calendars shortly before 830, which were very different from Byzantine and old Roman ones because they showed appropriate activities for the various months, like plowing, harvesting, wood chopping, and so on. The upshot was that vast areas of the Continent were settled for the first time; settlement in existing areas was intensified; and the visual landscape was changed as trees were replaced by farms, crops, and grass. In fact, the clearing of the forest by individuals and great domains, both lay and ecclesiastical, and the cultivation of the ill-drained and forested land—technically the "waste"—over much of western and central Europe was one of the most dramatic changes made to human landscapes anywhere and can be regarded as one of the great achievements of the medieval age.

The forest was woven into the cultural fabric and material existence of medieval society. For ordinary people, especially landless peasants, the forest was close to everyday life; it was not only a source of heat, materials, and arboreal by-products, like honey, wax, fowl, small animals, and grazing, but also a source of potential "new" land and, hence, food. Historical analogies are dangerous, but in these characteristics at least, the medieval frontier was similar to the neo-European frontier of the seventeenth to nineteenth centuries and bears no small resemblance to the frontier facing the landless peasant in the tropical rain forest today. The forest was then, as it is now, in the words of a Scandinavian proverb, "the mantle of the poor," and in its exploitation and probable destruction lay the means for survival and, even, social and economic advancement. Although the peasant wanted primarily to destroy the forest (yet paradoxically keep it for its products), there was no conflict in the minds of the nobility and royalty who wanted to preserve the land for hunting and game. Consequently, as clearing progressed, differences arose between the poor and the rich over rights of usage and delimitation. These complex and conflicting goals were played out like antiphonal themes against the backdrop of the forest.

The abundance and ubiquity of wood in medieval Europe was matched by an extraordinary endowment of other natural resources, especially constantly flowing streams and diverse and abundant minerals. Wood was essential for smelting metals, particularly iron, which became the universal metal of the age. The medieval peasant used unprecedented amounts of iron, and the smithy was integral to every village. Thus iron axes, plows, and implements go a long way to explain the massive extension of cultivated land from the tenth century onward. The harnessing of water power in mills had long been known, and the combination of many streams, together with the availability of wood and iron for construction, culminated in the erection of mills in nearly every rural settlement. First water power was applied to grinding grain; 5,624 mills in some 3,000 communities are enumerated in the Domesday Book of 1086 for England alone. But soon mills appeared throughout Europe for the mechanical fulling of cloth, for the treating of hemp, and for tanning, laundering, sawing, crushing, grinding, sieving, turning, polishing, and stamping almost anything. Perhaps most significant, from the early eleventh century onward, mechanical power was applied to operate the bellows of blast furnaces and to puddle and beat iron in blooms with trip hammers, to draw wire, and to cut metal. Cranks, flywheels, pendulums, and cams were all manifestations of medieval inventiveness. The inanimate energy of water mills marked the beginning of the breakdown of the traditional world in which humans had to depend on the power of animals and on vegetable sources of energy. Windmills were another manifestation of this use of inanimate nature.

It was the age of water, wind, wood, and stone, with some metal parts. The scale of operations was small, tools were crude and hand forged, production was restricted, and the market local. In this nexus, the forest and its products of agricultural land, timber, and fuel were important. As these were used, so the forest was either diminished or more valued, or both.

CAUSES OF CLEARING

The medieval age covered the best part of a millennium, so inevitably we must generalize. Little clearing occurred from the end of the Roman Empire, circa AD 500 to circa AD 700 (the Merovingian period), as there was no pressure of population. The lack of necessity was compounded by a lack of conviction. For many Germanic tribes the primeval forest was of religious significance and held in awe as the abode of the gods. While this did not necessarily forbid clearing, it was a hindrance. The age of Charlemagne (the Carolingian phase), from circa 700 to 950, was a period of economic expansion and population growth, compounded by the movement of the Scandinavian and Germanic tribes into the British Isles and western Europe and the Magyars in central Europe. Some food shortages occurred in the highly developed parts of western Europe, and the forest was attacked with vigor. The attack intensified during the energetic and ebullient High Middle Ages, after 1000 to circa 1300. This was a period of purposeful change, the heroic age *des grands défrichements* (of the great clearings), which lasted until the end of the thirteenth century when activity began to wane, and ended abruptly with the Black Death of circa 1350.

Within this general chronology of activity, changes in the cultural climate of society and its relationship to the land can best be divided conveniently, if not quite accurately, into three broad sorts: demographic, technological, and ideological. In many ways they are inseparable, and put together they formed a conjunction of circumstances that were uniquely favorable to the growth and expansion of settlement in the forests.

Population and Land Use

Undoubtedly the driving force or engine of change that generated such spectacular activity was the growth of Europe's population. It doubled from 18.0 million in circa 600 to 38.5 million in circa 1000 and then doubled again to attain a high point of 75.5 million in the early thirteenth century. The increase in the food supply, the improvement of diet, the reduction of famine, and therefore better health and lower mortality all contributed to this surge. Also, the absence of major outbreaks of disease, coupled with a warmer and more stable climate before 1250, when temperatures rose by between 0.5 and 1°C and rainfall decreased by approximately 10 percent, had an effect.

The technological changes that followed were most probably a response to that growth of population, but there is also some evidence that the presence of untouched forest that required only clearing was a spur to earlier marriages for the peasantry, an increase in the birthrate, and hence larger families. In whichever direction the relationship worked, however, the need to increase food production confronted the medieval farmer. He had a number of options: one was to "make" new land by clearing, the others were related to the use of technology for production; they were the wheeled plow, the harnessing of animal power, and the adoption of three-field rotation system, which shortened the fallow period.

Making New Land

In the making of new land, the impacts on the forest were broadly twofold and roughly sequential. First, increasing densities during the early centuries resulted in the colonization of what Lewis has called the "Internal Frontier" in the European Heartland of northern Italy, France, western Germany, the Low Countries, and south east England.[5] In these long-occupied areas, the large communal fields were expanded at the expense of the unsettled and lightly used "waste" of ill-drained and forested land. The "waste" was misnamed; it was a valuable resource, sometimes cultivated on an infield/outfield system, usually grazed, and always the source of fuel, wild produce, pannage, game, and fowl. Its use was defined by custom and communal control, and as reclamation proceeded boundaries were demarcated in it. Expansion was by clearing trees (plate 5.1) or making assarts (from the French *essarter,* "to grub up" or "to clear"), references to which abound in manorial documents from the sixth century onward. Also, periodic burning and heavier grazing caused the degrading of the woodlands, which were eventually cleared of stumps.

Plate 5.1 Cutting Wood. The manuscript comes from the eleventh century AD. (By permission of the British Library, Ms. Tiberius, B.V. pt. 1, fol. 6.)

Second, and latterly, outward expansion occurred in the "External Areas" of the true wilderness of unbroken forest (silva). Here completely new settlements were created in clearings, often by the ecclesiastical houses, which sought solitude, and by secular lords, who wanted to expand their rent rolls. Sometimes the two "Frontiers" were coincident and coterminous, such as in the massive Germanic colonization from the tenth to twelfth centuries of the sparsely populated Slavic lands of central and eastern Europe.

Internal or External, the result was the same; the forest contracted. Whereas in the sixth century, fields accounted for less than 5 percent of land use, by the later Middle Ages the figure was nearer 30–40 percent. By that time colonization had gained a momentum of its own, and multiple and positive feedback effects operated so that large stretches of primeval forest of central and western Europe, while not necessarily cleared, were certainly incorporated into the realm of human affairs.

It is all too easy to forget that these relationships represent the lives and aspirations of real people, not some abstract, impersonal group. We have no record, as in later centuries, of what "making" the land really meant in everyday terms. But we can be sure that making a clearing in the forest was slow and arduous, the product of "a daily blinding sweat, blood at times, a backbreaking toil with axe and spade and saw." [6] It was a major part of medieval life.

Plows, Horsepower, and Fields

Somewhere between AD 650 and AD 800, three broadly "technological" developments appear that partially account for the bursting vitality of deforestation throughout the Carolingian realm.

First, the continual expansion of colonists into forestland took them out of the areas of light, well-drained sandy, chalky, and loessic soils that could be scratched open with the lightweight plow known as an *ard,* to the stiff, heavier, damp (and usually heavily wooded) soils that were potentially more productive but more difficult to cultivate. The solution lay in the invention of the wheeled heavy plow that appeared in parts of Germany, the Low Countries, and northern France in the country between the Loire and the Rhine sometime during the seventh century.

The wheels of the plow controlled its height above the ground, its coulter (or knife) cut the soil vertically, while a plowshare sliced it horizontally and an angled moldboard turned it over. In one stroke, the heavy soils were conquered—weeds were buried, accumulated nutrients turned up, and labor saved. Because the plow was unwieldy and difficult to turn at the end of the furrow, land was plowed in long, narrow strips, or furlongs (furrow long), grouped in large, unfenced, "open" fields. These strips were normally plowed clockwise, with the sod being turned over and inward to the right, creating long, low ridges with an intervening depression—hence the typical "ridge and furrow" landscape of much of cultivated lowland Europe. Thus, even in the wettest years the heavy clay soils had a rudimentary artificial surface drainage system, and some crops grew successfully on dry land.

Second, while the action of the new plow in slicing and turning the sod increased friction, its effectiveness was augmented by the use of horses rather than oxen. The invention a little after the beginning of the ninth century of a harness with a rigid collar that rested on the shoulders and not the neck (which virtually strangled them) transformed the pulling power of horses four- or fivefold, and nailed horseshoes preserved their hooves in wet soils. As horses move faster than oxen and do about twice as much work in a day, the saving in human labor was great. Moreover, the swiftness of the horse made it particularly versatile in harrowing to cover seed, break clods, and smooth fields, an advantage in the uncertain western European weather. A new form of horse-drawn spiked harrow appeared in southern Germany sometime after 1050.

The disadvantage of the new plow was that more beasts were needed to pull it—up to eight oxen or four horses, which was beyond the means of most peasants. Beasts of a settlement were consequently pooled, which reduced individualism but encouraged cooperation and a strong system of self-government.

Third, more efficient plowing contributed to the shift from the traditional two- to the new three-field crop rotation systems, there being a close correlation between triennial rotation and the use of the horse for agriculture. This new system appeared in the ecclesiastical lands of northeast

France during the ninth century and spread steadily throughout most of Europe. In place of each field sown alternately with grain in the autumn with the other left fallow, now one field was planted in autumn with winter wheat, barley, or rye; the second field was planted in spring with new crops like oats, chickpeas, peas, lentils, or broad beans; and the third field was left fallow. At a stroke, fallow was shortened from 50 to 33 percent of the total period and total area, labor requirements were more evenly spread over the year, and oats were converted into horsepower. Leguminous crops like peas and beans fixed nitrogen in the soil and maintained its fertility, allowing larger numbers of livestock to be kept, thus reducing the chances of famine as well as providing more manure. In turn, the raised protein intake improved human nutrition and health, contributing to the explosion of population.

These innovations resulted in more land being brought into cultivation. Triennial cropping could not take place unless two "old" fields could be reorganized, which was rare, and it was far more likely that a new third field was carved out of the standing forest. Everywhere, improved horse-power eased and speeded up the task, and there is also some evidence of the development of an improved felling ax. The growing population and farming innovations converged, enabling Europe to enter its era of spectacular expansion into the untouched hardwood forest on its External Frontier.

Power and Piety

While the prime engine of change was the growth of population, accompanied by the reduction of famine and aided by technological innovations, other factors—broadly ideological but, more accurately, sociocultural and religious—also played a part. The extension of secular power and the cult of piety gave underlying motivation to many actions and decisions: practical reality was combined with mystic idealism to produce spectacular change.

The extension of territorial organization occurred as local lay and ecclesiastical rulers consolidated their political control for reasons of defense and personal gain. Gradually they assumed the right to dispose of wasteland like any monarch. They allotted the wilderness under their control to groups of colonists who agreed to clear and farm it. The interests of these rulers were the opposite of those of the old manorial system; rather than keep peasants confined to traditional areas of settlement in order to control them and garner greater rents, now, people and their labor were regarded as a source of wealth. Colonizers were released from feudal constraints and offered generous terms, which included ownership and disposal of land, personal freedom, and often no restrictive requirement to clear-cut and grub out the stumps, which enabled girdling, burning, and rapid occupation to take place. Money services gradually replaced labor services and payments in kind. Thus, forest clearing and land reclamation contributed in a general way to a new society of free and equal agriculturalists by providing a greater opportunity for advancement and freedom; it was an important step in the emancipation of the common man.

The link between Western Christian piety and land reclamation was a leitmotif running through medieval clearing. From classical times onward the ability of humans to alter and control the environment had been prevalent; the early Christian fathers, such as Tertullian, Philo, Saint Jerome, and Saint Augustine, had linked it with Christianity. Like Cicero, they believed that minds and hands gave humans a capacity to create their own environment through inventiveness and necessity. Consequently, they attempted to make Christianity more acceptable and less "other-worldly" by emphasizing the message of Genesis—that God had given man dominion over nature. In fact man was in partnership with God and acted as God's helper or steward on earth in finalizing creation, so that theology was linked with everyday life and a divine purpose was seen in human works. Early Christian writers thus raised humans to a supreme position, so that what humans did had divine sanction; and humans, in turn, in the execution of their many accomplishments, skills, and talents, came nearer to God. It was a way of defending the new faith and expressing unity with humans on earth. It probably also gave rise to the unparalleled technological creativity of medieval Europe.

Onto that basis of approval of man's works was grafted the recognition of, and respect for, the concept of the dignity of labor, which was an essential and integral part of the technological change. From Carolingian times onward the monks of western Europe were less classical and bookish than their southern and eastern brethren. Physical labor was not despised and left to slaves. The Benedictines, in particular, proclaimed that "idleness is the enemy of the soul. The brethren, therefore, must be occupied in stated hours of manual labour, and again at other hours in sacred reading." Work had justification in theology, even in such unsophisticated texts as Paul's exhortation to the Thessalonians (3:10): "If anyone will not work, let him not eat." [7] Work was its own spiritual reward and especially, so it seemed, if performed away from the world and sin. A wild landscape not hallowed by prayer and asceticism was said to be in a state of original sin, but once it has become fertile and purposeful, it was transformed.

Thus, the prayer book and the ax were the way to expiate "original sin" in man and in nature and a way to demythologize the dark wilderness. Aided and abetted by pious monarchs who made generous grants in order to extend secular control, the early religious orders sought isolated spots in which to create a paradise and glorify God. If these clearings were in previously pagan areas on the margins of Christendom, as in Slavic eastern Europe, then all the better.

The clearing work of the Benedictines during the seventh and eighth centuries was widespread, and there are well-documented accounts of the setting up of monastic sites deep in the forest. The elite of society allied itself with the movement (and their piety ensured their place in the afterlife), so that the fervor of the ecclesiastical houses had ample backing. The expansion of clearing provided the rents and tithes for the church, an aim that harmonized perfectly with the yearnings of the freemen and peasants for new property and independence. Thus, for example, on 12 January 744, the use of the site at Fulda in the northern Odenwald was granted to the church, together with approximately 16 square miles of land, and two months later Saint Boniface visited it with his followers who set about clearing trees, and praying, and it became the site of the great abbey of today. It is possible that the remoteness of Fulda and other places was a pious topos in order to exaggerate the spirituality and achievements of the actors. But having said that, many places were "blanks" on the map, and although the detail would vary from place to place, and from time to time, it was repeated in broad outline in St. Gallen, Lorsch, Hersfeld, and Werden-on-Ruhr and subsequently elsewhere hundreds, if not thousands, of times across the breadth of Europe. Each monastery systematically allotted forestland to colonists to clear and cultivate, so that in time the countryside was transformed from forested wilderness to farmland landscape.

Thus the religious orders were the shock troops of clearing. Between 1098 and 1675 the Cistercians founded 742 centers, of which over 95 percent were in existence already by 1351, and these constituted about half of all religious houses. Each was a nucleus of intensive forest clearing and farming. "Give these monks a naked moor or a wild wood;" wrote Gerald of Barri, "then let a few years pass away and you will find not only beautiful churches, but dwellings of men built around them." [8] Piety was an accompaniment of improving zeal, and the creation of new landscapes fit for Christian settlement gave a just reward for that piety.

The colonization movement, however, contained paradoxes. First, while medieval theologians stressed partnership and stewardship with nature, the destruction of the forest and the extension of cultivation were inevitable and an affirmation of human supremacy. Second, while it cannot be denied that colonization was an act of piety, it inevitably increased the influence and fortune of the monasteries, which became politically, economically, and socially important. In time they became large landowners; the sacred mission gave way to the secular, solitude gave way to civilization, and toward the end of the great age of clearing in the eleventh century, monastic houses came into conflict with neighboring lay and ecclesiastical estates, and even with the peasants, who murmured that the changes to the forest had been so drastic and clearing had gone so far as to deprive them of their valued common resource. This, together with the fact that the monasteries became more worldly—even corrupt—meant that they lost the respect they once had. But for all that, nothing could take away their immense contribution to the clearing of the European landscape over three centuries.

EXTENT AND PACE OF CLEARING

In measuring the extent of clearing, a rough but useful distinction can be made between the core of Europe—the British Isles, France, Germany, and eastern Europe—and the periphery—Russia and the Mediterranean lands. The core documents "swarm" with allusions to clearing, place-names, and field names that reveal new settlements.

The Core
Early Centuries

During the early medieval years the work of clearing went on largely un-recorded. Peasants nibbled away at the edges of the woodlands around the villages, and then the assart, or new clearing, would be added to the exist-ing field system. It was a process that must have been repeated thousands, possibly millions, of times across the Continent. We get some hint of what was happening in France in the sixth and seventh centuries, when deserted properties were being resettled and new land created in the waste zones between settlements. "Brabant" was the original name for these intermedi-ate zones, and the once wooded Belgian province of that name acquired hundreds of settlers as the great *Silva Carbonnaria,* or Charcoal-Burners' Forest, was cleared.

In the time of Charlemagne the ambitions of the emperor, secular lords, and church to extend their holdings coalesced with the needs of the peas-ants and small-holders everywhere, as Charlemagne ordered his agents to give forest to the able-bodied to cut down in order to improve the royal possessions. In the south, expansion of settlement moved into the forests of the alpine foreland in Bavaria and along the Danube, where the new stra-tegic settlements of Passua and Salzberg were pivots of colonization, and elsewhere, in the east, there was scattered, sporadic clearing. But nothing compared to clearing in the lands along the middle and lower Rhine in the center of the empire. The forests were in rapid retreat; the Ardennes were losing their primeval character, as was much of the hill country around the upper Rhine, while farther east the valleys of the great forest of the Oden-wald between the Neckar and the Main, which were untouched before 800, now had many assarts, or *Bifänge,* in them. These lands also displayed the first manifestations on the Continent of the typical forest row village, or *Waldhufendorf,* with its characteristic *"hufen,"* or long, narrow fields that were cut back into the forest behind each new holding. The *Waldhufendorf* was a sure sign of planned clearing.

The widespread and comprehensive colonization of these western forests at such an early date has been overlooked, as attention has focused on the colonization east of the Elbe during the thirteenth century, but it was no less spectacular. For example, the Odenwald colonization probably began in 764 with the founding of the imperial Benedictine monastery of Lorsch, 30 km south of Fulda. Charlemagne subdivided the royal forest among the Abbeys of Lorsch and Amorbach, the Bishop of Worms, and a half-dozen nobles in return for a variety of secular services including annual gifts, contributions to the royal budget, and most important, large numbers of mounted troops for defense. Lorsch set about methodically settling and clearing the forest with the establishment of *Waldhufendorf.* There seem to have been three sizes, which corresponded to their date of foundation and degree of independence (fig. 5.2). The earliest (ninth century) and smallest in the west were for dependent peasants who rendered services; much larger and later ones in the south and center were for independent peasants who rendered only fixed amounts of stock and harvest; and the very largest in the east and founded in the eleventh century were for the entirely free, who probably engaged in a regulated slash-and-burn tillage within the mass of smaller agricultural settlements. A systematic network of central places or *Villicatio* and castle settlements with manorial courts and markets were established. Thus the forested landscape was successfully transformed into a planned "cultural landscape." [9]

The significance of this planned experiment in the Rhineland was far-reaching; it may have been the "hearth" area of experimentation and the model for the colonization of the rest of the central European forest. The *Waldhufendorf* settlement probably originated in the upper Rhine and reached its first formal perfection in Odenwald before spreading to neighboring Spessart in the east, the Black Forest, and the Augsburg plains to the south. Eventually, with variations, it was adopted even farther afield in the massive forests of the Frankenwald, Thuringia, and Lower Saxony before becoming such a distinctive feature of the trans-Elbian colonization and forest clearing.

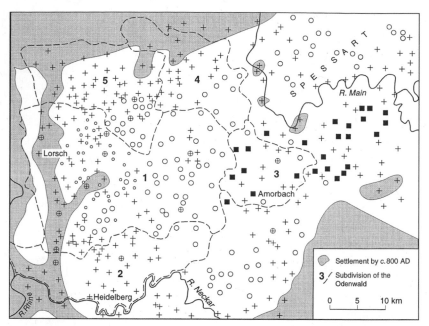

Figure 5.2 Forest clearing and village foundation in the Odenwald, eighth to eleventh centuries
AD. The subdivisions of the royal forest of Odenwald are as follows: (1) Abbey of Lorsch,
(2) Bishop of Worms, (3) Abbey of Amorbach, (4) Abbey of Fulda, and (5) Nobility. The subdivisions of the Odenwald settlement types are coded as follows: + = irregular (mainly early);
° = *Waldhufen*—short, small "*hufen*" (eighth to ninth centuries); ○ = *Waldhufen*—long,
large "*hufen*" (tenth century); ■ = *Waldhufen*—large, disconnected "*hufen*" (eleventh
century); ⊕ = administrative centers. (Source: after H.-J. Nitz, "The Church as Colonist:
The Benedictine Abbey of Lorsch and Planned Waldhufen Colonization in the Oldenwald,"
Journal of Historical Geography 9 [1983]: 105–23.)

Similar but far less systematic and extensive colonization is hinted at in
fifth- to ninth-century England, where the Anglo-Saxon poet described the
plowman as the "grey foe of the wood." [10] Here place-names are especially
useful, as they can be divided into a relative chronology indicative of early
and late stages of settlement. Names belonging to the first phase of settlement
that do not indicate woodland (e.g., those ending in *-ing, -ington, -tun, -cote,
-ham*) tend to occur on more easily worked light gravel and loamy soils.
Names belonging to the later phase of settlement that do indicate woodland (e.g, *-leah, -feld, -wood, -holt, -hurst, -weald*) occur on the deeper clays
that must have been wooded and hence cleared in order to be settled. Other
names indicate types of woodland, and yet others still the act of clearing such
as "sarts" from "assarts," "intak" or "intake," "stubbing" or "Brentwood"
for "burnt wood," and so forth.

The various strands of evidence come together nicely in Warwickshire (fig. 5.3), although other counties show the same pattern. The county is bisected from southwest to northeast by the River Avon, which divides the heavier clay of the famed Forest of Arden, from the lighter soils and open country known as the Felden, to the south. Arden shows considerable woodland in the Domesday Survey of 1086, as measured by its length and breadth in leagues; a concentration of place-names such as *-ley,* which is indicative of clearing; and also a concentration of defensive moated farmsteads, a distinctive feature of settlement in once-forested areas, here as well as in Essex and Norfolk. But the south is a complete contrast in all respects.

L'Âge des Grands Défrichements

As the eleventh century progressed, Europe entered two centuries of massive clearing as religious houses and lay lords actively encouraged colonization. In France and Germany in particular, the age of medieval prosperity is the age of land reclamation. The detail can be mind-numbing in its amount and complexity, and it is difficult to get an exact measurement of the total clearing that changed the face of the medieval world. It is best to look at some regional examples.

In France the early example of clearing set by the Benedictine monasteries in the Paris basin was expanded after 1125 with the efforts of the Cistercian order, which had a concentration of motherhouses in Burgundy in the east and north of the country from which numerous daughter settlements were founded, each a nucleus of "aggressive" clearing. Documents are full of references to clearings, or assarts; to pioneer settlements, or *hôtes;* to their crop-sharing arrangements, or *champarts;* to their tasks, or *tâches,* which were payments due from recently reclaimed land; and to *novales,* or tithes, levied on newly broken-up areas. The expansion of settlement during the twelfth century in the Middle Yonne Valley, southeast of Paris, is indicative of what was happening (fig. 5.4).

Frequently, completely new settlements were created: the *ville-neuves* of the north, the *bourgs* of the west, and the *bastides* of the south, all basically villages of 30–80 colonists or *hopites.* In order to encourage settlement and clearing, lords gave franchises, or freedoms of self-government, reduced dues, and abolished customary taxes, such as *chevage* (a yearly head tax), *formariage* (the prohibition of exogamy), *taille seigneuriale* (tallage), and the *corvée* (payments in labor). For example, Abbot Suger of St. Denis boasted that he had added 20 livres to the income of a nearby manor by settling 80 new *hôtes* on newly cleared land next to it.

Sometimes the new villages, like those in Normandy, partook of the morphological characteristics of the *Waldhufendorf,* but it is the place-name

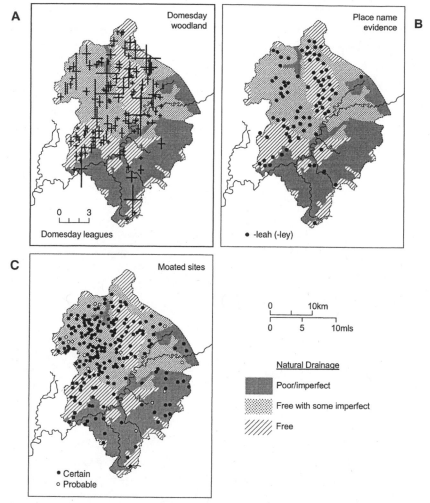

Figure 5.3 Landscapes of woodland clearing in Warwickshire, England. *A,* Extent of Domesday woodland; *B,* Place-names indicative of clearing; and *C,* Moated sites. (Sources: based on H. C. Darby and I. B. Terrett, eds., *The Domesday Geography of Midland England* [Cambridge: Cambridge University Press, 1971], 296; J. E. B. Glover and A. Mawer, *The Place–names of Warwickshire* [Cambridge: Cambridge University Press, 1936]; B. K. Roberts, "Moated Sites," *Amateur Historian* [later, *Local History*] 5 [1961–63]: 40; and W. A. D. Whitfield, *The Soils of Warwickshire,* Soil Survey Record no. 101 [Harpenden: Soil Survey of England and Wales. 1986], no. 6.)

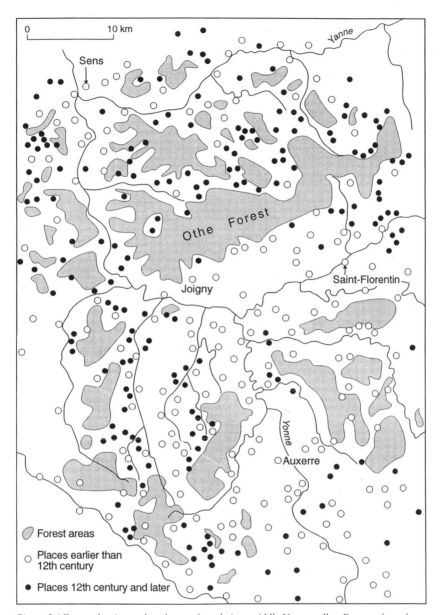

0   10 km

Sens

Yanne

Othe Forest

Joigny

Saint-Florentin

Yonne

Auxerre

⬭ Forest areas

○ Places earlier than
   12th century

● Places 12th century and later

Figure 5.4 Forest clearing and settlement foundation, middle Yonne valley, France, eleventh century AD. (Source: G. Duby, *The Early Growth of the European Economy: Warriors and Peasants from the Seventh to Twelfth Centuries,* trans. H. B. V. Clarke [Ithaca, N.Y.: Cornell University Press, 1974], 204.)

elements that are so indicative of origin. For example, there are those with *rue* in their name, meaning originally a breach in the forest (*rupta*), hence La Rue Doré (Val-d'Oise) or Rupt-sur-Saône (Haute-Saône). Far more common are *Villeneuve, Neuville, Neufbourg, La Villeneuve, Neuvy, Neuilly,* and so forth, followed by the name of the founder—king, bishop, duke, count, or the saint of the founding abbey church (e.g., Neuilly-Saint-Pierre), or a neighboring town. And there are those with exotic names taken from the Crusades, such as Jerusalem, Nazareth, or Jericho, or with assart in the name (e.g., Essarts-le-Roi), or with the founder's own name (e.g., Beaumarchais), and there are many others. Similar place-name evidence exists in other areas of western Europe. The "*-sarts*" ("assarts") in Flanders and the "*-rodes*" ("to grub up") in Brabant and Hainault were instituted by French and Flemish colonists, respectively.

Farther east, in the lands between the Rhine and the Elbe, the Great Reclamation, or *Urbarmachung,* was promoted vigorously by ecclesiastical and lay lords, and where the proprietors resisted, the peasants either encroached or took the forest by force. The map is peppered with ecclesiastical and diagnostic place-name suffixes such as those in the land between the Weser and the Harz Mountains that end in *-hagan,* which indicate settlement by Flemish colonizers; or elsewhere, names like *-wald* ("forest") and *-holz* ("wood"), which are indicative of prior vegetation conditions; or those like *-rode* ("grubbed up"), *-swend* ("burned"), and *-ho* (cut down), which tell of the process of clearing. Across the lowlands and the Alpine forelands the economy was changed and the appearance of the land transformed as fields and farms replaced forests. The upland massifs, such as the Harz, the Eifel, the Westerwald, the Thuringian Forest, and the Black Forest, were coming to look like great wooded islands in a sea of cultivation. But the change did not cease; writing in 1222 concerning the previous century, Ceasarius of Prüm, the great monastery in the forested depths of the Eifel, recounted that "during this long space of time many forests were felled, villages founded, mills erected, taxes ordained, vines planted, and an infinite amount of land reduced to agriculture." [11] Elsewhere in the upland forest, charcoal burners chipped away and thinned the stands for their daily consumption of wood for smelting the abundant silver/lead and iron ores, particularly in the Harz Mountains. One arm of colonization thrust southeast across the Alps, the Sudeten Mountains, and the slopes of the Erzgebirge, and down the Danube, to create Austria, and it culminated in many isolated pockets of German agricultural and mining settlements in Slav or Magyar territory in present-day Bohemia, Hungary, and Transylvania. It was virtually over by 1150.

Impressive as this great colonization was, it did not equal the great movement east that occurred during the twelfth century, which changed the map of the heart of central Europe, culturally and physically. Anywhere between 150,000 and 200,000 settlers moved east of the Elbe-Salle line, extending cultivated area into the forests to reach its greatest extent ever, so that little more was added until modern times. The advance was across the varied and poorly drained outwash sands, gravels, and clays of the northern German plain into what are now Mecklenburg, Pomerania, and Brandenberg and Silesia. The motives here were a mixture of the economic and the missionary as Germans sought to convert the Slavs. In addition, Slavonic lords wanted to emulate German methods of cultivation and organization with the heavy plow in order to prosper. Much of the movement was the uncoordinated migration of small groups of peasants who sought their own land and personal liberty. People came from all classes and from everywhere in "old" Germany; Flemings and Hollanders were especially sought out for the settlement of the swampy areas, although their reputation as pioneer colonizers made them desirable anywhere. Recruiting drives, with their promises of independence and wealth, were aimed at "westerners" to colonize the lands east of present-day Berlin. It was not unlike the booster literature used to lure settlers to the cutover lands of the Great Lakes states of the United States 700 years later.

Few of the new overlords had links with the west, and in any case, to get the best settlers and to plan the best type of settlement required an organization beyond their means. Therefore they employed "locators," middlemen whose job it was to find and negotiate with the migrants and arrange transportation, land allotment, and settlement layout. Their reputation for organization must have been a big factor in the readiness and confidence with which so many western peasants were prepared to travel hundreds of miles into the unknown of the east. Towns were established as nodes of communication and trade, and about 1,200 villages were created in Silesia alone, though some of these must have been additions grafted onto existing settlements.

Toward the end of the thirteenth century this episode of forest colonization had more or less played itself out, but there was one more scene to be enacted. In the early thirteenth century, the military order of the Brethren of the Sword had established an isolated and shallow outpost of fortified towns around Riga on the Baltic coast. Then, with the return of the Teutonic Knights from the Crusades, the systematic colonization began of the intervening lands, by all the means already perfected on the "old frontier," so that by 1346 all the territory fringing the Baltic—through Prussia West and East, Courland, Livonia, and Estonia, almost to the Gulf of Finland—was under their control (see fig. 7.6 for these locations). What they called *das Grosse Wildnis* was transformed, and by the end of the fifteenth century some 93 cities had been established, as well as 1,400 villages, many of which can be easily traced because they are *waldhufen* or street villages in the former forest or *marschufen* in the former marsh.

The clearing in central and eastern Europe was not solely a German enterprise, though they were the spearheads of change. Slavonic lords and peasants, sometimes under coercion but often through emulation, cleared forests and founded new villages, some of which were the distinctive *waldhufen* type. In the interior basin of Bohemia there are over 300 villages called *Lhota*, which means approximately "freedom" or "freeing"—a reference to exemption from rents and taxes for a number of years in return for establishing a new settlement and clearing. A little farther west in Slovakia the word appears about forty times as *lêhota,* and northward in eastern Poland some thirty times as *Logota,* which merge into over 1,500 places named *Wola* (again meaning "freedom") east of a line from Cracow to Kalisch. These examples could be multiplied endlessly, and added to with specifically Slavonic "clearing" names such as *kopanice, lazy,* and *paseky.* Although this clearing was usually later and more limited in extent than the German colonization, it meant essentially the same thing: the diminution of the forest cover.

An obvious question is, How much was cleared? But it will never be answered definitively because of the long time span and the absence of unequivocal evidence. But despite the technicalities of what forest meant, we can be sure that there was still a lot of woodland in Europe and much of it very dense. Roland Bechmann suggests that the forests of France were reduced from 30 million to 13 million ha between circa 800 and 1300, and still a quarter of the country remained covered.[12] In Germany and central Europe, Otto Schlüter's exhaustive and detailed enquiry into nearly 7,000 German and non-German place-names, plus the evidence of historical documents, soils, archaeology, vegetation history, and the actual sites themselves, resulted in his maps of the forest for over 1 million km² in central Europe in circa 900, and again a thousand years later. Perhaps 70 percent of the land was forest covered initially and about 25 percent remained by 1900 (figs. 5.5, 5.6).[13] We may vary these estimates here and there, but they are certainly within the correct level of magnitude. By any calculation, the medieval European experience must rank as one of the great deforestation episodes in the world.

Britain participated in much of the experience of the continental core, but as was so often the case, it stood slightly aside and was a faint echo of the bigger story. The rapidly growing population put pressure on woodland on the edges of cultivation everywhere, yet centuries of clearing had left a patchy cover that was already exploited. There was no concerted plan comparable to mainland Europe. Clearing was piecemeal by free peasants and

Figure 5.5 Forest cover in central Europe, circa AD 900. (Sources: H. C. Darby, "The Clearing of the Woodland in Europe," in *Man's Role on Changing the Face of the Earth,* ed. W. L. Thomas [Chicago: University of Chicago Press, 1956], 183–216, esp. 202, 203, simplified from O. Schlüter, *Atlas Ostliches Mittleuropa* [Belefield: Velhagen & Klasing, 1952], plate 10.)

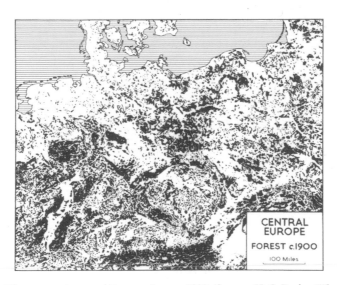

Figure 5.6 Forest cover in central Europe, circa AD 1900. (Sources: H. C. Darby, "The Clearing of the Woodland in Europe," in *Man's Role on Changing the Face of the Earth,* ed. W. L. Thomas [Chicago: University of Chicago Press, 1956], 183–216, esp. 202, 203, simplified from O. Schlüter, *Atlas Ostliches Mittleuropa* [Belefield: Velhagen & Klasing, 1952], plate 10.)

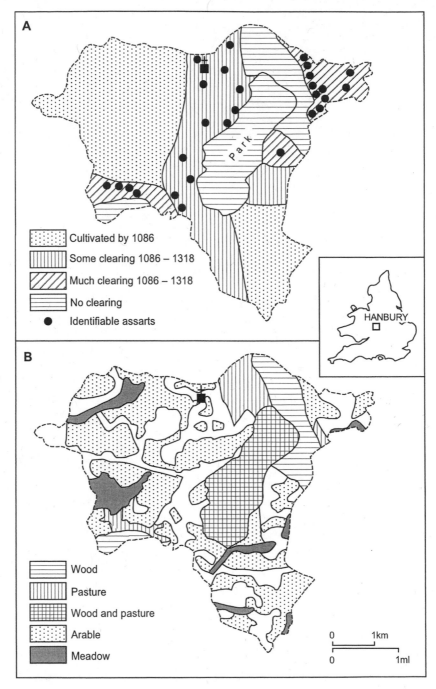

A

Cultivated by 1086
Some clearing 1086 – 1318
Much clearing 1086 – 1318
No clearing
● Identifiable assarts

HANBURY

B

Wood
Pasture
Wood and pasture
Arable
Meadow

0   1km
0   1ml

Figure 5.7 Hanbury, West Midlands, England. *A*, Settlement zones, AD 400–1318; and *B*, Land use circa AD 1300. (Source: after C. Dyer, *Hanbury: Settlement and Society in a Wooded Landscape*, Department of Local History Occasional Papers, ser. 4, no.4 [Leicester: Leicester University Press, 1991].)

tenants, some acting with a license from their lord, but most acting illegally. References are scattered and difficult to trace, even in large woodland areas; but just occasionally the story of individual effort can be reconstructed, as in the parish of Hanbury, in northeast Worcestershire, deep in the Forest of Feckenham. Figure 5.7 shows the incidence of assarts and the areas in which most clearance occurred in Hanbury, where the population rose from 266 to 725 by 1299. Small as the parish is, Hanbury must stand as a representative example of what must have happened hundreds, if not thousands, of times across Britain, and indeed the whole continent, during the great age of clearing. The detail might have varied from place to place, but the experience of clearing a small patch of woodland, breaking up the soil, and getting in and harvesting the first crop was one that millions of people shared from Land's End to the Urals.

The Periphery

Around the European core of innovation and transformation lay the peripheries: Russia to the east and northeast and the Mediterranean to the south. Clearing occurred for all the reasons mentioned already, but never with the same single-mindedness of purpose or overall impact.

Russia: "The Icon and the Ax"

Russia exhibited many of the characteristics of the core, but the experience was subtly different. From their homeland somewhere between the Carpathians and the Upper Dnieper, the Slavs moved westward into Europe but also eastward into the mixed-oak forest zone that lay in an elongated triangle pointing eastward toward Asia—its apex located on the Oka-Volga confluence (near present-day Moscow)—and wedged between the almost unbroken wall of the coniferous forests to the north and the steppe to the south. Kiev, near the extreme southwest corner of the mixed forest zone, was founded in the ninth century and traditionally lay "amongst forests" but is now surrounded by open steppe, which suggests extensive clearing. It was a frontier society, constantly battered by the onslaught of the Mongols, the battles of 1237–40 having a ferocity unequaled until the twentieth century. Consequently, the Slavic Orthodox Christian refugees moved north into the security of the forests, even as far as Moscow (founded circa 1147).

The material effort and religious zeal of the new settlers in the forest is symbolized by the icon and the ax—two objects that were traditionally hung together in a place of honor on the wall of every peasant hut and had enduring meaning to Russians. The ax was the indispensable means of subordinating the forest; the icon a reminder of the religious faith that gave

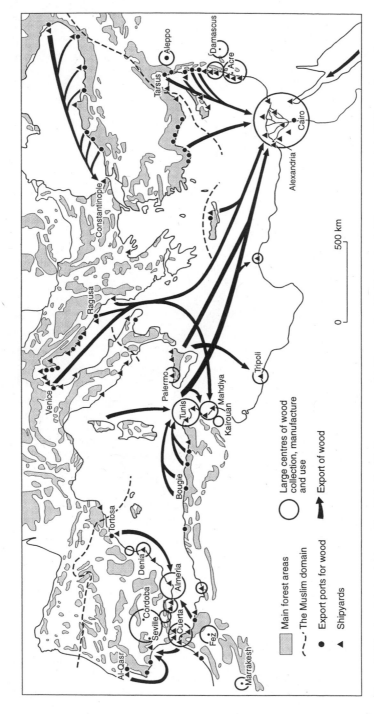

Figure 5.8 Wood and timber in the medieval Muslim Mediterranean world. (Source: after M. M. Lombard, "Une carte du bois la Méditerranée musulmane [VIIe–XIe siècle]," *Annales, Economies, Sociétés, Civilisations* 14 [1959]: 23–54.)

Map legend:

- Main forest areas
- The Muslim domain
- Export ports for wood
- Shipyards
- Large centres of wood collection, manufacture and use
- Export of wood

Labels on map: Aleppo, Damascus, Acre, Tarsus, Cairo, Alexandria, Constantinople, Ragusa, Venice, Palermo, Tripoli, Mahdiya, Kairouan, Tunis, Bougie, Tortosa, Denia, Cordoba, Almeria, Cuerta, Seville, Fez, Al-Qasr, Marrakesh

500 km
0

the refugee a sense of security and higher purpose and that was often the equivalent of a battle standard borne on high against the foe, whether that be the barbarians or the unbroken forest.

The progress of forest clearing was slow and the extent limited compared with the vigor and thoroughness of the trans-Elbean Germans at this time. There were reasons for this: Mongol raids continued, the dominant slash-and-burn cultivation did not lead to permanent clearing, and above all, the nobility and religious patrons were intensely feudal and autocratic and did not want the land to pass into the hands of independent farmers but that the farmers should remain as serfs. The feeling of freedom and emancipation that fired the energy and ambition of the western European forest settler was absent. Clearing was patchy, even as late as the eighteenth century the country around Moscow and on the road to Smolensk seemed "one huge forest, and the towns and villages in it as mere clearings." [14] In the coniferous forests farther north, furs, pitch, pine, tar, and wax were funneled through the merchant system of Novgorod, which moved increasingly into the orbit of the Hanseatic League, and from there out to the markets of the core of maritime western Europe. Small settlements developed into prosperous towns between Moscow and the White Sea, but it should not be overstated; it was a light settlement of slash-and-burn cropping with rye, flax, oats, and hemp and had little impact on the forest.

The Muslim Mediterranean

Initially the Muslim conquest of the Mediterranean was land-based, with expansion moving through Egypt and North Africa between AD 700 and 750. But repeated harassment and victories by Christian fleets from Byzantium against North Africa led to a change in strategy, and soon the Muslims were engaged in extensive shipbuilding. Defense shifted to offense, and raids occurred along the southern coasts of Europe and Asia Minor during the eighth and ninth centuries. These assaults culminated in outright conquest: Spain fell quickly during the eighth century, then Cyprus, and Sicily between 800 and 902.

Now the limited timber supplies for the Cairo and Tunis shipbuilding yards from the Atlas Mountains in North Africa could be augmented by the ample local supplies of Sicily and Spain, long-distance trading with the Dalmatian and Anatolian coasts, and even Malabar for the prized teakwood (fig. 5.8). But use was not confined to shipbuilding. Major concentrations of furniture and artisans' woodworking shops of all kinds grew up in major urban centers like Cairo, Baghdad, Tunis, and Acre; the Spanish cities of Seville, Cordoba, and Almeria; and new towns like Kairouan in Tunisia. The fuel demands in this generally wood-poor environment were ceaseless;

domestic fuel, metal smelting, mining, ceramics, and sugar refining all added to the drain on supplies.

By the thirteenth century, Byzantium had reconquered Crete, Cyprus, and much of Syria, and then Sicily fell, and Spain followed, and the Muslims' timber supplies dried up. The Arabs tried to organize supplies from the rich Venetian hinterland in Dalmatia and the Alps, but they either had to pay exorbitant prices or were denied access to supplies as the strategic nature of timber was appreciated, especially at a time when the Crusades to reoccupy the Holy Land were getting under way. By the end of the fourteenth century, the Muslim world was in comparative disarray and Venice was in the ascendancy. A new chapter in forest use in this part of the world was opening up.

COMPLEXITY AND CONFLICT IN THE FOREST

The forest was deeply embedded in the fabric of medieval life. Its size, its multiple uses, and yet its continuing diminution meant there would be a conflict of aims, a complexity of uses, and an ambivalence of motives. The issues were stark—few rural communities or towns owned the freehold of the forest on which they depended: that was the prerogative of royalty and, later, the nobility. Monarchs and aristocrats had reserved "forest" areas (whether densely treed or not) in which they had ancient rights for their own use, particularly for game and hunting. Yet the forest was close to the everyday life of ordinary people because of its multiple products and uses. It was not an abstract concept: it was simply the necessity of eating and keeping warm, of fencing land and pasturage (plate 5.2). It was a valued resource without which people could not exist. Consequently, from about the eighth and ninth centuries a vast body of rights, usages, and customary law had grown up about forest use that were gradually codified and regulated, and by the twelfth and thirteenth centuries were given precise definitions and delimitations.

For example, in France, over 350 places surrounding or within the huge Forest of Orléans had codified and defined usage rights. These were usually free or, if emanating from a religious house, granted in return for saying masses for the lord. There was *faucillage* or herbage, the right to cut grass and take it away; *champiage,* the right to graze animals on common pastures; *ramage,* the right to take branches and boughs for fences; *affouage,* the right take firewood; *maronage,* the right to cut timber for necessary repairs to buildings; and *ramas,* the right to collect litter for cattle, to name but a few. The Law of Beaumont (1182) granted free use of woodlands to over 500 mainly new towns created throughout the country, and the Law of

Plate 5.2 Swine Feeding in the Forest. The manuscript comes from the eleventh century AD. (By permission of the British Library, Ms. Tiberius, B.V. fol. 7.)

Lorris (1108–37) did the same for over 300 new towns created in the east and south of the Parisian basin.

In Britain, the forest was less extensive and all-pervasive in rural society, but even so, many peasants had the right to collect constructional timber (*housebote*), wood for fencing (*hayebote*—known collectively as "estovers"), grazing for cattle or pannage for swine, and the right to take fuelwood (*firebote*), which was often deadwood that could be got "by hook or by crook"—that is to say, such timber as could be knocked off or pulled down from standing trees, a concession paralleling the French right of *mort-bois* or *morbois*.

But hunting was the preserve of royalty and the nobility, who had an irresistible infatuation with it that went way beyond the attaining of meat (plate 5.3). Hunting was a symbolic ritual that mirrored both royal charisma and the political power of elites. The ritual display of "manners" and power made it an exercise in courtly ceremony, but at another level it was a ritualistic reenactment of the historical conquest of wilderness (literally, "the place of wild beasts"). Thus, the message was mixed: on the one hand the king or lord embodied a civilizing force, but on the other he also harbored a savage nature that ensured the protection of the territory. In a sense the king belonged to nature, returning periodically to ritualize its conquest.

These examples of forest control and use could be multiplied endlessly at different times and different places, and we have not even touched the abundant evidence of these practices for Germany and central Europe. So intricate was this body of custom and traditional rights in most rural societies that they were like strands that enmeshed individuals and institutions and constituted, suggests Glacken, "the medieval counterpart of the modern concept of culture" that bespoke of an organized society and that spanned the continent.[15]

Anything that lessened these rights and customs was bound to cause concern. Population increase during the thirteenth century, the demands of trade and towns, and the clearing and conversion of forest to farmland produced acute pressure on the resource. In addition, seigniorial pressure on the peasantry in order to maintain income led to the demarcation and regulation, or even prohibition, of certain forest rights. Thus, a tension arose between royalty and lords, each of whom wanted to preserve the forests for their own hunting, and between both of these and the peasants, who valued the products and privileges of forested land. It was a sort of conflict of interest between preservation and modification, though at times it is difficult to know who was preserver and who was modifier—king, lord, or peasant—though we can be certain that hunting was crucial in forest conservation.

As early as Carolingian times in the early ninth century, royalty attempted to regulate forest use by forbidding lords to make new hunting grounds, but much more commonly, lords limited peasant rights. These were usually enforced ruthlessly. Unauthorized dwellings were destroyed, and poachers mutilated or put to death. In England, William set up a severe forest regime with harsh penalties for poaching and assarting. As hinted

Plate 5.3 The Hunt in the Forest by Paolo Uccello, circa 1470. This unique painting depicts wealthy patricians indulging in the ritual of their favorite sport on a moonlit night. (Ashmolean Museum, Oxford.)

in figure 5.1, whole counties were scheduled as "forest" and hundreds of
families evicted. In time, peasants and nobles alike chaffed under the harsh
restrictions, and in 1217 the nobles wrung concessions out of Henry III with
the Forest Charter, which safeguarded the rights of their tenants and themselves. The charter was far-reaching in its implications and "took its place,"
said Doris Stenton, "alongside the Great Charter [Magna Carta] as part of
the foundations on which the English social scene was laid." [16] Simply, once
more, the forest played a role in the development of human affairs. Not only
did clearing it promote the social advancement of the common man, but the
establishment of forest rights was a precursor of human rights.

But as the colonization process waned at the end of the thirteenth century, many felt that clearing had gone far enough, if not too far. If it continued, where would the animals graze and where would the fuel come from,
especially as the development of the chimney and hearths in individual
rooms in houses increased the demand for fuelwood? The medieval frontier had closed, and the free profit of unused land could no longer enrich
monastery, lord, or peasant. Forest protection seemed a desirable aim. Both
lords and peasants alike cooperated more.

It is difficult to generalize about concerns of forest loss or preservation, but there are indicators. In France, an ever-increasing proliferation of
edicts throughout the thirteenth century defined usage rights more closely,
set up a special judiciary concerning forests, and culminated in 1291 in
an ordinance defining the role of the new officials, the masters of *Eaux et
Forêts,* that was repeated and strengthened by measures in 1317, 1319,
1346, 1355, and 1357. The agents were charged with visiting all forest
areas, investigating complaints and breaches of use, and having the forests
exploited with the purpose that they remained in a perpetually good condition. In Germany, similar though less comprehensive measures are evident.
In 1309 cleared and cultivated forest land either side of the Pegnitz River,
near Nuremberg, was ordered to be returned to forest by royal edict, and
clearings in Hagenauer forest phased out. In 1331 King Ludwig of Bavaria
promulgated more regulations that further restricted forest use, especially
the sale of wood that might be "harmful to the city" and its industries. [17]

The significance of these glimmerings of concern in the story of global
deforestation is that the forest was becoming valued, both economically and
culturally. Additionally, there was an awareness that the forest environment
was being changed radically and that not all change constituted "progress"
or was necessarily desirable. Finally, there was a consciousness of the need
to achieve a balance among the different and competing uses of the forest—agriculture, industry, and forestry. Timber was the indispensable raw
material of metal smelting, glass-making, furniture making, cooperage,

house building, and a dozen other manufacturing and fabricating processes. By about 1400, iron production alone throughout Europe was between 25,000 and 30,000 tons (plate 5.4). The ore deposits and the towns and their industries could not be moved when the supplies of wood ran out, but the supplies could be protected and growth encouraged. Simply, the forest was the lifeblood of the brisk and vigorous medieval economy, so an accommodation between various uses had to be found.

EUROPEAN EPILOGUE: PLAGUE AND REFORESTATION

The crisis in the forest never came; the exuberance of the medieval spring turned to the melancholy of dark winter. The spread of bubonic plague from Constantinople and across Europe between 1347 and 1353 wiped out at least one-third of the population in most of the West, and maybe one half in some places. Over 20 million people died, and the total population fell from 73.5 million in 1340 to about 50 million in 1450. In some areas the effect was compounded by deteriorating climate and unsettled weather, first evident during the late thirteenth century, which led to crop failure, disease in stock, and settlement retreat from marginal areas. The population surplus, which had caused an "agrarian crisis" through overcrowding on good lands, pressure on the forests, and conflicts over usage rights, was reduced at a stroke. Across the continent, between one-fifth and one-fourth of all settlements were abandoned, the "deserted villages" of England and France being matched by the *Wüstungen* of Germany, in both the "old" south and west as well as the "new" eastern trans-Elbean settlement. The abandonment of cultivated land has been put as high as 25 percent. The recolonization by the forest of once-cultivated land was rapid and extensive, and many present forests in Germany came into being only after the Middle Ages (fig. 5.9).

Conditions became no better in the succeeding century. War and pillage ravaged the countryside; the Hussite Wars (1419–36) devastated Bohemia economically and demographically, and similarly in the west, France suffered grievously during the Hundred Years War (1337–1453), which reduced the population by one-half to one-third in places. Settlements were reduced to a heap of ruins and abandoned fields invaded by brambles, bushes, and ultimately forest. For a while, the forest had been reprieved.

CHINA: A LAND OF "PONDEROUS UNKNOWNS"

The comparison between Europe and the even more densely populated and intensely humanized lands of China, where deforestation had been going on during the equivalent of Neolithic, classical, and medieval times, could not

Plate 5.4 Mining used up vast amounts of wood for shoring up the workings and, of course, for smelting. (From G. Agricola, *De re metallica* [1557], trans. H. C. Hoover and L. H. Hoover [New York: Dover, 1950].)

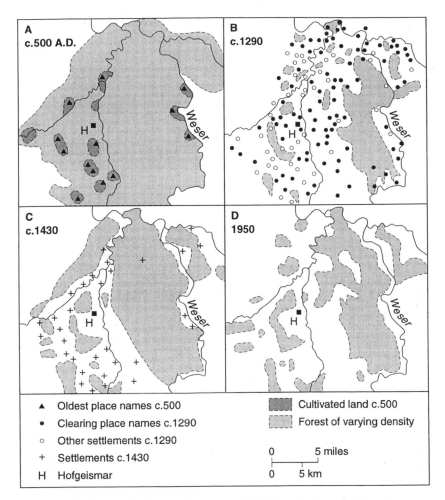

Figure 5.9 Woodland and settlement change around Hofgeismar in the upper Weser basin:
A, circa AD 500, to D, AD 1950. Source: Helmut Jäger, *Die Entwicklung der Kulturlandschaft im Kriese Hofgeïsmar* (Göttingen: Department of Geography, 195). Note the post-fifteenth-century settlements not shown in fig. 5.9C.

be starker. Whereas events in Europe are reasonably clear, those of China before the beginning of the Ming dynasty in 1368 are truly "dark." Our knowledge of deforestation is almost wholly confined to the musings of the third-century BC philosopher Mencius on the destructive nature of grazing and tree lopping for fuel that left "bald" mountains, the seventh- to tenth-century poems of the *Shih Ching,* and the workings of the iron industry. Compared to Europe, the information gap is immense, making China a land of "ponderous unknowns." [18] There is a paucity of information on the life of the peasants and middle classes but an abundance on the working of bureaucratic government, taxation, government agricultural policies, fiscal reforms, and development plans. Thus, material for a "bottom-up" approach or regional studies is missing, and interpretations of early Chinese rural society rarely carry the conviction of their counterparts in Europe. Nonetheless, there are hints of massive change.

The Clearing Process

The Chinese forest has a greater geographical variation than does that of Europe. It stretches from the Arctic tundra and steppes of Siberia to the tropical rain forests of Southeast Asia. Agricultural development was centered in the Yellow River (Huang-Ho) basin in the broad-leafed deciduous forests of the north, which merged into the loess plateau, and the grassland steppe beyond. Possible climatic change and millennia of agriculture had transformed these lands into a mosaic of different vegetation types, fairly thick forest around rivers and other permanent sources of water, sparse deciduous woodland on the plains, opening out into savannah grasslands with scattered trees or brush in the northwest. Denser deciduous woodland was found on the foothills of the mountains, merging into coniferous forest above about 1,500 meters, and then larch and spruce above that. The heavily forested northeast and tropical southern forests were probably also being cleared, but we know very little, if anything, about the process.

How these lands were occupied and improved predominantly by the Han is largely unknown. Nonetheless, the seventh- to tenth-century BC poems in the *Book of Odes* (*Shih Ching*) give us some idea of the labors and livelihood of ordinary people as they broke up new land:

> They clear away the grass, the trees;
> Their ploughs open up the ground.
> In a thousand pairs they tug at weeds and roots,
> Along the low ground, along the ridges
> There is the master and his eldest son,
> There is the headman and overseer.
> They mark out, they plough.
> Truly those southern hills—
> It was Yü who fashioned them;
> Those level spaces, upland and lowland—
> The descendant tills them.
> We draw boundaries, we divide the plots,
> On southern slopes and eastern we set our acres.[19]

The one unambiguous description of land clearing occurs in the *Ch'i Min Yao Shu* composed by Chia Ssu-Hsieh circa AD 535, and it refers to the reclamation of woodland and scrub that had grown up after decades of devastating warfare in North China in the post-Han period (after AD 220), which were to be cleared for civil and military colonies:

> When clearing land (Khai huang) in mountains or marshes for new fields, always cut down the weeds in the seventh month; the weeds should be set on fire once they have dried out. Cultivation should begin only in the spring. Larger trees and shrubs should be killed by ring-barking. Once the leaves are dead and no longer cast any shade ploughing and sowing may begin, and after three years the roots will have withered and the trunks decayed enough to be burned out.
>
> Once the ploughing of the waste is completed, draw an iron-toothed harrow across it twice. Broadcast millet and then run the bush-harrow over the field twice. By the next year it will be fit for grain land.

Roots and stumps were grubbed out with mattock and hoe. Clearing was certainly worth the effort, and it was a common saying that "even setting up in trade was not as profitable as clearing new land." [20]

In the forested hill slopes of the less densely populated tropical forests south of the Yangtze, a shifting cultivation system was practiced, in which the inhabitants were "ploughing with fire" and using axes and spades. This was satisfactory as long as the patch cleared was small and the rotation short; but problems arose after the third century AD, when the Han migrants with their clear-cutting techniques moved into the forested hill country from the overcrowded north. Overcultivation caused massive soil degradation, as well as siltation in the Yangtze by the thirteenth century.

By the end of the innovative T'ang dynasty (circa AD 923–36) the transformation of large parts of northern China was evident. Buddhism and Confucianism had not stopped the ascendancy of culture over nature; indeed, the high art of calligraphy had led to a demand for pine soot for making the ink for the vast Chinese bureaucracy, causing massive inroads into the pine forests of the T'ai-hang mountains between Shansi and Hopei. Paradoxically, it was the advantages of comfort and safety of the human-made world that engendered a greater awareness of the beauty and fragility of nature. Increasingly the government sought to protect forests against needless agricultural burning and excessive cutting in watersheds and reinforced respect for the surroundings of temples and tombs, though often in vain. As in Europe, some forests were reserved by the nobility for hunting.

In the north, dense forest was valued as a barrier to the marauding hordes of horsemen from the steppes of Central Asia who plagued the agricultural societies, and the strategic barriers of trees on the Wu-t'ai mountains in northern Shan-shi were still in place in the sixteenth century. The Great Wall begun in 300 BC completed what the forests could not accomplish in the drier regions. In the southern mountain region the mixed deciduous and evergreen broad-leafed forests were barely touched, and wild elephants and the rhinoceros roamed the malarial jungles of the province of Kuang-tung in the ninth century; but that was to change with migration from the north that reached a new momentum after the tenth century.

Urbanization and Industry

As always the detail of agricultural clearing is murky while the demands of urbanization and industry have some clarity. In particular, an iron and steel industry flourished in the Shantung region in northeast China during the ebullient and innovative Northern Sung, between AD 910 and 1126 (fig. 5.10). In what can only be called an industrial revolution, iron production reached 125,000–150,000 tons by the end of the Sung (AD 1078), which compares favorably with the total Western and Russian European output of 145,000–180,000 tons at the beginning of the eighteenth century and was a figure only just surpassed in England and Wales in 1796. The bulk of iron went into producing farm implements and armaments, metal coinage, and surprisingly, shipbuilding. The Shantung peninsula described in 845 as being so densely wooded that the widely spaced towns "were like single mounds in the wilderness" was severely denuded a few hundred years later.[21] What woodland remained was coppiced and pollarded in order to ensure supplies. Firewood and charcoal were "imported" from as far afield as Szechuan, Hunan, and Fujian in the south, together with food from the newly colonized irrigated rice fields of the great deltas. The Grand Canal constructed between 1266 and 1289 was the culmination of efforts to improve waterways and so secure fuel and food from the south. In addition, the early substitution of coal for charcoal suggests not only precocious technological development but also widespread forest devastation and shortages of fuel, which the manufacturing of salt, alum, bricks, porcelain, tiles, and liquor all exacerbated. But by 1300, Northern Sung iron production had declined by one-half—whether through exhaustion of fuel, the Mongol invasions, or some other factor is not known. Whatever the reason, the florescence of the Sung dynasty was over, and with it the glimmer of light that illuminated the deep past of the Chinese forests was extinguished.

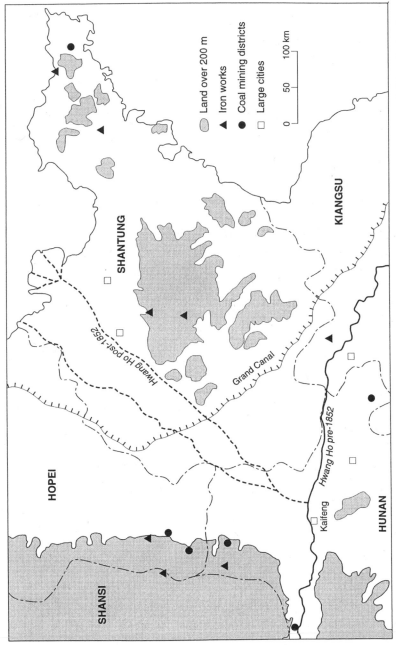

Figure 5.10 The iron industry of Sung China, circa AD 1100. (Source: R. Hartwell, "A Cycle of Economic Change in Imperial China: Coal and Iron in Northeast China, 750–1350," *Journal of Economic and Social History of the Orient* 10 [1967]: 102–59.)

The remarkable economic expansion generated massive urbanization, which, like the iron industry, had no counterpart in the European world at this time. By 1100 at least five cities had populations exceeding 1 million, including Kaifeng and Hangzhou, the capitals of the Northern and Southern dynasties, respectively, with a number of other trading and administrative centers on the southeast coast almost as large. The demand for building materials and fuel wood was immense. Cities counted fuelwood resources as one of their major essential "imports," together with food and water, and there is some evidence that carefully managed plantations for supplies were located on the edges of some cities. Nonetheless, the accumulated evidence of this and succeeding periods points to a severe energy crisis in China from 1400 until at least the mid-nineteenth century and shows that scavenging for combustible matter from stunted shrubs, grass, and leaves was a major preoccupation of the Chinese peasant until recent times.

When the subsequent histories of deforestation in Europe and China are compared, it is clear that the sheer press of population in China and the constant emphasis on agriculture for subsistence was to the detriment of extensive land uses, whether grazing or forests. The overwhelming peasant population had little choice but to alter and manipulate nature for its survival, and over the centuries it destroyed the environment on perhaps a greater scale than any other part of the world if only because there were so many more of them at it for so much longer. Europe, on the other hand, broke out of its vicious circle of subsistence when it was able to reach out and garner the resources of the wider world.

PART II

REACHING OUT: EUROPE AND THE WIDER WORLD

Chapter 6

Driving Forces and Cultural Climates, 1500–1750

Two things belong to this age [the sixteenth century] more than to all its predecessors: the discovery of the world and the discovery of man.
—J. MICHELET, *Histoire de France* (1855)

MEDIEVAL EUROPEANS may have used their forests rapaciously, but those forests had been the basis of an expanded agriculture, abundant energy, many new dwellings, and a vibrant metallurgical industry. Land and its biological resources were the basis for the creation of an innovative, decentralized, energetic, yet comparatively stable society that enjoyed a rise in the general standard of living. Indeed, before the end of the fifteenth century, Europe had climbed out of the abyss of plague and depression, pulled itself together, and was preparing for the long-term economic and cumulative development that Douglass North and Robert Thomas have termed "the rise of the Western world" or, as Eric Jones has aptly labeled it, "The European Miracle."[1] Perhaps it was even the beginning of what we call today globalization.

Therefore, although the Middle Ages signaled the end of the "deep past" of deforestation in a chronological sense, in a thematic sense they were merely a prelude to an even bigger episode that was yet to come, when Europe began "reaching out" across the wider world. This was the "age of discovery" par excellence, but it was also an age of intellectual ferment that encapsulated the Renaissance and the Reformation. Michelet put it nicely when he said that two things belonged to the sixteenth century "more than to all its predecessors: the discovery of the world and the discovery of man."[2] But there was a third characteristic to this period, and that was commercial expansion and enterprise, which flowered during the 250 years separating 1500 and 1750 and bridged the gap between feudal agricultural Europe and industrial Europe. Now the countries of the western rim of the Continent broke out of their geographical bounds and initiated a new phase

127

of change, far different in kind and greater in extent than anything known before. This phase was the start of what were probably the biggest transformations in natural vegetation of the world since the Ice Age. Of all the major types of land cover affected, perhaps the forest was altered most.

The alterations to the forest were of two kinds. First, a core of intensive (usually urban-oriented) land use emerged, in the sea-oriented, capitalist economies of western Europe. In the sixteenth century, there were Spain and Portugal, then in the next century Britain and the Low Countries and, to a lesser extent, France. Only later did the other countries of the European continent come into the picture. An increasing scarcity of wood, sometimes real but sometimes imaginary, led to the search and utilization of forest resources on the European margins and then, ultimately, overseas.

Second, in time, the countries of the core expanded their influence beyond the continent to exploit the global periphery. Successive waves or frontiers of settlement, together with the growing of new crops by new methods, extracted the wealth and stored energy of the peripheral environment for the benefit of the core. In that expansion, events were put into motion that had far-reaching consequences on the distribution of the world's peoples, plants, animals, and even diseases—but particularly on plants because forest clearing occurred in places where it had never happened before—all of which had direct effects on soils, hydrology, and other biogeographical phenomena.

The two locales of forest clearing and exploitation in Europe and subsequently in its overseas territories were related. For example, ships were built of timber and were the means of exploration and overseas expansion, and the lack of ships' timber precipitated the sea-faring nations' search for new supplies. Again, the forces that led to the European resurgence after the fifteenth century were also the forces that propelled them overseas in the sixteenth; the attitudes toward the forest that drove the desire to clear in Europe also drove clearing in the new settlements, especially in North America; and there are many more connections. Nonetheless, if only because of order and clarity, the two theaters of forest exploitation are best separated and dealt with in individual chapters, although their complementarities must be recognized. Of course, Europe and the territories it affected were not the whole world; there was a third major theater of deforestation in China and Japan.

THE CULTURAL CLIMATE OF THE AGE

Our knowledge about changes in the extent and composition of the forests between roughly 1500 and 1750 is, with few exceptions, surprisingly slight. In some parts of Europe probably less is known about clearing then than during the Middle Ages, if only because two forms of evidence that were so useful—place-names and settlement morphology—are no longer diagnostic of either the time or the conditions of first settlement. In the wider world, pioneer societies and initial settlers were not great record keepers; they had more pressing tasks of simple survival to keep them occupied.

But first we need to isolate those forces that most clearly linked land and its vegetation with economic growth and social change in European society during these centuries to produce a cultural climate for change. Some of these forces, like population numbers, are tangible and calculable, but others, like goals and attitudes, are more difficult to grasp. For the sake of brevity, only four are selected here, as they seem to have either generated or facilitated significant changes and affected underlying structures. These forces can be called conveniently, if not quite accurately, discovery, technology, modernity, and ascendancy and go a long way to explain the cultural climate of the sixteenth to early eighteenth centuries. This quartet of themes was obviously already appreciated by the opening of the seventeenth century (plate 6.1). They are not separate, independent topics with clear boundaries. For example, a great deal of interplay exists among territorial expansion and control, technology, the organization and conditions of material life, and attitudes of superiority over nature. In the great ferment of activity of the age, each intertwined and reinforced the other. Together they produced a cultural climate characterized by an ever-ascending spiral of increased production and consumption, economic change, and biome modification, leading to the permanent transformation of the land cover and land use of most parts of the globe. As never before, humans could now intervene and alter nature on an unprecedented scale, increase the production of all commodities to unparalleled levels, and move commodities in unheard-of quantities, all to cater to accelerating human needs.

DISCOVERY

The encounter with the Americas in 1492 is often chosen as a convenient date for dividing the Middle Ages from the early modern era, which began with the "Great Age of Discovery," the Renaissance, and the Reformation. But like all dates it is fairly arbitrary, and the history of expansion, ideas, and science show that there was no abrupt change, and even Columbus's remarkable discovery had its roots deep in the Middle Ages.

Europeans had been on the move for a long time; portents of what was to come were already in place in the fourteenth century. The *Reconquista* of the Iberian Peninsula, begun in AD 800 and largely over by 1300, was dramatic evidence of land expansion. The Norse explorations to Iceland (circa

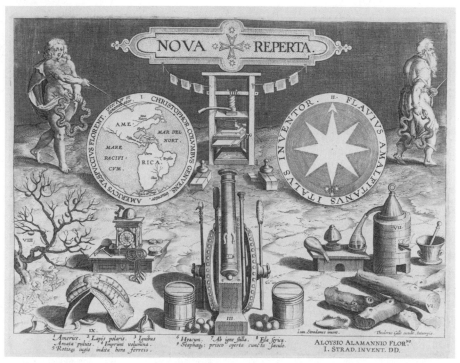

Plate 6.1 Frontispiece from Jan van de Straet's *Nova Reperta* [New discoveries] (Antwerp, 1600). (By permission of the Folger Shakespeare Library, Washington, D.C.) This etching is replete with the imagery of discovery, technology, modernity, and ascendancy. The unadorned young woman on the upper left could well represent modernity, while the bearded old man who is about to leave the stage might represent the old order. Modernity points to a map of the newly discovered Americas encircled by the inscription "I. Christophor Columus Genuens. Inventor. Americus Vespuccius Florent. Retector et denominator." The corresponding circle to the right represents a compass and is encircled by the inscription "II. Flavius Amalfitanus Italus Inventor." Between and beneath these are an array of symbolic technical inventions or discoveries: the printing press, for dissemination of information, and the cannon, for military power, stand central. On the left, the saddle with stirrups again represents military power, and the clock speaks of mechanical ingenuity and the triumph of science in ordering time and space. The apparatus of alchemy and smelting, as symbol of the conquest of the material world, are on the right. The logs are labeled *Hyacum* or *guaiacum,* a tree from the New World commonly thought to be an antidote to the one unwelcome import from the New World— syphilis.

AD 900?) and Greenland (AD 982) and almost certainly Newfoundland (AD 1000), while abortive in terms of permanent settlement, were spectacular evidence of what might be achieved through long-distance sea voyages. The exploits of the vigorous and aggressive politico-commercial networks of Genoa and Venice, which reached at least 1,000 miles across the Aegean to outposts in the Levant and the Black Sea, where they connected with all the great trade routes of western Asia, showed what trade could do. The Crusades were also a pointer to European mobility. Most significant of all, however, were the voyages of the ambitious Portuguese prince, Henry the Navigator (1394–1460), who wanted to penetrate beyond the Muslim world of North Africa to the fabled sources of gold in Africa; capture the spice trade from the Venetians; and search for new potential allies in the Christian struggle against Islam, which the fall of Constantinople in 1453 and the conquest of the Balkans and blocking of trade routes to the east emphasized. By the end of the century the Portuguese had made landings all down the west coast of Africa and were trading ivory, pepper, and gold from Guinea and the Cameroons. By 1488 Bartholomew Dias had rounded the Cape of Good Hope, and 10 years later Vasco da Gama had reached Calicut, a major spice port on the Malabar coast of India, by way of the east coast of Africa. Despite opposition from established Arab traders, cinnamon was soon coming to Europe from Ceylon (Sri Lanka), cloves from the Moluccas, nutmeg and mace from the Banda Islands, and later, porcelain and brocades from China. The Western preoccupation with the Orient had begun and was to open the first global epoch in human history.

None of these voyages would have been possible without the assimilation of Chinese knowledge of cartography and astronomy and without the use of the astrolabe and the compass, including the gyroscopic compass (all via the medium of the Arab world). These had greater utility in the wide oceans of the Atlantic (especially in establishing latitude) than in the narrow seas of the Mediterranean. Additionally, the improvement in shipbuilding and sailing technology during the twelfth century helped. Hinged stern rudders and the lateen sail that allowed ships to sail much closer to the wind were combined in the easily handled Portuguese caravel, which outperformed the contemporary square-rigged northern European cogs. Then within twenty years, during the middle of the fifteenth century, the best of both kinds of rigging were combined in the carracks, which were versatile, oceangoing ships with square sails, lateens, and jibs. By 1500 good portolan maps of sailing directions aided navigation. With the development of ship-mounted guns and lightweight field artillery, Europe achieved absolute and relative superiority even where its numbers were small, and it was now well placed to dominate the global seas and their coasts.

The significance of these voyages of exploration was many. First, before the fifteenth century, Europe was a peripheral appendage—a mere "peninsula of peninsulas"—of the civilized world, which consisted of the land-based empires of Ming China, Ottoman Middle East and North Africa, Safavid Persia, and Mughal northern India, in which contacts by sea were relatively unimportant (fig. 6.1).[3] The continents were isolated

c. 1500

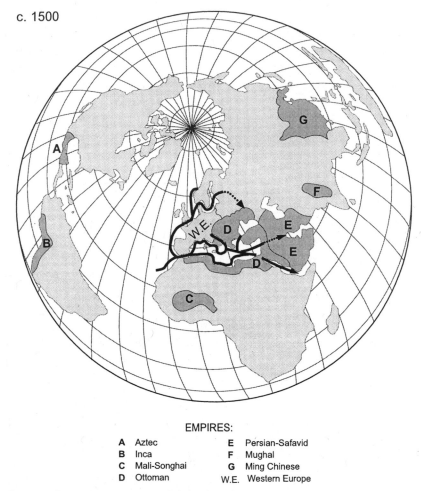

EMPIRES:

A	Aztec	E	Persian-Safavid
B	Inca	F	Mughal
C	Mali-Songhai	G	Ming Chinese
D	Ottoman	W.E.	Western Europe

Figure 6.1 European economy on a global scale, and other empires, circa AD 1500. (Sources: after F. Braudel, *Civilization and Capitalism, 15th–18th Century,* vol. 1, *The Structures of Everyday Life: The Limits of the Possible* [New York: Harper & Row, 1981], 26; and G. Barraclough, ed., *The Times Atlas of World History* [London: Times Publishing Co., 1978], 154–55.)

one from another, except for a few overland trading routes that linked Europe with India and Africa for the movement of high-value goods, such as tea, porcelain, indigo, spices, and pearls. But it was Europe that leaped ahead, breaking out of its land-based territory and turning the continents inside out by, in effect, reorienting them to face the sea. The exploits of the Portuguese established sea contacts between continents and started a process of cultural and economic expansion and domination by Europe over much

c. 1775

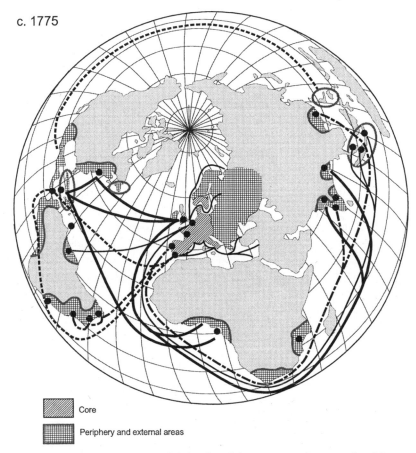

Core

Periphery and external areas

Figure 6.2 European economy on a global scale and the emergence of a core and periphery, circa AD 1775. (Sources: after F. Braudel, *Civilization and Capitalism, 15th–18th Century,* vol. 1, *The Structures of Everyday Life: The Limits of the Possible* [New York: Harper & Row, 1981], 27; and G. Barraclough, ed., *The Times Atlas of World History* [London: Times Publishing Co., 1978], 198–99.)

of the globe. From being on the periphery Europe now moved to be at the center, or core, of innovation, trade, and change to become the most powerful region of the world (fig. 6.2).

Naval supremacy and trade had a powerful internal effect on the nations engaged in it, even possibly creating a more open and entrepreneurial government and society in which merchant values, open consultative government, and greater tolerance prevailed. That archetypal discoverer, entrepreneur, colonizer and adventurer Sir Walter Ralegh was convinced of the preeminence of those "ascendant at sea" when he coined the dictum

"Hee that commaunds the sea, commaunds the trade, and hee that is Lord of the Trade is Lord of the wealth of the worlde."[4] "Lord of the wealth of the worlde": an awesome prediction of what was going to happen. The relationship between the inhabitants and their environment in the peripheral parts of the world was going to be shattered as Europe extracted the unused and stored-up potential of land and its vegetation for its own use.

But, in emphasizing the undoubted success of European traders on the global seas, it should not be overlooked that when they entered the Asian realm, in particular, they found extensive and well-organized regional trading systems that were handling basic commodities as well as luxuries. How large that trade was we do not know, but the work of Asian scholars suggests that it was not inconsiderable. However, despite the plea "to raise one's eye from the European scene," the fact remains that the global mass movement of bulky commodities and raw materials came only with European expansion.[5] There was an increasing separation of areas of production from areas of consumption, and the bulk of the trade ended up in Europe.

TECHNOLOGY

Much of the technological creativity of high medieval Europe had arisen in the forests; the heavy plow, the new field systems, and the horse had led to forest clearing. It marked, suggests White, "the moment of crisis in the history of mankind's relationship to the natural environment: it produced the 'invention of invention' of which the practical effects were soon felt."[6] The new technology of the early modern period (the Renaissance) built on that foundation and was the beginning of a cultural climate of ever-accelerating enquiry, change, and innovation with a renewed interest in experimentation, verification, and accuracy, which led to a pervasive and thoroughgoing transformation of all nature. Technology was more a facilitator of change than a driving force: without technology, change was less effective, but it created a certain momentum of its own.

It has been said that Europe showed not so much an inventive ingenuity as remarkable capacity for borrowing ideas and technologies and bringing them to a high pitch of perfection and practical use. In 1620, Francis Bacon observed that the three greatest inventions "which had changed the appearance of the whole world" up to Stuart times—printing, gunpowder, and the compass—had all originated in China; they had been received by Islam from China and then brought to Europe from the Levant during the Crusades.[7] He might have added the astrolabe, chain mail, the crossbow, methods of rigging, papermaking, and possibly clocks (to say nothing of mathematics and trigonometry). Borrowed or not, Europe assimilated and used these technologies to its great advantage, constantly improving, refining, and innovating on what it had assimilated.

Those inventions/discoveries that aided navigation, as well as gunpowder and mills, have been mentioned already, but printing and clocks have not, and they need fuller explanation.

Just as the full-rigged ship opened up the geographical world to Europe, so the printing press and cheap paper opened up the world of knowledge to the European mind. Gutenberg's invention of movable type, first used in his Bible of circa 1468, revolutionized learning and the dissemination of information. By 1500 it had reached every country except Russia. Widespread and increasing literacy, the prior invention of spectacles (AD 1280), and an openness in societies that contained a large secular section and on the whole did not impose censorship led to the growth of printing. By 1600 about 2,000 titles were printed annually; by 1815 it was 20,000. Probably 20 million books had been printed before 1500 alone, an impressive number for a population that was somewhere in the region of 70 million, much of it illiterate. The written word allowed the retrieval and dissemination of knowledge, precision, continuity of thought, and the revision of ideas through argument, and the result was incalculable in the story of Western intellectual and technological progress and, indeed, in Western domination. To imagine a world without books is to imagine a world without the continuity and disputation of ideas; the book was a potent force for change that altered society, its outlook, and its technology. Ultimately, of course, after the mid-nineteenth century, paper would be made from wood fiber and not rags, with devastating effects on the world's forests—but that is looking too far ahead.

The scientific and intellectual ferment of the age in Europe is neatly summarized in the number of new books, the number of universities as centers of learning and innovation, and the growth of population. These developments intersected at around 1650, when there were approximately 100 universities, 1 million books, and 100 million persons. It marks the end of one epoch (the Renaissance) and the beginning of another (the modern)—1650 seems to be a key marker date in the transition of cultural climates.

One other invention needs special mention. Mechanical clocks appeared in northern Italy by the middle of the fourteenth century and spread widely after that. Clocks radically affected mental and social attitudes. Their manufacture created a corps of skilled craftsmen, their existence aided the synchronization of production and processes in manufacturing generally, and they were a manifestation of an irrepressible interest in mechanical innovation that was a hallmark of modern European society. When the spring was invented toward the beginning of the fifteenth century, the miniaturization of domestic clocks and watches was possible. Instead of nature being the day's clock with dusk and dawn, time could now be divided finely, especially with the development of the minute hand. A new awareness of time arose; the clock was "the prod and key to personal achievement and productivity," and the novel concept of "saving time" arose. People now had

> time at home or on their own person and could order their life and work in a manner once reserved for regulated communities. In this way privatization (personalization) of time was a major stimulus to the individualism that was an ever more salient aspect of Western civilization.[8]

But clocks had a significance beyond the keeping of time, important as that was. The division of time was inseparable from the division of space on the globe and was also the basic explanation of the solar system. To understand the latter accurately was to eventually undermine the medieval religious cosmological view of the world. Keeping time became an invaluable, if not indispensable, tool of astronomical observation, and with modification the clock became the maritime clinometer, crucial for the calculation of longitude at sea. Delays at sea were shortened, landfalls found, cargoes saved, and the loss of crews through thirst and disease lessened. More accurate maps could be made. The story of the persistent experimentation between 1714 and 1773 by the lone mechanical genius, Thomas Harrison, to create frictionless, carefully balanced timepieces that had no pendulum, needed no cleaning, and were not subject to temperature differences or the movement of the sea (they were made of wood) is one of the great stories of patient invention that revolutionized life. It proved beyond doubt that then, as now in the age of satellite "fixes," it is time that determines where you are.[9]

But what has all this to do with the forests and their destruction? In answer, one could say, "a lot"; the end result was the development of the physical and mental equipment of the dynamic early modern capitalist world. The ever-accelerating quest for power over nature, the development of labor-saving mechanisms, the creation of new productive skills, and the evidence of dynamism and innovation, which started in about 1000, has continued ever since. By about 1450 European intellectuals welcomed technological progress approvingly. In its gadgetry as well as in its mentality, the later Middle Ages had provided the basis for the subsequent technological structure of the early modern age, which was the harbinger of the radical changes that came about with the Industrial Revolution. Lynn White has put the significance of these years more succinctly, if bluntly, by saying that the buildup of technological competence, self-confidence, and accelerated change during the Middle Ages enabled Europe after 1500 "to invade the rest of the world, conquering, looting, trading and colonizing."[10] In that process the forest was affected severely.

MODERNITY

Modernity describes those sweeping changes that began in Europe in the sixteenth century and then spread throughout the rest of the world, transcending geographical boundaries and binding disparate peoples, nations, and societies in a "paradoxical unity of disunity" under a global market.[11] Ever since the breakdown of feudalism in the late fourteenth century, Europe had been moving toward a more entrepreneurial, commercial, mercantile, profit-oriented market system—capitalism no less. The economic system and means of production were interacting with each other in an upward spiral of consumption and production.

The transition to modernity was not clear-cut. Dates as wide apart as 1510, 1600, 1650, and 1750 have been suggested, as if one could ever pick a specific year. What we are sure of is that compared to anything that had existed in medieval times, a qualitatively different social system, together with systems of production and distribution, had emerged during the late sixteenth century and was fully in place by 1650. Also, a new sociopolitical system emerged as state structures strengthened, especially in their ability to wage large-scale war. The sheer organizational tasks of war meant that successful monarchs could no longer act like surrogate gods but had to be more like the heads of corporations. Indeed, a large part of the dynamic of the state system was "the arms race." It may well be that Europe's polycentric, competitive state system was the key ingredient in the rise of the merchant empires.

Truly capitalist states involved in the new sort of international exchange economy emerged first, possibly in northern Italy during the late sixteenth century but most certainly in the Low Countries and then Britain during the mid-seventeenth century, with the concomitant rise of Amsterdam and London as international trading, financial, and information-exchanging centers. These regions were highly urbanized, dependent to an unprecedented extent on imported food and raw materials, socially varied but predominantly middle class, and enjoying an unusually high standard of living.

A monetary economy became dominant in Europe by the late sixteenth century. "Everywhere," said the Dutch historian Herman Van der Wee, "money was on the march."[12] The old economic relationships that were embedded in the connection between environment and society (as in peasant economies) were dissolved as the link between where one lived and what one consumed was broken. Money brought anonymity to the process of economic exchange and allowed profit to be extended through social interactions. Thus, barter as a means of exchange gave way to a monetary economy, initially based on metallic money boosted by the huge shipments of gold and silver bullion from Latin America after 1550. While enormous effort went into establishing, stabilizing, and regularizing metallic money, it did not hamper the development of credit, which was central to the new market economies. Credit required a financial infrastructure: fairs, bills of exchange, commerce manuals, checks, marine insurance, new methods of accounting—even, possibly, double-entry bookkeeping. All of these were present from the fourteenth century, if not earlier; however, they became increasingly sophisticated and flourished as never before.

The expansion of consumer credit was crucial to the new level of economic activity. This was especially so in overseas trade, where cargoes took months, if not years, to collect, dispatch, and sell. Usually no actual, physical money changed hands, so trust and honesty were essential in this new system of global interchange. Credit was conducted through the development of bills of exchange, bills obligatory, notes of credit, and other promissory instruments, often at the main international fairs, such as those at Lyons, Frankfurt, or Antwerp. The mobility of money was constantly being improved, both from place to place and temporally into the future.

Developing a legal and institutional framework in which transactions could function was also an important requirement for the successful working of the global interchange system. The refinement of banking, clearing, settlement days, and the fixing of exchange rates were crucial in making credit mobile. Institutional landmarks in the organization of money and credit were, for example, the bourses established in Antwerp (1531), London (1571), Seville (1583), and Amsterdam (1611). Epitomizing the new-style public banks were the Banco della Piazza Rialto (1587) and the even more successful Banco del Giro (1619) of Venice, which were the models for exchange banks elsewhere, such as the Wisselbank of Amsterdam (1609) and banks in Hamburg (1619), Rotterdam (1635), and Stockholm (1656). By 1697 there were 25 major banks in existence, of which the Wisselbank was preeminent until overtaken by London banks in the early eighteenth century. The foundation of the Bank of England (1694) was another landmark, as it functioned as a central bank, transferring funds, discounting bills of exchange, issuing "promises to pay on demand," or bank notes, and consolidating the national debt. At the same time, merchant law evolved to protect traders and entrepreneurs from unreasonable claims and nonpayments.

Symptomatic of the new organization needed was the rise of the trading, or joint stock, company, in which people ventured capital in hazardous overseas enterprises in return for monopolies guaranteed by royal charter.

Such were the English Muscovy Company (1550), the East India Company (1600), the Dutch East India Company (1602), the Dutch West India Company (1621), and later the Hudson Bay Company (1670) and the Royal Africa Company (1672), as well as many minor ones. The companies were the powerful and well-organized spearheads of long-distance trade and the precursors of colonial land empires. They were capital intensive, spread the risks and concentrated settlement, and combined the various tasks of conquest, settlement, investment, and defense all in one. In fact they acted like sovereign states, making peace and war at pleasure, administering justice, settling colonies, importing slave and indentured labor, building fortifications, levying troops, maintaining armies and fleets, and coining money. They were the transnational companies of the age.

In sum, the sixteenth century saw the adoption of efficient and flexible institutions and procedures that constantly lowered the cost of transacting, producing, and transporting goods and, thus, produced a continuous growth of productivity. Capital became more mobile, uncertainty was transformed into an actuarial, ascertainable risk, information was improved, and traders received better protection. The entrepreneurs who made the decisions and took the risks flourished in direct measure as they gained greater and more certain control of their environment, both socioeconomic and physical. Each development encouraged and eased another into being, and modernity was born.

The great companies and lesser traders could only function with ships. It is estimated that in 1600 there were between 600,000 and 700,000 tons of merchant shipping, quadrupling to 3.37 million tons by 1786, which translates into nearly as many tons of ship timber. How this tonnage was distributed between countries we do not know for certain, but of the 20,000-odd ships in 1650, three-quarters were said to be owned by the Dutch, until Britain usurped Dutch hegemony by the mid-eighteenth century. Perhaps two-thirds of the Dutch fleet were *fluyts,* or flyboats—light, fast, maneuverable, and unarmed cargo ships of about 200 tons that were cheap to build and maximized cargo-carrying capacity. They were constantly being modified in order to increase their speed and crew-to-tonnage ratio, which made them very profitable.

All these improvements in finance and shipping allowed the free and easy movement of goods in quantity and facilitated the ascending spiral of consumption and production. For example, the number of European ships outward bound for Asian ports stayed stable at between 50 and 90 per decade until 1590, then rose to over 250 per decade by 1620, stabilized, and then rose again dramatically to about 450 per decade after 1660 until the end of the century.

But questions remain: What caused the increased consumption? What goods were moved? And what was the effect on global forests? Undoubtedly the increase in Europe's population from about 82 million in 1500 to about 105 million in 1600 and 140 million in 1750 was a driving force that must have stimulated consumption. But rising numbers were of less significance than the increasing purchasing power of segments of the European population, a power aided by the influx of gold and silver bullion from the New World. For the rich of western Europe, all aspects of life improved considerably, as indeed they did for the expanding urban commercial and professional classes. The intermediate group of skilled artisans and small farmers was also marginally better off, and the ordinary man was beginning to emerge in importance as a consumer. The gulf between rich and poor may have widened, but life for the bulk of the population was more stable, safer, and more law-abiding, though in eastern and southern Europe it may not necessarily have been more comfortable.

Consequently, demand for all goods rose, putting increased pressures on land resources. In particular there was a shift from the medieval preoccupation with a land-based trade in small quantities of high-value luxury goods, such as spices (though pepper was a semi-necessity and associated with the vast increase in meat eating in Europe, particularly England), perfumes, porcelain, dyestuffs, and silk clothes and rugs from Asia and Africa, to a sea-borne mass trade of far bulkier commodities or staples from Asia, the Caribbean, and the Americas. These were destined for an increasingly widening segment of affluent people who consumed a disproportionate amount of resources. Immanuel Wallerstein typifies this shift as a move from "preciosities" from the largely unaffected "external arena" of contact in Africa and most of Asia, in contrast with the trade in lower-ranking goods from the "periphery" of the Americas and the East Indies, a trade that had led to social change, division of labor, and change in land use in those areas.[13]

Besides the textiles and china tableware, many of these "lower-ranking" goods were tropical products, the growing of which led directly to tropical forest clearing. Some, such as tea, coffee, chocolate, and sugar, were not essential, but they certainly varied diet; some, like silks and tobacco, were more purely optional. Later, potatoes and cotton were of more fundamental significance in that they related to basic needs for an easily cultivated, high-yielding food crop and for cheap and hygienic over- and underclothing. These tropical staples could now be added to the traditional trade staples of wheat, wood, wine, and dyes. For example, the stimulants and tonics of tea, coffee, and chocolate were introduced into Britain during the 1650s and the Low Countries a few decades earlier. Initially, these goods were regarded as expensive, exotic products or luxuries (even as aphrodisiacs) that only the wealthy could afford. But from the mid-seventeenth century onward, rising affluence for many, better global transport, and the consequent cheapening of commodities meant that their consumption filtered down through society, and they became the staples or commonplace necessities of the everyday material life of the masses.

The significance of these tropical products went beyond mere titillation of the palate, as they created a legacy of what Marshall Sahlins has called the West's "soft drug" culture. The impact of tea on British life was overwhelming; its acquisition was the basis of many imperialist adventures around the Pacific, and its psychological values and desirability functioned to deliver a "docile and effective working class into the maws of developing capitalism."[14] Sugar was probably even more significant. Geographically its cultivation was a means of financing colonial endeavors and a motive for the occupation of yet more territory; socially it fostered habits of consumption, changed dietary habits, and was a source of wealth and power; economically its production on the plantation system altered the distribution of populations globally through slavery and emigration. Said one eighteenth-century observer:

> Whether coffee and sugar are really necessary to the happiness of Europe, is more than I can say, but I can affirm—that these two vegetables have brought wretchedness and misery upon America and Africa. The former has been depopulated, that Europeans may have land to plant them in; and the latter is stripped of its inhabitants, for hands to cultivate them.[15]

The link between production and consumption was, of course, foreign trade, which, in a favorite metaphor of the time, was the great wheel setting the machinery of society in motion. Trade was a true driving force, and the ship was its symbol. Grain, copper, cattle, textiles, and wood dominated world trade, but by the early seventeenth century, 20 and 24 percent of all imports into the Netherlands and England, respectively, were tropical goods. By the middle of the next century the proportion had doubled in England but fallen a little in Holland. But who would have thought that so much tea, coffee, sugar, and silk could have been consumed?

When that transition in consumption got under way, the impact on the biomes of the world really began, as sugarcane, tea bushes, coffee trees, and numerous other crops replaced wild tropical vegetation. Peasant proprietors almost imperceptibly shifted from predominantly subsistence agriculture to an agriculture with a considerable cash-crop element in it; and the recent invention of the plantation (first fully developed by the British in the colonization of Ireland), with its subjugated and/or imported servile labor of slaves, left an indelible mark on huge expanses of the world. In a word, the "look" of the tropical world changed forever. From Java to Jamaica, Virginia to Assam, from Fiji to Malaya, Brazil to Congo, tropical regions were utterly transformed by the drive toward managed tropical agriculture. And when the purposeful movement of "settler societies" to the temperate lands of North America, Argentina, and southern Brazil got under way in later years, the impact on the global forests was devastating.

ASCENDANCY

It would be surprising if the age of discovery, which opened up the map of the world, and the Renaissance and Reformation, which opened up the human mind to new concepts, questions, and relationships, did not coalesce to bring about changed ideas of the habitable world and the human ascendancy over nature. Everywhere there was a broadening and deepening of intellectual life, in which printing played a major part. In time, science and technology created a great repository of knowledge of the physical world and the means for making it useful for humans.

A major factor in this new awareness was the European encounter with the Americas, which led to an intellectual confrontation with the geography, natural history, and ethnography of a "new" world. It was not only a bigger world than the medieval mind had encompassed but a more varied and complex world.

Nature

The Middle Ages had been a period of extensive environmental change, with clearing, draining, and domestication, and later hints of concern about overuse, especially of the forests. But the dominant idea, if any existed, was that because humans were blessed with the faculty of work, they assisted both God and themselves in the improvement of an earthly home—even if, in the Christian view of things, the earth was merely "a sojourners' way station."[16] The most compelling reason for studying nature was that it led to a greater understanding of God, and together with the new discoveries, was proof of his existence, of a varied, full, and designed world, and of the truth of Christianity and final causes.

Implicit in this teleology was the medieval physiotheological idea of the Great Chain of Being, whereby humans were seen as a part of a pyramidal hierarchy with God at the apex, followed in descending order by the angels, humans, animals, plants, metals, minerals, and the ground itself. On the face of it this was an essentially holistic, organic, and harmonious arrangement in which man was placed on earth as God's steward to tend and complete the creation, as interpreted by John Ray in his *Wisdom of God Manifest in the Works of Creation* of 1691.[17] Looked at another way, however, the Chain of Being could be interpreted as the reverse of humility to nature, and rather as a recipe for its domination. Increasingly, humans were seen as superior or ascendant to the other elements of creation, which gave them the right to exploit it.

The assumption that the earth had been created for the sake of humans appears to have grown stronger during this era, and it was rarely questioned or reflected on. There were precedents: classical writing from Aristotle to Cicero (now revived with the Renaissance) had urged man to use the earth because it existed in order to serve human interests of pleasure and profit, and Christianity reinforced these ideas. The narrative of Genesis (1:28) explained that the earth was a paradise prepared by God for man in which he had dominion over all living things. Admittedly, the Fall had caused God to make life more difficult with odious insects, troublesome weeds, sterile soil, wild animals, and the need for human toil, but even so, superiority over all other works of creation was assured. From about 1500, and well into the eighteenth century, theological writing provided a substantial moral underpinning for the ascendancy of humans over all other elements in the natural world.

Nonetheless, no age is uniform in its thought, and the growth of natural science had a curious twofold, even contradictory, effect on these ideas. On the one hand it underpinned religious thought; on the other hand it strengthened and gave new justification to human domination. By the sixteenth century, cracks were appearing in the unity of medieval theology. The Ptolemaic/medieval cosmological view of a geocentric universe, which centered on a stationary, motionless earth around which rotated the sun, planets, and stars, was shattered in 1543 by Copernicus with his simple suggestion that the position of sun and earth should be reversed and that the earth revolved in its own orbit. In what seems in retrospect to be a dizzying spiral of inquiry, reasoning, and explanation came the work and overlapping careers of Galileo Galilei (1564–1642), Johannes Kepler (1571–1630), and René Descartes (1596–1650). From then on, nature was more likely to be written in the language of mathematics than words, matter to be separated from mind, and rationality extolled over religion. Descartes was particularly influential; all nature, except the human mind, was a machine without feeling and therefore could be manipulated without scruple, and all received wisdom should be doubted systematically, as expressed succinctly in his dictum in his *Discourse on Method* (1637), "I think, therefore I am."[18] In place of the medieval unity of the trilogy of God, humans, and nature, Cartesian dualism now separated the mind from tangible, objective earthly matter; and science as a way of thinking grew in importance. As the centuries unfolded, the idea grew that nature was of less relevance as a teacher and that any technical problems could be solved by patient, systematic experimentation, accompanied by a growing faith in quantitative progress and greater production.

That the accumulation of knowledge, the waning of the human-nature unity, and the replacement of that unity by separation would increase the control of humans over nature seemed self-evident and, indeed, as we have seen, was fully underpinned by theology. But it was Francis Bacon (1561–1626) who, perhaps, first drew out the full implications. For him the most lofty and noble use of the new knowledge was not only to restore to man the dominion over creation that he had partly lost with the Fall but also to relieve the lot of humankind. Like Descartes's belief in technology, Bacon's belief in science was as a means of controlling nature and changing the environment. It was an altruistic enterprise in which the power of humankind over the universe was enlarged: it was a departure from the stultification of the past of Aristotle and the Scriptures and brought order out of chaos. Although Bacon was not the only one who expressed the view that the earth was made for humans, he put it particularly well:

> For the whole world works together in the service of man; and there is nothing from which he does not derive use and fruit . . . insomuch that all things seem to be going about man's business and not their own.[19]

From that time on, humans viewed their role less as John Ray saw it—as God's humble stewards on earth—and more as Sir Matthew Hale perceived it, as "the Vice-Roy of the great God . . . in this inferior World . . . and reserve to himself the supreme Dominion, and the Tribute of Fidelity, Obedience, and Gratitude, as the greatest recognition or Rent for the same."[20] Instead of nature being the tyrant that subdued humans, humans were fast becoming the tyrant that subdued nature. The transformation of the cultural climate was complete.

Purposive control meant that the world was to be used and its products could be exploited, sold, and traded—in a word, commodified—particularly the tropical world, which was perceived as being a place of such "exuberance" and plenty that Europeans need no longer face scarcities. The pursuit of profit—the logical end of capitalist enterprise—took Europeans a long way along the road to global domination. Perhaps, ultimately, this shift in attitude toward nature and their penchant to rationalize encounters with new lands and to develop the resources that they brought within their reach was more important to their success than the technology, the environmental advantages, and the voyages themselves. When that encounter with new territories got underway, the world and its forests were changed.

The Trees and the Forest

Of all the forms of plant life that were altered in this new, conscious domination of nature, trees and their assemblage in forests seemed to engender the most emotional comment and action. They were both detested and loved. Keith Thomas, in his brilliant survey of the human relationship to the natural world in England, makes the novel and perspicacious observation that the progression of attitudes toward trees has paralleled that toward animals, which

> had been divided into the wild, to be tamed or eliminated, the domestic, to be exploited for useful purposes, and the pet, to be cherished for emotional satisfaction. The early modern period has duly seen the elimination of many wild animals, the increased exploitation of domestic ones, and a rise in interest in the third category, the pet, maintained for non-utilitarian reasons.[21]

It is possible that the development of these attitudes was more pronounced in the lives of the well-to-do of seventeenth- to nineteenth-century England than in other countries of the European continent. But there is evidence that in time these attitudes permeated through the population at large and that they were most certainly transported with that population wherever it migrated, especially in the vast forests of North America.

From the time of the first farmers, almost anywhere in the world, forests had been seen as wild and hostile, and human progress had seemed to be viewed in some proportion to the amount of woodland cleared, or at least used. The Middle Ages in Europe had seen one of the greatest onslaughts on the forest ever witnessed, and although there was a hiatus in clearing during the *Wüstungen,* the attack was taken up with renewed vigor during the sixteenth century. By then religion and aesthetics found forests not only forbidding but also repugnant and repulsive, and a mythology or set of cultural mores had developed in which the acts of felling, firing, grazing, and cultivating turned them into civilized abodes. Forests were dark and horrible places where there were very real dangers from wild animals, particularly bears and wolves, and, in North America, snakes and ticks. The word wilderness etymologically was the "place of wild beasts," and it was almost synonymous with forest. In addition, the forests were places of terrifying eeriness, awe, and horror, where the imagination played tricks and the limbs of trees looked like the limbs of people, especially if animated by the wind. In that chaos, the hapless peasant was first be-wildered and eventually succumbed to license and sin.

The accumulation of folklore and tradition attests to these deeply held feelings. For the Greeks there were the genial dryads, but there were also the malevolent satyrs and centaurs; Pan was the Lord of the Woods, and his approach produced panic in unwary travelers. In northern and central Europe, popular folk culture abounded with trolls, sprites, dwarfs, ogres, witches, werewolves, child-eating monsters, and forest demons of all descriptions. The fears created by these creatures have been handed down to us in the terrifying "fairy tales" of, for example, "Hansel and Gretel," "Little Red Riding Hood," "Sleeping Beauty," "Tom Thumb," "The Three Little Pigs," and even "Snow White." These tales are all set in the somber, dark environment of the forest. Early Christianity, as we have seen, extolled the virtue of clearing the forest on two counts: the forest was associated with pagan gods and also equated with the devil and was, therefore, the abode of natural sin. But there were contradictions. Wild country was also a place to draw nearer to God, and it became a sanctuary against evil. Many a medieval monk had been motivated to make a clearing in the wicked waste as a means of purifying his faith. Yet if the forest was to be feared, its products were to be valued; piety and economic progress went hand in hand with the creation of "new" land that was akin to Paradise, an Eden, or, in North America, a New Canaan or New Jerusalem.

In addition to being places of original evil and wild animals, forests were also the abode of savagery and dangerous outlaws. *Wood* may have a common root with wild, and the word *savage* is derived from *sylva*—"a wood." The forest was dark, melancholy, and uninhabited, fit only for beasts, and therefore by implication those who lived in the forests were uncouth and barbarous. John Locke averred that experience showed that inhabitants of cities were "civil and rational," while those from "woods and forests" were "irrational, untaught." [22] In Europe, the forests were regarded, with some justification, as the abode of outlaws, brigands, highwaymen, smugglers, poachers, and the more benign, but no less feared, blackened charcoal burners and squatters. All this is to say nothing of wolves. Because of the many postmedieval disputes over rights of forest use, the forests were also areas of resentment, social conflict, and violence. Selwood Forest in England was felled largely to eliminate a refuge for criminals, and in France many a forest was felled alongside major highways in order to give a safe passage to travelers. In the twelfth century the Capetians had established 12 *villeneuve* and set up citadels in three established settlements along the road from Paris to Orléans that ran through the vast Forest of Orléans, and there are many other examples.

Nowhere was the notion of the relationship between forests and savagery more fully developed than in the forest settlements of seventeenth-century North America. The Plymouth colony was founded, said Governor Winthrop, in a "hideous & desolate wilderness," "where are nothing but wild beasts and beastlike men." Terror of the forest was reinforced by the way nature seemed to contrive to help the Indians in their attacks on the colonists, so that, said Increase Mather, "our Men when in that hideous place, if they did but see a Bush stir would fire presently, whereby 'tis verily feared that they sometimes unhappily shoot English Men instead of Indians." The forest was a dark and sinister symbol of man's evil where the Indians "were transformed into beasts" and where even a civilized man could revert to savagery because he was beyond the reach of redemption.[23] The fact that the Indian inhabited the forest and did not appear to clear it (which was not true) was proof of that. His "vegetative nature," said Arnold Guyot, kept him at the "lowest grade on the scale of civilization."[24]

Thus, social order and the Christian concept of morality seemed to stop on the edge of the cleared land; and in new territories at least, without the ameliorating regulations of organized communities, social cohesion, and the ties of positive Christianity, frontier man could become less civilized and degenerate into license and even savagery. J. Hector St. John de Crèvecoeur in his celebrated essay "What Is an American?" was quite explicit. In the "great woods, near the last inhabited districts" inland, dwelt the "off-casts" of society, where men "appear to be no better than carnivorous animals of a superior rank. . . . There remote from the power of example, and check of shame, many families exhibit the most hideous parts of our society." In time that "hitherto barbarous country" would be "purged" by the next wave of decent settlers and changed into a "fine, fertile, and well regulated district."[25]

It is evident in this amalgam of belief, superstition, and prejudice that the virtues of development, progress, and individual freedom were never far beneath the surface, as they were the logical outcome of the fight for survival. Increasingly, the tamed landscape became the ideal. In England this view went so far that "moralists who condemned enclosures made an exception for taking in and grubbing up trees" and even objected to trees in hedgerows, as they might hinder the ripening of crops. Tree clearing became something of a crusade: in 1683 John Houghton advocated the destruction of all forests within 12 mi of a navigable river or the coast in order that the land could be converted to more productive uses.[26]

In North America the experience came about a century later, but with much more intensity. The difficulties of the forested wilderness reinforced the Puritan New Englanders' belief that they were the Chosen of God and that the New Jerusalem would lie in America. Consequently, subduing the wilderness quickly became an exalted calling that tested and strengthened their faith. Increasingly, to fell the forest was almost to enter the kingdom of heaven on earth, as the making of new land seemed to demonstrate the direct causal relationship between it and righteous Puritan faith and, more broadly, moral effort, sobriety, frugality, industry, and material reward. Early American nature seemed full of implications for ethical and material betterment. By the early eighteenth century Benjamin Franklin identified the frontier of cultivation with opportunity and tended to measure moral and spiritual progress by progress in converting the wilderness into a paradise of material plenty. Half playfully, Franklin even attributed a cosmic influence to the clearing of the forest: "by clearing America of Woods" Americans were "Scouring our Planet . . . and so making this Side of our Globe reflect a brighter Light to the Eyes of the Inhabitants of Mars or Venus." But on the more mundane and day-to-day level the "great primary aim" of most pioneer farmers was, said William Cooper, "to cause the wilderness to bloom and fructify" so that the landscape would be converted from forest to

> fair cities, substantial villages, extensive fields, an immense country filled
> with decent houses, good roads, orchards, meadows, and bridges, where a
> hundred years ago all was wild, woody and uncultivated![27]

Thus, it is no surprise that when nearly every religious, aesthetic, practical, and even moral circumstance conspired toward the taming or elimination of the forest, great changes occurred in its composition and extent. Clearing was both a sacred and a secular process, a combination of motives that was particularly apparent in medieval Europe and early colonial North America.

The historian of medieval society and technology, Lynn White, has condemned Western Christianity as being the "most anthropocentric religion that the world has seen" and the font of the attitudes that have led to the environmental degradation of the present day.[28] But it would be absurd to infer from what has been said about forest clearing that Europeans were unique in their inclination to transform, manipulate, and so abuse the environment. Certainly they were no laggards, but the history of deforestation and subsequent soil erosion by, for example, the Greeks and Romans (chap. 4), native Indian societies in Central and North America (chap. 3), and Chinese society, despite all its avowed working with nature (chaps. 5

and 8), all without the assistance of Christianity, should effectively dispose of that notion. The ambivalent messages of Christianity, with its antithetical emphases on stewardship and domination, are also ignored in the charge of anthropocentrism. The important point is that at the start of our period, exploitation, not stewardship, was the dominant theme, though in time a more reserved attitude toward the modification of nature by humans emerged as Europeans and their overseas offspring moved into the second and third stages of their relationship with trees and began to preserve the useful and cherish the beautiful.

In summary, the Europe of the mid-eighteenth century and its place in, and impact on, the world was very different from the Europe of 1500. The little civilization of land-based states had spread across the world and was going to dominate it eventually. European rule was established in North America, Latin America, the Indian mainland, and portions of Southeast Asia and Africa; and the population of European communities overseas, particularly North America, now reached several million. Europe's ships traversed every ocean and entered every harbor, and its control over world trade was disproportionately great.

Chapter 7

Clearing in Europe, 1500–1750

No wood, no kingdome.
—A. STANDISH, *The Commons Complaint* (1611)

Trees had ceased to be a symbol of barbarism or a mere economic
commodity. They had become an indispensable part of the scenery of
upper-class life.
—K. THOMAS, *Man and the Natural World* (1983)

THE OUTREACH of Europe across the globe after 1500 and its eventual impact on the forests of the world did not mean that the forests of the Continent
remained untouched. Everywhere people were chopping, lopping, burning,
and otherwise altering the composition and extent of the forest, as well as
establishing and codifying rights about its use. It is not possible to generalize about these alterations and how much was left because the forest varied
with the physical and climatic gradation of the Continent from west to east
and from north to south, as well as with the intensity of economic activity
and agriculture from the core in the northwest to the more peripheral areas
elsewhere.

About 7.7 percent, or perhaps a little more, of England and Wales was
forest covered at the end of the seventeenth century and Scotland even less,
while Ireland was still 12 percent covered in 1600. Across the Channel,
the Netherlands had next to none and northern France might have been
16.3–18.0 percent covered, with the proportion increasing the farther east
one went until it was over 40 percent in Prussia even in the late eighteenth
century. One cannot be more precise than that. Nonetheless, these estimates
are important, as it seems that once the proportion of forest fell below about
one-fifth of the land in any country, alarm, both real and perceived, seemed
to set in that clearing had gone too far. It happened in Europe in various

places between the sixteenth and eighteenth centuries and in North America in the later nineteenth century.

A TIMBER CRISIS?

After the *Wüstungen* (village desertion) and retreat of cultivation during the late fourteenth and early fifteenth centuries, the attack on the European forests was renewed with vigor as population rose—from approximately 82 million in 1500 to 105 million in 1600, and then to 115 million a hundred years later. The demand for land for cultivation, and wood and wood-derived products in every branch of industry, transportation, and day-to-day life, was immense. The idea of a "timber scarcity" gained ground throughout the seventeenth and early eighteenth centuries, though in many ways the scarcity was more apparent than real. More and more of the forest was being claimed and reserved for hunting and game by seigniorial lords, royalty, and the nobility, thus reducing the amount available for general use, particularly in the more feudal societies of Germany and France.

Also, climate change was altering forest composition. After the wet and stormy Middle Ages Europe entered its "Little Ice Age." Glaciers and snow spread more widely and lasted longer, and rivers froze more frequently and for longer periods, with a consequent decrease in flow and lowering of groundwater. The growing season diminished, causing a general retreat from upland areas as far apart as Norway, Scotland, and the Alps. Even grain and olive production in southern France was affected and famine ensued. Insolation decreased by possibly as much as one-tenth, and the dominant cover of broad-leafed deciduous trees (e.g. beech, oak, chestnut, elm, ash, willow) could not cope with the colder, drier conditions and lowered water table and were replaced by conifers in upland Germany and the Rhine plains.

Shortages appeared in the economic core, first in England and the Netherlands during the later 1500s, but the scarcity was probably more local and limited than widespread. It was certainly intense around centers of industry and large urban areas, which were growing as a result of trade and commerce, such as London, Paris, Barcelona, Amsterdam, Antwerp, Milan, Venice, Naples, and Messina. By and large, there was no crisis in central and eastern Europe; local demands were not as intense, and the forest was still more abundant than in western Europe. Mediterranean Europe had always had less timber, and severe inroads had been made during the fifteenth and sixteenth centuries by the Venetian and Spanish shipbuilders. The forests of the Apennines, Calabria, Sicily, Monte Gargano, southern Spain, and the Dalmatian coast of the Adriatic were depleted of large timber, and only the highest and most inaccessible mountainous areas had substantial resources left.

Much of the evidence of an impending timber crisis and its solutions comes from the British Isles, one of the least wooded parts of Europe and the scene of some of the earliest depredations due to industrialization and urbanization. For the near-hundred years of the reigns of Elizabeth I and James I (1558–1649) dozens of government commissions investigated the shortage, which resulted in legislation prohibiting or restricting cutting. Even in remote and reasonably well-wooded Pembrokeshire in southwest Wales, a local topographer wrote in 1603 that "this Countrie groneth with the generalle complainte of other countries of the decreasinge of wood."[1] The comment in 1600 that the national forests had been "reduced to such a sicknesse and wasting consumption, as all the physick in England cannot cure, described a common perception of the situation."[2] Two other pieces of evidence have been cited to establish the shortage: the rising importation of timber from Norway and the Baltic for general construction and even for pit props in the mines and the rise in the price of firewood in London. From a base level of 100 in 1451–1500, the price index for firewood climbed roughly in line with the general index for all goods until the decade 1583–92, when it diverged markedly to ultimately reach 780 in 1633–42, more than double the general trend of the rise in prices of all goods. During this time the population of London grew from between 40,000 and 50,000 to about 340,000 (fig. 7.1).

But was it the "national crisis" subscribed to by some historians or merely a number of acute local crises? First, the propaganda about scarcity put out by special-interest groups was misleading and exaggerated, and the sweeping exemptions of the many acts made them "hollow" legislation. Second, the rise of the price in wood in London, even if correct, was subject to the demands around a uniquely growing and industrializing city and did not necessarily reflect the conditions in rural areas.

Similar revisionist arguments have been put forward about the perceived shortages in France and Germany. In France the forests had undoubtedly diminished. At the end of the seventeenth century the agricultural north of France was said to be "destitute" of wood, and by 1701 all riverside forests in the lower Loire Valley that could easily be transported had been removed. The causes of decrease were manifold and clear. An underpaid bureaucracy of foresters accepted bribes to cut and sell wood illegally; Louis XV wanted quick revenues and alienated 800,000 acres of royal forests; a growing population needed more grain and therefore cleared agricultural land; the peasants claimed their rights to use the forest to a degree greater than good silviculture could withstand; and mining and industry stripped some areas.

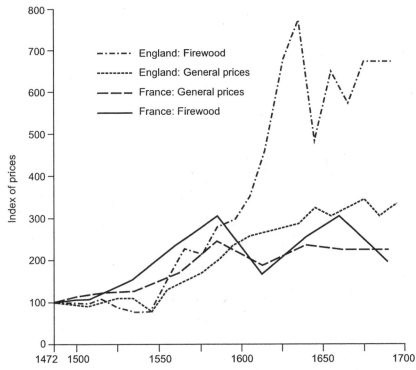

Figure 7.1 Indices of firewood and general price rises in England and France, 1451–1702. (Source: based on G. Wiebe, *Geschichte der Preisrevolution des XVI und XVII Jahrhunderts* [Leipzig: Dunder & Humblot, 1895], 375, 378.)

For example, there were complaints about *"déboisement"* around Nevers that led to the demolition of all forges within 4–5 mi of that town.

Nonetheless, it seems that the French forests provided sufficient wood for the majority of urban and rural needs well into the eighteenth century. The price of firewood in urban areas was either about the same or less than inflation, so that the spectacular climb that occurred in England after about 1600 never happened in France. Probably only the navy suffered a deficiency, and the peasant experienced some hardship but only locally as in, say, Brittany, whereas the urban dwellers and industrialists were barely affected at all. An enquiry in 1701 into the use of coal as a substitute fuel, and general treatises on the state of the forests during the early eighteenth century, suggest concern, but a general shortage was a long way off. The minute use of the abundant supplies of coal in France compared with Britain— 450,000 tons in 1789 compared with 15.2 million tons in 1800—is a clear indicator of this.

Similarly, Werner Sombart's thesis of a major timber scarcity (*Holznot*) in German lands has been questioned. Certainly there was a scarcity of charcoal and pit props at copper and silver mines in Bavaria in 1463 and Bohemia in 1550, and the number of furnaces in the Siegerland had to be halved between 1563 and 1616 due to high wood prices.[3] But the timber debate had more to do with protecting state-controlled resources (and the jobs of foresters) than with protecting the forests per se. The shift from timber to coal did not come until the middle of nineteenth century, and then it was a response to a need for a more efficient fuel for steam engines, not a lack of fuelwood.

Despite doubts expressed about a general crisis, it cannot be denied that shortages were becoming real enough in specific places and for specific sorts of wood. Scarcity revolved around four activities that destroyed the forest: first, clearing for agriculture and, second, for fuelwood, which were local and domestic; third for shipbuilding, which was basically foreign and strategic; and finally for charcoal for iron making and industry in general, which was both domestic and strategic. But the perception of, and emphasis on, each of these activities varied, largely because of the nature of the particular evidence. The first two were ignored in the historical record, while the record of iron furnaces and ships was official and published and, therefore, accessible and prominent, which made them loom disproportionately large as destroyers of the forest.

AGRICULTURAL CLEARING

The addition of about 60 million people between the *Wüstungen* and the end of the devastating religious wars of the seventeenth century (circa 1500–1750) made agricultural expansion the single greatest factor in the decrease of woodland and forest. The abandoned lands were reoccupied, and everywhere, cultivation nibbled away at the edge of the forests, which in western Europe, at least, were now reduced to relatively isolated patches. Rising grain prices reflected the competition for land, which was augmented by an overall increase in the number of horses and stock and their need for fodder. The pressure did not relax until the latter half of the seventeenth century, when prices fell, some cropland passed out of cultivation, and much land moved into grass as pastoralism and animal husbandry expanded.

The historical record is remarkably silent about these events, Agricultural clearing elicited little comment and even less record. It was a part of the day-to-day task of making and maintaining a farm or getting fuel that was left until the slacker parts of the agricultural calendar, usually winter. Clearing had become a part of the natural agricultural round of preparing, plowing, sowing, and harvesting and was now depicted as one of the typical monthly tasks in Books of Hours. It did not warrant special record unless it caused an infringement of someone else's property or rights, in which case it was challenged and brought before some form of arbitration or court. Agricultural clearing was individual, piecemeal, and, above all, approved of. It was imbued with virtue as the correct and time-honored thing to do in order to either perfect God's creation or contribute to the domination of nature. Hence it was "natural." The patient, backbreaking drudgery of clearing a few more acres every year was still an important element in widening the margin of subsistence, creating greater income, and conferring independence on millions of small-scale farmers and their families. It represented the application of a tried-and-true method and technology.

One of the clearest statements about the impact of agriculture on the forests came somewhat surprisingly from England, which is usually associated more with iron making and shipbuilding during this period. Its population had almost doubled between 1550 and 1700 to reach an overall density of about seven persons per acre, exceeded perhaps only by Holland and China at this time. Its people were still predominantly engaged in agriculture and dependent on homegrown grain. In 1664 in *Sylva; or, A Discourse of Forest Trees,* his celebrated enquiry into the shortage of timber and the extent of forest in England, John Evelyn was convinced that industry was of less importance in the demise of woodland than agriculture:

> It has not been the late increase of shipping alone, the multiplication of glass-works, iron-furnaces, and the like from whence this impolitic diminution of our timber had proceeded; but from the disproportionate spreading of tillage, caused through that prodigious havoc made by such, as lately professing themselves against root and branch . . . were tempted not only to fell and cut down, but utterly to extirpate, demolish and raze, as it were, all those goodly woods and forests, which our more prudent ancestors left standing for the ornament and service of their country.

To correct this devastation by letting nature take its course "would cost (besides the enclosure) some entire ages repose of the plough."[4]

Probably few of Evelyn's contemporaries agreed with him, but he was only echoing the assessments of other writers and travelers who were either ignored or conveniently forgotten. For example, in 1553 William Cholmeley described how "the unsatiable desyre of pasture for sheep and cattel" had resulted in the clearing of untold woodlands during the preceding thirty years.[5] With a few exceptions, the same amnesia about agricultural clearing applies even now.

Elsewhere in Europe, evidence of agricultural clearing is patchy. France had a considerable amount of forest left, firmly held by the unbreakable triad of crown, nobility, and church, which accounted for nearly one-third of the land. But the forests were under pressure from the burgeoning peasant population, which was either denied access or allowed to use (but not clear) one-third of their extent (the *tièrcement*). As in Germany, abandoned lands were recolonized during the fifteenth and sixteenth centuries—"we have ploughed up land that has lain waste as long as any man can remember," wrote a proprietor in the parish of d'Auzon (Yonne)—but there were limits.[6] The forest edicts issued by François I (1516, 1518, 1519) and the measures taken by the regional parliaments of Paris and Rouen to stop peasant incursions testify to that. Consequently, complaints of timber shortages were sporadic but frequent; for example, alarms were raised in the Franche-Comté region as early as 1588 and 1606 about the dearth of domestic supplies; wine merchants in Bordeaux complained that they did not have enough wood to make casks; and peasants blamed forges and foundries for the lack of fuelwood for baking their bread—a single forge using, it was claimed, as much wood as the whole town of Chalon-sur-Marne. The eastern borders of France were little better; the devastation and turmoil of the Thirty Years' War and the Frondist revolts of 1648–53 had left their mark. The Frondist agitation was initially a protest against excessive taxation but then became a power struggle between the nobility and the king. This led to much forest destruction, as peasants went on the rampage and took the wood they wanted, deforesting many hundreds of thousands of hectares.

Like France, the expanding peasantry of Germany chafed under the feudal oppression of the nobles and formed protest movements over their loss of hunting, grazing, and fuel rights and over the inroads made into the forest by industrial uses. These grievances contributed to, and culminated in, the Peasants Revolt of 1524–26, usually thought of as purely a sociopolitical movement. But because forests were so much a part of the peasants' everyday life, their list of demands—the Twelve Articles—included a call for the restitution of grazing and hunting rights, condemned the imparkation of forests by the nobles, demanded that all forest not bought fairly by nobles revert to the community, and evoked the common man's "divine right" to the products of the forest. Emboldened by the fervor of Lutheranism, the protest erupted into revolt. It was eventually suppressed, and even more forest was confiscated and removed from common use. More serious for forest extent was the intense religious turmoil of the Thirty Years' War (1618–48), fought mainly in Germany and spilling over into adjacent countries, which caused widespread domestic and civil havoc and a veritable holocaust of the population. This had two opposite results. Where population was decreased (by one half in places), forests reestablished themselves over marginal and abandoned land. In other areas, however, warfare and lawlessness resulted in deforestation. For example, the Swedes, who needed ready money to continue fighting, cut down large areas of forest on the light soils of Pomerania, which degenerated into sand dunes. But generally, it is thought that the forests expanded and that the destructive exploitation had been less than in the more-maritime west. By the middle of the seventeenth century, metallurgical and industrial uses of wood were rising again, and shortages did not appear. The impression is that wood was abundant, and large exports of hardwood timber still went to England and Holland during the eighteenth century.

Rapid economic growth in the core of western Europe had a remarkable effect on the forests and grain lands of other parts of the Continent. The southern shores of the Baltic were what Fernand Braudel called Europe's "internal Americas," awaiting economic colonization and integration into the buoyant economy of the core.[7] Rising demand for grain pushed up prices, so that in Poland and adjacent areas the landowning nobility responded to the opportunity for profits by forcing the peasants into a revived manorial agricultural system of large-scale cultivation during the summer and cutting and hauling timber during the winter. Between 1497 and 1660 exports of grain through the Baltic Sound (or Straits) averaged 60,000 tonnes/yr, most going to the Low Countries, and later, England. Between 1661 and 1787 it was an average of 95,296 tonnes/yr. Cereal exports of this magnitude translate into between 500,000 and 700,000 ha of grain lands extra to local needs, and these new fields were carved out of the forests alongside the frontages of the Oder, Vistula, and Niemen rivers and their tributaries. It was a giant food reserve for western Europe. In east Prussia, on the edge of the new area of exploitation, clearing was confined solely to the river edges, and inland forests remained largely untouched until the late eighteenth century.

In Russia the forest was even closer to peasant life than in France or Germany because it was more extensive and yielded copious supplies of deadwood for fuel, as well as furs, fish, small game, wax, honey, and quite overwhelming yields of mushrooms and berries, all of which sustained life in a harsh environment. Nonetheless the mixed hardwood forests were cleared steadily during the sixteenth and seventeenth centuries in much the same way as the hardwoods from the Loire to the Elbe had been cleared during the medieval period. Traditional slash-and-burn and long-fallow agriculture gave way to more sophisticated common two- and three-field systems. Some of the most spectacular changes occurred on the frontier south and southeast of the Muscovy heartland after the defeat of the Kazan Tartars in 1552. An influx of Russian settlers occupied the forests in the rolling hills and plains between the Dneiper and the Volga, while Ukrainian Cossacks moved east, bringing with them teams of oxen and heavy iron plows for cutting the matted sod. Forestland was parceled out to individuals, and ecclesiastical houses and clearing proceeded energetically. By the mid-seventeenth century, the pioneer frontier had reached the Grey Forest Earths, Black Earths, and the richer chernozem soils of the southern mixed forest/forest steppe, eventually transforming them into cultivated land. With the buildup of Tsarist military forces, especially after the renewed campaign of Peter the Great against the Kazan Tartars in the lower Don Valley in 1696, the scene was set for a massive expansion of Russian peasant agriculturalists into these areas. A successive series of defensive lines (the Zaseki, Belgorod, Izyum, and Simbrisk) were established, running roughly west to east across the new territory, and the forest was cleared along them to provide barriers of fallen trees and timber for forts and stockades (as well as open and easily defensible ground in front). Next the forests behind the fortifications were cleared ruthlessly (fig. 7.2).

Gradually, the density of population and percentage of land under cultivation increased in the six provinces of Tula, Ryazan, Orel, Tambov, Kursk, and Vorenezh, which straddle the deciduous forest, forest/steppe (parkland), and steppe zones. Whereas in 1719 about one-third of the land was in cultivation and population densities were about $10-15/km^2$, the comparable figures had risen to nearer one-half and $20-30/km^2$ by 1811; clearing and settlement went hand in hand.

Farther north, in the coniferous forests of Russia, Finland, and Sweden, poor glacial, ill-drained soils, together with a limited growing season, restricted agriculture. The northern lands were almost totally covered with coniferous forests, which, before the development of the pulp industry, had little commercial value compared with hardwoods. It was only after the opening of the White Sea route to the west by English Elizabethan merchants in 1533 that the forest became a source of strategic goods, such as masts, naval stores like pitch and tar, and furs. Yet here and there peasant settlers were felling and burning these northern forest margins. The system was primitive but effective—roughly four cycles of burning occurred in each century, so that in a hundred years the burned-over land would experience 20 years under grain (usually rye), perhaps 12 under rough grazing, and 68 under woodland grazing. In the long run, this practice of "burn-beating" destroyed the forest structure, and because it continued well into the twentieth century it has left permanent marks on the northern forests.

In southern Europe, the decline in forest after the Middle Ages was due less to the expansion of cultivation than to extensive migratory livestock grazing. In central Spain, the powerful organization of the Meseta, promoted by the unrestricted autocracy of the Castilian monarchs, pastured

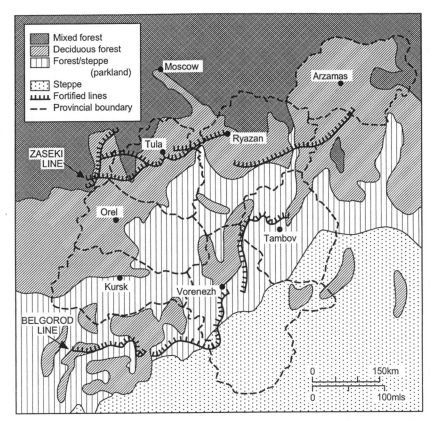

Figure 7.2 Provinces, main vegetation zones, and fortified lines, south-central Russia (note: the tsarist "governments" would have had slightly different boundaries to the postrevolutionary provinces shown here). (Sources: natural vegetation zones based on Central Department of Geodosy and Cartography, Council of Ministers, USSR [Moscow, 1975], 1:5,000,000; political administrative map based on Central Department of Geodosy and Cartography, Ministry of Geology [Moscow, 1966], 1:5,000,000; and lines after D. J. B. Shaw, "Southern Frontiers of Muscovy, 1550–1700," in *Studies in Russian Historical Geography*, ed. J. H. Bater and R. A. French [London: Academic Press, 1983], 1:123, 128.)

vast flocks of sheep that ran into the tens of millions. The hills of Castile were stripped bare of young trees for fodder; and annual burning to promote grass growth and close grazing of the sheep stifled tree regrowth. The same processes, though not so single-minded or severe, were at work in Languedoc, Provence, the Apennines, Calabria, and parts of the Balkans. Where subsequent erosion did not strip the soil, the forest vegetation was in the first stages of its degradation to the typical Mediterranean garigue scrub.

In sum, all the indications are that the agricultural landscape of Europe had undergone another period of intensive change by 1750 and that it was very different from that of the beginning of the sixteenth century. The change during those 200 years cannot be quantified with any certainty, but it must have been immense. But we know that by about 1700, there were about 100 million ha of cropland, one-third of that in Russia. Most of it had been created out of the forestland of the western, central, and northern portions of the continent.

FUELWOOD

Wood was the indispensable raw material of everyday life, and as necessary as food in a preindustrial society. The forests provided the major raw material for buildings, mills, looms, furniture, spinning wheels, plows, carts, and wheels; wood was even used in the gear wheels of clocks and watches. All tools and machines were of wood, except for the actual cutting or striking edge, which was of iron. Moreover it was calculated that a Russian farmhouse and yard took the timber of about 1.36 ha of forest to construct, and there were untold millions of farmhouses in Russia that had an average life of only 15 years. It was a "wooden" age, so we have to take the ubiquitous and universal use of wood for buildings, fencing, tools, and implements as given, and concentrate rather on the use of wood for fuel.

Wood fuel was vital during the intense central European winters, which had become significantly colder with the onset of the Little Ice Age; in addition, most food was unpalatable without the application of heat. Existence simply would have been impossible without wood to burn. The comfortably well-off peasant farmer in seventeenth-century southern Germany could reckon on using 50 m^3 (13.8 cords) per annum, though most rural dwellers had to be content with about half that amount. Cutting, gathering, and hauling wood were common wintertime activities that typified the busy countryside scenes of the late sixteenth-century Netherlandish painters Pieter Bruegel and Lucas van Valckenborch (plate 7.1). But the days were gone when the mass of the population lived in villages and small towns and fuel could be gathered freely from surrounding woodlands without payment. From the early sixteenth century onward, more and more people were living in larger and larger towns. If 40,000 is taken as a reasonable measure of an urban area large enough to make significant demands on its hinterland. Then there were 26 such towns at the beginning of the sixteenth century, 42 at the end, and 48 at the close of the seventeenth century, of which Amsterdam and Naples were over 150,000, and Constantinople, Paris, and London over 400,000 (fig. 7.3). Each urban conglomeration formed a node of collection, haulage, and consumption. The average family needed to spend about 7–10 percent of their annual income to get enough wood to keep a

Plate 7.1 Winter Landscape by Lucas I. van Valckenborch, 1586. Collecting and carting wood was a typical occupation during the winter months, when demand was highest and agricultural tasks at a minimum. (Kunsthistorisches Museum, Vienna.)

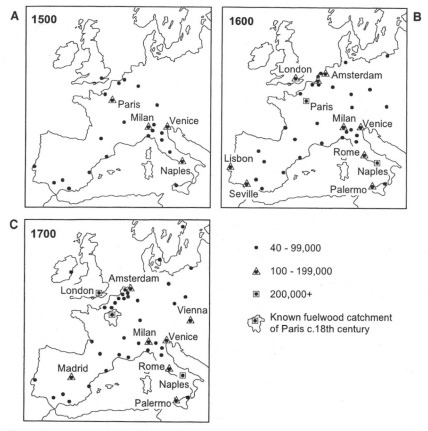

Figure 7.3 European towns whose populations exceeded 40,000. *A*, Circa 1500; *B*, Circa 1600; and *C*, Circa 1700. (Source: after R. S. J. Mols, "Population in Europe, 1500–1700," in *The Sixteenth and Seventeenth Centuries,* Fontana Economic History of Europe, ed. C. M. Cipolla, vol. 2 [Brighton: Harvester Press, 1977], 40–44.)

fire burning for part of the day in one room during the coldest weather, and that was probably only enough to keep them alive, not comfortable.

Clearly, the amount of wood consumed depended not only on the climate and weather but also on the availability of fuel and the income of the purchaser, as there was always wood to be had at a price. But the price was usually excessively high, as middlemen intervened at every stage between suppliers and dealers. Like fuel dealers anywhere and at any time, they hoarded stocks, delayed deliveries, created artificial shortages, especially in times of severe cold, pushed up prices, and still sold substantial quantities to rich and poor alike. Wood shortages were manufactured in an unscrupulous fashion. With the fatal combination of cold, food shortages, and epidemics, it is not surprising that William Harrison could say at the end of the sixteenth century that the poor "often perish for cold," while in Paris at the end of the severe winter of 1709 "people died like flies." [8] Death from exposure to cold as well as famine were still realities in early eighteenth-century Europe.

General shortages of fuelwood appeared first in 1300 in London, one of Europe's largest cities, even though it drew its wood from a radius of 80–100 km in all directions. By the 1500s concern became intense. The once flourishing medieval export trade from Essex, Kent, and Sussex across the Channel to the woodless Low Countries and agricultural northern France was long over, and descriptions of England in 1587 referred repeatedly to timber "want" and forest "decay." In France and Italy, local shortages appeared around larger towns such as Montpelier, Lyons, Paris, and Naples by the later seventeenth century. Thomas Platter, a Swiss student in Montpelier, noted the absence of forests around the town as early as 1595:

> The nearest is at the Saint-Paul glass works, a good three miles in the direction of Celleneuve. The firewood is brought from there in the winter and sold by weight. One wonders where they would get it if the winter lasted a long time because they consume an enormous quantity of it in their fireplaces, while shivering beside them. Stoves are unknown in this region; unlike at home, the shortage of wood is so great that bakers fill their ovens with rosemary, kermes-oak and other bushes. [9]

The shortage increased the farther south one traveled: in Medina del Campo in Spain, fuel was more expensive than the food that it cooked in the pot. Generally, the opposite was true in central and eastern Europe, where the forest was extensive enough to withstand domestic and industrial demands, though local shortages existed around metallurgical centers in Germany and Bohemia.

Examples of the fuelwood demand in individual European towns and cities can be enumerated endlessly. For example, Saint Petersburg in the eighteenth century consumed thousands of rafts of timber and thousands of cartloads of firewood every year. Even the boats bringing the wood were usually broken up and sold for their timbers. In Paris, wood for both construction and heating was transported down the Seine and its many tributaries from as far away as Morvan along the Cure and Yonne after the mid-1500s. But unlike London there was no eventual access to mineral fuel, and 12 years later the radius of collection had widened from 60 km to 200 km, with supplies coming down the Marne and its tributaries. This brought domestic fuelwood gathering into direct conflict with the iron industry in Lorraine, Haute-Marne, Haute-Sâone, and the edges of the Vosges forest (see fig. 10.1 below), and even possibly contributed to difficulties of food supply for the city. In the sixteenth century, charcoal reached Paris by way of Sens from the forest of Othe, but 200 years later it was coming from all over France, sometimes in carts or on pack animals, but usually by river, the boats "piled high, with hurdles along the sides of the boat to keep the charcoal in." [10] In sum, fuel supply to Paris was very different from the situation in London; it was truly "a tale of two cities."

How much fuelwood was consumed is not known; no one collected statistics about an everyday necessity. In any case, much of it was the by-product of agricultural clearing and was never enumerated. But an immense amount was needed. Annual per capita consumption in preindustrial northern Europe was about 1.6–2.3 tons of dry wood, say, 2 tons. Assuming a production of about 20–25 tons of underwood per square kilometer of intensively managed woodland, then a town of approximately 40,000 people needed the annual yield of between 3,200 and 4,000 km^2 (1,235 mi^2–1,544 mi^2) of managed woodland. These figures cannot be regarded as definitive, only indicative.

There were two ways around the fuelwood shortage: either improve the method of heating or find a substitute fuel. The traditional large, open hearth was used primarily for cooking but was a poor source of heat, irrespective of how much wood was piled on it. The two huge blazing fires in the admittedly vast Hall of Mirrors in the Palace of Versailles did not succeed in heating the room. It was advisable to wear furs for dining, and in February 1695 it was observed that "at the King's table the wine and water froze in the glasses." It was not an uncommon experience. Gradually, during the later seventeenth century, chimneys were made narrower and deeper, with the flue curved to prevent smoke from coming back into the room; the mantle was lowered; the hearth's dual purpose of cooking and heating was restricted to one function or the other; and the fire was raised off its brick base onto an iron grate to allow an updraft through the embers. Hearths were now more heat efficient and consequently spread widely. Stoves of brick or stone—usually covered with ceramic tiles—that were more fuel efficient still, free of fumes, and able to maintain a comfortable and even temperature, were not unknown in England or France, but they never caught on in the rest of Europe as they did in Germany and central, northern, and eastern Europe. One can begin to see the truth of the comment that by the early eighteenth century, "it was better to pass the winter in Cologne or Warsaw than Milan or Toulouse." [11] Cast-iron stoves did not appear until the end of the eighteenth century.

Coal was the substitute fuel. It had been brought by coasters from Newcastle to London and English east-coast towns since medieval times. Ease of sea and river transportation, favorable conditions of landownership, and the undoubted demand created by timber shortages gave the coal-mining industry an initial advantage and much encouragement. By the end of the seventeenth century, many coalfields had been opened, and only the most inaccessible places were solely dependent on wood (fig. 7.4). In round figures, coal production increased from about 210,000 tons in 1551–60

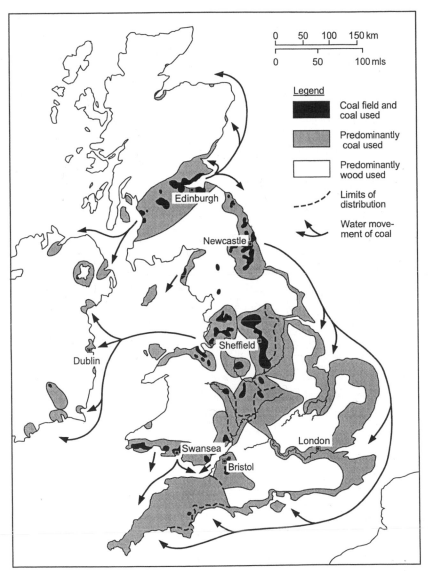

Figure 7.4 Coalfields and type of fuel used in the United Kingdom, circa 1680. (Source: based on J. U. Nef, *The Rise of the British Coal Industry,* 2 vols. [London: Routledge & Sons, Ltd, 1932], vol. 1, facing p. 19.)

to 2.9 million tons in 1681–90, and then to 10.3 million tons in 1781–90. Elsewhere at this time, only Belgium had few collieries of any importance. Even so it is doubtful whether by the end of the seventeenth century the entire annual production of the Continent amounted to more than a sixth of that of Britain. Despite its noxious smokiness, coal seems to have been well accepted for heating and cooking in the domestic households of all classes in Britain by the early seventeenth century, much to the astonishment and comment of Continental travelers. But it was not used for domestic purposes alone: soon it was being substituted for wood in suitable industrial processes with the notable exception of ferrous ore smelting. As a result, other than the remarkable example of eleventh-century northern China, Britain led the world in the conversion from vegetable to mineral energy sources, the process being well under way before 1600. Industrial consumption reached about 1 million tons before the end of the century, or about one-third of total output.

The shrill cries of a timber shortage, so common in the early decades of the century, die away from about 1670 onward. Fuelwood prices stabilize, and in the name of economic efficiency, many advocated the complete stripping of forests so that land could be used for growing food, timber could be imported, and coal used for fuel. Coal had penetrated nearly everywhere; in 1724 Daniel Defoe commented on its widespread use in London taverns and added, "T'is not immaterial to observe what an Alteration it [coal] makes in the Value of those Woods in Kent, and how many more of them, than usual are yearly grubbed up, and the Land made fit for the Plough." [12]

For the moment, at least, the pressure was off the British forests, as coal was plentiful and cheaper to produce than charcoal. The transition from wood to coal was probably the mainspring of Britain's leadership in the future "Industrial Revolution." Eric Jones makes the provocative suggestion that just as Europe obtained a "ghost wheat acreage" with the extension of cultivation in its overseas territories, so it obtained a "ghost timber acreage" with the extension of its resource frontier vertically by mining coal, thereby giving its economy a massive boost.[13] What this meant in terms of woodland not used has never been calculated, and there are many variables to consider. But if we take the simple rule of thumb that the heat generated by a ton of coal was the equivalent of the burning of 2 tons of dry wood, which might be the underwood output of an acre of well-managed woodland, then the 2.98 million tons of coal consumed as energy in Britain in 1681–90 was the equivalent of about 3 million more acres of forest than the country felled. By 1781–90 its "ghost timber acreage" would have risen in proportion to the 10.3 million tons of coal mined, or approximately 10 million acres, which was much greater than all the available woodland. This goes a long way in explaining why Britain was able to industrialize so early despite a shortage of wood.

CHARCOAL AND IRON MAKING

Compared to clearing for agriculture and fuelwood, clearing to make industrial charcoal and build ships was viewed differently. First, these activities represented outside interests that paid little regard to local rights and arrangements and, therefore, were often resented and opposed. Second, they were regarded as new, alien, "unnatural" intrusions into the forests. Charcoal burners, who formed a new set of forest dwellers, were particularly feared because of their peripatetic habits, blackened faces, and the general air of lawlessness that seemed attached to them (plate 7.2). The popular perception was that industry ravaged the woodland and led to its decline. Nevertheless, these activities had to be tolerated because the state dictated that they were of national and strategic importance. Without ships and armaments a country was in an inferior position in the new competitive arena that was emerging in the Europe of territorially aggressive, mercantilist nation-states, which jockeyed with one another for local and, increasingly, global supremacy. Arthur Standish put it pithily in 1611 when he said, "No wood, no Kingdome." [14]

Brick, glass, ceramics, and iron making, salt evaporation, lime burning, sugar refining, soap boiling, brewing, brimstone, and saltpeter needed in the making of gunpowder were taking prodigious amounts of timber, and their demands were year-round and growing. A lack of large timber for house building meant more brick and plaster, but it was one of the ironies of the age that the amount of wood needed to bake the bricks and burn the lime to build a house was greater than the timber to build it. A single glazier in London during the early seventeenth century burned 2,000 wagonloads of wood annually, while the average intake for a glass furnace was 60–70 cords a month. Brewers in London may have consumed as much as 20,000 wagonloads of wood a year in 1578. Wood use for salt making was prodigal: one of many salt furnaces in Nantwich in Lancashire consumed 6,000 cartloads of wood a year, collected from a 75-mi radius, and the great mines of Hall in the Tyrol might have used 1 million m^3 during the late fifteenth to early sixteenth centuries. Similar examples can be cited for Russia. When multiplied across the Continent by thousands of large towns and manufacturing units, for hundreds of years, the result is incalculable, and the drain on the forests must have been immense.

But it was metallurgy in general, and iron making in particular, that engaged the most attention as the destroyer of forests and the creator of a timber

Plate 7.2 Preparing and making charcoal. Woodcutters brought the wood to the kiln area, where the charcoal producers stacked it methodically in cone or beehive form and then covered all with a coating of clay or earth (*I*, this page). This kept the inner temperature at a minimum, so that the wood smoldered and was eventually converted to charcoal and not ash. After the cone was lit (*II*, 169, right foreground), the pile was progressively reduced in size until pure charcoal remained. (From D. Diderot, *Encyclopedie . . . Recueil de planches sur le sciences, les artes liberaux, et les arts méchaniques* [Paris, 1763], vol. 1.)

famine, largely because charcoal was essential in the smelting process. As the universal metal of the age, iron meant tools, implements, and even machinery. Above all it was crucial for armaments and, therefore, had a strategic importance out of all proportion to its domestic importance. Iron making was scattered across the breadth of Europe (fig. 7.5), wherever ores outcropped on valley sides or were easily stripped, and its location barely changed significantly until the late eighteenth century. Essential to the process were running water to move a wheel for the bellows and hammers and abundant supplies of wood. Most of the production was of a low-quality, soft iron, but a few places, such as northern Spain, the Dauphiné and Franche-Comté,

Plate 7.2 (continued)

Liege, Lorraine, the Rhineland, central Sweden, and later the Weald and
Sheffield, established a reputation for finer, stronger metals, and that meant
a degree of specialization. The technology of production was simple. Smelting was carried out on a hearth with a bellows, and alternate heating and
beating removed the impurities in the metal and made it stronger and harder.
The stone-built blast furnace, first invented in the later Middle Ages, greatly
increased the volume, quality, and speed of production.

   How much wood fuel the furnaces used, and therefore how much forest
was cut down, is difficult to calculate. It depends on so many variables, such as
the amount of wood needed to make a load of charcoal; the quantity of charcoal used to smelt the ore and then to refine the pig iron; the amount of pig
iron consumed to make a ton of bar iron; and the heat value of the wood, which
could vary enormously according to the species of tree used. Another problem is to disentangle the exaggerated, misleading, and incorrect information

put out by those with vested interests, such as shipbuilders and local inhabitants, in order to safeguard their supplies. The example of Britain's iron
industry is instructive. Although starting late in comparison with Germany
and France, it rose spectacularly in the later sixteenth century under government encouragement for reasons of national safety and self-sufficiency and
was soon being blamed as the main destroyer of the forests. Local petitions
against furnaces and complaints at the scarcity and rising prices of domestic
fuelwood in the Weald of southeast England were numerous. An added complication was that the navy saw the iron industry as its main competitor for
the limited areas of prime oak timber in the Weald and other royal forests, so
it sought to limit felling and discredit the ironmasters.

But was it such a destroyer? George Hammersley suggests that during
the 1620s, 59.4 m^3 of wood were required to produce 1 ton of bar iron,
and by the last decades of the century fuelwood requirements were down to
50.9 m^3 or less. The yield of the forest was variable, but early seventeenth-
century Crown Surveyors-General consistently rated coppices as yielding
30 cords/acre. If a Wealden cord equaled 2.464 m^3, then each acre of coppice yielded 73.92 m^3, or the equivalent of 182.85 m^3/ha.[15] If we now bring
the two calculations together, then even at the peak of iron production of
27,000 tons of bar iron, fuelwood consumption was somewhere between
1,603,800 m^3 and 1,374,300 m^3, which could be got from only 8,771 to
7,516 ha of woodland. Such a total is hardly enough to cause the crisis
that was so often said to be imminent, especially as the wooded area at this
time must have been well over 1.5 million ha, and also keeping in mind
that coppiced trees are not clear felled but regrow at rates approaching
3 m^3/yr.

In continental Europe, greater forest cover and declining pressure from
competing uses led to less comment on forest decline. Hermann Kellenbenz
suggests only 4 m^3 of wood was needed to produce 1 ton of pig iron and a
further 9 m^3 for 1 ton of wrought iron—in total, a surprising one-fourth
less than the amount produced by Hammersley's calculations above. Nevertheless, the closure of furnaces and foundries could still occur through
thoughtless cutting and, presumably, a lack of coppicing. The Slovakian
ironworks of Stare Hory and Harmanec were forced to shut down in 1560,
and the timber shortfall was only made up with "outside" supplies floated
down the River Gran to collecting points near Neusohl.[16] The rising consumption of timber there, and in the Siegerland in the Ruhr area, caused
a rise in the price of wood. Forestry corporations were formed to cultivate
trees for coppicing in order to ensure a constant supply of fuel and avoid the
expensive transportation of charcoal, which could amount to 70 percent of
the production cost of 1 ton of wrought iron. A more extreme solution by

many territorial rulers was to limit the number of foundries and forges in order to prevent forest destruction.

All in all, then, the picture of the impact of metalworking on the forests is somewhat confused. Yet the general conclusion must be that while each iron-working location (fig. 7.5) was a focus for local destruction that was often real and severe, the overall impact was exaggerated and much less than the inroads of agriculture and domestic fuel getting, which are usually ignored. It is estimated that the total European production of iron (type unspecified) was 40,000 tons in 1500 and possibly 145,000 tons or a little more in 1700. If Hammersley's most favorable calculations for the British iron industry are applied to these production figures, then approximately 11,135 ha of woodland would have been affected in 1500 and 40,364 ha in 1700. The effect could be dramatically less if Kellenbenz's figures are applied.

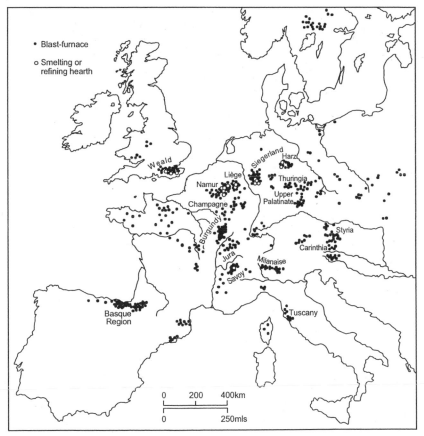

Figure 7.5 Iron making in Europe in the sixteenth century. (Source: after N. J. G. Pounds, *An Historical Geography of Europe* [Cambridge: Cambridge University Press, 1979], 50–53.)

The closure of ironworks—frequently said to be another manifestation of the timber crisis—was far more likely to result from sustained production at one site rather than a national shortage of timber. The cost of carting charcoal and its friability in transit over rough tracks limited its transport to a 5- to 8-km radius, which encloses approximately 20,000 ha, and a big furnace could exist on about a quarter of that if rotational coppicing was employed. Therefore, output everywhere had to adjust to the rate of regrowth in the economically accessible area of forest, and if production exceeded that, then one either waited for timber regrowth or imported fuel at great cost.

Whichever calculation we take, the forest would most likely have been coppiced and almost certainly not totally destroyed. To have done so would have been foolish; it would have upset production stability, raised transportation costs, jeopardized the investment in the plant, and undermined profits, especially in Britain, where there was intense competition from Swedish charcoal imports. It is often forgotten that while Evelyn deplored the "prodigious waste which these voracious iron and glass works have formerly made," he asserted elsewhere that his father's forge and mills "were a means of maintaining and improving his woods, I suppose by increasing the industry of planting." This was not an isolated example; in 1667, Andrew Yarranton commented on iron making in the Forest of Dean, Gloucestershire:

> If the Iron-works were not in being, these Coppices would have been stocked [pulled] up and turned into Pasture and Tillage, as is now daily done in Sussex and Surrey where the Iron-works, or most of them, are laid down . . . and so there would be neither Woods nor Timber in these places.[17]

Paradoxical as it may seem, while being among the first to exploit the woodland commercially, the ironmasters were also among the first to consider some form of forest management in the form of systematic cultivation and coppicing of hundreds of thousands of acres (plate 7.3). These practices cheapened the cost of fuel, protected the ironmasters' investment, and maintained profits. They were merely following an age-long practice, when many forest areas had been managed to produce fuelwood, a frequently overlooked practice in the heroic story of cultivation. Unlike the agriculturalists, the ironmasters did not uproot or plow up woodlands; neither did they graze the young shoots.

Finally, these figures for the amount of forest affected by iron making can be compared with those for complete clearing, primarily for agriculture. From 1650 to 1749 between 18.4 million and 24.6 million ha of forest disappeared in Europe. At the greatest level of production, the area affected by iron making was only a mere 12–16 percent of the amount cleared an-

Plate 7.3 Fuelwood cutters at work in a coppice, eighteenth century. (From John Perlin, *A Forest Journey: The Role of Wood in the Development of Civilization* [Cambridge, Mass.: Harvard University Press, 1991].)

nually during roughly the same period. If most iron-making impacts came through coppicing rather than the complete stripping that was done for agriculture, then iron making was a very minor element in the total picture of deforestation, accounting for a few percent, at most, of the annual wastage. Iron was not the devourer of the woods it was made out to be.

THE DEMANDS OF THE SEA

Homegrown Timber

Shipbuilding (plate 7.4) has always exerted a powerful influence on the perception and use of the forests because of its strategic and commercial significance in the life of nations that were born through overseas expansion and conquest. In addition, the requirement for special types of timbers—those resistant to rot, naturally curved in some fashion for the construction of hulls, or supple yet strong enough for masts—meant that different timbers were sought widely. During the early Renaissance period Venice, Genoa, and Catalonia launched great fleets at the expense of the Mediterranean forest. The Venetian Republic may have held "the gorgeous east in fee," but part of the price of that domination was the stripping of the forests from the mountains around the rim of the Adriatic and the Dolomitic Alps, the timber being floated downstream on sizable rafts. While the Venetian authorities had just about enough timber from its reserved forests, the private shipbuilders did not. By the end of the sixteenth century they began to buy from Venice's emerging rival on the Adriatic, Ragussa, which had plentiful supplies of oak for the time being, and from the Dutch, who were virtually mass-producing ships from Baltic timber. A new chapter was opening in European maritime activity as trade shifted from the Mediterranean to the Atlantic and the source of naval supplies shifted permanently to the Baltic. Even Spain in the days of the Armada was sending North American silver to the Baltic to buy suitable timber, masts, and naval stores.

Estimates vary, but a large warship of about 1,000 tons required between 1,400 and 2,000 oak trees, each at least 100 years old, which could not have grown on less than 16–20 ha of woodland; three masts of up to 130 feet; and numerous spars. Oaks were at a premium because of their resistance to fungal rot and because of the way in which they grew naturally to form the variously curved timbers for the hull: the "futtocks," "knees," "crutches," "catheads," and "ribs." Oak is indigenous to all the countries of western and central Europe from Spain to Poland, but firs are not; and from the thirteenth century at least, firs, together with such "naval stores" as pitch and tar for waterproofing hulls and decking, turpentine for preserving rigging, hemp for making ropes, and flax for making sails, had been imported from the Baltic lands.

In Holland the supply of oak was never adequate for the vast shipbuilding program, and from an early date it imported timber for both hulls and masts from the Baltic. In Britain supplies of oak seem to have been adequate, but concern about reserves was expressed after the early seventeenth century. The oak came mainly from the royal forests in the southern and east-

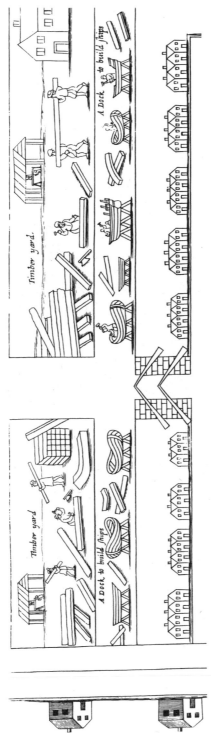

Plate 7.4 An eighteenth-century shipyard. (From Andrew Yarranton, *England's Improvement by Sea and Land* . . . [London: R. Everingham, 1677], 19.) (William Adams Clark Memorial Library, UCLA.)

ern counties, though private parks and estates could make up deficiencies from time to time (plate 7.5). The Dutch wars of the seventeenth century and the maritime wars of the eighteenth put a heavy and continuous strain on oak supplies. Samuel Pepys, secretary to the admiralty, could only write, "God knows where materials can be had." [18] In France the situation was better, delaying the crisis, but the geographer-silviculturalist Georges-Louis Leclerc, comte de Buffon predicted in 1739, "we are threatened with absolute want of it in time to come." [19]

In both Britain and France these statements have been taken as proof of widespread scarcity, but it is probably best to regard them as only warnings, based on an awareness of local scarcities. The continuing reduction of forest led many to exaggerate the extent and immediacy of deforestation, egged on by vested interests. The Admiralty's request for advice from the Royal Society, which led in 1664 to John Evelyn's *Sylva* and the almost contemporaneous enquiry by Colbert in France, which culminated in his Ordonnance des eaux et forêts (Ordinance of Waters and Forests) of 1669, were evidence of official concern. But despite the alarm and propaganda, the navies of both countries relied almost entirely on native timbers for more than another 100 years. For example, 90 percent of the 66,330 m³ of timber used annually between 1760 and 1788 in English dockyards was still homegrown, and French dockyards did not import large quantities of foreign timbers until after 1783, and then only as required.

All this supports the view that far from there being a timber famine, the supply of both timber and cordwood during the two centuries after 1550 was increased. Perhaps the real basis for anxiety was that the forests were not being replanted; the British experience was a dismal story of neglect and inadequate planning on the part of successive governments that never thought beyond their term of office.

The Baltic Timber Trade

Masts and naval stores were another matter. Masts demanded length, cylindrical straightness, strength, durability, and yet a certain elasticity—a combination of qualities that could only be obtained from the conifers of the Baltic forests, which set the standard of quality. But supply from the Baltic was always precarious. Each western consuming maritime nation wanted to deny supplies to its rival; each Baltic supplying nation was at pains not to alienate influential customers and lose essential revenue. Baltic timber was, said Robert Albion, "a matter for diplomats as well as traders." [20] The closure of the Baltic was a constant threat; it had happened during the First Dutch War in 1652. Exacerbating matters, Prussia, Sweden, Denmark, and

Plate 7.5 Timber being felled by ax and measured by dividiers (probably for shipbuilding) while the owner and his agent discuss the price with the timber merchant. (Frontispiece to Moses Cook, *The Manner of Raising, Ordering and Improving Forest Trees*, 1717 ed.) (William Andrews Clark Memorial Library, UCLA.)

Russia had occasionally levied additional customs duties on masts and naval stores. Naval powers like Britain and France did not want to be dependent on foreign powers for indispensable shipping supplies and, in time, looked elsewhere. France experimented with firs from its mountainous areas, and even trees from Quebec, although they were often of inferior quality. Britain tried its North American colonies with more success, but at the expense of raising the ire of its American colonists, with ultimately far-reaching political consequences.

Masts were only a relatively small part of the development of Europe's "internal America" of the Baltic, which was also the source for other everyday bulk commodities, such as timber, potash, grain, fish, furs, flax, and iron. Of these, timber was most important, as the Baltic timber trade was probably the first manifestation in the world of lumber (i.e., crude, undressed trunks) and mass-production techniques that were to be copied later in the forests of North America and elsewhere. Trading by the Hanseatic League had been going on since the Middle Ages, but colonization in Poland and Lithuania in the fifteenth and sixteenth centuries stimulated clearing for more extensive agricultural and urban needs, as well as for exports. Danzig, with its many water-driven sawmills, emerged as a major shipbuilding center and the hub of the export trade, which it soon dominated, dictating standards to Konigsberg, Riga, and other exporting towns in the "East Country." It was a complex story of shifting zones of exploitation, depending on rapidly changing political swings and alliances (see fig. 7.6). By the seventeenth century, a reasonably well-defined system for mass production emerged. A contract would be drawn up in, say, Deptford, Amsterdam, or La Rochelle, and credit advanced to a Baltic merchant house, which would engage middlemen to negotiate with forest owners to produce the required amount of timber and sometimes to transport the trunks to port, paying so much per tree. The growth of the grain trade under the Polish nobility was crucial to the new lumbering system, for armies of peasants worked in the fields during the summer and the forests during the winter.

The efforts to procure masts and naval stores, and find substitutes for these in North America, has always tended to overshadow the very substantial imports into northwest Europe from both the southern Baltic lands and Scandinavia of timbers other than those vital to naval strategy. General sawn timber imports were not a new phenomenon of the eighteenth century; during the great boom in domestic building in England in the sixteenth century, Baltic oak paneling, or "wainscot" (which referred to the way oak logs were shipped from Danzig and Riga with two sides hewn flat to save space in the hold), estriches (East Reichs), and spruce (from "sprusia," an Old English corruption of Prussia) were common, and deals, the 12-inch planking

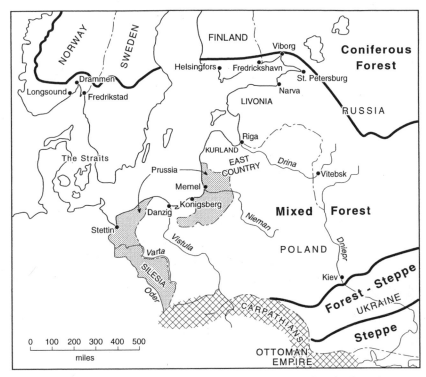

Figure 7.6 The Baltic and Scandinavian timber trade in the seventeenth and eighteenth centuries. It is impossible to show political boundaries with any certainty over this long period because of the frequent and substantial changes of states. For example, Sweden extended around the eastern Baltic and included Livonia until 1658; the two parts of Prussia were joined after 1720; and Poland did not exist as a separate state entity but was variously partitioned between neighboring states until 1810.

so common in English houses built before 1880, are mentioned frequently. The need to rebuild more than half of London after the Great Fire of 1666 resulted in massive felling in Norway, so much so that it was said that the Norwegian merchants "warmed themselves well at the fire." Exports of sawn timber came increasingly from the northern Bothnian-facing provinces of Sweden, which eventually replaced the southern Baltic ports as a source of supply for western Europe during the early eighteenth century.

Exploitation was aided by local topographical and climatic conditions. Gradients were gentle, felling could be done in the winter months when the sap was low, and the huge trunks then hauled out of the forest easily on horse- and ox-drawn sleds on the snow cover to the edge of the many substantial rivers that flowed across the northern European plain (fig. 7.6). With the spring thaw, individual logs were thrown into the smaller streams, to be collected at some strategic point for assembly into great rafts of over a thousand logs that could be navigated downstream. These rafts were piled high with smaller sawn lumber, fuelwood, grain, and also potash, the production of which consumed many millions of cubic meters of timber per annum.

At the Baltic ports, the rafts were floated into mast ponds and broken up. The choicest "sticks" were reserved for masts, and the rest sawn into whatever lengths and widths the market demanded: balks, planks, deals, battens. Lumber was originally sawn laboriously by hand, but productivity was stepped up manyfold when Dutch and German wind- and water-driven multiframe mills, each with up to 10 multiple blades per frame, were established before 1700 in the main south Baltic milling centers. The timber was loaded into comparatively small ships of 250–400 tons that drew shallow drafts and were preferred because of the many offshore spits and bars in the shallow and sandy Baltic ports. The whole system was a precursor of the timber transportation that evolved in North America during the eighteenth century.

Each river had a major transshipment port at its estuary, and each tapped specific supplies in its hinterland. The Stettin trade along the Oder and Warta was almost exclusively oak from central Germany and even Silesia, but fragmented political control upstream hindered development. The Danzig trade along the Vistula reached into Galicia and even the Carpathian edge, from where both oak and fir were obtained. Riga on the Drina specialized in masts from Livonia and later from as far east as Vitebsk, and with connecting canals it could draw on the fir and oak from as far south as the Ukraine on the Dnieper beyond Kiev, from where the famous "Riga wainscot" came. Memel on the Niemen was developed in the eighteenth century to exploit the areas of oak and fir not reached from either the Vistula or Drina. Saint Petersburg traded almost exclusively in fir; what little oak existed was used by the Russian navy.

For over 300 years these forests had been repeatedly cut over and culled for large mast timbers, so that by the sixteenth and seventeenth centuries, when the huge demands of the Dutch, English, and French navies came into being, the wave of exploitation was forced eastward into the less disturbed forests of the Russian borderland and, especially, Finland. Up until 1760 the Baltic supplied Britain with 84 percent of masts of all sizes every year. After that date, imports increased manyfold, but the bulk of the smaller spars came from Norway, which could not be blockaded, and only the irreplaceable "greats" came from the Baltic, which by that time meant almost exclusively Russia and its territories, and shipped mainly out of Riga. North America also supplied many "great sticks," but the War of Independence during the 1770s caused a dent in whatever trade there was. We do not know the situation for the Dutch and French mast imports, but presumably they must have followed a similar pattern.

The full flowering of the Baltic timber trade in the eighteenth century is considered later, but the important point here is that lumber was so indispensable a commodity that it was worth moving a great distance. The idea that a mast felled in the central Russian forest might be shipped to a naval yard in the Caribbean in order to refit a vessel at a distant station seems exotic, but because of its strategic and unique value is not surprising. But the idea that crude, unsawn lumber ("fir timber") might make almost as great a journey is rarely appreciated. It was not as if lumber were a high-value product; perhaps the nearest comparable commodity moved in bulk was wheat, and that was anything between four and six times more valuable than sawn lumber and 10–12 times more valuable than logs per unit weight—and even wheat was said not to be worth moving if the price was low. That lumber continued to be moved around the world irrespective of its bulkiness and low per-unit value was a measure of its essential nature. It is salutary to think that prosaic English drawing rooms constructed in the late sixteenth century were paneled with oak that came from Silesia and Galicia and, occasionally, with "Riga wainscot," oak that came from Kazan on the Russian forest-steppe edge. Timber had turned the bulk trade of the world upside down.

PLUNDER, PRESERVATION, AND PLANTING

The human modification of the earth that took place during the seventeenth and early eighteenth centuries seemed to be a fulfillment and vindication of Francis Bacon's prophesy that "all things seem to be going about man's business and not their own." Human actions seemed beneficent, and optimism prevailed. But the forests appeared to be an exception; the plundering of their timber threatened their very existence (plate 7.6A–D). And yet, how to stop that destruction defied solution, as the economic necessity for timber and fuel overrode concern. Advances in knowledge and crop-cultivation methods were discussed, disseminated, and acted on, but the idea that the same principles might be applied to trees—that trees were a crop—was a much rarer notion. "Wood," said Buffon, "appears to be a present from nature," and most people thought that they had to do "no more . . . but to receive it, just as it comes out of her hand."[21] The simplest methods of preserving forests and increasing their produce were still largely unknown, and he spoke with some knowledge as the keeper of the Jardin de Roi in Paris.

Plate 7.6 The consequences of deforestation, 1601. In this uniquely early set of sketches of a hypothetical mountain, Giuseppe Paulini, a forestland owner at Belluno in the mountains northwest of Venice, graphically portrayed the sequence and consequence of deforestation, especially as it affected the siltation of the Venetian lagoon. *A,* The tree-covered mountain in its preexploitation state. The runoff was slight and controlled.

Generally speaking, Buffon was correct in his observation, though there were notable exceptions. For example, measures had been taken in places to ensure supplies of particular types of wood for shipbuilding and, also, for fuel for local metal-smelting needs. In addition, a completely new element entered into the forest picture during the course of the seventeenth century, arising from a desire on the part of the English aristocracy to plant trees for a "complex mixture of social assertiveness, aesthetic sense, patriotism, and long-term profit."[22] In time, this new, multistranded motivation was to have a far-reaching influence on attitudes toward the forest in many parts of the world.

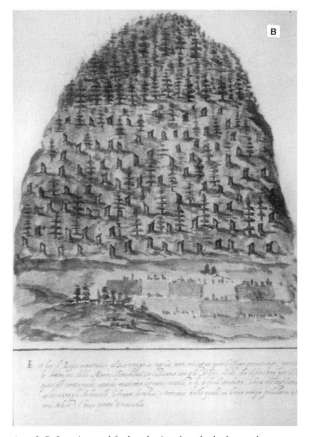

Plate 7.6 (continued) B, Logging and fuel gathering denude the lower slopes.

Preservation

During the fifteenth and sixteenth centuries, Venice had confronted the problem of diminishing timber supplies for shipbuilding, leading to some of the first known measures to preserve the forest. In 1470 it reserved oak forests in Friuli and Istria, and fir trees in the upper Adige and Cadore; but inevitably, so it seemed, this policy led to dispute, evasion, and resentment from villagers, who long had rights in the forests, and private shipbuilders, who had previously profited from felling. The policy failed to replenish the timber supply and, in fact, may even have hastened timber destruction by the peasants who thought the possession of oak trees would become a burden due to the obligation placed on them to supply timber at the command of Venice's giant ship-building factory, the Arsenal. A complete survey and mapping of oak forests was completed in 1568, and from then until 1660 the policy was more rigidly enforced in what were, in effect, state forests.

Plate 7.6 (continued) C, Shepherds and agriculturalists fire the remaining forest to enrich the herbage and the soil.

But this enlightened conception of forests management, in which the trees were regarded as a crop to be cultivated under a definite plan, rather than a mine to be exploited, was never pushed to its conclusion. It needed more policing than the state was willing to sanction, and in any case the decline of Venice as a maritime power and the availability of Baltic supplies effectively took all the resolve out of it.

One moderately successful manipulation of the forest on a sustained, long-term basis came with the iron industry in Britain. The ironmasters had learned the hard way that indiscriminate cutting was a waste of their investment in furnaces and foundries, which had to close if fuelwood supplies ran out. Coppicing and crop rotation were extensive to maintain a constant supply of fuel. It was claimed in one petition that 200,000 acres in the Weald alone was so managed, and it must have been more widespread than that.

Plate 7.6 (continued) D, The hill is denuded of trees. At this point, the lack of vegetation and humus causes a rapid runoff and snowmelt. The water sweeps away the topsoil, damages the pastures, and carries huge deposits to Venice, which silt up the lagoon. (G. Paulini, *Un codice veneziano dell 1600 per le acque e le foreste.*) (Original in Venice State Archives.)

Signs of purposeful, corrective action to counteract the unplanned and unsought consequences of environmental modification did not come about until the publication of Evelyn's *Sylva* and the French Ordinance of Waters and Forests of 1669, associated with Colbert. Both were prompted by the perceived dearth of naval timber and they represent a "divide" that separated centuries of abuse from a recognition of the need for positive forest conservation. Evelyn's *Sylva* was an appeal for a scientific approach to forest conservation and for a proper understanding of the competing demands of industry, agriculture, and forests. It abounds with technical details on planting, grafting, and other arboricultural advice and was a plea to the nobility to plant oaks. But in a broader sense it was less a forest manual and more an appeal for the rational use of all land, forest or not. Portions of the royal forests were reserved and some planting went on, but the government lacked all *esprit de suite* and the program of planting lapsed by the end of the century.

The 1669 Ordinance of Waters and Forests was different in purpose and design to *Sylva*. It sought to rationalize and codify the mass of ancient French forest law, which had become confused and unworkable, and to make forestry an autonomous branch of the state economy while ensuring the supply of timber for the navy. It was designed for the royal forests but was soon being applied to all forestland—ecclesiastical, community, and private. The details of this long document are less important than its general purpose and the fact that it was widely copied throughout continental Europe. It stipulated that kilns, furnaces, and charcoal making were to be restricted in forests, and a range of other woodworking occupations—such as coopers, tanners, woodworkers—had to be located at least 1.5 mi (2.4 km) away from the forest edge. Grazing by cattle, sheep, and goats was absolutely prohibited in forests, pannage was regulated annually by common agreement, and large trees and seed-bearing trees (the "stallions," or *balliveaux*) were marked and reserved. Not unnaturally the restrictions and severe penalties imposed for infringement of the Ordinance of Waters and Forests did not commend it to the mass of people, who lost privileges and individual freedoms, but the forests did prosper or, certainly, got no worse.

Over most of politically fragmented Germany, forestry was still largely subordinate to hunting, but where mining was important, forest planning became a necessity by the eighteenth century. By the early eighteenth century the planting of fast-growing conifers was recommended in order to replenish stocks, a policy that eventually spread through Silesia and Moravia. In the more western political units of Hesse-Darmstadt, Kassel, and Mainz, deciduous trees were favored, and many other experiments were conducted elsewhere. By the latter half of the eighteenth century a spate of forest manuals appeared, and forestry could be taught to cameral officials (princely advisers) as part of their science and administrative coursework in half a dozen universities. These were the foundations of the reputation that Germany acquired for the rational and scientific study of trees and the development of a sustained yield from even-aged woodlands.

Planting

In the preface to the 1679 edition of *Sylva*, Evelyn boasted that several million trees had been planted as a result of his book; but while its publication

Plate 7.7 Reforestation. (From G. Agricola, *A Philosophical Treatise on Husbandry*, 1721.)
On the left, tree stumps are being grubbed out; in the foreground, portions of roots and saplings are being prepared for replanting in pits that are protected by shields, seen on the hills in
the background and to the left. (William Adams Clark Memorial Library, UCLA.)

certainly raised awareness of the desirability of tree planting, there is reason to believe that the trend had begun earlier. The reasons for planting
(plate 7.7) were primarily economic. It paid well to grow large trees, if one
could wait the 50 or more years it took for them to mature. Trees were a
bankable asset that could be realized in times of emergency to pay unforeseen debts, and an economic necessity for the continuance of industry. But
along with these practical arguments went other, less utilitarian considerations. Ever since medieval times the forests had been the hunting grounds

of royalty, and large areas of the country were preserved for the recreational use of the few. Hunting, and the possession of the ground in which it could be undertaken, became an important symbol of social rank, and large land-owners increasingly copied the nobility and created their own deer parks. In time, deer parks became more ornamental and nonutilitarian as owners displayed their wealth by refashioning the landscape. There was a wide belief that wood added beauty and dignity to the scene. This belief was the genesis of the famed English landscaped park or garden.

To look favorably on trees as an element of landscape was a crucial new viewpoint somewhere between the second and third phases of the transi-tion of attitudes toward trees depicted by Keith Thomas—between that of exploitation and fond appreciation (see chap 6, p. 145). It was not that the first phase of taming and eliminating trees was over, or that the exploitation of useful trees was not still taking place; it was merely that these actions were now paralleled by a different set of values and aspirations that were to grow stronger as time progressed.

It is possible to see two strands in this development of a love of trees—or silvaphilia, if one may call it that—one rural, mentioned already in relation to the beautifying of deer parks, the other urban. In the urban sphere the cult of walking and promenading as a social exercise gathered momentum after the restoration of Charles II in 1660, and where better to do it than along formally laid out tree-lined walks and avenues modeled on Continen-tal examples? Fairly rapidly, the London parks and the gardens of Oxford and Cambridge colleges were transformed, and in due course virtually every town with any social pretension became prepared to vote money for a walk or avenue where local beaux and belles might stroll up and down under the trees to display their best clothes and exchange gossip, as a sort of outdoor assembly room.

Whereas the Romans had taken off their clothes and used great quanti-ties of wood at the baths in order to meet socially, the English donned their best clothes and planted a great number of trees to do the same.

In the country, trees were planted in hedgerows and thousands of acres of orchards established, but above all it was the scale of planting on the country estates that was so extraordinary (plate 7.8). Landowners vied with each other in the complexity and extent of their plantings of ornamental clumps and radiating avenues and, in so doing, subjected the surround-ing countryside to the impress of the authority of the landowner himself. Trees became the way to conceal, extend, ameliorate, enhance, or otherwise manipulate the view from the great country house and, in that process, to "appropriate" the view and, ultimately, one must add, the people. Trees

Plate 7.8 The cult of trees: "wood added beauty and dignity to the scene." Blenheim Palace, near Oxford, England, and its park, looking northwest. Built during the early eighteenth century, Blenheim was larger than most country houses. It was a gift from a grateful nation to John Churchill, first duke of Marlborough, for his decisive military victories over the French between 1704 and 1709. (Simmons Aerofilms Limited.)

even had a symbolic, patriotic quality, in that after the depredations caused by felling during the republican era of the Commonwealth, to plant trees was to express publicly and visually the planter's loyalty to the restored monarchy.

From that point on, trees could be regarded neither simply as evidence of barbarism and a cause of savagery nor purely as useful objects in nature. Through a complex mixture of social assertiveness, aesthetic sense, patriotism, and long-term profit, they had become, as Thomas says, "an indispensable part of the scenery of upper-class life." The important point is that here was one of the first manifestations of the value shift from extirpation, through utilitarianism, to aesthetic appreciation and a love of trees, so that ultimately trees achieved "an almost pet-like status."[23] In future years, more and more people across a broader social spectrum of the population would find pleasure in and revere trees, so that they would not only plant new ones but preserve the old—thereby starting a revolution in how the forest was viewed and used.

Chapter 8

The Wider World, 1500–1750

Hee that commaunds the sea, commaunds the trade, and hee that is Lord of
the Trade of the world is lord of the wealth of the worlde.
—Sir W. Ralegh (ca. 1603)

The internal Americas were not enough.
—I. Wallerstein, *The Modern World System I* (1974)

Such are the means by which North-America, which one hundred years ago
was nothing but a vast forest, is peopled with three million inhabitants. Four
years ago, one might have travelled ten miles in the woods I traversed, without seeing a single habitation.
—Marquis de Chastellux, *Travels in North America* (1789)

By the opening of the sixteenth century, Europe was not the world, but
it was certainly the most dynamic and potentially powerful part of it. With
bursting social energy and surging economies a few countries broke out
of their national confines and began to utilize the resources of the wider
world. The processes of conquest, colonization, and terrestrial and cultural
transformation that had created the European landscape and society during
the latter Middle Ages were now applied to the wider world. The European Christians who sailed to the coasts of the Americas, Asia, and Africa
already understood the problems of, and the solutions to, the settlement of
new lands, learned through long apprenticeship in Iberia, eastern Europe,
and Ireland. Moreover, they had a confidence and an ability to maintain
cultural identity. The expansion, particularly in the New World, gave Europe unprecedented windfalls of land, minerals, timber, and crops, as well
as fish and furs. As this flow of abundant and cheap resources gathered

191

momentum the process of land transformation in the modern world began, of which deforestation was a major part.

But Europeans did not affect all parts of the world. China, Japan, and, to a much lesser extent, India remained "outsiders." In China the Treaty Ports had little effect on life inland and existed, in Richard Tawney's words, as "a fringe stitched along the hem of an ancient garment"; Japan was barely penetrated until 1865.[1] Even the bulk of India, which was to become the model of successful Western expansion in Asia, remained untouched beyond the hinterlands of the coastal cities of Bombay, Madras, and Calcutta. However, internal, indigenous change was enormous. Populations were growing rapidly, and large-scale forest clearance and lowland reclamation were undertaken as new land was "made" to feed and keep warm the growing numbers. The forest experience of China during the sixteenth and seventeenth centuries was more akin to Europe during the Middle Ages than to anywhere else. That of Japan, however, was unique in every way.

Although the penetration of the wider world began about 1500, it took about another 150 years for the Europeans to grasp the real novelty of the "New World." The first colonists were obsessed with precious metals, the creation of landed estates, collecting revenues, and sharing out the spoils, as well as the conversion of the natives to Christianity. On the whole these activities did not greatly affect the forest. But when later colonists grasped the significance of the productive capabilities of the land they had occupied and the possibilities of trade, the impact became much greater. Perhaps the proverb of the Dutch colonial latecomers when they compared themselves to their Spanish predecessors summed it up well: "Jesus Christ is good, but trade is better." Step by step the Europeans advanced westward via the Atlantic islands, Brazil, the Caribbean, and the mainland of the Americas. Technical superiority and cultural assurance were critical in this expansion, but so too was disease, the harbinger of the new "ecological imperialism."

"ECOLOGICAL IMPERIALISM"

Disease

Before the late sixteenth century sea contact around the globe was minimal, and the continents were relatively isolated one from another; it was a world of separate peoples. It is true that long-distance oceanic voyages were being undertaken by mercantile-maritime communities; the exploits of Cheng Ho to India and East Africa, and generally within the south China seas, were an example of this. But in the larger intercontinental picture the significant developments were the forays of Breton fishermen to the Grand Banks off

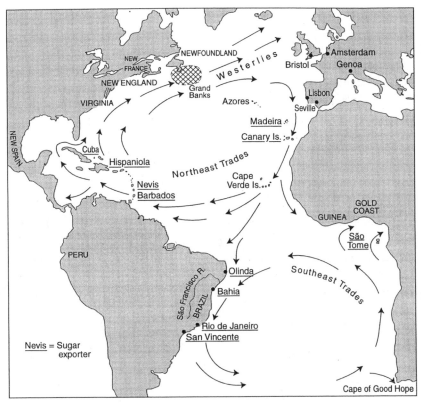

Figure 8.1 Circuits and stepping-stones across the Atlantic. (Source: after J. H. Galloway, *The Sugar Cane Industry: An Historical Geography from Its Orgins to 1914* [Cambridge: Cambridge University Press, 1989], 49.)

Newfoundland for their harvest of cod, and the exploration by Spanish and Portuguese sailors down the coast of Africa and out to the Atlantic islands of the Canaries, Azores, and Madeira. They found, and got to know, the currents and winds of these regions, which, compared with those elsewhere in the world, were remarkably constant and reliable. The northeast trade winds *did* carry them from Europe and down the coast of Africa to the Canaries and thence on to the Caribbean, and the return voyage *could* be made via the Westerlies and the strong sea currents, provided they first sailed northwestward in order to pick up the wind. Simply, environmental conditions aided long sea voyages from Europe to the Americas and back again, or hindered them elsewhere (fig. 8.1).

Because of the assured accessibility and contact, fresh infusions of people and supplies from the Old World were reasonably reliable, enhancing the success of the settlement process. But by the same token, too, there was an equally unfailing, constant, and unrelenting infusion of biological forces, such as plants, animals, and above all diseases, which gave an overwhelming advantage to the invaders. It was, says Alfred Crosby, an "ecological imperialism" far more effective and terrible than an imperialism of arms.[2]

Europeans carried with them many pathogens to which the native population had no immunity. For all their vastness, the Americas were no more than "an enormous island," and their long isolation had excluded exposure to Old World epidemic diseases (many of which had evolved with domesticated animals) and to which Europeans were all but immune. With these Old World pathogens the native populations met their "most hideous enemy."[3] First came influenza, then smallpox and measles, which were particularly virulent and deadly, and then mumps and pneumonic plague, followed later by diphtheria, trachoma, whooping cough, chicken pox, malaria, typhoid fever, cholera, yellow fever, and scarlet fever.

The evidence is fragmentary but abundant, and it parallels the well-documented experience of the susceptibility of isolated peoples in more recent times. The first manifestation of debilitating disease occurred in the Canaries, where resistance by the native Guanches to Spanish conquest suddenly buckled during the 1480s and they were completely subjugated by 1495. Then it reached its apogee in the Americas, where each new pandemic not only displaced or eliminated hundreds of cultural groups but also led cumulatively to a total demographic collapse. All resistance to conquest was undermined. A conservative estimate of the population for the hemisphere was 53.9 million in 1492, but only 5.6 million in 1650, an 89 percent drop; and in North America it fell from 3.8 million in 1492 to approximately 1 million in 1800, a 74 percent drop. Some people would put the original population for the hemisphere much higher, at between 100 and 113 million, which would merely make the decline even more dramatic. Whatever the exact numbers, the fact remains that depopulation did happen on a catastrophic level. Metal weapons—to say nothing of gunpowder and horses (the Amerinds had none of these)—though decisive in battles, were nothing compared to the biological advantages possessed by Columbus and those who followed him. "It was their germs, not the imperialists themselves, for all their brutality and callousness, that were chiefly responsible for sweeping aside the indigenes and opening the Neo-Europes to demographic takeover."[4] One could say, fancifully, that they triumphed through breath alone.

Plants and Animals

Over 50 million people cannot exist without drastically altering their surroundings, and the high densities in the forests caused major faunal changes.

Quite contrary to the denial of contemporary environmentalists, romantics, Native Americans, and Marxists, the New World was not a pristine wilderness. By the same token, however, the loss of up to 90 percent of the population also led to the widespread abandonment of agricultural land and an increase in forest extent and density, so that by 1750 America was probably more forested than it had been in 1492.

In the short term, as the population was eliminated, already cleared fields—and even at times, growing crops of plants such as squash, tomatoes, potatoes, and maize—were available to the newcomers. Both were a major factor in the colonists' ability to gain a successful toehold on the continent. In fact, they thought this bounty was part of a divine punishment on heathens and a God-given reward for their endeavors: said Governor John Winthrop of Massachussetts, "For the natives they are all neere dead of small Poxe, so as the Lord hathe cleared our title to what we possess." Little wonder a settler in tidewater Virginia could say, not altogether disingenuously, many years later:

> The objection that the country is overgrown by woods, and consequently not in many years to be penetrable for the plow, carried a great feebleness with it for there is an immense quantity of Indian fields cleared ready to hand by the natives, which, till we are grown over-populous, may be every way abundantly sufficient.[5]

While nutritious food crops were readily used, other flora and fauna disappeared and were replaced by opportunistic and aggressive Old World varieties. From the Saint Lawrence to the Rio de la Plate, ferns, thistles, nettles, and plantain (weeds we would call them), as well as the more common grasses and clovers such as bluegrass and white clover, found eco-niches on the bared and eroded ground of abandoned Amerind fields or new European clearings. Plants moved with feral stock in advance of people. In more tropical locations, as in the Caribbean, soils were changed as the humus layer was leached or destroyed, with detrimental long-term effects.

The ecological advantage of the Europeans over the indigenes, however, was not so much a matter of crop plants as of domesticated animals. Their multiplication was prolific, as they ran wild in a world without natural predators and competitors. In particular, pigs flourished in forested environments; they are omnivorous, and healthy sows can have litters of 10 or more piglets. The eight pigs brought by Columbus to Hispaniola in 1492 multiplied prodigiously in the wild, spreading to mainland Mexico during the late 1490s and soon said by the Spanish to be "*infinitos.*" Cattle were said to multiply tenfold in three or four years. Horses adapted more slowly, as did sheep. Slower they may have been, but the rate of increase was unimpeded. These feral goats, sheep, horses, pigs, mules, and cattle were the forerunners and forebears of the millions that were to populate the land from the prairies in the north to the pampas in the south. Felix Azara, an unusually keen observer of natural phenomena, calculated that the numbers of cattle in the pampas had reached 48 million in 1700—perhaps an exaggeration, but even if he got it only half, or even quarter, right, it was still a staggering number.[6]

All stock had a devastating effect on the land because of the need to create pastures and hence clear land, a process that had not been a part of the native economy. Stock also prevented tree regrowth by nibbling young shoots, trampling and overgrazing land, causing erosion, and, incidentally, aiding the spread of Old World crops and weeds. Old World stock seemed to do well, if not better, in their New World situations than in their homeland, and the Europeans benefited with better nutrition.

The breaking down of the biological isolation of the continents that had existed for millennia, and the replacement of one vegetation cover by another, was the supreme example of what Columbus's voyages really meant. Although the immigrant settlers had no understanding of epidemiology, processes were set in motion and soon augmented by many purposeful changes as large areas of the earth's surface were cleared of their vegetation and either cultivated or grazed more intensively. Within 250 years, virtually all land uses, land covers, and biota in the Atlantic islands and the Americas had been or were in the process of being changed dramatically, particularly the most prized land cover of all, the forests.

STEPPING-STONES AND CIRCUITS TO THE NEW WORLD

The Atlantic Islands

Tropical islands had long held a fascination for the European mind as a part of the myth of tropical exuberance. Not only were they sources of exotic products, but they were also perceived as island Edens. The Portuguese voyages of the fifteenth century stimulated fascination over the location of the biblical Garden of Eden. A literary tradition that stretched from Shakespeare's *The Tempest* and the poetry of Andrew Marvell, and subsequently to the novels of Daniel Defoe and Jean-Jacques Rousseau, bestowed tropical islands with a symbolic significance. They became paradisiacal utopias, idealized as places of plenty, and microcosms of a seemingly simplified and less sophisticated society. Paradoxically, they were also an allegory of the whole world. If Paradise could not be attained in a tropical island, then it was re-created and encapsulated in the botanical garden, an encyclopedia of common and exotic plants displayed in the open or under glass for all to see. Such gardens began to appear throughout Europe from the sixteenth century onward.[7]

Although not truly tropical, the three archipelagos of the Azores, Madeira, and Canaries in the eastern Atlantic were some or all of these things, but most important, they were stepping-stones on the way to the New World. By 1420 the occupation of Madeira was complete; by 1429 the Azores was occupied; and by 1492 resistance in the heavily populated Canaries was all but over. The Cape Verde Islands, São Tomé, and the islands of the Caribbean were added in time (see fig. 8.1). The first three were like "pilot programs" of colonization and acted as precedents for the new settlement and plantation colonies that were to come; the lessons learned were to last for centuries. Although not extensive, these pinpricks in the ocean had a significance out of all proportion to their size. They were microcosms of how the new, alien, commercial objectives of the Europeans, serving a worldwide market, unleashed a host of radical ecological and biogeographical changes in a short period.

The insatiable demand for sugar in Europe was the key to the settlers' success by providing a source of export income, and excuse for further expansion. Its cultivation led to extensive forest clearing for the crop, as well as for the fuel needed to refine it. One by one the Atlantic islands embraced the new crop, and their economies flourished wonderfully.

In Madeira the settlers found a lush vegetation: "there was not a foot of ground that was not entirely covered with great trees," hence the name given to it, *madeira,* meaning *wood.*[8] Despairing of their ability to clear enough land in time to get in food crops and sugar, they set fire to the forest and the conflagration blazed out of control for days. In 1540 slaves were introduced (probably Guanches from the Canaries) to clear and cultivate the land and to construct and tend the irrigation system. Besides forest destruction for clearing plots, prodigious amounts of wood were used to boil and refine the cane. In contrast, the Azores were too cool for sugar and some of the islands in the Canaries too dry, but not the upland, northern slopes of Tenerife and Gran Canaria. Although the evidence is hazy, it seems that a flourishing plantation sugar economy existed, peaking between 1520 and 1550. Far to the south, tropical São Tomé had more in common with the Caribbean islands. But there was no indigenous population, and African slaves were imported in large numbers to service the plantations. It was a harbinger of things to come.

In time all the Atlantic sugar islands succumbed to the lower-cost producers in the Americas. In addition, the scarcity and expense of fuel; the progressive deforestation of the islands, the stripping of the steep mountain slopes leading to soil exhaustion, erosion, and reduction of runoff, particularly in Madeira and the Canaries—to say nothing of slave revolts in São Tomé—all undermined production. There was no space for rotations or livestock; the islands were simply too small and their resources too limited to support such a scourging agriculture. By 1550 Madeira abandoned sugar and turned to viticulture to produce the sweet dessert wine for which it became famous, and in the Canaries the industry dwindled to be replaced by banana growing. São Tomé lingered on, but painfully. The colonies on the Atlantic stepping-stones declined before the massive production coming from Brazil, where land, fuel, and slaves were plentiful.

Brazil and the Caribbean

As the consumption of sugar diffused both down the social scale and outward spatially throughout Europe, all the new production from Brazil and the Caribbean was readily absorbed. The forests of Brazil were among the most extensive in the world; first encountered was the subtropical rain forest of 780,000 km^2, which stretched along the Atlantic coast from Recife (formerly Pernambuco) in the north to Rio de Janeiro in the south. The pre-Columbian Tupi-Guarani Amerind population of the forest practiced a shifting, slash-and-burn, swidden cultivation, and grew crops of manioc, maize, squash, beans, peppers, and peanuts. But by 1500 the Tupi were stricken by Western diseases and slave-raiding and were gradually replaced by a mestizo population. The concomitant introduction of iron axes and machetes and the herding of pigs and cattle intensified the preexisting shifting regime, and larger areas were cleared periodically.

Sugar was introduced from Madeira in about 1560, and cultivation was concentrated in a narrow coastal strip focused on Recife, Sergipe, and Bahia, with a minor concentration around Espírito Santo and Rio de Janeiro in the south. Considering sugar "ruled" Brazil for well over 100 years, it is surprising that so little information survives about its extent and methods of cultivation, compared to the detailed descriptions of the process of refining, rolling, and boiling at the mill or *engenho* (plate 8.1), and of the social life of the *senhor de engenho*. Despite the many paintings and etchings of mills, especially during the Dutch period of occupation around Olinda in the northeast from 1630 to 1654, there is only one crude drawing of an *engenho* in which the cane fields are also represented, though well over a dozen of the imposing residences. Nevertheless, it is clear that primary forest was always favored for planting, the clearing done by ax, hoe, mattocks, and fire by slaves who were each expected to clear 6.6 m^2 a day, and stumps

Plate 8.1 A water-powered *engenho* (sugar mill) with slaves at work, Olinda, Brazil, by Frans Post, mid-seventeenth century. (From Joaquim de Sousa-Leão, *Frans Post, 1612–1680* [Amsterdam: A. L. van Gendt, 1973], 150.) (State Historical Society of Wisconsin, Madison.)

grubbed out, which slowed the rate of clearing. Plows were rarely used to open up the soil, but gangs of hoe-wielding slaves worked in rows, falling back together and repeating the process through all the daylight hours. Then the cane was planted in trenches, and after three or more periodic weedings the crop would mature and smother weeds by shading them out, and after about 18 months would be ready for cutting and harvesting. At every stage it was backbreaking, arduous, repetitive work that was accompanied by force and brutality, and mortality among the slaves was high.

Because no thought was given to replenishing soil fertility, yields declined. But since cane is a fast-growing grass, it could be left in the ground for multiple cuttings and burned periodically in order to boost the yield. In time, however, the yield fell so low that the field was abandoned to pasture, a cycle that took between 12 and 15 years. New areas were cleared and cultivation moved on, destroying more forest. Erosion on steeper slopes was also a major problem and contributed to declining yield. Sugar growing was a system of profligate use based on abundant resources of land and labor.

Because extreme heat was required for boiling the cane syrup in order to crystallize it, the supply of firewood was a central concern and expense, amounting to about 20 percent of operating costs, and only occasionally exceeded by the cost of slaves. A rule of thumb was that 100 m^3 of fuelwood (and some would put it as much as four times higher) was needed to crystallize 1 metric ton of cane, and thousands of hectares of forest were cut out per annum. If anything, cutting for the mills caused more destruction than cutting to clear ground. Certainly clearing did not contribute to fuelwood, as the normal practice was to make planks for sugar crates out of the larger trees and burn the rest to ash.

By the first decade of the seventeenth century, there were over 140 *engenhos* in the northeast, and fuel supplies were becoming a problem that got progressively worse as the number rose to 180 by 1758. Measures of this deteriorating situation were the illegal cutting on neighbors' property, the relocation of plantations to be nearer forested areas, the cessation of sugar refining for weeks on end, the relocation of *engenhos* to river sites in order to increase the range of wood collection, and the late seventeenth-century decree that mills were not to be built within half a league (3.3 km) of each other, which was rarely observed. The appetite for fuel at the mills was voracious, and the use of bagasse (cane stalks left after pressing) for this purpose, common in the Caribbean, did not become widespread in Brazil until the next century. In the meantime, the forests were under pressure, though the crisis was more one of accessibility than availability.

The sugar industry was responsible for other clearing, as the need for oxen for carting, as well as for providing tallow for candles and meat for employees, encouraged wide-ranging cattle ranching in the sertão (or backblocks), especially along the São Francisco River. Ranches were large, exceeding 100,000 acres (approximately 41,500 ha), or 20,000 head of cattle, though usually smaller; and total numbers of cattle reached over 1.3 million by 1600. The cattle ranged freely through the forest, altering its composition by nibbling and trampling. Around the ranch headquarters the forest was fired indiscriminately to improve feed and provide pastures and arable land.

The Brazilian sugar industry was inefficient, and it wilted under the rising cost of slaves and competition from the Caribbean as the English, Dutch, and French founded their own sugar colonies. While the distinctive slave-sugar society on the coast lingered on into the nineteenth century, the center of gravity had now moved to the Caribbean islands, mainly to the English colonies of the little islands of Barbados and Nevis, where trading companies sponsored settlers on the land in order to grow sugar and stimulate trade.

Although the vegetation of the individual Caribbean islands varied in detail, most had a fairly dense cover of subtropical species, with a many-layered canopy of trees and lianas, which became denser in the higher centers. Jamaica was larger and more lushly tropical; it also had extensive savannas, which were probably old Indian fields abandoned when disease struck the island. Tobacco, cotton, and sugar were grown on the islands for trade, and food crops for subsistence, and the first season was a scramble to find food.

From Barbados, the message went back to England to send able-bodied axmen with "working tools, to cut down the woods, and clear the ground." When they came, patches of forest were selected and tall trees removed either by clear-cutting or ringbarking, followed by the burning of the debris and trees toward the end of the dry season. It was essential that "every hand employ'd therein must be furnished with an Axe, a Saw, and other Instruments for felling Timber, and grubbing up its Roots." Soon, more systematic clearing got underway and vast swathes were cleared, but as Richard Ligon, an early settler commented,

> the woods were so thick, and most of the trees so large and massie [massive], as they were not to be falne with so few hands; and when they were lay'd along, the branches were so thick and boysterous, as required more help, and those strong and active men, to lop and remove them off the ground.

Clearing proved so difficult that Indian methods of cultivation were adopted, and crops were planted between stumps and the trunks of felled trees.[9]

By 1647, about one-fifth of the rain forest and the secondary scrub along the coasts had been cleared, and fields for vegetables and sugar plantations had been established (fig. 8.2). The infusion of capital and importation of African slaves ensured the rapid expansion and profitability of the plantations and the systematic replacement of the remainder of the forest by cane fields. Slaves now took over from the white settlers and each were made to clear about 3 acres of ground a year. The method of clearing did not change—partial clearing, burning, an adventitious subsistence crop or two—leading eventually to a sugar plantation in about 7 years. By 1665 the once forest-covered landscape of Barbados was dominated by large sugar estates and was almost totally open except for forest on the highest peaks. "There is not a foot of land in Barbados that is not employed even to the very seaside," said Governor Atkins in his report to London in 1676.[10] Though small in area, it was a measure and portent of things to come elsewhere in the wider world when commercial plantation agriculture really got underway.

In nearly every Caribbean island, the 15 years before 1665 had been called "The Great Clearing," and by 1672 the same devastation and transformation had happened in St. Kitts, Nevis, and Montserrat. It was said that most of the islands were destitute of timber, with the exception of Antigua. By 1690 the same was true of Martinique, Guadeloupe, and Montserrat, and Jamaica was becoming that way along its coasts. Throughout the Caribbean the severity of clearing was highlighted by soil erosion and by the

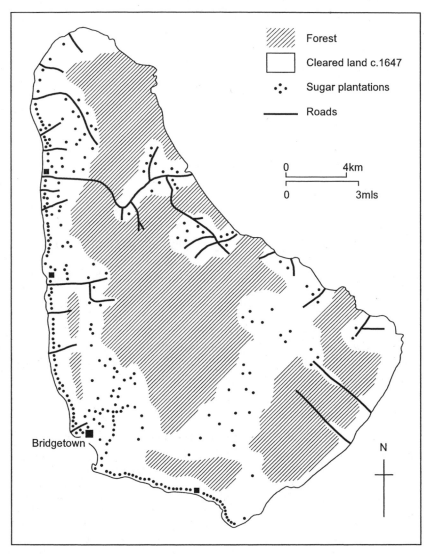

Figure 8.2 Forests and plantations in Barbados, 1647. (Source: after D. Watts, *The West Indies: Patterns of Development, Culture, and Environmental Change since 1492* [Cambridge: Cambridge University Press, 1987], 185.)

scarcity and high price of timber for construction and fuelwood, particularly for refining the sugar. By the 1660s there was not enough wood in Barbados to boil the sugar, and coal was imported from England. But that was not a satisfactory solution and soon timber was flowing from North America. And yet despite the almost complete stripping of vegetation the vigor of nature to reclaim once-cleared land was astounding; Sir Hans Sloane stumbled on an abandoned Spanish settlement and cacao grove on the north shore of Jamaica where the cocoa trees were now 70 ft high and the town site studded with mature trees. " 'Tis a very strange thing," he remarked, "to see how short a time a Plantation formerly clear'd of Trees and Shrubs, will grow foul." [11] But that was a rare sight; far more forest was being felled during these centuries than ever reverted to its natural state. The great clearing of the eighteenth century was about to begin.

The Emerging Atlantic Timber Trade

The success of the English settlements in the Caribbean initially overshadowed the ultimately larger and more significant settlements in North America. Even by 1642 the 80,000 Caribbean Englishmen outnumbered the 49,000 American Englishmen by nearly two to one, a ratio that did not change much: the flow of migration to New England dried up after 1640, when conditions improved in England after the Long Parliament. Lack of constant contact with, and a dearth of finished goods for, New England caused a local crisis, the solution to which was to export its surplus of timber for the essential manufactured goods it lacked.

The first overseas export ventures were with Spain, Portugal, Madeira, the Canaries, and the Azores, where supplies of ships' timbers and timber for wine casks were diminishing rapidly, especially the timbers that enhanced the flavor of wine. Consequently, white-oak pipe staves for wet casks were shipped east in the tens of thousands, together with some general timber cargoes, fish, and provisions. Then New Englanders turned their attention to timber-starved Barbados, exporting timber in exchange for cotton. Soon many of the poorer independent and tenanted Barbadian farmers migrated from the overcrowded island to New England, especially after the introduction of slaves in the middle of the 1650s completely transformed the economy and society of the island and turned it into "one large sugar factory." [12] The New England economy flourished with its immense timber exports; general lumber, white-oak staves for rum casks, and red-oak pipe staves for sugar and molasses casks flowed from north to south. Although places like Jamaica had abundant timber, it could not compete, and even finished casks could be made in Boston and sold in Barbados more cheaply than locally assembled ones.

Trade patterns strengthened throughout the seventeenth century, with less going to the "Wine Islands" over time and more to the Caribbean, together with a lively trade to Newfoundland, where over 20,000 fishermen exploiting the Grand Banks fisheries required wood supplies. Beyond lay the European market, but timber could not stand the costs of transportation across the Atlantic when compared with the cheapness of supplies from the Baltic, except for specialized woods, like mahogany, brazilwood, and dyewoods, and masts, which had strategic value.

The commodities that linked the three continents in an emerging pattern of trade were basically sugar and timber. There are many examples, but one must suffice. It was easy for New England vessels to go out filled to capacity with timber, but difficult for them to return fully loaded. Therefore, they called into places like Tortunga to pick up salt or the Gulf of Campeche for logwood (mahogany), which was then reexported from Boston. In time slaves entered into the pattern. The forests around the western Atlantic were slowly becoming enmeshed in new circuits of trade that were going to grow enormously in future years, but which, even at this early date, were contributing to their exploitation and destruction.

THE ENCOUNTER WITH THE NORTH AMERICAN FOREST

Since the early seventeenth century, political and religious refugees had sought their freedom in the land around Boston, while even earlier adventurers like Ralegh had experimented with settlement in Virginia. After some initial adjustment, the Plymouth Colony had quickly adapted to the forest environment, and once the bonus of abandoned Indian fields was exhausted, its colonists started to clear land for farming. From these "hearths" and many others along the eastern seaboard, European settlers edged forward for the next two centuries into the vast forests that covered the interior of North America from Florida in the south to Maine and Quebec in the north. Figure 8.3 shows the spread of settlement by 1700, 1760, 1790, and 1810, when the total population reached about 0.25, 1.6, 3.9, and 7 million, respectively, and the spread can be taken as a measure of the human impact on the forest at these different times. Settlers were not occupying a totally un-humanized landscape, it is true, but the prior advance of disease had ensured that it was a depopulated one, which was probably in the process of reverting to a denser forest than existed previously.

Backwoods Life

Compared to previous European forays overseas, the settlement of North America displayed many new characteristics that were to have a profound impact on the forests. The ideals of agricultural living, freehold tenure, dispersed settlement, "improvement," and personal and political freedom were extolled and were novel and potent driving forces in the cultural

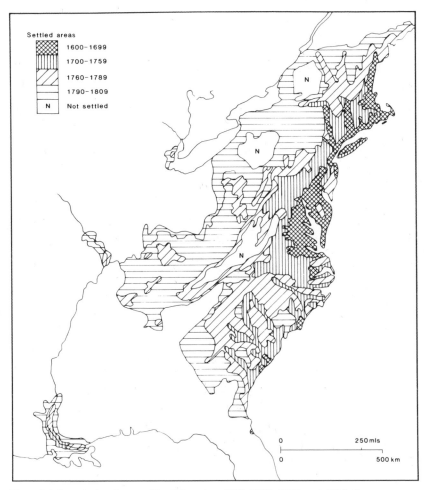

Figure 8.3 Spread of settlement, North America, 1700, 1760, 1790, and 1810. (Source: after M. Williams, *Americans and Their Forests* [New York: Cambridge University Press, 1989], 54.)

climate of the new settler empire. Similarly, the pioneer's self-sufficiency, thrift, independence, and resourcefulness were virtues that were lauded. But for them the reality, as they cleared the land, was more likely to have been isolation, drudgery, unremitting toil, and worry. A distinctive American "backwoods" culture evolved in the forests (plate 8.2), producing the largest transformation of forest landscapes seen in the world since the high Middle Ages. Also, it was probably the best documented account of forest clearance and occupation ever. By the middle of the eighteenth century, America was, as Thomas Pownall put it, "as yet a new World

Plate 8.2 Backwoods Life in New England, 1770. (From the anonymous work *One Hundred Years of Progress in the United States* [Hartford, Conn.: L. G. Stebbins, n.d.], 21.) (State Historical Society of Wisconsin, Madison.)

to the Land-workers of Europe." But soon the forest experience of the "land-workers" was to become the basic element in the geography and history of the continent. The marquis de Chastellux, who traveled extensively in America, said that the sight of "the work of a single man who in the space of a single year" had cut down several acres of woodland and built himself a house in the clearing was something he had observed

> a hundred times. . . . I have never travelled three miles without meeting a new settlement either beginning to take form or already in cultivation. The combined tasks of clearing, of building a house and fences, and even of

making a road to his clearing could take a settler's lifetime, during which he
was less a farmer and more a builder.[13]

Before a pioneer could clear land he had to acquire it. In the early tightly
knit village communities of New England, that was a carefully controlled
communal affair, but with the removal of the Indian harassment after about
1760 and the relaxation of religious oversight, regular surveys were made
in townships away from the villages, and settlement and clearing spread
rapidly. In contrast, in the later frontier areas of New York, Pennsylvania,
Tennessee, Kentucky, and Virginia, it was a relatively simple matter for an
enterprising man to move into the forest beyond his neighbor in true backwoods fashion and squat without legal title. A cabin and a clearing of a
few acres were sufficient to establish title for the land. After 1790, regular
surveys in Ohio and western New York resulted in more orderly westward
expansion, which was fortunate, as the new forest dweller was usually a
migrant who came many hundreds of miles, often from New England. He
got his information about land sales from newspapers and broadsheets; he
might even have a preliminary look at the land, buy it, go home, and return
the next winter with ax, gun, blanket, provisions, and ammunition. He
would then start to clear it in preparation for his family, who might follow
one or even two years later. Such dissemination of information and personal
mobility were without precedent and were a foretaste of the dynamic forces
being unleashed on the world's forests.

Although farmers in the South pioneered in the traditional manner, the
rise of the plantation system gradually forced individual farming into the
background. The system that had developed on the island stepping-stones
across the Atlantic now took hold on the American mainland. Large blocks
of land of 500–1,000 acres or more were needed for cotton and tobacco
growing, and slaves replaced European pioneer farmers.

Clearing

Everywhere, old Indian fields initially reduced the amount of clearing
necessary and heightened the chances of survival. Soil quality was judged on
tree size and, perceptively, on the prevalence of particular species. For example, pitch and other pines meant dry, sandy soils; oak, chestnut, walnut,
and hickory meant good arable soils. Every region, it seemed, had its plant
indicators.

In the northern and middle colonies, clearing was accomplished by
either clear-cutting or ringbarking, both followed by burning. Clear-cutting
was common enough in New England and New York to be known as the

"Yankee" method; ringbarking, or girdling, was known as the "Indian" method. There was little to recommend one over the other, for girdling merely deferred the expenses of time and labor, though it at least allowed the pioneer to get on with cropping. Stumps were a problem with both methods, and most were left in the ground to rot, with cultivation carried on around them. Grass, potatoes, tobacco, flax, and maize were no problem, as they could be planted "Indian style" on mounds between the stumps, and then either harvested by hand or grazed by stock (see plate 8.2). Stump clearing only became necessary once wheat or rye were sown and harvested.

The individual experience of clearing is difficult to capture, but the simple yet powerful poem of a Pennsylvania farmer as he clear-cut his farm in 1692 comes very near it:

> When we began to clear the Land
> > For room to sow our Seed,
> And that our Corn might grow and stand,
> > For Food in time of Need,
> Then with the Ax, with Might and Strength
> > The Trees so thick and strong,
> Yet on each side, such strokes at length
> > We laid them all along.
> So when the Trees, that grew so high
> > Were fallen to the ground
> Which we with Fire, most furiously
> > To Ashes did Confound.[14]

Pioneers rarely cleared more than 10 acres during the first year; it would simply have been too arduous. Few cleared more than 30 acres if a comfortable subsistence was their aim. Clearing was a combination of sweat, skill, and strength, and the pioneer farmer was seen as the heroic subduer of a sullen and unyielding wilderness that needed taming.

In the Southern colonies girdling was common, but in any case, stump grubbing was rarely worthwhile because of the need for constant crop rotation. Tobacco exhausted the soil and led to soil toxicity, and cotton was only a little less demanding. Manuring was rarely resorted to: "We can buy an acre of new land cheaper than we can manure an old one," said Thomas Jefferson, and manuring was regarded as more irksome than cutting down trees. Three or four tobacco crops were taken before turning the clearing over to a few crops of wheat or maize and then abandoning it to the forest. "After twenty or thirty years," commented one observer, "the same land would be cleared and put under a similar scourging tillage."[15] To accommodate these constant shifts, estates had to be large and widely spaced, and the impression they created was of islands of cultivation in a sea of forests. Thomas Anburey, who traveled through the South in 1789, said:

> The house we reside in is situated upon an eminence commanding a pros-
> pect of nearly thirty miles around it, and the face of the country appears
> an immense forest, interspersed with various plantations, four or five miles
> distant from each other: on these there is a dwelling house in the centre
> with kitchen, smoke house, and out-houses and from various buildings each
> plantation has the appearance of a small village.[16]

The plantations had their own seasonal labor rhythm. It was a common slave task to clear 3 acres during the fall, split the timber for huts and rails, and then prepare the ground for planting in March. While the cutting of trees on 1 acre was considered a day's task of eight slaves, lopping and burning during the evening was an extra task. The cost of clearing had to take into account the cost of buying, housing, and feeding slaves, which was not inconsiderable; consequently, clearing in the South was far more commercially oriented than the essentially subsistence farming in the North. What the northern farmer paid for with hard labor the southern planter paid for with hard cash.

Whichever part of North America one was in, however, the process of land clearing and farm developing was widespread, universal, and an integral part of rural life, continuing well into the latter years of the nineteenth century. "Such are the means," marveled the marquis de Chastellux in 1789,

> by which North-America, which one hundred years ago was nothing but a
> vast forest, is peopled with three million of inhabitants. . . . Four years ago,
> one might have travelled ten miles in the woods I traversed, without seeing
> a single habitation.

The clearing in the forest on the frontier with its log cabin was the ultimate American symbol, the place where the pioneer created the world anew, as if in some latter-day Genesis (plate 8.3). Benjamin Latrobe's seemingly extravagant comment, that "the American axe may well rank with maize and steam as one of the three things which have conquered the western world," may have more of a ring of truth for North America.[17]

Other Backwoods Forest Uses

Beyond the clearing lay the unfenced, unclaimed range of the forest that provided free feed for stock and the raw material for many of the essentials of everyday life, including houses, fences, fuel, and the generation of cash.

Plate 8.3 The Beginning. (From the anonymous work *One Hundred Years of Progress in the United States* [Hartford, Conn.: L. G. Stebbins, n.d.], 19.) (State Historical Society of Wisconsin, Madison.)

Overwhelmingly stock meant swine, and the wild razorback hog dominated the woodland grazing regime; cattle only challenging swine during the later nineteenth century. Consequently, pork was the most widely consumed meat, either as fresh meat or salted down and packed in barrels. The full pork barrel was a symbol of plenty, and when its bottom could be seen it was a symbol of starvation—one was literally "scraping the bottom of the barrel."

Large feral cattle herds roamed the forests of the South, particularly the Carolinas. The forest and its clearings were fired continuously in order to maintain the growth of young grass. Cow pens were constructed in strategic places so that the wild herds would return at night to suckle their calves. With the establishment of more permanent dwellings, along with branding, rustling, and roundups (often with black "cowboys"), we can perceive the prototype for the western range, except that closed forest replaced the open grassland.

The presumption was that fences were essential only if the aim was to keep the stock out of fields, not in them; therefore, the onus of responsibility lay with the cultivator, not the forest stock owner. Given the number of other tasks the pioneer farmer had to do, fencing was not too high on his list of priorities, and hence many makeshift fences of piled-up stumps or brushwood served until straight-grained logs could be split, postholes dug, and posts notched and holed for cross rails. A common and favorite pioneer expedient was the Virginia, worm, or zigzag fence, which was constructed by laying horizontally six to 10 slender, 12-ft poles or rails in such a way as to interlock with one another at right angles. It was expensive in its use of land and wood (for example, a square field of 160 acres required about 15,000 rails) but took little time to construct and, therefore, was adopted widely. By as late as 1850, zigzag fences still accounted for 79 percent of the 3.4 million miles of fencing in the United States, and post-and-rail and plank fences another 14 percent, mainly in the prairies, where timber was expensive. Wood was the overwhelming fencing material well into the nineteenth century and was not replaced by barbed wire until after the 1860s.

As with fencing, the dominant building material was wood. The archetypal domestic structure was the log cabin, both an emblem of frontier life in the forest and a metaphor for pioneer hardship, hope, and virtue. So simple was this dwelling that little can be said of it, except that its origins have been traced to northwestern Europe and that after its introduction into the Delaware area by the Swedes it diffused widely and mutated vigorously throughout the length and breadth of the country. All that was needed to build a cabin were 80 or so logs between 20 and 30 ft long for the walls, split planks for the floor, and grass, straw, and mud for filling the gaps between the logs. Depending on the help received from neighbors, the whole structure could be raised in between one and three days. Not until the Indian threat diminished and sawn timber from mills became readily available did clapboard frame houses appear. But the log cabin took a long time to disappear; there were still over 33,000 in New York in 1855, housing one-fifth of all farm families. Four-fifths of Americans lived in timber houses of one sort or another at the turn of the nineteenth century.

The forest yielded two other "domestic" products, the volume of which is difficult to calculate accurately but which were of immense value: potash and fuel. Potash produced an alkali solution used for many industrial purposes, including soap and glass-making, tanning, bleaching, calico printing, medicines, and gunpowder. It sold readily, and provided a steady cash income for farmers. It was claimed that one-half or two-thirds of the expense of clearing land in New York was repaid from making potash; the cash earned helped to buy land, hire labor to clear it, or purchase the necessities that could not be produced on the farm. Potash was in great demand in Europe, and by the late eighteenth century it ranked sixth in value among American exports.

In the north of the country, fuel was indispensable for the very preservation of life for 7 or 8 months, and it was scarcely less crucial during the southern winter, so that slaves never dared return from the fields without bringing back a load of firewood. "So much of the comfort and convenience of life," said Benjamin Franklin, "depends on the article of *fire*." The answer was to pile on the wood, which was plentiful enough, and great blazing fires halfway up the chimney were a common sight in farm homes.[18]

Fuelwood was measured in cords, a cubic measure of $4 \times 4 \times 8$ ft, or a total of 128 ft³ (3.625 m³). Consumption varied according to the combustible quality of the wood (hardwoods usually burning warmest), the size of the house, and the habits of a family, but each year a typical rural household might well have consumed between 20 and 30 cords, which is between 72 and 109 m³, some of which might well have been sold to urban centers for cash. Fuelwood demand rose with the growth of cities on the eastern seaboard; by 1750 there were 435 sizable urban centers on the coast, and the populations of Boston, Philadelphia, New York, and Baltimore were all over 50,000. There are plenty of examples of measures of scarcity (and hence destruction), particularly during the punishing winter months: the emergence of fuel dealers, price increases and seasonal "gouging," municipal regulation, and wood charities for the urban poor, along with the increasing use of iron or tin-plated draught stoves, or "Franklins," as they were known after their inventor. Whereas wood had once been "at every man's door," it now had to be trundled overland from pioneering districts well over 100 miles distant or brought down the coast in sloops from Maine and New Hampshire to Boston, up from New Jersey to Philadelphia, and down the Hudson to New York. So bad was the situation that by the winter of 1775, fuelwood was said to be just as dear as it was in timber-starved England!

How much wood was cut for fuel will never be known because of the variability of, among other things, the yield of forests, the amount of regrowth and recutting (it might be cropped four or five times in a century), the population, and the fact that fuelwood was a cheap and plentiful byproduct of agricultural clearing. But it is possible that by the end of the eighteenth century, a total of some 812 million cords had been consumed. At a yield of 100 cords per acre (a high figure), this equals 8.12 million acres, which is more than the amount of land cleared for agriculture at the time, so there must have been a great deal of repeated tree "cropping." Regrettably, we will never know the amount of land cleared purely for fuel; the wood used for fuel was so commonplace that no one wrote about it or collected statistics about it.

Commercial Uses of the Forest

To make a distinction between the impact of agricultural clearing and the impact of commercial cutting and exploitation is difficult, as the two over-lapped in so many ways. On the one hand, the infant settlements needed to clear land in order to grow food to live; on the other, they needed to export surplus products to exchange for essential manufactured goods. Thus pot-ash and fuelwood—incidental products of clearing—were crucial to the profitability of farm making, and similarly, agriculturalists supplied much of the wood that went into the general domestic lumber business and even the export trade. At some indeterminate point, the pioneer agricultural set-tler arranged his life and activities in such a way that he purposely supplied the outside, distant market, rather than his own and local needs. At that point, the pioneer economy shifted away from self-sufficiency, and the ex-ploitation of the forest began to have a distinctly commercial orientation.

It is impossible to summarize the detail of the commercial use of the forest, such as naval stores, masts, shipbuilding, timber production, and charcoal making, but suffice it to say that while these products and processes were important locally, they were mere pinpricks in forest destruction compared with farm making and domestic fuel consumption. If collectively they amounted to as much as 10 percent of the drain on the forest resource by the mid-eighteenth century, it would be surprising; and the percentage was probably much less. Yet American naval stores and masts had a strategic significance for England because of the precarious nature of supplies from the Baltic. The gathering and manufacture of pitch, tar, turpentine, and resin were fairly unsystematic, scattered, and tied in with southern planta-tion agriculture and were far more expensive than their Baltic counterparts. But under the stimulus of subsidies, production in the Carolinas reached over 82,000 barrels in 1718, accounting for nearly 90 percent of Britain's total imports of these commodities.

While Britain's policy of utilizing its colonies as a source for raw ma-terials and a market for its manufactured goods worked reasonably well in the South, it went wildly awry in the North. Increasingly the Yankees were building boats and transporting timber and other products for trade (particularly to the "Wine Islands" and the West Indies), and in the pro-cess achieving some sort of economic independence. From about 1660 on-ward, true conflict arose over mother country and colonial demands for shipbuilding timber and over the claim by Britain under the White Pine Act of 1722 to reserve and exploit exclusively the choicest timber for masts, the so-called Broad Arrow Policy. While the number of masts exported was very few—rarely more than 15 percent of total Royal Navy needs—most of their diameters were over 20 in, and many over 27 in, sizes that the depleted German and Russian forests could no longer supply. However, to get these the British placed a blanket ban on the felling of all white pines growing outside the townships. Resentment ran high at these unworkable restrictions—at the high prices the contractors received and the low prices the local woodsmen got; at the speculation in land prices that the higher value of the pines helped to promote; and at the many "paper townships" in Maine that were created by speculators in order to get the pines. The years between 1722 and 1776 are muddled with illegal cutting on the part of the woodsmen, duplicity on the part of the Crown agents, and conniving on the part of the contractors.

New England merchants carried on a thriving trade in masts and timber with Spain and Portugal because better prices were to be had from those countries, even though they were officially at war with Britain. What John Evelyn called the "touchy humour" of those Yankee colonies culminated in the "woodland rebellion" against the timber restrictions that had all the ingredients of the conflict of 50 years later that brought about American independence. Timber and forests were too important an ingredient in the life and livelihood of colonial North America to be dealt with lightly.

From the very beginning, shipbuilding was an integral and fundamental part of the whole timber and trade economy of New England and in scattered ports as far south as Georgia. We will never know exactly how many ships were built, but all the evidence is that it ran into many scores per annum and that most were of small capacity (approximately 100 tons) to suit the coastal trade and the seasonal nature of the West Indies trade. Because of timber shortages at home, British merchants began to place orders in American yards for larger transatlantic vessels, and so successful were the Americans with this production that by the eve of the Revolutionary War a startling 40 percent of all British tonnage was being built on the eastern seaboard.

The "woodlands revolt" highlighted the fact that indigenous American commercial timber production was well developed by the eighteenth century. Every settlement, almost without exception, had its small water-powered sawmill that was considered an indispensable adjunct to pioneering life, and nearly every farmer was a part-time lumberman. Logging did not usually extend for more than 5 or 6 mi from the mill; logs were snaked out of the forest and then carted to the settlements.

The insatiable market for timber in the growing urban centers on the eastern seaboard meant that a more regular long-distance method of transportation had to be devised, and sometime during the early 1700s cooperative rafting became popular. Although rafts had been used on European rivers for centuries, it was the immense rafts on the American ones that foreign travelers and native Americans alike never ceased to comment upon. During the 1750s Anne McVickar Grant witnessed some "very amusing scenes" on the banks of the Hudson where the new settlers had cut planks and logs and brought them down to the river edge:

> And when the season arrived that swelled the stream to its greatest height, a whole neighbourhood assembled, and made their joint stock into a large raft, which was floated down river. . . . There is something serenely majestic in the easy progress of these large bodies on the full stream of the copious river. Some times one can see a whole family transported on this simple conveyance; the mother calmly spinning, the children sporting about her, and the father fishing at one end and watching its safety at the same time. These rafts are taken down to Albany, and put on board vessels there for conveyance to New York.

Soon raft building spread to all the east-flowing rivers and the tributaries of the St. Lawrence. It was the cheapest way to convert timber into cash to purchase the essential items needed in the pioneer land-clearing settlements inland.[19]

Timber production was widespread and regarded as a necessary part of everyday living that required no comment. Only where timber entered into overseas trade is there a record of cutting. Every port from Falmouth in Maine to Sunbury in Georgia was exporting sawn lumber, staves, and shingles, mainly to the Caribbean at this time. The New England ports tended to dominate the sawn lumber trade, the southern ports the stave trade. Only the Piscataqua inlet with its felling and shipbuilding and the Albany–Glen Falls region on the Hudson with its many mills seemed to be emerging as distinctive timber production centers.

Like timber production, charcoal production for iron smelting was early, widespread, and commonplace in colonial America because of the huge need for equipment and tools. It is possible that pig-iron production reached 30,000 tons on the eve of the Revolution, of which 3,000–5,000 tons was being exported to Britain. Wood fuel was rarely a locational factor in production, as it was abundant and ubiquitous, but iron ore deposits and moving water to drive trip-hammers and bellows was significant. Furnaces dotted all the Atlantic states, with major concentrations in the oak forests of northern New Jersey and adjacent southern New York, western Connecticut and Massachusetts, most of Pennsylvania, and the pine barrens of New Jersey.

From permutations involving cords per acre, bushels per cord, and charcoal per bushel, it can be calculated that efficient high yielding–low consumption furnaces needed about 150 acres of woodland to produce 1,000 tons of pig iron, and if inefficient low yielding–high consumption furnaces were in operation, the amount of forest affected could multiply tenfold. In reality an intermediate figure of 500 acres per 1,000 tons seems more likely and is substantiated by contemporary accounts of the size of forest reserves needed for a 20-year rotation of cutting. These estimates have to be placed against the comments of Johann Schoepf, who traveled through Pennsylvania in 1783 and noted the lack of timber supplies in the country around the Schuylkill, where the forests were "everywhere thin," because the ironworks "could not but ravage the woods to their own hurt"; and there were plenty of examples of furnaces in northern New Jersey and the Housatonic Valley in Connecticut said to have been abandoned because of timber depletion.[20]

The impression is that, like seventeenth-century England, local depredations could be severe but their overall impact might be greatly exaggerated. The alien, disruptive intrusion of industry into the quiet and traditional regimes of the forest and agricultural life was still a literary topos. At its least, charcoal making was destroying a mere 4,500 acres per annum and at its greatest, 45,000; the actual figure was most likely about 15,000 acres, a mere drop in the ocean of forests that clothed the eastern United States. Unlike England, the lack of interest in substitute fuels for nearly another 100 years suggests no shortages. The retention of the old fuel technology was both a reflection of the superabundance of wood and a widespread preference for the type of versatile iron that charcoal made.

CHINA: "A DARK AREA IN SPACE"

China has one of the longest-settled and most intensely humanized of landscapes and, as such, must have been a major part of the "wider world" of deforestation. But its story is obscure—it is a true "dark area in space." In all the uncertainty, two basic statistics stand out—population and area of cultivation. At the beginning of the Ming dynasty in circa 1400 there were between 65 and 80 million people, and the area cultivated was about 24.7 million ha. By 1770 there were 270 million people and 63.3 million ha of cultivated land, and by 1893, 385 million people and 82.7 million ha of land in cultivation—a fourfold increase from 1400 to 1770, and a five- to sixfold increase by the end of the nineteenth century.

The population was never well fed, but it survived disasters and multiplied, being one of the most rapidly growing of any in the early modern world, averaging 0.4–0.5 percent per annum. Given our knowledge of comparable societies at comparable times, it seems inconceivable that this huge increment of over 300 million people and 58 million ha of "new" agricultural land did not have a dramatic effect on the natural forest vegetation. Submarginal land on forested slopes in southern and central China, dry land on the northern fringes and Inner Mongolia, and wetland in the river bottoms and deltas were transformed first. The raising of yields through the selection of better seeds, double-cropping, and better water control and fertilizing tended to follow later, but the transition was never that clear-cut.

Information about the extent and clearing of the forest is sparse. Works on agricultural and rural life in China can be scoured for information but not one reference to forests, woodland, timber, or fuelwood can be found, despite their essential nature for the very existence of the inhabitants up until recent times, and they are by no means irrelevant today. For most of the Ming and Qing dynasties (1368–1912), if not before, the story of deforestation can almost only be told through the medium of traditional first millennium BC poetry and the observations of foreign scientists and travelers of the late nineteenth and early twentieth centuries. It is as if one is combining Homer with the technical reports of field officers of the U.S. Department of Agriculture or some similar organization.

Mandarins and Peasants

In addition to the great number of people, the one thing about the Chinese past of which we can be reasonably sure is the form of governance, though what to call it—Oriental Despotism, Bureaucratic Feudalism, Imperial Bureaucracy, or the Asian Mode of Production—is an open question. The label is of less importance than the characteristics, which had their effects on the clearing process. An all-powerful mandarin bureaucracy dominated a multitude of autonomous village communities. While the state did not attempt to interfere in the daily affairs of the villagers, it ensured its dominance over society through the management of public works and took an active role in migration, land clearance, and reclamation, sometimes through enforcing corvée labor. Despotic rule did not seem to hinder agrarian economic growth, but commercial developmesnt lagged, and the country remained obstinately feudal. The peasantry labored hard but were lightly taxed and relatively unfettered and did much as they liked; the state directed major developments of irrigation, drainage, and clearing as part of a dynastic concern for the welfare of its subjects and the feeding of an expanding population.

The example of the 210,000 km² of Hunan Province in south-central China during the Ming dynasty (1386–1644) and the early part of the Qing

(1644–1911), as it changed from an underpopulated periphery to part of the densely settled core of the country through state-encouraged immigration, helps one to understand the process of deforestation in a significantly large part of the country.

In circa 1386, the population was between 1.87 and 2.08 million, spread over some 695,000 ha of agricultural lowlands around Donting Lake on the central Yangtze, where the Yuan, Xiang, Li, and Zi rivers meet. The lowlands comprise about 15 percent of the land surface of the province, with the remainder consisting of steeply sloping land on the ridges and ranges between the rivers and high mountains (over 1,500 m) in the southern, eastern, and western edges of the province. During the Ming period, officials encouraged in-migration from more populated areas in the lower Yangtze by giving exemptions on loans for tools, seeds, and animals as incentives to clear the land or drain it. Concern for the welfare of people and the desire to raise the tax base were intermixed. By 1582 the population had increased to between 5.1 million and 5.6 million and cultivated land to 1,885,200 ha, but there was still room for further expansion.

The impressive progress of settlement was completely disrupted by widespread internal conflict and destruction during the transition from the Ming to Qing dynasties (circa 1640–70). There was great loss of life and local depopulation, with many fleeing to the hills; and only 27 percent of the land registered in 1581 was still being cultivated in 1679. With the restoration of peace, a program of land settlement through immigration was renewed to restore the population to its pre-Qing level, again with loans for implements, seeds, and animals and with tax exemptions. Cultivation revived quickly, even bypassing previous totals. Population rose to 14.9 million by 1776 and registered cultivated land to 2.6 million ha; consequently, Hunan "filled up," with the population reaching 20 million by 1842. Land around Donting Lake was reclaimed, and there was a shift in the lowlands to intensification, particularly double-cropping. Immigrants were now forced into the steeper, forested, surrounding slopes of Hunan and started extensive clearing, an experience repeated throughout the mountainous areas of southern China.

The demands for fuelwood were also immense, especially in the colder northern half of the country. Major cities counted fuelwood resources as one of their major essential "imports," together with food and water, though some towns had managed fuelwood plantations on their edges. Nonetheless, everything points to a severe energy crisis in China from 1400 until at least the mid-nineteenth century and that the collection of grass, leaves, and any other combustible matter was a major preoccupation of the Chinese peasant until recent times.

The Landscape of Clearing

While lowland farmers dyked and ditched the plains for paddy rice, the hill-slope farmers cut the forest, periodically clearing small patches by ax and fire, and then moving on every 3 or 4 years when fertility ran out or erosion was out of control. Rainfall could be torrential, and the yield was always poor and frequently failed. The early introduction in the mid-sixteenth century of New World crops like peanuts, corn, and sweet potatoes and their widespread acceptance enabled further colonization of those upland areas. However, they contributed to worsened erosion and lowland siltation, especially maize and potatoes, which were invariably sown in straight furrows up and down the slope. Up to a point, fertilizer provided a solution to low yields, and in the lowlands its steady supply was easily maintained by the waste from hogs and humans. But in the hills it was almost impossible, so that where timber could not be easily shipped out, lumbermen burned entire hillsides and collected the ashes to sell farther downslope, with devastating effects on soil stability.

Late eighteenth-century descriptions of Hunan make it quite clear that the deforestation had been dramatic and had upset the precarious ecological balance. Hillsides were "stripped of trees," and there was a scarcity of firewood:

> When there are too many people there is not enough land to contain them, there is not enough grain to feed them, and there are not enough wealthy people to take care of them. . . . Water rushes down violently from the mountains and the mountains became bare; earth is dug out . . . and the rocks are split; there is not an inch of cultivable land left.

With forest cover gone, the "earth was loose; when the big rains came, water rushed down from the highlands and mud and silt spread out below. Fertile areas near the mountains were ruined as they were repeatedly covered with sand and abandoned."[21]

In the north of the country the lower foothills of the mountains of Shen-hsi and Shan-hsi Provinces experienced some clearing during the economically energetic Sung dynasty (960–1127). However, officials sought to protect the forests as a barrier to the penetration of the nomadic invading horsemen from the Mongolian steppes; the Wu-t'ai mountains in northern Shan-hsi were still a forested wilderness in the early sixteenth century. But within a few decades a Ming scholar reported:

> At the beginning of the reign of Chia-ching [1522–66] people vied with each other to build houses, and wood from the southern mountains was cut

without a year's rest. The natives took advantage of the barren mountain surface and converted it into farms. . . . If heaven sends down a torrent, there is nothing to obstruct the flow of water. In the morning it falls on the southern mountains; in the evening, when it reaches the plains, its angry waves swell in volume and break embankments causing frequent changes in the course of the river. . . . Hence, Ch'i district was deprived of seven-tenths of its wealth.

A gazetteer of 1596 reported the following:

When the timber by the streams was gone the wood cutters went into the midst of the valleys in crowds of a thousand or a hundred, covering the mountains and wilderness; axes fell like rain and shouts shook the mountain. . . . [Eventually] the beautiful scenery of Ch'ing-liang became almost like a cow or horse pasture.[22]

With the erosion of land and even territorial security at risk, an imperial edict was passed in 1580, prohibiting further timber felling, which aided in some forest regrowth. But when imperial control waned again in the later nineteenth century, farmers and graziers moved in and stripped the timber.

The overwhelming impression is that there was a steady process of environmental degradation throughout much of China. Yet while that was true overall, one must recognize the periods of respite and examples of conscious forest protection. There were over 100 hunting reserves, the largest of which was the great imperial hunting enclosure of the Mulan Weichang, which covered over 10,400 km² in northern China. There were also temple and monastic forests, community forests, and trees grown as a part of agroforestry systems, particularly for silk production. But these exceptions, while interesting, do not amount to much; and one must conclude that throughout the seventeenth and eighteenth centuries the Chinese moved inexorably toward the almost total deforestation of their portion of the earth—leaving forests only in the remote wild mountainous parts, which were not suited for agriculture.

JAPAN: "THE FOUNDATIONS OF THE HEARTH"

Our ignorance of forest clearance and usage in China is not repeated in Japan, where the picture is clearer and the outcome is markedly different. In stark contrast to China, Japan is one of the most densely forested countries in the world today, and the seeds of that plenitude were sown during the sixteenth century.

The impacts on the forest accelerated in pace and extent as the population of the archipelago approached 12 million by 1600 and doubled to 26 million by 1720, while the amount of cultivated land rose from 1.49 to 2.94 million ha during the same period. By the end of the sixteenth century an industrious society of subsistence cultivators had already occupied most of the limited area of the alluvial lowlands (approximately 20 percent of all land) that were sandwiched between the high, steep mountains and the sea and were busy clearing forests and making terraces on the lower valley sides and headwaters. Above, the forests of the higher upland slopes were exploited for green fodder for stock and fertilizer for the intensively cultivated fields. For any given area of rice, between 5 and 10 times as much mountain land was needed to supply the grass, scrub brush, leaf fall, and small branches that were either trampled into the flooded paddies or fed to stock. In addition, demand for forest resources was increasing in line with a growing economy and a rising level of affluence as families were consciously limited. Iron smelting, salt making, ceramic production, and building all expanded, and the demand for both domestic and industrial fuelwood grew.[23]

Like everywhere else in the world, the record is silent about the essential tasks of getting fuel and green fodder—it was simply taken for granted. Land cover conversion is equally unrecorded, even though conflicts over common woodland resources were one of the most frequent causes of intervillage disputes. But a few hints about forest use can be gleaned. The unique diary of the Ishikawa family in Mushai Province for 1728 suggests that 45 person-days were spent gathering fuel on the mountainsides, but by 1804 the figure had dropped to eight days, presumably because the family now bought most of its fuel. A similar shift in labor expenditure is seen as commercial fertilizers of dried fish, oil cakes, and night soil replaced the green fodder, and the time saved in fodder and fuel collection went into silk manufacture and more intensive arable cultivation.

We are on much surer ground, however, when considering the forest used to satisfy the egos and ambitions of the ruling elites. They indulged in an almost peculiarly Japanese passion for grandiose and monumental building projects that consumed vast quantities of prime timber and that had few counterparts other than in, perhaps, Imperial Rome, although the latter built predominantly in stone and brick.

During the fifteenth and sixteenth centuries, the 250-odd major regional military and feudal lords—the *daimyō*—were constantly feuding with each other. Indeed, the early name for Japan—Sengoku—meant simply "a country at war." In this ceaseless struggle for supremacy, the *daimyō* built wooden defensive regional fortresses with barracks, watchtowers, gates, and residences that often became the nuclei of urban settlements. Between

1467 and 1571 over 111 were constructed, and during the next 8 years another 90. In addition, because of the usefulness of timber and its essential military nature, many *daimyō* strengthened their control over woodland and appointed officials to ensure that timber and bamboo groves (the latter valuable as an obstacle against cavalry) were properly maintained, even to the extent of forbidding peasants to fell trees and engage in slash-and-burn agriculture. In this way military and defensive needs ensured that large areas of forest were protected, just as hunting ensured the protection of forests in medieval and later Europe. Additionally, forests were simply a ready source of wealth.

The chaos of the constantly feuding *daimyō* and their samurai warriors were replaced during the late sixteenth century by the hegemonic rule of the new shogunate, or *bakufu*. First, and outstanding, was Hideyoshi (r. 1582–98), followed by Tokugawa Ieyusa (r. 1598–1616), who established the Tokugawa or Edo period in Japanese history, which lasted from 1603 to 1868. Both rulers imposed a tight control over many of the *daimyō*, who became vassals and, by a complex system of alliances with others, extended their power throughout most of the islands and demanded massive contributions of timber.

Many *daimyō* and their domains (*han*) paid a timber tribute to the shogun. Outstanding was Hideyoshi's levy for his monumental castle at Osaka and numerous grandiose temples and shrines, as well as for the building and equipping of two armadas of troop carriers for the conquest of Korea and China. The buildings required large, high-quality timbers that could be found only in the untouched forests. Thus, Hideyoshi established direct control and organized the systematic exploitation of stands on the Yoshino and Kiso river valleys in Shikuko and the east-central Honshu Islands, respectively, and placed pliant overlords to control other timber resources in the Tenryū Valley and farther north around Akita (fig. 8.4).

The exploits of Ieyusa were probably more spectacular than those of Hideyoshi. His monumental castles at Edo, Sunpu, and Nagyoa used wood lavishly and must have consumed over 2,750 ha of prime woodland. As supplies became more distant and more difficult to obtain, Ieyusa was forced to improve the means of long-distance timber transportation. Small timber came on horseback as usual, but larger pieces were moved along improved rivers in rafts and collected at booms, in a manner reminiscent of late eighteenth-century American logging practices.

In order to ensure *daimyō* compliance, the new *bakufu* required each warlord to keep his wife and main heir in a residence adjacent to the shogunate castle in Edo; consequently, each of the *daimyō* built ostentatious

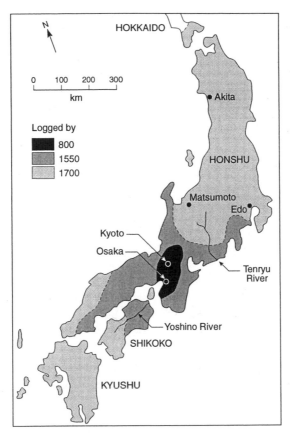

Figure 8.4 Forest exploitation in Japan. (Source: based on C. D. Totman, *The Green Archipelago: Forestry in Pre-Industrial Japan* [Berkeley and Los Angeles: University of California Press, 1989], fig. 2.)

mansions (often several of them) for their families in the capital. In the country they vied with one another and with the shogunate in constructing elaborate castles, shrines, and many towns, cutting wide swathes through the mountain forests. Fairly accurate records of this destruction exist for a number of places, including Matsumoto in west-central Honshu and Tosa on eastern Shikoku.

After about 1660 a class of entrepreneurial commercial loggers emerged to supply the timber for an increasingly sophisticated urban market. Most seemed to rise from fairly humble rural beginnings, and a few became spectacularly wealthy merchants, buying up stumpage and anticipating demand, especially after the devastating fires that periodically wiped out individual

structures and whole cities and created a ceaseless cycle of repair and replacement. The best documented of these fires were in Edo (Tokyo), which
grew to about half a million people by 1660. There were 93 major fires
between 1601 and 1866, and so frequent and spectacular were they that
they earned the name "the flowers of Edo." The conflagrations of 1657
and 1772 were particularly devastating: over 100,000 people were killed
in the holocaust of 1657, and because the city was rebuilt immediately, it
required, by the most conservative calculation, the timber from hundreds of
thousands of hectares of forests from throughout Japan. Kyoto and Osaka
were barely smaller than Edo, and sections frequently went up in flames, as
did those of many a smaller town.

Paradoxically, the imposition of peace among the feuding *daimiyō* encouraged a long century of unbridled and profligate timber use in the construction of extravagant ecclesiastical and other monumental buildings;
burgeoning urban development; a surge of population that demanded food,
fuel, fertilizer, shelter, ever-intensified methods of tillage; and an expansion
of industry. Everywhere, the forests were in precipitous decline. The number of logs sent down the Tenryū and Yashino rivers fell off radically by the
end of the eighteenth century, and the wasteful "free float" of hundreds of
thousands of individual logs was replaced by mass floats that were carefully
supervised, and eventually even these were replaced by a few rafts. The last
of the large, old-growth timber accessible to streams, coast, and roads had
been cut out everywhere. Loggers were moving into the interior high forests
in search of exploitable timber and employing new transportation methods
in order to log inaccessible stands. Scarcity and price rises were common
after the 1660s, which led to the substitution of inferior pieces and the use
of alternative materials. These examples could be multiplied endlessly, but
they all add up to an incontrovertible story of overexploitation and timber
paucity. As Kumazawa Banzan, a Confucian scholar and severe critic of
ecclesiastical extravagance, lamented, "Eight out of ten mountains in this
nation are deforested." [24]

It was fortuitous for Japan that, unlike China, the pressure of population and the consequent colonization, clearing, and cultivation of the upper
mountain slopes did not occur before consciousness of the need for conservation became widespread. What followed during the eighteenth century
was an era of purposeful regulation, silviculture, and planting, unprecedented in Asia and, indeed, perhaps anywhere in the world.

The increasing concern about the mountain forests is captured in the
remarks of Nobumasa, the fourth *daimyō* of Tsugaru *han,* who wrote during the 1660s about the essential nature of forests to everyday life. They

encapsulate the ethos of care and sensitivity about the forests that began to pervade Japanese society:

> One must take care for the family line and one's heir. One's third consider-
> ation is the mountains. To elaborate, man is sustained by the five elements
> [wood, fire, water, earth, and metal]. In our world today neither high nor
> low can survive if any one of the five is missing. Among the five, water and
> fire [heat] are most important. Of the two fire is more crucial. However, fire
> cannot sustain itself; it requires wood. Hence wood is central to a person's
> hearth and home. And wood comes from the mountains. Wood is funda-
> mental to the hearth; the hearth is central to the person. Whether one be
> high or low, when one lacks wood one lacks fire and cannot exist. One must
> take care that wood be abundant. To assure that wood not become scarce,
> one cherishes the mountains. And thus, because they are the foundations of
> the hearth, which nurtures the lives of all people, the mountains are to be
> treasured.[25]

By about the middle of the eighteenth century, the lineaments of nine-teenth- and early twentieth-century global deforestation were becoming discernible. China, and to a much lesser extent southern and western Europe, were nearly bankrupt of stock; Japan was embarking on an exciting experiment in preservation; and northern Europe was still acting as a great reservoir of supplies. America was beginning the great clearing that would transform the continent and act as the model for European colonists everywhere. In the tropical areas, the pinpricks of European influence were soon to grow—with less obvious impact than in their temperate settler empires, it is true, but ultimately with about just as much effect. The forest biomes of the world were changing irrevocably.

Chapter 9

Driving Forces and Cultural Climates, 1750–1900

Consumption is the sole end and purpose of all production.
—A. SMITH, *The Wealth of Nations* (1776)

Americans are insensible to the wonders of inanimate nature, and they may
be said not to perceive the mighty forests that surround them till they fall
beneath their hatchet. Their eyes are fixed upon another sight . . . peopling
solitudes and subduing nature.
—A. DE TOCQUEVILLE, *Democracy in America* (1838)

THE FORCES unleashed during previous centuries were suddenly put into
high gear after about 1750 and accelerated with the onset of the Industrial Revolution. Within the span of scarcely three generations, from 1750
to 1830, the face of the globe changed, and the relatively simple world of
plants and animals, of water and wind power that had previously existed became the world of machines, of inventions, of inanimate energy use, of rapid
communication, and of the movement of goods in bulk as humans gained
control of the world and its resources. With these changes went changes in
ideas and attitudes toward nature, which were to affect the forest.

Of course, none of these changes happened overnight for the roots of the
Industrial Revolution were already evident in the earlier age of commercial-
ism and incipient capitalism. By 1500, the foundation had been set for global
trade and political domination by Europe, an inquisitive attitude toward all
knowledge, an arrogant appropriation of the natural world, and the spread
of Western peoples and their civilization over the "thinly or weakly peopled
parts of the earth." [1] Then, with the passing of the eighteenth century, one
epoch in Western civilization's relationship with the natural world ended
and another of a new and different order began. It was based on machinery
and energy use and was informed by specialized knowledge, which resulted

in the accelerated transformation of nature. The traditional rural occupations and activities persisted, but it would not be long before urban and
industrial ones transformed the scene.

Industrial technology allowed a greater human control over the material world (nature) by increasing production, by extracting wealth from the
earth, by going faster or lighting the darkness. Technology also allowed
one group to gain a greater control over other groups by defeating enemies,
outwitting competitors, and controlling the vanquished. It radically altered
the pace and character of the life, livelihood, and the structure of society for
a large number of people. Europe was first, and then its appendages overseas—North America, Australia, New Zealand, and select parts of Latin
America. Aspects of the same technology, coupled with European exploitation and domination, had equally dramatic effects in Asia, Africa, and the
bulk of Latin America, overturning ancient ways of life, opening the way
for a new global economy, and unbalancing world relations. Everywhere,
land cover and land use experienced a dramatic transformation, of which,
perhaps, the forest was affected most of all, followed in time by changes in
grasslands (fig. 9.1). The years between 1750 and 1900 witnessed the most
extensive changes to the vegetation of the world since the Ice Age.

The need is to isolate these new driving forces, and five are selected: (1)
industrialization, (2) population and migration, (3) colonization, (4) transportation and communication, and (5) domination, preservation, and regulation. On the face of it, they may seem disparate, but they go a long way
to explain global domination and the transformation of the earth's forest
cover. Increasingly, measures of change can be displayed statistically in long
time series, which in some tables in this chapter are continued up to the near-
present for the sake of completeness.

The division used up till now between a European core and "the wider
world" no longer serves as a satisfactory organizing structure, if only because
parts of the periphery, such as North America, Australasia, and eventually
Russia and Japan, become increasingly a part of the core. It is now more
accurate to distinguish a temperate and a tropical world, each with its own
deforestation story, which intensifies with time. The temperate becomes
broadly synonymous with the core and the tropical broadly synonymous
with the periphery. Later the distinction gets new names: developed, and
less developed, developing, or third world.

INDUSTRIALIZATION

Whereas it is possible to select individual technological changes that
affected forest clearing in Europe during the Middle Ages, such as plows,

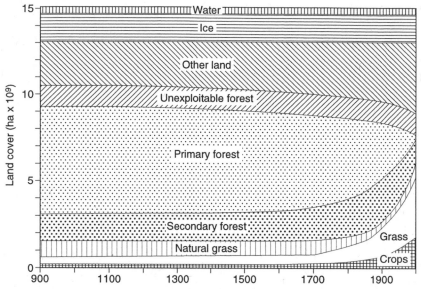

Figure 9.1 The transformation of major global land covers, AD 900–2000. (Source: after P. Buringh and R. Dudal, "Agricultural Land Use in Space and Time," in *Land Transformations in Agriculture,* ed. M. G. Wolman and F. G. A. Fournier, Scope Publication no. 32 [Chichester: John Wiley & Sons, 1987], 9–44, esp. 15.)

horses, harnesses, and field systems, it becomes less easy to do that for the middle of the eighteenth century onward when there were more complex congeries of interrelated changes, some technological but others financial and attitudinal. Crucial questions about the fundamental nature and connecting links of the Industrial Revolution are legion. How and why did it happen? Why and how did it begin, and why did it begin specifically in Britain? The role of population growth, agricultural expansion, mechanization, and capital accumulation are just some of the elements that are juggled in order to explain the sequence of causal links that might explain the origins and connections of the Industrial Revolution, with many different answers. The Industrial Revolution is probably one of the most written-about topics of all time. In all this complexity the simple and straightforward contemporary statement of Natalis Briavonne as to what was going on in 1839 is probably sufficient for our purposes:

> The sphere of labor grew larger; the means of production were in the process of being multiplied and simplified each day a bit more. Population grew consequently through the diminution of the mortality rate. The treasures found

in the earth were exploited better and more abundantly: man produced and consumed more; he became more rich.[2]

We must be content with the idea that the revolution was basically a process of "industrialization," to which must be added massive urbanization. But how, specifically, did it affect the forests of the world?

Pace and Location

The location and movement of the Industrial Revolution are important in the story of global deforestation. Table 9.1, which shows the total industrial potential from 1750 to 1980, helps to pinpoint some of the main sequences of timing and diffusion. Industrialization began in England, especially Lancashire and the Midlands, between 1750 and 1830 with one indigenous product, iron, and one exotic product, cotton. At its peak in 1880 the United Kingdom had increased manufacturing output by 36 times over 1750 and accounted for 22.9 percent of the global manufacturing total. Then, with the application of steam to stationary engines and after 1830 to locomotion, industrialization diffused into other parts of western Europe. Not until the later nineteenth century did it spread to Germany and the United States (13.2 and 23.6 percent, respectively, by 1900) and then, later, to Russia and Japan. This sequence was accompanied by a less familiar one: an absolute decline in manufacturing in the less developed world, which fell from 73.0 percent of the global share in 1750 to 6.5 percent in 1953. The implications for deforestation are clear: Western imports replaced local manufactures and were paid for by exports of primary raw materials, of which timber and the plantation crops that replaced the forest were major items.

Income and Consumption

It would be true that nearly all the inventions and changes encapsulated in industrialization had an effect, directly or indirectly, on the vegetation of the world, but from this great array we must select only those that had a direct bearing on the forests. Foremost was the increased consumption that accompanied the increased wealth, itself the result of economic growth. Real incomes per head accelerated, often in fits and starts but always upward, exceeding 1 percent per annum in many European countries. For example, they averaged 1.25 percent in the United Kingdom after 1780; probably the same amount for France; 0.8–1.6 percent for Germany from the 1850s to 1880s; and 2.5 percent for a brief period from 1860 to 1914 in Russia. In the United States and "Europe's overseas descendants," high growth was more

Table 9.1 Total industrial potential, 1750–1980 (index: UK = 100 in 1900)

	1750	1800	1830	1860	1880	1900	1913	1938	1953	1963	1973	1980
Developed												
UK	34	47	73	143	253	481	863	1,562	2,870	4,694	8,452	9,718
Germany	2	6	18	45	73	100	127	181	258	330	462	441
France	4	5	7	11	27	71	138	214	180	330	550	590
Italy	5	6	10	18	25	37	57	74	98	194	328	362
Russia/USSR	3	4	4	6	8	14	23	46	71	150	258	319
Japan	...	1	5	16	47	128	298	528	1,378	1,804	3,089	3,475
	5	5	5	6	8	13	25	88	88	264	819	1,001
Less developed												
China	93	99	112	83	67	60	70	122	200	439	927	1,323
India	42	49	55	44	40	34	33	52	71	178	364	553
	31	29	33	19	9	9	13	40	52	91	194	254
Total world industrial potential	127	147	184	226	320	541	933	1,684	3,074	5,138	9,359	11,041

Source: P. Bairoch, "International Industrial Levels from 1750 to 1980," *Journal of European Economic History* 11 (1982): 292, 299.

consistent, with the United States achieving a steady 1.55–1.76 percent increase between 1839 and 1959 on an already high base level to become the richest country in the world by the 1890s, and Canada and Australia were not far behind.

Increasingly affluent populations in the economic "core" consumed a rising amount of timber products for housing and construction (and, in some countries, for fuel), as well as the food and fiber products that came from tropical and subtropical forested environments. The one well-attested example of timber consumption was the United States, where per capita use of lumber (saw timber) rose from approximately 220 bf (0.51 m^3) in 1850 to 510 bf (1.2 m^3) in 1910. Per capita consumption for all timber products, which included fuelwood, was 157 ft^3 (4.445 m^3) in 1910. Although this level of consumption was higher than in any other country, the general upward trend was common everywhere in the industrializing world. Britain, for example, did not build wholly in wood or use much wood fuel after the conversion to coal in the eighteenth century, but consumption was still 40–50 percent that of the United States.

Mechanization and Motive Power

The harvesting and manufacture of lumber was the perfect example of what the Industrial Revolution really meant. The scale of operations, the interrelated inventions, and business and labor organization were geared to mass consumption. Increased consumption in urban and industrial markets meant greater logging activity in the forests and the development of improved methods for handling and moving the bulky raw material. In the mills, timber needed to be processed more quickly and at a greater capacity in order to feed the demand. Consequently, a concatenation of inventions and improvements to existing machinery came into being to boost production.

Log handling and sawmill technology had not changed much since the Middle Ages. A marginal improvement in productivity came when the old water-powered, single-bladed, up-and-down saws that cut 500–3,000 bf a day were replaced by finer, multibladed gang saws and, later, by light, fast-moving muley saws that doubled output (table 9.2). These were introduced into the Baltic lumber industry in the later seventeenth century. But the big changes came in the early nineteenth century. Circular saws, invented and used in English shipbuilding yards as early as 1777, were adopted slowly at first because they overheated and wobbled at high speed, had easily breakable teeth, and their thick plate iron wasted an enormous amount of wood in the "kerf" or "bite." For example, a saw "bite" of five-sixteenths of an

Table 9.2 Increasing productivity of saws, seventeenth to nineteenth centuries

	Sawmill Output per Day (bf)
Hand-powered pit saw	100–200
Water-powered single blade (1621)	500–3,000
Water-powered single sash (1621)	2,000–3,000
Water-powered muley saw (circa 1780)	5,000–8,000
Water-powered circular saw (1844)	500–1,200
Steam-powered gang saw (circa 1850)	40,000+
Steam-powered circular saw (1863)	40,000+
Steam-powered band saw (1876)	20,000+

Sources: A. J. Van Tassel and D. W. Bluestone, *Mechanization in the Lumber Industry: A Study in Technology in Relation to Resources and Employment Opportunity.* National Research Project Report no. M-5 (Philadelphia: Works Project Administration, 1940), 8; R. C. Bryant, *Logging: The Principles and General Methods of Operation in the United States,* 2d ed. (1913; reprint, New York: John Wiley, 1923). 3; and J. E. Defebaugh, *History of the Lumber Industry in America,* 2 vols. (Chicago: American Lumberman, 1906–7), 2:8, 58.

inch could turn 312 bf (8.83 m³) into dust for every 1,000 bf (28.3 m³) of boards sawed. If the bite could be reduced to only one-twelfth of an inch, then the waste was only 83 bf (2.39 m³). Some improvement came in 1846, when Spaulding of Sacramento, California, invented a curved ratchet that held hard-tempered replacement teeth, with the result that the saw could be easily repaired by the insertion of a new tooth. But when thinner, heat-resistant steel and better welding procedures were adopted during the 1870s the saw took off and production increased enormously. Finally, the band saw, which had been invented in France in the early nineteenth century, eventually pushed up productivity even further.

Water was the main motive power and was subject to all the vagaries of climate and associated river flow, which included drought but more commonly freezing, as most major timber-producing areas were in high-latitude coniferous softwood forests. But it was the application of steam to cutting that eventually shifted productivity to a new high level. Nonetheless, its adoption was surprisingly late—even in 1870 in the United States there were still 16,562 water wheels in lumber mills generating 327,000 hp compared with 11,204 steam engines generating 314,000 hp. Steam power was not universal until the last decades of the century.

In Europe the adoption of steam was patchy. As production for export declined on the south side of the Baltic and shifted firmly into Scandinavia proper, the multitude of water-power sites, where the rivers tumbled off the Scandinavian Shield and Norwegian mountains, were systematically utilized to produce hydroelectricity. Consequently, steam made relatively little headway in this region, but electricity achieved the same acceleration of the manufacturing process and fed the rising demand—but later.

Saws and steam were only part of the picture of industrialized logging; there were a host of other inventions as well. The United States led the way with inventions to speed the movement, preparation, and finishing of the timber. In the mill, friction feeds, wire feeds, and direct steam-powered carriages increased the speed at which the logs were transported past the saws. New labor-saving devices included the accurate setting of head and side blocks, and a machine for turning the logs for the saw. Now the men hardly touched the logs. In 1863 a Wisconsin lumberman patented the endless-chain method of moving logs from the sorting ponds into the mills, and few years later the automatic carrying of the sawdust to fuel the steam engines boilers was perfected. Double edgers and gang (multiple) edgers expedited the finishing of the wood, and shingle-, stave-, and slab-making machines made it possible to utilize awkwardly shaped material and reduce waste.

In an ever-expanding and ever-more-discriminating consumer market, the rapid and standardized finishing of timber began to assume as much importance as the quantity of raw timber produced. Edgers for squaring boards had been invented in 1825. In 1828, William Wordsworth of Poughkeepsie, New York, invented and patented a planing machine that had an impact on the lumber industry second only to that of the saw. By 1850 it had evolved into numerous specialized forms adapted to all sorts of finishing purposes and final products. Inventions and modifications to lumbering and woodworking machinery flowed through the U.S. Patent Office in ever-increasing numbers, and leadership in lumber manufacturing lay unequivocally in the United States. In 1854 a visiting British Parliamentary Committee of Inquiry viewed the developments and was astonished at the energy, inventiveness, and specialization that characterized wood manufacture.

> Many works in various towns are occupied exclusively making doors, window frames, or staircases by means of self-acting machinery, such as planing, tenoning, mortising, and jointing machines. They are able to supply builders at a cheaper rate than they can produce them in their own workshops without the aid of machinery. In one of these manufactories 20 men were making paneling doors at the rate of 100 per day.[3]

The steam engine not only provided the motive power for these developments but it had the added tendency to centralize operations into increasingly larger mills with increasingly more workers. Mills with an average production ranging from 1.5 to 5.0 million bf/yr were the norm in the mid-1850s in Michigan, but 30 years later, 10 million bf was common, with some mills even achieving outputs of between 50 million and 60 million bf (i.e., 118,000 m³), making them among the biggest businesses of the day. Generally mills were smaller in northern Europe.

The new inventions and increasing size of plant boosted production by speeding up the flow of wood through the mills to produce a better, more standardized product at a cheaper cost than before, which both fed and fueled greater consumption in more-affluent and consumer-oriented populations. Change begot change in a cumulative and self-sustaining advance in technology and output. Gains in productivity in one field exerted pressures on related industrial operations. Not only was more produced faster, but products were manufactured that could not have been produced by the craft industries of the past, which were now waning.

Material changes promoted nonmaterial changes as the factory system dominated lumber production. In the past, mills had usually been one-man or single-family affairs, but as the size of plant increased with the concentration of power sources and machinery, the gap between owner and worker widened, and jobs became more specialized as labor became divided. In the forest, individual and neighborhood logging ventures gave way to lumber camps, which were formed to concentrate the productive labor of the male workforce. Whole lumber towns—special settlements devoted entirely to the manufacture of lumber—appeared and then disappeared as the lumber was cut out.

On the business front, there was a rapid evolution of corporations and the establishment of monopolies and trade associations. Most significant was the vigorous pursuit of vertical and horizontal integration by acquiring large tracts of timberland, or stumpage. This ensured adequate supplies of raw material and a continuous, uninterrupted, and profitable flow of produce from forest to retail outlet. It also helped to eliminate rivals, as increasing size, takeovers, and amalgamations were part of the monopolizing concentration process. All this was accomplished by a relentless quest for greater efficiency, greater competitiveness, tight contractual agreements based on the time element, and the mass production of a standardized manufactured end product.

Wood was (and is) crucial to the industrialization process, and it still played a significant role in the process in late twentieth-century Brazil, India, and China. Coal only substituted for wood first in Britain, the most treeless country in Europe, where 17.6 million tons were mined in 1816 compared with only 942,000 metric tons in fairly well-forested France. In the United States, fuelwood dominated in domestic hearths, in charcoal furnaces, and in mechanical and locomotive engines as late as the closing years of the nineteenth century, and it only became less significant when alternative sources such as coal, oil, and natural gas came onto the scene. Fuelwood still accounted for four-fifths of all energy use as late as 1867, and not until the mid-1880s did coal overtake it as the principal source. By 1900 fuelwood was probably contributing only 21 percent of the nation's energy needs, and by 1920 a mere 7.5 percent, by which time coal had passed its peak and oil and natural gas were making their impact felt. But even if the relative contribution of wood to energy needs was diminishing, it was still large in absolute terms; and even a share of 5.4 percent in 1940 was probably the equivalent of nearly 4 billion ft³ (113.2 million m³) of timber—still more than in any year in the nineteenth century, with the exception of 1899 (fig. 9.2).

POPULATION AND MIGRATION

Since 1700 the population of the world has shown a nearly unbroken upward trend, and the increase in numbers has had a severe impact on the world's forests. The global total was 769 million in 1750, and within 100 years it had nearly doubled to 1,260 million, to double again to reach 2,515 million by 1950 (table 9.3). The relationship between the total number of people in a given territory and deforestation has been shown time and again to be a positive one; it is perhaps the one driving force that we can be absolutely sure about. The increment of 270 million people in 150 years and their inevitable spread meant a need for more land to grow food, more timber to provide shelter, and more fuelwood to cook food and to keep warm. Rotational bush fallow systems were shortened and intensified, and elsewhere the forest was felled to make way for intensive plantation or commercial peasant cultivation. The weight of population numbers did, and still does, hang heavily on the forest.

The increase in population was first noticeable in the industrialized and urbanized countries of the world, where political stability and improved nutrition were aided by more productive agriculture, an increase in imported foodstuffs and plants, and improved animal husbandry. Better sanitation, hygiene, clothing, and housing, plus better transportation and storage of foods to combat times of dearth, all added up to a major change in mortality. The old demographic regime in which high fertility and high mortality were in rough accord, leading to little increase in population, was increasingly replaced by one of lower mortality, leading to an increase in total population. As affluence increased and spread during the nineteenth century, so the demographic character of populations changed. Although fertility was

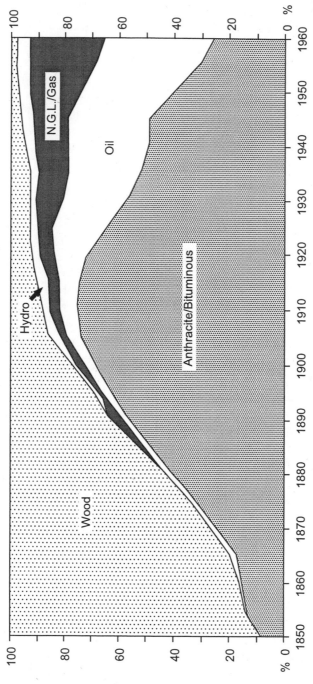

Figure 9.2 Energy sources in the United States as a percentage of total consumption by 10-year periods, 1850–1960. (Source: based on S. H. Schurr and b. c. Netschert, *Energy in the American Economy, 1850–1975: An Economic Study of Its History and Prospects* [Baltimore: Johns Hopkins University Press for Resources for the Future, 1960], 36–37.)

Table 9.3 World poulation by major regions (millions), 1700–1985, and projection to 2020

	1700	1750	1800	1850	1900	1950	1985	2020
Africa	107	106	107	111	133	224	587	1,441
Asia (total)	435	498	630	801	925	1,375	2,834	4,680
China	–	200	323	430	436	555	1,060	1,460
Japan	–	30	30	31	44	84	121	130
Rest of Asia	–	268	277	340	445	736	1,653	3,090
Europe[a]	92	109	145	208	294	393	492	514
USSR	30	35	49	79	127	180	277	343
North America[b]	2	3	5	25	90	166	265	327
Latin America[c]	10	15	19	34	75	165	404	719
Oceania	3	3	2	2	6	13	25	37
World total	679	769	957	1,260	1,650	2,515	4,853	8,061

Source: After P. Demeny, "Population," in *The Earth as Transformed by Human Action,* ed. B. L. Turner II et al., (Cambridge: Cambridge University Press, 1990), 42.
[a] Not including USSR.
[b] USA and Canada.
[c] South and Central America, Mexico, and the Caribbean.

controlled and highly responsive to changing economic conditions, it was still high enough to cause a rapid increase in the overall population. In 1750 the population of Europe and Russia was 144 million, and at each successive 50 years between then and 1900 it rose to 194, 287, and 421 million, representing 18.8, 20.3, 22.8, and 28.5 percent, respectively, of the world population. After the beginning of the twentieth century, the proportion fell off.

The increment of over 200 million people in Europe not only put pressure on the forests of that continent but also on those overseas. Between the late 1840s and early 1930s, at least 52 million migrants left Europe and Russia. The majority went to the United States, which grew from 3 million in 1750 to 90 million in 1900, but many also went to Latin America (15–75 million) and Oceania (3–6 million) during the same span of years. There were other significant European settlements in southern and northern Africa, and eastward from European to Asiatic Russia. Altogether, the area of European settlement in Europe proper and in the formerly thinly populated "neo-Europes," which comprised barely 20 percent of the world's population in 1700, rose to 36 percent of the world total by 1900.

Generally, by 1900, the shift in demographic behavior had not yet reached the rest of the world; the population of Africa barely moved, but because Asia already had a high base population, 427 million were added by 1900. Most remarkable was the spectacular expansion in China between 1750 and 1800, when its annual rate of population growth averaged 1 percent, nearly double that of Europe. Expansion continued until about 1850, after which it came to a near halt. China's share of the world total had risen from 26 percent in 1750 to 34.1 percent in 1850, only to fall to 27 percent by 1900.

The population changes occurring after 1900 are left for consideration in later chapters where they are more relevant, but the point can be made here that sometime after 1900 most of the areas suitable for human settlement under the then existing state of technology had become inhabited. Towns, of course, were going to grow or be established all over the globe, but the outer edges of the great grasslands had more or less been defined, and irrigation in the semiarid areas although amenable to some extension was very limited. The only great reserve of "unused" land capable of growing more food lay in the forests, which had the added advantage of providing a bonus of raw material and fuel. Consequently, it was the global biome of the forest that was to feel the full weight of human numbers during the twentieth century.

COLONIZATION

The nineteenth century witnessed an unprecedented escalation of change in the world's vegetation as European industrial technology interacted with European imperial territorial ambitions to colonize large areas of the world. In Europe, sharpening political rivalries, "land hunger," and the pursuit of spheres of influence led to rapid overseas expansion, either by formal annexation and colonization or by imposing informal commercial ties over weaker peoples. In this competitive process for territory and global influence, Britain became supreme, ousting France from the Western Hemisphere after the signing of the Treaty of Paris in 1763. Europe now occupied or controlled approximately 35 percent of the world's land surface; by 1878 that proportion had risen to 67 percent; and on the eve of World War I it was 84 percent—more than four-fifths of the globe. Between 1800 and 1878 the average rate of imperial expansion was 216,000 mi^2 a year. Nowhere was too small, too remote, or too barren not to be incorporated in the new nationalistic empires. According to David Landes, "This was the high-water mark of the expansion of Europe that began in the eleventh century on the Elbean plains, the plateau of Castile, and the waters of the Mediterranean."[4]

The new global territorial control was broadly of two kinds. First there was the continued settlement and exploitation of the neo-European temperate lands of the United States, Canada, southern Africa, Brazil, Argentina, and then Australia and New Zealand. For all intents and purposes these were simplified social and political offshoots and replicas of the European mother countries, which resembled one another in that they were vigorous neo-European settler empires that took on a life of their own. They experimented with, and exploited, their resources just as vigorously as had their ancestors back home, particularly the soil and its vegetation. Where the settlers were unable or unwilling to do the work themselves, as in the Caribbean, Brazil, or the U.S. South, they imported slaves. But whatever the social make-up they became firmly incorporated into the periphery, and then, in time, some became an integral part of the core. Some, like the United States, freed themselves of their colonial ties and were politically independent by the end of the eighteenth century. Brazil and the rest of Latin America were not far behind.

But the significant difference of the nineteenth century compared to previous ones was the concentration of European attention on the tropical world, particularly Africa and Asia. These were the "external arenas" of intermittent contact into which forays had been made in the past to create coastal way stations and trading points. These previous contacts had been shallow in depth, temporary in duration, and rarely the basis of settlement and control. They contrasted with the older "periphery" of the Americas and Caribbean, which had been an active theater of colonization and settlement, as well as exploitation. Now Europe attempted to create colonies and "nationalistic" empires in Asia and Africa that were politically submissive and economically profitable to them in crops, minerals, and other raw materials.

Concomitant with global territorial control went the vigorous, expansive spread of European industrial technology, with its omnivorous demand for raw materials, its need for expanding markets, and its development of even more efficient tools for overcoming distance and conquering peoples. A dazzling array of interacting inventions and discoveries made contact with the existing colonies easier and quicker and made the conquest of new territories cheaper in cost, cheaper in lives, and more effective than ever before. These "tools of empire," as Daniel Headrick calls them aptly, were of various kinds; some used natural resources, some integrated economic systems, and some allowed a greater manipulation and control of lands.[5]

In the new tropical territories two overriding problems made political control and colonization difficult. Disease was a major obstacle to penetration in Africa, though less so in Asia, where the major impediments were the sheer number of people and a preexisting, organized political state system that was resistant to change. In Africa, dysentery, yellow fever, typhoid fever, and, above all, malaria caused enormous mortality among European settlers, missionaries, and traders; before death rates were in the order of 250–750/1,000. But technological solutions were at hand. The discovery in 1830 of the prophylactic use of quinine, extracted from cinchona bark, counteracted malaria, and between 1820 and 1840 European mortality dropped dramatically to 50–100/1,000. Although mortality was still 10 times higher than for similar groups in Europe, and there were still many years to go before 1897 when the *Anopheles* mosquito would be identified as the vector of these diseases—Africa was no longer "the white man's grave."

Now that a territory's interior could be penetrated, its political control was facilitated by arms. In succeeding decades steamboats (often gunboats) were introduced on the navigable rivers and sheltered coastal waters of Africa and Southeast Asia, China, the Persian Gulf, and India. These were often transported in pieces to these locations and then reassembled in situ. Gunboats came into their own with devastating effect in China during the First and Second Opium Wars of the middle decades of the century, where they demonstrated their effectiveness as a "political persuader." Another key tool in establishing early superiority was the development of the breech-loading gun during the 1860s, followed in time by the machine gun. As a young subaltern, Winston Churchill witnessed the confrontation between the British under Kitchener and about 40,000 Dervishes at Omdurman, Sudan, in 1898 in one of the last great colonial wars of the century:

> [The infantry] fired steadily and stolidly, without hurry or excitement, for the enemy were far away and the officers careful. Besides, the soldiers were interested in the work and took great pains. But presently the mere physical act became tedious. . . .
>
> . . . on the other side bullets were shearing through flesh, smashing and splintering bone; blood spouted from terrible wounds; valiant men were struggling on through a hell of whistling metal, exploding shells, and spurting dust—suffering, despairing, dying.

At the end of that day, 20 Britons and 20 of their Egyptian allies were dead, but so too were 11,000 Dervishes.[6] Political domination had replaced political "persuasion," and the control of the Sudan was absolute. The "arms gap" between colonizer and colonized was awesome.

TRANSPORTATION AND COMMUNICATION

Perhaps more than any other single factor the improvement in transportation and communication, both nationally and globally, was the key to success. Space and time were compressed by steam locomotives, steamships, and eventually the electronic technology of submarine cables to allow an integrated global exchange of people, goods, and knowledge. The vast resources of timber, grain, meat, and other products of the neo-Europes were developed and drawn into the world economy, and the previously backward, isolated subsistence economies in the tropics became primary producing areas for the consuming core. Everywhere, the network of communications meant that goods could be transported more cheaply, and electronic information flows meant instant price fluctuation, adjustment, and fine-tuning. All required financial infrastructures, banking, credit, and a reliable monetary system, which developed as fast as did production.

In the tropical world, transportation facilitated political control, which usually resulted in land survey and subdivision and the imposition of a taxation system. Taxes could only be paid by selling crops for cash (which usually meant expanding cultivation and cutting down trees) and, in time, the commercialization of peasant agriculture in order to increase production and lower costs. One incidental but momentous effect of these developments in tropical territories was that greater security, more assured food supplies, and a growing demand for labor stimulated population growth, which was to have dramatic effects on the transformation of the land cover.

Transportation improvement had two broad impacts on the forest. First, the new wood-producing or wood-destroying territories in the periphery were tied across the world to the consumer cores, and second, it boosted the movement of timber out of the forest. The distinction between these two types of movement is a fine one, and there was much overlap at times; but broadly speaking, the first was global in extent and was often imposed as a part of some imperial strategy. It also affected all primary commodities, from cotton to coffee, wheat to wool, and tea to timber. The second was national in extent and specifically affected the movement of lumber.

Across the World

Despite the undoubted power of gunboats and machine guns as "political persuaders" in the new colonies, ultimately they counted for nothing if the conquered territory was not connected effectively to the metropole. Economic networks were established and new techniques developed in order to exploit these territories. Goods, information, and reports were the lifeblood of the new global thrust, and European countries acquired the means to communicate almost instantly with their remotest colonies and, also, to engage in an extensive trade in bulky goods despite their freight costs.

On both land and sea, steam—the most characteristic and pervasive invention of the Industrial Revolution—lowered costs and made it more worthwhile to transport low-value goods over greater distances than before, decreasing the price, which in turn increased consumption and encouraged greater specialization in those places of primary production that had natural

advantages. Transportation became quicker, safer, more reliable, better handled, and more punctual, reducing insurance and inventory costs for goods
and ensuring greater comfort and safety for people.

On land, the railway era got under way after George Stephenson's locomotive successfully operated the Stockton-to-Darlington line in 1825, and
it lasted for over 100 years. Railways were not cheap to build, but the expenditure was justified by the improvements they brought: compared with
human portage and animal haulage they cheapened costs by anything from
30 to 10 times less; they sped up delivery by between 10 and 30 times; and
it was variously calculated that a fairly small train did the work of between
13,000 and 20,000 human porters. Railways were dependable and, unlike
canals and rudimentary roads, were not affected by the weather. Moreover,
as goods and people were moved their economic and social effects rippled
through society, making them a spearhead for change and modernization.

Table 9.4 shows the development of permanent track by continent
and major country from 1840 to 1960. Railways started in northwestern
Europe, diffused throughout the rest of the Continent by 1840, and made
massive strides in eastern North America. Both these regions were covered
by a dense web of main and feeder lines, so much so that by 1900 nearly 78
percent of the world's track was in these two continents. Elsewhere, in less
industrialized and less populated territories, railways either connected main
towns or, as in the case of colonial territories in Africa and parts of Asia
and Latin America, simply linked coastal ports with continental interiors
to create worldwide trading systems. Among these countries India was a
special case, with a fairly dense network linking major centers by 1900. The
transcontinental lines completed in the United States after 1869, Canada
after 1885, and Russia after 1903 had a political as well as an economic
significance.

The same revolutionary changes occurred in the world of shipping. The
opening of the Suez Canal in 1869 (itself the first major manifestation of
the application of steam to earthmoving) marks a convenient watershed in
the development of steam shipping. Before that steam was regarded as a fast
and punctual but expensive alternative to sail. But progressive improvements
in multiple-cylindered engines that used less coal; the substitution of iron and
then steel for wood for stronger, more durable, and more commodious hulls;
and the demonstrated efficiency of the propeller over the paddle all combined
to increase speed and carrying capacity while lowering costs. After 1870 and
for the next 40 years, world steam tonnage increased from 2.7 million to
26.2 million tons, and freight costs were halved during the same period.

The days of moving only "preciosities" and high-value products, such
as coffee, tea, silks, and tobacco, were over. Now vast quantities of bulky,

Table 9.4 Length of rail way line open (in thousands of km) by continent and major country, 1840–1960

	1840	1860	1880	1900	1920	1940	1960
Europe	4.0	49.8	156.8	262.8	336.2	413.4	421.7
UK	2.4	14.6	25.0	30.1	32.7	32.1	29.5
Germany	0.5	11.1	33.8	51.7	57.5	62.0	52.2
France	0.4	9.2	23.1	38.1	38.2	40.6	39.0
Italy	0.2	2.4	9.2	16.4	20.4	22.6	21.3
Russia/USSR	–	1.6	22.8	53.2	71.6	106.1	125.8
Rest of Europe	0.5	10.9	42.9	73.3	115.8	150.0	153.9
North America	7.0	52.5	161.1	339.7	469.4	444.2	421.0
USA	4.5	49.2	150.1	311.2	406.9	376.1	350.1
Canada	2.5	3.3	11.0	28.5	62.5	68.5	70.9
Australia and New Zealand	–	–	7.7	25.0	46.6	50.5	47.7
Latin and Central America	–	1.4	11.1	77.5	111.5	132.9	139.6
Argentina	–	–	2.3	16.8	35.3	41.2	43.9
Rest of region	–	1.4	8.8	60.7	76.2	91.7	95.7
Asia	–	1.3	15.3	55.8	103.6	117.0	156.5
Japan	–	–	0.2	6.3	13.6	25.1	27.9
India	–	1.3	14.5	39.8	59.6	66.0	57.0
Rest of Asia	–	–	0.6	9.7	30.4	25.9	71.6
Africa	–	–	4.6	14.9	47.6	70.9	71.6
South Africa	–	–	1.6	7.0	16.3	21.4	20.5
Rest of Africa	–	–	3.0	7.9	31.3	49.5	51.1
World total	11.0	105.0	356.6	775.7	1,114.9	1,228.9	1,264.4

Sources: B. Mitchell, *International Historical Statistics: Africa and* Asia (New York: New York University Press, 1982), 496–508; Mitchell, *International Historical Statistics: The Americas and Australasia* (Detroit: Gale Research Company, 1983), 666–67; Mitchell, *International Historical Statistics: Europe, 1750–1988* (New York: Stockton Press, 1992), 655–64; and Mitchell, *International Historical Statistics: The Americas, 1750–1988* (New York: Stockton Press, 1993), 528–39.

low-value goods such as ores, coal, wool, wheat, raw textile materials, and timber, as well as perishable commodities like fruit and meat, were worth shipping to and from distant places. For example, in 1860 alone Britain imported about 1.7 billion bf (4 million m³) of squared and sawn timber from the Baltic and Canada, and amounts increased substantially afterward. After 1880 refrigeration made it worthwhile to ship meat and butter from Australia and New Zealand, with devastating effects on their forests. All the while, consumers benefited: they paid less, consumed more, and enjoyed rising standards of living.

Together, railways and steamships increased cargo loads and reliability, made human travel comfortable, and above all reduced time and hence costs. For example, before 1830 a letter and its reply sent between London and Calcutta could have taken up to 2 years by the time the monsoons had been taken into account. With the opening of the Suez Canal, the same process took about 30 days. With the advent of the telegraph and telegram a few years later, a message and its reply would take 1 day. By 1924 the submarine cable network allowed a message to circle the globe in 80 seconds. Each successive invention or development facilitated or deepened global contacts through a constant flow of goods, people, and ideas, and buyers were put in direct contact with sellers. Isolated subsistence societies with limited trade relationships imperceptibly became part of a single world market. Industrialization, population growth, territorial acquisition, and mechanical energy (particularly steam), together with medicine and agricultural modification of land, shattered traditional relationships and laid the foundations for a worldwide transformation of the land cover. Globalization was truly underway.

Railways not only speeded the flow of people, goods, and ideas but also created a new and enormous demand for timber. Putting aside any demands for construction, rolling stock, and fuel, the railways needed crossties, and many of them. It was calculated that every new kilometer of track required 1,640 ties, which needed to be renewed approximately every 7 years or so, and that because of the special requirements for selecting ties, no more than about 494 were gathered from every hectare of forest (table 9.5). From

Table 9.5 Crossties used and estimated ha of forest cleared, world, 1840–1960

	Km of Track (thousands)	Annual Tack Increment (thousands)	Ties Used in New Track (millions)[a]	Ties Renewed Annually (millions)[b]	Total Ties[c] Used Annually (millions)	Ha of Forest Cleared (thousands)[c]
1840	11	11	18	2	20	41
1860	105	94	154	23	177	358
1880	357	252	413	78	491	992
1900	776	419	688	169	857	3,414
1920	1,115	339	556	242	798	1,617
1940	1,229	114	187	267	454	1,122
1960	1,264	35	58	275	333	674

Sources: Based on table 9.4. Conversion factors used as in table 10.5.
[a] 1,640 ties/km of new track.
[b] 217 ties/km of track renewed.
[c] 494 ties/ha of forest.

1865 onward there was never a year in which at least 500,000 ha of forest were not destroyed for ties; between 1881 and 1945 it never fell·below 1 million; and between 1888 and 1915 it never fell below 2 million ha/yr, with the peak of 3.4 million ha coming in 1900. These are clearly average figures and could vary enormously, but even if they are only half right the effect on the world forests would have been staggering. The contemporary American view that the railroad was "the insatiable juggernaut of the vegetable world," though a little exaggerated, was essentially correct.[7]

In the Forest

Wood is a heavy and bulky commodity of intrinsically low value. Much of it is found in inaccessible, uninhabited places and has to be transported many hundreds, if not thousands, of miles to its market. From the mid-eighteenth century onward, transportation costs in the large-scale lumbering areas accounted for between one-half and three-quarters of production costs, the remainder being made up of milling, sawing, and stumpage, so that the actual trees were a very small proportion of the total. Transportation controlled or influenced most other factors of production such as capital investment, forest land purchase (stumpage), and the availability of markets, finance, and labor. A cheap system of transportation was therefore essential to feed the growing appetite for timber, and it also had to be flexible enough to accommodate changing sources as supplies were cut out.

Transportation was the major pivot around which revolved the entire process of converting the standing trees to lumber. Like the developments in milling and finishing machinery, the majority of modern innovations originated in the United States, which became not only the biggest producer and consumer of lumber in the nineteenth century but also the leader in the "industrialization" of the forest. Of the many new methods of getting the logs out of the forest, three deserve special mention: the log drive, the integration of the continent's rivers, and the application of steam.

The Log Drive

Rivers had always been used for the movement of bulky timber from classical times onward. But the new mass-production methods that emerged during the early nineteenth century demanded a more comprehensive mode of exploitation, and that was the log drive, whereby the whole river catchment and its watercourses were regarded as the venue for extraction (plate 9.1). Said to have originated in 1813 in the headwaters of the Hudson, the log drive started as a means of allowing the new high-production mills and saws to be fed adequately via a mass of individual, part-time farmer-loggers

Plate 9.1 Industrial logging: the log drive. A logjam in a river in Minnesota, the result of the unregulated felling activities of innumerable individuals and companies. (Forest History Society, Durham, N.C.)

by extending the area of raw material supplies. Each logger cut during the winter and hauled and stacked his logs near the water's edge to await the spring flood. With the spring thaw the logs were thrown into the swollen rivers and carried downstream to the mill. The log drive became a complex and, by necessity, highly organized operation, analogous to cattle ranching. Each logger used an elaborate identifying log mark (over 20,000 were registered in Minnesota alone) for his logs, which was "driven" downstream to the millponds, where it was sorted out in enormous "pens" or booms (plate 9.2) to ensure a ready supply of lumber to feed the new high-production mills.

The system required cooperation and/or regulation. Driving, river improvement, and boomage charges were levied at the rate of so many cents per thousand board feet (hereafter mbf) delivered to the mill, and strict laws enforced the start date of the log drive, the methods of sorting, the disposal of "strays," and penalties for "log lifting." There were also charges for building splash dams, which stored water to be released at critical times to increase the volume of the spring flood.

Plate 9.2 Sometimes the products of the individual log drives could be collected within a towable boom. In this view the boom is being towed by steam tug across Rainy Lake, Ontario, to the mill of the Minnesota and Ontario Paper Company at Fort Frances. (Forest History Society, Durham, N.C.)

The first well-documented boom was built on the Androscoggin in Maine in 1789, and soon they spread to all the rivers of New England, New York, and Pennsylvania. Maine's Penobscot boom of 1825 was renowned for its size, as was Pennsylvania's Williamsport boom on the Susquehanna constructed in 1846. By 1860 booms existed on all the major rivers in the new lumber-producing areas of the Great Lakes states of Michigan, Wisconsin, and Minnesota and, later, spread to rivers in Florida and Alabama that flowed into the Gulf of Mexico.

Without the spatial system of the log drive as part of the new lumber production pipeline, the new high-output, steam-driven mills could not have met demand. Even if there were boomage and driving charges, and some logs were lost or damaged, the disadvantages were more than offset by the increased quantity of lumber processed.

The Continental System

While the log drive operated locally, a river transportation system evolved at the continental level. Using major rivers to link areas of lumber surplus and

Plate 9.3 Industrial logging: rafting yellow poplar logs on the Big Sandy River, Ohio, circa 1920s. This was a small operation in a minor timber-producing area, but it illustrates the principle of fixing logs together, which on the larger rivers of the continent produced rafts of up to 5 acres in size, pushed and nudged along their journey by steam-powered riverboats. (Forest History Society, Durham, N.C.)

lumber deficiency had been a common practice in watercourses as far apart as the Tiber, Rhine, Vistula, Seine, Adige, Pontus, and Delaware. Groups of logs were lashed together into rafts (and often piled high with smaller timber, fuel, or potash), which were floated down to the mill, market, or shipyard (plate 9.3). The continental system became best developed in the United States. By the late 1830s the industrialized and urbanized eastern seaboard states were experiencing timber deficiencies and consequently bringing in timber via the coast from Maine, then from Ottawa, Canada, then by raft and steamer from the Great Lakes states, to be off-loaded at Buffalo and Tonawanda on Lake Erie. From there it was sent by the Erie Canal to Albany, which grew to be the largest wholesale lumber center at the time, and then down the Hudson to New York. To the west, Chicago after about 1845 became the gateway through which the lumber of eastern Wisconsin and western Michigan went into the largely treeless prairie states of the Midwest that were being settled at this time. During the 1860s and 1870s lumber from Minnesota and western Wisconsin was floated down the Mississippi in enormous 5-acre rafts, to be broken up at west-bank ports for milling, the planks then distributed over the plains to the emerging settlements in Kansas, Iowa, and Nebraska, and even as far west as Colorado.

Steam in the Forest

In the vast forests of the cold northern continents, the log drive had disadvantages. It depended on an early freeze, heavy snow for skidding out the logs, and then the spring thaw for moving the logs down to the mills, all of which became more difficult as logging moved farther away from the rivers and, certainly, when it moved into warmer regions. Therefore, in time, new transportation methods were introduced to speed up and even-out lumber production throughout the year and, thereby, reduce costs.

A solution for nonsnow months was to replace the "snaking out" of individual logs by bullocks with the "go devil," a sled that lifted the front end of a log to stop it from digging into the ground. This was soon replaced by the "bummer cart," a self-loading skidder in which a carriage with huge wheels was linked to a long tongue that acted as a lever, so that with forward movement one end of the log was hitched up under the wheels. More applicable to the northern coniferous forests was the simple and effective solution of ice roads. Developed after 1872, these graded, permanent ways were sprinkled with water over which sleighs could be pulled with a minimum of friction by horses with spike shoes. Four horses could move 30,000 bf of timber, or 120 tons, with little effort. The quantity of timber moved increased further by developing steam traction engines, with caterpillar-like treads to cope with the ice. By 1901 A. O. Lombard's steam locomotive was capable of moving loads of 120,000 bf, or about 500 tons, on linked sleds.

The independence of logging from snow and ice and an even more certain and controllable means of timber supply could only come with the adaptation of the railway to the operation. If the main-line or common carriers, as they were known, had lines passing near the forests or mills, then all was well; but more often than not the forests were remote from the main urban and industrial areas. Thus the construction of logging railroads as feeders to the common carriers took off in the Great Lakes states after about 1875. These logging "roads" were lightweight, small-gauge lines that could be laid quickly to exploit the forest resource thoroughly, and when the trees were cut out, pulled up and relaid in another locality. When industrial exploitation moved into the forests of the nonfreezing South and West of the United States, as well as tropical areas in other parts of the world, the logging railroad reigned almost supreme.

In every way, the railroads and their versatile feeders revolutionized forest exploitation (plate 9.4). At the local level, exploitation penetrated the uttermost extreme of forest stands, and by the late 1880s river booms became

Plate 9.4 The railroad provided mass movement, versatility, and speed to the industrial logging process and was particularly important in the largely riverless areas of the South, as depicted in this photograph taken in Arkansas circa 1904. (Forest History Society, Durham, N.C.)

empty as more and more timber was delivered directly to the mills. At the continental level, movement of timber by the river system was replaced by the main-line carriers, which linked all areas and came to dominate lumber distribution. Chicago, the biggest lumber market in the United States, must stand as an example of these changes; in 1882 the railway contributed a mere 13 percent of the intake of 1.9 billion bf (4.5 million m³) to the city. As the decade progressed, however, the proportion of lumber arriving by rail increased steadily, whereas that arriving by lake and river declined, so that by 1900 more lumber was received by rail than by lake. By 1907 the railroad was supreme, responsible for 82 percent of the total of 2.4 billion bf (5.66 million m³) delivered.

There was one more stage in the transportation revolution in the forest. In time, spur rail lines were constructed from the main lines without any break of gauge, thereby quickening and maximizing forest exploitation. Simultaneously, mill owners found it profitable to install drying kilns to assist in seasoning the wood and planing mills to finish off products that could then be transported directly to the customer. They even began to produce ready-to-assemble houses, churches, stores, barns, and other buildings in a multiplicity of styles that could be ordered from a mail-order catalog such as that produced by Sears, Roebuck and Co. Timber—and in abundance—was now one of the necessities of life, and the industrialization of the forest was complete.

FOREST DOMINATION, PRESERVATION, AND REGULATION

The revolutionary economic, technological, demographic, and territorial changes of the latter half of the eighteenth and the early part of the nineteenth centuries had their intellectual and attitudinal counterparts. The age was rich in ideas and debates about a range of issues, such as national character, human history, culture, and environmental influences, and downplayed religious ideas, the individual, and humans in the abstract. The discovery of the wider world of natural history and ethnography by Linnaeus, Banks, Cook, and later Humboldt and others, and the widespread dissemination of its details and peculiarities through publication, prompted endless questions about primitive peoples, the influence of the environment, and the stages of civilization. It was not that the debate about a divinely designed world was dead; physiotheologians still found evidence of God's divine plan in the creation, but they were now buffeted by the new ideas of people like Hume, Goethe, and Kant, who questioned teleology in nature, nature's immutable laws, and the relationship of humans to it.

There were two main thrusts to this new questioning: by the middle of the eighteenth century, Montesquieu in particular (but there were others of the Physiocratic school) wondered about the influence of climate on the course and character of civilization. He suggested that the environment determined these and many other human endeavors. The other branch of enquiry emanated from people like Condorcet and Godwin, who enthused over the political triumphs of the French Revolution and were convinced of the consequent progress and perfectibility of humankind in a limitless earth. But Malthus, in his first *Essay on Population* (1798), dissented from this view. The earth set limits, and checks to growth were the natural order as the weight of humankind pushed against the limits of subsistence, making human progress uneven and uncertain. Whatever one thinks about the moral and practical implications of his argument, Malthus was the first to bring together the two facts of population numbers and resources. This Malthusian "equation" is still a powerful and relevant concept today. One consequence was that almost every country in Europe began to engage in inventories of natural resources and empirical studies of forests.

This is a mere hint of the richness and volume of literature generated during these and succeeding years about human relationships and attitudes toward nature. The writings accelerated and increased throughout the nineteenth century, especially after Darwin questioned the whole edifice of Western ideas about the origins of humankind.

But there was also another dimension to the Enlightenment. Knowledge and speculation about the character and human alteration of the New World offered opportunities for comparison, of which the most striking was that between long-settled Europe and yet-to-be-settled America. In particular, the spectacular expanse of forest in the United States, and its equally spectacular clearing, gave rise to a literature about forests and their relationship with soils, disease, erosion, and climate. The physical environment of the New World was like a "great outdoor laboratory for scientific study." It was also the place where some of the early concerns about preservation began.[8]

Domination: "The Epoch of Man"
In the Mind

The speculations of Montesquieu and others could be said to have taken place in the mind, while on the ground the forest was still being cleared at a ferocious rate for its timber, fuel, and land. These writers recognized that humans were agents of change but gave it little further thought, and they were certainly not concerned specifically with the forests. The one major exception was George-Louis Leclerc, comte de Buffon, whom we have met before in relation to the culture of trees. Buffon was a great synthesizer of the new knowledge of the natural and physical world that was unfolding during his lifetime. Between 1749 and 1804 he wrote the massive 44-volume *Histoire naturelle générale et particulière,* an account of changes to the environment made by humans as a result of the growth and migration of population, the expansion of cultivation, and the domestication of plants and animals. Buffon had no romantic illusions about nature or, for that matter, about primitive societies; and while he thought nature a part of a divine creation, he also believed its power to be immense, living, inexhaustible, and even hostile. Humans brought order to nature by controlling it—by draining, clearing, embanking, domesticating, and otherwise altering it. "Wild nature is hideous and dying; it is I, I alone who can make it agreeable and living," he wrote. Man was "king on earth" and master of nature and, by his activities, brought order out of chaos and "improved" nature by turning forests, thickets, and swamps into meadows and arable fields. In this way the processes of nature were improved, so that it was brought to its current state of magnificence.[9]

In volume 5 of *Histoire naturelle,* entitled *Des époques de la nature,* Buffon examines what he calls the epochs of creation and change. The seventh and final epoch, "The Epoch of Man," begins with early humans assuming control of their environment through the use of fire and clearing, thereby making lasting and widespread changes to the forest and the world. Unwittingly, he had written the epitaph for the coming age. On the face of it the early writing of Buffon, the concerned forest cultivator, conservationist, and botanical expert, and the later writing of Buffon, the forest destroyer and extirpator, seem inconsistent. But the apparent contradiction can be explained when one realizes the degree to which his theory of the formation of the earth was influenced by the debate about the relationship of forests to other natural phenomena then going on in the New World.

Ever since Christopher Columbus had said that he knew "from experience" that the clearing of the forest cover of the Madeira, Canary, and Azores islands had reduced their rain and mist, the relationship between forests and climate had run sotto voce through debates about clearing, nowhere more so than in America.[10] Hugh Williamson suggested in 1770 that forest clearing had made the winters less harsh and the summers cooler during the preceding forty years. Noah Webster (of dictionary fame) in 1799 found no evidence of long-term change in climate but conceded that clearing could make significant changes by exaggerating extremes. For Buffon, the key was heat, for it was essential to life on earth, and anything that increased it was good. Forests harbored and safeguarded moisture (and possibly also harbored disease) at the expense of heat, which was necessary for the multiplication of life, so forests were inimical to nature and civilization. Therefore, in the New World, large areas of forest had to be cleared to make the earth habitable, but in Europe too much had gone on already. In either case, in a "modern" country the forest had to be tended with care and foresight and restored. Buffon's commitment to forest restoration was not in doubt, and in addition to his forest culture tracts, he was also involved in campaigns to increase the use of coal for smelting in order to lessen the demands on woodland.[11] The philosophical foundations had been set for seeing human agency as formative in the fashioning of the natural world.

On the Ground

It is doubtful whether any of the pioneer settlers in North America, or anywhere else in the world, whose actions on the ground were causing this debate, had heard of Buffon let alone read him; but intuitively they had come to very similar conclusions for somewhat different reasons. On a physical level the forest was an immense, hostile, and uncomfortable environment that was a threat to survival; on a symbolic level, as we have seen before, it was repugnant, being dark, sinister, devoid of order, and the abode of wild beasts and wild men. The settler had little time or value for the beauty and novelty of the untouched forest, which was worth contemplating only when it lay felled by the ax. His was a strictly utilitarian view, so the forest was good only inasmuch as it either became improved land or lumber or became the site of settlements—and quickly at that. The forest stood in the way of progress.

Alexis de Tocqueville caught this mood brilliantly when he described frontier life in Michigan in 1831:

> The pioneer, living in the wilds . . . only prizes the works of man. He will gladly send you off to see a road, a bridge, or a fine village, but that one should appreciate great trees and the beauties of solitude, that possibility completely passes him by.

Generally, Americans, like pioneers everywhere, were

> insensible to the wonders of inanimate nature and they may be said not to perceive the mighty forests that surround them till they fall beneath their hatchet. Their eyes are fixed upon another sight . . . peopling solitudes and subduing nature.[12]

Just like their Puritan forbears, the Promised Land or Paradise was within their grasp, provided the obstacle of trees was first cleared by back-breaking work and toil.

But even to these hard-bitten pioneers the act of clearing was not without its subconscious imagery and symbolism. Clearing was an act of redemption, and the destruction of the forest was uppermost in their minds in the making of their new, common wealth. In emphasizing the hardships and temptation of the forest environment, the pioneers fulfilled two aims: first, the struggle to clear the forests tempered the spiritual quality of those who faced it, and they were better, humbler beings for that; second, it was a reminder to later generations of the magnitude of the accomplishment and the character of those who achieved it.

Above all it was the sheer size of the forest that astonished and frustrated the New World pioneers. The forest was impersonal and lonely in its endlessness; consequently, clearing was likened to a struggle or battle between the individual and the immense obstacle that had to be overcome in order to create a new life and new society. If the immigrant Anglo-Saxon farmer in England, the ancestor of so many early Americans, could be described in the chronicles of about AD 800 as "the grey foe of the wood," then within another 800 years it was the American pioneer who was reenacting the role. The image of the heroic struggle to subdue the sullen and unyielding forest by hand, and to make it something better than it was, was a legacy of feeling, thought, and imagery that was handed down over the centuries. For Francis Parkman in 1885, the forest was "an enemy to be overcome by any means, fair or foul," and Frederick Jackson Turner, the inheritor and brilliantly successful interpreter of these deeply held images, echoed these ideas and attitudes in his account of early pioneer life. The forest frontier, and subsequently the wider frontier, was the ultimate American symbol and the place where the pioneer created the world anew.[13]

Thus, although the motive for clearing the forest was virtually sacred, increasingly it came to take on secular overtones as well. The concepts of progress, development, and ultimately of civilization itself had never been far beneath the surface even from the beginning of settlement because they were the logical outcomes of the fight for survival. However, from the eighteenth century onward the concept of controlling nature and making it more useful gained strength. The ideal was the rural, domesticated, agrarian landscape that many extolled, and the making of it was replete with ethical betterment. The link with virtue was pointed out explicitly in President Andrew Jackson's second annual address (1830), in which he asked, not for a moment doubting the answer,

> What good man would prefer a country covered with forests, and ranged by a few thousand savages to our extensive Republic, studded with cities, towns, and prosperous farms, embellished with all improvements which art can devise or industry execute, occupied by more than 12,000,000 happy people, and filled with all the blessings of liberty, civilization and religion?[14]

If the forest and the Indian were swept aside in the process, then so be it. Not only was progress good; it was also inevitable.

The detail of motivation and action can be varied here and there; it was writ large in North America, but for the most part it was the same whether in Europe itself or in any of the neo-Europes and territories that were colonized. But it was not a specifically "European" phenomenon; we merely know more about it than clearing, say, in China, or elsewhere. Wherever humans needed land to grow food or timber to cook, keep warm, or to construct a shelter, the forest was in retreat.

Preservation

Destruction of the forest reached new levels of intensity and extent during this era, but there were some countervailing tendencies that would lead in time to its preservation in parts of the world. Concern about the forest focused on two broad issues: Did clearing affect the "harmonies of nature"—in other words, did it have an environmental effect? And was the presence of forests a "tonic" for the new industrialized and urbanized population—in other words, did it have an ethical effect?

The Harmonies of Nature

Nothing like the American environment had been experienced before, and the possible alteration of its soils and climate through agricultural clearing came under increasing scrutiny. Perhaps too much could be cleared with unforeseen and deleterious consequences? In 1804, Count Volney mounted a sustained inquiry; he was convinced that the alteration of the climate was "an incontestable fact" and had occurred "in proportion as the land has been cleared." Moreover, if stream flow was directly related to the amount of forest cover and hence humus accumulation, then clearing could not but reduce stream flow and bring about eventual aridity. Humans, therefore, were the agents of change who upset the harmonies of nature.[15]

More thoughtful still was John Lorain's *Nature and Reason Harmonized in the Practice of Husbandry* (1825). Lorain saw nature as having a system or cycle of decomposition, growth, and change that returned humus to the soil, but continual plowing and cropping were the "hand of folly" that destroyed that cycle. Moreover, by destroying the protective vegetative cover, humans interfered in the process of runoff from the uplands and hence deposition in the lowlands. In one blow, two fundamental processes in nature were affected. To illustrate his point Lorain contrasted the clearing practices of the New England and Pennsylvanian farmers. Both were destroyers of the forest, the New Englander slightly less so because he tried to increase livestock and hence grass cover and manure. However, his destructive use of burning ultimately matched the Pennsylvanian's continual cropping and lack of manuring. Lorain concluded:

> Perhaps a better method could be devised for clearing the woods, or a more profitable first course of crops be introduced, if it were not that by far the greater part of the animal and vegetable matter which nature had been accumulating for a great length of time, is destroyed in a day or two, by the destructive and truly savage practice of burning.[16]

He had come to what was really a momentous and far-reaching conclusion: whereas nature had long time processes, humans had short ones. Rather than merely conquering and controlling nature, humans were destroying it at a rate that was more rapid than their ability to adjust their activities, leading to permanent damage to the environment. Buffon's "Epoch of Man" was truly upon the world.

It was on such building blocks as these that George Perkins Marsh built his magnificent edifice published in 1864, *Man and Nature; or, Physical Geography as Modified by Human Action*. Marsh was a sheep farmer and mill owner from Woodstock, Vermont, but he was also an extremely observant and learned man. In 1845, when was asked to address the farmers of Rutland at their annual fair, he moved beyond economic concerns about the shortage and price of fuelwood to talk of other things. Everywhere in the state, he said, "the signs of artificial improvement are mingled with the tokens of improvident waste." Denuded hilltops and slopes, dry streambeds and ravines furrowed out by torrents, had all followed agricultural clearing. If a middle-aged farmer returned to his birthplace, Marsh continued, he would look upon "another landscape than that which formed the theatre of his youthful toils and pleasures." [17] In short, the visual world had changed markedly through human action.

In 1861 Marsh was appointed U.S. ambassador to the new kingdom of Italy, and it was there that he wrote *Man and Nature*. Drawing on his early Vermont experience, stimulated by the examples of the devastated landscapes of Mediterranean Europe, and drawing on a vast historical, philosophical, and scientific literature now available to him, he compiled a highly readable account of the human impact on the environment through time. The theme of the injury to earth by humans dominates the work. More than one-third of the book deals with forests and is a painstaking review of the literature on forest influences on temperature, precipitation, soil formation, fauna and flora, and human health and disease and on the role of forests in maintaining the flow of springs and retarding erosion and flooding. Marsh's conception of the forests went far beyond their value for timber production, and he adumbrated a concern for the total forest ecosystem.

The change of emphasis in the deforestation argument from purely economic to environmental concerns by Marsh was a tremendous intellectual leap. Although humans had always intervened in nature, that intervention had always been considered a beneficial—rarely, if ever, a detrimental—act. Marsh was certain that nature was in a state of equilibrium except for the disturbances made by humans, though just as humans could disturb, they could mend. He ended his book by asking "whether man is of nature or above her?"—a question that was as crucial to the forest then as it is in a global sense now. In a sense, *Man and Nature* was a philosophical treatise documented with technical details. The findings of emerging science and technology were converging with the seventeenth-century conception of nature as divinely designed harmony. [18]

Here, then, were some of the first stirrings of environmental awareness and the conservation movement, as it became known in the Western world. It started in the forest, and as we shall see in chapter 11, it drew on various experiences from around the world, including India—but it certainly came to its fullest fruition in America.

Tonics for Civilization

Trees, provided they were not in endless, gloomy forests, had always held a fascination for some people. Sacred groves, druidical temples, and individual trees associated with particular historical events and heroes had been venerated and protected for millennia. But as we have already seen, midst the destruction, the latter part of the seventeenth century saw the emergence of a more sympathetic attitude toward trees, both individually and en masse; trees were assuming an emotional importance.

The new sensibility had a number of sources. In England, the idea of tree planting as opposed to tree cutting was gaining ground. Many landowners were finding pleasure in planting trees and had moved beyond the needs of the navy, construction, and fuel, important as they were. Planting was becoming an integral part of the landscape cult as well as the public display by a landowning class of its power and wealth. That power was compounded by a sense of immortality, as trees were an enduring monument of the continuity of the families that planted them and, thus, provided a visible symbol of human society. Avenues and clumps of trees adorned the private parks, and new exotic species such as poplar, plane tree, cedar of Lebanon, sequoia, spruce, fir, and larch and a variety of shrubs such as rhododendron, acacia, buddleia, and hydrangea, to mention only a few, became part of the new landscape furniture of ornament, amenity, and display.

But the significance of trees went even further than domestication, as they "gradually achieved an almost pet-like status." The gathering momentum of the Romantic movement saw grandeur, even sublimity, in trees; "The love of woods," said Joseph Addison in 1713, "seems to be a passion implanted in our natures," and William Gilpin, the arch exponent of the picturesque, thought trees "the grandest and most beautiful of all the productions of the earth."[19] Besides their intrinsic beauty, trees—particularly oaks—symbolized continuity, strength, and even patriotism (they were the raw material of the navy, the source of British power), and these positive associations meant that they were cherished and worshipped as sources of pleasure and inspiration. In time they even assumed a religious tinge as the analogy between groves and religious architecture became firmly etched in peoples' minds. In another century the American elm would achieve the same status in the United States.

In contrast, hostility and repugnance toward the forest remained the dominant feeling in America, as the bulk of the population was still confronting it and clearing it. But in time, as in England, the forest began to find new champions among those who found aesthetic values in it and even associated its primitive, primordial condition with the works of God. The advances of eighteenth-century science had produced a new wonder and awe of nature and a feeling that God showed his power and excellence in such untouched environments. Moreover, as the proponents of the picturesque were at pains to point out, nature's "roughness" had a certain pleasing quality about it.

Others went further: wild nature was sublime, and disordered, chaotic scenes could please and exalt just as easily as the comfortable, well-ordered landscapes of cleared and made land. If God and his beauty could be found in the forest, then would not humans be more perfect if they were in touch with that environment? From Daniel Defoe's *Robinson Crusoe* (1719) to Jean-Jacques Rousseau's *Emile* (1762), there had been a suggestion that the primitive life, despite its disadvantages, produced a happiness and wholesomeness that was not found in manmade agricultural landscapes, let alone cities. Innocence was contrasted with sin and guile, the natural nobility of the person brought up in "nature" with the product of the new urbanized society.

Deism, sublimity, the picturesque, and the primitive fused in the multistranded Romantic movement, which also emphasized the strange, the solitary, and the melancholy. Consequently, Byron's "there is a pleasure in the pathless woods" and Wordsworth's "one impulse from a vernal wood will tell you more of man" were more than mere lines of pretty nature poetry; they were a revolution in thinking about the natural world and a substitute for moral philosophy. An early expression of romanticism in America was in the writing of the vicomte de Chateaubriand, who said that he was seized with "a sort of delirium" when he found so little evidence of civilization in his travels in 1791 and 1792. In contrast with "manmade" Europe, his imagination "could roam . . . in this deserted region, the soul delights to busy and lose itself amidst the boundless forests . . . to mix and confound . . . with the wild sublimities of Nature." And Philip Freneau was not speaking for himself alone when he said that he found "something in the woods and solitudes congenial to my nature." [20]

Admiration for what had once been rejected was bolstered by yet another change of attitude that can best be called the "patriotic." The quest for something distinctively and uniquely American compared to the antiquities of the Old World was fulfilled by the seemingly pristine wilderness of forests, plains, and mountains. Although America had little that was old, its forests were the equivalent of monuments and ancestors. Diarists and naturalists, as well as fiction writers and artists, drew on this vein of feeling to contribute to "a proper feeling of nationality."

By the mid-nineteenth century the significance of the uniquely American character of the continent's scenery took another twist with the writings of Ralph Waldo Emerson and particularly of Henry David Thoreau. Both expounded the transcendentalist philosophy that the experience of nature in general, and forests in particular, produced a higher awareness and sense of reality than did one's everyday, manmade, artificial surroundings, particularly cities that were dominated by exploitation and expansion. Forests, on the other hand, were "God's first temples." Unlike their Puritan forebears, who thought that morality stopped on the edge of the clearing, the transcendentalists thought that it began there. The argument went further. If the forests and other wilderness areas were uniquely American, and if God's purpose was made more manifest in such places, then the very spirit of America and its creativity came from the forests, from whence came, said Thoreau, "the tonics and barks which brace mankind." "In the woods," echoed Emerson, "we return to reason and faith." The environmental agenda now contained a semitheological component.[21]

Regulation

Somewhere between the elimination of the forest by agriculture and logging and its preservation through planting and for aesthetic enjoyment lay its regulation for the maximum production of wood. These categories correspond almost perfectly to Keith Thomas's trilogy of human approaches to the natural world: the elimination of the wild, the worship of the beautiful, and the domestication of the useful.[22] Of course, the forest in the older, settled parts of the world had been "domesticated" for centuries as a source of wood, wild browse, and game, and uses and rights elaborately codified, but the purposeful alteration of the forest composition for maximum yield had never been attempted. However, the Enlightenment approach of quantification and rationality that flowered in Europe from the mid-eighteenth century onward was to change all that. Foresters now attempted to maximize the output of wood, an attitude and approach that was ultimately to have a global influence.

Forest regulation was especially the product of the many princedoms of eighteenth-century Germany. Almost without exception they sought to make amends for the widespread devastation of the Seven Years' War (1756–63). The specter of wood shortages, particularly fuelwood, seemed very real and caught the attention of a group of enlightened bureaucrats and conscientious foresters. A new science arose, known as the cameral sciences, a term derived from the *kammer* (chamber) in which the princes' advisers traditionally debated issues of economy, forests, finances, administration, and policing as well as manufacturing, agriculture, and trade. All these activities seemed amenable to a "rational economic regulation," and because the forests were so significant in the wealth of the princedoms, they were particularly singled out for this treatment. Forests could be "managed" quantitatively and rationally, but that required training. Specialist schools and university courses were set up to teach "forest science" and "forest economy," thus establishing Germany's reputation for originating these approaches. The publication of Wilhelm Gottfried von Moser's *Principles of Forest-Economy* in 1757 was especially significant, and it became the bible of the new cadre of "patriotic" foresters who replaced the old *jäger*, or honorary forest officials, who tended to preserve the forest primarily for hunting.

With the declared aim of treating the forests as a cash crop, the calculation of the mass or volume of their yield replaced the old area-based systems of measurement as the basis of quantitative forest management. The awkward shape of the tree trunk led to its being regarded as a cone, a concept that was endlessly refined statistically to become an almost abstract representation of the *Normalbaum*, or "normal tree," which was the basis of inventory, growth, and yield. From this calculation of woody fibrous mass it was a short step to regarding the standing forest as capital and its yield as interest; and one could complete the chain of conversions from wood to units of measure, to units of currency, and then estimate the worth of a forest and predict its tax yields and future income.

The notion of a regulated forest filled with "standard" trees was soon translated into management practices that reconstructed the forest to grow only "standard" trees.[23] This required a minimum diversity of species to simplify the calculation of the forest "balance sheet," which would be harmonized with the state financial balance sheet. Completing the trilogy of quantitative principles was the idea of sustained yield, the cutting of sufficient trees to meet the state balance sheet—a concept that became one of the cornerstones of forest management then and in the future. Sustained yield also brought the element of time into forest science, so that the foresters' role moved from that of measurer to that of curator of the stock. The domestication of the trees and regulation of the forest was complete.

The monocultural, even-aged forests of Germany and many other parts of the world are the outcome of the cameral tradition. Order was imposed on disorderly nature, geometric perfection replaced the ragged edges of natural growth, and sustained yield became the forester's guiding principle. Wherever the aim was to "manage" the forests for timber production, these principles dominated and denoted a well-managed forest. When the Americans, the French, the Australians, the British in India, and even Forestry Commission members in Britain wanted a more professional, scientific forest corps and a better conservation and management of the forest in order to stave off any impending timber "famine," they imported German ideas, and the German foresters who had the reputation for knowing what to do. In the United States it was Carl Schurz, Bernhard Fernow, and even Gifford Pinchot, who was trained in the German school; in British India it was Dietrich Brandis, Berthold Ribbentrop, and Robert Troup; in Britain it was William Schlicht; and in Australia it was Berthold Ribbentrop and Frederick Mueller.

Of course, other national experiences have been subtly different from those of the United States, Britain, and Germany, and much has yet to be written about the cultural significance of the forest and trees for different peoples. But the themes that run through the British, American, and German stories, ranging from repugnance and destruction to love and protection, from the practically environmental and excessively regulatory to the irrationally aesthetic, and from the moral to the patriotic, all have their counterparts in other countries to some degree. And because of the global and intellectual dominance of these countries during the last 200 years, their attitudes and experience have spread far and wide. Of one thing we can be certain: these conflicting attitudes and aims of preservation, domestication, and regulation will always encompass the economic, the environmental, and the ethical requirements of the society affirming them. They are always in a state of tension, and which goal dominates greatly depends on the degree to which the forest is essential to survival for a large part of the population. That is the dilemma that we must attempt to unravel in succeeding chapters.

Chapter 10

Clearing in the Temperate World, 1750–1920

America is glutted with its vegetable wealth, unworked, solitary.
—A. Guyot, *The Earth and Man* (1849)

If mere cultivation be not beauty, it is closely allied to it. . . . Every acre, reclaimed from the wilderness, is a conquest of "civilized man over uncivilized nature."
—A. Hodgson, *Letters from North America* (1823)

The late eighteenth and the bulk of the nineteenth centuries were a period of maximum deforestation in the temperate lands of the world. All the trends and forces noted before worked with ever-accelerating speed, intensity, and effect as populations grew, affluence increased, and steam power and other industrial methods were applied to timber extraction, transportation, and processing. It was during these centuries that the new "settler empires" of North America, Australia, and New Zealand really came into their own, and vast areas of forest were felled and put under cultivation. Even older settled areas in Europe, particularly Russia, saw millions of hectares of forest disappear before the plow. In China, the expansion of the peasant population gobbled up the remaining vestiges of forest. Everywhere, agriculture expanded at the expense of the forest, and industrial logging aided the process.

Some idea of the magnitude of agricultural expansion is given in table 10.1, which shows land use in the temperate areas of the world for 1700, 1850, and 1920, as far as can be reconstructed. The amount of cropland increased by 238 million ha between 1700 and 1850 and a further 243 million ha during the next 70 years to 1920; and the forest decreased by 180 million and 135 million ha, respectively, during the same periods, a total decline of 315 million ha. The figures for forest conversion in North America

Table 10.1 Cropland and land cover change (in millions of ha), temperate world, 1700, 1850, and 1920

	Cropland			Cropland Change		Forest Change		Grassland Change	
	1700	1850	1920	1700–1850	1850–1920	1700–1850	1850–1920	1700–1850	1850–1920
Europe	67	132	147	65	15	−25	−5	−40	11
Russia	33	94	178	61	84	−71	−80	10	−4
North America	3	50	179	47	129	−45	−27	−1	−103
Pacific developed	5	6	19	1	13	0	−6	−1	−8
Subtotal	108	282	523	174	241	−141	−118	−32	−104
China	29	75	95	46	20	−39	−17	−7	−3
Total	137	375	618	238	243	−180	−135	−39	−107
Temperate total, 1700–1920				481		−315		−146	

Source: After J. Richards, "Land Transformation," in *The Earth as Transformed by Human Action*, ed. B. L. Turner II et al. (Cambridge: Cambridge University Press, 1990), 164.
Note: The estimates for 1700 were drawn from Richard A. Houghton et al., "Changes in the Carbon Content of Terrestrial Biota and Soils between 1860 and 1980: A Net Release of CO_2 to the Atmosphere," *Ecological Monographs* 53 (1983): 235–62 and table 1 (p. 237). The remaining values were taken from *World Resources Review* 1987 (New York: World Resources Institute, 1987), table 18.3 "Land Use, 1850–1980" (p. 272), based on additional modeled information supplied by Richard A. Houghton and David Skole. Besides the addition of the 1700 data, Richards's 1990 table differs from the *World Resources Review* table in three main respects: different values for grassland and pastures in North America and for China and for forest and woodland in Europe.

Plate 10.1 Land Improvement. (From George H. Andrews, *Modern Husbandry: A Practical and Scientific Treatise on Agriculture* [London: Nathaniel Cook, 1853].)

are conservative, as detailed work shows that the amount of "improved land" (plate 10.1)—in other words, cleared land in forests, which was always more than cropland alone—rose by 92.2 million ha after 1850, not the mere 27 million ha listed in the table above. Before 1850 three-quarters of the cropland came out of forest and woodland areas, but after 1850 the proportion dropped to a little over one-half as it was many times easier to prepare the open grasslands of the prairies for cultivation.

In all countries, shipbuilding, the refining and conversion of clay, lime, and metals (particularly iron), and the manufacture of beer, sugar, and bread all formed nodes of intensive wood use, drawing in their supplies from a wide radius. Coal substitution affected only Britain, parts of western Europe, and the eastern seaboard of the United States. Wood still accounted for the bulk of energy needs in most parts of the world well into the twentieth century.

As the demand for constructional and general timber rose, so timber deficits occurred in western Europe and even on the eastern seaboard of the United States. They were alleviated only by the importation of timber in unprecedented quantities from the northern coniferous forest belts of Scandinavia, Russia, Canada, and the United States, meshing these countries together into a new Atlantic and Baltic system of production and consumption.

The toll of industrial logging on the northern forests was relentless, and land cover was transformed dramatically.

EUROPE: THREE STORIES OF CLEARING

During the late 1860s the amount of land covered by forest in European countries showed a wide variation. Other than the largely agriculturally untouched coniferous wildernesses of the Scandinavian countries and Russia, centuries of clearing had reduced the area of land covered by forests to less than 30 percent. Germany was just over one-quarter forest covered; France, Switzerland, and Sardinia, a little more than 12 percent; and the rest of Europe had very little woodland. Nonetheless, given the long centuries of exploitation, it was surprising that so much remained.

There was no common deforestation experience among these countries, and only a few individual ones can be singled out because of the way they contribute to the wider story. In Europe, France was experiencing mounting tension about forest destruction, while Russia practiced unrestrained clearing. Britain had little forest left, but its industrialization generated timber deficits, substitution, and trade, which inextricably linked it to Scandinavian, Baltic, and Canadian stands where industrial logging provided copious exports. Although not examined here Germany seemed to achieve a desirable balance between forests and other land uses through "scientific" forestry methods and the creation of even-aged stands.

France
Agricultural Clearing

With 8.8 million ha of forest, France was one of the most wooded countries of western Europe, with marked concentrations of forest in the eastern and northern parts of the country. Henry Colman, writing about his travels in 1848, was "constantly impressed with the immense tracts of land which are in forest." [1] Yet large as they were, they had undoubtedly been as much as halved during the previous 100 years. After the French Revolution the peasants wrought a terrible revenge on the nobility, aristocracy, and church by appropriating forests for pasturage and cultivation or ravaging them as they had the châteaus, to express their fury at the old order and the symbols of authority. In the chaos that followed after 1789, even the restraints that existed over their own extensive communal forests were ignored, with particularly disastrous results in the uplands. The reforms of 1791 decriminalized the occupation of privately owned woodlands, and *défrichement* for agriculture was common. The demand for land was there: the population had increased from approximately 19 million in the early eighteenth century to 26.3 million in 1790, and 35.8 million in 1851. Those 17 million new people had not been absorbed into industry, as France remained predominantly rural in livelihood and needed to grow its own food. Widespread food riots and speculative prices throughout most of the later years of the ancien régime were evidence that the country was on the brink of national agricultural disaster.

Woodland destruction was evident everywhere. Shipbuilders in Toulon and the Mediterranean ports scoured the country for supplies to supplement the traditional sources of timber in the Vosges. Woodlands were thinned or eliminated around large towns like Lyon and Saint-Etienne in the south and the emerging industrial centers in the northern areas of Flanders and Picardy. Paris grew phenomenally, from 524,000 in 1789 to 713,000 in 1821, and sucked in supplies of constructional timber and domestic and industrial fuel from a wide radius. Colman saw "immense arks of charcoal and wood" floating down the Seine, while there were "piles of wood in the city covering acres of ground and on a level with the highest houses."[2] Agricultural expansion, spurred on by a constant demand and high cereal prices, nibbled away at forest edges everywhere, and even whole forests, like Bellecombe forest in Haute-Loire was felled. Woodland was even cleared to create rough pasture in Limousin, which was an improvident waste.

Although as much as 500,000 ha might have disappeared between 1800 and 1860, not a great amount by world standards, but important in the total land-use budget of a country with limited supplies. As ever, the details of agricultural and pastoral expansion were ignored unless they were accompanied by other noteworthy phenomena, such as catastrophic floods, which then triggered political action. In contrast, the details of fuelwood consumption and the impacts of furnaces and forges were publicized and loomed far larger in the record.

Iron Smelting and Fuelwood

By midcentury the long-established French iron industry produced only around 500,000 tons from a multiplicity of scattered small-scale units of production relying on the equally scattered woodland (fig. 10.1). Whether fuel supply was a limiting factor in this low total is a matter of debate. Did the wanton depletion of the forests during the ancien régime mean a widespread and constant crisis that retarded the economic development, or did the lack of coal mining and burning mean an abundance of fuelwood? The answer, of course, was neither; it was not a national crisis so much as a regional one, and French ironmasters were never faced with the choice between innovation or extinction. Admittedly, there were serious fuelwood

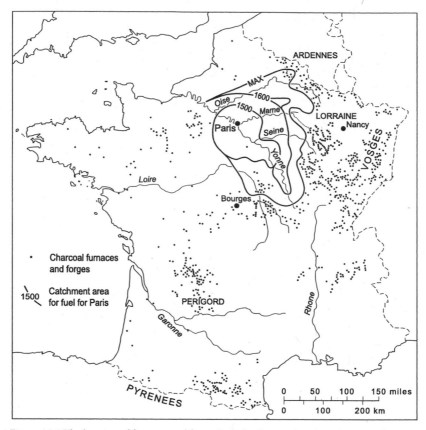

Figure 10.1 The location of furnaces and forges in early nineteenth-century France and competition for fuelwood supplies in the Paris basin, 1500, 1600, and at its maximum in circa 1800. (Sources: after B. Gille, *Les origins de la grande industrie métallurgie en France* [Paris: Éditions Dormat Montchrestien, 1947]; and J. Boissière, "La consommation parisienne de bois et les sidèrurgies périphériques: Essai de mise en parallèle [milieu XVᵉ—XIXᵉ siècles]," in *Forges et forêts: Recherches sur la consommation proto industrie de bois*, ed. D. Woronoff [Paris: L'École des Haute Études en Sciences Social, 1990], 212.)

shortfalls in a few areas of production, but supplies were sufficient elsewhere. Initially, coal only penetrated into nearby iron-producing districts where transport costs were low. But later, rapid economic expansion raised demand and prices, and coal made greater headway as a fuel, probably equaling the contribution of charcoal by the late 1820s and possibly fueling 70 percent of total iron production by 1848.

The price of fuelwood was a matter of national concern and it formed part of a special enquiry in the French national statistical report of 1831. Price reflected factors of forest growth and yield, which varied widely with the age and type of trees, and local environmental conditions as much as

Table 10.2 Population, fuelwood used, and per capita fuel consumption, Paris, 1815–1900

Year	Population	Fuelwood Used (m³)	Per Capita (m³)
1815	c. 670,000	1,200,000	1.80
1865	1,668,000	756,000	0.45
1900	2,661,000	552,000	0.20

Source: H. Clout, *The Land of France, 1815–1914* (London: George Allen & Unwin, 1983), 132.

with good or bad management in the past. Royal and state forests were better managed and cutting restrictions more strictly enforced than for communal forests, and consequently yields were higher. Some well-managed areas produced 13–16 m³/ha, others, either near large towns or in the overgrazed upland communes, a mere 1.0–1.5 m³/ha. All departments produced more than was consumed, with the exception of four with modest deficits and Seine (Paris) with an annual deficit of 1.2 million m³. Prices were highest in the areas of greatest demand around Paris (16 francs/m³); a variety of places in the cooler, industrial north; the Lyonnais and Rhône valley and delta; and in the sparsely wooded Mediterranean peripheral around Marseilles and from Narbonne to Mountauban. Later, canals and then railways evened out distribution and rectified deficits; and by the 1860s coal was being substituted for wood in the north and in Paris, as indicated by table 10.2. But France's energy crisis rumbled on in more remote areas, and many rural areas still relied on fuelwood and charcoal well into the twentieth century.

The Déboisement of the Uplands

Deforestation was much more serious in the communal lands in the mountains of the Pyrenees, Alps, Causse, and even farther north in the Jura and Vosges. Particularly badly affected were the provinces of Dauphine and Provence in the departments of Var, Basse-Alpes, Hautes-Alpes, Vaucluse, and Drôme in the extreme southeast of the country. Population numbers had been rising steadily and had reached a crisis point in the early eighteenth century. In places, clearing was total: woodcutters took any wood fiber available, and what lopping and fire did not accomplish, goats and sheep finished off.

Peasants trudged up to 5 hours daily to collect whatever they could, or they scraped leaves off the ground and uprooted heather. Dried cow dung was commonly used to keep warm and bake bread, and during the winter they moved in with the cattle to keep warm.

With vegetation cover and even the roots gone, runoff accelerated on the steep slopes; the soil moved, and the once-fertile valleys became covered with coarse deposits and boulders. Heavy and sudden downpours of rain turned the once-placid streams into raging torrents. In the lower courses of the rivers sediment clogged channels, navigation was impeded, and malaria throve around sluggish watercourses.

Descriptions of the uplands abound with phrases and words like "landscapes of desolation," "blasted," "terrible aspect," and "terrible nudity of bare and sterile rocks," and the reports of Henri Baudillart in 1831, Adolphe Blanqui in 1843, and many others were sprinkled with descriptions of *déboisement* (degradation), *défrichement* (clearing), disaster, and devastation. Everywhere yields and flocks decreased and the local economy went into decline. "The country," wrote André Surell, "is being depopulated day by day. . . . There may be seen on all hands cabins deserted or in ruins, and already in some localities there are more fields than labourers."[2]

Fancifully it was predicted that within 50 years France would be separated from Savoy by a desert, as Egypt was from Syria. Syria, Algeria, and deserts were very much in the French mind because of colonial expansion, and the specter of the rise and decline of Rome permeated the imagination and the rhetoric. But bad as conditions were, it is likely that there was much overstatement in the descriptions. It was more a case of slow degradation than outright clearing and, consequently, only needed less intense use to regenerate. However, the words tended to be used interchangeably and the severity of the situation exaggerated. But no one doubted the rapidity of change. Marsh, who was not prone to exaggeration, soberly announced that "a single generation has witnessed the beginning and the end of the melancholy revolution."[3]

Reforestation was the answer, and one of the earliest known efforts anywhere occurred in these uplands. It was not a "protogreen" movement but a struggle between the state and the peasant, between technocracy and tradition, between private and communal property, and it was a manifestation of opposing cultural constructions of the nature of alpine France. The realities of the peasant agro-pastoral economy were not understood—and even deliberately misunderstood—by a bureaucracy of foresters and engineers who had been trained in the semimilitary atmosphere of the new École des Eaux-et-Forêts, founded in Nancy in 1822. All public forests passed under their control, and in 1827 a more efficient code of management came into force. In the atmosphere of national revival that pervaded the Second Empire (1852–70), along with the atmosphere of concern over the torrents, agricultural production, and wood supplies, reforestation became almost a "moral awakening." The mountains, like the pastoralist peasants, appeared

disorderly and anarchic and had to be tamed and controlled. Indeed, thinking went so far as to imply that the peasantry should be ejected, transformed,
or otherwise altered so that the mountains would return to an idealized
greenery.

Reforestation was fiercely resisted by the peasant pastoralists because
they thought it would change their way of life and reduce their livelihood even
further. Open rebellion in the Guerre des Demoiselles in Ariége in the Pyrenees in 1829, when the rioters disguised themselves as women, and similar
outbreaks elsewhere in the Jura, Pyrenees, and Alps, seemed a confirmation
of peasant anarchy. The cause of reforestation was put back severely, and
it was only at the very end of the century that significant progress was
made to reforest these upland regions.

Patriotic fervor for afforestation was greatest in the wastes of the lowland agricultural districts of Champagne, in the departments of Marne and
Aube in the Vosges, and particularly in the coastal sandy departments of
Landes and Gironde north of Bordeaux, where the forest area nearly doubled from 127,000 ha in 1821 to 225,000 in the late 1830s to become the
basis of what is still claimed to be the biggest human-made forest in the
world. Overall, France came out of its intensive and often fraught forest
experiences with more forest than it had started, and between midcentury
and 1907 the forest area had risen from 7.6 million to 9.2 million ha. It was
an impressive record for a country in timber-starved western Europe.

The *déboisement* of the uplands and consequent torrents had a broader,
more global, significance than the local area alone. Humans appeared to be
at the center of a complex relationship between uplands and lowlands. Simply put, the torrents showed that social conditions, and even ancient customs, could be directly affect physical processes; humanly induced change
had led to the permanent loss of soils and the irreversible change in river
courses. It is little wonder that the "Torrents of the Var" was the penultimate topic in Clarence Glacken's magisterial work on nature and culture in
Western thought because it signaled a new appreciation of what humans
could do to the environment and contained a "far more pessimistic idea
than the simple warning about damage to a single holder or a commune."[4]
Knowledge about the interconnectedness of things was growing.

Russia

The richly textured detail about the French forest does not exist for the
continental extent of the Russian forest. What happened where and when
is largely unknown, nevertheless, the overall picture of great destruction is
reasonably clear, even if the estimates of the amount of clearing vary. A huge

expansion of 145 million ha of cropland occurred between 1700 and 1920, most of which came out of former forestlands. In a detailed study of each province between 1696 and 1914, Tsvetkov put the figure for clearing lower than those in table 10.1—at about 67.1 million ha, or 28 percent of all forests. The difference between the two figures might be explained by the fact that table 10.1 refers to the whole Russian state, while Tsvetkov's concerns European Russia only. Thus about half of the difference of 78 million ha can be accounted for, but we simply cannot be more positive than that.[5]

What we do know, however, is that by any measure the amount of clearing was immense (fig. 10.2). In the six central provinces of Tula, Ryazan, Orel, Tambov, Kursk, and Vorenezh looked at already in figure 7.1, the ever-increasing density of population and percentage of land under cultivation, first evident during the eighteenth century, continued in the nineteenth. From roughly one-half of the land in cultivation and a population density of between 20 and 30/km^2 in 1811, two-thirds of the land was in cultivation and population densities had risen to 27/km^2–36/km^2 by the mid-nineteenth century. Toward the end of the century anything between two-thirds and three-quarters of the land was cultivated, and rural densities reached between 40 and 50/km^2. In 1847 the novelist Ivan Turgenev commented that in his native Orel Gubernia, "the last of the woods and copses will have disappeared five years hence"; sometime later a landowner, Golenishchev-Kutuzov, told a congress of forest owners that "the Tartar invasion did not inflict greater evil on us than we ourselves have done, robbing our descendants by the cutting and devastation of forests."[6]

But nothing tells the story of agricultural clearing more vividly than the changing land cover in the Arzamas region on the Volga right bank, east and slightly south of Moscow and situated almost wholly in the deciduous forest belt of oak, beech, and hornbeam. The maps (fig. 10.3A–C), which are based on the general survey of large estates of 1696 and subsequent cadastres, show the dramatic decline of forest between the mid-sixteenth and late eighteenth centuries, and again by 1947. In contrast, the vast forests of Siberia in Asiatic Russia were virtually untouched by agriculture, except for "burn-beating," but they were reduced by industrial logging.

Agriculture was not the only cause of the forest destruction. With a population by 1890 of about 110 million, fuelwood must have been cut in prodigious and almost incalculable amounts during the long, severe Russian winter. If the citizens of Paris—in the warm western periphery of Europe, where the mean January temperature did not go below freezing—needed an average of 1.80 m^3 per capita to keep life and limb together in 1815, then the citizens of Moscow—in the heart of continental Europe, where the mean January temperature was −10 to −20°C—must have needed many

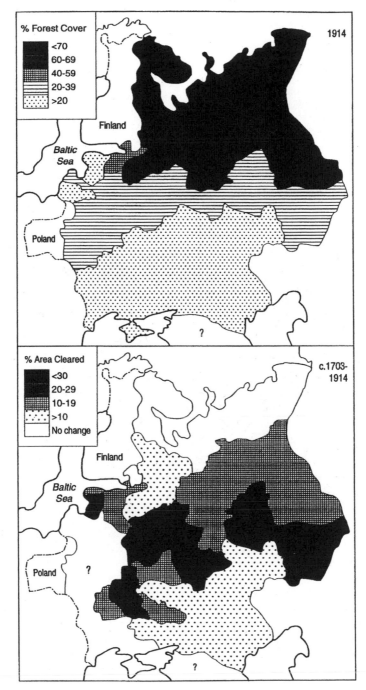

Figure 10.2 Change in forest cover of European Russia: land in forest in 1914 and percentage of area cleared, circa 1703–1914. (Source: R. A. French, "The Making of the Russian Landscape," *Advancement of Science* 20 [1963]: 4–56.)

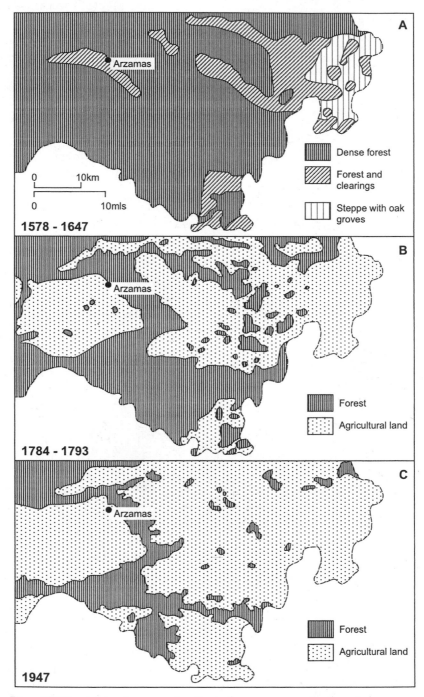

Figure 10.3 Forest cover, Arzamas region, Russia, from sources covering the period
(A) 1578–1647; (B) 1784–93; and (C) 1947. (Source: R. A. French, "The Making of
the Russian Landscape," *Advancement of Science* 20 [1963]: 47–48.)

times that amount. In addition, the millions of rural buildings were made of wood, and they lasted no more than about 15 years, each one consuming the timber of 1.36 ha of forest. River barges, of which there were over 5,000, consumed about 500 trees each. Moreover, the Russian navy was growing in an attempt to dominate the Baltic, and iron making (using 17.5 million m³–20.4 million m³ of timber per annum by 1880), potash making, and salt making all took their toll on the forests.

The export of timber for ready cash increased markedly during the eighteenth century, with British merchants being in the forefront of exploitation. One such company, Gom, operated in the White Sea area around Archangel during most of the eighteenth century, and by 1830 was said to have caused so much destruction that the forest "wounds" would "not quickly heal." Another company, Pitt and Forster, working in the Belorussian forest along the Pripyat' from the late eighteenth century onward, stripped and exported all the merchantable timber and sold the land as cleared estates. But its speculative operations were so rapacious that local landowners protested, the tsar intervened, and the company was forced to stop operations.

With the construction of railways to the Baltic and Black Sea ports, improved accessibility to western markets securely locked Russian supplies into the global timber trade. Russian timber landowners indulged in an orgy of destruction on their estates, and "strove," commented Tsvetkov, "in every way possible, as it were to overtake each other in wiping out their forests as fast as possible." The emancipation of the serfs in 1861 had undermined the economic viability of estates, and landowners also wanted to raise capital to invest in industry, railways, and the newly opened Donbas coalfields. Contractors were given the right to cut without limitation, over a specified period, so that most of them tried to scalp the land, a process that was usually followed by stock grazing over the cutover area, thereby stopping any regrowth. By 1897 over 1.6 million tons of logs and an almost equal number of tons of sawnwood were exported annually, mainly to Britain, Germany, and Holland, a total that had risen to 2.9 million tons by 1908.[7]

One could go on recounting endlessly statistics of consumption in this and that industry, here and there, from time to time. The best summary view is that given by A. F. Rondski and N. I. Shafranov in their exhaustive enquiry into the Russian wood- and timber-using industries of 1890. With a mixture of complex calculations interspersed with inspired guesses, they arrived at a total consumption of 543.9 million m³ destroyed annually by that year, an amount that rose to 869.2 million m³ if the higher estimate for export figures is accepted (table 10.3). Whatever the exact figures, the point was that the Russian forest was under a widespread and sustained attack

Table 10.3 Consumption of wood and timber products (in millions of m³), Russia, 1890–91

Use	Million m³	Total
Industrial:		
Woodstuffs in chemical and mechanical operations, including shipbuilding	19.4	
Mining (salt, iron, metals)	24.2	
Railways (fuel, sleepers, and construction)	7.8	
Steamboats	2.9	
Manufactures and works	18.5	72.8
Domestic:		
Domestic fuelwood @ 3.23 m³/capita	359.3	359.3
Exports:		
Low estimate	436.0	
High estimate	543.7	
Total consumption (low est.)		795.3
Total consumption (high est.)		903.0

Source: A. F. Rondski and N. I. Shafranov, "Forestry," in *Agriculture and Forestry,* vol. 3 of *The Industries of Russia,* ed. and trans. John Martin Crawford (St. Petersburg: Department of Agriculture, Ministry of Crown Affairs, 1893), 311–52, esp. 334–40. *Note:* Original figures are in the traditional measure of sagenes³, which have been converted to m³ and rounded up to the nearest million.

from agriculture and industry, from which it was not to recover for many decades, if at all; it was one of the great episodes in global deforestation. In the central provinces forests became "a mere dwindling reminiscence of the past, and preserved as a luxury." [8]

Britain

Britain did not figure prominently in the story of European deforestation in the same way as did France or Russia; it had hardly any forest left to chop down, although here and there, as at Hainault Forest in about 1851, remnants of woodland were cleared and heavy clay lands tile-drained as part of enclosure and agricultural improvement. (See plate 10.1.) But that very lack of wood supplies was vitally important in stimulating interest in inventions, substitutes, and trade as ways of making up deficiencies. Apart from the early example of Sung China, the move to substitute fossil fuel for vegetable fuel occurred first in the British Isles, both in the domestic and industrial spheres. Britain (and to a lesser extent, Holland) was the focus, organizer, and carrier of the world timber trade, which was a precursor of present patterns of global exploitation.

Coke for Charcoal

Contrary to popular opinion, the use of coke to smelt iron ore by Abraham Darby of Coalbrookdale in Shropshire in 1709 neither was the first attempt to smelt with it nor did it herald the revolution in iron production that is sometimes suggested. At least 20 attempts had been made to substitute peat or coal for wood in iron making during the preceding 150 years, and it was already being used successfully for smelting copper and making glass and bricks. Darby's achievement was to make two great technical discoveries: that coal could be freed from sulphur and other impurities by coking, and that coke made good iron castings; and although coke made poor pig iron he had, incidentally, taken the first step toward the production of commercial coke pig iron. The lack of headway made by these experiments suggests that coal and coke were not cheaper than charcoal and that the shortage of timber was overstated. Coke pig iron did not become consistently cheaper than charcoal pig iron until after 1770 or coke bar cheaper than charcoal bar until about 1800. Charcoal iron persisted throughout the eighteenth and nineteenth centuries, even against cheaper Swedish imports; and as the manufacturers did not ask for subsidies for planting or special conditions in woodlands, supplies of timber must have been there to support it. By the middle of the seventeenth century, coppicing had become almost universal and was producing high calorific wood. As already concluded, the ironworks were not the devourer of the woods that they were made out to be.

Therefore, the proposition that scarcity was the spur to inventiveness and resource substitution clearly did not occur except on a local scale. But when overall demand for iron reached new heights during the industrial upheaval of the late eighteenth century, the concentrated, large, and accessible supplies of coal came into their own and were able to compete successfully and economically with charcoal. Additionally, while charcoal iron technology did not improve, coke iron technology did—for example, readily adopting the steam engine after 1775 for blasting and forging. It was lack of organization and inertia in a new dynamic age that left the charcoal iron industry behind, so that, concluded Hammersley, it "rather fell than was pushed."[9] The great shift occurred after 1780, when for the first time the number of coke furnaces exceeded charcoal-fueled ones, although the shift in the balance of production had occurred about 20 years earlier. The "fall" occurred much earlier in Britain than elsewhere in Europe, where the problem of charcoal supplies was less acute. It was not until after 1850 that smelting with coke became common in France and Germany.

The Hub of the World

As the Industrial Revolution got under way, Britain's towns grew, and naval power expanded. It drew in great quantities of timber from overseas and created patterns of global exploitation in the forests of the world. The importation of resources, and their subsequent reexportation as manufactured goods, had ensured steady growth during the eighteenth century, which had not really been affected by the loss of the American colonies. The Napoleonic Wars were a trying time, but after Waterloo in 1815 a new century of prosperity opened up: population increased from approximately 15 million in 1801 to 29 million in 1861; enhanced conditions of material life meant improved shelter, better food, and more fuel. Increased affluence turned luxuries into necessities, of which abundant timber was one. Between 1811 and 1831 alone, when it was said that half the expense of building a house was in the cost of the timber, over 750,000 new houses were built, and between 1831 and 1851 the railway extended from a few hundred miles to over 6,000.

With the fuel problem more or less solved, the national forests still had to provide sufficient timber for the two other great demands of a premier world power and industrializing society: shipbuilding and general constructional needs. But there was an enormous shortfall of supplies. Britain was becoming the driving force in, and hub of, the world timber trade.

Although it is convenient to look at shipbuilding and general construction separately, in reality they were intimately interrelated as the source, organization, and trade of both types of timber were often identical. The major difference was that ships' timbers and masts were of strategic importance, valuable, and moved in relatively small quantities, whereas general constructional timbers were commonplace, of low cost and high bulk, and moved in vast quantities. Both were moved over great distances.

Ships and Masts

The political precariousness of the Baltic countries as a source of raw materials for sustaining British sea power had long been appreciated, but the situation became critical during the conflict and long blockade of the Revolutionary and Napoleonic Wars from 1793 to 1815. Every port in Europe was closed to British shipping, and the price of timber trebled or more. Britain might just have survived on its own reserves of oak, but at roughly 50 acres (20.23 ha) of mature oak per 74-gunner, and considering the number of ships launched annually, one can understand why near panic set in. More critically, it lacked the masts and naval stores that were essential to its very survival. Of all the British possessions, Canada seemed the most promising alternative source of supply. However, the forests of Nova Scotia had been culled for masts since 1721, so there were few left, and attention turned to New Brunswick and then Ontario. With the imposition of the Baltic blockade, the annual shipment of a few thousand masts from North America increased dramatically to over 10,000 between 1804 and 1812. But when the blockade was lifted, the mast trade swung back to the Baltic and more or less remained there.

In the meantime Britain scoured the world for alternative constructional naval timbers—stinkwood and yellowwood from the Cape of Good Hope, teak from Sierra Leone and India, kauri from New Zealand, jarrah from Australia, mahogany from Honduras and Madagascar, and Demerara greenheart (*Ocotea rodiaei*) from British Guiana. But nearly all ventures foundered due to imperfections in the timber, unfavorable transportation rates, or local difficulties in extraction, such as tropical disease and labor supply. It was still easier and more satisfactory to raid enemy cargoes in foreign ports like Genoa, Copenhagen, and Flushing for supplies.

Only one viable alternative existed, and that was teak from the Malabar coast of southwest India, which had long had a reputation for durability. Also, it did not corrode iron as did oak, which allowed shipbuilding to be simplified by using spikes instead of wooden nails. The prize was worth war: Portuguese and Dutch interests in Malabar were eliminated; the local ruler, Tippoo Sahib, who favored the French, was deposed; and by the beginning of the century the supply of teak went to the British. While little teak was actually moved to British yards because of protectionism at home and high transportation costs, many ships were built in Calcutta and particularly in Bombay by the expert Pharsee shipbuilder, Jamsedjee Jeejeebhoy, ensuring British supremacy in the South Seas and Southeast Asia.

The timber problem remained acute for all European navies, but changes were at hand. Iron gradually began to enter into ship construction, its advantages of lesser weight and greater strength, and hence bigger payloads, becoming apparent, especially since steam began to be used for propulsion after 1830. Initially, wooden frames were clad in iron for protection in warfare, or iron frames were sheathed in wood, as with the fast-sailing clippers built during the 1850s and 1860s. In both cases teak came into its own because of its noncorrosive qualities. But by 1840 wood had practically been superseded by iron except in the United States and Canada, where supplies were still abundant. One of the great icons of nineteenth-century British art, J. M. W. Turner's painting *The Fighting Temeraire* of 1838 (plate 10.2) depicts the battered, de-masted hulk of the massive wooden fighting ship being dragged up the Thames at sunset to the breaker's yard by two nondescript steam-powered iron paddle tugs. It sums up dramatically the passing of the age of wood at sea. Perhaps the decisive event in the death of the wooden

Plate 10.2 "The Fighting Temeraire" Tugged to Her Last Berth to Be Broken Up by J. M. W. Turner, 1838. (National Gallery, London.)

ship occurred on 9 March 1862. On that day the Battle of Hampton Roads in the American Civil War demonstrated the superiority of the iron-clad fighting ship. From that moment the drain on the world's forests that had gone on for thousands of years stopped suddenly and dramatically.

General Constructional Timber

While strategic considerations dominated thinking about overseas sources of supply, it was inevitable that much was learned about the rest of the forest resources. The "mast-getters" slide easily into the role of "timber-getters" to satisfy the growing demand for general constructional timber, or lumber. Lumber was imported as large, crudely squared-off logs known as "fir timber" if from the Baltic or "ton timber" if from Canada or as smaller planks, deals, and battens, in abundant amounts, and as cheaply as possible. A secondary, minor demand was for selected quality timbers such as mahogany, brazilwood, and rosewood for ornamentation, furniture, and interior finishing, which came from the tropical world and constituted barely 3 percent of imports. The general-purpose timber came initially and overwhelmingly from the Baltic, which became so enmeshed in the British

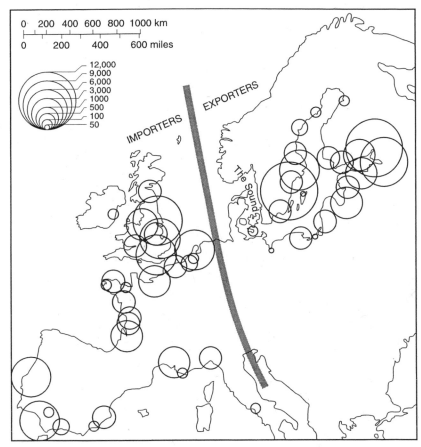

Figure 10.4 The geography of the European trade in Baltic "deals" (planks) for the year 1784. (Source: based on S.-V. Ånström, "English Timber Imports from Northern Europe in the Eighteenth Century," *Scandinavian Economic History Review* 18 [1970]: 31–32.) The map shows shipments originating in the Baltic and customs-cleared through the Baltic Sound. The unit of measure is the long hundred, or 120 pieces, up to 20 ft long.

trade that it became, suggests Arthur Lower, "a semi-colony" of Britain, just as Canada was to become "Great Britain's woodyard" in later years.[10]

To get an overview of the flows and amounts is difficult. First, the prosaic planks and blocks of timber often went unrecorded unlike the more glamorous masts and naval supplies that excited official interest. Second, they came in a large number of different measures, and the record is frequently discontinuous—some relate to ships cleared at the exporting port, others at the importing port, or, in the case of the Baltic trade, through the Baltic Sound. Of the many possible geographies of trade, only one—the export and import of deals of various sizes for 1784—is shown in figure 10.4, and it must stand as an example of the complexity of production and consumption of timber around the world.

Britain was the main consumer and destination of flows, with London taking up to 60 percent of the total imports. However an increasing share was being taken by the provincial ports of Hull, Liverpool, and Newcastle, entry points adjacent to the newly emerging industrial areas in the North of England.

The picture is one of gradually rising consumption of all types of wood but particularly of general-purpose fir timber after about 1750, from approximately 42,476 m³ to 223,704 m³, the total amount being initially equal to, and then surpassing by some fourfold, the imports to the Netherlands, where demand stayed relatively stable. The per capita consumption rose steadily to 190 bf (0.45 m³) by the end of the century, although it was still only about one-half to two-fifths that of the United States. The domestic cut supplied barely a tenth or twelfth of the demand. And yet, in the total picture of all imports, timber did not loom large; it never exceeded 1 percent before 1820, and masts are put into perspective when one realizes how relatively unimportant they were even in that timber component. By 1871 imports had risen to 5.9 million m³ and then climbed steadily to 13.4 million m³ by 1901, but despite the rising volume timber still rarely exceeded 5 percent of U.K. imports and most commonly hovered around 3–4 percent.

Before 1760 all imports came primarily from Norway, that part of Scandinavia nearest to Britain and unhampered by the political vagaries of the Baltic Sound. But the big timbers had gone after centuries of exploitation, and increasingly the forest could supply only smaller pieces. Therefore, after 1760 fir timber and spruce deals ("spruce" meaning from Prussia, and not necessarily *Picea abies*) came increasingly from the "East Country," which meant the rivers converging on Memel and Riga, and the hinterlands of St. Petersburg, Viborg, and Narva. Like the east-flowing rivers of the United States, huge rafts with houses on them brought timber downstream. Robert Johnston saw them on the Niemen River in 1815: "They also bring along with them carts, horses, poultry, etc. When the cargo of wood is disposed of, they return, by land with the horses."[11]

It was remarkable that despite the Napoleonic Wars the bulk of imported timber (roughly three-quarters) still found its way through the Baltic Sound. From about one-third of the total in 1780 it rose to nearly a half in 1790 and then rarely fell below two-thirds or four-fifths from then on. The other main supplier was, of course, Canada, where the British government had encouraged the investment of private capital in order to promote exploitation of strategic supplies. In Ontario in particular, private firms developed facilities and sawmills for the supply of oak timbers and masts, which rivaled those of Riga and Danzig. Inevitably, in order to make the most of their investments they moved into the general timber trade, and soon hundreds of ships were sailing eastward with cargoes of crudely squared pine trunks, deals, and planks, much of it coming down the St. Lawrence from Vermont. Mindful that, after the war, trade might swing back to the nearer, cheaper (and generally better-quality) wood of the Baltic, as it had with masts, the Canadian firms pressured the government to impose stiff duties on Baltic timber imports so that they were several times the cost of the wood at the port (the ratio was 5:1), and these punitive restrictions were not removed until 1857. Canada concentrated on "ton" timber and deals and dominated while the differential tariff operated between 1820 and 1846. But when the tariff was lifted, the flow of Baltic supplies resumed, eventually to surpass Canadian imports. Britain absorbed them all in ever-increasing quantities, especially when the railways started up with their demand for sleepers. Despite its prominence, Canada was "only an episode" in the history of the bulk lumber trade—a large one, to be sure, but an episode all the same.[12]

Despite the complexities and variations of what may be called the many different lumber trades, a number of generalizations can be made. First, timber ranked with grain, tea, sugar, cotton, and wool as a major commodity in world trade, all the more remarkable because of its great bulk and low value, which attests to its indispensability. Second, the general timber trade was very much the product of individual entrepreneurs and rarely of governments. In 1800, London had 75 timber merchants whose yards lined the Thames between Greenwich and Southwark, Liverpool had about a score, as had the other major importing ports. Many of the firms had local agents, skilled in foreign languages and local politics, whose sole job was to scout out supplies, arrange deals with local cutters to ship the lumber, and generally to send back market intelligence. The merchants were key players in the operation and dominance of the consuming market of the metropolitan core. Rarely did they engage directly in the cutting, only in the movement of the timber. They were the facilitators, not the producers, but they were a crucial link in the exploitation of the world's forests.

Finally, to translate the quantities of timber moved internationally into the area of forest cut or thinned is impossible, but the outcome most certainly was depleted forests that could not supply the big timber. The destruction seemed worse in the newly settled countries, where a pioneer mentality of "cut out and get out" existed, whereas in the old, settled countries forest exploitation tended to be integrated more fully into other ways of life and may even have proved a general stimulus to the economy and an aid to protoindustrialization, as perhaps happened in Finland, southern Sweden, and parts of the south Baltic coast. But in the New World the forest was both enemy and wealth, and it was plundered. Writing about New Brunswick in 1825, one observer, Peter Fisher, speculated that a reasonable person would have expected all this trade to "produce great riches to the country; and that great and rapid improvements would be made." But instead of towns, farms, elegant houses, extensive stores, and mercantile conveniences, the "capital of the country had been wasted" and the wealth had gone elsewhere. The shippers and merchants were

> strangers who have taken no interest in the welfare of the country; but have merely occupied a spot in order to make what they could in the shortest time possible . . . the forests are stripped and nothing left in prospect, but the gloomy apprehension when the timber is gone, of sinking into insignificance and poverty.[13]

This picture was overdrawn: by 1850 approximately 640,000 acres had been cleared and 193,000 people lived and farmed where once forest had been. But the forest still dominated and there was little industry. New Brunswick was a microcosm of clearing in the temperate New World. Lumbering meant the destruction or degradation of the forest resource, and even if a territory was lucky enough to retain some of that plundered wealth in the form of farms and settlements, it meant that the forest had gone. It was a dilemma: at best, new land could only be created at the expense of the old forest; at worst, old forest was destroyed and left a wasteland.

CLEARING A CONTINENT: THE UNITED STATES

By the latter part of the eighteenth century, all the ingredients were in place in the United States for one of the greatest episodes of global deforestation ever seen. Millions of immigrants swarmed into a continent so wooded that Arnold Guyot described it as "glutted with . . . vegetable wealth."[14] The population reached 23.2 million by 1850 and 74.8 million by 1899. By 1848 13 new states had been created in the trans-Appalachian West, and Texas was annexed. The bustling, expansive, industrial nation of the end of the nineteenth century was a very different country from the tiny agricultural one that had hugged the plains and hills of the eastern seaboard for so many generations before.

The Process and Extent of Clearing

Farm making stayed basically the same as in earlier centuries; for the pioneer farmers it was still hard, backbreaking work with the ax. But not all pioneer farmers stayed permanently on their cleared land; there was a class of backwoodsmen who merely did preparation work because they knew that there were plenty of pioneer farmers ready to take up part-cleared land. "It is considered here a small affair for a man to sell, take his family and some provisions and go into the woods upon a new farm, erect a house, and begin anew," said the Reverend John Taylor of early nineteenth-century New York.[15] Perhaps for the first time ever in the world, clearing was not a purely subsistence activity but was becoming a commercial, even speculative, proposition, characterized by high mobility and impermanence.

Obviously some farmers had capital, and the prospect either of acquiring a partially cleared farm or of hiring a labor gang to chop down the trees and prepare the land for a crop, even to build a temporary shelter and some fences, was attractive and far more common than is supposed. The "setup" men were usually itinerant laborers, traveling great distances, armed only with their axes and grubbing hoes, and usually asking about 50 cents a day, the prevailing wage for unskilled labor. It was arduous work; some skilled axmen claimed that they could clear an acre in three to seven days, but that was the work of a professional, and a strong one at that, and the rapidity of clearing also depended on the density and size of the trees. Sometimes the setup men were farmers who had bought a farm but could not clear enough land in time to get in a crop and thus needed the cash to pay for food and other essentials for the family. The permutations of who was clearing for whom were endless.

The problem of "how to subdue the land," as Jeremy Belknap put it, remained, and methods of clearing did not change—it was either clear-cutting or girdling, with both involving burning.[16] Girdling cost about eight dollars an acre (approximately $20/ha) and took 13.5 man-days, whereas clear-cutting cost between 10 and 12 dollars an acre (approximately $25–$30/ha) but took between 16.5 and 20 man-days. Because tasks like collecting fallen timber were deferred in girdling, the conclusion is that the costs in terms of labor and cash were ultimately about the same. Both methods left stumps that were either left to rot or had to be grubbed out with axes, levers, spades, chains, and oxen, all of which took about as long as the initial tree-clearing effort. But by the end of the nineteenth century, stump removal had probably dropped to between four and six man-days as geared stump removers, primitive gasoline flamethrowers, and above all, dynamite, were employed. But however done, the hacking, grubbing, and burning went on until the farmer had as much land as he could handle. It was a job not of a few years but of a generation.

No tally was kept of the amount of forest cleared because, among other things, clearing was regarded as the first step in the "natural" process of land

Table 10.4 Amount of land cleared and man-years expended in forested and nonforested areas, United States, circa 1650–1909

Date	Forested		Nonforested	
	Acres (in millions)	Man-Years (in thousands)	Acres (in millions)	Man-Years (in thousands)
Before 1850	113.7	12,633	0.5	2
1850–59	39.7	4,268	9.1	48
1860–69	19.5	1,973	19.4	68
1870–79	49.3	4,243	48.7	122
1880–89	28.6	2,471	57.7	139
1890–99	31.0	2,486	41.1	68
1900–1909	22.4	1,705	51.6	86
Total	304.2	29,779	228.1	531

Source: M. I. Primack, "Farm Formed Capital in American Agriculture, 1850–1910" (Ph.D. diss., University of North Carolina, 1963)a, tables 3, 4, 7, 8.

"improvement," which was so obvious and commonplace as to be barely worth comment or record. Nevertheless, in the counties of the densely forested eastern half of the country, the amount of "improved land" returned in the federal censuses after 1850 is a good indicator of the amount of land cleared (table 10.4). Before 1850 it is probable that over 113.7 million acres (46 million ha) had been cleared, only a very small amount coming from either natural or Indian clearings (fig. 10.5A). At the very least about 100 million acres (40.5 million ha) represents the culmination of two centuries of pioneering endeavor in the forests.

In the 20 years between 1850 and 1869 a big upswing in clearing occurred when a remarkable 59.2 million acres (24 million ha) were affected, equivalent to roughly one-half of all the clearing that had gone on before; and it was concentrated in the northeastern and northern Midwest states of New York, Ohio, Indiana, Illinois, and Wisconsin (fig. 10.5B), where every field was won by ax and fire. During the turbulent decade of the Civil War the amount of forest cleared and settled dropped to 19.5 million acres (7.9 million ha). But in the 20 years from 1870 to 1889 it rose again to its highest amount, when a colossal 77.9 million acres (31.5 million ha) were affected (fig. 10.5C).

After the 1880s got under way, more acres of open prairie land were settled than forested land. The invention of the improved steel-tipped plow by John Deere in 1837 reduced the time taken to prepare prairie ground for cultivation. A mere 1.5 man-days of labor were now needed to break and plow an acre of prairie, compared with a total of about 32 man-days to

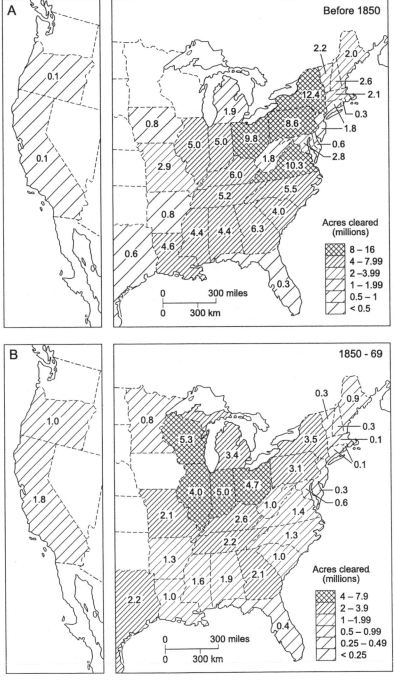

Figure 10.5 Millions of acres cleared in the United States, by state. *A*, before 1850; *B*, 1850–69; *C*, 1870–89; and *D*, 1890–1909. (Sources: based on M. I. Primack, "Farm Formed Capital in American Agriculture, 1850–1910" [Ph.D. diss., University of North Carolina, 1963], and U.S. Bureau of the Census for appropriate years.)

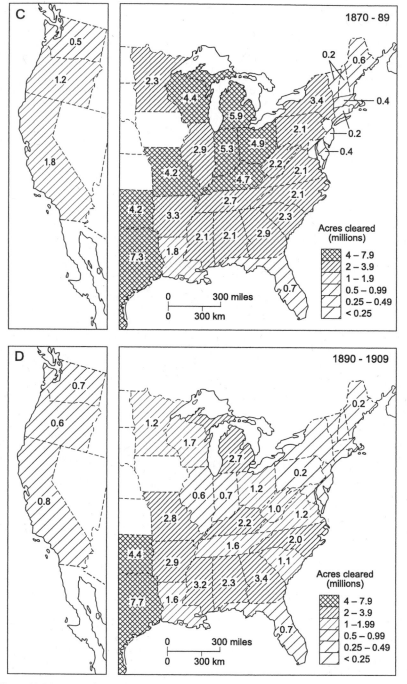

Figure 10.5 (continued)

clear an acre of forest completely. Henceforth, forest clearing as an element in the formation of the landscape diminished in importance, both actually and in popular impression, as the glamour of the open range, cowboys, and in fact everything that made up the amorphous concept of "the West" overshadowed the harsh, grinding labor of forest pioneering. But the war on the woods was by no means over: from 1880 onward, clearing continued, mainly in the southern states (nearly 29 million acres, or 11.7 million ha), with a little in the Pacific Northwest; and the old areas still contributed a significant amount to decadal totals, which still hovered between 22 million and 31 million acres (8.9–12.5 million ha) (fig. 10.5D). In all, some 300 million acres (121.4 million ha) of forest were eliminated by the turn of century, after which time forest reversion became a more dominant process than forest removal.

This necessarily generalized view of clearing based on the crude statistics of counties and states gives a good overall picture of the pace and extent of the process, but it gives little sense of the realities of everyday life for the forest pioneer, which are difficult to pinpoint and understand. Perhaps the essence of the experience is conveyed best in a series of four sketches made to illustrate Orsamus Turner's *History of the Holland Purchase of Western New York* and based on the sequence of events he had actually experienced and seen (plates 10.3–10.6).[17] In plate 10.3, the pioneer and his wife have

Plate 10.3 The First Six Months. (From Orsamus Turner, *A Pioneer History of the Holland Purchase of Western New York* [Buffalo, N.Y.: Jewett Thomas, 1849].) (State Historical Society of Wisconsin, Madison.)

Plate 10.4 The Second Year. (From Orsamus Turner, *A Pioneer History of the Holland Purchase of Western New York* [Buffalo, N.Y.: Jewett Thomas, 1849].) (State Historical Society of Wisconsin, Madison.)

been on the block for six months. He has cleared a patch to "open out" the forest and has gotten logs for his cabin. The cows and sheep browse on whatever vegetation they can find. His nearest neighbor is miles away. After two years (plate 10.4), the pioneer has cleared a few more acres and enclosed them with rail and brush fences. Corn, potatoes, and beans have been planted among the stumps, and in the background his scattered and distant neighbors have formed a "logging bee" to help him clear his land. In the foreground, his wife holds their first child. Ten years on (plate 10.5), 40 acres have been cleared, and stumps in the background indicate that more clearing is underway; the fields contain crops of corn and grass. The log cabin still stands but has been expanded and improved with a new clapboard barn. In the upper left we can discern a church and schoolhouse in the nearby growing village. In the final scene—"The Work of a Lifetime" (plate 10.6)—the surrounding forest has been cleared by the farmer and his neighbors, so that only the ridge tops remain as woodlots. The house has been extended and "beautified," and a railway passes near the village.

The detail of these four sketches, which are like "stills" clipped out of the continually moving picture of forest settlement, may be varied here and there, but the scenes portray the essential truth of an experience that was repeated many millions of times in the eastern portions of the United States until the opening years of the twentieth century. Indeed, these unique scenes can

Plate 10.5 Ten Years Later. (From Orsamus Turner, *A Pioneer History of the Holland Purchase of Western New York* [Buffalo, N.Y.: Jewett Thomas, 1849].) (State Historical Society of Wisconsin, Madison.)

Plate 10.6 The Work of a Lifetime. (From Orsamus Turner, *A Pioneer History of the Holland Purchase of Western New York* [Buffalo, N.Y.: Jewett Thomas, 1849].) (State Historical Society of Wisconsin, Madison.)

stand as a microcosm of forest life almost anywhere in the temperate world, at almost any time during the last 300 years.

Rapidity of change was the overriding characteristic of American clearing, which seemed so speeded up as to achieve a dreamlike quality. The sudden creation of towns and farms "in the centre of the forests," said Adam Hodgson, "in whose solitudes, within a very few years, the Indian pursued his game, appears rather like an enchantment than the slow result of those progressive efforts, with which, in the old world, savage nature has been subdued." The edges of time and space were blurred, so that what was "stage" and what was "place" were difficult to disentangle. "In successive intervals of space," Hodgson noted,

> I have traced society through those various stages which in most countries
> are exhibited only in successive periods of time. I have seen the roving hunter
> acquiring the habits of the herdsman; the pastoral state merging into agricul-
> ture; and the agricultural in the manufacturing and commercial.[18]

The sensation was overwhelming that time was being telescoped as the process of runaway clearing rapidly reduced distance and space; and rather than taking decades, new landscapes and geographies seemed to emerge overnight. If forest clearing could be described as "perhaps the greatest single factor in the evolution of the European landscape" during historical times, the same could be said without qualification for the North American landscape.[19]

The Landscape of Clearing

It was the rawness of the newly made scene and the wanton destruction of nature and prodigal waste of wood that especially struck the travelers from Europe. Of the many descriptions, perhaps that of Basil Hall, a British artist and writer, is the most revealing. The girdled forest was grotesque:

> Some of the fields were sown with wheat above which could be seen nu-
> merous ugly stumps of old trees; others allowed to lie in the grass guarded,
> as it were, by a set of gigantic black monsters, the girdled, scorched and
> withered remains of the ancient woods. Many farms are still covered with
> an extricable and confused mass of prostrate trunks, branches and trees,
> piles of split logs, and squared timbers, planks, shingles, great stacks of fuel,
> and often in the midst of all this could be detected a half smothered log hut,
> without windows or furniture, but well stocked with people. At other places
> we came upon ploughs, always drawn by oxen making their sturdy way

Plate 10.7 Newly Cleared Land in America. The scene is Oak Orchard Creek, 40 miles west of Rochester, New York. (From Basil Hall, *Forty Etchings from Sketches Made with the Camera Lucida in North America in 1827 and 1828* [Edinburgh: Cadell, 1829], plate 9.) (State Historical Society of Wisconsin, Madison.)

amongst the stumps like a ship navigating through coral reefs, a difficult and tiresome operation.

In addition to this splendid description of cleared land, Hall later sketched the new cutover areas (plate 10.7) and appended the following caption to his etching, which taken together are a vignette of newly cleared land anywhere, at any time:

> The trees are cut over at the height of three or four feet from the ground and the stumps are left for many years till the roots rot;—the edge of the forest, opened for the first time to the light of the sun looks cold and raw;—the ground rugged and ill-dressed . . . as if nothing could ever be made to spring from it. The houses which are made from logs, lie scattered about at long intervals;—while snake fences constructed from split trees, placed in a zig-zag form, disfigure the landscape.

The scene, said Hall, had invariably a "bleak, hopeless" aspect, which had "no parallel in old countries." [20]

Yet to the American pioneer the beauty of the forest and its destruction was of little consequence. The aesthetics of the scene were subordinate to practical problems of clearing—simply, trees and stumps meant toil;

cleared land meant production, food, and neighbors; and work now meant the sacrifice of current well-being for a more glorious future. "The sight of wheat field or a cabbage garden," said Isaac Weld,

> would convey pleasure far greater than the most romantic woodland views. They [American pioneers] have an unconquerable aversion to trees; and whenever a settlement is made they cut away all before them without mercy; not one is spared; all share the same fate and are involved in the same havoc. . . . The man that can cut down the largest number, and have fields about his house most clear of them, is looked upon as the most industrious citizen, and the one that is making the greatest improvements in the country.

Ever perceptive, Adam Hodgson thought that clearing was an essential step in the development of the Americans' moral imagination:

> If mere cultivation be not beauty, it is closely allied to it . . . Every acre, reclaimed from the wilderness, is a conquest of 'civilized man over uncivilized nature'; an addition to resources, which are to enable his country to stretch her moral empire to her geographical limits.[21]

Simply, clearing *was* America.

But the clearing was not quite as indiscriminate as the travelers would have one believe. Remnants of forest were left on the steeper slopes, poorer ground, and the extremities of the farms. Even as late as 1900, up to half or more of the farmland in the South and the northern Great Lakes states was still in woodland, as was 10–20 percent in the Middle West and Middle Atlantic states. To clear more would have been ecologically impossible, given the regrowth rate, and economically unsound, given the value of wood to the farmer. The woodlot was a valuable source of rough grazing and browsing for stock (especially in the South), shelter from cold winds and heat, construction timber, and above all, fuel. It has remained a prominent feature of the landscape.

It was not until the settlers entered the Midwest, where the forest ended and the prairie began, that the value of trees was truly appreciated. Initially, half a mile was said to be too much to haul timber for those settlers who had been used to trees growing at their door; but in time, 3–6 mi seemed reasonable. Eventually huge quantities of lumber were floated down the Allegheny, Ohio, and Mississippi from as far away as Upper New York State or, after 1834, from the newly exploited forests of southern Michigan and Wisconsin via Chicago, all at vast cost. The linking of the Illinois River with the Chicago River by the Illinois-Michigan Canal in 1847 halved prices almost overnight, and lumber now flowed easily into the prairie lands. Yet whatever the cost of imported timber, it was more than compensated for by the absence of tree felling and by the speed and ease of breaking up the sod with the steel-tipped plow. Compared with "making" a farm in the forest, "making" one in the prairie took less than a twentieth of the time and effort, thereby signaling a massive shift in human endeavor and resources and a partial reprieve for the forest.

Domestic Fuel

The transformation of nearly 300 million acres of forest into improved land after 1750, and the scores of millions of acres cleared as a result of industrial logging from circa 1850 onward, provided an enormous amount of wood for energy. If it was not burned on the spot, a little was used for fences and houses, and some went into the manufacture of potash, but most must have been burned for heating the home.

Considering the magnitude of this commodity and its importance in the economy and life of the nation, it is surprising how little we know about its production, consumption, and distribution. Fuelwood dominated as a domestic and industrial energy source until well after 1885 (see fig. 9.2) and constituted the greatest drain on the forest until overtaken by the general timber production in about 1860 (fig. 10.6). Even in the warmer South, woodcutting was a profitable sideline for the pioneer farmer and an indispensable aid to the making of a farm. The profits were said to provide enough cash for the purchase of provisions and stock, and sometimes even the hire of setup men. The forest, then, was both task and capital. Rural diaries suggest that anything between one-eighth and one-fourth of a farmer's time was spent in chopping, splitting, hauling, and stacking firewood. An annual consumption of 20–30 cords (72.5–109 m³) was common for a rural household, and larger farms used twice that amount.

Fuelwood was needed in every home, rural industry, and town. There was also an intense demand alongside the main river courses, particularly the Ohio, lower Missouri, and the Mississippi down to New Orleans, to feed the hundreds of steamboats that plied the rivers after 1820. The boats consumed about 500 tons on a 20-day, 3,000-mi voyage from New Orleans to Louisville and took on fuel twice daily, so that "wooding" stations lined the rivers, and the forests were cleared for many miles inland. Even so it was less than 1 percent of total fuelwood used.

The overwhelming demand was domestic, which accounted for over 95 percent of all use, and of that over half was in the urban centers on the eastern seaboard. For example, New York, which had a population of

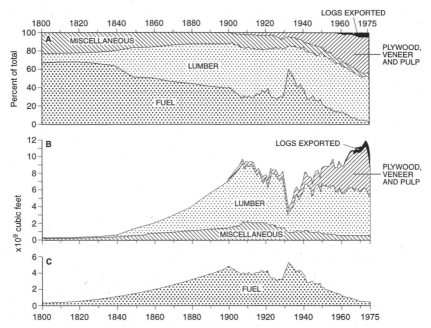

Figure 10.6 The uses of timber in the United States, 1800–1975. *A*, Timber in different uses as percentage of total; *B*, All timber used, other than fuel; and *C*, Timber used for fuel. Note: 1,000 ft^3 = 28.317 m^3. (Sources: based on M. Clawson, "Forests in the Long Sweep of American History," *Science* 204 [1979]: 1168–74, and Clawson, personal communication.)

79,000 in 1800, grew to 696,000 by 1850 and 2.5 million by 1890. Boston, Philadelphia, and a host of other cities also grew rapidly. Thus it became profitable to haul supplies from farther and farther away. Fuelwood came by boat along the Atlantic coast from Maine and New Jersey, down the Hudson, and increasingly along the Erie Canal, which had opened in 1825 and penetrated the forests in the Genesee country in upstate New York, the region Basil Hall had seen being cleared. By 1845 New York was said to be consuming over 4 million cords (14.5 million m^3) per annum, and despite the rise in the price of fuelwood and some penetration of coal and anthracite, especially in Philadelphia after 1820, wood still accounted for over three-quarters of the energy used and was still the cheapest fuel by some 12–25 percent.

The only other possible solution was more efficient heating. Wide, roaring, open hearth fires lost nine-tenths of their heat up the chimney, so their replacement by more efficient enclosed stoves was advocated. But the early stoves (known as Franklins after their inventor, Benjamin Franklin) were smoky, inefficient, and inelegant, and as long as wood was reasonably plentiful and/or cheap they made little headway. Moreover, to cut wood small enough to fit into the stove required extra effort, and time was the one commodity the pioneer did not have. Over 800 patents for stoves were taken out between 1790 and 1840, most no more than stylistic tinkerings of previous designs, and it was not until better iron-casting techniques came in after 1820 that stoves moved into mass production to become so common and accepted in towns that they were no longer a topic of comment after 1850. By 1860 nearly half a million were being manufactured annually.

Anthracite was the main competitor of wood as an energy source in urban areas and came into its own after 1850, when boilers for central heating were installed in the cellars of multistoried urban buildings. Compared with anthracite, wood was bulky and heavy (by a factor of four to five times) and difficult to store in urban cellars. In time, anthracite also spread west into the less well-treed plains (fig. 10.7). However, wood fuel consumption continued to grow. Coal may have constituted about 60 percent of all fuel used in 1900 (fig. 9.2), but wood still comprised the bulk of the rest of the expanding energy needs. The drain on the forests continued: rural families still sat in front of their great, blazing open hearths, and with a burgeoning economy and concomitant energy needs, more wood was cut in almost each successive year until the late 1930s.

Railroads: "The . . . Juggernaut of the Vegetable World"

Fuelwood consumption was boosted by the growth of the railroads and factories (about 2.5 percent of use). The railroad was a voracious devourer of forests, and wherever it went, wood became scarce. Wood use diminished rapidly throughout the 1870s and 1880s with the availability of coal, which was less bulky to store on the train, with about 1 ton of coal replacing 4 tons of wood. But it was gradually realized that it was the timber needed for general railway purposes, such as buildings, stations, telegraph poles, fencing, and especially ties, that was likely to reach astronomical proportions if the length of track constructed continued to expand at the rate it had in the past. Track length tripled from 32,600 mi in 1860 to 100,000 mi in 1880, and it was set to double during the next decade and again during the next. Each mile of track needed between 2,200 and 3,500 prime heart-of-oak ties, but most commonly 2,640, which had to be replaced every six to seven years because of decay.

How much wood the railroads actually consumed was one of the great debates in forestry and the timber trade during the middle and latter half of the nineteenth century. Like charcoal furnaces, the railroad was singled out by some as a major factor in woodland destruction because it was an

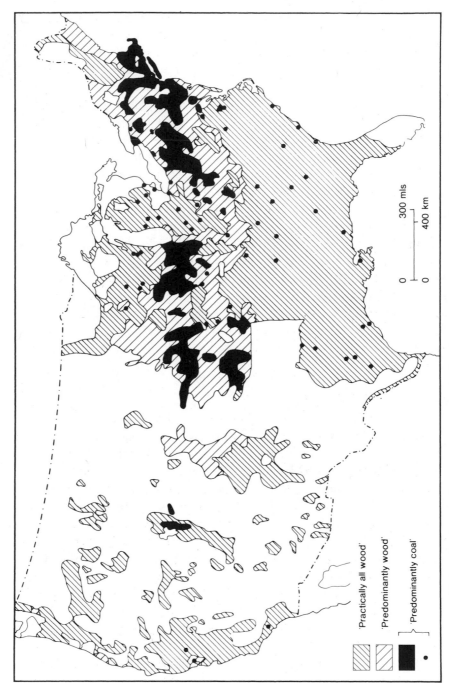

Figure 10.7 Types of fuel used in the United States, circa 1880. (Source: based on C. S. Sargent, *Report on the Forests of North America (Exclusive of Mexico)*, vol. 9 of *Tenth Census of the United States (1880)* [Washington, D.C.: GPO, 1884], 488–89.)

'Practically all wood'

'Predominantly wood'

'Predominantly coal'

alien intrusion into the idyll of American rural life: it was the harbinger of rapid change and truly "the machine in the garden."[22] Others could not laud it enough; it was the spearhead of modernization and civilization in the wilderness, and the uniter of the continent. In 1876, Daniel Millikin, who had lately witnessed the forest destruction caused by the many railroads built across his native Ohio, thought it difficult "to conceive of the demands which this new invention will make upon the woods" and that it would lead to more forest destruction than had agriculture.[23] The advent of the transcontinental lines that thrust across the treeless plains at a rate of up to 8 mi per day raised timber-depletion consciousness. Nathaniel Egleston, director of the fledgling Forestry Division of the Department of Agriculture, hazarded a guess that 3 million acres (1.2 million ha) had been destroyed for existing track and 472,400 acres (191,173 ha) were needed annually just to keep up maintenance, which estimate he raised to 567,714 acres (229,746 ha) a few years later. A more exact and sober investigation by M. G. Kern, an agent for the division, suggested that existing track had consumed 3.1 billion ft^3 (87,782.7 m^3) of timber and that maintenance and extension needed another 0.5 billion ft^3 (14,158 m^3), the equivalent of 300,000 acres (121,406 ha) of forest per annum.

Whatever the precise figures, the preference for the heart of white and chestnut oaks—and to a lesser extent, black locust, which had the requisite qualities of strength, elasticity, and resistance to rot—meant selective but highly destructive and wasteful felling throughout the hardwood forests of the Appalachians. A mere 6-ft railroad tie required a minimum of 75 ft of good timber, and it only stopped when the creosoting of ties under high pressure became accepted in the later 1890s and, ultimately, when railroad expansion stopped. Kern's calculations were substantially upheld by the more finely worked-out estimates of the Forest Service in 1911, to which must be added the timber used in the construction and replacement of buildings, rolling stock, bridges, and so on.

If the calculations in table 10.5 are correct, then the railroads were using at least one-fourth to one-fifth of the annual U.S. timber production during the latter part of the century, so the contemporary view that the railroad was "the insatiable juggernaut of the vegetable world," though exaggerated, was essentially correct.[24] Multiplied on a world scale, the effect on the forests was staggering (see table 9.5).

Charcoal-Made Iron

Although the last charcoal-fueled iron furnace ceased operation in Britain in 1810 when all were being fired by coke or coal, not one coke furnace had

Table 10.5 Crossties used and acres of forest cleared, United States, 1870–1910

	Miles of Track	Ties Renewed Annually (in millions)	Ties Used on New Construction (in millions)	Total Ties Annually (in millions)	Acres of Forest Cleared (in thousands)
1870	60,000	21	18	39	195
1880	107,000	37	21	58	290
1890	200,000	70	19	89	445
1900	259,000	91		91	455
1910	357,000	124		124	620

Sources: S. H. Olson, *The Depletion Myth: A History of the Railway Use of Timber* (Cambridge, Mass.: Harvard University Press, 1971), 12; and U.S. Bureau of the Census, *Historical Statistics of the United States,* rev. ed. (Washington, D.C.: GPO , 1977), vol. 2, table 392.

been built in the United States. The charcoal iron industry died a very slow death. Not until 1835 were the first experiments made with coke, and not until 1945 was the last charcoal furnace shut down. The sheer abundance of wood was an obvious factor in the survival of this traditional technology, but charcoal-made iron also had positive qualities. It was heat resistant, tough, and retained a good cutting edge, yet it was also malleable, making it a versatile all-purpose iron for use on the frontier in making boilers, tools, and implements.

In 1865 there were 560 iron furnaces, of which 439, or 78 percent, were still fueled by charcoal. These were concentrated in the Hanging Rock district of southern Ohio, the Allegheny valley northeast of Pittsburgh, the Juniata valley in south-central Pennsylvania, and the Berkshires on the New York–Massachusetts-Connecticut borders. The remainder of the furnaces burned anthracite and were concentrated in eastern Pennsylvania. In time, most of these charcoal furnaces were either abandoned or converted to coal of some sort, but iron making by means of charcoal lingered on in the South and, particularly, in northern Michigan and Wisconsin until as late as the mid-1940s, in conjunction with the mining of high-grade ores of the Lake Superior ranges.

Large supplies of wood were needed for these furnaces, and iron "plantations" or forested estates of between 30,000 and 100,000 acres around the furnaces were common. The area cleared for smelting iron depended on the density of the trees and the efficiency of the furnaces. But if the modest estimate of 150 acres for every 1,000 tons of pig iron produced is accepted, then the acres affected could have been as low as 25,000 in 1862 and as high as 94,000 in 1890, although many "iron forests" were cut over at

25- to 30-year intervals, or sometimes less. Either way, taking the larger or the smaller estimate, the amount cut had relatively little impact on the forest as a whole. Even if we total all the known charcoal iron production between 1855 and 1910 (20.4 million tons), it would have consumed only 4,800 mi² (12,432 km²) of woodland, or 3,000 mi² (7,770 km²) if a 25-year rotation had been employed. This is a mere 1.3 percent (or 0.8 percent if regrowth is considered) of the amount of land cleared for agriculture during the same period. Having said that, however, charcoal iron production was concentrated, so the effects on the immediately surrounding forest were noticeable. The furnace and the cut forest were visually prominent, so that charcoal iron, rather like fuel for locomotives, could be pointed to as a great destroyer of the forest. But nationally it was a mere pinprick, as it was upon forests throughout the world.

Lumber Production

By the early decades of the nineteenth century the intertwining of lumbering activity and agricultural clearing began to unravel as the pioneer farmer–cum–part-time lumberman gave way to large-scale, specialized, commercial logging. New England and New York assumed the same relationship as raw material suppliers to the urbanizing, industrializing eastern seaboard as the Baltic did to northwest Europe. But there were significant differences. Whereas the Baltic still relied on peasant labor and production methods, U.S. exploitation was the epitome of industrial capitalism in the forest. Second, while distances were often as great as the 1,200 mi from the Baltic to Britain, sources of supply in the United States were internal and could be linked by river, lake, and canal and, eventually, by rail. Third, U.S. forests were supplying not only a rapidly growing and urbanizing population in the same territory, but one that after about 1840 was expanding and colonizing the treeless plains of the West. The population leaped from 7.2 million in 1810 to 31.5 million in 1860, and then more than doubled to 74.8 million by 1899.

Wood and wood products permeated American life so thoroughly that in 1836 James Hall could say truthfully, "Well may ours be called a Wooden country; not merely from the extent of the forests but because in common use wood has been substituted for a number of most necessary articles, such as stone, iron, and even leather."[25] Also, its roles as a producer of energy and creator of agricultural land were paramount.

From a mere 0.5 billion bf (1.2 million m³) in 1801, the amount of lumber cut rose and accelerated with each successive decade to a form a new, upwardly sloping curve that peaked at nearly 46 billion bf (108.5 million m³) in 1906, an amount never reached since (fig. 10.8). The ability to supply

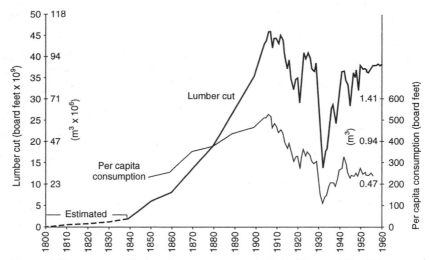

Figure 10.8 Lumber cut and per capita consumption in the United States, 1800–1960.
(Source: U.S. Bureau of Census, *Historical Statistics of the United States,* rev. ed. [Washington,
D.C.: GPO, 1977], tables L.87–97 and L.113–21.)

these enormous quantities of lumber rested on a host of new inventions,
methods of transportation, and forms of business organization, all at a new,
larger scale of operation. The lumber and forest products industry, like industry everywhere in the United States, was entering a new phase of vigorous expansion in an era of industrial capitalism.

Many of the technological developments affecting mechanization, transportation, and business organization have been outlined already in chapter 9,
but suffice it to say that steam power meant the concentration of industrial
activity, high and continuous output, and the beginnings of corporations
and monopolies; steel meant better and more efficient tools and machinery; the railroad meant reliable, fast, and more flexible transportation; and
all these meant increasing specialization of activity, concern for efficiency,
cutthroat competition, and the mass production of a standardized manufactured end product of known quality. The factory had moved into the
forest, where the systematic cutting of large areas replaced the cutting of
individual trees, and the large-scale ownership of standing timber allowed
monopolistic exploitation to take place. The old scale and style of cutting
was swept away; the only significant borrowing of a past technology was
the use of river transportation, now boosted by the development of the log
drive and by tugboat rafting on the continental rivers.

The vast sweep, complexity, and rapid changes of the American lumber
story are difficult to encapsulate in a few words, but a number of points can

be made. First, lumber was so essential to life in the United States during the nineteenth century that nothing was allowed to stand in the way of its acquisition. If stands ran out in one place, or were better and cheaper to acquire, transport, and market in another, the timber industry moved on. The continental shifts were enormous. By 1860 the supremacy of lumber production had passed from New York and New England to the Great Lakes states. Although New York, Pennsylvania, and New England were still important producers, Michigan, Wisconsin, and Minnesota now cut greater volumes and values of timber. Lumbering in the South began to achieve prominence by 1890 and carried on well into the twentieth century. And the Pacific Northwest was beginning to rank high in national production by 1900, when the Great Lakes states were in decline.

Second, each locality/phase of lumber production (they were almost one and the same thing) had its own distinctive characteristics (see fig. 10.9)— never exclusively so as there was overlap, but distinctive enough if only because of factors of terrain, climate, and technology. Each diagram in figure 10.9 is a composite picture drawn from many accounts of the salient features of each phase. The first (fig. 10.9A) was characteristic of New England, New York, and the early Great Lakes states and was common during the first half of the nineteenth century. Although the log drive dominated, it was later augmented by transport over ice roads. The second (fig. 10.9B) was common in the later Great Lakes states forest exploitation from about 1850 to 1880 and the early years of the southern logging industry. The advent of the railroad during the 1860s caused a shift in sawmill sites to the intersections of mainline track and major river. Specialized lumber camps and lumber towns emerged to house the workers and their families. The third phase (fig. 10.9C) straddled the years 1880–1920 and was especially characteristic of the nonfreezing South. The light logging railroads were laid and relaid to ensure maximum exploitation of the stand, and in time spur lines were constructed from the main lines to overcome the break of gauge and integrate mills in order to speed up and maximize production. The fourth stage (fig 10.9D), which occurred after 1920 and was characteristic of the Pacific Northwest. There was an emphasis on road haulage and high-wire logging that took the logs across intervening forest or broken terrain. Subsequently it became the norm everywhere.

During the final decades of the century the lumber industry was exploitative in the worst sense of the word, and the Great Lakes states, and later the South, where industrial methods of logging and transportation saw their first and fullest flowering, were the epitome of that plundering. It was the first time that the world had seen the deleterious environmental effects produced when steam, steel, and business enterprise combined with capital,

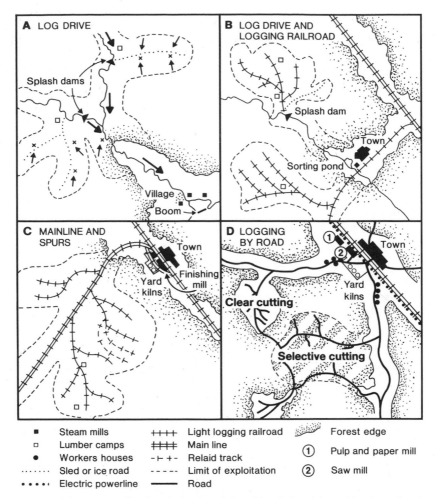

Figure 10.9 Four stages of lumber production. *A,* Log drive; *B,* Log drive and logging railroad; *C,* Main line and spurs of the logging railroad; and *D,* Logging by road. (Source: M. Williams, "The Clearing of the Forests," in *The Making of the American Landscape,* ed. M. P. Conzen [London: Unwin Hyman, 1990], 146–68.)

rising affluence, and increased demand. It was an experience that, regrettably, was going to be repeated in one form or another in many other forests of the world in the future.

The heady boom of cutting the stands of the much-prized white pine in the Great Lakes states doubled lumber production from about 4 billion bf (9.4 million m³) annually in 1870 to over 9 billion bf (21.3 million m³) in 1890, only to fall from then on to a mere 1 billion bf (2.4 million m³) by 1920. Cutting left behind a landscape of depletion and devastation. Although many sawmills turned to other types of wood, especially hemlock and hard-woods, dozens of once-flourishing settlements went into decline and even disappeared. Some of the more enterprising, like Eau Claire, Oshkosh, and La Crosse in Wisconsin or Grand Rapids in Michigan, managed to diversify into manufacturing, and a whole array of wood-using industries such as door, blind, sash, and furniture making sprung up using the new industrial woodworking machinery. But many more were like Cheboygan and Alpena in Michigan, which became ghosts of their former selves. During the heyday of the cutting boom in 1886, Cheboygan had been a bustling town of over 6,000 inhabitants, 16 mills, and numerous woodworking industries, but by 1916 there were only two mills left and the number of employees in the indus-try had fallen to barely 1,000. Alpena suffered similarly. Whereas the town had seemed once to be "made of saw dust," now it scratched for a living:

> Mills that formerly selected only the stoutest pine trunk now welcome the slender log, the crooked log, the rotten log, and the sunken log fished up from the river bottom. In place of beams for the western railway bridge or huge rafters for the Gothic church, Alpena busily turns out planks, shingles, spools, pail handles, veneering, and the wooden peg for furniture. It also makes manila paper out of hemlock pulp. It brings hemlock bark to its tan-nery. It combs its brains for inventions to utilize by-products, as does the Chicago pork-packer.[26]

There were two other consequences of excessive logging. First, a thick carpet of combustible slash waste remained on the forest floor after the cut-out-and-get-out exploitation that made the forest highly susceptible to fire. The Peshtigo fire of 1871 in northeast Wisconsin devastated over 50 mi^2 and killed at least 1,500 people, and the Michigan fire of the same year consumed over 4,000 mi^2 of prime pine timber. In 1894 the great Hinkeley fire in Minnesota claimed 418 lives, and so it went on almost annually, and with increasing frequency.

Second, there were the wastes of the aptly named cutover areas, stretch-ing for over 600 mi across the middle and northern parts of the three Great Lakes states, from the Red River in Minnesota in the west to Lake Huron in the east, and probably totaling over 50 million acres (20.2 million ha) by the end of the century. Unlike the hardwood forests of the South, much of which had been taken up for agriculture once cleared, these lands were cli-matically and agriculturally marginal. Cutting had been careless; the ground was strewn with debris and massive stumps remained, often cut many feet above the ground. The soil was mainly poor glacial outwash sands and gravels, and the climate averaged only 100–130 frost-free days, a period much too short for growing corn but just sufficient for grass and hay. Most of the cutover area was simply too far north for successful agriculture.

But the timber companies wanted to wring the last penny out of the land and, moreover, wanted to get rid of it because it was liable to state taxes. It could be abandoned, of course, but that threw an intolerable burden on surrounding taxpaying areas. The railway companies wanted settlement because new farms would increase revenues, and state governments, imbued with concepts of progress and improvement, were not prepared to allow the northern portions of their states to become a wilderness with the passing of the lumber industry. Consequently, all three advertised the virtues of the cutover areas widely in America and Europe, particularly in Scandinavia. The literature was boosterish; it sidestepped the difficulties of the once-forested environment and promoted an image of a productive rural paradise. Thousands of unsuspecting immigrants came and struggled to make a living. There was a high rate of failure, and the survivors hung on to lead a wretched life, trying to eke out an existence. The cutover areas were (and still are in places) dotted with derelict fences and sagging, unpainted farmhouses, some mere tar-paper shacks. In the deserted fields occasionally one still sees a lilac tree or a heap of stones where a chimney once stood, both markers of an abandoned homestead, the whole scene a mute and melancholy testimony to abandoned hopes in the former forested lands. The really hard sell occurred just before World War I, and it was only after the mid-1930s that efforts were made to return the land to the crop it grew best—trees.

When the output of the Great Lakes states began to decline after 1880, the wave of forest exploitation moved south to the extensive evergreen longleaf, slash, and loblolly pine forests of Georgia, Alabama, Mississippi, Louisiana, and eastern Texas. Here exploitation was possibly even more ruthless and thorough, and it was almost entirely railroad focused. Main-line railroads stretched across the continental United States from southern ports to northern markets, with many spur lines into the pine forests of 40 or 50 mi in length. Mill sites would be preselected at 3- to 5-mi intervals along the spur lines, the sawmills sometimes being built ahead of the railways (the equipment trundled in by mule) so that a stock of lumber was immediately ready for market once the connection was made. The mills themselves were generally larger than those in the Great Lakes states and exclusively steam powered. Timber haulage was mechanized, usually by massive steam-operated skidders that ran on railway tracks. These had long grappling arms and derricks from which steel cables were run out into the surrounding forest and attached to logs, which were then dragged to the trackside and hoisted onto the trucks. As the skidders pulled in the logs in a circle around them, so they ripped out all the young growth that might have allowed the forest to regenerate and scraped the thin soil bare. In one parish in Louisiana the cutover areas

> stretched wearily away from the rusting rails of the mainline track. Those nearest the mill, which had been cut last or had been gone over a second time during the recent era of high prices, were desolate indeed. No living pine tree remained on acre after acre. The extraordinary demand for every stick of timber . . . the pitiless system of taxing annually every board foot in standing trees, and the sweep of slash fires had done their work.

This description, said Reginald Forbes, was not "sensational" but "commonplace." Indeed, for some of those foresters and lumbermen who fought in the trenches in the Flanders during World War I, the desolation of the shell-shattered and denuded landscape had a familiar look—it reminded them of the cutover areas back home in the South.[27]

Just as the big lumber monopolies owned the land and the trees—in fact whole counties—so they owned the towns, and their inhabitants too. There were hundreds of little company towns with rows of identical houses or shacks with a central commissary, the sole, company-operated store, where the employees bought their food and goods at inflated prices, by coupons paid in lieu of wages. Most laborers were either ex-slaves or poor whites coming off low-income farms. No all-male lumberjack camps with the aura of rugged and heroic individualism existed in the South. Lumber settlements were populated instead by a docile labor force of family men in small houses and small towns who could not protest about their isolation and exploitation. The description of them as a new form of "feudal" town was apt; they were mere cogs in the new machinery of industrial lumbering. With important social differences—and usually without the river—the characteristic landscape of lumber exploitation in the South conformed to the generalized pattern depicted in figure 10.9C.

When the forest was stripped bare, the lumber companies moved their mills and a few of their key workers and let the town die. The mills, once the "pulsing hearts" of the settlements, sagged at their foundations while the railroads rusted from disuse. In the towns, grass began "to grow from the middle of every street and broken window lights bespoke deserted homes." The mill had "sawed out."[28] What the skidders had not ripped out, wildfires in the slash debris finished off. By 1907 it was said that an astounding 79 million acres (32 million ha) were left as cutover in the South, of which a mere fifth was being restocked with trees. In 1920 the figure was revised downward to 55.4 million acres (29.5 million ha), of which just over one-half was restocked. Whatever the truth, however, one thing is certain: as in the Great Lakes states forests, logging had left a vast area of derelict land through the forests of the South. Much of the cutover areas was going to be invaded naturally by scrub oak of little commercial value; rapacious logging had led to a permanent pauperization of the forest.

The abundant detail of the North American deforestation is without parallel. At the most conservative estimate, over 350 million acres (142 million ha) of forest were cleared for agriculture and another 20 million acres (approximately 8 million ha) for industry, communications, mining, and urban sprawl. The effects of lumbering were immense. In all, by 1900 the destruction must have eliminated one-half of the original forest cover of the country, which should give us pause when we condemn the present deforestation of the tropical world. Yet, while much was lost, much was gained. Some of the first stirrings of the conservation movement as we know it in the Western world today began in the U.S. forests just prior to and just after the Civil War. And there is no doubt that the widespread availability and abundance of wood and land were the mainsprings of the country's agricultural supremacy, industrial might, and high standard of living that first became evident during the second half of the nineteenth century. Simply, without its wood, the United States would not be the country it is today.

THE PACIFIC RIM: COMPLEXITY AND CONTRAST

In contrast to the temperate lands around the Atlantic, which were culturally and economically linked and had a largely similar deforestation experience, the experience of the temperate lands of the Pacific was different and disparate. Australia and New Zealand were soon to be in the throes of pioneering agricultural settlement in the forest, similar in kind to that in North America but vastly different in scale. Japan had entered an era of purposeful regulation, silviculture, and reforestation that was unprecedented anywhere in the world. China was more or less written off as a hopeless case of extreme deforestation for which there seemed neither remedy nor promise. The northwest Pacific coast of North America, however, was gearing up to be one of the great global exporters of timber, supplementing the resource deficiencies of territories elsewhere around the Pacific. It was a complex story.

Japan

In Japan the excesses of town and monument building, illegal cutting, and cultivation on steep slopes were evident before the end of the seventeenth century. The great stands of virgin timber had gone, disputes over forest use were common, flooding and sedimentation of the cultivable lowlands were causing alarm, the quality of timber had deteriorated, and scarcity was widespread. It was remarkable that these multiple problems were recognized so early by the shogunate and the vassal military lords, or *daimyō*, and that both took positive measures to control and alter forest use. It is difficult to generalize about the remedial measures—the Tokugawa shogunate lasted for over 250 years and there were 250-odd *daimyō*—but in general one can say that the administration devised what Conrad Totman has called a "negative regimen," a comprehensive, if uncoordinated, body of regulations that in total constituted a complex and moderately effective system of rationing.[29] Administrative rules were evolved for both the protection of the forests and the safeguarding of products. Because the concept of land "ownership" did not exist, the emphasis was on "rights"; and those of the villagers and lords, and the forest domains in which exploitation could take place, were carefully delineated and codified. For example, regulations were devised to control the areas open to harvest, the number of days and number of workers who had access to the area, the size and type of tools to be used, the number of loads that could be produced, and the inspection of the movement of timber goods, of building size, and of timber to be used. Sumptuary regulations prohibited the use of certain prized woods such as *sugi* (*Cryptomeria japonica*), *hinoki* (*Chamaecyparis obtusa*), or Japanese cypress, except for specific items. Protection was extended to lowland basins, and the Office of Erosion Control was even created to supervise excessive cutting in the Kinai basin. In many ways the "negative regimen" solved nothing during an era of growing population, but it was an essential prelude to raising awareness and knowledge. Moreover, it "bought time" for the introduction of more effective policies of silviculture and the purposeful planting of trees to produce the "green archipelago" that Japan is today, rather than the ruined land that it might have been.

To understand this remarkable precocity in forest matters, we can dismiss explanations such as a national "love of nature" or Buddhist, Confucian, or Shinto sentiment for natural objects; the Japanese sensibility toward nature was always refined and delicate, but recreational and urban in orientation, and trees were considered crude and rural. And in any case, these religious values had not saved the forests of the pre-Edo era. Rather, the concerns of the restorers were intensely practical: forests helped supply raw materials, fuel, and fertilizer, concerns that were alleviated by the natural succession of deciduous trees, which replaced coniferous trees. Also, the connection between forest cover, run-off, and erosion and the stability of the lowland paddy rice seemed to be appreciated early. In all, a form of conservation ethic resulted. Additionally, for unknown reasons wheeled vehicles and crosscut saws were rarely permitted in forested areas; this constraining of technology probably helped preservation, as did the absence of sheep and goats. The overriding concerns of the Tokugawa administration to preserve peace and avoid foreign contacts focused attention on the resources to hand and prevented the introduction of alien, destabilizing technology. Therefore, it was a unique social and environmental situation in which a disciplined and literate society sorted out its priorities: people of all classes knew that resources were limited and that they simply had to make do with what they had. The fact that population increase stabilized after 1750 certainly took pressure off the forests, and the search for protein and resources shifted from the land to the ocean. As a result, the total demand for woodland actually decreased.

China

The contrast between China and neighboring Japan could not have been starker. Everything we know about that vast country (and it is precious little for this period) suggests the existence of an impoverished peasant society, subsisting in a deforested, denuded, and eroded landscape. For all western observers it was the example par excellence of a denuded landscape. Substantial timber reserves remained only in the coniferous forests of remote Manchuria and northwest Mongolia, and the evergreen broad-leaved forests of the hilly and remote subtropical and tropical south.

The primary cause of the denudation was, of course, agricultural clearing to feed a population that grew from about 300 million in the early eighteenth century to reach 430 million by 1850 and 500 million by 1900. In the northern and central lowlands, rice cultivation leveled the land; in the more mountainous south, the forested uplands were colonized by renewed bursts of migration from the overcrowded lowlands of Hunan and Szechwan during the eighteenth century. As in the case of the Hunan colonization, the New World crops of maize and of sweet and Irish potatoes were suited to and productive in these marginal highland environments where the previous crop mix had not been. It was now an old story: slash-and-burn cultivation stripped the hillsides. The sequence was outlined graphically during the early nineteenth century by a local official:

> The mountain people fell trees and cultivate in the shade of the dead trees. The fertility of the soil will double the grain for one or two years. After the fourth of fifth year, the soil is already gouged and slack, the mountain is steep and the fierce water of the sudden rains in summer and autumn leave only stone "bones" everywhere. They must again seek land to cultivate. The

original land, left vacant, gradually grows grasses, shrubs rot and become mud, or are felled and burned to ash; only then can it be tilled again. One cannot rely on the old forests for a steady living but must move on to seek one's livelihood; thus the mountain people cannot but wander.

These mobile "shed" or "shack" people, as they were quite accurately known, disrupted the stability of the land as surely as they disrupted the stability of existing society.[30]

The severity of deforestation was manifest in two other ways, which added greatly to the hardship of peasant life. First, soil erosion and swollen, silt-laden rivers plagued lowland agricultural productivity; and second, the scarcity of fuel was a constant worry, particularly in the cold north of the country. These problems caused a vicious downward spiral in which the grubbing-up of every piece of combustible material removed the last remnants of vegetation that held the soil together and/or helped to manure it. China's fuelwood crisis had lasted since at least 1400 and showed no signs of abating. The old and the very young, in particular, were sent out to scour the village surrounds for leaves, roots, and stalks and to beat the dried leaves off the trees until not one piece of combustible matter remained. The alternative was to economize on domestic heating and go without hot meals, as many did, with grim consequences for health and life.

The overwhelmingly Confucian ethos had not stemmed deforestation in China any more than it had in pre-Edo Japan, except for the vicinity of a few temples and sacred sites. In fact it may have been a contributory cause; the elite of the Ming and Ching dynasties were drawn largely from the cultured Confucian scholars of the country who found aesthetic pleasure in the temples and manicured gardens that they were fortunate enough to experience but left the mundane problems of administration to lower-ranking officials who had little or no vision or experience to combat the land pressures created by unremitting population growth. Whatever the reason, China's deforestation experience was the very antithesis of neighboring Japan's, and there was a dire scarcity of timber everywhere.

Australia and New Zealand

Australia's dense eucalypt forests are located in the humid areas in the extreme southern and eastern portions of the continent. As rainfall decreases inland, large trees give way to open savanna forest, which in turn merge into scrubby trees, often the distinctive mallee vegetation—multiple-stemmed, drought-resistant eucalypts with massive lignotuber roots. Beyond that, yet again, lay mulga scrub and grassland and, finally, stony and sandy deserts. In

Plate 10.8 A selector's homestead cleared out of the dense eucalypt forests of Victoria. (From *The Illustrated Handbook of Victoria, Australia Prepared for the Colonial and Indian Exhibition, London,* 1886.)

round figures, between 238 and 244 million ha, or a quarter of the continent, was tree covered, of which only about 30 million ha (3–4 percent) could be considered forest in the commonly accepted sense of the word and, therefore, suitable for timber exploitation. Compared to other continents, Australia had no extensive green mantle to deforest. The rest was scrubby low forest and woodland. That these forested areas were also the areas suitable for agricultural settlement meant their widespread destruction as pioneer farmers and timber-getters during the late eighteenth and most of the nineteenth century cut down trees indiscriminately to cater for immediate needs (plates 10.8, 10.9). Simply, Australia was no different than other new countries.

Just as in other areas of the world information on agricultural clearing is tantalizingly slight. There is no easy way to get an overall view of clearing, as no comprehensive statistical series exists. One attempt has been a study of land-cover modification. Starting with generalized maps of natural vegetation and of land cover, changes between the two were calculated for nearly 900 statistical areas using LANDSAT (land surveillance satellite) images (fig. 10.10). Although the picture confirms in a general way what we know intuitively, the data and method have limitations, particularly the

Plate 10.9 Pastures of the future. These once mighty forests of the Gippsland region in Victoria were reduced to dairy cow pastures. (From *The Illustrated Handbook of Victoria, Australia Prepared for the Colonial and Indian Exhibition, London,* 1886.)

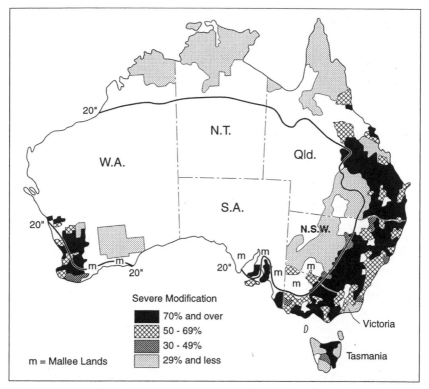

Figure 10.10 Australia: percentage of vegetation severely modified since 1780, by rural local government area. (Source: K. F. Wells, N. H. Wood, and P. Laut, *Loss of Forests and Woodland in Australia: A Summary by State Based on Local Government Areas,* CSIRO Technical Memorandum 84/4 [Canberra: CSIRO, Institute of Resources, Division of Water and Land Resources 1984], foldout map and table.)

interpretation of this early satellite imagery and the generalized nature of the evidence. For example, the mallee scrub woodlands of Western Australia, South Australia, northwest Victoria, and western New South Wales are excluded because of their sparse, intermittent, and generally low level of forest, but we know that vast areas of these woodlands were cleared for wheat growing. This is acknowledged, and it is thought that South and Western Australia are greatly underrepresented. Nonetheless, the overall conclusion is that 87.6 million ha were cleared or "modified" (table 10.6), with the greatest changes occurring in the tall and medium-height forest (46–58 percent affected), and less drastic changes occurring in the woodlands and tall scrubland (29–31 percent). One cannot be more precise than that.

Clearing was an especially physically demanding task because of the dominance of hardwoods, the constant regeneration of suckers, and the

Table 10.6 Australia: minimum area of vegetation severely modified since 1780, by state/territory (in millions of ha)

State/Territory	Modified	Original wooded	% Modified
New South Wales	30.7	61.5	50
Victoria	11.3	16.3	69
Queensland	29.6	83.8	35
South Australia	2.3	5.6	41
Western Australia	11.7	36.7	32
Tasmania	2.0	5.3	37
Northern Territory	0.01	34.4	. . .
Australian Capital Territory	0.1	0.2	60
Total	87.6	243.9	36

Source: K. F. Wells, N. H. Wood, and P. Laut, *Loss of Forests and Woodland in Australia: A Summary by State Based on Local Government Areas,* CSIRO Technical Memorandum 84/4 (Canberra: CSIRO, Institute of Resources, Division of Water and Land Resources 1984), foldout map and table.

ability of eucalypts to regenerate after even severe fire. Consequently, ring-barking followed by the firing of the deadened trees was common, and stumps were left in the ground, either to rot or to be grubbed out when time was available. In the more open savanna forests, ringbarking was resorted to exclusively. After 1875 clearing was brutal and complete in the high-rainfall areas containing rain forest and wet sclerophyll forest along the coasts of Queensland, New South Wales, Victoria, and Western Australia and in the dry sclerophyll of the Western District of Victoria, the southeast of South Australia, and much of Western Australia south of Perth. The "Big Scrub" astride the New South Wales–Queensland border was a semitropical rain forest of well over 4 million ha, which was described when first encountered as "all but impenetrable jungle, a lush profusion of vegetable growth." But between 1880 and 1910, over 2.8 million ha of forest had been cleared for dairying, sugarcane growing, and lumber. At about the same time, an equally large area in the Strzlecki and Otway ranges in Gippsland, Victoria (plate 10.9) was also cleared for dairying. Everything was burned on the spot and nothing disposed of profitably because no transportation links had been developed to markets. The equivalent of the American woodlot was never seen. "Here the axe is set to every tree, and often not a shrub is left for shelter or cover."[31]

The expansion of dairying and the destruction of the forest in both Victoria and New South Wales–Queensland had much to do with butter making, which flourished after the perfection of the refrigerator (1880), the cream separator (1883), and the Babcock milk-testing machine (1892), together with the railways that eventually opened up these regions. Increasingly, the technological advances in one sphere of activity had repercussions in others, so that, for example, a direct connection existed between the butter that British families spread on their toast for breakfast and the destruction of the great trees of the forests of the Otway and Strzlecki ranges, via the refrigerated holds of the fast steamships that brought the previously perishable goods from one part of the empire to another.

One might have thought that the massive eucalypt trees in the pastoral savanna lands would have been spared for shade and even fodder during times of drought and that even the popular folk idea that trees encouraged rainfall would have favored their retention. But the opposite idea gained ground: that tree destruction was the best and cheapest way of promoting good grass growth, with devastating consequences for millions of acres of forests. While it is true that trees competed successfully with grass during times of moisture stress, the enthusiasm of the advocates of the "murderous practice of ringbarking" went so far as to suggest that the destruction of the forests improved the flow of streams.[32] It was for actions like this that Australians came to have the unenviable reputation of being mindless tree hackers.

The radically different character of the mallee scrubland throughout much of South Australia, northwest Victoria, southwest Western Australia, southwestern New South Wales, and inland areas of Western Australia demanded a different method of clearing. Even if the many stems were axed down, the massive lignotuber root just below the surface remained fully alive and ready to sprout a thicket of saplings the next spring. Technological innovations were developed in South Australia that facilitated the clearing and cultivation of these scrubland forests. In 1866 Joseph Mullens, a settler on the plains north of Adelaide, devised, first, a heavy horse-drawn rake-cum-harrow, then later, a primitive roller, to knock down the slender scrub stems prior to burning and sowing in the ashes. Then in 1875 J. B. Smith, a settler from Yorke Peninsula, invented the stump-jump plow, whose hinged and weighted shares kicked up harmlessly over the rocks and mallee roots of the newly cleared land. These two folk inventions were the key to the opening up of the lightly wooded areas of the continent, from the mallee lands of the south to the similar brigalow scrubs of southern Queensland. From 1870 onward, many millions of hectares were cleared and cultivated throughout the southeast states. Horse-drawn rollers could clear up to 16 ha a day, which by the next century could be achieved every hour when a heavy chain linked between two crawler tractors was dragged across the ground, knocking down all before it.

The linkage between technology, food supply, global markets, and forest clearing already noted in the clearing of the Gippsland ranges of Victoria was even more evident with the development of dairying and pastoralism in remote New Zealand, probably the farthest corner of the habitable globe from Europe. Between 1840 and 1900 the remaining forest cover of that country was reduced from just under a half to about 25 percent, most of that occurring during the last decade of the century, when 36,000 km², or approximately 14 percent of the entire country, was cleared in order to establish a pastoral economy of pioneer family farms. The products of these New Zealand pastures were mutton, butter, and cheese, which became a byword of quality in England. The world was shrinking as surely as were its forests.

In these fledgling pioneer societies of only a few million—which took over continents greater in size than the United States—huge quantities of timber were consumed for fencing, railways, smelting, and fuelwood. Toward the end of the century, especially after the boom of the Victoria Gold Rush of 1850, there was not enough millable wood for housing and general construction. This had happened during the short space of barely 70 years. In later years the cheap and abundant timber of North America increasingly filled the shortfall of the countries around the Pacific basin. With the stimulus of railroad construction, the demand for Californian termite-resistant redwood for ties complemented the demand for Oregon pine for general construction. In addition to Australia, such places as China, Hawaii, and even Peru and Ecuador proved to be lucrative markets for the enterprising Pacific Coast lumber entrepreneurs. Perhaps only New Zealand was an exception with its own flourishing timber industry. Now, the Pacific basin, like the Atlantic basin, was fully enmeshed in the global timber trade.

Chapter 11

Clearing in the Tropical World, 1750–1920

Nothing was heard but groaning, cracking, crunching, and splintering . . .
it appeared as though the whole of the forest-world about me was tumbling
to pieces.
—J. CAPPER, "Old Ceylon" (1878)

BY ABOUT 1700, the temperate and tropical worlds were roughly evenly matched in terms of population totals and hectares of land in cultivation. The temperate world (including Japan and China) contained 324 million people and had 137 million ha in cultivation; the tropical world, 355 million people and 128 million ha in cultivation. But the huge changes in Europe, and its expansion overseas, dramatically changed that rough parity. By 1850 the population of the temperate world was about half as much again as that of the tropical world (775 million compared with 485 million) and the area of cultivated land was almost exactly double—357 million ha compared with 180 million ha (compare tables 10.1 and 11.1). By the opening years of the twentieth century, the population gap was virtually unchanged, but the difference in the area of cultivation shifted even more decisively in favor of the temperate world: 618 million compared with 295 million ha.

Most of the expansion was at the expense of the original biomes. Between 1700 and 1920 a total of 537 million ha of forest disappeared under cropland—315 million ha in temperate areas (greater if the evidence of the "land improved" in forested counties in the United States is taken into account), and 222 million ha in the tropical areas. In the grasslands, 146 million ha were changed into cropland in the temperate world, whereas in the tropical world a staggering 56-million-ha net of forest was so permanently damaged by burning, grazing, and shifting cultivation that it was transformed into grassland, thus adding to the net area of this biome in the tropics.

Table 11.1 Cropland and land-cover change (in millions of ha), tropical world, 1700, 1850, and 1920

	Cropland			Cropland Change		Forest Change		Grassland Change	
	1700	1850	1920	1700– 1850	1850– 1920	1700– 1850	1850– 1920	1700– 1850	1850– 1920
Tropical Africa	44	57	88	13	31	−22	−61	9	30
North Africa and Middle East	20	27	43	7	16	−4	−7	−4	−7
South Asia	53	71	98	18	27	−18	−28	0	1
Southeast Asia	4	7	21	3	14	−1	−5	−2	−9
Latin America	7	18	45	11	27	−25	−51	13	25
Tropical Total	128	180	295	52	115	−70	−152	16	40

Source: After J. F. Richards, "Land Transformation," in *The Earth as Transformed by Human Action*, ed. B. L. Turner II et al. (Cambridge: Cambridge University Press, 1990), 164.
Note: South Asia = Afghanistan, Bangladesh, Bhutan, Myanmar, India, Nepal, Pakistan, and Sri Lanka; Southeast Asia = Brunei, Cambodia, East Timor, Indonesia, Laos, Malaysia, Philippines, Thailand, and Vietnam. The data are derived from *World Resources Review, 1987* (New York: World Resources Institute, 1987).

Tropical forest destruction stemmed from two broadly different sets of driving forces and processes of change: first, the expansion of indigenous agriculture, which needed to support the addition of approximately 300–400 million people during these 170 years; and second, the impact of European colonialism and capitalist commercialization. Inevitably this division is blurred at the edges, as when indigenous overlords extracted tribute from the peasants or when colonial "modernization" seemed to unleash a fury of entrepreneurial activity in previously subsistence peasant societies, but it is a useful distinction.

INDIGENOUS USE OF THE FOREST

Nearly all the world's tropical forests were inhabited from earliest times and were being transformed as shifting cultivators and peasant agriculturalists changed them to cropland and grassland, by chopping, cropping, burning, and grazing. And yet the idea has grown that the forests were barely touched before the coming of the exploitative European invaders because the native peoples were "ecologically noble savages" who lived in harmony and balance with their surroundings. Precontact America, in particular, has been perceived as "a place as close to an ecological paradise as humans are likely to come."[1] But this earthly paradise evaporates when confronted with the evidence of the social complexity, antiquity, and obvious manipulation of the environment in the Old World, especially Asia. Any picture of an ecological, precolonial, precapitalist golden age of common property rights, sustainable resource use, and a happy peasantry is overdrawn, hopelessly romantic, and barely plausible. If sustainable societies existed, then they depended on very low population densities, abundance of land, and little or no involvement in a market economy, local or regional, all of which were rare.

Shifting Agriculture

The indigenous impacts in the tropics came mainly through the widespread use of burning to clear land for agriculture, improved grazing for domestic stock or attracting of game, and driving away predatory animals and pests. But clearing caused problems. Leaching, iron pan formation, erosion, and weed infestation all took their toll on soil fertility; therefore, cultivators typically shifted from place to place raising crops in temporary clearings. With only minor variations this system existed throughout the tropical world. In Malaysia and Indonesia it was called *ladang;* in Central America, *milpa;* in parts of Africa, *chitemene;* in India, *kumri;* and in Sri Lanka, *chena.* Only the largest trees were spared, or chopped high up where their girth was less; the rest were felled or deadened, with the debris burned during the dry season and the land cultivated for one, two, or maybe four years at most before being abandoned.

Only the crops were different in different parts of the world. In central and northern Latin America maize and beans were common; in Brazil, manioc; in the Southeast Asian realm, upland rice; in Africa, small grains usually called "millet" or sorghum—but even these differences were being obliterated by crop exchanges after the eighteenth century. For example, maize, manioc, sweet potatoes, pineapples, and tobacco came from the Americas to Africa and Asia, and conversely sugarcane and rice quickly established themselves in the Americas. If burning was too frequent and the "forest fallow" reduced, then the land quickly became overgrown with tough perennial grass that inhibited further cultivation.

There are many excellent contemporary accounts of this agricultural method, especially in Asia, but however much they varied, the observers all found the flames of the final month-long blaze, wasteful, astounding, yet sometimes exciting as they displayed "a scene of most majestic beauty, which certainly equals, and probably surpasses, the burning of the grass of the plains of North America."[2] Unlike Asia, there appears to be no early recognition or description of the shifting, or *milpa,* system in Central and South America until the writing of Orator Fuller Cook in the early part of the twentieth century. The Indians were cutting and burning vast areas of forest, which frequently got out of hand. "At night in the farm clearing season," he wrote, "the burning mountain slopes gleam with lines of light like the streets of distant cities. By day the sky is darkened and the air is heavy with smoke." *Milpa* agriculture had "long been at work," so that like tropical forests everywhere, those of Central and Latin America were "far from [being in] a virgin state" and bore the marks of a long history of clearing and its many stages of regrowth.[3]

Almost without exception, the European sensibility toward nature revolted at the unequal exchange of magnificent trees for a small plot of ground soon to be abandoned. Shifting agriculture seemed to be not only primitive, backward, inefficient, and unproductive but also wasteful and destructive to the point of irrationality. Marsden writing in Sumatra in the 1780s lamented:

> I could never behold this devastation without a strong sentiment of regret. Perhaps the prejudices of a classical education taught me to respect those aged trees, as the habitation or material frame of an order of sylvan deities, who were now deprived of existence, by the sacrilegious hand of a rude, undistinguished savage. But without having recourse to superstition, it is not difficult to account for such feelings, on the sight of a venerable wood, old as the soil it stood on, and beautiful beyond what pencil can describe, for the temporary use of the space it occupied. It appears a violation of nature in the exercise of too arbitrary right. . . . Trees whose amazing bulk, height, and straightness would excite the admiration of a traveler, compared to which the masts of men of war are diminutive, fall in the general ruin.[4]

The feeling that Europeans could make better use of the land was not just a matter of different cultural perceptions; it could have serious, practical ramifications. It was a potent rationale for justifying timber exploitation and the consequent dispossession of the indigenes from their native lands, particularly in the Americas and Africa. However, the gulf was not as great in Asia, where complex, structured societies and economies already existed. Nonetheless, even here two themes prevailed. First, European rule and organization were perceived to be beneficial, as they brought tranquility, stability, and prosperity—which was frequently true—and therefore agricultural expansion was encouraged. India was the supreme example of this. Second—and perhaps colored by the European experience of timber shortages—trees were thought to be more valuable than anything other than the most intensive cultivation. In India, this meant excluding the traditional users from the forests.

Permanent Agriculture

Clearing for permanent agriculture was largely of two kinds: the cultivation of irrigated land and the cultivation of groves and gardens for vegetables and spices, much of which entered into world trade. Both were of great antiquity, and very extensive. For example, Aceh Province in Sumatra and western Java had supplied the Chinese, Indian, and Muslim worlds with cinnamon, mace, cloves, nutmeg, and particularly pepper for literally thousands of years, and after about 1600 the trade with Europe grew to a great volume. During the nineteenth century, pepper production was about 20,000 tons, which required 57,000 ha of land. But because of pepper's exhausting nature, regular and widespread rotations were practiced, and more like 475,000 ha was cleared, which rarely reverted to forest but usually became grassland. If "new" forestland was not available, then the nutrient level in existing fields was kept high with animal and human excreta, vegetable "waste" from the village, and especially with green leaves from the forest.

Irrigated rice land depended on an elaborate system of water impoundment in either valley flats or terraced hill slopes. By the early eighteenth century it was certainly well developed in the lands of South and Southeast Asia, which abounded with dense populations in favored floodplains or where level land was limited, in spectacular rice terraces, as in Java, Sumatra, parts of south China, and the Bontoc in Luzon, which were miracles of peasant engineering. These permanent irrigated rice fields, or *sawah,* contrasted with the dry-land rice fields, or *ladang,* of the shifting agriculturists.

Often the two forms of cultivation were combined, producing mature and picturesque tropical landscapes. Village centers with intensive horticulture and groves were separated by bamboo hedges from surrounding permanent *sawah* cultivation, and beyond that lay the forest. But to achieve that landscape, devastation had been significant. By the mid-seventeenth century, the Javanese forest had been so reduced that it was no longer able to sustain elephants. Looking from the summit of the Dempo volcano in the Pelambang region of south Sumatra in 1885, Henry Forbes was amazed at the vast extent of treeless land. The forest of Sumatra, as in Java, was "rapidly disappearing," as each year saw "immense tracts felled for rice fields" and gardens wantonly consumed by "wilful fires." Trees of the rarest and finest timber were cut, half burned, and then left to rot, only to be replaced by worthless secondary forest and grasses. He lamented that "our children's children will search in vain in their travels for the old forest trees of which they have read in the books of their grandfathers." [5]

Contrary to accepted views, similar scenes of "busy" landscapes of villages and farms surrounded by fields and palm forests were seen along the sides of the rivers in West Africa, in present day southern Liberia, and farther east in Côte d'Ivoire, Ghana, and Togo.

The ownership and use of the forest resource by traditional societies was vastly more complex than is commonly supposed. From Madagascar to southern India the elite controlled the forest for economic gain and prestige. Small farmers, lessees, servants, laborers, or slaves were allowed occasional use but had only a tenuous grip on it. Everywhere the forest was under intense pressure, and equilibrium did not exist. For example, Uttra Kannada was one of the successor states to Mughal rule on the southwest coast of India and is now part of Karnatak State. During precolonial times the Muslim rulers imposed an autocratic state control on the forests to raise revenue. There was a complex hierarchy of rights and access similar to that of late medieval Europe in which usage was not necessarily accompanied by legal ownership but which, in time, implied de facto ownership, leading to greater commercialization of the resource. The sultans guarded their exclusive rights to teak (its strategic value for shipbuilding being understood), blackwood, sandalwood, and ebony; established teak plantations; and traded in wild and cultivated peppers and cinnamon. The indications are that Uttra Kannada was representative of many other areas, like Travancore, Cochin, and the Maratha states.

Across the plain, mainly Hindu village chiefs and headmen (*patel*) controlled the local agriculturalist proprietors and their tenants through taxation, land allocation, and access to the forest. The agriculturalists basically had free use of the forest for collecting firewood; cutting constructional wood for road building, housing, implements, and fencing; and grazing stock. They also chopped green fodder for cattle and for fertilizing the coastal rain-fed paddy rice fields and the irrigated, terraced paddies on the slopes. Tracts around the villages were freely burned and cleared in order to provide grazing for cattle and to create a buffer zone of safety from wild animals and fires in the forest. In some localities, forest use was controlled by village councils, which limited timber removals. These rights to fuel and green manure did not extend to the non-Hindu tribal shifting cultivators in the upland forested areas. These "tribals" had no rights and the uncontrolled fires associated with *kumri* were always feared.

In the north the forests fringing the Gangetic plain was being pushed back on all fronts; strips and corridors of woodland connecting them with the Himalayan foothills were disappearing under a fierce agricultural onslaught of permanently cultivated cropland. Tigers had disappeared, and similarly, elephants could only have roamed the forests of Gujarat in the seventeenth century where there were unbroken belts of forest extending to the east. But some time before 1760, the intervening ground had been cleared, barring the westward movement of elephants from central India. In places, clearing went too far and degradation ensued, with once-cultivated land being abandoned or subject to uncontrolled fires. For example, the country between Cuddapah and Hyderabad was littered with the ruins of villages and remnants of field divisions; in the view of naturalist Benjamin Heyne, it would "in a short time be a dessert [sic], in which no human being will be found except some straggling lombardies with their herds." He put the degradation down to the autocratic behavior of the Muslim overlords toward the vegetation: "Destruction is the delight of the pious Mussleman—he is the destroying angel." The signs of ecological deterioration were to be seen on every hand.[6]

The precolonial forest, then, was neither an untouched, pristine Eden nor a community resource shared equitably by all; nor was it used by everyone in the same way. As one Indian scholar has put it recently, "arable expansion, elite hunting and land colonization existed long before the Company Raj and the making of the British Empire." The imposition of colonial rule and the implementation of imperial programs of timber production, while vast in scope, were not the radical break seen by some but, rather, displayed "broad continuities in the policies adopted by Indian rulers and their British successors."[7]

Grazing and Burning

Our knowledge of the impact of the first farmers (chap. 3) should leave one in no doubt about the ability of humans to convert forests to grassland, and the transformation of 56 million ha of forest to grassland in the tropical world between 1750 and 1900 is one of the striking features of global land-cover change. Of that total area of grassland about 54 percent was in Africa, 45 percent in Latin America, and a mere fraction in Southeast Asia.

Many Western writers and observers affirmed confidently that the transformation was caused by the cumulative effect of deleterious native agricultural practices. Generally they were correct; however, the savanna–forest edge in semi-arid areas was not explained so easily. André Aubréville, who wrote extensively about forest retreat in francophone West Africa, was a leading advocate of the hypothesis that the savanna and grassland were an anthropogenic formation as centuries of short fallows, fire, and overgrazing reduced the forest to a sea of grass or even desert studded with remnant islands of fire-resistant trees, change being accelerated by periods of climatic deterioration.[8] However, although he realized that this could not be proved historically, he could not see how else the degraded forests had come about. Many others argued along the same lines.

Many assumptions were built into this conventional wisdom that, among other things, some "baseline" vegetation exists against which modern change can be measured; that there was little change before circa 1900; that the climate has been deteriorating progressively; and that forest clearance has been partly responsible for that. But much of this reasoning is flawed. The processes were far more complex and have not been all one way; much new forest has been created; and forest composition is the result of active management of particular trees. In addition, there has been regeneration of old fields back to forest after the depopulation consequent on the slave trade over centuries.

A similar story of exaggeration and preconceived assumption leading to a dominant discourse is true of Madagascar. The island is held up as an example of rampant deforestation and ecological mayhem through erosion. Leading French botanists in the 1920s, drawing on remnants of fossils (particularly of pygmy hippopotamuses and *Aepyornis*, a large, moalike flightless bird), concluded that the whole island had once been 90 percent forested, rather than approximately 30 percent. Similarly, these botanists suggested that the grassland was a result of repeated burning of forestland for cattle grazing, and the spectacular gully erosion was the outcome of this misuse, rather than the natural phenomena they are. This is not to deny that deforestation occurred with logging after colonization in 1893. Of the 58 million ha of the island, by 1920 about 20 percent remained in primary forest, and by 1949 it was 8.6 percent; 10.3 percent was in *savoka*, second-growth bracken fern with bamboos; and the rest was in grass and savanna. Consequently, the Malagasy were not the ecological vandals as commonly portrayed but quite careful land managers who treasured the forest. What was traditionally referred to as "the robe of the ancestors" was not the hopelessly tattered garment that it was popularly described as being, though there were some big holes and tears in it.[9]

In contrast, the ample rainfall of the tropical countries of Southeast Asia ensured that grassland created as a consequence of deforestation did not degenerate into semidesert but was often utilized productively (table 11.1). In fact, overall, grassland declined at the expense of cropland. For example, in Sumatra most areas of *lalang* (*Imperata* grass) became productive rubber and tobacco plantations.

But South and Southeast Asia were a mere pinprick compared with Latin America where the *campo cerrado* (literally, "closed field") or simply *cerrado,* covers an enormous area of interior Brazil and the drier northeast coast—from near the mouth of the Amazon as far west as the Tocatins River. The implication is that large parts of its margins were once forest. But how much is manmade or natural, aided perhaps by climatic changes, is not entirely clear. The longevity of human occupation is enough to have produced these changes, especially as active European involvement in this region dates from as early as 1500. The Portuguese grew sugarcane along the coast and ran cattle inland and, uniquely, intermarried rapidly with the native Indian population, thereby often altering traditional Indian ways. The mixed mestizo population and the introduction of iron axes and machetes meant that traditional swidden cultivation was intensified, many fold. In addition, pigs and cattle added a dimension to forest destruction that had been absent before. The forest did not regenerate easily, and any open ground was colonized by exotic grasses, ferns, and weeds.

CAPITALIST PENETRATION: THE PASSAGE TO INDIA, 1750–1850

European capitalist exploitation and colonial expansion in the forests of the tropical world after 1750 had many motives. One was the need to cater to the newly acquired European taste for exotic tropical products, such as cotton, tea, sugar, coffee, chocolate, and pepper. Plantations and trading stations sprang up on the Caribbean islands, and foothold settlements were established on the coasts of the tropical land masses (plates 11.1, 11.2).

Although mere pinpoints in the ocean, the islands served many important functions. They were strategic stepping-stones; they provided fresh water and provisions for passing ships; they acted as experimental precedents for a more penetrating settlement of the mainland masses; they conjured up engaging images as places of plenty and comfortable Edens or paradisiacal utopias; and because of their small size and confined area, the consequences of environmental deterioration were spotted early. Ascension, St. Helena, and Mauritius—together with the Cape of Good Hope, an enclave in a vast continent and an "island" in all but name—were the crucial stepping-stones on the passage to India before the Suez Canal was excavated in 1869.

In St. Helena, for example, deforestation, soil erosion, and stream-flow variation were all noted, and government officials tried to protect the remaining forest and corral destructive grazing animals but with little ultimate effect. Similar problems plagued the Dutch and French in Mauritius, and the island's diminishing role as a supplier of ship timber was another concern. The widely traveled Pierre Poivre, who was appointed Commissaire-Intendant of Mauritius in 1766, was convinced that deforestation caused a decline in rainfall and affected the incidence and spread of disease. He tried to establish reserves in order to protect plants and animals (all to no effect with the dodo) and also created the island's celebrated botanical garden. The changes on these tiny islands had at least three practical outcomes

Plate 11.1 Clearing Mahogany down the Rapids in Cuba. (From Chaloner & Fleming, *The Mahogany Tree . . .* [Liverpool: Rockriff & Sons, 1851].) (State Historical Society of Wisconsin, Madison.)

Plate 11.2 Cutting and Trucking Mahogany in Honduras. (From Chaloner & Fleming, *The Mahogany Tree . . .* [Liverpool: Rockriff & Sons, 1851].) (State Historical Society of Wisconsin, Madison.)

that were transported to India. First, Poivre's inferences about the role of tropical forests in influencing rainfall and runoff came to have a widespread currency. Second, the regulations for forest management and reservation devised for Mauritius were later applied to St. Helena and, eventually, became a model throughout the tropical world, especially India. Third, the famed botanical garden (the captured Eden in miniature) of Mauritius was emulated in St. Helena, and then Calcutta in 1788, and many other tropical locations in later years. Rare species were brought together, awareness of tree growth and management was stimulated, as was the value of exotic species for food and manufacturing. In short, the course of empire and the management of the Asian tropical forests owed much to the experience gained in these minuscule islands.[10]

But these islands were as nothing compared to the prize to be won in India, which must rank high as the best documented and most outstanding example of all tropical colonizations and deforestation episodes. By 1805 the hegemony of the imperial trading organization, the East India Company (EIC), straddled much of the peninsula, where the population stood at about 197 million in 1800. The EIC remained in control until the administration of the country was taken over by the British government in 1857. Increasingly, India's administration, survey and land revenue system, trade, transportation, and communications were fashioned and focused by its colonial overlords. The three presidencies based in Bengal (Calcutta), Bombay, and Madras and their surrounding territories were mini-empires in themselves. (For their extent, see fig. 11.3 below.) It was the largest, most populous (285 million people by 1901), most diverse colonial territory the world had ever seen.

Britain undoubtedly gained much economically from the control of this vast empire, but immense sums of capital were invested in Indian infrastructure, especially railways, communications, irrigation, and public health works. The exercise of imperial power was authoritarian and frequently repressive, but it was tempered by a concern for stability, prosperity, adequate food supplies, public health, and an intellectual curiosity at the cultures encountered. Consequently, political turmoil, predatory raiding, banditry, and endemic warfare were replaced by relative tranquility, political unity, and the stability of reasonably predictable administration and laws. Energies were diverted to more peaceful pursuits, and the entrepreneurial native society responded dynamically to the imposed political framework and stability, especially within agriculture, from which many benefited.

The creation of a market for land and a vast revenue system to support the public works and the British raj penetrated all levels of economic activity and social intercourse. An elite was created of professionals and employees of the colonial administrators, and the rural propertied classes probably benefited at the expense of the mass of producers. It is debatable as to what extent the peasants were caught up in a vicious circle of increased revenue demands, deeper debt, greater taxation, and therefore the need to clear more land in order to raise cash crops and increase productivity. The forest *did* come under pressure and was reduced in size; "it was," said Bertold Ribbentrop, "the watchword of the time to bring everywhere more extensive forest areas under cultivation," and what remained was reserved for timber production.[11] One thing is certain: the reliance of both the sedentary and the traditional shifting agricultural economies on the "free" bounty and safety valve of an abundant forest, in times of stress or need, was diminished by agricultural expansion and forest protection.

A distinctive aspect of the story of India deforestation was the activity and "networking" of some of the 800-odd influential and botanically well-versed surgeons of the EIC. Edward Balfour, Hugh Cleghorn, Alexander Gibson, John McClelland, William Roxburgh, and John Stocks were the intellectual offspring of the Scottish scientific, medical, and philosophical "enlightenment" and usually men of a radical social and political persuasion. They had respectability and permanence in the structure of the EIC and exercised enormous local influence. They knew about St. Helena and Mauritius as well as the works of Humboldt, Boussingault, Count Volney, and early American writers on the relationship between forests and climate.

Increasingly these surgeons became commentators on environmental and ecological matters in the subcontinent, and they kept up a relentless campaign to intervene and halt forest destruction, not only because it led to timber shortages but also because they thought that it affected climate, health, and food supply. So concerned and confident did they become that on several occasions they were prepared to bypass the conservative and lethargic EIC by appealing directly either to its directors or to scientific forums in Britain. In 1851 Hugh Cleghorn did just that, and reported to the British Association meeting in Ipswich about "the probable effects in an economical and physical point of view of the destruction of tropical forests." Despite the popular image of India as having "interminable jungles," much, said Cleghorn, had been cleared. His report, a catalog of acts of "indiscriminate havoc," shortage, and impending "deficiency" and "timber famine," became the basis for most subsequent colonial responses to problems of environmental degradation in India.[12] In order to understand how this startlingly contemporary concern came about more than 100 years before its modern counterparts, we need to look in turn at the twin questions of teak supplies and the relationship between deforestation and climate, food supply, and health.

The Teak Forests

Since at least the ninth century, Arab traders had prized the teak (*Tectona grandis*) timber of the Malabar coast for shipbuilding and general construction and had carried timber back to the Red Sea and the Gulfs of Persia and Kutch (chap. 5). Little teak was shipped to Britain because of the protectionism at home and high transportation costs, but vast amounts were used in the yards of the Parsi shipbuilders of Bombay and Calcutta who built ships for the British. Continued cutting of teak by local entrepreneurs and indigenous rulers deprived the EIC of valuable revenues and strategic materials, so in 1805 it reserved the teak forests for its own use and appointed the first "Conservator of Forests," legitimizing the takeover by citing the previous princely control as a precedent and justification. But by 1822, Sir Thomas Munro, governor of Madras, criticized the EIC severely for restricting "sensible" local trading and cutting with regulations that he thought "worthy only of the times of the Norman Forest Laws." Eventually, restrictions were relaxed, and deforestation accelerated. But clearing continued despite the restrictions, the use of elephants—the most versatile logging machine ever devised—being a major factor in the removal of large trees.[13]

When Cleghorn reported on forest destruction 29 years later, exports of teak were hovering between 11,000 and 18,000 tons per annum; the forests of Malabar had "fallen to a deplorable state"; the tribal *kumri* shifting agriculturalists had cleared the forests of Canara "to a most destructive extent"; and the teak of Mysore had "well nigh disappeared" as forest rentiers let out tracts for cutting to the highest bidder, and thousands of "floats" went downstream every year. Already by midcentury, the west coast forests as far east as the Ghats were said to be largely cut out of big trees, and the focus of cutting had shifted to the "glory of the Tenasserim forests" in Burma, annexed in 1826. But even there, "wanton destruction . . . by fire" and the chopping up of large timbers for ease of transport depreciated the value of the original trees to one-tenth of the amount they would have realized whole as ships' timbers. Undoubtedly this account was exaggerated in order to make a particular case for action, but there was a large measure of truth in it.[14]

Clearing, Rainfall, Famine, and Health

Concern about deforestation shifted from one of basic timber depletion to a more complex and sophisticated consideration of the relationship between forests, rainfall, and runoff, and the moral duties of food supply and health of India's rapidly growing population. Undoubtedly the famines of 1837–39 in the Doab and Bengal, and subsequent civil unrest, and the start of the Irish famine of 1846 gave this concern a political and practical urgency.

The EIC's interest in these environmental relationships was stimulated by the work of one of its surgeons, William Roxburgh, who collected meteorological data relating to the 1780 and 1789–93 famines in the coastal zone between Madras and Calcutta. He concluded that local drought seemed less significant for famine than tenurial uncertainty and the widespread clearing, of which there was abundant evidence.

Two other regions loomed large as areas of concern. One was the Doab, the broad strip of land (circa 80–120 km wide by 500 km long) between the Ganges and Jummna, from the Himalayas southeast to the confluence of the two rivers at Allahabad. Depletion of the forest cover of the southeastern section of the region beyond Delhi were of concern. In 1800 thick Dhak (*Butea frondosa*) forests were said to cover over half the land surface, in wide continuous belts on the low interfluvial ridges. Even in the agricultural areas, up to one-fifth of the land cover was still forest. But with direct colonial rule after annexation in 1805, high revenue assessments were imposed and the expansion of more internationally valuable cash crops, such as cotton, sugarcane, and indigo, was encouraged, often at the expense of subsistence food crops. A vicious circle arose of raised taxation, deepening debt, and expanding agriculture accompanied by forest destruction and deteriorating ecological conditions, all exacerbated by demographic pressures and increased economic activity with brick-making and general construction. The upshot was the almost complete annihilation of the forest in about 25 years (see figs. 11.1A–C and 11.2A–B). Salinization became common, water tables dropped, many wells were abandoned, drainage channels dried out or were silted by moving soil, and malaria spread. The drought of 1837–38 was the final blow to the area. Colonization and deforestation seemed to go hand in hand.

The other focus of concern was the forests of the Ghats and the plains of Canara to the west, spearheaded during the 1840s by Alexander Gibson, another of the EIC's surgeons and later director of the Bombay botanical gardens, and Blane, collector of taxes in Canara. Their report was a powerful statement about forest destruction and deteriorating climate, calculated to cause alarm and prompt action. In Canara, "within thirty or forty years the forests had receded from the coast to within a few miles of the Ghats," and large areas of country that were known to have been once forested now hardly "carried a stick large enough for firewood." In the neighborhood of Mangalore on the coast, the destruction was so great that firewood, "formerly

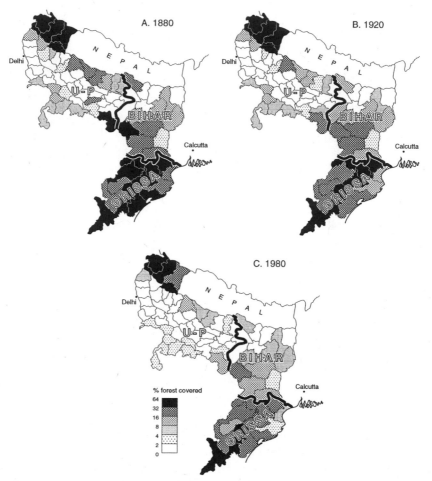

Figure 11.1 Percentage of land in forest in Uttar Pradesh, Bihar, and Orissa. *A,* 1880; *B,* 1920; and *C,* 1980. (Source: J. F. Richards et al., "Changing Land Use in Pakistan, Northern India, Bangladesh, Burma, Malaysia, and Brunei, 1880–1980" [Report to Carbon Dioxide Research Division, Office of Basic Energy Sciences, U.S. Department of Energy, Washington, D.C., 1984].)

so abundant, is now one of the chief items of expense to the poorer classes of society." The scarcity was a result of the

> improvidence with which the wood was treated, every tree and bush being felled at first, and the shoots and saplings which would have grown up and supplied their places being cut down every year until the roots die off, leaving nothing but the bare laterite hills which will remain for ever afterward utterly sterile and useless.

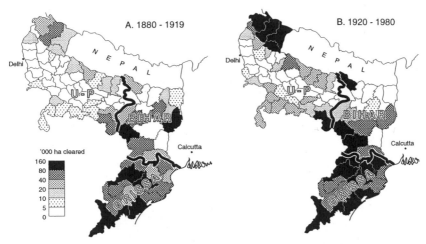

Figure 11.2 Forest decrease in Uttar Pradesh, Bihar, and Orissa. *A*, 1880–1919; and *B*, 1920–80 (in thousands of ha). (Source: J. F. Richards et al., "Changing Land Use in Pakistan, Northern India, Bangladesh, Burma, Malaysia, and Brunei, 1880–1980" [Report to Carbon Dioxide Research Division, Office of Basic Energy Sciences, U.S. Department of Energy, Washington, D.C., 1984].)

They made a special study of the "wasteful and improvident" *kumri* shifting agriculture and recommended that the forests be protected from its ravishes by being alienated and put into reserves.[15]

Because of his status, Gibson bypassed the heads of the Bombay and Indian governments and took his complaints directly to the directors of the EIC in London. And his advice was heeded, and in 1847 the Bombay presidency decided to form a Forestry Department, with Gibson as its conservator. The immemorial rights of the *kumri* shifting cultivators were extinguished; the ad hoc clearing of the permanent agriculturalist peasants was banned; and private capital interests, both Indian and European, were excluded from timber felling in the valuable teak forests.

The Gibson-Blane report disturbed the neighboring Madras government, which feared that famine would follow the deforestation evident within its confines. Like Bombay it was anxious to establish a Forestry Department but was thwarted by a lukewarm response from the Indian government. Consequently, it sponsored the publication in 1849 of a report by another of the surgeon-environmentalists, Edward Balfour, entitled "Notes on the Influence Exercised by Trees in Inducing Rain and Preserving Moisture." He explicitly affirmed that deforestation caused a cycle of drought, famine, and death and developed a sustained critique of colonial revenue-raising policies as a contributing factor. He also introduced a public health

argument into the debate by asserting that deforestation increased the incidence of disease through defective water supply, especially in the rapidly
expanding urban centers like Calcutta, a concern he developed later during
the 1870s, when he was surgeon-general of India. A further survey of the
teak forests of Burma and their destruction in the late 1840s by the surgeon
John McClelland, and the appearance of Hugh Cleghorn's report in 1851,
pushed everything into high gear. As a result, the Madras presidency established a Forestry Department in 1855, appointing Hugh Cleghorn, the arch
political activist, as its conservator.

But there were far-reaching contradictions in what happened. While the
surgeon-environmentalists and their scientific allies showed precocious and
spectacular intellectual curiosity, engaged in much astute political maneu-
vering, and expressed admirable moral concern about the welfare of those
over whom they had assumed control, with few exceptions they were blind
to the long-term environmental effects of the interventionist policies they
were advocating. The condemnation of *kumri,* the "settling" of people, the
reservation of forest tracts, and the raising of taxes to pay for public works
probably contributed to local hardship and encouraged widespread deforestation in the teak, sal, and other commercially valuable forests. The Forest
Conservation Department founded in 1857, of which the Bombay, Madras,
and Sind conservancies were experimental forerunners, was a remarkable
achievement, and, India the first major country of the world, outside the
nascent German state, to boast an efficient and widespread forest administration. But it was also going to be a source of future trouble.

COLONIAL CONSOLIDATION: INDIA, 1850–1920

The subcontinent was pivotal in the British imperial system, and the aim was
to consolidate imperial rule by bringing order, stability, and efficiency into
the sprawling physical, economic, and social diversity of the subcontinent.
Railway development, financed largely by British capital (and the opening of the Suez Canal in 1869), welded India together more effectively and
enmeshed it in the trade of the wider world. Survey, well under way by the
midcentury, created knowledge and control over the land and was the basis
of the cadastre and the taxation system. The ponderous EIC was replaced
by direct rule with a judiciary and civil service composed of British officials,
who intervened directly in such matters as tenurial systems and property
rights; the initiation of irrigation projects, road building, and a comprehensive forestry policy; and the prohibition of customs they considered in-
humane. There can be little doubt that the extension and intensification

of the "modernization" project had a profound effect on the land cover. Better communications, more commercialized farming, and greater land control, together with an increasing population, all interacted with one another to unleash a fierce onslaught on the forest. Peasants tried to extract more products out of the forest, yet the firewood, forage, green fertilizer, thatching grass, building material, honey, game, and medicinal cures, and the use of the forest for gathering, hunting, and grazing, all became less accessible and abundant. Increasingly, they lost access to emergency supplies and found themselves forced to purchase products that had formerly been there for the taking.

The Amount and Locale of Clearing

If the destruction of the forest seemed bad before 1850, it was nothing compared with what followed. The comments of Sainthill Eardley-Wilmott, who entered the Indian Forest Service in 1873 and became inspector-general in 1908, summed it up:

> Nature's forces cannot be expected to contend against the cattle that destroy the seedlings, against fires that kill saplings, and against the axe that removes the seed-bearers. Persistent attacks by these enemies, ever increasing in strength with the increase in population must result in the deterioration and ultimate disappearance of the forest, and these are just those forces which have been active ever since the time when men were few and forests overwhelming. And now . . . the position is reversed, and forests are restricted while men are all-powerful.[16]

We will never know the exact amount of forest that disappeared. Table 11.1 gives a broad view of the major land-use change in the regions of the tropical world, and it shows that in South and Southeast Asia during 80 years between 1850 and 1920, crops increased from 78 million to 119 million ha (net change of 41 million ha), forests and woodland declined by 33 million ha, and grasslands declined by a net 8 million ha. The extension of the railways, the increment of 236 million people between 1850 and 1920, and the commercialization of agriculture (exacerbated by increased taxation), all fed off one another in an unquantifiable but undoubtedly positive way to increase the area of cultivation by over 7 million ha and the destruction of the forest. Forest policy was not a cause of deforestation, but a response to real and perceived shortages, which contributed to the shortfall of forest products for the Indian farmers.

The Railways and Their Impact

The construction of railways was an integral part of British colonial military and commercial policy. They strengthened the control of British rule by facilitating the speedy movement of troops and armaments—a point emphasized by the Mutiny of 1857—and second, they augmented British wealth by facilitating the import of British manufactured goods and the export of Indian raw materials. The Lancashire and Glasgow cotton manufacturers were a powerful lobby group for railways, especially after the "cotton famine" of 1846, which underlined their precarious dependence on American supplies. With startling clarity and self-assurance they saw that a railway from Bombay inland was simply "nothing more than an extension of their own line from Manchester to Liverpool." [17] It would be far speedier and more efficient than bullock wagons, which took months to trundle down from the Deccan, with the cotton bales often being ruined by dust and rain.

The manufacturers had a strong ally in the reformist first governor-general, Lord Dalhousie, who replaced the lethargic administration of the EIC. He thought that the railway, together with the telegraph and uniform postage, would be one of "three great engines of social improvement." For him food production and famine alleviation were paramount, and the railways would promote agricultural intensification in remote areas and move surpluses to areas of need. But he was also conscious of the multiple, beneficial, "modernizing" effects of railways. Certainly, Indian society and economy were transformed radically as its millions took amazingly readily to the railways. Social and cultural barriers were broken down, local markets were ruptured, self-sufficiency was upset, and local handicraft industries went into decline. Construction of lines began in 1852 from Bombay inland to the foot of the Ghats and from Calcutta to the Raniganj coalfields 195 km away. Construction burgeoned, and by 1867, 19 of India's 20 largest cities were linked. India's network increased rapidly, so that by 1900 its 40,396 mi were surpassed only by those of the United States, Russia, and Germany, and by 1920 its 61,957 mi were exceeded only by the United States, Russia, and Canada.

Despite halving transportation costs and guaranteeing access to global markets, it seems that the new railway network did not have such a drastic effect on food supply as is commonly supposed; there was neither a marked rise in incomes nor a radical shift in cropping patterns. New tax regimes may have produced a far more radical change. Cotton acreage rose slightly from 6.4 to 9 percent of cultivated land under the stimulus of higher prices after the American Civil War. Food grains showed no major drop by the end of the century (they increased in many cases), and production did not appear to fall below consumption levels, except in the more extreme famine years. The peasants did not become commercialized; many were already commercialized in the precolonial market economies. Thus, by the time the railway came, millions of peasant proprietors were not the passive pawns of market forces, as they are sometimes portrayed, but canny opportunists who saw the chances for profits that the new agriculture provided and, consequently, who were drawn into the global commercial market.

One example where change was evident was the upland plateau of the Deccan and Karnatak, east of Bombay, where the extension of the railway to Nagpur during the early 1860s cut transportation times to the coast from three months to three days. Between 1856–60 and 1871–75, the amount of cultivated land rose from 6.3 million to 8.3 million ha (15.5 to 20.5 million acres) and within that total the acreage of cotton increased from 322,125 to 614,708 ha (796,000–1,519 000 acres). Almost imperceptibly the cover of dry deciduous Babhul forest (*Acacia arabica*) dwindled, and by 1878 no tracts of potentially cultivable land lay unused. By the 1890s, fuel, pasture, and fodder supplies were in short supply everywhere, and because of the removal of the tree cover, flooding, silting, and erosion were becoming common.

In contrast with this almost imperceptible land-use change, the impact on the forests in the immediate vicinity of the railroads was usually stark and severe. This was especially true of the early lines, which were designed to link large cities, which then consumed whatever supplies of adjacent fuelwood were available. Ribbentrop was in no doubt about the relationship: "Railways spread and forest growth disappeared with incredible rapidity within reach of the lines" in a "reckless and wasteful manner." The railways, said Robert Wallace in 1887, had caused large areas to be "shamefully and wastefully denuded." [18] Typical was the line from Madras to the southwest coast that passed through the

> wooded country occupying the notch [The Palghat Gap in the Ghats, in reality about 20 mi wide] between the Koondah and Anaimalai ranges [which] was famous for wild elephants, but the extended cultivation along the line, and the increasing demand for wood, have jointly contributed to clear the primeval forests, and there is now only a thin scattered jungle.[19]

In the timber-scarce Punjab the situation was worsened by the competition for fuel by the riverboats on the Indus and its tributaries.

As was the case everywhere in the world, the railways received far more attention as the destroyer of the forest than did the diffuse and difficult question of their effect on cultivation, which must have been much greater.

But how much forest fell directly to the railways? Ties are probably the easiest to calculate. Every mile of railroad required between 1,760 and 2,000 ties, each of at least 3.5 ft^3 or more. However, because ties rotted or were eaten by termites they had to be replaced regularly. Teak was said to last for 14 years, sal and deodar 13 years, but other timbers six years. Ten years might be a reasonable average life, and therefore one-tenth of the track had to be replaced every year (table 11.2). As the network expanded rapidly, shortages became acute, and imports from the Baltic were considered at one point in the 1870s, and then iron ties, and then creosoting the softer pines from the Himalayas. All were prohibitively costly. In the meantime, the forest was being destroyed steadily at a rate of some 70,000 acres (28,611 ha) per annum during the 1860s and 1870s; then the rate nearly doubled to between 122,000 and 130,000 acres per annum in the 1890s and 1900s during the peak of railroad construction activity. Many variables might enter these computations to alter them one way or another, but whatever way they are looked at, the impact was nothing compared with the difficult-to-define but relentless clearing by peasant proprietors and commercial farmers. In all, about 700,000 acres (286,118 ha) of forest must have been destroyed to supply the ties, a sizable amount in one way, but a mere pinprick (about 4.5 percent) compared to the total destruction of over 6 million ha by agriculture over the same period.

The same was true of fuelwood, which was the main source of energy for over 80 percent of engines throughout the nineteenth century. It was commonly thought that with a 17-year cutting rotation, plantations devoted solely to railway fuel would be required near lines at the rate of 20 acres per mile of line. At that rate, about 544,000 acres (approximately 220,000 ha) were needed in 1890 and 1,056,000 acres (approximately 427,000 ha) in 1910, though coal was making inroads by this time. Certainly, forest tracts of 3,000–8,000 acres were reserved or planted near railway lines.

Peasant Cultivation

The felled forests, the new railway earthworks, bridges, and tunnels, and the gangs of itinerant railroad laborers had a dramatic impact on the lands and livelihoods through which they slowly passed, crushing all that got in their path like some crashing, noisy juggernaut. But away from the lines, peasant farmers were largely untouched by it. Life went on in its inexorable and timeless way: the seasons of planting and harvesting, the cycles of birth and death, and the constant battle to provide enough food for a slowly increasing population occupied the minds and muscles of these village dwellers.

Table 11.2 Estimate of sleepers (crossties) used and acres of forest cleared, India, 1850–1940

	Miles of Track	10-Year Increment	Ties in New Construction (in millions)	Ties Renewed Annually (in millions)	Total Ties (in millions)	Acres of Forest Cleared (in thousands)
1850	0					
1860	1,542	1,542	2.8	0.3	3.1	15.5
1870	8,637	7,095	12.8	1.3	14.1	70.5
1880	15,764	7,127	12.8	1.3	14.1	70.5
1890	27,227	11,463	20.6	2.1	22.7	113.5
1900	40,396	13,169	23.7	2.4	26.1	130.5
1910	52,767	12,371	22.3	2.3	24.6	123.0
1920	61,957	9,190	16.5	1.7	18.2	91.0
1930	70,565	8,608	15.5	1.6	17.1	85.5
1940	72,144	1,579	2.8	0.3	3.1	15.6
Total						715.6

Source: Track miles from M. D. Morris and C. B. Dudley, "Selected Railway Statistics for the Indian Subcontinent (India, Pakistan and Bangladesh), 1853–1946/7," *Artha Vijnana* 17 (1975): 193–96.

In the vast plain of the Ganges and its tributaries that stretched from beyond Delhi in the west to nearly Calcutta in the east—in the states of Uttar Pradesh, Bihar, and Orissa—the production of food reigned supreme. By 1880 half the land in Uttar Pradesh and Bihar was in cultivation, but Orissa was much more forested. In the three states together, some 44 percent of the land was in cultivation, 20 percent in forest, and 12.1 percent in interrupted woodlands. Only on the upland margins did the proportions change significantly, with forest accounting for a quarter to a third of the land, and even up to nearly all land in the Himalayan provinces of northern Uttar Pradesh, although it too was being cleared. Down the coast, through Orissa and toward Madras, forest was more widespread and accounted for half or more of the land, but agricultural expansion and the cutting of the sal for the expanding railway system was causing massive destruction.

During the next 40 years the population increased from 79.8 million to 86.1 million, and arable land from 27.5 million to 30.8 million ha. The bulk of this newly cultivated land was taken out of the forests of Bihar and Orissa and the margins of Uttar Pradesh, which decreased from 12.5 million to 10.8 million ha. Another 0.3 million ha came out of interrupted woodland, 0.6 million out of grasslands, and another 0.7 million out of other land uses. Little expansion occurred on the plain, as there was no more forest to fell. The changes are shown in figure 11.1A–B, which shows the extent of forest in 1880, 1920, and 1980. The annual rate of clearing from

1880 to 1920 was 42,500 ha, most of this coming out of eastern Bihar and Orissa, where individual provinces showed declines of 50,000–100,000 ha (fig. 11.1A). It was a complex picture of transformation and change that hints at but hides many local stories of peasant clearing.

Global Crops: Plantations and Commercial Farming

In contrast with the incremental and largely undetected expansion of agriculture by millions of peasant farmers, there were a few areas where commercial plantation cropping for mainly tea and coffee for a global market reached spectacular proportions. These areas did owe their existence to rapid accessibility and cheap and efficient transportation links with the wider world, and to that extent they can be said to have been created by the railways and steamships.

In favorable spots throughout the foothills of the eastern Himalayas in Assam, tea cultivation replaced forest. Darjeerling became a household name in England and was synonymous with "Breakfast Tea." After 1833, foreigners were allowed to buy land in India, and by the end of the century British speculators had amassed over 253,000 ha in about 764 large estates, of which about one-third was cultivated at any one time. Tea was a lucrative crop: during the early 1850s it yielded, on average, about 445 rupees per ha, compared with 30 for rice, 52 for cotton, and 90 for opium. Only sugarcane, at 475 rupees, exceeded it. Such high profits encouraged exploitation in difficult terrain, and bridges and roads were built to aid exploitation.

Similarly in the Wynaard Plateau and Nilgiri Hills of Kerala in southern India, the semi-independent, indigenous princes and landed elite encouraged British administrators and planters to colonize uncultivated tribal hill forests in order to increase their revenues. Clements Markham knew the area well and observed in 1865 that "within the last 20 years a great change has come over the forest-clad mountain districts, in the establishment of many English planters. . . . In all a total area of 180,000 acres of forest has been cleared for coffee, tea and chinchona plantations." Blight in coffee in 1868 caused a major shift to tea cultivation. But not all was good; while the planters had "brought great material blessings to the natives" their "extensive clearings of trees . . . have brought about a deterioration of the climate," and he resuscitated all the arguments and observations about decreasing rainfall in the western Ghats region.[20]

In more distant Ceylon (Sri Lanka), the same processes were at work with ruthless efficiency (plate 11.3), and by the end of the 1880s, nearly 600,000 acres (243,000 ha) were felled for tea plantations, which was

Plate 11.3 The New Clearing, Ceylon (Sri Lanka). (Plate 4 of V. M. Hamilton and S. M. Fasson, *Scenes in Ceylon,* 1881.) (Bodleian Library, Oxford.) This sketch had an accompanying verse:

> The ruthless flames have cleared his lands;
> No trace remains of green
> When lost in thought our Planter stands
> And views a sterile scene.
>
> In dreams he sees his Coffee spring,
> Fed by the welcome rain
> And berries many a dollar bring
> To take him home again.

replacing coffee. On one of his many global journeys, novelist Anthony Trollope bemoaned the passing of the forests:

> The lovely sloping forests are going, the forests through which elephants have trampled for we do not know how many more than 2,000 years; and the very regular but ugly coffee plantations are taking their place.[21]

How those plantations were created some decades before is recounted vividly by John Capper in a splendid, if lengthy, account of clearing that must stand as an example of the "industrial" clearing of the tropical forest:

> Before us were . . . fifty acres of felled jungle in wildest disorder; just as the monsters of the forest had fallen so they lay, heap on heap, crunched,

splintered into ten thousand fragments. . . . The "fall" had taken place a good week before, and the trees would be left in this state until the end of October by which time they would be sufficiently dry for a good "burn."

He and his companions clambered through the "fall" to the steeper forested slopes, "where the heavy click of many axes told us there was a working party busily employed." In front of him were some 40 Sinhalese laborers "plying their small axes with a rapidity and precision that was truly marvellous," but leaving enough of the stem uncut to keep the tree just standing upright. A few hours later, Capper climbed to the top of the slope and looked down on the vast area of almost cut-through trees that were ready to knock down one another like a series of upturned dominoes:

> The manager sounded the conch sharply . . . forty bright axes gleamed high in the air, then sank deeply into as many trees, which . . . groaned heavily, waved their huge branches to and fro, like drowning giants, then toppled over and fell with a stunning crash upon the trees below them. Nothing was heard but the groaning, cracking, crunching, and splintering . . . it appeared as though the whole of the forest-world about me was tumbling to pieces.

When he recovered from the overwhelming experience, Capper commented wryly that the small axes may have "rang out a merry chime—merrily to the planter's ear—but the death-knell of many fine old forest trees." [22]

Another purposeful transformation came with the colonization, reclamation, and settlement of the 18,000–20,000 km^2 of the Sunderbans, the floodable marshes of the Ganges-Brahmaputra delta (and similar but small deltas on the Mahanadi, Godavari, Krishna, and Penner rivers). The seaward side of the delta was covered with the largest area of mangroves in the world, while on the inland drier side were dense stands of *kanazo* (*Heritiera fomes*) forests, with trees up to 45 m high. It was the natural habitat of the Bengal tiger, the crocodile, and a rich assemblage of monkeys and snakes.

As early as 1793 the Sunderbans was declared "state" owned, and from 1816 onward a commissioner was appointed to oversee the extraction of fuelwood (mangrove and *kanazo*) for the growing urban area of Calcutta and its jute mills. In addition he was to encourage private owners to settle and drain the land by embanking, clearing the forest, and growing rice in order to build up export and emergency famine stocks. Taxation and tenure were manipulated to encourage settlement; large areas were made available free of charge on long-term leases that were inheritable and transferable, provided 25 percent of the land was under cultivation within five years. After 20 years, 75 percent of the land was liable to normal taxation. These regulations, together with formal land survey after 1830, guaranteed private property rights and unleashed a rush of peasant entrepreneurial energy. By 1870, 2,790 km² had already been cleared and embanked and, by 1920, about another 5,000 km². The Bengal tiger was becoming as rare a beast as its watery forest habitat.

Shortages and Forest Policy

By the early 1860s, everything was moving inexorably toward a state of alarm about the reduction in the area and quality of the forest, and the pressure on its many "free" products. An extra 38.3 million people between 1880 and 1920, an almost equal addition of cows, and all-too-frequent famines showed that the quest for more land could never be relaxed. In the absence of intensification of agriculture, expansion into the forest was the only possibility and was a deliberate part of British land policy, especially as it helped to maximize revenue. Indian rural life was affected in other ways. The widespread dependency on livestock was not possible unless forested forage lands were available. But common rights to browse diminished as the area of the forest was reduced and greater restrictions were placed on its use. Fuelwood supplies were similarly affected. The spread of the railways, and their insatiable demand for timber of all kinds, caused "havoc" in the forests alongside the lines and reduced local supplies. The radius of fuelwood procurement was widened and the demand was so great that in the villages supplies were being drawn "from remote districts which as yet have hardly heard the axe." [23] The alternative to wood fuel was to burn cow dung, which was half the price. That had a disastrous effect on the already low yields in existing cultivated lands; it was a vicious circle of degradation.

In highlighting the general timber shortage and the role of the railways as causes for a nationwide forest policy, it is easy to forget other complex official concerns. First, the search for teak and other useful timbers within the broader strategic view of empire led to the reservation of particular stands of trees. Second, uncultivated land was regarded as "waste," and the abode of the unruly and disorderly, from the murderous thuggees to run-of-the-mill thieves. The elimination of the forest meant an end to lawlessness, as well as unproductive land and population. Finally, from at least the late 1840s the surgeon-environmentalists saw the "vagabond habits" of the itinerant *kumri* cultivators in the hills and their rotational burning as the prime cause of forest destruction, decreasing rainfall and increasing desiccation, famine, and declining health—not realizing that the regeneration of the timbers they prized so much was dependent on periodic burning. The suppression of *kumri* seemed essential for environmental health and reflected the wider concern about revenue and labor supply because uncontrolled patterns of settlement and production betokened a lack of colonial control. Both actually and metaphorically, the shifting cultivators needed to be kept in their place. It was a circular, self-reinforcing, and self-justifying argument that the stewardship of the forests, and the control of the hill people, seemed essential for the survival and welfare of the mass of Indians and the forests.

Therefore, the British authorities began one of their great "modernizing" projects: to set aside forest reserves for preservation and management by professional foresters. The expertise was found in the German-trained Dietrich Brandis, who was appointed inspector-general of Indian forests in 1864. Brandis had been a regional superintendent of forests in Pegu, Tenasserim, and Martaban, where he initiated forestry policies described as the outcome of "a master-hand and mind." An outstanding organizer, he built up a massive administrative and management structure based on scientific management and sustained-yield principles. By the end of the century the Forest Department had within its remit slightly over one-fifth of the total land of the subcontinent (fig. 11.3).[24] The Forest Act of 1865 was controversial. The Madras presidency resisted it vehemently until 1882, contending that it was a usurpation of native rights and a prescription for further shortages, rural hardship, and even social instability and crime. It was not alone; commentators in Britain condemned the "excessive zeal" of the Indian government, which had "put on the screw in . . . limited areas," and they specifically singled out the injury done to the agricultural population in denying forest lands for cattle grazing. Others, like the autocratic and influential B. Henry Baden-Powell, dismissed the notion of customary rights and wanted the state to be supreme. Customary rights would be allowed only if "proof" were available in writing, something that even European peasants could rarely do. Like suttee or smallpox, the indiscriminate cutting of trees was "an evil that must be suppressed."[25] Brandis attempted to steer a middle course between these extremes, favoring annexation of areas vital for commercial or climatic purposes, and wherever possible leaving village rights untouched. But in the end Baden-Powell's views prevailed.

The 1865 act allowed only a tenuous control over the continent's forests, and the Forestry Department sought stricter and more comprehensive legislation. Brandis and his forest officers, aided by Baden-Powell's formidable knowledge of Indian land rights, drafted the New Indian Forests Act, which became law in 1878. In reality the new legislation of 1878 was not as devastating as feared because not all uncultivated lands were annexed. In any case, the impact depended on three other widely varying conditions: the type of forest, the applicability of the legislation, and local tenure. In the

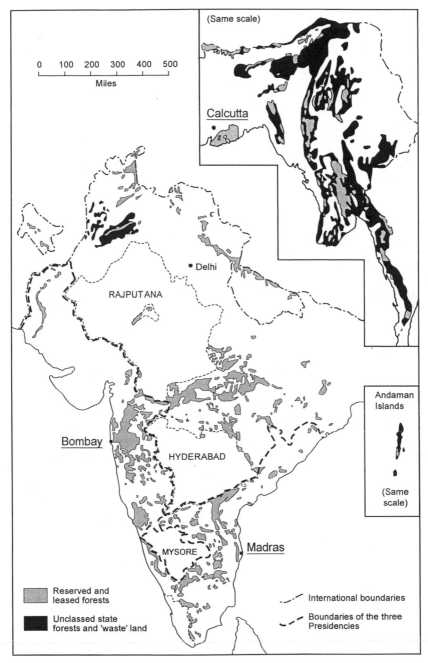

Figure 11.3 The extent of reserved and leased forests and unclassed state forests and wasteland under British control in the three presidencies of Madras, Bombay, and Bengal (Calcutta), India, 1899. (Source: B. Ribbentrop, *Forestry in British India* [Calcutta: Office of the Superintendent of Government Printing, India, 1900].)

legislation a distinction was made between forested lands, which were either reserved or protected and unclassed forests or "waste" land (fig. 11.3): in the former, no rights could be acquired unless ceded by a provincial government; in the latter, rights were recorded and permitted, but land was not settled. But all forests were protected to secure timber, and it was now possible to exclude rural land users and promote the growth of commercially valuable species.

But the end result was a terrible paradox. An admirable and massive administrative edifice had been constructed for the rational use of the timber resource, which had no parallel in the world for decades to come. It was one of the administrative jewels in the Imperial Crown, a model for the rest of the world, and a highly efficient and profitable enterprise. But it was also going to prove to be one of the festering sores in the body of the Indian Subcontinent that has still not been healed. The foresters and their regulations became the face of alien power, which pervaded Indian rural life just as surely as any military, judiciary, or political administrative framework. The process of colonization was far more complex than political domination alone. Its cultural, social, economic, and even psychological ramifications cut deeply into the fabric of traditional life—in this case the forest—carrying with them rapid and sometimes deleterious change.

MAINLAND AND INSULAR SOUTHEAST ASIA

With few exceptions, the wealth of detail that accompanied forest destruction and policy in India is not paralleled throughout the rest of Asia, which was not under the efficient and precise administration of British officials, who bequeathed such an archive of information. But the forces of change were different too. Population densities in mainland Asia (Burma, Thailand, Cambodia, Laos, and Vietnam) in 1880 were a mere one-sixth of India's (0.12 compared with 0.73 persons/ha). Production was beyond subsistence needs, and clearing catered to external rather than internal demand. Pioneer peasant farmers attacked the lowland and delta forests aggressively to grow rice and feed the greater world beyond, encouraged by an extended period of favorable terms of trade and rising land and commodity prices.

For example, in Lower Burma, British interest had revolved initially around the extraction and conservation of teak and ironwood for ships, first in coastal Arakan and Tenasserim and later along the Sittang and Salween rivers. Then Lower Burma was annexed in 1852, including the 35,000–40,000 km^2 of *kanazo* forests of the Irrawaddy delta. At midcentury no more than 3,200 km^2 were in cultivation, but with the experience of the Sunderbans in mind, officials regarded the delta as ideal for growing wet rice that would produce revenue and surpluses to alleviate famines, as had occurred in Bengal. When Burma became a part of the empire in 1886, pioneering peasant migrant cultivators were deliberately encouraged to clear the *kanazo* and mangrove for rice growing, and "the pioneer's axe . . . [was] heard daily as the forests are cleared and prepared for the rice crop." Canals, embankments, roads, railways, and mills were built, and steamship routes established. Peasant migrants flocked in, and the delta population rose from 1.5 million in 1852 to over 4 million in the early 1900s, and with over 12,000 km² of wet rice it became one of the main rice-exporting regions of the world. So swift and complete was the deforestation that by the early 1920s "scarce a tree was to be seen" in the delta, which had once been dense jungle.[26]

Similar stories of reclamation and deforestation of coastal deltas can be told for the 12,700 km² of the Chao Phraya in Thailand, the Mekong in Cambodia, and other, smaller deltas, but details are few; however, we do know that in Thailand, in particular, royal patronage and state aid, under the stimulus of British imperial hegemony, were directed toward encouraging peasant rice cultivators. It was the Irrawaddy story all over again: canals were dug to facilitate communications, Dutch hydraulic expertise was brought in to plan the draining, Bangkok grew as the major rice processing and refining center, and the wetland forests disappeared.

Clearing before 1920 was equally widespread in insular Southeast Asia, the third of the regions under discussion here. Cultivated crops increased by a phenomenal 9.4 million ha, and over 10.3 million ha of forest was cleared, the largest amount in any of the three Asian regions. But the detail of how that happened is virtually unknown. In Indonesia, for example, copious records exist of the changes in the policies and conservation measures of the Vereenigde Oostindische Campagnie (United [Dutch] East India Company) in precolonial Java—up to 175,000 teak logs were being cut annually by the mid-1860s—but this gives only a limited view of the forest changes. Obviously the expansion of cash crops like coffee, indigo, tobacco, and sugar for the European market meant large-scale land clearing, but as ever the multitude of individual and incremental clearings for subsistence by peasant proprietors remains unrecorded. In addition, the 6,400 mi (9,300 km) of railway constructed between 1873 and 1920 demanded clearing for track rights-of-way, and timber for crossties.

Knowledge of clearing in the Philippines is slightly better, especially around the core of early settlement in the plains of central Luzon. Here the legacy of over 300 years of Spanish settlement had created a domesticated landscape of large estates and smaller farms, which were gradually encroaching on forests of the slash-and-burn cultivators on the upland margins. Forest cover declined from about 90 percent of the island in 1521 to about 70 percent by 1900, and most of that in central Luzon. A rising population and the spread of commercial crops such as tobacco, abaca (manila hemp, used for ships' rigging), and sugarcane integrated the local economy into the world system. A microcosm of the process is provided by the example of the province of Nueva Ecija, just north of Manila, between 1800 and 1920, "the great era" of forest clearance. Sugar was grown on large feudal-like estates owned by elite Filipinos and Chinese mestizos, and abaca on smaller peasant farms. Sugar estates were clear-cut and were voracious consumers of fuel for refining the sugar. Wherever these two plantation crops were not grown, rice and ranching took over the land.

But away from the Luzon plain, the rest of the Philippines were almost untouched. As late as 1917 it was said that there were vast stretches of unmapped and sparsely inhabited forests that were not exploited because of the lack of transport. The only destruction was by the shifting agriculturalists. Once more, Western perceptions were at variance with local adaptations, and the elimination of the shifting agriculturalists (who were merely clearing to live) and the promotion of "development" were seen as the keys to unlocking the wealth of the forests. When the American-backed transportation links came after 1920, the Philippine forest began its long and rapid descent to near oblivion.

BRAZIL AND THE "LONG JOURNEY TO EXTINCTION"

The Continental Picture

With the notable exception of Brazil, the forests of Latin America were barely touched before 1900 and only marginally so by 1920, other than by shifting cultivation. Of the 51 million ha cleared from 1850 to 1920, approximately half disappeared before 1900 and half in the following 20 years, the bulk of it in Brazil (see table 11.1). But clearing was not a prelude to agricultural expansion. Of the 27 million ha of cropland created by 1920, about two-thirds of it was in the temperate grasslands of Argentina, Uruguay, and Chile. Mexico and Brazil accounted for about another 12 percent each, and the rest was scattered in small amounts in all other countries. Over half of all clearing must have been either for grazing or an outcome of destructive exploitation by careless and/or rapacious cultivators.

In every country a few tracts of 100,000 ha or more disappeared as large estate (latifundia) owners, and some individual pioneer settlers, lumberers, and fuel procurers, set about their work. But clearing was marginal in the development of these territories. In the Pacific-facing countries of Chile, Peru, Ecuador, and Colombia, remoteness and high transportation costs militated against lumbering and commercial cropping for overseas markets. What agriculture there was existed mainly in either the treeless Sierra upland or the irrigated coastal plains. Bolivia and Paraguay were landlocked.

The Atlantic-facing countries of Uruguay and Argentina utilized their extensive grasslands for cattle raising and then wheat cultivation largely for the European market. In Venezuela and Atlantic-facing Colombia, coffee and cacao cultivation had made limited inroads into the tropical forests of the plains and foothills. Deforestation was far greater in Cuba, which was a slave society and plantation colony par excellence with over 500,000 ha in sugar. The larger area of the intensely peasant and agricultural society of Mexico is more of an enigma. The estimated precontact population of 25 million had dropped to 3.8 million in 1650 and existing clearings had reverted to forest, thereby increasing its size. The next three centuries were a long process of recovery from that demographic disaster, and the population did not regain its precontact level until roughly 1950. The only evidence of commercial impacts on the forest was sporadic lumbering for mahogany in coastal Yucatan. It was not until the expansion of railways (1,080 km in 1880 to 20,447 km in 1912) that the remoter forested areas, particularly in the south, were opened up, but again not until after the turn of the century.

Brazil: Elites and Exploitation

Brazil was utterly different. The devastation of the great Atlantic coastal forest was early, extensive, and severe and had much to do with the peculiar social system that developed with initial colonization. During the seventeenth century the racial and social makeup of the colony took shape and became a stratified, caste system. The more obviously white population sought and received royal (Portuguese) patronage over land and forest rights, and progressively they occupied land illegally. If they had enough money and/or influence, they had their occupation legitimized by receiving *sesmarias*, royal land grants 1 square league (4,356 ha) in size. Ownership of land was the basis of social position and privilege; it had almost no monetary value and was rarely sold, which meant that little care was taken of it.

Those natives who survived disease and were captured, as well as the vastly expanded mestizo population, were segregated into *adelias* (government-sponsored villages often under the administration of missionary Jesuits and Franciscans). This captive underclass formed a pool of labor for the large estates, supplemented after 1550 by African slaves. Consequently, the forest frontier was rarely one based on small pioneer settlers but instead was founded on latifundia, slave labor, and coercion. The boundaries, let alone locations of the *sesmarias* were often unknown, which led to unbridled lawlessness, fraud, and violence. It was a recipe for future social disaster and ecological mayhem.

The enormous size of the *sesmarias* meant an extravagant use of the forest in a modified form of slash-and-burn agriculture. When the soil became "tired," the next piece of forest, and even the next *sesmaria*, was occupied. This meant a saving in labor, but in the meantime the use of the once-and-for-all fertility of the soil maintained the population at a subsistence level. Imported pigs, sheep, chicken, goats, and above all cattle ran wild and multiplied wonderfully in the absence of natural predators. They soon filled the available grasslands and invaded the forests of the *sertão* (internal backwoods). It is possible that the cycle of cultivation was well under 30 years and that the forest had little chance to grow back except as very degraded secondary woodland (*capoeira*), especially now that animals grazed it. The eventual outcome was often that the woodland ended up as grassland.

By about 1700 the population in the Portuguese-controlled section of the forest probably numbered about 300,000. They occupied an astounding 65,000 km² of the forest at very low population densities (two to five persons per km²), all in various degrees of clearing. Pockets of sugar cultivation along the coast near Recife, Salvador, Espirito Santo, and Rio de Janeiro led to the clearing of about 1,000 km², and at least another 1,200 km² had been cleared or degraded to supply fuel for the refineries.

The influx of over 100,000 miners into the interior with the discovery of gold and diamonds in Minas Gerais during the early eighteenth century had far-reaching effects on the vegetation. Around the mines the forest was stripped and the land scarred and eroded. "As far as the eye can see," said one contemporary observer, "the earth is turned over by human hands," and perhaps 4,000 km² ended up looking like a lunar landscape.[27] The miners ate prodigious amounts of beef, which meant an expansion of herds on the natural pastures and degraded subsistence plots. Incapable of being grazed so intensively, the pastures were quickly replaced by less palatable species and less nutritious introduced African grasses. In order to encourage new succulent growth, fire was applied indiscriminately, but with devastating effects where it reached the forest edges. The cattle bred freely on the unfenced range, creating *minas de ganado*—"mines of livestock." The cattle were afflicted by vampire bats and gadflies, and in order to avoid these debilitating pests they invaded the forest margins, trampling saplings and spreading grass seeds. Everything seemed to transpire to shift the cattle from grassland to forest edge, especially where forest had previously been farmed, opened up, and then abandoned on the *sesmarias*. Furthermore, the continual and aggressive use of fire, especially during the dry season or during droughts, led to uncontrollable fires in the forests themselves. These fires were much more frequent and on a much grander scale than those of the swidden farmers and were, consequently, far more devastating.

Cattle raising created a permanent change to the human landscape and its vegetation and, together with mining and farming, may have eliminated another 30,000 km² of trees in the southeastern sector of the forest in a 300–400 km arc inland from Rio and Santos. The Zona da Mata, or Forest Zone, of Minas Gerais was disappearing, and the Atlantic forest was at the beginning of its "long journey to extinction."[28]

Brazil: "Green Gold"

The scientific curiosity of the late eighteenth/early nineteenth century about the natural world barely touched colonial Brazil because of royal suppression of any enquiring mind, which was equated with subversive political and social concepts. The prohibition of printing presses and public libraries was indicative of the insecurity and paranoia of the ruling elite. Nevertheless, some trees, plants, and forest products were identified and their commercial properties recognized—for example, brazilwood, cochineal, indigo, and rubber. Generally, however, the sentiment was that the Brazilian forest was of little value, although Brazilian plants like cashews, papaya, passion fruit, and pineapples were quickly adopted when introduced to the cuisine of Goa and India generally, and from there spread to the wider world. Greater emphasis was placed on growing and then exporting exotic Asian crops like cinnamon, hemp, and chinchona, but with little success.

Timber suitable for oceangoing vessels was initially sent to Lisbon, but later commandeered for Portuguese vessels built at Bahia. In an act reminiscent of the British in North America, the Portuguese authorities tried to reserve all hardwoods suitable for shipbuilding that grew between the coast and the inland escarpment, although centuries of cutting in the forests meant few were left. Faced with shortages, they quickly learned the realities of the subtropical Atlantic forest: unlike the temperate forests, trees did not grow back from stumps; they rarely grew at all unless in a forest environment; and growth took generations. Planting of hardwoods in homogeneous stands was not feasible, and there was no comprehension that an adequate supply could come only through carefully selective logging and conservation. But such biological niceties were of little concern to the loggers who forged ahead into the forest wherever possible, until they came into conflict with the colonial landholding elite. To make matters worse, the landholders could no longer legally fell trees on their own land because of the royal reservation policy, and indignant at their loss of freedom they simply cut down as much of the surrounding woodland as possible to get around the restriction. The forest was always the loser.

In the end it was easier and cheaper to import wood for shipbuilding and construction from the United States, just as, later, jarrah railroad ties came from Australia. There were shortages everywhere, even on the forest frontier, where it might least be expected. Here the backwoods farmer (*caboclos*) set fire to the woods for a few seasons of manioc raising and never considered replanting. One naturalist, a native of Minas Gerais, José Vieira Couto, vividly and memorably depicted the *caboclos* as devastating vast areas as he held a "broadax in one hand and a firebrand in the other":

> [He] gazes upon one or two leagues of forest as though they were nought, and hardly has he reduced them to ashes but he extends his view still further to carry destruction to other parts; he harbors neither affection nor love for the land he cultivates, knowing full well that it will probably not last for his children.[29]

The rapid advance and incessant burning left behind a stunted and pauperized woodland, sparsely settled and almost invariably changing to grassland and cattle grazing.

In 1815 Brazil became a separate kingdom and, by 1821, independent of Portugal; but the great political upheavals of these years did not signal a change of attitude toward the forest. If anything, the destruction became worse as the elite did everything to maintain its privileged position. Slavery was not abolished until 1888, by which time another 1.25 million African slaves had been transported, enough to service the plantation system until the end of the century; any restriction on gaining land for nothing was resisted; the removal, enslavement, or servitude of indigenous peoples continued; and any restrictions on forest use was opposed. The elite wanted the right to convert this vast stockpile of wood into cash as quickly as possible. Everywhere, profligacy, exploitation, shortages, and violence were rampant.

In their search for a more enduring prosperity, the colonial aristocracy cast about for a staple crop to export to the consuming nations of the Northern Hemisphere. Experiments with tea were a failure, and the demand for rubber was not yet on the horizon. Sugarcane cultivation was revived and spread south into the coastal plains around Santos, Rio, Campos, and Vitoria. It may have consumed up to 7,500 km^2 of forest by the mid-nineteenth century, along with another 900 km^2 for the fuel to refine it. But because of cheaper competitors, the colonial elite's hoped-for prosperity never materialized from sugar cane. Salvation came in the form of an entirely new crop—coffee—which proved to be their "green gold." Although coffee had been introduced from East Africa in 1727, its value was not recognized until the end of the eighteenth century. Coffee *fazendas* covered the hills around Rio, later spreading into the Paraibo Sul Valley and the surrounding São Paulo highlands. By the 1840s the extensive forests of Minas Gerais and adjacent portions of Espirito Santo were succumbing to the crop. Coffee became Brazil's main income source and remained the principal export commodity until 1964, reaching its apogee in 1925, when it accounted for three-quarters of the country's export earnings.

Occasionally coffee was planted on ground already thinned by fuel gathering or sugar cultivation, but usually it was planted on heavily forested ridges, as it was commonly thought that it would not yield unless grown on land originally covered by "virgin" forest. Because coffee was particularly sensitive to frost damage, the bushes/small trees were planted in rows up and down the steep hills in order to facilitate the drainage of cold air. The result was devastating erosion, which hastened crop abandonment and migration to new tree-covered areas. Although the bushes could yield for many decades if tended carefully, they were usually neglected, as in the time-honored Brazilian tradition, it was easier to claim that the land was "tired," apply for a new *sesmaria*, and shift onto the next piece of forest-land, clear it, fire it, and plant again. The forest was felled in a restless cycle as the coffee frontier moved continuously inland, and the land resembled "some modern battlefield, blackened, smouldering and desolate."[30]

The construction of the Santos–São Paulo railway over the obstacle of the Serro do Mar in 1867 allowed a new wave of exploitation to be unleashed in the interior uplands (fig. 11.4*A*, *B*), and during the next two decades railroads fanned out in all directions from Campinas to southern Minas Gerais and the "Paulista West." The fertility of the decomposed basaltic-derived red soils, or *terra roxa*, encouraged the massive expansion of the *fazenda* frontier northeast between 1885 and 1900; but depletion of even these soils meant yet farther migration west onto the interfluves of the many rivers flowing toward to Paraná River.

The coffee *fazenda* was founded originally on slave labor, and indeed, the newfound wealth provided by coffee was the excuse for slavery's retention and extension. But the construction of the railroad in 1867 unleashed social and economic changes that led to the crumbling of the old regime. The slaves were finally emancipated in 1888, and their place on the plantations was taken by over half a million Italian, Spanish, and Portuguese migrants. The migrants came in and the coffee went out through the new port of Santos. Forest destruction increased as the railways grew from 6,000 km in 1900 to approximately 12,000 km by 1929. They needed timber for their construction, they facilitated the movement of fuelwood to the cities,

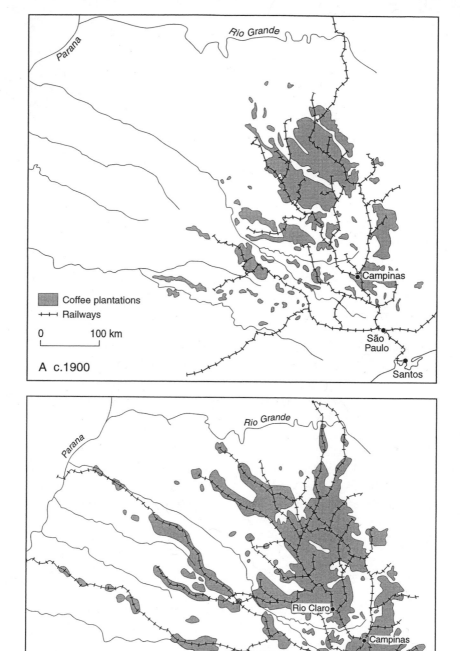

Figure 11.4 Extent of coffee plantations, Brazil. *A*, End of nineteenth century; *B*, 1929. (Source: P. Monbeig, *Pionniers et planteurs de São Paulo* [Paris: Librarie Armand Colin, 1952].)

and they helped the spread of coffee cultivation. If the land in coffee is used as a surrogate measure for the area of forest destroyed, then at least 4,000 km² could have been cleared by 1900, 7,980 km² by 1920, and 140,000 km² by 1931.

Throughout the southeast region the rural and urban population climbed steadily with the coffee boom, from about 1 million in 1808 to 6.4 million in 1890; Rio alone became a bustling metropolis of 500,000. The appetite for wood was immense. More land was cleared for food crops, and domestic fuel consumption was at least half a ton per capita per annum, or more. With over 40,000 dwellings in Rio in 1890, about 400,000 tons of fuel would have been needed, the equivalent of 200 km² of secondary forest, to which must be added the demands of the bakeries, forges, and numerous factories. In

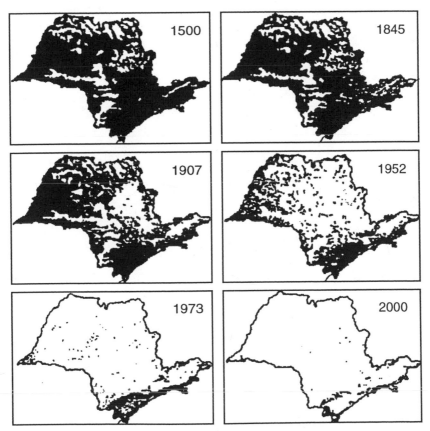

Figure 11.5 Forest clearing in São Paulo State, Brazil, 1500, 1845, 1907, 1952, 1973, and 2000. (Source: K. Oedekoven, "The Vanishing Forest." *Environmental Policy and Law* 6 [1980]: 184–85.)

addition, the construction of each dwelling would have used about 100 tons of fuel for the firing of bricks and the burning of lime for plaster. Further, the iron forges of Minas Gerais would have consumed 40 km² a year.

The *caboclos* in the *capoeira*, or secondary forest, and in the true forest remained persistently itinerant. They had no security of tenure, tenancy being discouraged by the plantation elite because it might endanger the slave society; also by being itinerant they avoided arbitrary impressment into the military, which was employed as a means of suppressing opposition. Thus, the displaced *caboclos* moved on to the forests of the drier western frontier—cutting, burning, planting an occasional crop, and running a few stock. Farther inland the big cattle ranchers, their trade boosted by the coffee boom, continued to transform the grassland-forest border by repeated, large-scale, and indiscriminate burning to repress woody growth, ultimately reducing the productive capacity of the grasslands as well as eliminating the western forest margin and the gallery forests that extended along the rivers. All these forces were reducing the forest, particularly in São Paulo, to a mere shadow of what it had once been (fig. 11.5). The virtual elimination of the Atlantic coastal forest must rank as one of the most rapacious, complete, thorough, and ultimately perhaps needless and senseless episodes in the annals of the deforesting of the earth.

CONCLUSION

In 1776, Adam Smith said that "the discovery of America, and that of a passage to the East Indies by the Cape of Good Hope, are the two greatest and most important events recorded in the history of mankind." [31] Whether or not that was true, the two geographical events certainly meant radical changes to the societies and economies of the tropical areas of the world and, ultimately, to their vegetation cover. The forests of southern and southeastern Asia, and particularly those of Brazil, while still extensive, underwent massive transformations as their people and produce were drawn into the global economy. Over 222 million ha disappeared by the beginning of this century, and crops and grasslands took their place. In John Capper's memorable words, "the whole of the forest-world . . . was tumbling to pieces." It was to be nothing, however, compared to what was to follow in the second half of the twentieth century, which was the era of true tropical deforestation.

PART III

THE GLOBAL FOREST

Chapter 12

Scares and Solutions, 1900–1944

If the present rate of forest destruction is allowed to continue, with nothing to offset it, a timber famine in the future is inevitable.

—T. ROOSEVELT, "The Forest in the Life of the Nation" (1905)

PROBABLY ALL centuries end on a pessimistic note as people reassess the past and look toward the next century with a mixture of trepidation and hope. But compared with the hubris of the nineteenth century, the 1890s was a period of particular introspection. For Europe the space for colonization had all but gone, and the glitter and brilliance of *"la belle epoch"* seemed too brittle to last. For the United States a similar sense of limited space accompanied Frederick Jackson Turner's announcement that the frontier had "closed," and the Gilded Age was over. The phrase *fin de siècle* was coined; more than a reference to the last decade, it resonated: *decade, decayed, decadence.*

Yet the pessimism seemed to be contradicted by signs of "progress." The development of railways, steamships, industry, and world trade had led to a booming world economy, with western Europe and the eastern United States as its twin cores, and imperialism and "white" expansion were at their peak. The world had been parceled out among the "Great Powers"; Africa had been partitioned and China seemed to be going the same way. Of course, the great discontinuity was not the end of the century but the outbreak of World War I in 1914. It produced the chasm and yet bridged the gap between the age of European predominance and a new era of global affairs and politics. When the events of World War II, a mere 21 years later, are added, then the whole era from 1914 to 1945 became a new "Thirty Years' War" that tossed the assured world of the nineteenth century upside down. It was, said Carl Sauer, "the end of what we have been pleased to call modern history [1492–1918], the expansion of western peoples and civilization over the thinly or weakly peopled spaces of the earth." [1]

Inevitably, these became years of reflection and adjustment. There was concern about the limits, availability, and ownership of some of the earth's key resources, particularly land, timber, soil, and water. This led to the quest for "conservation," and a concern for ecology emerged in the discourse. Ecological thinking provided coherence and focus for fusing concerns about resources and their scarcity by providing a contextual and holistic biology that would heal the land and society's relations with it. Both of these concerns were characterized by a shift from local and regional thinking to a more global view.

DESTRUCTIVE EXPLOITATION OF GLOBAL RESOURCES

The very progress that ensured the prosperity, territorial control, and power of the developed Western world had also increased resource competition and exploitation. Timber and land were the greatest concerns. For all the steam, steel, and speed of the era, it was still a "wooden age" for many industrialized countries. Even up to 1950, assured supplies of timber for construction and fuel were a high priority in some countries, with timber's strategic position being akin to that of petroleum later on. It was widely believed that a predicted "timber famine" would become so severe as to undermine civilization.

Concern about natural resources was not new, but what distinguished the turn-of-the-century views from earlier observations was that exploitation was seen increasingly as being worldwide and deleterious. In 1901 the Russian physical geographer, Alexander Woeikof, was concerned about the emergence of a "world civilization" that had led to "the growing disassociation of man and the earth." Humans had became more urbanized and industrialized and, consequently, had lost contact with their surroundings, which were then altered unthinkingly and irrevocably. Most affected was the earth's vegetation, which in turn affected hydrology, erosion, and climate and could well lead, he thought, to the ultimate destruction of civilization. Three years later, the German geographer, Ernst Friedrich, went further and suggested that European global expansion and resource gathering was based on an exploitative and destructive economy (*Raubwirtschaft*) that had already destroyed the flora, fauna, and soils over vast areas. And there the matter lay until 1938, when unexpectedly Carl Sauer produced a biting critique of the destructive social and environmental impact resulting from Europe's predatory outreach overseas, based on Friedrich's ideas. Sauer's experience of Latin America and knowledge of its history suggested a devastating and permanent impoverishment of land and of culture and society. The Spanish Conquest had led to the ravishing of New World societies by disease, warfare, and enslavement and the total disruption of their traditional value systems. Thus, humans and their culture could be abused by the thoughtless exploitation of new and technologically superior societies, just as much as physical resources could be.[2]

Somehow, humans had to rise above this mindless, short-term exploitative mode and acquire what Sauer later called "an ethic and aesthetic under which man, practising the qualities of prudence and moderation, may indeed pass on to posterity a good Earth."[3]

The complex idea of ecology ran sotto voce throughout many of the narratives. The word "ecology" itself was coined in 1866 by Ernst Haeckel, a German biologist, to describe the web of linked organisms and their surrounding environment. But it is an enigmatic concept that changes continually, and it became loaded with multiple meanings, such as "economy," the avoidance of waste and disorder, and the efficient use of "energy." Its most obvious manifestation was in the Clementsian ecological climax–equilibrium concept within biology, which implied a steady state, stability, interacting community, and no change, which appealed because it mirrored earlier and older states of society that were supposedly more stable and happier. Aldo Leopold's "Land Ethic" added yet another dimension to this ecological mystique.[4] The destruction of the Great Plains during the dust bowl era and the crash of Wall Street all seemed to point to the same thing—a need to sustain the community and its environment in stable equilibrium.

Ecology was the one conceptual contribution of the age to resource use and environmental management. In time, ecology and scientific conservation became a proof of right thinking and came to represent a moral yardstick that emphasized desirable qualities such as balance, order, harmony, diversity, and benign care, compared to the materialism of the production-oriented, industrialized world of the early twentieth century.

But if nature was best when altered least, difficulties were going to arise with forests. The alternatives were stark—either use them and clear them or leave them alone. But experience had shown that there was a third way and that some forests, at least, had a long history of conscious, manipulative conservation management along ecological lines and were thus capable of yielding a harvest of timber while staying intact enough to grow another day. The experience of the global forests during the first half of the century revealed these contrasting philosophies in all their complexity, with the debate driven by the specter of a predicted "timber famine." From this debate eventually arose some of the first glimmerings of global awareness of forest resources.

THE COMING TIMBER FAMINE

Many countries in Europe had long since faced up to the fact that they did not possess enough timber for their needs and had overcome their deficiencies by securing colonial supplies and/or establishing an elaborate system of reforestation. But when the specter of a timber famine hit the United States, by any measure the biggest producer and user of timber in the world, scarcity assumed both urgency and importance. Timber became the key resource issue, and it was replete with all sorts of environmental implications.

"The Day Is Coming": The United States

Timber shortages had not affected the United States, but in 1866 Andrew Fuller sounded an alarm: "The day is coming," he warned, "if not already here, when her people will look to the time when forests were wantonly destroyed." [5] By the late 1870s or early 1880s, the day seemed to have come. Whereas supplies of lumber and land had always seemed obtainable by the opening up of a new region, the public domain was closing. Admittedly, settlement was moving into the forested areas of the Rocky Mountains and Pacific Coast, which contained about one-third of the known forest stand, but this was the last timber frontier; there was no more after that. Increasingly, the words extinction, timber famine, and timber starvation were bandied about to describe the perceived impending crisis, and because the American economy and way of life were so dependent on wood, many were prepared to believe it.

The United States needed every bit of wood it could get. In 1906, lumber production reached 46 billion bf (108.5 million m³), nearly two-thirds of the world's output and an amount never equaled since. Per capita consumption was 525 bf (1.24 m³), which was not even remotely equaled anywhere else in the world then or since. The total U.S. consumption of all wood products reached its highest point of 13.38 billion ft³ (31.6 million m³) in 1907; 1906 had been the third highest and 1910 the second highest totals. Of this total consumption, over one-third was fuelwood (5 billion ft³, or 11.8 million m³), which still accounted for about 21 percent of energy needs in 1900. Also, a million tons of pig iron were still being made from charcoal. At the same time as these industrial demands were being made, agricultural clearing had reduced the forests by a further 108.9 million acres (48.1 million ha) between 1869 and 1899. [13] It could not go on like this for much longer.

Well before the time in 1877, Carl Schurz promoted the idea of forest preservation and conservation, and with the help of pressure groups and forestry professionals the goal eventually came to fruition with the creation of the Division of Forestry. Then, by a series of bizarre events (and even some illegalities) in Congress, the Forest Reserve Act was passed in 1891, conferring on the president the power to reserve land from the public domain. This legislation was followed by the Forest Management Act of 1897, which provided for forest administration. About 47 million acres (19 million ha) were reserved almost immediately (fig. 12.1), and the 1897 act allowed further reserves to be created to improve and protect the forests or to assist water flow and to provide a continuous supply of timber. Nonetheless, the country remained concerned about the rapacious laissez-faire economy and the destructive exploitation of the "cut-out-and-get-out" lumbermen. In addition, the Western states were becoming anxious to preserve forested watersheds in order to integrate irrigation, domestic water use, and hydroelectric power. The forests became an emotive issue for everyone—the tree lover, the rainmaker on the plains, the sportsman, the wilderness preservationist, the aesthete, and the Western developer—while the man in the street was concerned about timber scarcity and high prices.

It was against this background that Gifford Pinchot was appointed head of the Division of Forestry in 1898. Pinchot was a remarkable person; he was rich, young, energetic, intensely ambitious, and displayed a great insight into issues as well as an adroitness in manipulating public and congressional opinion. The epitome of the technical "expert," Pinchot sensed brilliantly the uneasy mood of the public and also that of the loggers themselves, who were frightened by the dwindling supply of timber, the frenetic shifts of price, output, and location, and their inability to manage the forests for a more sustained yield.

Pinchot concentrated on the forests of the western public lands in order to establish his management program of "wise use," basically a Utilitarian philosophy of resource extraction that embodied concepts of "the most productive use for the permanent good of the whole people" and of "the greatest good for the greatest number for the longest time." Conservation was simply "good business," he said; every other consideration was secondary to economics.[6] In addition he had three other aims—(1) transfer the forest reserves from the Land Office to his Division of Forestry (renamed the Forestry Bureau in 1901), (2) raise the status of the Forestry Division in the federal hierarchy, and (3) add even more forests to the reserves. Pinchot's campaign coincided with the presidency of Theodore Roosevelt, whose interests in the out-of-doors and flamboyant personality complemented those of Pinchot perfectly. They understood each other intuitively, and both were imbued with the same crusading zeal to change the current way of looking at land and its resources. Roosevelt embraced the "timber-famine" thesis and used the phrase many times in his speeches—probably because Pinchot ghost-wrote them. In 1905 the president said, "If the present rate of forest destruction is allowed to continue, with nothing to offset it, a timber famine in the future is inevitable." [7] It was claimed that Roosevelt consulted Pinchot more than any other person in Washington, so Pinchot was able to behave like a benevolent autocrat, confident that he had presidential approval and a large measure of public support behind him. The upshot was that Pinchot achieved all his aims, created a powerful federal agency in the Forest Bureau, and almost doubled the number of reserved forests to a massive 150 million acres (60.7 million ha) by 1906. (See fig 12.1.)

Using his influence and his own money, he bankrolled a lavish Governors' Conference in Washington in 1907, a spectacular and unprecedented gathering of politicians, experts, and big business at which his philosophy of conservation would be proclaimed before the people, bypassing an unwilling and increasingly hostile Congress. Although stage-managed down to the last detail, Pinchot found it difficult to get recommendations out of the conference and, as a compromise, steered it toward the idea of a National Resources Inventory, to be compiled by a National Resources Commission with himself as chairman.

In later years Pinchot and his associates continued to create a climate of anxiety about supplies. Several times he predicted that the supply would end in 30–35 years' time. His most eloquent statement was in his short but influential book of 1910, *The Fight for Conservation,* in which he brought the timber issue down to the individual home by saying that the country had "already crossed the verge of a timber famine so severe that its blighting effects will be felt in every household in the land" through scarcity and rising prices. The forests were failing as a result of the "suicidal policy of forest destruction" which everyone had allowed. That such dire warnings came from the chief forester, confidant of the president, and a prominent public figure in the heart of government meant that they were treated seriously.[8]

With his alarmism and actions, both autocratic and arbitrary, Pinchot made many enemies. Congress resented his overly intimate association with the president, rival federal departments were jealous of Forestry's spectacular success, and the public at large tired of his moral crusade and began to distrust his alliance with big business. When Roosevelt's second term ended and Taft was elected, Pinchot lost his independence and much influence. In 1910 he was dismissed on a relatively insignificant charge of insubordination over the Alaska coal-holdings case, the so-called Ballinger-Pinchot affair.

Although out of federal office, never to return, Pinchot continued to act as goad, spur, and agitator for another 35 years as leading spokesman for the Progressive Party, from 1910 to 1917, and as governor of Pennsylvania

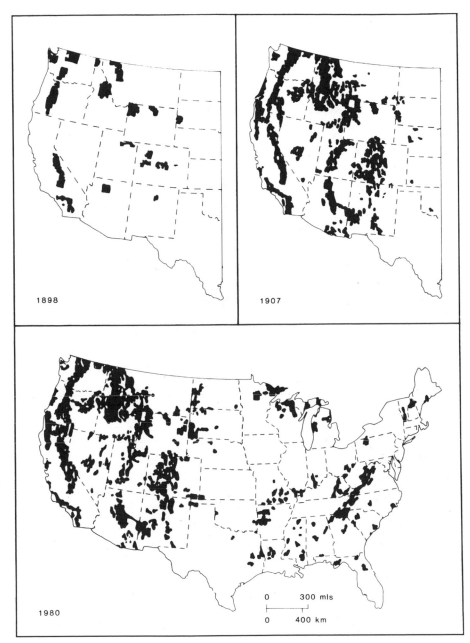

1898

1907

1980

0   300 mls

0   400 km

Figure 12.1 The national forests of the United States, 1898, 1907, and 1980. (Sources: M. Williams, *Americans and Their Forests* [New York: Cambridge University Press, 1989], 408, based on National Archives GRG 95, container 108 and official maps.)

from 1923 to 1927 and 1931 to 1935. But he was walking an intellectual tightrope: conservation could not be both a moral crusade against materialism and a wise-use policy of maximum use. Pinchot's "gospel of efficiency" would inevitably bring him into conflict with aesthetes like John Muir, who drew on the romanticism of transcendentalism and the "wilderness" experience. In time, considerations of aesthetics and beauty would loom as large, if not larger, than those of utility when it came to judging the "conservation" of trees.

In the immediate post–World War I period, Pinchot became increasingly vociferous. In order to whip up support for his apocalyptic vision of shortages, he cast his successors in the Forest Service—Henry Graves and William Greeley—together with the Society of American Foresters and the lumbermen as the enemies within, who were creating the "blighting famine." "Forest devastation . . . threatens our national safety and undermines our industrial welfare," thundered Pinchot, so that "without the products of the forest, civilization as we know it would stop." His call for the nationalization of the forests stirred up enough support in Congress for the Senate to institute an enquiry, *Timber Depletion, Lumber Prices, Lumber Exports and Concentration of Timber Ownership,* commonly known as the Capper Report, issued in 1920. But although the thinking and phraseology of the report were permeated with the "five Ds"—devastation, depletion, deterioration, decay, and disappearance—it did not advocate a national takeover of the forests and the lumber industry. The lumber industry had had a narrow escape.[9]

Although attributed to Chief Forester William Greeley, the Capper Report was largely written by Earle Clapp and Raphael Zon of the newly created Research Section of the Forest Service. It was more sophisticated than any previous reports in that it emphasized the dynamics of growth of the forest and not simply the area. It calculated that growth was 6 billion ft^3 but that the drain on resources was 26 billion ft^3, which meant that mature, high-volume original stands were being plundered at 4.3 times the rate of growth, and inferior timber used for fuel and smaller products was being depleted at 3.5 times the rate of growth. It was, said Greeley, "a steady wiping out of the original forest resources of the country. Three-fifths of primeval forest are gone." In addition, about 81 million acres (32.8 million ha) of the cutover trees—an area greater than the combined forested areas of France, Germany, Belgium, Holland, Denmark, Switzerland, Spain, and Portugal—were periodically swept with fire and were contributing nothing to the growth budget; and of the 5.5 million acres (2.2 million ha) of merchantable timber being cut annually, well over half did not restock and were being added to the cutover. And yet, for all the emphasis on the productive

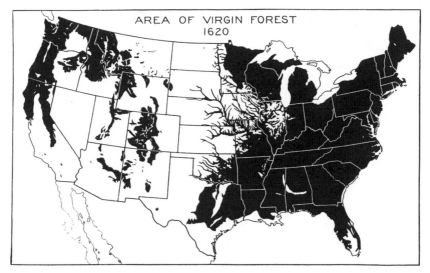

AREA OF VIRGIN FOREST
1620

Figure 12.2 "Area of virgin forest," United States, 1620. (Source: W. B. Greeley, "The Relations of Geography to Timber Supply," *Economic Geography* 1 [1925]: 4–5.)

dynamics of the forest, there was still an obsessive concern by Greeley on the area of mature or virgin forest, as he called it repeatedly. For him virgin trees represented the major, perhaps the only true, resource remaining in the forest. Although it is true that virgin trees are the source of large merchantable timber, they do not represent a source of growth; they are, as E. A. Zeigler said, "non-producing capital" having reached maturity. But Greeley did not seem to recognize the difference, and he stoked the fires of concern by later compiling three maps of the declining area of virgin forest, 1620, 1850, and 1920, which were alarming in their stark and seemingly simple message of denudation (figs. 12.2–12.4). The mathematical precision and detail of the dots reinforced the certainty of his enterprise. It looked as though the predictions of the doomsday men were correct: the day was coming when the country would experience a timber famine.[10]

"Segments of a Greater Whole": World Supplies

If U.S. timber needs could not be satisfied by the nation's own forests, where could the supply come from? The question had already been asked by the Research Section of the Forest Service. By 1910, Zon had already completed a preliminary assessment of global timber resources followed by a detailed study of those of Latin America. This was then followed up by *The Forest Resources of the World*, a landmark publication of 997 pages that for the

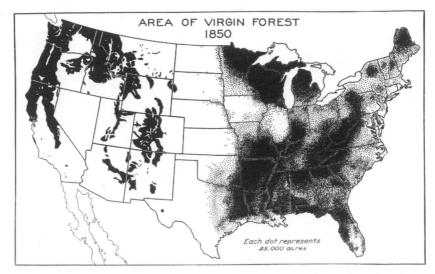

Figure 12.3 "Area of virgin forest," United States, 1850. (Source: W. B. Greeley, "The Relations of Geography to Timber Supply," *Economic Geography* 1 [1925]: 4–5.)

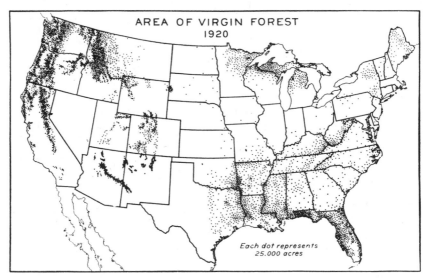

Figure 12.4 "Area of virgin forest," United States, 1920. (Source: W. B. Greeley, "The Relations of Geography to Timber Supply," *Economic Geography* 1 [1925]: 4–5.)

first time attempted to survey the forests globally and comprehensively—
a difficult task, considering the almost total absence of statistics on area,
growth, consumption, and production.[11] For the first time, maps were produced of four different types of forest (coniferous, temperate hardwood,
mixed hardwood and coniferous, and tropical hardwood). Calculations

were made of the area, productivity in terms of growth, production (saw timber and firewood), and drain and depletion of remaining resources. Ownership, consumption, and trade were also discussed. It was not going to be replaced as a sourcebook for half a century.

Forest Resources of the World had a foreword by Gifford Pinchot, then governor of Pennsylvania: it was vintage stuff with its doom-laden aphorisms and slogans. The wood problem was "a world problem"; "the need for wood is increasing, the forests are decreasing"; even the "last great bodies of soft woods—those of the Pacific Coast—will soon be gone"; Asiatic Russia was the only undeveloped source left. Furthermore, World War I and U-boat warfare had shown how global conflict adversely affected the movement of goods, so that the establishment of peace and the abolition of trade barriers were indispensable to solving America's timber shortage. Pinchot, always with an eye to the "big show," called for an international conference to prepare an inventory of all global resources, with himself, no doubt, as a prime player.[32] It was his first, and last, gambol into global forests.

Zon owed much to Pinchot, who was his patron, but he did not adopt the same strident, alarmist tone, and his work was sober and methodical. He was not one for the limelight; perhaps he had had more than enough after being arrested for political activity as a student at Kazan University in tsarist Russia. Sentenced to imprisonment, he escaped and finally made his way to the United States. He entered the Forest Service and in 1914 was appointed head of the Office of Forest Investigations.

Zon set out the interrelated economic, social, and environmental benefits of forests, which he considered seriously impaired once their area fell below the magical figure of 30 percent. He calculated that the global area of forests was 30.3 million km^2, or 22 percent, of the extrapolar regions. He was aware that the area of world forests had been drastically reduced over the ages and that the process was continuing. The greatest decline had possibly been in China, but no one knew for sure. Next came Europe, where most of the original land area of 10.1 million km^2 had been forested, but now only 3.1 million km^2, or about one-third, remained, most of that in Scandinavia and Russia. In the United States the original forest had shrunk more than 40 per cent in the course of three centuries.

Zon's country-by-country calculations are regrouped in table 12.1 into the two major categories of developed and less developed, which correspond largely to the temperate and tropical world. The figures are undoubtedly flawed in detail, as he had little hard fact to draw on; but whatever their imperfections in absolute terms, they did pinpoint for the first time the relative magnitude of forest area, use, and destruction, and the contemporary perception of the potential of the global forests. Slightly less than

Table 12.1 World forest area (in millions of ha), production (in millions of m³), and deficits (in millions of m³) by major world regions, circa 1923

	Area (in millions of ha)	Production (in millions of m³	Average Annual Cut (million m³)			Excess of Growth over Consumption
			Saw Timber	Fuelwood	Total	
Developed:						
North America	502.7	120.8	421.0	338.5	759.5	−638.7
Europe	132.7	272.6	142.6	133.6	276.2	−3.6
USSR	640.2	367.0	116.8	88.5	205.3	+161.7
Other	80.5	85.0	13.5	57.9	71.4	+13.6
Total developed	1,356.0	845.4	693.9	618.5	1,312.4	−467.0
Less developed:						
Asia	346.4	95.2	25.2	79.7	104.9	−9.7
China	76.9	55.8	8.1	47.8	55.9	−0.1
Central and Latin America	524.1	15.5	7.8	53.8	61.6	−46.1
Brazil	404.7	36.8	2.8	34.0	36.8	0.0
Africa	322.1	28.0	1.8	18.5	20.5	+7.5
Other	. . .	0.3	0.0	0.2	0.2	0.0
Total less developed	1,674.2	231.6	45.7	234.0	279.7	−48.1
World	3,030.2	1,007.0	739.6	852.5	1,592.1	−515.1

Source: Based on R. Zon and W. N. Sparhawk, *Forest Resources of the World* (New York: McGraw-Hill Book Co., 1923), 4–12, 37–43.

half (44.75 percent) of the forest was in the developed world, but because these forests were well managed they contributed over three-quarters of the growth. However, the drain of cutting for sawed timber and firewood was so great that the balance sheet of growth versus consumption showed a massive deficit. The annual drain was in the order of 56 billion ft³ (1592.1 million m³) of which 46.4 percent was sawed timber, and the remaining 53.6 percent was firewood. The total sawed timber cut worldwide exceeded growth by one-half, of which the United States accounted for nine-tenths. The country was clearly heading for a timber famine.

Zon was aware that the growth figures were "guesstimates," but the one statistic about which he was certain was that of the timber trade. The six western European countries of the United Kingdom, Germany, France, Netherlands, Italy, and Belgium (in order of magnitude) took nearly half of the world's imports, and the United States another 15 percent. The imports were supplied largely from the coniferous forests of Russia, Canada, the three Scandinavian countries of Norway, Sweden, and Finland, *and* the United States, which, paradoxically, exported as well as imported timber. This pattern of consumption and supply was not going to vary markedly over the next half century, other than the addition of Japan, and with only minor variations, such as the emergence of the market in China, will probably continue well into the twenty-first century.

Taking "a look into the future," Zon thought that the reduction in forest area would continue as world population increased (particularly in the tropics) and required more land for agriculture. Reforestation in Europe and reversion of abandoned farmland to forest in the United States were not great enough to compensate for clearing in these continents. On the plus side were the untouched reserves in Siberia and the tropical world, enough to supply the needs of America and the rest of the world for many decades to come. But exploitation of the tropical forests was difficult. They lacked communications, transport was expensive, and their biological diversity made extraction uneconomical and difficult; it was hardly possible to find two or three trees of the same kind in a single acre. Also, the wood was so hard that softwood sawmill machinery could only achieve about one-third of the output when applied to South American timbers. In any case, when the tropical areas developed economically, their forests would be exploited just as wastefully as all other forests as their timber consumption rose in line with a rise in standards of living. As fast as the consumption of fuelwood decreased with substitute energy sources, so new uses arose, such as paper, packaging, railroad ties, and telegraph and telephone poles. The world timber famine, therefore, could be averted only by boosting the production and management of the coniferous forests.

Whatever the future held, one thing was becoming abundantly clear— after 1920, forests everywhere in the world were coming under scrutiny and being assessed. What happened in one part of the world had repercussions in another part. That had always been true, but now it was clearly recognized that individual forests were "only segments of a great whole." The forest was now being looked at as not only a global resource but also as a large-scale conceptual entity that could be visualized, managed, made productive, and "economized."

CLEARING IN THE LESS-DEVELOPED WORLD

While Zon's speculations about the future of the world's forests were not all that accurate they were discerning. Particularly astute was his recognition that population growth in the tropical world was on an upward trajectory and, combined with slowly but steadily growing economies, would be likely

Table 12.2 Net forest change (in millions of ha) and annual rate of
change (in millions of ha), tropical and temperate worlds, 1700–1995

Date	Tropical	Temperate	Total	Rate/yr
1700–1849	109	180	−289	1.94
1850–1919	70	135	−205	2.97
1920–49	235	99	−334	11.52
1950–79	318	18	−336	11.57
1980–95	220	6	−226	15.10

Sources: J. F. Richards, "Land Transformation," in *The Earth as Transformed by
Human Action,* ed. B. L. Turner II et al. (Cambridge: Cambridge University Press,
1990), 164; and amendments by M. Williams, "Forest and Tree Cover," in *Changes in
Land Use and Land Cover: A Global Perspective,* ed. W. B. Meyer and B. L. Turner II
(Cambridge: Cambridge University Press, 1994), 97–124.

to cause massive deforestation in the future—indeed, between 1900 and
1920 another 40 million ha were cleared. In contrast, he underestimated
the extent of abandonment of farmland in the marginal areas of the developed world and its reversion to forest, so that the 40–44 million ha cleared
between 1900 and 1920 was matched almost exactly by the same amount
of forestland gained, especially in Europe. Even in the eastern United States
the pioneering urge had waned and forest reversion was well under way.

But Zon could never have forecast the magnitude and extent of clearing
during the next 30 years, when the expansion of cultivation at the expense
of all types of natural vegetation was relentless (table 12.2). In the tropical
world an additional 235 million ha were cleared between 1920 and 1950,
almost half as much again as the 179 million ha of the long two centuries
before. Even in the temperate, developed world a net 99 million ha disappeared, most of that destruction caused by timber extraction, though
the total might be offset somewhat by further land abandonment and forest reversion. In other words, the 50 years between 1900 and 1950 saw a
complete reversal of the eighteenth- and nineteenth-century pattern, where
the temperate world had surpassed the tropical in terms of deforestation.
The other startling fact was that the overall rate of clearing had risen from
nearly 3 million ha/yr between 1850 and 1919 to a staggering 11.5 million
ha/yr between 1920 and 1949, an amount only fractionally less than during
the opening three decades of the highly publicized "great onslaught" after
World War II.

The regional detail of clearing between 1900 and 1950 is tantalizingly slight. With few exceptions the sources seem to be either absent or
fragmentary—a classic example of what has been referred to before as a

Table 12.3 Cropland and land-cover change (in millions of ha), tropical (developing) world

	Cropland			Cropland Change		Forest Change		Grassland Change	
	1920	1950	1980	1920–50	1950–80	1920–50	1950–80	1920–50	1950–80
Tropical Africa	88	136	222	48	86	−87	−114	+39	+28
North Africa and Middle East	43	66	107	23	41	−9	−4	−15	−37
South Asia	98	136	210	38	74	−38	−71	0	−3
Southeast Asia	21	35	55	14	20	−5	−7	−9	−13
Latin America	45	87	142	42	55	−96	−122	+54	+67
Total	295	460	735	165	276	−235	−318	+69	+42

Source: After J. F. Richards, "Land Transformation," in *The Earth as Transformed by Human Action,* ed.
B. L. Turner II et al., (Cambridge: Cambridge University Press, 1990), 164.

"dark age" and a "dark space" in the history and geography of deforestation. In general, though, what happened seems to be more a continuation
of past events and localities of deforestation rather than anything startlingly
new. Peasant agriculture continued to expand, caught up increasingly in the
world economy, as did plantations and commercial farming for cash. The
millions of individual, incremental actions by peasant farmers to clear a few
square meters of forest here and there meant widespread destruction. The
whole was driven by a massive population increase in the tropical world
compared to the temperate world. Over half a billion were added between
1900 and 1950, on a base of about 1.1 billion (see table 9.3).

In summary, over 70 percent of the 235 million ha taken from the tropical forests between 1920 and 1950 went to make new cropland, with the
remainder reverting to grassland (table 12.3). Cutting for firewood rose
in line with population increase (table 12.1). In addition, lumbering could
now be added to the impacts on these forests, although compared with
temperate lumbering it was still a mere one-fifteenth of the volume (approximately 3.1 million m³), barely increasing until the export trade developed after 1950. It is true that Britain in particular, and Europe in general,
had always imported special tropical timbers for special purposes, such as
mahogany, rosewood, and brazilwood for furniture and teak for ships and
jetties, but now the tropical forest was beginning to be regarded simply as
a source for wood regardless of type. As far as the forest was concerned, it
was one world.

Plate 12.1 A coffee plantation in Brazil. (From G Pieraccini, *Emigrazione agricola al Brasile: Relazione della Commissione Italiana, 1912* [Bologna: U. Berti & Co.].) (State Historical Society of Wisconsin, Madison.)

Central and South America

In the Western Hemisphere, the United States regarded the forests of its southerly tropical neighbors in Latin America and the Caribbean as an "untouched storehouse." [12] In their global survey, Zon and Sparhawk calculate how long supplies would last in the face of vigorous domestic agricultural clearing, something they did not do for any other part of the world. Destruction was most severe in Central America, and their country descriptions are peppered with phrases like "much clearing"; a "great deal of the original forest . . . has been swept away"; "large tracts are under plantation crops"; while the coastal forest of Brazil was "much reduced" (plates 12.1 and 12.2).[13] There was very little hard fact about the extent of forest change, though there was a suspicion of great activity.

These qualitative assessments were supported a few years later by Tom Gill who toured the Caribbean to assess its forest prospects, but paradoxically also to promote conservation. He found a forest that was well used and severely degraded in places, and he was both amazed and depressed by

Plate 12.2 Deforestation for a coffee plantation in São Paulo State, Brazil, with a *fazenda* plantation in the background. (From *Le brésil: Ses richesses naturelles, ses industries,* vol. 2 [Paris: Librairie Aillaud & Cie, 1910].) (State Historical Society of Wisconsin, Madison.)

the devastation wrought already by indigenous and colonial agriculture. Fire and *conuco,* or shifting agriculture, had made massive inroads into the forest, always with the same result:

> The land has been cleared and is now abandoned. Trees have been cut and destroyed. Usually worthless jungle takes its place; a thick growth of brush springs up that will probably prevent forestation by valuable species for many years to come. Worse still, coarse, rapidly growing grasses may capture the field and prevent any form of forest cover re-establishing itself.

He deplored the "waste" of good trees and the permanent degradation of the forest. If the native people were removed, then the forest might "slowly, but surely, regain the ground that it had lost through long centuries." However, it was far more likely that the population would multiply and "drive back the forest to the very Atlantic." Around the cities, forests had been "cut away for miles." Along the coasts and inland along accessible rivers,

American and European loggers had "laid waste" great areas of forest. Only British Guiana, parts of Venezuela, Colombia, and southern Mexico possessed a "wealth of useful products" and were a source of wood for the future; the rest had gone.[14]

The Atlantic coastal forest was fast becoming "little more than a memory" as coffee, cotton, cattle, colonists, *caboclos*, and industrial and domestic fuel users ensured its rapid destruction. It must have constituted a considerable part of the 96 million ha of the Latin American forest that disappeared between 1920 and 1950 (table 12.3). During these years the population in southeast Brazil grew phenomenally, from approximately 7 million to 22 million, generating "boom" conditions. In addition to overseas migrants, hordes of internal migrants from the drought-prone and impoverished northeast flocked into the cities. Surveys in São Paulo State showed that forest decreased relentlessly, from about 34 percent of land use in 1905 to a mere 15 percent by 1950. Overall it was disappearing at rate of 3,000 km²/yr, with an overall probable loss of 150 percent since 1910. The remaining patches of the original forest became reserves, and the remnants of the native population were rounded up into reservations or eliminated. There was no public forest left. Scarcely anyone objected, as everyone's prosperity and comfort were bound up with the exploitation of the forest.

As long as it was believed that coffee growing was most productive in "virgin" forest, then the frontier of deforestation was going to advance inexorably to the south and west. So valuable did untouched forest become that land values were reversed, uncleared land commanding a premium in contrast to cleared land. But increasingly, it was domestic and industrial fuel needs that put most pressure on the remnants of the forest. For example, it took 4.5 m³ to produce a ton of pig iron, and 4.2 million tons were produced by 1950. At a reasonable growth of 200 m³ for secondary (*copoiera*) forest, that would equal 2,650 km² of woodland cleared in that year alone. Similarly, if railroads used 12.5 million m³ in 1950, then that was the equivalent of 620 km² of forest. Domestic and small industrial establishments, metal works, and other uses may have amounted to at least 1,000 km². A total, then, something approaching 4,000 km²/yr (less, if some form of rotation was in play), was a formidable drain on the forest that it simply could not sustain, especially when as late as 1979, 79 percent of Brazil's energy needs were still supplied by wood. Some attempt was made to meet fuel needs with fast-growing Australian *Eucalypts*, and although millions were planted between 1911 and 1953, it is doubtful if even "3 hectares had been planted for every 10,000 that had been cleared."[15]

On its southernmost extremities the semitropical forest merged into the temperate stands of the easily worked softwood, *Araucaria augustiflora* or

Paraná pine, a widely spaced (approximately 25–65 trees/ha—but at least uncomplicated by other species), tall, thick conifer. These forests consisted of about 44 percent (25.3 million ha) of the total land area of the 58 million ha of the states of Paraná, Santa Catarina, and Rio Grande do Sul. It was all too attractive to remain intact. After about 1920 immigrant European and Japanese farmers cleared the land to create small, intensive, and highly mechanized holdings growing temperate crops for export; and U.S. lumbermen cut systematically to supply this straight-grained and easily worked pine to the burgeoning towns on the treeless pampas, such as Montevideo and particularly Buenos Aires (up from 750,000 in 1893 to 4 million by 1940). Over 17.7 million tons of logs were exported, and probably double that amount illegally, but it was only a fraction of the potential 1.5 billion m^3 that the forest could have yielded. By 1980 it was estimated that this once extensive forest had been reduced to a mere 445,000 ha. It was a typical Brazilian story of "stupendous" waste. Similarly, to the east, in the northern Argentine provinces of Chaco, Formosa, Tucuman, Santigo del Estero, and Sante Fe and in adjacent parts of the limitless Chaco Boreal of Paraguay, the easily worked hardwood, *quebracho,* was being cleared at the alarming rate of over 200,000 ha/yr.

Africa

Although it is probable that 87 million ha of forest were cleared for agriculture in tropical Africa between 1920 and 1950 (table 12.3), little is known about it. With the exception of the extremes of the continent in French North Africa and British South Africa, the colonizing powers had hardly got a sufficient grip on their new territories after "the scramble" of the 1880s to know how much forest existed, let alone recognize and explain deforestation. Africa was a "dark continent" in more ways than one. Even as late as 1945 the second edition of Lord Hailey's authoritative *An African Survey* still devoted less than one of its 1,800-odd pages to African forests and thought that forests were more important in conserving water and ameliorating climate than supplying timber. By the third edition of the *Survey* in 1957, the forest occupied 23 pages; but deforestation, other than as a vague background fact, was still neither analyzed nor commented on.[16]

The only comments or explanations of forest change were dominated by the conventional wisdom that, as ever, the greatest enemy of the forest was the native farmer, who cut down virgin forest, cropped, and fired the ground for a few years. Consequently, every year "thousands of square miles of forest are ruthlessly cut down for a few years' crops." Climax theory, much in vogue at the time, predicted a progressive and inevitable deterioration to park-like savanna, grassland, increased soil erosion and exhaustion, and eventual desertification.

The indigenous cultivators were likened to parasites, and the only way to stop them was to declare forest reserves and exclude them, though where they would go was never suggested. For the hard-liners, the natives were likened to willful and destructive children who did not know the value of their possessions:

> A child is not allowed to play with fire, although it may very much like to see the flames; in the same way . . . [the local administration] . . . cannot allow the inhabitants . . . to play fast and loose with their priceless treasures, the African forests, well knowing that the country will be permanently injured thereby.[17]

It was the Indian story all over again but with a vengeance, always working to the detriment of the shifting agriculturalist and indigenous farming practice and denying the peoples' livelihood and history.

Nowhere was this ignorance more pronounced than in West Africa. The vegetation graded in belts of varying width from south to north from tropical and mangrove forests on the coast, to forest savannas, grasslands and then finally the Sahel, as rainfall and its reliability decreased northward. Because there were quite large "islands" of dense, lush, semideciduous forest in the forest-savanna belt, successive French botanists, from 1911 to 1948, designated it a natural forest formation that had become degraded through constant cultivation and fire. It became, therefore, a "derived" savanna incapable of reestablishing itself because presumably rainfall had decreased. Such alarmist explanations of humanly induced degradation were not confined to francophone Africa. The experience of the dust bowl in the United States during the 1930s was taken up enthusiastically by British foresters, who thought that the deserts were "on the march" into the grasslands of northern Nigeria.[18]

This idea of degradation was reproduced and elaborated through each generation of the scientific, forestry, and administrative communities. They evoked the notion of a climatic climax—an ultimate stage of succession that represented the "natural" vegetation against which the degree of current degradation could be measured. In time it became the dominant discourse and hegemonic explanation of forest destruction in the continent. However, recently it has been shown that the forest "islands" are far from being relics of a once greater forest but are the outcome of intensive cultivation and fertilization, so that fallow areas have become progressively more woody. Population growth has implied more forest, not less; it is a landscape "half-filled

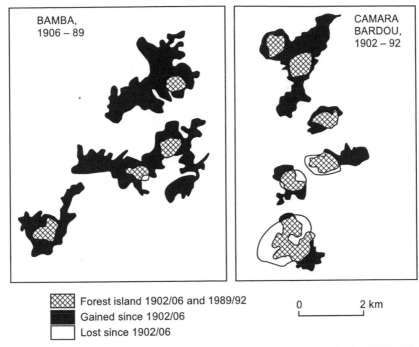

Forest island 1902/06 and 1989/92
Gained since 1902/06
Lost since 1902/06

0   2 km

Figure 12.5 Growth of forest "islands" at Bamba (1906–89) and Camara Bardou (1902–92), Kissidougou area of Guinea. (Source: J. Fairhead and M. Leach, *Misreading the African Landscape: Society and Ecology in a Forest-Savanna Mosaic* [Cambridge: Cambridge University Press, 1996], 71.)

and filling with forest, not half-emptied and emptying of it" (fig. 12.5). History has been read backwards and conventional explanations of deforestation, in this part of the world, at least, turned upside down.[19]

If this analysis is extended to the bulk of the West African forest belt in Sierra Leone, Liberia, Côte d'Ivoire, Ghana, Benin, and Togo, then the startling conclusion is that views on deforestation have been unilineal and have obscured more complex histories. The extent of the forest in the past has been exaggerated, thus making any diminution appear greater. Depopulation and population shifts that have ensured forest regrowth have been ignored, recent historical climatic change favorable to tree growth has been discounted, and it has not been appreciated that many forests in the open savanna are human creations based on intensive cultivation and settlement and are not relics of a forest lost through misuse. This is not to deny that there has been quite extensive deforestation, but it is not as great as is supposed. The West African story is a cautionary tale that needs to be remembered when grappling with the contemporary rhetoric about deforestation.

Time and again, whether in seventeenth- and eighteenth-century Europe or nineteenth-century United States, the impact of metallurgy has been invoked to explain deforestation, and the same is true of the indigenous iron industry of West Africa but as is usual, although locally dramatic and visually spectacular, it was nowhere as devastating or widespread as agricultural expansion and intensive cultivation. It was a mere pinprick and probably accounted for no more than a few thousand hectares.

Far more destructive was land clearance for commercial crops, which replaced subsistence plots. Peasant proprietors experimented with commercial cropping of cotton, coffee, cocoa, palm oil, and rubber and production flourished. In the rain forest of Asante (Ashanti) around Kumase in Ghana, the local council became alarmed at the destruction, bemoaning in 1938 that "almost all the forests . . . have been converted to cocoa farms and that all attention has been diverted from the cultivation of foodstuffs." Within two generations much of the forest in Nigeria, Benin, and Ghana had changed from unappropriated forestland, roamed by elephants, lions, and monkeys, "in which tribal wars were fought and hunters wandered over large tracts, to settled and cultivated land over which families and individuals claimed more or less exclusive rights." The whole process of conversion was going to accelerate rapidly after 1945.[20] And, as it took at least 75–100 years to reestablish a reasonably mature forest, and over 250, if ever, to get back to primary forest, the forest could never win against humans.

South and Southeast Asia

Forest destruction accelerated in South and Southeast Asia between 1920 and 1950, as the population of the region rose by 192 million and livestock numbers by 89.4 million. A mosaic of different patterns and motivations emerges. While some land began to be cropped twice, the easiest solution was to convert forestland to arable, so that 35.8 million ha of forest of all types was affected. In British India it was official policy to sacrifice forest for crops, even in hilly and mountainous districts, as on the Himalayan slopes and in Orissa Hills (see fig. 11.2B), but railways and fuelwood demands continued to take an enormous toll.

In mainland Asia, pioneering peasant farmers cleared land for cultivation of wet paddies, especially in Thailand's Chao Phraya delta region and surrounding country, and because population densities were low, the resulting surplus of rice became the basis of a thriving export industry. In insular Southeast Asia, Indonesia and Malaysia expanded cultivation but also plantation crops, especially rubber, and with Borneo indulged in quite rapacious logging of timber for the export market. It was a prelude to the great logging exploitation for global markets that was to come later.

CLEARING IN THE DEVELOPED WORLD

During the first half of the twentieth century, the great bulk of the world's commercial timber came from the softwood coniferous forests that stretched across the northern parts of the Eurasian and American landmasses, with important offshoots of other softwood production in the Pacific coast and the South of the United States. Although a little less than half (44.75 percent) of all forests, they contributed a staggering three-quarters of global production. The experience of exploitation in three of the core countries of production, the United States, the USSR, and Sweden, was very different. In the United States laissez-faire capitalism ran riot until tempered by regulation and self-interest; in the USSR a nominally planned economy resting on Marxist-Leninist ideology plundered the forests in the name of production; while in Sweden the semiregulatory, cooperative approach of a liberal socialist administration produced a forest about as regulated, artificial, and productive as any in the world. Together these three countries form a wide spectrum of experiences and approaches regarding the perception of the coming timber crisis, the attempt to sustain production, and the problem of deforestation.

The United States: Laissez-Faire Capitalism and Self-Interest

Even as Pinchot and his clique were proclaiming the coming timber famine, the forest was making its comeback in the eastern half of the country as farmland was abandoned. In addition, programs of fire suppression and afforestation and changing patterns of consumption augmented stands. Most important, investigators and commentators seriously underestimated the regenerative power of the forest and did not detect the trend toward regrowth.

The Forest Balance Sheet

In 1905 James Defebaugh had pointed out that in the past the country had been "drawing on the surplus," but now it was starting "to draw down on the capital funds." [21] His analogy of a financial statement or balance sheet in describing the forest resource was a good one because everyone wanted to be able to see the debits and credits. The debits or drains were reasonably well known; the credits or growth were a mystery. In order to produce a forest balance sheet, two major investigations had to be carried out that had a significance far beyond the United States alone. First, the location and extent of the forest had to be determined in order to calculate the stock, and second—and dependent on the first—the volume of timber and its rate of growth or depletion also had to be calculated, problems that Zon had grappled with, but not solved, in his world survey.

By the beginning of the century the mapping of the forest was almost complete and its size could be calculated with some reasonable accuracy (table 12.4). The original forest was estimated at between 950 million and 1 billion acres (384 million and 405 million ha), of which 850 million acres (344 million ha) was commercial forest and 100–150 million acres (40.5–60.7 million ha) noncommercial forest. By 1907 William Greeley estimated that only 515 million and 65 million acres (208 million and 26 million ha), respectively, remained, and although later estimates varied considerably, there was little doubt that the forest had diminished by between 300 million and 350 million acres (121–142 million ha) by the beginning of the century. The future looked just as bleak: projections of past trends carried forward by Greeley to the year 1950 suggested that another 100 million acres (40.5 million ha) would disappear in new farms and that lumbering would create an unproductive cutover area of 182 million acres (74 million ha), leaving something like a mere 230 million acres (93 million ha) in forest. It was an alarming prospect that struck at the very heart of America's self-image as the storehouse of boundless resources; the nation might be reduced to the state of some impoverished and denuded Mediterranean country. The message of dearth was underlined by the publication of Greeley's misleading maps depicting the diminishing acreage of "virgin" forests between 1620 and 1920. The fact that second- and third-growth forests more than compensated for the decrease in "first"-growth forest was ignored.

But the area of a forest really tells one little about its productive capacity, its stock of timber, and its rate of growth. Such calculations were (and are) fraught with difficulties. Subjective assessments, differing measures, deliberate underestimates by large companies to avoid taxation or competition, and the changing value of different timbers all led to pessimistic interpretations and underestimates of the forest resources. The best estimates showed a volume of 635 billion ft^3 (17.96 billion m^3) of standing timber in the original forest, which was reduced to between 167 and 208 billion ft^3 (4.73 billion and 5.89 billion m^3) by the end of the nineteenth century (table 12.4). In these varied estimates, the work of E. A. Zeigler was important because he pointed out something that was known intuitively but rarely acknowledged: that timber harvest could not exceed net timber growth indefinitely,

Table 12.4 Estimated area of commercial and noncommercial U.S. forest and standing saw-timber volume

Date	Commercial Forest (in millions of ha)	Noncommercial Forest (in millions of ha)	Standing Saw-Timber Volume (in billions of ft^3)
1630	344	40	635
"Original"	344	61	433
1895	227	. . .	192
1902	200	. . .	167
1907	208	26	. . .
1908	223	. . .	208
1920	188	61	185
1930	200	49	139
1944	187	66	133
1952	200	100	201
1962	206	101	203
1970	202	103	202
1977	197	102	214

Source: M. Clawson, "Forests in the Long Sweep of American History," *Science* 204 (1979): 1168–74.

neither could net growth exceed harvest for very long because the standing timber accumulated to a level where no further growth occurred unless young growth was stimulated after storm damage, fire, or decaying trees. Not only did Zeigler dismiss Greeley's fixation with "virgin" timber as unrealistic in terms of growth, but he went so far as to suggest that if all mature timber were removed and replaced by second growth, then yields would be raised by between 30 and 100 ft^3/acre/annum, depending on the species and location.[22] In other words, careful production management could increase yields and be the answer to the impending famine. This, of course, was not a revolutionary suggestion, having had its origins in the German tradition of total forest management; but the significance for the United States was that the "bounty" of a supposedly pristine nature could no longer be relied on; humans would have to intervene and alter "the wilderness."

All this debate on area, stock, and growth fed into the calculation of the overall balance sheet of growth and drain. Although Zeigler had estimated that annual growth was 6.75 billion ft^3—which was barely more than one-fourth of the estimated annual drain—it remained for Greeley in 1920 to refine the ideas and calculations further (table 12.5). The result was more alarming than the estimates of the number of acres being cleared. Growth

Table 12.5 Estimated forest volume and annual growth and drain, United States, 1909–77 (in billions of ft³)

	1909 Zeigler	1920 Greeley	1933 Copeland	1950 Forecast (I)	1950 Forecast (II)	1952 F.S.	1962 F.S.	1970 F.S.	1977 F.S.
Stock of all standing timber	545	746	486	634	634	603	648	680	711
Growth per annum:									
Actual	6.75	6.0	8.9	...	...	13.9	16.7	19.8	21.7
Potential:									
Cutovers restocked	...	19.5	...	...	...	...	...	...	...
Virgin timber cut	...	8.2	...	10.6	21.4	27.5	...	...	≈36.0
All forest well stocked and managed	...	27.7	...	...	...	...	...	...	...
Drain:									
Firewood and lumber	23.0	24.3	14.5	15.3	15.3	11.8	12.0	14.0	14.2
Fire and insects	≈2.0	1.7	1.8	1.2	1.2	3.9	4.3	4.0	3.9
Total	25.0	26.0	16.3	16.5	16.5	15.7	16.3	18.0	18.1
Ratio: growth to drain	1:3.5	1:4.3	1:1.8	1:1.5	1:0.77	1:1.13	1:0.97	1:0.90	1:0.83

Note: F.S. = U.S. Forest Service.

was down to 6 billion ft^3 and the drain was up to 26 billion ft^3, or 4.3 times the rate of the growth. Greeley's gloomy scenario never eventuated, however, and the balance between growth and drain shifted by the time of the Copeland enquiry of 1933 into the nation's forests when the ratio between them was down to 1:1.8. Copeland's projections to 1950, based on various mixes of extensive and intensive management strategies, suggested that growth could exceed drain and redress the ratio to parity or even below. By 1950 the lower of the two estimates of 20 years before had been surpassed. In 1952 the actual annual growth was 13.9 billion ft^3, and it rose steadily to 22.5 billion ft^3 in 1986 (fig. 12.6). Pinchot's prediction of nil stock by 1940 proved wrong; the forest famine and the specter of forest death were over, and the rebirth of the forest had begun. Its potential growth is currently thought to be 36 billion ft^3.

From Death to Rebirth

The remarkable turnaround of the forest after the 1930s was a combination of changes and trends that were happening to forests throughout the developed world. First, the enormous growth of trees was possible only because the old forest had been removed and allowed to recolonize the cutover area with second growth. Second, a vigorous program of fire control was initiated under the Clark-McNary Act of 1924, which provided funds for federal and state schemes of cooperation. From a staggering annual burn of 53 million acres (21.4 million ha) in 1931 alone, the number of acres affected annually dropped steadily to less than one-tenth of that amount by the 1960s. Third, reforestation was encouraged under a number of federal-state cooperative initiatives, which were also extended to private landowners under soil conservation programs. Most significant of all, the lumber companies realized that it was no longer feasible to abandon old plant and move on to new stands (even if there were any); it was cheaper to maintain the expensive capital equipment and its economic and social infrastructure and replant the surrounding forests. How much forest was replanted is hard to say, but it must have been at least 1 million acres (approximately 405,000 ha) per annum. Fourth, per capita consumption of lumber has dropped phenomenally, from a peak of 82 ft^3 in 1906 to a little less then one-third of that amount, with the increasing use of substitute materials such as aluminum, steel, and (later) plastics, despite a doubling of the population. Fuelwood consumption fell even more dramatically with conversions to natural gas, oil, and electricity, although plywood and pulp consumption have both risen.

Most important, throughout the eastern half of the country farmland was being abandoned and reverting to forest. From as early as 1840, farmers

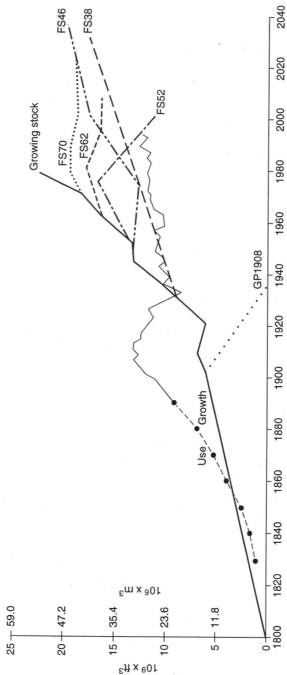

Figure 12.6 Annual net growth and use of timber in the United States, 1800–2040. *FS* denotes Forest Service; *GP* Gifford Pinchot, followed by date of projection. (Sources: M. Clawson, "Forests in the Long Sweep of American History," *Science* 204 (1979): 1108–74, with additional information from USDA, Forest Service, *An Analysis of the Timber Situation in the United States, 1952–2030*, Forest Resources Report no. 23 [Washington, D.C.: GPO, 1982]; and *An Analysis of the Timber Situation in the United States, 1989–2040*, Rocky Mountain Forest Range Experimental Station, General Technical Report RM-199 [Fort Collins, Colo.: Rocky Mountain Forest and Range Experimental Station, 1990].)

were leaving land in New England that was difficult to farm and either moved to better (often non-tree-covered) farmland farther west or migrated to the urban industrial centers. The process moved into the Middle Atlantic states of New York, Pennsylvania, and New Jersey after 1880 and affected the east-central states of Ohio, Indiana, and West Virginia after 1920. Later still, the same happened in the South as old cotton and tobacco fields reverted to pine forest. Knowledge about abandonment is remarkably sparse. In a society imbued with the frontier ideals of development, progress, and the virtues of forest clearance, abandonment was retrogressive, difficult to comprehend, and even sinful to contemplate and, therefore, ignored tactfully.

Although there were hints in the Copeland Report of what was happening, the implications for forest growth were never spelled out. However, an analysis of census data in the 31 easternmost states (table 12.6) shows that the net loss of cleared land between 1910 and 1959 was 17.7 million ha (43.8 million acres), with 26.5 million ha (65.5 million acres) having been abandoned mainly in eastern Ohio, western Pennsylvania, New York, New England, and the whole southern Piedmont, but 8.8 million ha (21.7 million acres) gained, largely out of the forest, mainly in Florida, Minnesota, Iowa, Arkansas, and Louisiana. In other words, 362,000 ha (894,000 acres) have been lost to agriculture and added to the forest in every year

Table 12.6 Cleared farmland, United States, 1910–79 (in millions of ha)

	Conterminous U.S.: Total Farmland	Thirty-one Eastern States		
		Total Farmland	Farm Woodland	Cleared Farmland
1910	356.7	198.4	58.4	140.0
1920	388.0	193.4	52.8	140.7
1925	374.0	180.4	44.0	136.4
1930	400.7	179.4	44.6	134.9
1935	426.7	192.0	53.5	138.5
1940	431.0	186.1	42.9	143.2
1945	462.0	189.2	48.0	141.3
1950	470.0	190.4	55.0	135.4
1954	468.7	184.1	54.0	130.1
1959	453.3	168.1	45.8	122.3
1965	447.9	160.3	38.7	121.6
1969	428.8	149.5	31.6	117.8
1975	410.2	139.0	31.4	107.5
1979	. . .	142.1	29.3	112.7

Sources: J. F. Hart, "Loss and Abandonment of Cleared Farmland in the Eastern United States," *Annals, Association of American Geographers* 58 (1968): 417–40; and U.S. Bureau of the Census, *Agricultural Census* (Washington, D.C.: GPO, 1965, 1969, 1975, 1979).

between 1910 and 1959. During the next 20 years the trend has continued with another 9.55 million ha (23.6 million acres), giving a significantly higher rate of 477,500 ha (1,180,000 acres) lost to agriculture and added to the forest every year.

These figures are mind-boggling in their millions and hundreds of thousands and are, therefore, difficult to comprehend, a problem compounded by the fact that the pattern of regrowth is just as individual, piecemeal, and difficult to detect as was initial clearing in the forest during the last three centuries. But the trend still continues. A map of a single county tells the story better than any words can (fig. 12.7). Carroll County is about 30 miles southwest of Atlanta, Georgia, and between 1937 and 1974, 8,496 acres of forest succumbed to agriculture and a further 515 to urban expansion; but 90,807 acres of once-agricultural land reverted to forest and a further 6,171 acres to urban uses. It is a story that has been repeated thousands of times in the eastern states; after 1974 even more land has been abandoned, so that the forest is coming back.

The Soviet Union: The State Supreme

The forces of change unleashed during the mid-nineteenth century as landowners attempted to recoup their losses after the 1861 emancipation of the serfs (see p. 275 in chap. 10) were augmented as the country entered on a new and unprecedented era of capitalist industrial expansion at the century's end. Anarchy prevailed as government, aristocracy, mining enterprises, military authorities, and private landowners plundered the forests, and at least another 3–4 million ha were destroyed during the next two decades. Undoubtedly, the sheer size and ubiquity of the country's forest, which comprises one-fifth of the world total, nearly a quarter of its growing stock, and just over half the volume of all coniferous forests, engendered a sense of their endless bounty, which encouraged profligacy and waste.

And it got no better in revolutionary times. Conflict caused destruction. The depredations of World War I and the ensuing civil war were recklessly augmented by even more rapacious cutting. During World War II the wholesale logging and transport of lumber from Russia to Germany, the scorched-earth policies, and the general destruction, especially around the Pripyat marshes and north to Leningrad, may have led to the destruction of another 20 million ha of forest in Nazi-held territories, from the Baltic to the northern Ukraine. Savage Japanese exploitative logging in Sakhalin Island, Manchuria, and Inner Mongolia must be added to this toll.

But even if these catastrophic and unusual events are acknowledged, it was the Soviet system of centralized planning, introduced in 1928, that

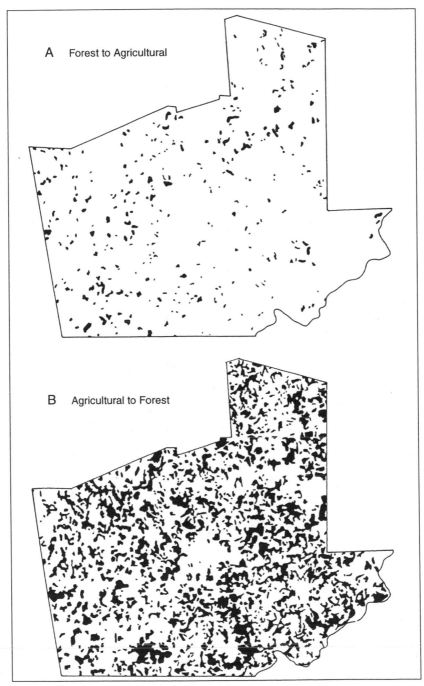

Figure 12.7 A, Conversion of forest to agricultural land; *B*, Abandonment of agricultural land to forest, Carroll County, Georgia, 1937–74. (Source: J. F. Hart, "Land Use Changes in a Piedmont County," *Annals, Association of American Geographers* 70 [1980]: 492–527.)

initiated a new era of state plundering that led what Boris Kamarov called the "destruction of nature." [23] With centralized planning, tsarist indifference was replaced by cynical Communist mismanagement. Doctrinaire Marxist-Leninist ideology sanctioned human interference with nature as laudable and correct, so that environmental outcomes were considered minor and temporary aberrations that were inevitable but irrelevant in the goal of creating a superior economic and social system. In addition, the system of financial rewards and production bonuses to state managers and producers meant that there was simply no incentive to behave in the long-term interest of the resource, the state, or society at large or of the ultimate efficiency of the production unit. A multiplicity of state organizations and departments (about 34), along with over 10,000 logging units, worked either in ignorance of or deliberately against each other in order to reach production targets. Targets went up with each Five-Year Plan and production rose to meet them (table 12.7), irrespective of the ability of the forest to sustain such cutting. Areas of supply (Siberia) effectively got more distant from areas of consumption (Europe); and on a more local scale, the reckless cutting of forests around new giant, expensive wood chemistry plants at Zima, Birusa, Yurty, Tulun, and Chunsky in Irkutsk Province led to reverse journeys of

Table 12.7 Industrial and domestic timber removals (in millions of m³), USSR, 1913–83

	Industrial Removals			Domestic Removals			All Removals
	Roundwood	Fuelwood	Total	Roundwood	Fuelwood	Total	
1913	27.2	33.4	60.6	28.0	204.0	232.0	292.6
1928	36.0	25.7	61.7	27.0	215.0	242.0	303.7
1930	96.7	50.5	147.2	NA	NA	NA	...
1935	117.0	93.1	210.1	22.0[a]	201.0[a]	223.0[a]	433.1
1940	117.9	128.2	246.1	6.0	130.0	136.0	382.1
1945	61.6	106.8	168.4	10.0	130.0	140.0	308.4
1950	161.0	105.0	266.0	8.0	92.0	100.0	366.0
1955	212.1	122.0	334.1	7.0	63.0	70.0	404.1
1960	261.5	108.0	369.5	10.0	30.0	40.0	409.5
1965	273.6	104.5	378.1	6.0	32.0	38.0	416.5
1970	298.5	86.5	385.0	7.0	30.0	37.0	422.0
1975	312.9	82.1	395.0	6.0	29.0	35.0	425.0
1980	277.7	78.9	356.3	NA	NA	NA	NA
1983 (est.)	274.0	83.0	357.0	NA	NA	NA	NA

Source: B. Barr, "Perspectives on Deforestation in the USSR," in World Deforestation in the Twentieth Century, ed. J. F. Richards and R. P. Tucker (Durham, N.C.: Duke University Press, 1988), 230–61.
[a]Record for domestic removals is for 1932.

supplies from Europe to Siberia. Deforestation was neither acknowledged nor problematized, and even as late as the 1950s it appears that there was ignorance of basic sustained-yield management. Thus, defective and divided administration, poor managerial practices, and ignorance, together with the problems of war, survival, and social upheaval between 1917 and 1945, led to a progressive deterioration of the quality of the growing stock. As a consequence, throughout the European Soviet Union there were extensive areas of relatively unproductive and uneconomical forest land.

The comparison with the United States from the 1920s to 1940s could not have been starker. The considerations of efficient management among capitalist entrepreneurs and sheer self-interest, guided by enlightened federal intervention, which eventually promoted better forest management and conservation measures, never emerged in the USSR. Despite the superior size of the Russian forest, it was producing only a fraction of the wood of the United States. And even with the apparent increase in the area of forest (e.g., 738 million ha in 1961 to 792 million ha in 1978) as more distant areas were drawn into national inventories, supplies actually diminished. Even putting aside disastrous fires, about 40 percent of the annual harvest of approximately 400 million m^3 was lost in various stages of production, a little less than 10 percent was used as scrap fuel, and only half reached the customer. Consequently, by 1950 the Soviet Union was suffering from a unique form of deforestation. It was not brought on by the pressure of peasants seeking land, the influx of unemployed urban dwellers into forested areas, or plantation agriculture but by the unwieldy centralized planning apparatus, where the size and multiplicity of forest cutters caused destruction over vast areas while paralyzing production that never satisfied needs.

Little has improved in the post-Soviet era. The legacy of overuse and unsustainable exploitation, together with the collapse of the previous network of command and transaction, shortage of capital, decaying plant, and political chaos, has contributed to a plummeting output. At present the Russian forest is an underused and wasting asset.

Sweden: "Negotiated Order"

At some intermediate point between the laissez-faire capitalism of the United States and the doctrinaire communism of the Soviet Union lay the forest experience of Sweden—a mixture of state intervention and private cooperation—which produced what Per Stjernquist has called aptly "a negotiated order" of exploitation.[24] By the end of the eighteenth century the oak, hazel, and beech forests of southern and southeastern Sweden were severely affected by the inroads of peasant agriculture and iron smelting. The practice of burn-beating to improve fertility on poor soils in order to get an occasional crop of rye and hay had reduced much of the deciduous forest to heather, which was then colonized by birch and alder. Elsewhere, fuelwood procurement and cattle grazing in commonly held forests had thinned and altered the forest.

With a rapidly expanding population after 1820, forest use grew so great that it was no longer self-replenishing, especially as the iron industry required about 1 million m^3 of wood in the mines and 3 million m^3 for charcoal for smelting. Glass, lime, and tar works all added to the drain on the forest.

The lowering of the British import tariff on Swedish timber in 1840 caused a boom in the coniferous forests of Norrland as both national and particularly foreign companies indulged in a free-for-all, cut-out-and-get-out exploitation of the old-growth stands. The frontier of exploitation pushed north between 1840 and 1875; sawmills were set up on every convenient break of slope on the eastward-flowing rivers, which funneled the timber to the Gulf of Bothnia. Soon supplies from Norrland dwindled, and the lumber companies began to buy up farms and the forest common. This was particularly worrisome because it meant the gradual elimination of forest grazing, which had made farming in these northern marginal areas just about possible. The precarious nature of farming was an emotive issue striking at the very heart of the concept of being Swedish, especially from the 1880s onward, when famine and migration of landless rural workers to North America was reaching massive proportions. The demographic vitality, skills, and talents of the nation seemed to be hemorrhaging.

Bit by bit the state intervened to counteract these trends, and by 1903 had set up regional forestry boards composed of rural landowners and staffed by trained foresters. Their job was to promote the multiple use of the forest and to stop or regulate purchases of rural land by lumber companies so that the traditional farming practices of forest grazing could be stabilized. To this end, forest ownership was "frozen" in proportions that are still in force today—namely, approximately 25 percent each to companies and to the state, and the remaining half to private owners. Gradually, the agrarian aims changed, and it was realized that the land grew trees best. Private farm owners were cajoled and persuaded to abandon forest farming and accept the forest as the single-purpose producer of wood, particularly in the south, where the time required for tree regeneration is approximately 75 years, half of what it is in colder Norrland. Further acts followed in 1918, 1923, and 1948, consolidating state regulation with the avowed aim of a gradual but firm public direction of private forestry. In the process, productivity has increased as deciduous woods have been replaced by coniferous forests (down from 40 percent of southern forests in 1920 to 14 percent in 1977), spruce has replaced pine (*Pinus sylvestris*), and more recently the high-yielding American lodgepole pine (*Pinus contorta*) is replacing all other trees. The forest is no longer a wilderness of old-growth mature timber but an almost totally managed human artifact of even-aged, even-spaced exotic trees. It is manipulated by thinning and fertilizing, disease, and fire control.

Rather like the United States, Swedish conservation measures have been driven by anticipated dearth and supported, it must be admitted, by local and regional shortages. But when reliable records became available during the 1920s, it was found that the volume of wood extracted was less than the volume added by growth, something that lasted up to the present (fig. 12.8). Current growth may also be due to a higher density of introduced spruce, but others suggest, controversially, that the increased flow of nitrogen through atmospheric pollution probably acts as a fertilizer. Some trees may even be growing to death because other necessary nutrients are no longer able to match the intake of nitrogen. Even the acidification of

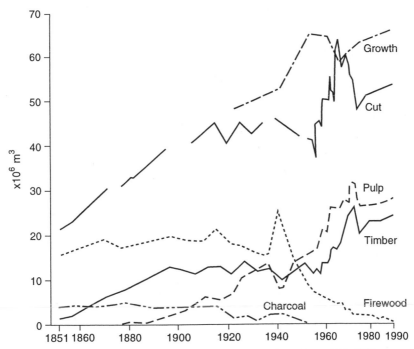

Figure 12.8 Swedish forest budget: annual growth and cut, and wood use, 1851–1990. (Source: T. Hägerstrand and U. Lohm, "Sweden," in *The Earth as Transformed by Human Action*, ed. B. L. Turner II et al. [Cambridge: Cambridge University Press, 1990], 616.)

the soils may be leading to the leaching out of deleterious nutrients in the bedrock, enhancing the relatively poor soil.

* * *

WHEN THE midpoint of the century was reached, the world forests were broadly divided into two kinds. There were those that were managed carefully for production and/or environmental protection and leisure, though often unwittingly at great sacrifice to their ultimate diversity and ecological viability, and there were those that were hacked and felled either to create land to grow food or to provide a source of ready cash. There was nothing new in this division; in some form or another it had already been in existence for several hundreds of years. What was new was the broad and fairly consistent relationship of surplus in temperate forests and dearth in tropical forests. What the temperate world lacked it bought with its superior wealth from the tropical, often, as in the case of Japan and several European countries, in an effort to conserve national timber supplies and forests while depleting those of the exporting countries. Of all the countries of the developed world, only the United States had timber in such abundance that it was both importer and exporter. Global solutions had been found for the scares of a timber famine that had characterized the opening years of the century, but they were not going to suffice in the closing half of the century when considerations other than the supply of timber began to alter the discourse on deforestation. The era of global warming and biodiversity was dawning.

Chapter 13

The Great Onslaught, 1945–95: Dimensions of Change

The destruction in modern times of a forest that is millions of years old is a major event in the world's history. It is larger in scale than the clearing of the forests in temperate Eurasia and America, and it will be accomplished in a much shorter time.
—P. W. Richards, "The Tropical Rain Forest" (1973)

The one process now going on that will take millions of years to correct is the loss of genetic and species diversity by the destruction of natural habitats. This is the folly our descendents are least likely to forgive us.
—E. O. Wilson, *Biophilia* (1984)

The cataclysmic events of World War II altered the world's forests more surely than any "end of the century" of about 50 years before. But it was not the five years of conflict, devastating as they were, that caused deforestation; rather, it was the aftermath of change that they unleashed that was rapid, far-reaching, and caused a disruption of global biomes. The nature and intensity of change reached worrisome levels of pace, magnitude, and environmental significance compared to anything that had gone before.

Its signs were already present; during the hitherto ignored 1920s and 1930s, global clearing was just above 11 million ha per annum, at least 70 percent of that in the tropical forests. But after 1950 the rate went up slightly and was wholly in the tropical forest. Paul Richards got it just about right when he said in 1973 that tropical deforestation was "a major event in the world's history" that was "larger in scale than the clearing of the forests in temperate Eurasia and America, and it will be accomplished in a much shorter time."[1] Between 1950 and 1980 an estimated 318 million ha[2] disappeared in the tropical world (table 12.2), and a further 11 million were cleared in China. In contrast, the forests of the developed countries of the temperate world declined by a mere net 7 million ha, those of the USSR and the developed Pacific countries falling by 11 million and 12 million ha, respectively, but those of the United States and Europe rising by 3 million and 13 million ha so that the amount of land in forests has remained essentially the same. Thus, a global total of 336 million ha net had disappeared, almost all the clearing being accounted for by the expansion of cropland, with some conversion to pastures. Since 1980 deforestation has accelerated again, so that perhaps another 220 million ha have been eliminated, at a rate of over 15 million ha (150,000 k^2) a year. In a little under half a century, approximately 555 million ha have gone, and there is no end in sight. In the whole history of deforestation there has been nothing comparable to this.

Deforestation is a seemingly simple issue, but in reality it is one fraught with difficulties. Despite the overwhelming amount of new information that is being added to daily there is much uncertainty about how, why, when and where current deforestation is happening. In an attempt to answer these basic questions the next two chapters, examine, first, the forces that drive current change and their various dimensions, and second, the regional locations and incidences of that change.

The forces that drive deforestation probably have three major dimensions that can be summarized as cause, concern, and calibration. First, what has caused "the great onslaught"? Answers to that vexed question lie in the political, economic, technical, and demographic changes that have occurred since 1945 in a globalizing world. Increasingly, national explanations are inadequate and the global view is the only way to understand events. Second, how and why did deforestation move from being, at best, a national concern to become a global environmental crisis? More specifically, how did traditional concerns of diminishing timber supply, lack of self-sufficiency, and land destabilization that were almost wholly confined to the developed world become replaced by new concerns of wider significance, such as deleterious climatic change, rising sea levels, and the loss of biodiversity, which affected the developing world in particular? Finally, how is change calibrated or measured, and how accurate is it? It is this intertwining of cause, concern, and calibration that forms the essential background to the story of contemporary tropical deforestation.

THE CAUSES OF CHANGE: "A WORLD LOSING SHAPE"

World War II sent out political, economic, technological, and demographic ripples that reached every part of the globe, whether it was involved in actual conflict or not. In that portion of the world dominated by tropical rain forests, change meant mainly one thing—the alteration and destruction of the dominant land cover.

Political and Economic

One of the most obvious changes after 1945 was the end of empire as the European powers retreated from their overseas possessions, which were predominantly in the tropical world. Some disengagement had already happened before World War II, but war weariness, postwar economic weakness, rising local nationalism, and a general sentiment against the colonial system turned halting moves into a sustained retreat after 1945. Between 1947 and 1948 Britain quit its Indian empire, which became India, Pakistan, and Burma, and the Dutch quit Indonesia. The bulk of Africa and the small Caribbean and Pacific island territories shifted to self-rule between 1954 and 1965, many in the short space of the four years between 1958 and 1962. The Portuguese empire in Africa (Angola and Mozambique), the oldest of them all, was the last to collapse, in 1975.

Political independence did not necessarily bring economic independence. The power of Europe in global political and economic affairs, while still significant, was now augmented and even overshadowed by that of the United States. Additionally, the postwar rivalry between "the West" and the Eastern bloc led to the notion of a "third world," nominally independent but courted and cajoled by both camps. With very few exceptions, third world countries were African or South and Southeast Asian, excolonial, underdeveloped, and tropical. It was these newly emerging countries, with all their special problems, that saw the greatest impacts on their forests. Whatever economic gains had been made since independence were reduced or swallowed up as their population soared. Consequently, strains on the forest increased as it became one of the last sources of new land for food and for fuelwood for heating, cooking, and even industry. Moreover, spontaneous migration—and planned settlement schemes, as in Brazil, Indonesia, and Malaysia—ate into the forest. Latin and Central America were a little different. Although ostensibly independent, most of these countries were deeply in the thrall of the United States, and most displayed at least some of the third world characteristics of poverty and underdevelopment, all tinged with a special Latin American character of deeply polarized social classes. Added to all this the economies of the West, which recovered after about 1960, and had a voracious demand for timber and other resources for reconstruction and expansion, as did a few selected countries in the developing world (such as Japan), where rising affluence boosted consumption.

Generally, third world governments were prepared to meet the "Western" demand for timber by mining their forest stock mercilessly in the form of whole logs, sawn timber, and wood chips in order to gain sorely needed hard currency to aid development. Trees were cash and their replacement by tropical plantation crops was perceived also as cash, but with a more frequent turnover than trees. Even if governments did not acquiesce in mining and stripping the forests, powerful minority elites, sometimes in collusion with the military or government, plundered them for their own gain. Thus, deprivation, stark economic necessity and inequality, and the apparent remedies for these, were all forces that "drove" deforestation.

Technological and Demographic

The unprecedented strain on the world's forest resources was exacerbated by a few simple but significant technological changes. The development of gasoline-powered motors and their widespread use after 1945 in trucks, tractors, and chainsaws introduced mobility and versatility, thereby altering the scale of production. From now on exploitation did not have to be carried out by big business and heavy capital investment, though they often were. Now the individual settler/logger with a bit of cash or credit to purchase a saw and truck could wreak high-tech havoc (plate 13.1). Consequently, almost nowhere in the world was too remote to be exploited, and because of the perfection of techniques to reconstitute vegetable fiber into boards and packaging paper/cardboard, no wood was too inferior to be harvested and used.

Far less obvious, but of far greater importance than the technological, political, and economic changes was the wholesale implementation in the developing world of Western medical technology to eliminate diseases and epidemics and alleviate obvious misery, suffering, and mortality. After 1950, better medicine, improved sanitation, and pest control led to better general public health, causing a demographic explosion that was to be a major driving force underlying all change.

Although these demographic changes were gathering momentum during the 1950s and early 1960s, they were largely ignored, or underplayed. Population numbers were not high on the international agenda, as there was a widespread faith that the science and technology which had created the increase would also cushion it. A few people sounded a warning, but these "lugubrious wailing . . . Neo-Malthusian Jeremiahs" were more than canceled out by the boosters.[2] Demographers seemed more preoccupied with the Western "baby-boom," which was to last for only about a decade before reproduction subsided to mere replacement level, or even below. But the

Plate 13.1 One person with a chain saw can create high-tech havoc in a forest. Parabara, Guyana. (Jevan Berrange, South American Pictures.)

precipitous decline of deaths, and the phenomenal rise of numbers even in the poorest countries of the developing third world largely passed them by.

Not until the publication of the *Population Bomb* by Paul and Anne Ehrlich in 1968 was the full extent of population growth realized, and even then it was discounted by some as alarmist.[3] The reality was that between 1950 and 1985 the world population nearly doubled, from 2,515 million to 4,853 million (see table 9.3), and the developing world's proportion of that total rose from two-thirds to three-quarters (from 67 percent to 76 percent). Still, the scale of change was ignored: projections of future growth were based on the assumption that the developing world would go through the same demographic transition (delayed and protracted, to be sure) as had the Western world as affluence increased and births fell. The expectation was for a modest growth of population of between 1 and 1.5 percent per annum, rather than the 2–3 percent that was soon to rage across Africa, Latin America, and Southeast Asia. In 1949 Fairfield Osborn had thought that the total world population might reach 3.6 billion by the end of the century, when the "limits of the earth" would be clearly visible.[4] But even in his pessimism he was far too optimistic; it passed 6 billion in 1999, and quite credible projections to 2020 suggest that it will be 8 billion, of which 80 percent will be in tropical countries (see table 9.3), which will put intense pressure on their forests.

The "Multilayered Cake" of Causes

From time immemorial expanding population numbers and increased technological abilities to promote change have placed people in competition with all other life forms. More land goes into cultivation, shifting agriculture is extended, fallows are shortened, and more livestock are grazed more intensively. Timber extraction and fuelwood gathering are promoted. It is a simple land use problem and is particularly evident wherever there is a significant subsistence element in the economy. And this basic demand has not changed much in recent decades, except that marginally greater affluence and the improved technology of farming, clearing, and felling has accelerated change, which leads to a greater consumption of wood products for construction, warmth, and energy.

But more recently the simple central facts of numbers, affluence, and technology have been augmented by other underlying causes. For some it is not population numbers per se that are the problem but the emphasis that one places on the numbers and their complex interplay with other socioeconomic factors. The debate is driven by much emotional heat along with political and intellectual agendas. Broadly speaking, neo-Malthusians see global population increase as leading to environmental degradation, while cornucopians think that population growth stimulates technological and social change, and even enhances the environment. Neoclassical political economists think that costs are not allocated correctly, so that effects and solutions are distorted, while neo-Marxists and like-thinking political economists, in addition to totally rejecting neo-Malthusian arguments, think that the capitalist quest for profits and accumulated capital requires unsustainable exploitation, socioeconomic difference, and the creation of inequality and poverty. Consequently, underdevelopment is not merely a result of deforestation but a cause of it. The differences in these positions reflect less the conflicting evidence than the conflicting interpretations of the same evidence because all approaches are ideological and underpinned by a definite set of assumptions.

But beyond population numbers, other causes and the emphasis that should be placed on them are questions that are vigorously debated. Thus, lack of employment opportunities, inequality of distribution of assets (particularly land), exploitative private enterprise and weak government control, misguided past policies of aid agencies, national indebtedness, poverty, and corruption of the elite groups who have economic and political control in society and accumulate profits through the extension of commercial logging have all been cited, and validated, as causes for deforestation. Also national and international policies toward forest use are often ill devised and imprudent and have "failed" through undervaluing the environmental functions of the forest resource. Inadvertently—or even intentionally—they aggravate losses by encouraging inefficient forest industries and, therefore, promote undue exploitation. "Usually," concludes Erik Eckholm, "uncontrolled deforestation is a symptom of society's inability to get a grip on other fundamental development problems." [5]

In contrast with these largely theoretical statements, over a dozen empirical, econometric analyses support some of the relationships, particularly that of deforestation with population growth and density, but a weak relationship between agricultural expansion and deforestation. Others find a positive relationship between wood use and logging and deforestation, while yet others have emphasized the impact of agricultural export prices, devaluation of exchange rates, or the rising burden of repaying debts in inducing agricultural expansion. In yet another study the positive relationship between population density and deforestation was augmented by a positive relationship with gross national product because the latter leads to greater demand for food. On a different tack it has been suggested that there is a strong negative correlation between the rate of tropical deforestation and the level of democracy and development of democratic institutions.

Somewhere between the two extremes of the "hard" numerical data of these quantitative analyses and the "softer" social values of the qualitative explanations is the judgment of three major international organizations, the World Resources Institute (WRI), the World Bank, and the United Nations Development Programme, which cite the expansion of agriculture as the biggest cause of deforestation, exacerbated by socioeconomic inequality and unequal land distribution and pressure on land. In recent years the

WRI seems to have deemphasized the sociopolitical arguments and stressed more the environmental. Degradation of land and forest with intensified land use on poor tropical soils and from logging are seen as the leading causes of deforestation. More recently still, it has come down on the side of population growth, buffered or increased by "government policies, the legal system, access to capital and technology, the efficiency of industrial production, inequality in the distribution of land and resources, poverty in the South and conspicuous consumption in the North," all compounding "the environmental impact of human activity."[6]

The realization that deforestation is a complex and multifaceted process operating at various scales, in various places, and with a multiplicity of variables has given rise to more holistic and global explanations rather than reliance on one, or a few, testable variables alone. One such attempt to model the process is illustrated in figure 13.1. Deforestation is conceptualized as an interrelated system of negative and positive feedback loops in which an important twofold distinction can be drawn between "types of forest exploitation" and "mechanisms of deforestation." "Forest exploitation" consists of any form of land use that modifies or replaces forest cover, either temporarily or permanently, such as shifting cultivation, or pastoralism, or permanent agriculture (cropping or ranching), or the creation of settlements, or logging. However, all these are essentially a reflection of the entire socioeconomic framework that constitutes the second portion of the causation, the "mechanisms of deforestation." These include population increase, rising per capita incomes, accessibility, and environmental considerations.[7] In this analysis it is these latter "mechanisms" that control the "types" of exploitation and hence the rate of deforestation. Thus, for example, rising per capita consumption of food could lead to a positive response in the expansion of the cultivated area at the expense of the forest but, ultimately, to a negative feedback as soil degradation culminates in cropland abandonment and reforestation.

Out of the bewildering complexity of the debate as to which human causes drive deforestation, a number of things seem clear. First, whatever driving force is in play it can either augment or lessen deforestation change. For example, rising interest rates or an increase in agricultural prices will increase deforestation because they provide an incentive for further clearing. At the same time, however, they decrease soil erosion on cultivated land, as it pays to conserve the soil. Second, there is no global, let alone regional, uniformity of deforestation; different causes can have the same effect. For example, deforestation in Borneo and parts of the Philippines stems from logging for export; in peninsular Malaysia it is due to agricultural clearing. Third, even if the underlying causes are agreed on, no one is prepared to agree on what constitutes a sufficient explanation for why this is so.

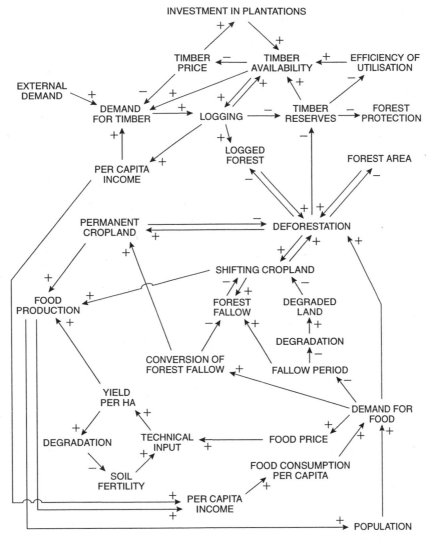

Figure 13.1 The causes of deforestation: a causal loop diagram of a systems model of national land use. (Source: A. Grainger, "Modelling Deforestation in the Humid Tropics," in *Deforestation or Development in the Third World?* ed. M. Palo and G. Mery [Helsinki: Finnish Forestry Research Institute, 1990], 3:55.)

Perhaps the last word on the complexity of the processes comes in the perceptive and biting critique of Nicholas Guppy during the early 1980s. He likened the attempt to explain the sudden acceleration of deforestation to "slicing into a multilayered cake." On the surface are the obvious factors—population growth, increased need of land for agriculture, stock raising and settlement, the wish to raise capital for development, and a rapidly growing demand for forest products. Yet these are not necessarily decisive or even important causes because

> underneath are other layers—of social mores, of political expedients, of national and global economics, and of ideological conflict . . . [so that] almost everywhere destroying rainforest is a means of avoiding tackling real problems by pursuing chimeras: a "license to print money" which yields quick cash at the cost of ultimate catastrophe.

These underlying layers included cropping of unsuitable soils, ignorance of the environmental benefits of forests, inequitable landownership, the political entrenchment and aggrandizement of local elites, and the lending policies of Western governments and financial agencies (such as the World Bank) that allowed such elites to remain in power and even to get more affluent and autocratic. In addition, the cult of giantism in development, dependency on foreign finance and expertise, the inevitable debt and then even greater plundering of the forest resource at the expense of the population at large, all generate unrest and repressive government and, inevitably, environmental degradation. In short, Guppy's analysis of causes stresses the international nature of processes, and it is an indictment of the global capitalist system's quest for profits. When "the deepest layer of the cake" is reached, then "what Oscar Wilde would have called Cynicism—knowing the price of everything and the value of nothing" was encountered, as prices and values were not identical. In this way "the world loses shape," and the tropical forests dwindle.[8]

Indeed, the "multilayered cake" of deforestation is made up of a complicated mix of ingredients; it has layers of different thicknesses and different flavors, some of which peter out here and there, all of which are assessed according to the consumer's ideological taste buds. Efficient policy instruments for the management and reduction of deforestation tend to fix on one or, at best, a couple of causes, but on the whole if they have had any effect it is merely to slow down the rate of increase rather than to stop clearing altogether. In the meantime important issues are avoided, deforestation surges ahead, and concern about the process deepens.

CONCERN ABOUT CHANGE

In the past there was no reason for people to lament the passing of the tropical forests unless their aesthetic senses were offended by the felling of the noble "giants" or their economic interests were threatened by a lack

of valuable timbers. To be sure, a few travelers, commentators, and foresters had expressed some concern. For example, in 1888 Henry Forbes had
wondered what future generations would know of Java's once great forests,
and during the 1920s Thomas Gill had lamented "the passing of the Great
Mother Forest" of the Amazon.[9] But these were mere islands of concern
within a sea of apathy and ignorance.

In the immediate aftermath of World War II, utilitarian and commodity
considerations dominated concern about the forest, and the new Food and
Agriculture Organization (FAO), established by the United Nations, began
annual inventories of resources. In 1948 it calculated that there were 3,978
million ha of forest worldwide, of which a mere two-thirds was classed as
"productive," of which only 36 percent were softwood conifers in the temperate regions, and the rest were broad-leaved forests, dominantly in the
tropical regions. But wherever located, this acreage was seen, perhaps for
the first time as "one forest," a unitary, interdependent resource, something
that the title of FAO's new journal—*Unasylva*—symbolized. Yet thinking
was still dominated by questions of the sufficiency of timber for wood, fuel,
paper, and other products, and the idea that forests were environments,
habitats, biological and aesthetic resources, or integral parts of bigger geo-
bio-chemical systems and cycles did not enter into the picture. Indeed, the
whole history of deforestation was still seen as contributing to "improvement,"
"civilization," and "progress." Rarely were any negative or malign consequences of clearing mentioned, only the progressive, utilitarian, and benign
ones. The social and environmental benefits of leaving forests untouched
and unchanged were rarely appreciated, and they came late. It was not until
the early 1980s that deforestation became a "problem" that moved from a
fairly restricted debate in scientific and conservation journals to coverage in
the large-circulation media. After 1987 the concern became general.

The positive benefits of leaving the forests untouched were fivefold and
emerged in a roughly chronological order. They revolved around issues of
social benefits, rainfall, ecological stability, climate change, and biodiversity, the last being so crucial that it deserves special attention.

Social Benefits

The social benefits of intact forest commons, and the game, fodder, fuel,
forage, and small timber they provided, had been important in the Western
countries until at least the end of the eighteenth century, and much later in
the rest of the world. Forests cushioned the marginality of subsistence life
and augmented income by offering greater diversification and an opportunity to counter seasonal shifts in the economy and employment. But as the

forest and its products were expropriated, divided, and felled, and substitutes found for some of the products, the social benefits counted for less. When Europe came to dominate the world during the nineteenth century it tended to subordinate the social benefits of "the commons" to what seemed like the more obvious economic benefits of individual ownership and the production of timber for the global market. In the Indian forests, for example, foraging by tribal groups and peasant settlements near the forest edge was forcibly restricted by the British who reserved forests for timber production. The social benefits of trees as cultural symbols and sources of aesthetic improvement and enjoyment made only marginal inroads into consciousness by the nineteenth century, although their function as a recreational milieu was to become important after about 1875.

Rainfall and Trees

Whereas the perception of the socioeconomic benefits of forests diminished as the nineteenth century progressed, the perception of their ecological/environmental benefits grew stronger. Initially these revolved around the effect of forests in promoting rainfall and, consequently, protecting the earth from excessive runoff and erosion. The trees, in other words, "kept the land together." These links had long been suspected, though never proven conclusively; but the belief in a connection was a remarkably persistent theme in the history of the attempt to comprehend the effect of humans on earth. So ancient was it that it became entrenched in folk belief and was incorporated into conventional wisdom as the cause of the decline and fall of Rome and a contributory factor in the dimming of the "glory that was Greece." Deforestation and consequent aridity was one of the great "lessons of history" that every literate person knew about.

The idea gained new currency with the settlement of that great outdoor laboratory for scientific study—the forests of North America. During the late eighteenth century, commentators speculated on the changes and extremes in seasonal humidity and temperature that clearing apparently brought about, and during the first half of the nineteenth century a long line of writers equated changed runoff regimes with changed rainfall as a result of clearing. The message had a fairly worldwide currency. For example, the surgeon-environmentalists of early nineteenth-century India and the intelligentsia in the Russian forest-steppe zone, like Dr. Astrov in Chekov's *Uncle Vanya*, knew that

> every year thousands, millions of trees are cut down. . . . Our climate is
> being tampered with in a way we don't understand at all. Our magnificent

landscape is mutilated forever. Our rivers grow shallower and will ultimately dry up. And the natural habitat of animals and birds is so disturbed that they may never be reinstated.[10]

But if clearing the forest caused a decrease in rainfall and a drying-out of the land, then would not the planting of trees increase rainfall? That was a message that the boosters and settlers of the North American western frontier wanted to hear. Obviously, the plains only needed trees to convert them into the "middle landscape" of well-tended land with the correct proportion of arable, pasture, and forest. Thus tree planting flourished as a means of turning the "Great American Desert" into the "Garden of the World." It culminated in the Timber Culture Act of 1873, whereby settlers were granted 160 acres free of cost provided they planted trees, and it remained in operation for 18 years. But prolonged drought in the plains during the early 1890s showed that the clumps of trees had no effect on rainfall, and the experiment of tree planting to promote rainfall was pronounced a failure. "It was a beautiful dream," wrote Benjamin Hibbard in his classic study of public land policies, "but the substance of the dream was for the most part as unreal as such visions usually are."[11]

By the end of the century the argument that forests influenced climate was almost dead, but the forestry profession could not let it go and flirted with this will-o'-the-wisp; if only it could be proved, what a boost to forestry it would be! In particular, Raphael Zon, chief of the Research Service branch of the U.S. Forest Service, in his report of 1912—"Forests and Water in the Light of Scientific Investigation"—concluded that although forests did not prevent floods, they could ameliorate their destructiveness; and then, in an almost throwaway remark, went on to say:

> Forests increase both the abundance and frequency of local precipitation over the areas they occupy as compared with that over adjoining unforested areas, amounting in some cases to more than 25 per cent.[12]

The rainfall connection was repeated halfheartedly again in 1927 and even as late as 1945, but the idea became so discredited that Zon pursued it no further.

Nonetheless, the notion will not lie down. By 1984, the prospect of widespread deforestation in the Amazon basin prompted scientists to predict a decrease in rainfall of up to 200 mm per annum, others putting it three times higher. But it is still controversial, as is the assertion that deforestation is accelerating or decreasing runoff and consequently aggravating flooding in the Amazon River, though there is much less doubt concerning the possible link between deforestation and higher sediment loads arising from soil erosion.

But there is one effect that forests have on the environment about which there is little doubt, and that is shelter—protecting houses and crops from the force of the wind, stopping snowdrifts on highways and railroads, and providing shade for houses and stock during the summer. Drought in the United States during 1910–11 brought about a greater appreciation of the value of trees as windbreaks, which culminated in the Shelter Belt project of the 1930s across the Great Plains.

Ecology and Order

The persistent but difficult to prove forest-rainfall connection was overtaken during the 1930s by the bigger and more tangible experience of the dust bowl, one of the defining moments in American and global environmental history and thinking. The dust bowl was the human hand on nature writ large and clear: simply, within a few decades the plains had been reduced to dust by excessive plowing, though there are divergent explanations as to the exact causes.

The equilibrium model of ecology with its concept of succession-to-climax, developed by Frederic Clements and others during the 1920s, helped explain the dust bowl and other environmental disasters. Contrary to all previous ideas, the lesson was that technology was not necessarily benign and passive and did not necessarily improve or perfect some unfinished nature but, more than likely, debased and destroyed it. Interference with nature became suspect and its conservation and preservation became idealized. Then flora and fauna could reach maximum diversity and stability. The records of ancient history did not need plundering for corroboration; abundant contemporary examples told the story of the link between destructive exploitation and land degradation all too well. Contemporary clearing in the tropical moist forest showed that the natural rate of soil erosion could increase by anything between seven and 50 times depending on whether the disturbance was through shifting cultivation or clear-cutting followed by cultivation with crawler tractors.

The ecological climax-equilibrium suggested a steady state, stability, balance, harmony, an interacting community, and no change to the environment, and the concept appealed because it mirrored earlier states of society that were supposedly more stable and happier. Although most ecologists have abandoned these ideas as scientifically untenable, they are still embedded in ecological texts and certainly appear in much contemporary environmental rhetoric. Thus, by the end of World War II, ecology and scientific conservation became a proof of right-thinking, and within that paradigm forest clearing was the quintessential environmental change having the multiple ramifications of land-cover change, agricultural practice, soil stability, climatic change, biological diversity, and landscape alteration. The forest was perceived as most fruitful when it was altered least. But that was not possible in the world of expanding numbers and needs that ensued during the second half of the twentieth century.

Climate Change and Trace Gases

The ability of humans to alter local climate by clearing forests had long been suggested but difficult to prove. The most common effect was assumed to be decreased rainfall and changed hydrology, but more recently the idea has grown that global temperatures may be increased by the changed albedo. However, the increase may be only a fraction of 1 percent. In contrast, the ability of humans to affect atmospheric quality by the emission of fumes from coal-burning has been known for centuries. The formation of local smog by petrochemical exhaust came later during the 1950s, and two decades later again the long-range transport of emissions to produce acid rain seemed incontrovertible.

Whereas these effects were local, or at most continental or regional, the idea of any global effect seemed unlikely, if not impossible. The conventional wisdom was voiced by one researcher: "How can little creatures like us compete with those titanic forces that drive the winds of the atmosphere and the ocean currents?"[13] However, during the mid-1960s a sneaking suspicion arose within the scientific community that the "little creatures" en masse were in fact altering the global climate. It was established that emissions from fossil fuels and from land-cover change, of which deforestation was the most important component, could absorb the infrared radiation emitted by the earth's surface and by trace gases like methane (CH_4) and nitrous oxide (N_2O), both of which interact radiatively in the atmosphere. This could trigger alterations in the heat balance of the earth and, hence, temperatures, atmospheric moisture amounts, and even sea levels. Predictions have been made that global temperatures could rise by between 0.8 and 4.1°C (the rise being greater at the poles than at the equator), although because of the time lag they might not be evident until the end of the twenty-first century. By the mid-1980s, the so-called greenhouse effect and associated climatic change were firmly established as worldwide concerns after two major international scientific gatherings. By 1990 the Intergovernmental Panel on Climate Change was set up to coordinate research and results, and after a run of the driest summers ever during the early 1990s, it

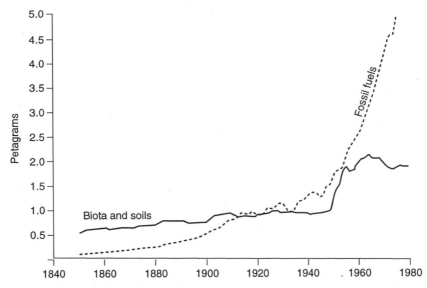

Figure 13.2 Annual releases of carbon from changes in land use and emissions from fossil fuel combustion, 1850–1980. One petagram $= 1 \times 10^{15}$ g (1 million billion grammes) = 1 billion metric tons. (Source: R. A. Houghton and D. L. Skole, "Carbon," in *The Earth as Transformed by Human Action,* ed. B. L. Turner II et al. [Cambridge: Cambridge University Press, 1990], 398.)

declared unequivocally in 1996 that humans had altered the atmosphere to bring about the biggest changes in the global climate since the Pleistocene ice age, which, it is salutary to learn, was triggered by an approximate decrease of a mere 4°C from the average.

The contribution of the forests to the damaging emissions and trace gases is rarely acknowledged but probably quite large. About 50 percent of all terrestrial carbon is stored in the vegetation and soils of the world's forests, with the remainder being in other vegetation. There is, of course, an uncalculated amount of carbon in the world's oceans and the atmosphere. With forest clearing, the carbon is released through decay and particularly burning, and it could constitute anything between 10 and 50 percent of the total amount sent into the atmosphere. Certainly land-cover change has dominated the release of carbon throughout the bulk of human history, being surpassed only by fossil fuel emissions after about 1910 (fig. 13.2), as well as 25 to 80 percent of all methane (CH_4) released, which has doubled since 1800, and 70 percent of nitrous oxide (N_2O) released. When population declined and cultivated land reverted to forest, as during the Great Plague of the late medieval period, carbon release appears to have gone into reverse.

There is also the possibility that climatic change could have disastrous effects on biodiversity, the other new major cause for concern, by causing the extinction of peripheral populations, geographically localized and impoverished species, poor dispersers, and some animals and communities in arctic, montane, and alpine locations. In addition, rising sea levels would engulf coastal species. That these events, in turn, could trigger humanly relevant "knock-on" effects, such as crop failure, crop shift, water shortages, and economic refugees, gave the deforestation debate a new dimension.

Given the magnitude and practical relevance of these emissions, the need to incorporate human land-cover change into global circulation models and into even policy predictions was clear, and it provided much of the rationale and many of the resources during the past 15 years for understanding deforestation and its effects on climate. The urge to calibrate all aspects of timber removal shifted deforestation from being the preserve of a few academic geographers and historians interested in the evolution and formation of landscapes and societies in the past to a matter of global scientific and governmental environmental concern.

But a note of caution is needed here. Some commentators have questioned the validity of the basic premise. First, they believe the assumptions that are built into the climate-change models are flawed and that the changes are within the realm of natural perturbations. Second, they point out that the problem is socially constructed, whereas the research is politically motivated and financially driven. Third, the amount of deforestation may be inflated. We know from the case of West Africa, for example, that deforestation has been exaggerated and has become a new orthodoxy. Colonial predictions of native profligacy and forest loss have become so accepted that research programs have been constructed (and their funding justified) against a backdrop of this decline. Consequently, deforestation may provide no more than "a cultural script for action" or a simplified narrative that facilitates action in research and policy formulation.[14] These qualifications aside, however, the evidence does seem to be mounting that something is happening to our climate. Is it anthropogenically induced, or is it within the natural perturbations of the planet, which have happened before? The consensus is that it is humanly induced. If so, then the "little creatures" have created "titanic forces."

THE RISE OF BIODIVERSITY

The destruction of the world's botanical abundance and diversity—the bulk of which lies in the tropical moist forests—has been the most important factor in the rising awareness and concern about deforestation. Indeed, it is almost synonymous with deforestation. Within about 10 years, between 1986 and 1996, biodiversity moved from being an unknown term to becoming a global byword and the subject of an international convention signed by over 150 nations. But unlike climatic change, the story of how and why biodiversity became an issue of global concern is untold because it has not had the full power of a vast international research machine to chart its progress.

The neat, encapsulating, "glitzy" buzzword—biodiversity—is, in reality, a complex concept of multiple meanings. It is the place where species, habitat, and ecosystem-based concerns meet, and where biological, economic, and socially and ethically driven motivations merge. Biodiversity is a rallying call for those who want to change science, conservation, cultural habits, human values, ideas about nature, and, perhaps, even nature itself.

In order to understand how this particular social construct has evolved, we need to appreciate how its diverse aspects have become woven together and how they relate to forest destruction. To do that, at least three questions need answering:

1. What are the reasons for the belief that biodiversity is an important feature of nature?
2. How and why was the concept conceived?
3. How did it become linked indissolubly with the loss or retention of forests?

The answers to these questions lie in the "archeology" of the word/concept, which reveals that new discussions, or "discourses" in a Foucaldian sense, arose during the 1940s to 1980s. Parallel, adjacent, and seemingly different but closely related events, facts, and ideas were defined, redefined, and transformed to combine and give new meaning and significance to the word.[15] In short, the knowledge of biodiversity has been socially "produced."

The origin of the concept of "biodiversity" probably lay in evolutionary biology, ecology, and conservation and meant a scale-dependent mixture of heterogeneities essential for the functional integrity, adaptiveness, and even stability of biological systems. The germ of the idea had been about for a long time. Charles Darwin was convinced of the necessity of variability for natural selection; by 1953 Aldo Leopold felt that "keeping every cog and wheel" in nature was the "first precaution of intelligent tinkering"; by 1958 Charles Elton was advocating conservation measures based on the diversity/ stability hypothesis; and by 1960 Rachel Carson was deploring the destruction via pesticides of nature's intricate processes.[16]

But biodiversity was an imprecise, "umbrella" concept with multiple meanings. It can, for example, include the number of species, the variety of habitat, genetic variation, or the general heterogeneity of nature. This creates confusion because most users assume that everyone else shares the same intuitive definition. Confusion is compounded because biodiversity is both a descriptive term that explains a structurally visible and measurable variability and an abstract term that describes a concept of great complexity. In its second, more abstract, meaning are at least two key ideas:

1. Variability and heterogeneity are a necessary condition for the existence of human life.
2. The significance of diversity can be reduced to two general metaphorical arguments: first, it provides buffers or functional resilience against unexpected shocks and perturbations; and, second, it provides the raw material for adaptive change and evolution—in other words, the selection function.

The arguments for these claims are many, diverse, and involved, and the answers lie deep within biological research.

But during the last 40 years the focus of the discourse has shifted from a scientific to a human concern that overrides the idea of the necessity for biological heterogeneity that is important in the conservation discourse. Simply, human disquiet stems from a concern to maintain a habitable earth and to preserve its beauty and variability; it amounts, no less, to the "irreducible complexity of the totality of life." Thus, several new and interdependent discourses have arisen, of which the conservation discourse is only one and is paralleled by an

> "economic discourse" on the economic value of biodiversity, [a] "management discourse" on the methods and means of maintaining biodiversity in human-modified environments, . . . [and an] "ethical discourse" on the relevance of biodiversity to the human relationship to nature.[17]

The evolution of these discourses from the 1940s to the present has come from five different sources of concern that have a roughly sequential development and over time become increasingly overlapping and interdigitating: (1) a recognition of the abundance and diversity during the 1950s; (2), an understanding of speciation and genetic diversity of the environment during the 1960s; (3), a recognition of the pace and irreversibility of change during the 1970s; (4), the publicizing and popularizing of these terms from 1979 to 1981; and (5), from the mid-1980s onward biodiversity arrived as a part of the international lexicon and environmental agenda. Gradually concepts have become polarized, so that some ideas are "good" (e.g., biodiversity) and some "bad" (e.g., deforestation).

1950s: Abundance and Diversity

The "jungle" had always been popularly described as rich, fertile, prolific, lush, luxuriant, complex, teeming with life, and quick to revert if cleared, even indestructible; but its true species abundance, diversity, and resilience were only guessed at. One of the first people to confront these issues was Eldred J. H. Corner, a mycologist in the Singapore Botanical Gardens, who commented in 1946 on botanists' ignorance of the true variety of tropical forest. He marveled at the "hundreds of thousands" of plants in the Malay Peninsula that needed to be recorded. But time was not on one's side; during the last two or three decades,

> more primeval forest must have been destroyed botanically—cut over, extracted, alienated, improved, converted, to use departmental terms—than in any other generation. . . . I fear lest all the virgin lowland forest of the tropics may be destroyed before botany awakes; even our children may never see the objects of our delight which we have not cared for in their vanishing.

Much of the forest destruction was "wanton through careless or corrupt control, without provision for the future." The thud of the ax and the crash of the trees as they hit the ground, followed by the "silencing of birds and monkeys, and the crackle of the flames," was enough to tell one that "Artemis has fled where Plutus starts to reign." [18]

The theme of thoughtless biological loss was taken up by Paul Richards in 1952 in his classic text, *The Tropical Rain Forest*. He was, perhaps, the first person to juxtapose the idea of millions of years of stability and genetic evolution producing diversity with the short, rapid period of destruction. A 2-ha plot in the Malay Peninsula contained more than 200 tree species, compared with 10 in an equivalent area of New England, and that did not include smaller trees, vines, orchids, herbaceous plants, ferns, epiphytes, mosses, liverworts, algae, fungi, and lichens. He blamed Western imperialism and the spread of plantation monoculture for forest change and destruction. Also, settled government had encouraged population expansion and even more widespread clearing for subsistence agriculture. With rare insight he likened the destruction of tropical forest to

> the clearing of the European forest by agricultural people beginning in the Neolithic period, except that the one process has been accomplished in a few decades, while the other lasted for thousands of years. [19]

Richards's comments went largely unheeded by those who said they were concerned with the environment. In the 1950s it seemed as though worries about tropical rain forest destruction were for scientific ignoramuses and crackpots only, and it is difficult to find specific elements of concern in early "environmental" texts such as those by Fairfield Osborn and William Vogt.[20]

1960s: Speciation and Genetic Diversity

If the tropical rain forest had such an abundance and variety of species, then why and how had that come about? A new slant on this question came in 1964 when the Russian scientist A. Fedorov suggested that species variation and the evolution of new species was not connected with habitat or site differentiation, which created variation through natural selection, but by "random genetic drift"—a completely new ecological concept.[21] Two basic characteristics of rain forest structure seemed to support this hypothesis: the widespread occurrence of groups of closely related species, and the relatively low densities of the most abundant species, with individuals of any given population separated spatially. In addition, the lack of seasonality in the tropics led to irregular flowering between these sparse populations, making self-fertilization important, and the complex fauna-flora dispersal synergies were also probably significant.

The response to Fedorov's hypothesis was understandably varied. Paul Richards clung to natural selection in niche or site, Thomas Ashton believed that complexity resulted from the great age of the forests in areas of climatic and geological stability, which led to selection for mutual avoidance, with the increasing specialization creating increasingly narrow ecological amplitudes. J. L. Stennis suggested that the bare soil of the rain forest was a free-for-all environment for seeds that offered a moist macrobiotope in which every plant had a chance. Later, Daniel Janzen thought that the great number and mobility of herbivores affected species variation. Tim Whitmore thought speciation a combination of some or all of the above. The tropical rain forest, commented Philip Stott wryly in an extensive review, was becoming "nearly as rich in theories concerning speciation . . . as they are in species!"[22] But the variety and validity of the theories were of less importance than the fact that they had been advanced. Each opened up new hypotheses about the undoubted genetic abundance and variety that increasingly became listed and categorized, thereby stimulating research into how tropical breeding systems worked.

While this was going on, an unrelated but parallel debate arose about the need to conserve genetic resources. This was a classic case of adjacency of an independent issue with a strong "family resemblance," which ulti-mately crossed over, melded, and transformed the nature of concern about the tropical rain forest.

By the early 1960s the rapid increase in the world's population became a matter of concern because of its implications for food supply. In 1964 an International Biological Programme (IBP) was set up to explore ways of collecting and maintaining plants and germplasm that could aid fur-ther development of plant breeding and the propagation of higher-yielding and/or disease-resistant varieties. Before the mid-nineteenth century, when purposeful individual plant selection was carried out, any variation had occurred in areas that were relatively stable and with a large natural vari-ability—in fact, those dominantly tropical areas that 40 years before had been designated centers of agricultural domestication by Nicolai Vavilov (see chap. 3). These gene centers were mainly in low latitudes where more than half the world's population lived under conditions of serious under-nutrition. With the exception of the Middle East these were in the tropical forested regions. The possibility of recombining old plant varieties with new to increase productivity had been proven with improved strains of wheat from Mexico and rice from the Philippines that were to engender the "Green Revolution," but their very success highlighted the possibility of the threat that the treasuries of variation in the centers of genetic diversity could disappear. The participation in this endeavor of historically minded plant geneticists, notably Jack Harlan and Daniel Zohary, linked and wid-ened the concern for diversity with that of domestication, social anthropol-ogy, and the very beginnings of agricultural on earth. At the instigation of the International Council of the Union of Scientists in 1972, the aims of the IBP became incorporated in a *Declaration on the Human Environment* that came out of its Stockholm conference of that year, and the conservation of genetic resources became an internationally recognized concern. With the collaboration of FAO, a network of germ plasma banks was created, of which there are now about 40 around the world, as part of the Interna-tional Board of Plant Genetic Resources.

The idea that genetic diversity was connected with the very evolution of human life and likely to be of practical value gave the concept a new dimen-sion that transcended the purely biological. At the simplest, utilitarian level, which could be easily grasped by the average layperson, the tropical forests were "a source-book of potential foods, drinks, medicines, contraceptives, abortifacients, gums, resins, scents, colorants, specific pesticides, and so on, of which we have scarcely turned the pages." In subsequent years the pages were being turned rapidly and detailed inventories were compiled of tropical genetic resources.[23]

1970s: Pace and Irreversibility

The immediate postwar apathy about the felling of the tropical rain forests gave way to a new level of concern during the later 1960s as it became increasingly evident that bulldozers and power saws were replacing axes and machetes and causing massive change. Drawing on a lifetime experience, Paul Richards revoiced his concerns of nearly 15 years earlier in a popularly written school text; the forest's "wonderfully varied life" was worth saving not only for economic reasons but for "compelling scientific reasons" as well because if it were destroyed before it could be studied, "whole chapters of biology may never be written." [24]

This plea was reiterated three years later in his article in the *Scientific American* targeted specifically at the scientific and thinking lay public. It was, perhaps, the first piece written in the recognizably modern idiom of "genetic diversity" and "species richness." Richards introduced an ethical/uniqueness argument and emphasized the idea that all living creatures were "a source of wonder, enjoyment and instruction to man" and should be preserved before they disappeared. He compared ancient forests to ancient buildings, which were becoming increasingly valued by the public as structures worthy of preservation because they were a source of national pride:

> Although the cost of preservation is sometimes high, it is considered to be justified by the insight such monuments give into the life and thought of past civilizations. The tropical rain forest is also a monument, far older than the human species. [25]

And there the issue might have lain had it not been for the emergence and interposition of another parallel concept that became linked to the idea of abundance and its increasingly rapid loss: the idea of nonrenewability and the long-term survival of the tropical forest, which was probably the precursor of another key concept of the era—sustainability. Most people thought that the forest was exuberant, resilient, and indestructible, but by 1972 Arturo Gómez-Pompa and his Mexican colleagues had become convinced that it was not. They did not have all the scientific evidence to prove their case, but they were sure that if one waited for further research, "there probably will not be rain forests left to prove it." The intensification of tropical agriculture and its extension to keep up with population growth had disrupted and eliminated natural processes that favored primary species, and only favored secondary species, which were preadapted to disturbance, flourished. Because of the new and widespread intensive use of tropical land, "ecosystems are in danger of mass extinction." Not only did

Gómez-Pompa emphasize nonrenewability, he also stressed the delicate adaptation of traditional shifting agriculture to the complex and intricate species regeneration systems that had evolved over millennia. Given these botanical conditions, shifting agriculture seemed the natural and most beneficial way to use the regenerative properties of the rain forest because it retained the genetic pool of primary trees that were the main raw material of the successional process.[26] This was a revolutionary viewpoint, and it reversed the centuries-old conventional wisdom of the Western discourse on the destructive effect of "native" agricultural systems on the tropical forest that they were a curse and would doom these forests (especially in Africa) to become either an unproductive grassland or even a desert.

The prediction of obliteration seemed well on the way to reality a few months later, when the geographer William Denevan forecast the seemingly outrageous idea of the "imminent demise" of the Amazon rain forest, which "within one hundred years . . . will have ceased to exist," as development projects and subsidized agricultural settlement caused the "most intensive destruction of extensive forest in the history of the world."[27] A few years later the publication of the survey of the world's tropical moist forests by Adrian Sommer seemed to provide the objective proof of these speculative assertions. Using FAO material and land-use and vegetation maps, and a detailed study of 13 countries representing some 163 million ha, or 18 percent of the world's tropical forests, Sommer calculated that 2.16 million ha were being lost annually, a figure that if extrapolated to the rest of the global rain forest would be "at least 11 million ha per annum," or 20.9 ha per minute. At this rate, the tropical forest would be irreparably damaged and would soon disappear.[28]

1979–81: Publicizing, Popularization, and Cultural Survival

Sommer's figures provided the link that united the three themes of deforestation, species loss, and nonrenewability. More and even higher estimates of forest destruction during the closing years of the 1970s (see fig. 13.3), together with a high-profile conference on tropical deforestation in Washington, D.C., in 1978, fueled the debate in which the various strands of concern for the environment now fused and linked with climatic change to create "an extremely serious problem."[29] Tropical deforestation had become identified and "problematized," and the "problem" was appropriated by the international research machine, which now moved into high gear.

Just as the official adoption of the "problem" as part of the international research agenda publicized deforestation, so an increasing emphasis on the economic and ecological value of biological diversity popularized it.

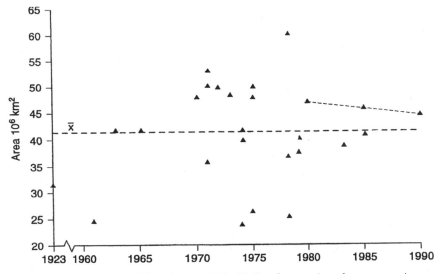

Figure 13.3 Estimates of world forest extent, 1923–90. (Based on a variety of sources, ranging from R. Zon and W. N. Sparhawk's *Forest Resources of the World* [New York: McGraw-Hill Book Co., 1923] to the World Resources Institute, *World Resources: An Assessment of the Resource Base That Supports the Global Economy*, World Resources Institute and International Institute for Environment and Development [New York: Basic Books and Oxford University Press, 1988–89].) The three totals—for 1980, 1985, and 1990—by the World Resources Institute are joined by a dashed line and suggest a steady decline.

The words *deforestation* and *diversity* achieved an almost sloganlike, charismatic status among an increasingly environmentally aware population, which accepted uncritically the simple and easy-to-understand associations that one was a "bad thing" and the other a "good thing." "Save the rain forest" became a rallying cry for conservationists, and in time would be taken up by "politicians, pundits and rock stars."[30] Advocacy scientists capitalized on the public's worries about uncertainty and irreversible loss. Thus, between 1978 and 1981 the debate moved from being an almost private one carried out in the journals of academic disciplines and learned bodies to being a public one on the popular bookshelves. Norman Myers's *The Sinking Ark: A New Look at the Problem of Disappearing Species* (1979) and Paul and Anne Ehrlich's *Extinction: The Causes and Consequences of the Disappearance of Species* (1981), for example, explicitly made a causal link between the increase of population and the systematic modification and elimination of habitats on which species depended, thereby leading to species loss. The rate of species loss was modestly estimated at about three per day, but was later raised to 11–16 per diem. In time the rate of loss became a token of faith in one's belief in environmental deterioration and riveted the attention of the concerned.[31]

These publications achieved wide circulation and notoriety, especially when their neo-Malthusian message of ever-depressing impoverishment and genetic decline was likened to nuclear winter, a much discussed idea at the height of the cold war years. Now the idea of diversity loss intersected with that of national security. Barring an actual nuclear conflict, Paul Ehrlich predicted, using the words of T. S. Eliot, civilization would disappear before the end of the twenty-first century, "not with a bang but a whimper." [32] One way or another, mass extinction seemed around the corner. Out of this general concern, conservation biology was formalized as a separate academic subdiscipline.

At about this time a previous parallel concern became prominent again. Gómez-Pompa's assertion that native dwellers of the rain forests had a better appreciation of the variety and potential of biological diversity than did the farming immigrants, and that they indulged in more ecologically friendly and sustainable practices, blossomed with greater awareness of cultural variety. The newly dubbed ecosystem people had learned to live more sustainably within their natural ecosystem habitat than had the biosphere people, who drew on the resources of the global economy or entire biosphere. Undoubtedly a part of the belief stemmed from the Western Romantic literary view that had idealized "primitive" societies and created the concept of the "noble savage." But during the 1970s and 1980s social anthropologists, ethnobotanists, and even plant geneticists began to argue not only that instinctive ecological harmony made the savage noble but also that local in situ knowledge was indispensable to plant genetic evolution. After all, coevolution had created plant variety and maintained it through conservation in the first place and had even encouraged plant mutation.

The greatest concentration of biological utility and diversity appeared to lie in those habitats with the greatest concentration of indigenous cultural diversity. In Latin America, for example, a strong positive correlation was most evident in the "base ecoregion" of the tropical moist forest and was also strong in tropical dry broad-leafed and tropical and subtropical forests but generally weakened in more temperate climes.

Up to that point the discourse on biodiversity had been fairly low key and diffuse, but gradually the idea grew (and with some justification) that not only were the species in danger of mass extinction from deforestation but so were those in most contact with them—the rain forest dwellers. Thus both cultural diversity and biological diversity were endangered; the mass extinction of species was paralleled by, and connected to, the annihilation of cultures and languages. The forest may have covered only 7 percent of the earth's surface, but it probably contained about half of the 1.4 million known living species (although there is much uncertainty as to numbers) and the key to further plant evolution. Edward O. Wilson was convinced that the loss of diversity through the destruction of natural habitats would "take millions of years to correct" and was "the folly our descendents are least likely to forgive us."[33] Similarly the forest might only contain a fraction of 1 percent of the world's population, but some 30–40 percent of all known languages. Biological and cultural diversity now went hand in hand.

Mid-1980s: Biodiversity Arrives

This new concern about change in the forest rose rapidly during the middle and closing years of the 1980s and was increasingly described as a loss of "biodiversity" (often rendered initially as *BioDiversity*), a neologism, which Edward O. Wilson claims was coined by Walter G. Rosen in 1986 and incorporated in the title of the National Forum on BioDiversity sponsored by the Smithsonian Institution and the National Academy of Sciences in Washington in September of that year. Certainly before 1986 "species variety," "variety of life," "genetic diversity," and increasingly "biological diversity" (all meaning slightly different things) described the concept. Now they were being rapidly replaced by the single word—biodiversity. Biodiversity was subsequently used throughout Edward Wilson's edited volume of the proceedings of the National Forum and contributed to the decision of the Library of Congress in September 1987 to enter "biological diversity" in its cataloguing with a cross-reference to "biodiversity." [34]

Thus, although biodiversity is an amorphous, even abstract, idea, and certainly one that has many meanings, within a few years after its circa-1986 invention it became a concept that was so firmly established in scientific and popular literature that it achieved buzzword status. Biologists are still attempting to count, measure, differentiate, and manage biodiversity, while on the more human side the original utilitarian concerns about the loss of "wonder" drugs and plants have been supplemented by a new discourse in which deforestation and irreversible habitat and species loss have became defined and redefined, understood, accepted unquestionably, given an ethical dimension, and condemned. Biodiversity loss has become socially constructed and "problematized," and it has become almost synonymous with deforestation. Moreover, the concept has other resonances that have led to its widespread acceptance as inherently "good." In the social sciences, diversity and heterogeneity were being promoted as desirable political and social ideals for Western societies that are becoming more ethnically, culturally, and sexually pluralistic and diverse. Biologically, the rise of the idea of a global "heritage" of genes and species that demanded preservation just as surely as do the Pyramids or the Taj Mahal meant that biodiversity was an idea whose time had come.

If ecology was the token of all right-thinking people during and after World War II, then the desirability of biodiversity is the token of all right-thinking people in the 1990s and early twenty-first century. It has become one of the most prominent and popularly understood environmental issues among the half a dozen or so major ones that have dominated the environmental debates during the last 20 years. Biodiversity has become officially mythologized and adopted as the charismatic cry of the environmental activist. Its acceptance has been little short of amazing; in 1992 it was the basis of the Rio International Convention designed to stem diversity loss, which was signed by 158 countries. With tropical deforestation as the universal metaphor for environmental and habitat change, the process of tree removal could never be the same again.

CALIBRATING CHANGE

When I started this book in Los Angeles in 1994, there was a large electronic billboard above the Hard Rock Cafe at the Beverly Center, just off Beverly Boulevard. It flashed its message day and night. Its row of figures represented the area of the global tropical rain forest in the hundreds of millions of ha. The last digit kept on flicking over and decreasing; it was counting backward, signaling the minute-by-minute destruction of the forest. It fell at about 20 ha (approximately 50 acres) per minute, at which rate there would be no rain forest left by the end of the twenty-first century. The flashing, ever-diminishing total was an arresting and disturbing reminder of what was happening. But it induced a strange mixture of reactions—indignation, concern, but more often a shrug of the shoulders as one realized the difficulty of "doing anything" about it. Then you dived into the mall to do your shopping and get on with your own life.

Whatever one's reactions to the display, at least three questions about it need answering: Was the total amount of rain forest shown correct? What exactly is "deforestation"? And is the rate of destruction true? Despite the undoubted importance and magnitude of deforestation as a key process in the transformation of the earth, our knowledge of these three elements is marked by an astonishing uncertainty. Definitions are disputed; basic data are either uncertain or found wanting; and the calibration of change is contested.

Extent and Area of World Forests

Before change in the forest can be measured, its extent and area must be known; and even more basically, before either can be delineated, a "forest" must be defined, something that has not been attempted until recent years. Intuitive experience suggests that a broad distinction can be made between closed and open forest, and that is commonly accepted. The Food and Agriculture Organization defines closed forest as "land where trees cover a high proportion of the ground and where grass does not form a continuous layer on the floor" and open forest (sometimes called woodland) as "mixed forest/grasslands with at least 10 percent tree cover and a continuous grass layer." More recently FAO says a forest is an ecological system with minimum crown coverage of 10 percent, and wooded land is a part of nonforested land.[35]

Despite conflicting definitions, attempts have been made to map the distribution of the world's forests and woodlands, but all suffer from being an aggregation of small-scale map data, and incorporate implicitly all their inherent problems of diverse aims, subjective classifications, and boundary delimitation.

The quest to overcome these problems and to get a statistical measure of the area and change in the global forests has been pioneered by climatic modelers, who want objective measures to incorporate in global circulation models and other calculations. Data sources have been analyzed digitally, with at least four attempts at statistical measure having been made during the 1980s. For our purposes the most important is the study by Elaine Matthews, who attempted to make vegetation mapping applicable to a variety of climatically related research, such as primary productivity, surface roughness, and ground hydrology, in addition to albedo and biomass. Two separate databases were constructed, one of "natural" vegetation, the other of current land use. In the vegetation base an attempt was made to reconstruct the preagricultural vegetation, and the land-use database was used to calculate the amount of vegetation remaining. Both databases were constructed on 1° latitude × 1° longitude cells so that they could be quantified. The vegetation classification used was the United Nations Educational, Scientific, and Cultural Organization (UNESCO) hierarchical system based first on life form and, then, subdivided into density, seasonality (evergreen or deciduous), altitude, climate, and vegetation structure, and it was compiled from over 40 atlases, with all the problems inherent in that. Of the potential 225 vegetation types, 178 were used, together with 119 land-use types.[36]

As the extent of the forest is largely the outcome of the accurate delineation of its distribution, there has been little agreement about the amount of the "contemporary" forest. Between 1923 and 1985 there have been at least 26 calculations of closed-forest land, and these are arranged chronologically in figure 13.3. Ranging from 60.5 million to 23.9 million km², they are randomly distributed around a mean of 41.27 million km². They are estimates compiled from different sources, utilizing different definitions, and cannot, therefore, be used as an indicator of current deforestation rates. However, there was a general firming up of the estimates during the 1980s as being between about 47 million and 37 million km², still a wide variation.

The only long time-series data for forest area come from the FAO returns of land cover (not land use) for the 35 years between 1950 and 1985. However, the FAO figures from the third and erstwhile second worlds must be used with caution. First, forest and woodland in the *Yearbooks* is defined as "land under natural or planted stands of trees, whether productive or not, and includes land from which forests have been cleared but will be reforested in the foreseeable future." But when is the "foreseeable future," will there be replanting, and what about regrowth? Second, it has been shown conclusively that the *Yearbooks* of 1976, 1981, and 1986 contain retrospective 10-year estimates that give totals that differ from each other and do not tally with the totals for individual years before 1975, making the FAO data another set of imperfect estimates. However, on face value the data suggest that temperate forests (North America, Europe, Mainland China, USSR, and Oceania) are in a steady state with slight increase, and tropical forests are declining slightly. However, the aggregate total masks many regional fluctuations.

The distinction between closed and open forest becomes more critical as the scale of analysis shrinks. For example, table 13.1 shows four calculations ranging between 1980 and 1987 for the three major continental areas: North America, Africa, and Latin America. There is little agreement except in a most general way. Similarly, estimates of a subset of the above—tropical moist forests—range from 935 million ha 1976, to 1,756 million ha in 1990, with a sprinkling of other estimates in between.

Definitions and Pathways of Deforestation

The definitional problems and measurements of the deforestation process are compounded by three basic questions: What is deforestation, how does it happen, and how much is occurring? It is not a simple set of binary opposites of "trees" or "no trees" but, rather, everything in between. In reports and publications, deforestation is often qualified with words like *clearance, conversion, modification,* and *disturbance,* but these are not quantified and are even unquantifiable.

Table 13.1 Estimates of closed forest and open woodland (in millions of ha) in three continents, 1980–88

	1980	1984	1987	1988
North America:				
Closed	470	470	419	459
Open	176	176	215	275
Total	646	646	634	734
Africa:				
Closed	190	217	218	221
Open	570	486	500	499
Total	760	703	718	720
Latin America:				
Closed	530	679	692	693
Open	150	217	250	240
Total	680	896	942	933

Sources: G. O. Barney, *Technical Report,* vol.2 of *Global 2000 Report to the President: Entering the Twenty-First Century,* Council for Environmental Quality and U.S. Department of State (Washington, D.C.: GPO, 1980), 118; S. Postel, "Protecting Forests," in *The State of the World, 1984,* ed. L. Brown, Worldwatch Institute (New York: W. W. Norton, 1984), 75; World Resources Institute, *World Resources Review 1987* (New York: World Resources Institute, 1987), 59; and S. Postel and L. Heise, *Reforesting the Earth,* Worldwatch Paper no. 83 (Washington, D.C.: Worldwatch Institute, 1988), 8.

Logging and shifting cultivation present particular problems and confusion. For example, Alan Grainger asserts that selective logging does not "lead to forest clearance and so does not constitute deforestation," whereas Norman Myers thinks that logging is crucial because, although it may only affect a small proportion of trees per hectare, it damages wide areas and is the precursor of penetration by the forest farmers:

Along the timber tracks come subsistence peasants, able to penetrate deep into forest zones that have hitherto been closed to them. Clearing away more trees in order to plant their crops, they soon cause far more damage if not destruction than the lumberman ever did. Thus, the "commercial logging/ follow-on cultivator" combination is the "primary" cause of tropical forest conversion.[37]

Perhaps an even bigger problem lies in the role of rotational, shifting agriculture in causing either permanent change or merely disturbance, although ultimately both lead to ecosystem change and degradation. Possibly only between 60 and 70 percent of land cleared for agriculture remains permanently without trees, the rest becoming fallow and returning to some form of forest. When one realizes that the number of shifting and "shifted" (displaced) agriculturalists might be 250–300 million and that they may be affecting as much as 190 million ha, then their total impact on the forests is not negligible. An illustration of the problem of disentangling their role is given in figure 13.4, one of many possible scenarios. From a stock of untouched closed broadleaf forest, an annual amount of 70,000 km² is "deforested" annually, of which 51,000 km² is cleared totally and passes into the land-use category of permanently cleared, while the remaining 19,000 km² goes into the category of fallow (shifting) closed forest. At the same time, there is some 34,000 km² of forest that is left fallow and open as a result of the annual cycle of shifting. But as population increases, cropland is overtaxed and fallows are shortened, so that 101,000 km² of that open forest is converted annually to permanently cleared land. In fact the net reduction of

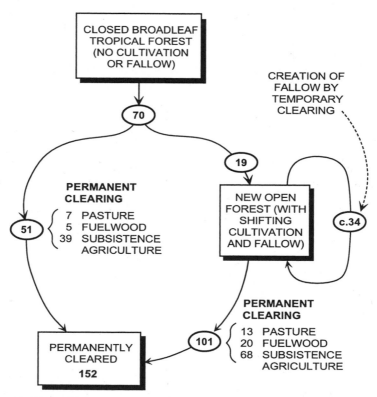

Figure 13.4 Tropical forest: annual pathways of conversion (× thousands of km²). (Source: based on R. A. Houghton, R. D. Boone, J. M. Melillo, et al., "Net Flux of Carbon Dioxide from Tropical Forests in 1980," *Nature* 316, no. 6029 [1986], 617.)

the fallow forest category is only 82,000 km² because of the annual addition of 19,000 km² of newly disturbed nonfallow forest. If this pathway of change is correct, then a total of 152,000 km² is being cleared annually in the tropics, with 51,000 km² coming from the nonfallow forests and 101,000 km² coming from the fallow forests that were once a part of the shifting cultivation cycle. The internal dynamics of the pathways of change are critical to calculating rates of deforestation but are imperfectly understood.

Rates of Change

When Adrian Sommer produced his inventory of tropical moist forests and estimate of the rate of deforestation in 1976 it was to counter what he called the almost universal "euphoric belief" of the unlimited extent and growth of those forests. But he also fired the first shot in what was to become a vast international endeavor to turn firsthand impression and experiences of devastation into hard statistical data. But as figure 13.5 shows, over a quarter of a century later we are probably no nearer to knowing the rough—let alone the exact—rate of tropical deforestation over the globe, which remains contentious.

Sommer had no illusions about the accuracy of his survey, which was based on incomplete data and a number of assumptions, and would ultimately yield only "rather rough results." He arrived at a figure of "approximately 11 million hectares" based on the average percentage deforestation rate for

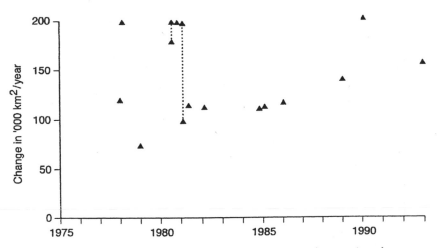

Figure 13.5 Estimates of annual rate of deforestation, 1978–93. (Based on a variety of sources ending with that of K. D. Singh, "The Tropical Forest Resources Assessment," *Unasylva* 44 [1993]: 10–19.)

just 13 countries (Bangladesh, Colombia, Costa Rica, Ghana, Ivory Coast, Laos, Madagascar, Malaysia, Papua New Guinea, the Philippines, Thailand, Venezuela, and North Vietnam) for which unattributed estimates of rates were available and, then, extrapolated those to all tropical moist forests.[38]

By the time of the Eighth World Forestry Congress in Jakarta in October 1978, Edouard Saouma was suggesting a rate of 12 million ha. In the same year Gerald Barney in the *Global 2000* report thought it was about 6.4 million ha and then, in a later volume of the report, inexplicably chose to use the high figure of 18–20 million ha and proceeded to treat that figure as if it were totally reliable. Two years later, Myers produced his report to the U.S. National Academy of Sciences, and it rapidly became a definitive study in deforestation. On the basis of unspecified estimates for 13 countries (Brazil, Burma, Colombia, Indonesia, Laos, Liberia, Madagascar, Nicaragua, Papua New Guinea, Peru, the Philippines, Thailand, and Zaire), he calculated that the rate of deforestation for them was 7.8 million ha, which he extrapolated to 11 million ha for the world, which was the same figure as Sommer's. But on the penultimate page of that report Myers suggested that if forest farmers and their increase in numbers were included, then the figure might rise to over 21 million ha, which a few years later was revised to give an annual loss of 7.5 million ha of closed forest and 14.5 million ha of forest fallow.[39] The contrary assessments continued with the publication of the massive 1,500-page FAO/United Nations Environment Program (UNEP) report of 1981 based on deforestation rates for 76 countries, of which 13 had supplementary satellite data. This put a figure of 7.3 million ha for the clearance of closed forests between 1976 and 1980 and a forecast of 7.5 million ha for 1981–85. During the next 15 years assessments continued to fluctuate widely.[40] Suffice it to say the rough parameters of magnitude (7.5 to approximately 20 million ha/yr) have been set. The lower figure is generally acknowledged to represent the complete removal of trees, and the upper figure might include modification to some degree. Thus, an area equal or even nearly double that destroyed could be severely disturbed or degraded.

Finally, the latest and most authoritative assessment by FAO in 1990 is far more elaborate than anything done before and is based on a continuous monitoring record, using a combination of ground-level and remote-sensing data and Geographical Information Systems (GIS) mapping for 90 countries. Its data are displayed in table 13.2 which shows that between 1981 and 1990 the annual rate of deforestation (i.e., the depletion of the tree crown cover to less than 10 percent) has been 15.4 million ha (compare with the rate of 15.1 million ha in table 12.2, arrived at by different calculations).[41]

Table 13.2 Estimate of forest area and deforestation, tropical areas, 1980 and 1990

Continent and Subregion	No. of Countries	Total Land Area (in millions of ha)	Forest Area (in millions of ha)		Annual Deforestation (in millions of ha)	Rate of Change (%/yr.)
			1980	1990		
Africa:						
West Sahelian Africa	9	528.0	43.7	40.8	0.3	−0.7
East Sahelian Africa	6	489.7	71.4	65.3	0.6	−0.8
West Africa	8	203.8	61.5	55.6	0.6	−0.8
Central Africa	6	398.3	215.5	204.1	1.1	−0.5
Tropical Southern Africa	10	558.1	159.3	145.9	1.3	−0.8
Insular Africa	1	58.2	17.1	15.8	0.1	−0.8
Total Africa	40	2,236.1	568.1	527.6	4.1	−0.7
Asia:						
South Asia	6	412.2	69.4	63.0	0.6	−0.8
Continental Southeast Asia	5	190.2	88.4	75.2	1.3	−1.5
Insular Southeast Asia	5	244.4	154.7	135.4	1.9	−1.2
Pacific Islands	1	45.3	37.1	36.0	0.1	−0.3
Total Asia	17	1,650.1	349.6	310.6	3.9	−1.1
Latin America:						
Central America and Mexico	7	239.6	79.2	68.1	1.1	−1.4
Caribbean	19	69.0	48.3	47.1	0.1	−0.3
Tropical South America	7	1,341.6	864.6	802.9	6.2	−0.7
Total Latin America	33	1,650.1	992.2	918.1	7.4	−0.7
Total Tropical World	90	4,778.3	1,910.4	1,756.3	15.4	−0.8

Source: K. D. Singh. "The Tropical Forest Resources Assessment," *Unasylva* 44 (1993): 10–19.

By 1985, international agencies had responded to the worldwide concern about these figures of forest loss by compiling a large-scale plan setting out possible courses of action for lessening the rate of deforestation. This was followed two years later by a policy document entitled *The Tropical Forestry Action Plan*. But the main thrust was aimed at regulating forestry, so it said little about the destruction caused by subsistence agriculture.[42]

Roger Sedjo and Marion Clawson were highly critical of the assertions about the rate of deforestation and the programs that ensued and while not denying that local effects of rapid deforestation may be severe, resulting in the clearing of about 7 million ha per annum, did not think that the evidence supported the view "that either the world or the tropics are experiencing rapid aggregate deforestation." Maybe it is higher than they suggest, but they are not the only commentators who are skeptical about the extreme claims.[43]

In all this debate, it is salutary to realize that between 1976 and 1998, only two primary sources of data have been produced—those made by FAO/UNEP and those made by Myers, one incorporating some objective satellite-measured data, the other relying on the expert assessment of an individual. All other estimates, including those made to date by the World Resources Institute, have been derived from these estimates, and their secondary nature makes them less reliable. Their variability depends on definitions of what deforestation is and what conversion is, the role of logging and shifting agriculture, the types of forest considered (closed or open), and whether they are specific measurements by remote sensing or subjective judgments or a combination of both. Some are extrapolations from sample areas, some are averages, some are actual, and some potential. In addition, it does not take too much imagination to realize that there may be good reasons to either exaggerate or play down the rate of deforestation for national political or economic ends, and even for personal professional reasons in the race for funding and status.

Thus, we are left with the knowledge that the exact magnitude, pace, and nature of one of the most important processes in the changing environment of large portions of the earth is largely unknown. In all this uncertainty we can be sure that the debate on the rate of deforestation is not over. As for the electronic sign over the Hard Rock Cafe, it is no more. The management dismantled it a few years ago—it had lost its appeal and impact, and someone had told them that the whole thing was suspect anyhow. Both of those are true, but we do know that if it were still functioning, even if it had been calibrated incorrectly, nothing was going to stop it counting down.

Chapter 14

The Great Onslaught, 1945–1995: Patterns of Change

Peasants felling trees in a rain forest cut poignant figures in the late twentieth century. Aspiring yeoman farmers, they struggle to better themselves by destroying an ecological treasure.
—T. K. RUDEL, *Tropical Deforestation: Small Farmers and Land Clearing in the Ecuadorian Amazon* (1993)

The pace of change in Amazonia has to be seen to be appreciated: 6 years at the frontier can transform an area as much as many decades or even centuries in other parts of the world.
—P. M. FEARNSIDE, *Global Environmental Change* (1997)

JUST AS the factors that drive people to cut down trees are clouded by uncertainty, the same is true about where they do it. In that respect most contemporary tropical deforestation is no different from deforestation at any other time. It is diffuse and difficult to detect; it is made up of the uncoordinated and unrecorded individual actions of tens of millions of small-scale decision makers and land managers. A good example of the difficulties of detection comes from a large area of roughly 45,000 km² in eastern Thailand (fig. 14.1). Between 1973 and 1976 sedentary cultivators had nibbled away at the edges of the forest in order to create more land to grow food, while in the forest itself, expanding numbers of shifting cultivators had shortened crop rotations, leading to permanent clearing. While the edge of the forest succumbed first in a piecemeal fashion, the thinning from the interior of the forest was almost impossible to detect, a problem that holds true for other parts of the world.

Amid all the unknowns, however, some parts of the earth show distinct signs of clearing, which are amply documented and in which definite forces for change appear to operate strongly—or at least have been better

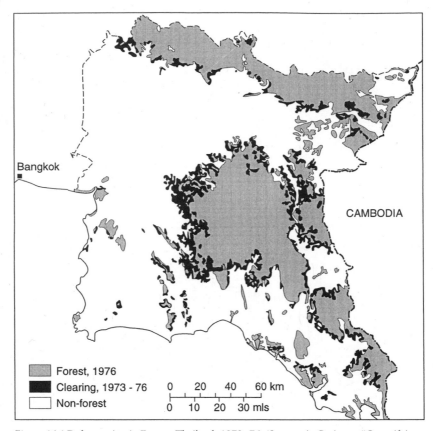

Figure 14.1 Deforestation in Eastern Thailand, 1973–76. (Source: A. Grainger, "Quantifying Changes in the Forest Cover in the Humid Tropics: Overcoming Current Limitations," *Journal of World Forest Resource Management* 1 [1984]: 3–63.)

documented than elsewhere. Here, the rationale of the principal actors, their attitudes, prejudices, and economic strategies, are known, and this information lends understanding to the current great onslaught. These examples, therefore, give the pattern of deforestation a reality and a superficial regional emphasis.

Broadly speaking, deforestation is associated with four kinds of motives or forces, though in reality the forces of change are more varied and less clear-cut than this, and they tend to operate in varying combinations to produce clearing. They are:

1. Agricultural expansion, associated with population increase/resettlement resulting in either planned or spontaneous colonization schemes is

universal but is particularly important in Amazonia, Indonesia, and Malaysia.

2. Ranching and pasture development are significant in Central and Latin America.

3. Fuelwood gathering is most important in Africa and, to a lesser extent, in India.

4. Logging is noteworthy in South and Southeast Asia and of declining importance in West Africa.

Some of these regional manifestations of predominant/proximate reasons for change are examined in more detail below.

AGRICULTURAL DEVELOPMENT

Amazonia: "The Great Mother Forest"

Among the papers of Thomas Gill, traveler, conservationist, and American commercial timber scout, is a manuscript of an unpublished short story or popularly written article about the Amazonian forest (the genre is difficult to determine, as so much of Gill's handwriting is illegible). Written sometime in the early 1930s, it is entitled "The Passing of the Great Mother Forest." Its opening is disturbing and prophetic:

> The perfect forest, men called it, but the Amazon Indian knew it as the Great Mother. Certainly it is the richest, the most complex expression of all life, unique and certainly old. Yet in all likelihood it will become little more than a memory before the century ends. And when it is gone we will never know again the same luxuriant out flowing of life.[1]

About 25 years later not much had changed in Amazonia; the "aggressive immensity" of 5.4 million km² of forested lowland that Bill Denevan saw in the early 1980s, extending "unbroken for hours beneath the plane" as he flew across its southwest corner from Porto Velho to La Paz in Bolivia, was still largely intact. But as he was well aware, its "demise" was only "a matter of time given present pressures."[2]

Of course, the forest was not entirely unbroken, untouched, and uninhabited. It contained about 150,000–200,000 Amazonian Indians, a fraction of the original 2–6 million that had been wiped out through disease, enslavement, and deliberate extermination from the beginning of the sixteenth century onward. The population had fallen to about 1 million in 1900 but fell again to a remnant of 200,000–300,000 by 1957. More than a third of the 220 tribes had passed away during the same period, and by the late 1950s it was predicted that the native Amazonians were destined to vanish. Also populating the forest were untold thousands of rubber tappers, some independent migratory workers, and some overlords with vast estates or territories of millions of hectares with thousands of Indian workers and tappers—slaves in all but name. But none of these inhabitants had had any discernible permanent effect on the forest: their impact was small scale and intermittent, and they all worked within the natural decay and regeneration cycles of the forest.

But changes were already underway around the edges of the Amazon River basin. By the mid-1960s about 4 out of every 10 ha cut in the tropics of the world was cut in this region, so its clearing burst on Western consciousness to provide a dramatic focus of concern about deforestation. From the west and the north in the overpopulated highlands stretching from Peru to Venezuela, peasants who scratched a bare living from thin soils began "overflowing from the Andes down to the Amazon plains . . . like a slow burning fire, concentrating along a narrow margin between the land they . . . [were] destroying and . . . about to leave behind, and the forests lying ahead of them." From the south and the east, Brazilian peasants from the heavily populated coastal lands, and the drought- and poverty-stricken northeast, were looking inward at their bigger territory. "The historical reluctance to settle the more humid life zones of the Americas is at an end," said Joseph Tosi and Robert Voertman in 1964.[3] From all sides, so it seemed, everything was conspiring to attack, maim, and reduce the "Great Mother Forest."

East of the Andes

Brazil and the Amazon forest seem synonymous, but it is not commonly recognized that one-third of the 5.4 million km² of the basin lies in the national territories of the Andean countries, which stretch from Bolivia in the south to Venezuela in the north (table 14.1). In contrast to the largely uninhabited forested lowlands, between 34 and 79 percent of the population of Peru, Bolivia, and Ecuador is located above 2,500 m (8,200 ft) in the *tierra fría*, or cold country, while the proportion in Venezuela and Colombia, though less, is still significant.

The economic, political, and social marginality of this Andean population has been of long standing. Repression, violence, and poverty, either controlled or exacerbated by entrenched elites, endemic fatalism, and the fact that Spanish is still a foreign tongue to the majority of the peasantry, have created a critical socioeconomic situation. "The circle of life and hope has been so small and so tight," said Raymond Crist and Charles Nissly in 1973, "that it has been impossible for the individual to escape from the

Table 14.1 Extent of Amazonian tropical lowland and extent of land over 2,500 m, and % population living over 2,500 m, by country

	Amazonian Lowlands			Andean Uplands (land over 2,500 m)		
	Amazon Area (in thousands of km²)	% of Total Area	% of National Territory	% of National Territory	Population (in millions)	% of National Population
Brazil	3,560	65.9	54	. . .	. . .	. . .
Peru	785	14.5	61	5.6	13.6	43
Bolivia	510	9.4	47	3.7	4.7	79
Colombia	309	5.7	27	5.7	22.2	26
Ecuador	139	2.6	48	2.0	6.0	33
Venezuela	100	1.9	9	0.1	10.8	1
Total	5,403	100.0				

Source: After E. F. Moran, ed., *The Dilemma of Amazonian Development* (Boulder, Colo.: Westview Press. 1983), 5; and M. A. Little, "Human Populations in the Andes: The Human Science Basis for Research Planning," *Mountain Research and Development* 1 (1981): 149.

immemorial way of life, or even think of wanting to escape"—that is, until new roads enabled migration to the urban centers or down to the unsettled forested lands of the east.[4]

Travel eastward across one of the largest mountain chains in the world had always been difficult. Precipitous terrain, deep ravines, and raging torrents meant that it was far more difficult to go overland from, say, Lima to Pucallpa in the humid lowlands 542 km to the east, than to take a ship via the Panama Canal to Belém, transfer to river steamer, and travel over 2,600 km up the Amazon and its tributary the Ucayli, via Iquitos. Nonetheless, by the 1940s a few roads had been constructed across the high Andes to the *tierra templada,* or temperate lands, lying between about 3,000 and 6,000 ft. Fewer still had penetrated the *tierra caliente,* or hot lowlands, of the tropical rain forest to reach the eastern national boundaries in the Amazon basin proper.

The eastward drive stemmed from a number of factors. The urge to consolidate all territory within the national confines loomed large, especially after the bitter conflicts among Peru, Ecuador, Colombia, and Brazil over their eastern boundaries during the early 1940s. This strategic military involvement was heightened by valuable oil and gas discoveries in all eastern provinces during the early 1960s. Additionally, the rapidly expanding population of the high Andes (over 3 percent per annum, i.e., doubling in 21 years) after the mid-1940s, as mortality tumbled, strained available agricultural resources to the point of environmental deterioration. Migration and colonization seemed a reasonable solution. By 1963, President Balaúde

Figure 14.2 The Carretera Marginal de la Selva and areas of active colonization, east of the Andes, 1950–70. (Source: based on R. E. Crist and C. M. Nissly, *East from the Andes: Pioneer Settlements in the South American Heartland* [Gainesville: University of Florida Press, 1973].)

Terry of Peru took the lead in proposing a 3,500-km highway that would link the two dozen or so eastern trans-Andean highways from Caracas in Venezuela to Santa Cruz in Bolivia. As its name implies, the Carretera Marginal de la Selva skirted the "high jungle," or *selva,* in order to open up the *tierra templada* and act as a springboard for future colonization of the low-land humid tropical forest (fig. 14.2). Financed liberally by international backers who saw it as an imaginative developmental project to even out population pressures, the highway was constructed piecemeal over the ensuing decades.

The copious commentary on the settlement and pioneer colonization that preceded and followed the Carretera from the late 1950s to the mid-1970s was couched in optimistic, heroic, and boosterish terms. The rain forest was no longer "the enemy, but rather the haven for those with the will to work." True, farming in the tropics did present problems, but most thought the criticisms were overstated and none were prepared to pass a judgment on the wisdom or efficiency of the process.[5]

In time, caution and then pessimism prevailed as the evidence steadily accumulated that many of the new settlements came at high social and ecological costs. They were haphazard in their implementation and ill-suited because of lack of funds; poor social infrastructure; lack of planning, markets, and technical knowledge; and an overly bureaucratic administration, all compounded by the social upheaval and destabilization caused by the oil discoveries. Moreover, directing or encouraging the spontaneous movement of ignorant peasants from the Andes to the rain forest made them no less ignorant, and they remained trapped in a peasant economy. For some commentators the fact that the peasants had come from the "treeless landscapes of the Costa or Sierra" made matters worse; it meant that when they moved into the Oriente, "their desire to create open country knows few limits," and they indulged in an orgy of clearing (plate 14.1). Further, it was realized that the native Amerind lowland people were bound to suffer in any contact, via disease, altered values, and labor coercion.

However, in spite of its problems, colonization was uncontroversial as it was a substitute for more radical and much-needed land reform that was politically difficult to enact because of entrenched interests. But it fell far short of even its own goals; rather than creating small farms, colonization created large, unproductive, essentially speculative ones characterized by semifeudal labor relations. Moreover, as in the Brazilian Amazon, Andean Amazonian colonization was dominated by cattle raising. Ranching required little labor, did not need complex transportation infrastructure, paid well, and conferred social status. The result was massive deforestation and negative long-term environmental consequences. Between 1972 and 1987 the lowland population of the Peruvian forest had risen from 1.3 million to 2.2 million, and more than 6 million ha of forest had been cleared in addition to the 1.2 million lost prior to 1972. In the Colombian Amazon 2 million ha had been cleared (7 percent of the total forest). Everywhere the humid tropical forest at the foot of the Andes was being cut down ruthlessly and transformed into pasture for cattle-grazing.

Plate 14.1 East of the Andes, Bolivian Lowlands. A migrant peasant family clearing their patch of forest and erecting a crude dwelling. (Tony Morrison, South American Pictures.)

Brazil: "Growth without Development"

Unlike their eastern neighbors, the Brazilians had always regarded the humid, moist forests of the continent as a grim fact of existence, which like an "interminable green monster . . . [shut] out the sun of heaven." From the mid-sixteenth century, the growing of sugar, cotton, cocoa, and coffee and the raising of cattle had only been possible by felling and burning the trees of the Atlantic coastal forest. The people of Brazil, thought Roy Nash in 1926, "always have considered the forests as a communal possession which they felt free to hack, burn and abandon at will," so that even then he thought that at least 30 percent of the precontact forest had disappeared:

> If one could hover over Brazil in a balloon and get a bird's-eye view of forest after forest as each comes to the end of its dry season, he would see myriad smokes curl heaven-ward year after year, and century after century. Farming by fire—shifting agriculture—is as much the mode of life of the nomads of the Brazilian forests as of the Fangs of the Congo.[6]

But in addition to its vast forest, Brazil was in a class of its own in other ways. Settlement and territorial expansion had long been accompanied by a history of exploitative behavior and violence that had few counterparts. Wide social differentiation, undemocratic politics, illegal squatting, the segregation—and even elimination—of native populations, and vast grants of land, all shot through with a staggering lawlessness, corruption, and contravention of the rule of law, were hallmarks of Brazilian society. The forest peasantry, or *caboclos,* had always devastated large areas with "broadax in one hand and a firebrand in the other," but now the shifting backwoodsmen were aided, encouraged, and even replaced by much bigger players.[7] The army, government agencies, transnational companies, even the state were the new *caboclo.* Deforestation after 1960 becomes a story of superlatives: of vast areas and long distances, of swirling population shifts by the millions, massive deforestation, breathtaking change, contradictory claims, and international reaction and condemnation.

The Generals' Plan

The impetus for Brazil's post–World War II accelerated deforestation was its obsession with economic development. The aim was to stimulate capital accumulation and industrialization through aggressive central planning in order to achieve a high rate of economic growth that would give the country world-class status while promoting the positive virtues of independence, self-realization, and the banishment of backwardness and poverty. Postwar exuberance worldwide had led to the notion that the global "periphery" could compete successfully with the "core" of the industrialized world; hot war and cold war policies from 1940 onward aided this notion and led to the propping up of the Latin American economies. "Economic development was more than a government policy," said Warren Dean; "it amounted to a social program of vast scope, energy and originality." The subsequent high-powered public relations campaign penetrated the consciousness of every citizen and was made to justify everything that was done to society, nature, and the forest.[8]

But development was a chimera; the strategy did not achieve its aims. Wealth was redistributed not to the poor but to the rich; the crucial issue of agrarian reform for the small landholder was avoided by diverting attention to the colonization of the Atlantic and Amazon forests, which tended to favor the large landholders. Brazil's forests were squandered in an exploitative binge that undervalued the rich resource, which was bartered cheaply for "development." As far as the Amazon was concerned, it was "growth without development."[9]

Initially the transformation took place in the Atlantic coastal forest, and from about 1950 to 1970 investment and development were concentrated in and around the "industrial triangle" of São Paulo, Belo Horizonte, and Rio de Janiero, where the return on investment was high. The remnants of the Atlantic forest were further reduced. All this was achieved, however, amid much political instability and volatility, with marked swings to the Left and to the Right. In the poisoned atmosphere of the cold war years and with the specter of a Communist ascendancy raised by the Cuban Revolution of 1959, such instability could not be tolerated, and military intervention followed in 1964 with the overthrow of the government of President Goulart. For the next 24 years "the Generals" ruled supreme, obsessed with the development imperative, dreaming of national destiny, suspicious of populism or any collective action—whether by peasant farmers, environmental activists, or banks—paranoiac about foreign designs on the Amazon and wary of overseas criticism of the loss of cultural and biological diversity.

The grand strategy envisaged for Amazonian colonization was a combination of military-strategic and geopolitical aims designed to secure national boundaries, promote economic development, and exploit unused resources. Central to the geopolitical was the development of roads to link the vast hinterlands "waiting to fulfill their historic destiny" from the core or "manoeuvring platform" of the developed south (fig 14.3). The roads would also aid in the "total war" that the Generals foresaw would have to be waged against internal and even external—particularly neighboring—subversion, which certainly had attracted U.S. aid in the Alliance for Progress program. The threat of the "internationalisation" of the Amazon voiced either in the insensitive overseas comments about relieving global population pressures and resettling tens of millions in the basin, or in lamentations over environmental degradation, also figured in their calculations.[10]

Between 1964 and 1967 the new government committed itself to developing the whole subcontinental region and integrating it into the rest of Brazil with a series of acts and decrees, known collectively as Operation Amazonia (fig 14.3). Central to this policy was the acquisition of state land by the federal government for a road-building program, which had three aims:

1. integrating the poverty-prone and isolated northeast around Recife into the rest of Brazil and siphoning off the excess of the 30 million inhabitants (a severe drought in 1970 merely laid bare an agony of poverty long evident);
2. promoting colonization in the northwestern states of Rondônia and Acre in order to counteract active colonization by Peru and Venezuela in these thinly populated upriver forested areas; and
3. creating a major east–west road, running roughly parallel to the River Amazon in order to protect the frontier, "inundate the Amazon forest with

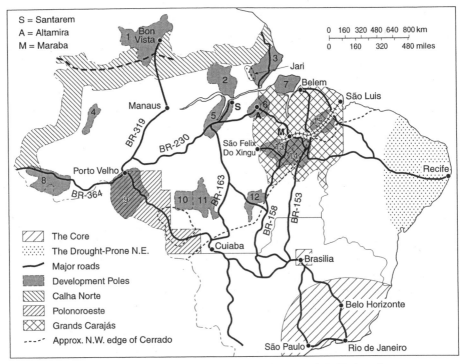

Figure 14.3 The Generals' Plan: slicing up the Amazon basin. (Source: S. B. Hecht and A. Cockburn, *The Fate of the Forest: Developers, Destroyers and Defenders of the Amazon* [London: Verso, 1989], 127–28; various.) The growth poles in the Polo Amazônia and their rationale are as follows: *1*, Roraima: livestock and some mining in a frontier zone; *2*, Trombetas: bauxite deposits; *3*, Amapa: agriculture and livestock in a frontier zone; *4*, Juruá: logging and later, oil; *5*, Tapajós: agriculture and livestock, later gold mining; *6*, Altamira: agricultural and livestock farming on Trans-Amazonian Highway; *7*, Marajó: livestock, timber, and oil; *8*, Acre: agriculture and livestock in frontier area; *9*, Rondônia: agriculture and livestock in frontier area; *10*, Aripuná: forest research and logging; *11*, Juruena: livestock and agriculture; later, gold mining; *12*, Xingu-Araguaia: livestock and meat; *13*, The Carajás: iron and gold mining, and center for later Projeto Grande Carajás; *14*, Araguaia-Tocantins: livestock, logging, goldmining, and general commerce; and *15*, Livestock, but later focused on railway line, Sao Luis to Carajás iron mine.

civilization" and link the newfound mineral resources (e.g., iron ore) with the coast.[11]

In 1960, the Amazon region had only 6,000 km of roads; two major cities, Belém and Manaus; and a scatter of small towns and villages along the major lines of communication, which consisted of the Amazon and its hundreds of tributaries. That isolation ended with the building of BR-153 from Belém, the 1,900-km road slashing through the savanna, scrub, and tropical deciduous forests of the Tocantins valley to the new capital, Brasília, which had been opened in 1960, itself a part of the overall strategy to shift the focus of the country from the overcrowded coasts to the interior. Construction of the Belém–Brasília road had actually begun in 1958 under the previous civil administration, which had also created SPVEA (Superintendency for the Economic Valorization of the Amazon), the first of the many acronymic bodies set up to develop the Amazon.

The success of the Belém–Brasília road and its feeders in opening up the forest was to be proved again and again as paved roads unleashed the spontaneous and uncontrollable spread of settlement. Small peasant holdings, but particularly cattle ranches, sprang up everywhere on the low-quality pastures created on cheaply deforested land, bolstered by the government's generous tax and credit incentives to attract private enterprise. The population increased from about 100,000 in 1960 to 2 million 10 years later, and more significantly the cattle population rose from nil to over 5 million in the same period. Feeder roads lead to the rapid occupation of the adjacent country. For example, on either side of the parallel road PA-150 in southeast Pará, a stretch of 4.7 million ha (about the size of Switzerland) had 30,000 ha cleared in 1972, 170,000 ha in 1977, and 820,000 in 1985 (fig. 14.4) and must serve as an example of what some commentators later called "explosive deforestation." [12]

The array of financial incentives for settlement and clearing was astounding. For example, up to 50 percent of corporate tax liability for 12 years (later extended to 17 years) could be invested in already existing Amazonian projects, thus allowing taxes to become, in effect, venture capital. Up to 75 percent of capital costs would be supplied by the government through its special credit bank, BASA; and credit was available for the purchase of land with no repayment for between four and eight years at interest rates of about 10–12 percent. Without these tax incentives the cattle ranches would not have been profitable. But with them—and with inflation running at well over 100 percent a year—it was a license to chop down trees and print money.

In addition to the incentives to invest, the costs of production were low because little labor was needed, and in any case, workers could easily be hired from the hordes of refugees from the drought-stricken northeast. The final product—meat—could be walked to market and was always readily salable whatever its quality given the Brazilian addiction to beef eating. In what was to become indicative of future developments, cattle reigned supreme: of about 950 projects approved by the Superintendência de Desenvolvimento da Amazônia (SUDAM), 631 were in the livestock sector, mainly in South Pará and northern Mato Grosso, with at least 60 percent of the investment coming from large industrial and agro-industrial enterprises in the

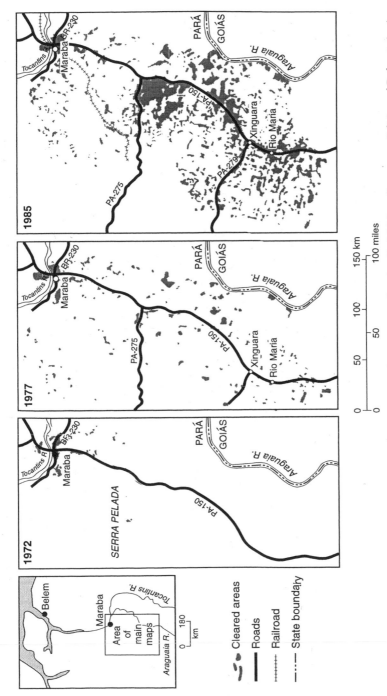

Figure 14.4 Deforestation in southeast Pará State, Brazil, 1972, 1977, and 1985. (Source: based on D. J. Mahar, *Government Policies and Deforestation in Brazil's Amazon Region* [Washington, D.C.: World Bank, 1989], 14.)

São Paulo region, which saw cattle raising as a tax-efficient investment. In the 8.4 million ha of SUDAM-approved cattle ranches, the average size was about 24,000 ha, and one (the Suia-Missu in northern Mato Grosso) was 560,000 ha. On every count the little farmer was being squeezed out.

Encouraged by the success of the Belém–Brasília road, the military government moved quickly to create the Program for National Integration (PIN) with the aim of building the 1,800-km north–south Cuiabá–Santarém road (B-163). More important was the symbolically significant east–west Transamazonia highway, BR-230. In total it was 5,400 km long, of which about 3,300 km were in Amazonia and aimed directly at the movement of the poverty-stricken northeasterners away from the south-central area around São Paulo and toward the interior (see fig. 14.3). Like the U.S. Homestead Act of a century before, the settlement project distributed free land with the aim of creating a class of prosperous, independent small farmers. Settlements were planned in contrast with the spontaneous settlement along the Belém–Brasília highway, which the Generals branded as "disorderly." The aims were ambitious: a hierarchical set of planned and serviced cities (*ruropolis*) for about 1,000 families; towns (*agropolis*) for about 300 families; and agro-villages (*agrovila*) for 48–60 families were envisaged at varying distances along and around the main highways. The goal was the gradual occupation of the empty spaces by moving 100,000 families in the first five years, though that would have hardly made a dent in the demographic problems of the northeast. More strategic than these two roads was the construction of a parallel Northern Perimeter Road to stop any chance of incursion into Brazilian territory by Venezuela and Colombia and to act as a counterbalance to the threat posed by the developmental Marginal Forest Highway (Carretera Marginal de la Selva) built by the Andean countries.

But because of the severe effects of the 1973 oil crisis, many of these plans were shelved. The Perimeter Road was never built and was replaced by the more limited and overtly strategic Calle Norte. Along the Transamazon Highway the policy of encouraging small farmers was abandoned in 1974 in favor of large-scale entrepreneurs. Of the 100,000 families that PIN had hoped to settle, perhaps only 8,000 came, and very few of the planned settlements eventuated. In addition, because the cost of cutting the subsidiary feeder roads was about three times greater than envisaged, thousands of kilometers were never built, which relegated the would-be settler to isolation and poverty, as the forest plots could yield no produce. In any case the initial enthusiasm about the fertility of most of the Amazonian soils was dispelled when their true lateritic nature was revealed after clearing. The declared aim of PIN to provide "a land without men for men without land" was all but over. All it had done was to unleash a fury of speculative clearing; it had created a land without trees but full of cattle.[13]

Rondônia

One of the most remote and inaccessible areas of the Amazon—indeed of the world—before 1970 was the border country with Bolivia and Peru, in the states of Acre, Rondônia, and northern Mato Grosso. Its 85 million ha of tropical moist forest contained about only 70,000 rubber tappers and an unknown number of Indian tribes people. From Rio or São Paulo, it took about six weeks to reach by oceangoing ship up the Amazon to Manaus, and then by steamer 1,100 km down the Madeira River to disembark at Porto Velho. In 1968 the geography of the region was revolutionized: Highway BR-364 was constructed to link the 1,500 km between Cuiabá and Porto Velho (see fig. 14.3), and the wild, remote, forested frontier could now be reached by three to four days' hard, but not unreasonable, coach journey.

As with the Belém–Brasília highway, the completion of BR-364 was followed by a wave of spontaneous migration, which rose from a few thousand per annum during the early 1970s, when the road was first opened, to a yearly average of 160,000 between 1984 and 1988. The rush into Rondônia stemmed from "pull" and "push" factors. First BR-364 traversed some areas of good soils (approximately 10 percent of the area, compared with an average of 3 percent over all Amazonia), a feature that was publicized and exaggerated. In addition, 100-ha plots with roads and services could be purchased cheaply via several colonization companies established by INCRA (National Institute for Colonization and Agrarian Reform). But as the decade progressed, migrants came not from Brazil's perennial problem area of the northeast as had been expected but from the country's richest agricultural area of the state of Paraná, 1,300 km to the south of Cuiabá at the far southern end of the highway. These settlers had a dramatic effect on Rondônia's forests.

Paraná had been a thriving agricultural area in the immediate postwar period with a reasonably healthy mix of tree and field crops—primarily coffee and maize, rice, and beans—and by Brazilian standards, it was a prosperous and egalitarian rural society. But coffee tree disease, soil erosion, and overproduction had caused severe problems, and the government's solution was to reduce the number of trees. The generous provision of compensation to the former coffee growers meant that more coffee trees were uprooted than had been anticipated: about 400 million were eliminated between 1961 and 1969, and what remained were devastated by a killing frost in 1975. The economy never recovered fully. Labor was shed as former coffee-growing areas were converted to mechanized soybean crops, for which there was a ready international market as livestock feed. Small farms (less than 50 ha) fell by 109,000 units between 1970 and 1980, with a loss of 890,000 ha of land, whereas during the same period large farms (over 1,000 ha) increased by 450 units, with a gain of more than 1 million ha. As coffee acreage halved and then halved again, land in soybeans rose from a mere 172,000 ha to over 2.3 million ha.

The loss of employment was catastrophic: over 2.5 million small farmers and laborers migrating out, with at least a third going to Rondônia. The establishment of a regular coach connection between Paraná and Rondônia completed the process of change. All that was needed was a ticket to ride the bus, and three or four days later the aspiring migrants arrived in the promised land, initiating one of the most rapid and extensive deforestation episodes of modern times.

The agricultural workers were given temporary accommodations and inoculated against malaria and gastrointestinal diseases and worms, which were rife. Those who had money attempted to buy land. The rest waited up to two years to be allotted a plot, by which time they had drifted into the squatter settlements on the edge of the burgeoning towns, become sharecroppers to established landholders, or illegally staked out claims in the forest edge and hoped for an eventual title to their land. The flow of migrants was so great that INCRA soon recognized illegal settler claims, but it was overwhelmed by the demand. In an attempt to control and cope with the flood of people, a new scheme—Polonoreste (the Northwest Brazil Integrated Development Program)—was set up in 1981 with World Bank backing to benefit an additional 20,000 families expected to come to the region, in addition to the 15,000 awaiting land. The program emphasized the planned provision of services and a sustainable system of farming consisting of protective tree crops like coffee, cacao, and rubber, along with a reduction of pasture development. But after 1984 when BR-364 was made into an all-weather road, the flood of migrants was overwhelming. The flow of newcomers rose to a yearly average of 160,000, fanning out along the branch roads, chopping, burning, and planting, hoping for a brighter future (plate 14.2, fig. 14.5).

The sheer press of people made the government's task unequal to the resources available, but just as important was the fact that many of the banks and SUDAM favored pasture development over small landholdings. This meant that by 1985 over a quarter of all the "improved" land was in pasture, a figure that has probably tripled since then. In fact, more land was cleared for speculative purposes than for producing food. Any land cleared of its trees was regarded as "improved," and the "improvement" could be sold, so that with the rapid rise of land prices a frenzy of deforestation and

Plate 14.2 An aspiring migrant family in the promised land of Rondônia State, Brazil. (Tony Morrison, South American Pictures.)

real estate speculation ensued. Consequently, it was possible to garner a net US$9,000 for clearing 14 ha of forest, plant some pasture, get a few crops for a couple of years, and then sell to a new settler, a process enhanced by the fact that the 25 percent capital gains tax was rarely collected. The implication of this level of profit for small landholders, let alone those with tens of thousands of hectares, was clear, and rising land prices were the engine that drove deforestation.

As was the case almost everywhere in Brazil, everything ultimately favored the clearing of the forest for pasture, and probably as much as 85 percent of all land cleared in Rondônia is occupied by livestock (plate 14.3). The positive benefits of cattle raising, such as high social status, low labor costs, and relatively good returns, are clear, as are the credit and tax incentives. Again, with a rate of inflation that has varied between 20 and 200 percent per annum, land has served as a hedge against the faltering value of the Brazilian currency. These advantages far outweigh the abysmally low productivity of pastures, which rarely exceed one beast per 2.4 ha. But in a country of—to put it mildly—uncertain land titles, which "rest on shameless fraud" and violence, a plot cleared of its vegetation is evidence of "effective use" (which has some legal standing) and substantiates and denotes ownership. At the very least it has readily recognizable boundaries that might dissuade

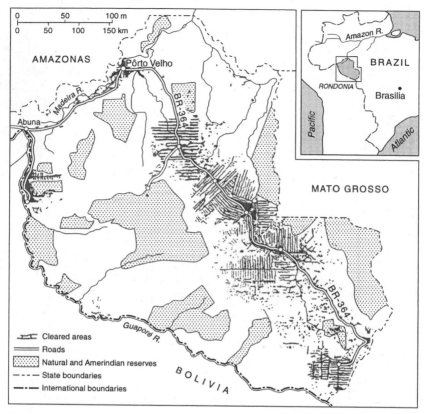

Figure 14.5 Rondônia State, Brazil, and the herringbone pattern of clearing. (Source: based on D. J. Mahar, *Government Policies and Deforestation in Brazil's Amazon Region* [Washington, D.C.: World Bank, 1989], 32; see also P. M. Fearnside, "Spatial Concentration of Deforestation in the Brazilian Amazon." *Ambio* 15 [1986]: 74–81.)

the gunmen of the big landowners from trying to take it over. Thus cattle substitute for other traditional ways of making money—through speculation and fraud. Once government subsidies are stopped, livestock raising is abandoned, as has happened with many of the SUDAM projects.

Other Schemes

Agriculture and ranching are not the only ways in which the forest is being destroyed. A naive faith in "giantism" has penetrated into other Brazilian schemes with devastating effect. The Fordlandia rubber plantation along the Tapajós River, just south of Santarém, was begun in 1927 only to be abandoned in 1945 after poor local planning, unsuitable soils, plant diseases, labor problems, and local corruption made it impossible to carry on. In an eerie replay of that experience, Daniel Ludwig, an American shipping

Plate 14.3 Rondônia State, Brazil. Banana plants replace the cleared tropical forest (remnants of which are in the background) while the ubiquitous white Brahmin/Zebu cattle roam over improvised pastures and degraded scrubland. (Tony Morrison, South American Pictures.)

billionaire, launched the rashly ambitious Jari scheme in 1967 with Japanese financial backing (fig. 14.3). About 2.5 million ha of forest were cleared and planted with the fast-growing *Gmelina arborea* trees from eastern India in order to supply an anticipated shortage of wood fiber. But again, poor planning, unsuitable soils, diseases to trees, labor problems, and an inability to get clear title to the land from the state government meant that the project failed, closing down in 1982. Everywhere, scores of plans and schemes for dams to generate hydroelectric power have inundated many thousands of square kilometers of forest because the generally flat terrain does not provide ideal locations for effective dam building.

Finally, the massive Grande Carajás Project (see fig. 14.3), a major regional plan for some 825,000 km² south of the Transamazon Highway and east of the Xingu River, involves the development of mining, forestry, agriculture, hydroelectricity, and transportation. Mining is concentrated on the exploitation of the vast deposits of copper, nickel, manganese, bauxite, and particularly iron ore. Although the mining per se has little impact on the forest (except to create some of the largest holes ever made in the ground), the 25 or so industrial furnaces use local charcoal. Plans to plant eucalypts have foundered because of their ecological unsustainability in the lowland rain forest, and fuelwood supplies are being garnered from an ever-increasing circle, consuming many hundreds of square kilometers of forest a year.

Life on the Forest Frontier

Almost everywhere in the world the colonization of the forest has been the means of social advancement and improvement for the landless peasant—the "little" man and his family. It was true, for example, on the frontiers of Rome during the first centuries BC and AD, of medieval Europe, eighteenth- and nineteenth-century America, nineteenth-century New Zealand and Australia, large parts of colonial India and Burma, and even, from what little we know, Ming China, especially in the southern part of the country. Even in Brazil, small- and medium-sized holdings were created successfully during the late nineteenth and early twentieth centuries out of the forested lands of the eastern parts of Rio Grande do Sul, west Santa Catarina, west and north Paraná, south Mato Grosso, areas of central-west São Paulo, the Doce valley in Minas Gerais, and a large part of Espírito Santo. But with very few exceptions the same has not been true of the colonization of the great Amazonian forest after about 1960. Despite the rhetoric "to give people with no land a land with no people," the reality has fallen far short of the ideal. Migrants have been lucky if they have farmed the land "for two or three years—if at all," according to Joe Foweraker in his aptly entitled 1981 study *The Struggle for Land*, which focused on south Pará, western Paraná, and south Mato Grosso. "Land on the frontier is taken over by large holdings and large enterprises dedicated more often than not to cattle raising . . . the cattle grow fat . . . while the people go hungry," he says. Thus, the colonization of the forest did not result in social betterment but social impoverishment, and the situation has fared no better in the subsequent 20 years.[14]

Many of the reasons for this paradox have been mentioned already. After the early 1970s there was a unique convergence of national and international economic and political factors that distorted the aims of natives and newcomers alike. Prolonged military government and its strategic aims, a drive to industrialize, an insensitive and corrupt bureaucracy, conflicting policies, a collapse of sponsored colonization schemes, increasing fiscal and credit incentives to international and national enterprises—all led to the penetration by monopoly capital not people. As always it was the poor, the potential beneficiaries of the mantle of the forest, who suffered most. Colonization was beyond even the reach of those with some resources to invest. They found it impossible to secure a firm title to the land they claimed or to establish the minimum conditions for long-term investment of time and labor. Even if they did, they faced a hostile physical environment of deteriorating soils and yields, and an even more hostile social environment of violence, intimidation, takeover, and murder as cattle ranchers and land grabbers (aided and abetted by corrupt local police and administrators) made their life one of fairly unrelieved toil, poverty, and injustice. If resistance became too great the military was called in to quell "a national security problem," of which the "Araguaia War" was a notorious example. In all, many thousands were killed. Thus, while the big sweep of the story of Amazonian deforestation is reasonably clear, the voices of the little people—"the men with the machetes" who "are ahead of the road builders trying, in the honest tradition of the pioneer, to carve a home from the forest"—are often difficult to hear in the din and turmoil of this new forest frontier. In fact, they have often been muted or extinguished.[15]

Books have been written attempting to explain the paradoxical nature of Brazilian agricultural development, and it would be superfluous to reiterate in detail what they have to say. One example must suffice. For 15 years Marianne Schmink and Charles Wood followed the lives and fortunes of migrants in the frontier settlement around São Felix do Xingu, a small frontier town on the Xingu River in South Pará State at the end of B-279, about 300 km west of the junction at Xinguara on the B-158 (see fig. 14.3).[16] By the middle of the 1970s most of the small farmers had been driven off the land they had cleared.

> The dispossessed faced a difficult and uncertain future. Many moved on down the road. Others ventured back into the bush, only to fall victim again to expropriation. Thousands of families drifted from one work site to another, temporarily employed by labor recruiters . . . who had been contracted by ranchers to clear land for pasture during the dry season.

If they had enough money, some went back to their home states, but many more lost their land and were too poor to return, so they sought refuge in the new shanty towns that sprang up on the outskirts of cities like Marabá, Xinguara, or Redenção. "In as little as two or three years places that held only a handful of people suddenly exploded into makeshift towns of fifteen to twenty thousand." Marabá grew at a staggering rate of 21 percent per annum between 1960 and 1980, and was well over 100,000 by the mid-1980s. Not surprisingly, these "boom" towns lacked sanitation, medical and educational services, regular employment, or any means of support for the uprooted.

The people of São Felix do Xingu experienced a measurable deterioration in their living standards between 1978 and 1984. Food consumption had decreased, the choice of foods had narrowed, and infant and child mortality had risen. To make matters worse, "Sao Felix was the third or fourth place where they had tried unsuccessfully to find a piece of land to support themselves." Some got employment during the dry season in the small sawmills that sprang up everywhere, but these were temporary, makeshift affairs. Once the mahogany was logged (which represented a minuscule part of the total timber available), the rest of the forest was cleared, burned, and converted to grazing land. The vision of the better life that the cleared forest offered was a chimera, and the hapless settlers were now literally and metaphorically at the "end of the road."

Opposition and resistance, exemplified by the protests and subsequent murder of rubber tapper Chico Mendes, sparked national and international condemnation, and the presence and savvy of the Kayapó Indians on their vast reserve west of the region impeded the exploitation of people and vegetation, but Schmink and Wood had no wish "to wax romantic about grassroots movements . . . which remain small and perched at the edge of power." Nor do they have any reason to believe that deforestation would abate, at least not as long as the incentives for it remained—a dismal conclusion to reach, but undoubtedly realistic.

How Much Deforestation?

Given the speed and extent of clearing in the Amazon region and the evidence of large, and long-lasting forest fires, it would not be surprising if the questions "how much?" and "how fast?" were asked. Like everything else about the Amazon, the answers come in emotive superlatives as the "dialectics of destruction" tumble out; the forest is in a state of "systematic demolition" or "imminent demise." The immigrants are "torching" the forest and creating "a burning season" (plate 14.4), while the large landholders indulge in murder and violence in order to dominate the frontier. An analysis of air photography images by a São Paulo–based research institute "conservatively estimated" that over 200,000 km^2 of the forest, or 4 percent of the Amazon region, were burning during an 80-day period, between July and October 1987. "The skies over western Brazil," reported *Time* magazine in 1989, "will soon be dark both day and night. Dark from the smoke of thousands of fires as farmers and cattle ranchers engage in the seasonal rite of destruction." The destruction of the Amazon rain forest was one of the "great tragedies of all history," and the country had acquired a reputation, "especially among the young" said the *Economist,* "as the world's environmental thug." [17]

The Amazon, of course, is not just an example or a microcosm of the bigger picture of tropical deforestation; it is a very sizable chunk of it, so that the pace and extent of clearing not only reflects but affects the global trend. All the problems of calibration and accuracy noted earlier are present. Official

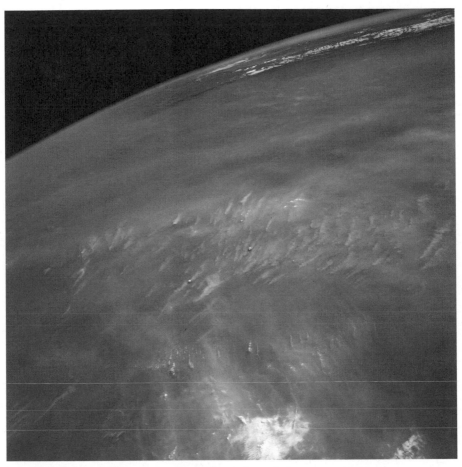

Plate 14.4 Rondônia and Mato Grosso States, Brazil, during the burning season, August 1984. The thermal plumes of smoke from clearing activity reach up above the smoke haze toward the Space Shuttle camera. On the horizon are the snow-covered peaks of the Bolivian/Peruvian Andes, which stand above the smoke pall, and Lake Titicaca beyond. (NASA STS41D-40–0022.)

data are incomplete and often out of date, and estimates "vary sharply" while data from different forms of satellite surveillance (e.g., LANDSAT, AVHRR [Advanced Very High Resolution Radiometer] satellite sensors) are open to different interpretation—in particular, the clearing of forest, or *cerrado*, and its regrowth are difficult to detect. During the early 1980s it looked as though the rate of clearing was such that if continued it would explode exponentially. In that case, all states of the Amazon would have been completely stripped clear of trees by now. This obviously has not happened, and as the end of the century has come and gone the forest is still far from becoming

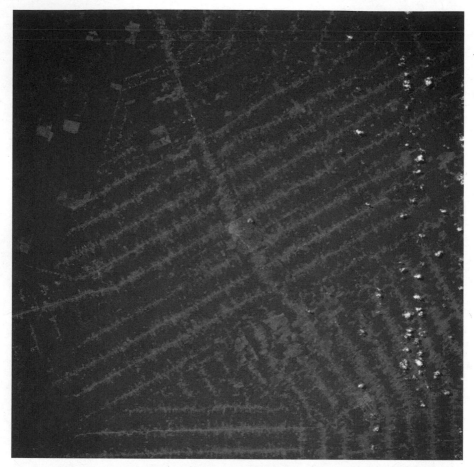

Plate 14.5 The distinctive "herringbone" pattern of clearing in Rondônia State, Brazil, as settlers fell the forest to create pastures and agricultural plots either side of the lateral roads, has made it one of the most photographed pieces of the earth's surface from space. Here the main road, Highway B-364, snakes diagonally across the picture, and roads branch out every 2–3 mi (4–5 km) into the tropical rain forest, shown as solid dark color. June 1985. (NASA STS51G-34–0060.)

what Tom Gill had predicted as "little more than a memory." By 1985 Philip Fearnside had abandoned the exponential argument and the prediction that the forest would disappear by a particular year, saying instead that deforestation was "explosive," especially in Rondônia, where the mass migration of smaller settlers after the paving of highway BR-364, made it a laboratory for studying deforestation.[18] Rondônia became one of the most photographed and remote-sensed patches on the earth's surface as paper after paper analyzed changes and made familiar the images of the progressively

Plate 14.6 An adjacent area 7 years later. The amount of clear-cut now exceeds the remaining rain forest stands. August 1992. (NASA STS046–078–026.)

thickening herringbone pattern of clearing along main and subsidiary side roads (plates 14.5, 14.6), so that it became a popular and universal symbol of forest destruction. Starting from virtually no land cleared in 1970 within its 230,104 km², the area of forest destruction climbed steadily to 13,995 km² in 1983, and to nearly 58,000 km² in 1988.

Over the whole of the 5 million km² of the Legal Amazon the picture looked only fractionally better.[19] Despite inconsistencies, problems, and the controversy of interpreting data, "best estimates" suggested that 345,000 km² had been deforested between 1970 and 1988 (including old clearings), or 8.2 percent of the forested four-fifths of the Legal Amazon, a total which might be raised by another 115,000 km², or 9.6 percent, if the area originally under forest and in cerrado was included. The rate of new clearing was staggering—20,000 km²/yr or 39,000 km² if the cerrado was included. With new data it was suggested by Salati that the total was even greater: up to 1988 over 598,921 km², or 12 percent, had been cleared.[20]

And there the matter lay, shrouded in uncertainty and speculation, until David Skole and Compton J. Tucker produced a detailed and widespread analysis. Using photographic images from LANDSAT Thematic Mapping Data and a GIS computer program, they mapped changes between 1978 and 1988 at a spatial resolution of 16 × 16 km², small enough to allow the identification of individual plots of forest, regrowth, crops, and pasture. Not only could the area of deforestation in the closed-canopy forest over the total Brazilian Amazon be identified but also the degree to which the forest had become fragmented and degraded, that is to say, the amount of forest that became isolated and the length of forest edge that was exposed through deforestation.[21] By 1978 some 78,000 km² had been cleared, which had risen to 230,000 km² by 1988 (table 14.2), giving an average annual rate of clearing of 15,200 km² over the intervening 10 years. The amount of forest degraded or fragmented rose from 208,000 km² to 588,000 km² in 1988.

Skole and Tucker's new total of 230,000 km² by 1988 is considerably less than the 345,000 km² calculated by Fearnside, and markedly less than the 598,921 km² suggested by Salati or, indeed, amounts put forward in a host of other more recent studies. Similarly, the rate of clearing at 15,200 km²/yr is considerably less than the 21,000–80,000 km²/yr suggested elsewhere, all of which has implications for the global total. Wherever the truth lies, it is evident that as in the tropical world at large uncertainty reigns and that there is much hype about it. That is not to say that the amount or rate is insignificant but that it is not as great as was commonly thought. At a constant rate of clearing of 15,200 km²/yr, it will take about 276 years for the 4.1 million or 4.2 million km² of the Great Mother Forest to disappear, even assuming that abandonment and regrowth will not reclaim a considerable portion of the old forestland, as all experience shows it will. What the Skole and Tucker study does supremely well is to locate change geographically for the whole Legal Amazon in a way that has only been hinted at before, or known only for small sections of spectacular change such as Rondônia and the Belém–Brasília highway (fig. 14.4).

But nothing stands still. Even as I write, the spotlight has swung back onto Amazonia. The headlong drive for development has picked up again with a vengeance, as Brazil attempts to dispose of its debts. Clearing surged to over 24,000 km² a year between 2002 and 2004. "The present rate is roughly equivalent to an area the size of New York's Central Park disappearing every hour, or of Belgium being razed and burnt each year."[22]

Table 14.2 Predeforestation area of forest, *cerrado*, and water, and deforested and isolated and edge forest (in km²), Brazilian Amazon

	Predeforestation				1978			1988			1988
	Forest	Cerrado	Water	Total Area	Deforested	Isolated and Edge	Total Disturbed	Deforested	Isolated and Edge	Total Disturbed	As % Total Area
Acre	152.4	0	0.4	152.8	2.6	4.5	7.1	6.4	24.1	30.5	20.0
Amàpá	137.4	1.0	1.1	139.5	0.2	0.4	0.6	0.2	0.7	0.9	0.6
Amazonas	1,531.1	14.4	29.8	1,575.3	2.3	6.5	8.8	11.8	36.9	48.7	3.1
Maranhão	145.8	114.7	1.3	261.8	9.4	13.8	23.2	32.0	30.3	62.3	23.8
Mato Grosso	527.6	368.7	4.2	900.5	21.1	26.2	47.3	47.6	73.7	121.3	13.4
Pará	1,183.6	28.6	49.5	1,261.7	30.5	52.0	82.5	95.1	123.5	218.6	17.3
Rondonia	212.2	24.6	1.5	238.3	6.2	18.7	24.9	24.0	54.8	78.8	33.0
Roraima	172.4	51.5	1.8	225.7	0.2	0.8	1.0	1.9	5.2	7.1	3.1
Tocantins	30.3	244.0	2.9	277.2	5.7	6.9	12.6	11.4	8.2	19.6	7.1
Total	4,092.8	847.5	92.5	5,032.8	78.2	129.8	208	230.4	357.8	587.8	11.7

Source: D. L. Skole and C. J. Tucker, "Tropical Deforestation and Habitat Fragmentation in the Amazon: Satellite Data from 1978 to 1988," *Science* 260 (1993), 1906.

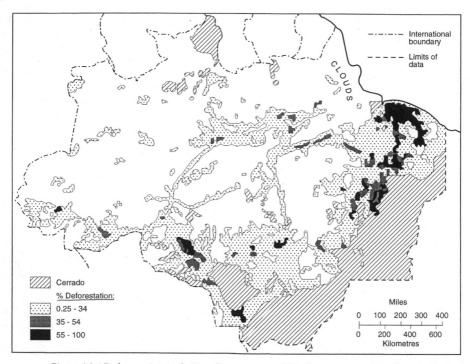

Figure 14.6 Deforestation in the Brazilian Amazon, 1988. (Source: generalized from D. Skole and C. J. Tucker, "Tropical Deforestation and Habitat Fragmentation in the Amazon: Satellite Data from 1978 to 1988," *Science* 260 [1993]: 1905–10, esp. 1907.)

Beyond Amazonia there is hardly any part of the Latin American continent where there is not some evidence of clearing, both planned and spontaneous, though much of it is only know about vaguely. In the Zona Central of Paraguay, for example, it is claimed that the 40,000 km² of tropical rain forest that existed in 1945 has been reduced to about 13,000 km² today, while the borderlands with Brazil have also been cleared for agriculture and pastureland. But the total continental picture remains blurred.

South and Southeast Asia

Planned and deliberate governmental schemes to promote agricultural development and resettlement for the alleviation of population pressures are not confined to the Amazon basin; they also have been prominent in Indonesia and Malaysia. But in neither of these countries are the agricultural development programs as large or grandiose, nor have they received the same publicity or research investigation. In any case they have been directed far more at peasant agricultural clearing.

In Indonesia the government initiated a Transmigration Project, which has attempted to shift over 2 million peasant farmers from overcrowded Java (where population densities reach as much as 3,000/km^2) to "empty" forested lands in Sumatra, Irian Jaya, and Kalimantan, although the schemes themselves have also proved to be the catalyst for larger, spontaneous migrations. But the true magnitude of the schemes and the clearing is lost in the fragmented locations of change in scores of islands, the spontaneous movements within a population of over 200 million people, and the cloak of secrecy with which the government has covered its activities. An added complication is that much of the movement is not to forests but to undrained or partially drained tidal wetlands, so we have no clear idea of the area of forest involved. Nonetheless, estimates suggest that perhaps as much as 6,000 km^2 have been cleared by planned or spontaneous movement, less than a quarter of that of the Amazon deforestation.

Attracting much less attention, but equally as devastating, are the activities of the Federal Land Development Agency (FELDA) and associated government agencies in peninsular Malaysia, which have embarked on a deliberate policy of expanding primary production of food and cash crops—particularly oil palm—in order to increase national wealth and create a prosperous rural middle class. In the process some 250,000 people have been resettled. About 73 percent of the land surface of the peninsula was forested in the early 1950s; a considerable amount having already been cleared during the early years of the century for rubber plantations and small peasant farms. During the early 1960s the annual rate cleared was about 80 km^2/yr, which rapidly rose to over 350 km^2 during the late 1970s. By 1966 the forest has been reduced to 64 percent of the peninsula (84,832 km^2) and by 1982 it was 51 percent (67,351 km^2; fig. 14.7). At least another 10 percent will be cleared before government aims are fulfilled in the mid-1990s. But the ability of the government of Malaysia, or anywhere, to put a brake on associated spontaneous clearing is doubtful, and the evidence is that it has already overshot its target. Already the forest, which once stretched in an almost continuous mantle over the peninsula, is fragmented into a southern remnant and two large northern blocks, and in many places the dominant landscape is no longer one of forest but of cultivation.

In all this discussion of the grand plans in Brazil, Indonesia, and Malaysia, the forest has been seen as wealth to be garnered for the advantage of the state, and as Nicholas Guppy forecast nearly 20 years ago, clearing is often a surrogate measure for other, more pressing, but much more

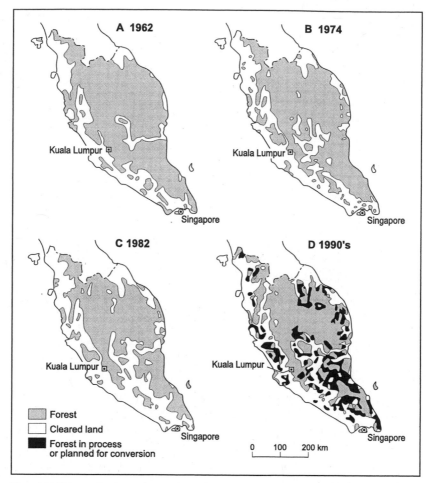

Figure 14.7 Forest clearing in peninsular Malaysia. *A,* 1962; *B,* 1974; *C,* 1982; and *D,* 1990s. (Source: H. C. Brookfield, F. J. Lian, K.-S. Low, and L. Potter, "Borneo and the Malay Peninsula," in *The Earth as Transformed by Human Action,* ed. B. L. Turner II et al. [Cambridge: Cambridge University Press, 1990], 506.)

difficult social reforms. But in many parts of the world the peasants have taken the initiative and have gone ahead and cleared the land in the time-honored fashion, bit by bit, year by year, making enough new ground to establish themselves and feed a family. In toto this massive, undocumented movement is thought to be one of the greatest impacts on the forests of the tropical world (see fig. 13.6). It is their activities that go a long way to explain the decline of forested lands between 1950 and 1980 by some 50.9

million ha, over half of which is in mainland and subcontinental Southeast Asia.

"HOOFPRINTS ON THE FOREST": RANCHING AND PASTURE DEVELOPMENT

In Central America, pasture development is probably the major cause of forest loss and may well be the primary cause of deforestation everywhere in Latin America. Pasture establishment is a relatively new phenomenon because the lack of livestock in pre-Columbian times gave no incentive for the American Indians to establish pastures, which in any case quickly reverted to some sort of forest. But that situation has changed rapidly since 1945, with the advent of bulldozers for road making.

Even though the stated aim of many of the development projects has been the resettlement of peasant proprietors on small plots of land, a whole amalgam of economic, social, and fiscal reasons work toward the new clearings eventually being converted to pasture. By the mid-1980s, the experience of Douglas Shane, as he hiked through the Ecuadorian tropical forest for hours on end and accidentally stumbled on "a distinct line of a path" that he followed for another hour, was to become common.

> Suddenly a wall of vegetation sprung up before me. I assumed I had come to a river, for only where the forest ends at such a feature does one usually find such thick growth. I approached the green wall and pushing through the curtain of vines, branches and weeds, to my astonishment I entered into a clearing of several hectares. Directly across the clearing, over the charred stumps and logs . . . [was] the shack of the colonist whose ax had felled the forest. And to my left, plodding about among the debris were a dozen cattle.

It was, as he said colorfully, the impress of these "Hoofprints on the Forest" that was so radically transforming and destroying the tropical forests in Latin America.[23]

Small farmers, as well as large, succumb to the lure of cattle. Pasture is the easiest means of keeping the land from reverting to secondary forest, cleared land has a speculative value far in excess of crop production in high-inflation economies, pastures are encouraged by tax laws, and cleared land is the surest title to ownership amid chaotic land title registration and corruption. Moreover, to be a cattle raiser is congenial to the Latin value system: "*Ganadero,* like *caballero,* is a term of respect," noted Jim Parsons. "It carries prestige, and it implies an attractive way of life that is easily entered."[24]

Practicalities support social mores: cattle provide versatility and additional income in the form of milk and calves, they even-out risk, and they require much fewer labor inputs than rice or maize. They can be walked to market, where they are not subject to gluts in the same manner as are crops. What is more, in a way cattle raising conforms to the realities of the environment because (as even Rondônia showed) newly cleared and planted fields of crops go out of production in about three years, at which time they are turned over to grass because cattle provide a marginal return, which, however little, is crucial to the struggling small landholder. In time the declining fertility and weed invasion of his plot are compensated for by clearing a new area or letting part of a holding go to bush, then cutting and burning it to give a flush of nutrients. Whatever is done, however, the result is the same: more of the forest is felled, and secondary regrowth takes over in abandoned plots or is fired constantly.

Cattle are excellent converters of cellulose to protein and do so relatively cheaply. In Central America their number has risen phenomenally from a few thousand to millions, and much of the final product—beef—finds a ready export market, mainly in the United States for pet and fast foods. This link between deforestation and consumer lifestyles and consumption a continent away has been dubbed the "Hamburger Connection" by Norman Myers, though its magnitude may not be as great as is thought.[25]

As early as 1972 Jim Parsons warned about what was happening: "The once limitless forests of humid tropical America are rapidly being converted to grasslands," he wrote, and "it must now be considered an important question whether . . . [the forest] will long endure." Wherever roads penetrated, agriculture followed, but it was only a temporary stage in the process by which the forest was converted to *potreros*. After a few years of cropping and declining soil fertility, aggressively colonizing African grasses formed "artificial" pastures. The small landholder was forced to sell out to the next wave of settlers or speculators that followed, who consolidated the smallholdings into larger ones in order to raise beef cattle; or he became a laborer for the hacienda owners, who owned disproportionately large areas of land and wanted to clear and acquire even more. The change in the landscape was striking: Parsons had done fieldwork in many parts of Latin America over decades and could now barely recognize places:

> Where once stood great tracts of lowland forest—along the Pan American Highway in Mexico and Central America, the northern coast of Colombia, on the Andean spurs of eastern Venezuela, in the Interior of Brazil, on the islands of the Greater Antilles—today one sees pasture lands stretching to the horizon, interrupted only by scattered palms, remnant woodlots or rows of trees planted as live fences.[26]

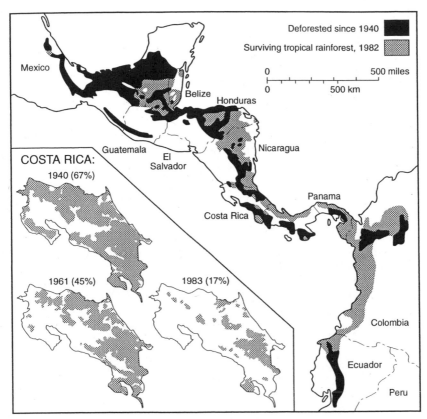

Figure 14.8 Forest clearing in Central America, 1940–82, and the detail of Costa Rica, 1940, 1961, and 1983. (Source: M. Williams, "Forests," in *The Earth as Transformed by Human Action,* ed. B. L. Turner II et al. [Cambridge: Cambridge University Press, 1990], 192, after J. D. Nations and D. I. Komer, "Indians, Immigrants and Beef Exports: Deforestation in Central America." *Cultural Survival Quarterly* 6 [1982]: 8–12.)

The evidence of air photography and remote sensing more than supports this observation (fig. 14.8), with the situation in Costa Rica having been particularly well monitored over the decades.

Even by the mid-1970s Parsons thought that "more than enough of the forest resource has been cleared already. . . . It is time now to pause in this mad assault on nature, time to think more in terms of saving what is left. We are rapidly running out of both time and forest."[27] But the "mad assault" never stopped, and perhaps as much as 25,000 km² have been cleared annually for cattle ranching. The transformation of the Central and South American forests continues unabated and much of the original forest cover has gone.

FUELWOOD AND CHARCOAL

Throughout the history of the human use of the forest, four broad uses of this resource have dominated: to create land for growing food, to supply timber for constructing dwellings, to build ships for the strategic and economic power they brought, and to provide fuel for warmth. In the latter half of the twentieth century the demand for land for food rose with devastating effect. The demand for timber for construction is unabated and significant, but in the temperate world, at least, it is often replenished by reforestation. The other two uses of timber, shipbuilding and fuel, seem to have been relegated; neither wooden ships nor, indeed, any sorts of ships hold the key to world supremacy in trade and influence anymore, and in many countries coal and petroleum seem to have eliminated the need for wood burning for warmth and energy.

But the perception that fossil fuels have supplanted wood is erroneous: in the developing world, wood and charcoal for personal warmth, for the preparation of food, and even for industrial energy is of long standing and still looms large. It took the 1973 hike in oil prices by OPEC (the Organization of Petroleum Exporting Countries) and the near panic in the developed world about the basis of its mobility, industry, and heating to remind people of what Erik Eckholm called in 1975 "the other energy crisis." [28] Approximately 2.5–3 billion people (40–50 percent of the world's population) rely on wood, not only for warmth but for the daily preparation of the very food they eat. In fact, wood comprises more than 70 percent of the national energy consumption in more than 40 countries. Deficiencies in this resource are particularly acute in Andean Latin America, the Caribbean Islands, most of the Indian Subcontinent, and particularly Nepal (fig. 14.9),

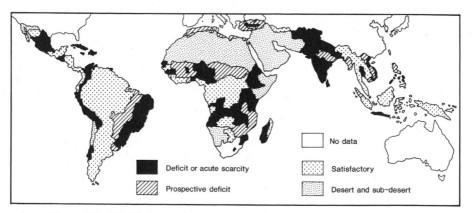

Figure 14.9 Global fuelwood deficits. (Source: FAO, *Yearbook of Forest Products* [Rome: FAO, 1983].)

but the shortfall appears to be most marked in Africa, which depends on wood for up to 58 percent of all energy requirements, and where in many savanna areas depletion far exceeds the rate of growth.

In these and adjacent parts of the developing world, fuel is scarcer and more expensive than food, and occasionally consumes one-fifth to one-half of the monetary budget of urban households, and up to four-fifths of the annual working year are given over to scouring the countryside for the last remnant of woody fiber to burn. This is particularly true around urban and industrial areas. For example, the closed forest cover within a 100-km radius of 30 major Indian cities was reduced from 96,625 to 72,278 km² between 1972 and 1982, although about 8,000 km² of the loss probably ended up as second-growth degraded open forest.

The collection and distribution of fuelwood and charcoal is one of the most important facets of the infrastructure of any large third world city. Hyderabad, for example, has 3.5 million inhabitants, and just over 100,000 tons of wood were "imported" into the urban area annually, coming from distances of up to 154 km away. Once in the city, the wood was handled by six major wholesalers and a diverse assemblage of 472 firewood retailers, who then auctioned it out to households. Rural dwellers, in contrast, rarely cause the same sort of absolute deforestation; rather, they collect deadwood or cause a "thinning" of the forest, though in the extreme that too can become complete deforestation, especially in the drier, more open forests.

Currently just over half (55 percent) of all wood known to be extracted from the forests of the world (1.8 billion m³) is fuelwood (fig. 14.10), and just as demand has doubled during the last 20 years, so the eminently predictable increase in world population makes it unlikely that the demand will slacken in the future. Indeed, predictions are that it will reach 2.4 billion m³ by 2010. Energy is essential in a developing economy, as the story of fuelwood use in the industrial and transportation growth of the United States during the eighteenth and nineteenth centuries shows clearly, and which has been repeated with variations in twentieth-century Brazil. As nearly 85 percent of the demand for fuelwood is in the developing world, the sharp rise of oil prices in the 1970s caused much hardship as competition for fuelwood increased; and although oil became cheaper during the 1990s, it has now risen again, causing new concerns. A switch to alternative fuels, such as petroleum and kerosene, by the 2.5–3 billion fuelwood burners is feasible in terms of the extra amount of these fuels consumed—a mere 4 percent of the current world petroleum production—however, the income and the hard currency needed to pay for this are usually difficult to come by.

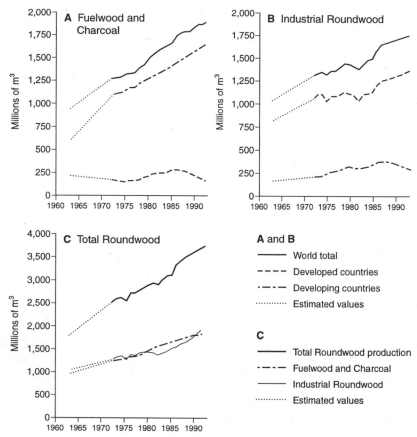

Figure 14.10 A, Fuelwood and charcoal production, 1963–85; *B,* Industrial fuelwood production, 1963–85; *C,* Total roundwood production, 1963–85. (Source: FAO, *Yearbook of Forest Products* [Rome: FAO, 1997].)

Although much of the fuelwood comes from trees that have in effect been coppiced and regrow in time, much comes as a by-product of land clearing. Nevertheless, it is thought that as much as 20,000–25,000 km² of woodland and forest are destroyed specifically for fuelwood gathering each year. The accuracy of this estimate is open to question, but one thing is certain: cutting for fuelwood in the forests is a problem that won't go away.

TIMBER EXTRACTION

In the first-ever attempt to calculate the drain on global forest resources, William Sparhawk and Raphael Zon in 1923 thought that slightly less saw timber was being extracted than firewood—739.6 million m³ compared with

852.5 million m³ (see table 12.1). In the post-1945 world, the expectation was that despite an increase in world population, the rapid substitution of steel, concrete, brick, and plastic for many purposes that had previously used wood would result in a relative decline in sawnwood use compared with fuelwood use. But that has not happened; in fact the very reverse has occurred. Since 1923 sawnwood and roundwood consumption has increased 2.59 times, to 1.9 billion m³ (and that does not take into account significant new extra uses of wood for paneling and paper, amounting to 363 million m³) while fuelwood consumption has increased 2.18 times, to 1.8 billion m³, and is forecast to rise steadily again in line with world population increase. Currently about 1.8 billion m³ of sawnwood is cut annually, and the rate is increasing by about 25 million m³ every year. In terms of value, the world export trade in wood products was worth over $135 billion in 1997. Next to petroleum and natural gas, wood is the third most valuable primary commodity in world trade.

In the developing world in particular, industrial roundwood or sawnwood is seen as the source of foreign exchange and an essential element in the quest for advancement. Regrettably, however, there are few well-managed forests and plantations, so that the extraction is at the expense of the standing stock. Also, the process is often monopolized by large companies and/or influential individuals, often in corrupt political alliances with government and the authorities. At the same time, in the industrial economies of the developed world, extraction and regeneration are roughly in equilibrium: regrowth exceeds extraction in Canada, New Zealand, and Scandinavia but probably only marginally so in the United States, western Europe, the Russian Federation, and Japan. But this internal conservation is often achieved at the disadvantage of producers in the tropical world, who are ready to supply hardwood for hard currency, even if they do not get the full resource value of the timber.

If the major softwood exporters such as Canada, Finland, and Sweden (and the United States and Germany) are excluded, then the next largest are the hardwood tropical exporters, Indonesia, Malaysia, and Brazil. Table 14.3 gives a "still" in the ever-changing, kaleidoscopic pattern of world trade. The exporters and importers that have a net trade in excess of $1 billion are ranked by volume. The biggest importers are predictably the most economically advanced countries in Europe and Japan, but China (now including Hong Kong) and South Africa have entered their ranks. The decline of production in Indonesia, Thailand, and the Philippines through sheer overexploitation is now being played out again in Malaysia and the Indonesian territories of Sabah and Sarawak, where the rate of extraction is roughly two to four times the natural regrowth. It is estimated that in Thailand the forest

Table 14.3 Global export, import, and net trade of forest
products, ± $US million, 1997 (in millions of $US)

Country	Exports	Imports	Net Trade
Net exporters + 500:			
Canada	25,081	3,189	21,892
Finland	10,394	707	9,687
Sweden	10,260	1,379	8,881
Indonesia	5,093	286	4,102
Malaysia	4,025	988	3,037
Austria	4,440	2,116	2,324
Russian Federation	2,892	688	2,204
Brazil	2,874	1,294	1,580
Chile	1,431	200	1,231
New Zealand	1,376	308	1,068
Net importers:			
Mexico	440	1,463	−1,023
Germany	10,727	12,037	−1,310
Denmark	435	1,801	−1,366
Netherlands	2,759	4,725	−1,966
Spain	1,664	3,704	−2,090
Korean Republic	1,512	3,813	−2,301
France	4,049	5,257	−3,217
South Africa	1,282	5,321	−4,039
Italy	2,632	6,776	−4,144
United Kingdom	2,116	10,009	−7,893
United States	15,698	24,003	−8,305
China	3,641	12,380	−8,739
Japan	1,639	17,160	−15,521

Source: FAO, *Yearbook of Forest Products* (Rome: FAO, 1997).

cover has fallen from 53 percent in 1961 to 25 percent or even less in 1986. In Cambodia illegal timber exports have been the means of sustaining various factions and warlords, like the infamous Khmer Rouge, while the world turns a blind eye to where the timber comes from in order to secure supplies. Similarly devastating economic and political crises have torn Indonesia apart in recent years and in the resultant "resource anarchy" the "protected" forests of the bulk of lowland Indonesia are being logged mercilessly, so that it is predicted that little forest will remain in another decade.

Although the valuable hardwoods account for only as little as 1 or 2, at most 10, percent of any unit area of the forest, careless and indiscriminate logging destroys up to 60 percent, and the soil is compacted or eroded. For example, a study of selective logging in the Paragominas region of Pará State in Brazil found that while only 1–2 percent of the trees were purposefully harvested, 26 percent were killed or damaged (12 percent lost their crowns, 11 percent were uprooted by bulldozers, 3 percent suffered substantial bark scarring) and the forest canopy was reduced by almost one-half. Logging roads also scar the forest and become pathways for exploitation by spontaneous migrations of slash-and-burn cultivators. Further degrading the ecosystem is the threat of fire sweeping through the logged area because it "escaped" from small landholders' clearings and careless logging companies or was set deliberately by large landholders, in the hope of driving out small cultivators and eventually taking over their land. When these occurrences coincide with drought brought on by El Niño oscillations, the result can be catastrophic. It happened in East Kalimantan in 1983, when about 3,500 km² were destroyed or heavily damaged and, again, in the disastrous fires of Indonesia and Kalimantan in 1992, 1993, and especially in 1997 that put most of Southeast Asia under a pall of smoke for months on end, disrupting traffic and life and causing a severe health hazard.

Various models have been constructed to predict the worldwide consumption of wood products, and all conclude that future demand will exceed the maximum level available from the forests on a sustainable basis. More regionally based models for 1980–2020 suggest that timber supplies would peak during the first decade of this century and then fall. Then, timber sources would shift from South and Southeast Asia as supplies are cut out and demand rises, to untapped but expensive sources in Africa and, very significantly, Latin America. Africa's Côte d'Ivoire already is a substantial exporter.

It is possible, however, that the calculation of the scale of deforestation is based on the erroneous exaggeration of the extent of the precolonial forest, which itself was based on the conventional wisdom that the native peoples had degraded and severely reduced the forest in the past. For example, the original forest cover of Côte d'Ivoire is more likely to have been approximately 7–8 million ha rather than the approximately 14.5–16 million ha, so that the 2.7 million ha remaining in 1990 represents a loss nearer to 130,000/yr than 330,000/yr—still great, to be sure, but nearly a third less. The same might well be true for other parts of West Africa.

Whatever the exact figures in this or that country, it is thought that about 44,000 km² of the tropical forest is logged over annually and largely destroyed or degraded, in addition to the approximately 110,000 km² cleared for agriculture. Such a scale of loss will lead to a permanent diminution of the tropical forest as the "mad assault" goes on.

EPILOGUE

Backward and Forward Glances

> The global problem of deforestation provokes unlikely reactions of concern
> these days among city dwellers, not only because of the enormity of the scale
> but also because in the depths of cultural memory forests remain the correlate
> of human transcendence. We call it the loss of nature, or the loss of wildlife
> habitat, or the loss of biodiversity, but underlying the ecological concern is
> perhaps a much deeper appreciation about the disappearance of boundar-
> ies, without which the human abode loses its grounding. . . . Without such
> outside domains there is no inside in which to dwell.
> —R. P. HARRISON, *Forests: The Shadow of Civilization* (1992)

TWENTY-FIVE years ago, when I first visited the United States, I started to
think and write about what I saw—or, perhaps more correctly, about what
I could no longer see. What had happened to the forest that once covered
so much of the country? How, when, and why had a people wrought such
a massive change to their landscape and their environment, and with what
consequences? Those questions resulted in *Americans and Their Forests*.
I have asked the same questions and used the same methods and inductive
approaches in the present book, but this time for the whole world through
all time—how satisfactorily, one can only guess.

As we enter the opening years of yet another century and cross the
threshold of a new millennium it is instructive to glance backward at what
has passed and forward a little to what is to come. What does this account
tell us about the process of deforestation? Undoubtedly the next thousand
years will be significantly different from the last thousand years, but would
an observer of, say, 1800 have been able to even come anywhere near visu-
alizing the world of 2000? It is difficult enough to sum up the complexity of
the past of human existence, let alone the unpredictability of its future.

Of one thing I am sure, *Deforesting the Earth* makes no claim to solve the profound problems of the transformation of global land cover, which is continually changing. Books and reports on deforestation abound and are published at a bewildering rate. A random glance at my study shelves reveals that in the first six years of the 1990s a dozen books emerged, all with arresting titles such as *The End of Nature; Who Will Save the Forests?; The Struggle for Land and the Fate of the Forests; Bad Harvest? The Timber Trade and the Degradation of the World's Forests; The Vanishing Forest; Logging the Globe;* and there are many more.[1] And this says nothing about, for example, the biennial World Resources reports of the World Resources Institute; the five-yearly reports of the FAO, *The State of the World's Forests;* and the numerous articles in environmental and forestry journals. A memorable passage in the book of Ecclesiastes more or less sums up the telling of the global deforestation story: "Of the making of books there is no end." And because there is no end to this continuous process of global transformation, many more books will be written about it in the future.

Consequently, *Deforesting the Earth: From Prehistory to Global Crisis* is just that: an account of how humans have related to their forests over at least seven millennia. It is not a compendium of solutions but an attempt to make sense of a very long, drawn-out, and momentous process of change. If in the writing I have pointed out how various societies and cultures have managed to do something with their forests other than destroy them, then these examples will have some value in extending our knowledge about possible solutions. This book can only be an invitation for reflection, not a prescription for action. That I leave to others.

Nevertheless, to reiterate something I mentioned at the beginning of chapter 12, there have been strong advocates for extreme action over forests—either they are to be used and cleared or they are to be left alone. But experience has shown that there is a third way and that some forests, at least, have had a long history of conscious, manipulative conservation management along ecological lines and are, thus, capable of yielding a harvest of timber while staying intact enough to grow another day. Examples abound in the developed world of western Europe and North America, and there are smaller but significant examples in parts of West Africa and India, in the developing world. The acceptance of the inevitability of human impact on the forests without the inevitability of their wholesale destruction is the experience of many parts of the world, and is, I believe, better than cordoning them off from any human exploitation for them only to change inevitably through natural causes.

A few things about the future are reasonably certain. World population will continue to rise and, depending on a variety of assumptions, will stabilize at between 9 and 10 billion by 2100. The bulk of those 3 or 4 billion extra people will be in the developing world, primarily in the tropical forest zone. It is inconceivable that they will need any less land to grow food, unless some miracle of genetic engineering of high-yielding foods comes to their (and the forest's) rescue. Cultivation has always been the greatest devourer of the forests, and inevitably many more millions of hectares will be destroyed. Similarly, the demand for fuelwood will remain immense for the poor of the world. Many of the additional people will be born in urban areas or will migrate to them, but those living in or near the tropical forest will still hope that it will continue to be "the mantle of the poor." The impoverished will want to use it; others will wish to restrict its use and preserve it.

The population of the developed world will barely increase over the next century, but real incomes will do so dramatically. Steady rises of about 2 percent plus per annum are common, and during the 1990s the United States, the biggest consuming country of all, was achieving an unprecedented 4–5 percent, rates (which are currently being matched or surpassed by China). Such rates of growth cannot be sustained without even greater demands on the world's resources, of which wood and pulp are still important. During the last few years raw material and energy prices have rocketed. More dwellings are being constructed, invariably with a large component of wood in them. Wood as a furniture and interior finishing material still has a workability and aesthetic acceptability that is unlikely to be wholly replaced by any synthetics, especially as standards of living rise. Wood-burning fires are a sign of "the good life" among many, and consumption of wood for energy is rising.

Moreover, the much-vaunted electronic age has not diminished the consumption of paper. If anything it has created new demands for the product, and a more profligate use. Books, newspapers, and magazines are being produced in ever-greater numbers as literacy increases. Similarly, e-commerce puts an even greater emphasis on packaging for transportation. Currently every 1,000 people in the developed world use about 160 tonnes of paper products per annum, compared with about 25 tonnes in the developing world. Just as wood has served humankind well in the past, it will continue to do so in the future.

The FAO has attempted to forecast what the demand for these wood products might be like by 2010 (table E.1). Overall global consumption of industrial roundwood, sawnwood, and panels will rise from 2,069 million to 2,553 million m³, a 23 percent increase, while pulp, paper, and cardboard will rise from 463 million to 602 million tonnes, a 30 percent increase. It is thought that the forests can meet these demands if, among other things,

Table E.1 Current and forecast global production/consumption of wood and paper products

Products (in million of m³)	Production/ Consumption 1996	Production/ Consumption 2010	Total Growth 1996–2010	% Increase
Wood:				
Industrial roundwood	1,490	1,872	382	
Sawnwood	430	501	71	23.4
Wood-based panels	149	180	31	
Total wood products (in millions of tonnes)	2,069	2,553	484	
Pulp and paper:				
Pulp	179	208	29	30.0
Paper and paperboard	284	394	110	
Total pulp and paper products	463	602	139	

Source: FAO, *Yearbook of Forest Products* (Rome: FAO, 1999), 50.

the older plantations of countries like Australia, Chile, New Zealand, South Africa, the United Kingdom, and the United States start to produce the saw logs needed, and all countries of the developed world recycled fibers and recovered paper in order to boost paper and pulp production. Clearly, with a predicted increase of approximately 25 percent over a span of 15 years, the pressure on the global forests will continue to be relentless.

In addition to more people and more products calling for wood, other threats to forests loom on the horizon and are not easy to predict or prevent. For example, acid rain pollution, caused by gaseous emissions and heavy metals, produces forest death, or *Waldsterben*. The many possible processes and biological pathways of this phenomenon are not fully understood; nevertheless, it is incontestable that between 70,000 and 100,000 km² of coniferous forests in central and eastern Europe are affected, and it is possible that three times that amount are at risk—perhaps as much as one-fifth of all forests there. Climatic stress after the recent spells of exceptionally dry years and mild winters during the 1990s, accompanied by pollution from eastern Europe, has also endangered broadleaf forests throughout western Europe. Acid rain is becoming evident in Canada, as well as in the United States in the northeast, the Appalachians, and the coastal ranges of California. It has even been detected in China, Malaysia, and Brazil.

The decline of the world's forest stocks has been countered, albeit slightly, by reforestation, but ascertaining the extent of this practice is difficult. Whereas deforestation is often concealed or underestimated in many countries, reforestation is publicized, exaggerated, and optimistically assessed as a positive and desirable part of public works programs. Moreover, many trees that are planted do not survive, anything up to 20 percent dying. Of the millions of hectares said to have been planted in China, it is unlikely that more than a fraction have come to maturity. Therefore, some announcements have to be treated with caution and even skepticism, so that the claim that the average annual amount of recorded reforestation during the 1980s was about 150,000 km², almost exactly the same as the amount of deforestation, is possibly not as comforting as it sounds. Of that total, 128,420 km², or 85.6 percent, were in the cool coniferous, temperate mixed, and warm temperate moist forests of the Northern Hemisphere, including China, Japan, and Korea, and the forests of South Africa, Australia, and New Zealand. In the tropical world, Brazil had an annual reforestation rate of 5,610 km², but the only other countries rated above 1,000 km² were India (1,730) and Indonesia (1,640). The optimistic implication of these figures is that depletion is being matched approximately by replanting and careful forest management in the cool coniferous forests of the major exporting countries of Canada, the United States, the Russian Federation, and Scandinavia. But depletion in the tropical forests, where trees are more difficult to propagate anyhow, is not being offset by replanting.

So much for the future, what about the past? How does it relate to the here and now? First, the enormity of past change means that the past must be taken seriously. Too often history is dismissed as irrelevant by policymakers and publicists living in a world of the "present" as though it were stable, normal, unchanging, and unchanged. Second, this book shows that almost as much forest was cleared in the past as has been cleared in the last 50 years, so present concerns are not new. Possibly between 7.4 million and 9.14 million km² have disappeared, perhaps up to half of that before 1950. Third, the continuity of this process of terrestrial transformation does help to illuminate our understanding of what is happening.

In a reflexive way, therefore, the causes and nature of past deforestation throw light on present processes, and the present situation throws light on past processes. For example, time and again we have seen that it is the underlying social, economic, and political makeup of society at any given time—its "cultural climate," no less—that causes deforestation. However, we know far less about what brings deforestation under control, except that experience suggests the need for strong government institutions to implement stated policies and resist elite groups who have traditionally pursued the exploitation of the forest. In addition, in the tropical realm (and, perhaps, post-Soviet Russia), such governments would also have to be responsive to popular concerns about the deleterious effects of deforestation, such as flooding, mudslides, landslides, smoke pollution, and high fuelwood prices. For a government to carry through these policies requires a high degree of democratic function and a certain amount of socioeconomic growth to raise standards of living. Of course, benevolent despots have existed—perhaps the Forestry Department in British colonial India was as near as one would get to that—but the likelihood is that absolute power will lead to absolute corruption, as has been true in Cambodia. What is needed are governments that are strong enough to be pluralistic and that listen to the concerns of the people.

Attempts by developed countries, international agencies, and NGOs (nongovernment organizations) to force the reforestation process are frequently viewed with suspicion by the developing countries. Criticism of deforestation seems like antidevelopment rhetoric and hypocrisy from countries that have already "made it," often on the basis of the profligate use of their forests in the past (plate E.1). Calls for conservation seem like neo-imperialism, and even debt-for-nature swaps are not immune to these negative impressions. Two items from two U.S. newspapers from March 1989, when concern about Brazilian deforestation was at its height, perhaps sum up these points of view. Regarding the North American historical experience, which could apply equally as well to Europe, Tom Wicker of the *New York Times* said the following:

> Now there's little left of the vast tree cover that once stretched from the Atlantic to the Mississippi and beyond. . . . Thus has the United States done throughout its history what a righteous world denounces Brazil for doing today: no wonder Brazilian leaders point to the United States as their role model in deforestation.

A few days earlier, another article in the *Chicago Tribune* quoted a Brazilian official:

> If the world wants oxygen, let them pay for it. We're not going to stay poor because the rest of the world wants to breathe.[2]

As revealed by the debate over deforestation rates, the whole topic of deforestation and the part it plays in the balance of forest resources is underresearched. We lack significant amounts of hard data, and that which we have is open to varying forms of interpretation. But over and above all that, it is difficult to separate the rhetoric from the reality of what is happening to the global forests. This is true about *Waldsterben*, reforestation, the effects and reality of climatic change, the controversy over carbon emissions and

Plate E.1 Deforestation is perceived differently by people and governments in developed and developing countries. (Scott Willis, Copley News Service, 1989.)

the Kyoto Treaty, and the truth of reduced biodiversity. Moreover, in the past we have seen repeatedly how deforestation has been exaggerated in order to serve special interests and pressure groups, and the same may be true today. In the developed world the wrong culprits, such as iron making, shipbuilding, or railway enterprises, were usually the deforestation scapegoats, whereas land clearing for permanent agriculture was so normal, so essential that it was excused, overlooked, or ignored. In the developing world, the myths of wilderness and of the destructive nature of swidden agriculture by the "backward" natives have justified authoritarian conservation policies based on outdated ecological notions of climax vegetation and a mistrust of fire, which have decoupled local people from their livelihoods.

The flood of books, often by environmental advocacy groups, continues— each one with a seemingly more alarming message than the last. For example, one of the latest, arrestingly entitled *The Last Frontier Forests: Ecosystems and Economics on the Edge*, claims that only 13.5 million km² remains of the earth's 62.2 million km² of "Frontier Forest." On a casual reading it seems as though that is the only forest remaining, until one realizes that the subject is "large, ecologically intact, relatively undisturbed natural forests" harboring maximum biodiversity—a narrowly defined subset of the total remaining 33.4 million km² of all forests.[3] The other 19.9 million km² of "non-frontier forest" includes those of all of Europe, almost the whole of the United States, the southern half of Canada, most of Australia, and massive chunks of Asia, the Russian Federation, and Africa, and they are ignored. Yet, people know they see and enjoy these forests and, consequently, are less impressed than perhaps they should be at the bad news. Deforestation and biodiversity loss are stories that sell, but they can leave an uneasy impression a little like Greeley's "virgin timber" maps of 1925 at the height of the "timber scare" era: amid the concern over the environment, special interests are being served as they jockey for power, influence, and funds.

Perhaps for reasons like this, a commensurate response to many environmental statements does not seem to exist. Is the public losing interest in the issue and becoming more skeptical—or is it just accepting the inevitable? One gets the sense that with the end of the cold war and the emergence, during the mid- to late 1990s, of real, televisual ethnic and religious conflicts, famines, mass global migration, and latterly, global terrorism, a sort of "environmental crisis fatigue" has set in. Consequently claims of disaster around the corner are being treated with some skepticism and weariness. Meanwhile, the pricing out of environmentally detrimental practices that affect peoples' comfort and mobility are meeting increasing resistance from the public. Town and rural dwellers alike are apprehensive about the new orthodoxy and discourse that tells people what to do with their lives and smacks of a kind of "ecofascism."

Deforestation is no longer a purely economic issue, though it is supremely that, as it is also fast becoming a matter of humanitarian concerns mixed with long-term environmental ethics. Unless forests are either regarded as "sacred" in some way or, as Robert Harrison suggests, an essential "outside domain" that defines the "inside" in which we dwell and that must be bought and/or wisely used, the forest will continue to diminish.[4]

One thing the past does tell us clearly is that the process of land-cover transformation and destruction is never ending. In a decade or so, perhaps another chapter will have to be written, outlining how humans grappled with the problems of the use and abuse of their incomparable heritage—a global green mantle of forest.

ACKNOWLEDGMENTS

THIS BOOK arose from a conversation with Penny Kaiserlian, formerly associate director of the University of Chicago Press, who put the idea to me over lunch in the campus Quadrangle Club many years ago. It was, I protested, simply too big for one person, encompassing as it would the whole earth through all time. Later she returned to the idea and suggested that I might know more about it than many. I agreed to try, having become convinced in the meantime that while it was probably a topic too big to be mastered, it was one that was too compelling to be ignored. I hope the result justifies her support and patience. During its production, staff at the press were superbly helpful and made it all a far less painful experience than I anticipated. In particular I am grateful to my previous copy editor, Sandy Hazel; my illustrations editor, Jennifer Howard; and my editor, Christie Henry. For this edition, Yvonne Zipter continued the tradition of helpfulness and service for which the Press can be justly proud.

My debts to individuals are many and include Michael Conzen, Andrew Goudie, David Harris, David Lowenthal, Norman Myers, Sheryl Oakes (librarian of the Forest History Society, Durham, North Carolina), John Perlin, Stephen Pyne, John Richards, Andrew Sherratt, Pete Steen, Phil Stott, and Richard Tucker. Jane Battersby did wonders with the tables and bibliography, and Ailsa Allan skillfully and patiently produced the many maps, which are a special feature of this book.

The British Academy generously supported the original work, and the University of Oxford and Oriel College gave me that most precious of commodities, contiguous time to travel, to think, and to write.

The original book was very big, and it was barely six months old when Christie Henry put forward the suggestion for a shorter version. For obvious reasons it soon got dubbed "Little Brother" alongside its "Big Brother." Then my first granddaughter was born and Christie had a daughter at about the same time. "In the circumstances" she said jokingly, "should we now say "Little Sister"? I liked that idea. I hope that what has become known as "Little Sister" retains something of the sense of excitement and wonder about the fascinating story of deforestation (and reforestation) that I felt when writing about her older and larger sibling.

As ever, my final deepest thanks are to Loré, who once more made it all possible.

LIST OF MEASURES, ABBREVIATIONS, AND ACRONYMS

AREA

The most common measure in this book relates to area. Metric measures of hectares and square kilometers dominate the world of international land use and land-cover literature, and I have tried to keep to these. However, acres are commonly used in the United States and until recently in Britain, and certainly were the common measures historically. Occasionally I have inserted equivalents. In order to facilitate comparisons, a few equivalents are listed below.

> 1 ha = 2.47105 acres
> 100 ha = 1 km^2, or 247.105 acres
> 1000 ha = 10 km^2 or 2471.05 acres (or 3.86 mi^2)
> 1,000,000 ha = 10,000 km^2 or 2,471,050 acres (or 3861 mi^2)

Reversing the conversion:

> 1 acre = 0.404686 ha
> 100,000 acres = 40,468 ha, or 404.68 km^2
> 1,000,000 acres = 404 686 ha, or 4046.8 km^2

TIMBER/LUMBER VOLUME

Contemporary timber/lumber volumes are similarly expressed as cubic meters (m^3); 1 m^3 = 1.308 yd^3.

An older measure common in the United States is the board foot (bf): 1 ft × 1 in; 12 bf equals 1 ft^3; and 1 million bf = 2,360 m^3.

One cord of wood (a common measure for fuelwood) = 4 × 4 × 8 ft, a total of 128 ft^3, or 3.625 m^3.

Reversing the conversions, 1 ft^3 = 0.028313 m^3, and 1,000 ft^3 = 28.317 m^3;

mbf = 1,000 bf.

OTHER ABBREVIATIONS AND ACRONYMS

t/yr = tons per year

BP = Before Present (conventionally taken as 1950 AD)

CLIMAP = Climate: Long-Range Investigation, Mapping, and Prediction

GIS = Geographical Information Systems

IBP = International Biological Programme

LANDSAT = land surveillance satellite

FAO = Food and Agricultural Organization (Rome)

PIN = Program for National Integration (Brazil)

SPVEA = Superintendency for the Economic Valorization of the Amazon (Brazil)

SUDAM = Superintendência de Desenvolvimento da Amazônia (Brazil)

UNEP = United Nations Environment Programme

WRI = World Resources Institute (Washington, D.C.)

NOTES

Preface

1. H. C. Darby to P. Fejos, 19 July 1954, Sauer Correspondence, Bancroft Library Archives, University of California, Berkeley.

2. W. G. Hoskins, *The Making of the English Landscape* (London: Hodder & Stoughton, 1951).

3. F. Braudel, *Civilization and Capitalism, 15th–18th Century*, vol. 1, *The Structures of Everyday Life: The Limits of the Possible*, trans. S. Reynolds (New York: Harper & Row, 1981).

4. L. White, Jr., "Cultural Climates and Technological Advance in the Middle Ages," *Viator: Medieval and Renaissance Studies* 2 (1971): 171–201, esp. 171.

5. C. Darwin, *The Origin of Species by Means of Natural Selection* (1859), ed. William Benton (Chicago: University Press of Chicago, 1952), 166.

6. The quote is from E. E. Evans, "The Ecology of Peasant Life in Western Europe," in *Man's Role in Changing the Face of the Earth*, ed. W. L. Thomas (Chicago: University of Chicago Press, 1956) 217–40, quote on 217.

Chapter 1

1. G. P. Marsh, *Man and Nature; or, Physical Geography as Modified by Human Action* (New York: G. Scribner's Sons, 1864), 36.

2. Because the amount of carbon in the atmosphere has varied over time, ^{14}C tends to underestimate the age of samples. Precise dates can be achieved by plotting ^{14}C dates against the sequence of annual growth rings in wood remains of trees (e.g., Irish bog oaks or Californian bristlecone pines) over the last 9,000 years. If the radiocarbon age corresponds exactly to the calendar and dendrochronological age, then the two coincide, but a gradual falloff of ^{14}C after 2,500 occurs. By 5,000 BP the actual calendar age should be about 5,800 years. However, throughout this book dates are given in uncalibrated years.

Chapter 2

1. O. C. Stewart, "Fire as the First Great Force Employed by Man," in *Man's Role in Changing the Face of the Earth*, ed. W. L. Thomas (Chicago: Chicago University Press, 1956), 115–33.

2. S. J. Pyne, "The Keeper of the Flame," in *Fire in the Environment: The Ecological, Atmospheric and Climatic Importance of Vegetation Fire*, ed. P. J. Crutzen and J. G. Goldammer (Chichester: John Wiley and Sons, 1993), 245–46.

3. Pyne, "Keeper of the Flame," 249.

4. J. Golson, "Cultural Change in Prehistoric New Zealand," in *Anthropology in the South Seas,* ed. J. D. Freeman and W. R. Geddes (New Plymouth: Avery, 1959), 29–74, quote on 29.

5. J. R. Flenley, A. S. King, J. T. Teller, M. E. Prentice, J. Jackson, and C. Clew, "The Late Quaternary Vegetational and Climatic History of Easter Island," *Journal of Quaternary Studies* 6 (1991): 85–115, quote on 112.

6. J. Cook, *A Voyage towards the South Pole and Round the World* (London: Printed for W. Strahan & T. Cadell in the Strand, 1777), 2:88.

7. I. G. Simmons, "The Earliest Cultural Landscapes of England," *Environmental Review* 12 (1988): 105–16, quote on 113, reprinted in *Out of the Woods: Essays in Environmental History,* ed. C. Miller and H. Rothman (Pittsburgh: Pittsburgh University Press, 1997), 53–63, 324–25.

8. J. Iversen, The Influence of Prehistoric Man on Vegetation," *Danmarks Geologiske Undersøgelse,* ser. 4, 3, no. 6 (1949): 1–23, quote on 6; and J. Troels-Smith, "Ertebølletidens Fangsfolk og Bønder," *Fra Nationalmuseets Arbejdsmark* (1960), 95–119, quote on 102.

9. E. Peacock, "Historical and Applied Perspectives on Prehistoric Land Use in Eastern North America," *Environment and History* 4 (1998): 1–30, quote on 8.

10. S. Shetler, "Three Faces of Eden," in *Seeds of Change: A Quincentennial Commemoration,* ed. H. J. Viola and C. Margolis (Washington, D.C.: Smithsonian Institution Press, 1991), 255–47, quote on 226.

11. W. M. Denevan, "The Pristine Myth: The Landscape of the Americas in 1492," *Annals, Association of American Geographers* 82 (1992): 369–85 quote on 370.

12. M. Catesby, *The Natural History of Carolina, Florida and the Bahama Islands,* 2 vols. (London: Benjamin White, 1747), 1:ii.

13. T. Morton, *The New England Canaan of Thomas Morton* (1627), ed. C. Adams Jr., Publications of the Prince Society (Boston: John Wilson & Sons, 1883), 172–73.

14. F. H. Higginson, *New-England's Plantation; or, A Short and True Description of the Commodities and Discommodities of That Country* (London: T.C. & R.C., for M. Sparke, 1830), 9, reprinted in *Tracts and Other Papers,* ed. P. Force (Washington, D.C.: P. Force, 1836–41), 1:12; and W. Byrd, *History of the Dividing Line between Virginia and Other Tracts, 1728–1736,* in *The Papers of William Byrd, Virginia, Esq.,* ed. T. H. Wynne (Richmond, Va.: n.p. 1866), 2:15–17.

15. A. White, "A Relation of the Colony of the Lord Baron of Baltimore in Maryland, near Virginia," in *A Narrative of the Voyage to Maryland by Father Andrew White* (1644), 18, reprinted in *Tracts and Other Papers,* ed. Force, 4:12; and J. Smith, *Travels and Works of Captain John Smith,* ed. E. Arber, 2 vols. (Birmingham: n.p. 1884), 2:77–80.

16. E. Johnson, *Johnson's Wonder-Working Providence of Sion's Saviour in New England, 1628–1681,* in *Original Documents of Early American History,* ed. J. F. Jameson (New York: Charles Scribner & Sons, 1910), 5; and A. Hodgson, *Letters from America Written during a Tour in the United States and Canada,* 2 vols. (New York: Samuel Whiting, 1823), 1:273.

17. H. Maxwell, "The Use and Abuse of the Forests by the Virginia Indians," *William and Mary College Quarterly* 19 (1910): 73–104, esp. 94–96.

18. A. Gray, "The Characteristics of the North American Flora," *American Journal of Science,* 3d ser., 28 (1884): 323–40, quote on 337.

19. T. Dwight, *Travels in New-England and New York in 1821*, 4 vols. (New Haven, Conn.: T. Dwight, 1821–22), 1:90; and Catesby, *The Natural History of Carolina*, 1:xii.

20. R. C. Anderson, "The Historic Role of Fire in the North American Grassland," in *Fire in North American Tallgrass Prairies*, ed. S. L.Collins and L. Wallace (Norman: University of Oklahoma Press, 1990), 8–18, quote on 14.

21. C. O. Sauer, "Grassland Climax, Fire and Man," *Journal of Range Management* 3 (1950): 16–21, quote on 16.

22. P. Richards, *The Tropical Rain Forest: An Ecological Study* (Cambridge: Cambridge University Press, 1954), 404; C. O. Sauer, "Man in the Ecology of Tropical America," *Proceedings of the Ninth Pacific Science Congress 1957* 20 (1958): 104–10, quote on 106–7; and G. Budowski, "Tropical Savannas, a Sequence of Forest Felling and Repeated Burnings," *Turrialba* 6 (1956): 22–33.

23. D. A. Posey, "Indigenous Management of Tropical Forest Ecosystems: The Case of the Kayapó Indians of the Brazilian Amazon," *Agroforestry Systems* 3 (1985): 139–58, quote on 141.

24. J. G. Myers, "Savanna and Forest Vegetation in the Interior Guiana Plateau," *Journal of Ecology* 24 (1935): 162–83, quote on 162.

25. J. G. D. Clark. *Prehistoric Europe: The Economic Basis* (London: Methuen & Co., 1952), 91–92.

26. Denevan, "The Pristine Myth," 375.

Chapter 3

1. J.-J. Rousseau, *Jean-Jacques Rousseau: The First and Second Discourses* (1755), ed. R. D.Masters, trans. R. D. Masters and J. R. Masters (New York: St. Martin's Press, 1964).

2. E. Evans, "The Ecology of Peasant Life in Western Europe," in *Man's Role in Changing the Face of the Earth*, ed. William L. Thomas (Chicago: University of Chicago Press, 1956), 217.

3. A. de Candolle, *Géographique botanique raisonée* (Paris: de Candolle, 1855), 1–50; N. Vavilov, "Studies on the Origins of Cultivated Plants," *Bulletin of Applied Botany and Plant Breeding* 16 (1926): 1–245; and J. R. Harlan, "Agricultural Origins: Centers and Noncenters." *Science* 174 (1971): 468–74.

4. D. R. Harris, "Vavilov's Concept of Centers of Origin of Cultivated Plants: Its Genesis and Its Influence on the Study of Agricultural Regions." *Biological Journal of Linnean Society* 39 (1990): 7–16.

5. D. R. Harris and G. C. Hillman, eds., *Foraging and Farming: The Evolution of Plant Exploitation* (London: Unwin Hyman, 1989); and D. R. Harris, ed., *The Origins and Spread of Agriculture and Pastoralism in Eurasia* (London: UCL Press, 1996).

6. R. S. MacNeish, *The Origins of Agriculture and Settled Life* (Norman: University of Oklahoma Press, 1992).

7. J. Grahame D. Clark, *Prehistoric Europe: The Economic Basis* (London: Methuen & Co. 1952), 92.

8. H. N. Jarman, "The Lowlands," in *Early European Agriculture: Its Foundation and Development*, ed. M. R. Jarman, G. N. Baily, and H. N. Jarman (Cambridge: Cambridge University Press, 1982), 131–202, esp. 133–34.

9. A. Sherratt, "Plough and Pastoralism: Aspects of the Secondary Products Revolution," in *Patterns in the Past: Studies in Honour of David Clark*, ed. I. Hodder, G. Issac, and N. Hammond (Cambridge: Cambridge University Press, 1983), 261–306, esp.

275–87, and "The Secondary Exploitation of Animals," *World Archaeology* 15 (1983): 90–104, esp. 94–95.

10. S. A. Gregg, *Foragers and Farmers: Population Interaction and Agricultural Expansion in Prehistoric Europe* (Chicago: University of Chicago Press, 1988).

11. P. I. Bogucki, *Forest Farmers and Stockholders: Early Agriculture and Its Consequences in North-Central Europe* (Cambridge: Cambridge University Press, 1988), 49.

12. W. Bray, "From Predation to Production: The Nature of Agricultural Evolution in Mexico and Peru," in *Problems in Economic and Social Archaeology,* ed. G. de G. Sieveking, I. H. Longworth, and K. E. Wilson (London: Duckworth, 1976), 73–96.

13. E. R. Craine and R. C. Reindorp, eds. and trans., *The Chronicles of Michoacán* (*Relación de Michoacán*) (Norman: University of Oklahoma Press, 1970), esp. 11, 13, 20, 24–25, 101, 130, 173.

14. S. L. O'Hara, F. A. Street-Perrott, and T. P. Burt, "Accelerated Soil Erosion around a Mexican Highland Lake Caused by Prehispanic Agriculture," *Nature* 362 (1993): 48–51.

15. A. Metraux, "The Revolution of the Ax," *Diogenes* 25 (1959): 28–40.

16. H. Jones, *The Present State of Virginia from whence is inferred a Shorter View of Maryland and North America* (1753), ed. R. L. Morton (Chapel Hill: University of North Carolina Press for the Virginia Historical Society, 1956), 55.

17. John Smith, *The Generall Historie of Virginia, New England, and the Summer Isles,* in *The Travels and Works of Captain John Smith,* ed. Edward Arber, 2 vols. (Birmingham: n.p., 1884), 2:363, new ed. by A. G. Bradly, Burt Franklin Research and Source Works Series, no. 130 (Philadelphia: Burt Franklin & Co., 1925).

18. William Strachey, *The Historie of Traivell into Virginia Britannia* (1612), ed. Louis B. Wright and Virginia Freund, Hakluyt Society, ser 2, vol. 103. (London: Hakluyt Society, 1953), 67.

19. J. Lederer, *The Discoveries of John Lederer in Three Marches from Virginia to the West of Carolina and Other Parts of the Continent, 1669 and 1670* (1672), comp. and trans. Sir W. Talbot (Rochester, N.Y.: n.p., 1902), 24. Winslow and Hopkins are quoted in A. Young, *Chronicles of the Pilgrim Fathers of the Colony of Plymouth from 1602 to 25* (Boston: C. C. Little & J. Brown, 1841), 206–7.

20. F. Cook, ed., *Journals of the Military Expedition of General John Sullivan against the Six Nations of Indians in 1779* (Auburn, N.Y.: Knapp, Peck & Thompson, 1887), 301; B. Hawkins, *A Sketch of the Creek Country in the Years 1798 and 1799,* Collections of the Georgia Historical Society, vol. 3, pt. 1 (Savannah: Georgia Historical Society, 1848), 22, 27, 33–35; and W. Bartram, *The Travels of William Bartram,* ed. M. van Doren (New York: Facsimile Library, 1940), 68.

21. J. N. B. Hewitt, "The Iroquoian Cosmology," in *Forty-third Annual Report of the Bureau of American Ethnology, 1925,* pt. 2 (Washington, D.C.: Government Printing Office, 1926), 449–63, esp. 461–62; and Hawkins, *A Sketch of the Creek Country,* 30.

22. A. L. Kroeber, *Cultural and Natural Areas of Native North America,* University of California Publications in American Archaeology and Ethnology, no. 38 (Berkeley: University of California, 1939), 131, 166; C. Heidenreich, *Huronia: A History and Geography of the Huron Indians, 1600–1650* (Ontario: McClelland & Stewart, 1971), 195–200; Denevan, "The Pristine Myth: The Landscape of the Americas in 1492," *Annals of the Association of American Geographers* 82 (1992): 370–71, H. Dobyns, "Estimating Aboriginal American Populations: An Appraisal of Techniques with a New

Hemispheric Estimate," *Current Anthropology* 7 (1966): 395–449; and Maxwell, "The Use and Abuse of the Forests by the Virginia Indians," *William and Mary Quarterly* 19 (1910): 81.

Chapter 4

1. Sophocles, *Antigone,* in *The Complete Greek Tragedies,* ed. D. Grene and R. Latimore (Chicago: University of Chicago Press, 1959), 2:362.

2. Theophrastus, *Enquiry into Plants,* trans. Sir A. Hort, 2 vols., Loeb Classical Library (New York: G. P. Putnam's Sons, 1916), 4.1.4, 4.5.5, 5.8.1–2; and J. D. Hughes, "Theophrastus as Ecologist," *Environmental Review* 4 (1985): 291–307.

3. Homer, *The Illiad of Homer,* trans. W. C. Bryant (Boston: Houghton Mifflin & Co., 1895), 16.794–97; Horace, "Epistles," in *Satires, Epistles, and Ars Poetica,* trans. H. R. Fairclough, Loeb Classical Library (London: William Heinemann, 1926), 2.2.185–88; and Sophocles, *Antigone,* 338–41.

4. Lucretius, *Titi lucreti cari de rerum natura libra sex,* trans. C. Baily, 3 vols. (Oxford: Clarendon Press, 1947), 5:505.

5. Marcus Terentius Varro *De re Rustica* 1.2.6.

6. Strabo, *Geography,* in *The Geography of Strabo,* trans. H. L. Jones, 8 vols., Loeb Classical Library (London: Heinemann, 1923), 14.6.5.

7. Ibid., 5.4.5; and Livy, *History of Rome,* trans. B. O. Foster, 5 vols., Loeb Classical Library (Cambridge, Mass.: Harvard University Press, 1924–29), 9.36.1.

8. Lucius Junius Columella, *De re rustica,* trans. H. B. Ash, 3 vols., Loeb Classical Library (London: William Heinemann, 1941–55), 2.1.3–6.

9. Strabo, *Geography,* 3.4.11, 5.1.12.

10. Ibid.; and Pliny the Elder, *Natural History,* trans. H. Rackham, 10 vols., Loeb Classical Library (London: Heinemann, 1960), 16.2.5; S. Schama, *Landscape and Memory* (London: Harper Collins, 1995), 83, 86.

11. Quoted in A. J. Toynbee, *Greek Historical Thought from Homer to the Age of Heraclius* (London: J. M. Dent & Sons, 1924), 291–92.

12. For Plato's description, see ibid., 169.

13. T. A. Wertime and S. F. Wertime, *The Evolution of the First Fire-Using Industries,* Seminar Papers (Washington, D.C.: Smithsonian Institution, 19–20 April 1979), 135–36; and T. Wertime, "The Furnace versus the Goat: The Pyrotechnologic Industries and the Mediterranean Deforestation in Antiquity," *Journal of Field Archaeology* 10 (1983): 445–52, esp. 452. For Cyprus, see G. Constantinou, "Geological Features and Ancient Exploitation of Cupriferous Sulphide Ore Bodies in Cyprus," in *Early Metallurgy in Cyprus, 4000–500 BC,* ed. J. D. Muhly, R.Maddin, and V. Karageorghis (Nicosia: Pierides Foundation, 1982), 13–24, esp. 22.

14. E. Gibbon, *The History of the Decline and Fall of the Roman Empire* (1776), 6 vols. (New York: Harper & Brothers, 1850); and E. A. Poe, "To Helen" (1831), in *The Complete Poems and Stories of Edgar Alan Poe,* ed. A. H. Quinn, 8 vols. (New York: Alfred A. Knopf, 1946), 1:42.

15. D. Attenborough, *The First Eden: The Mediterranean World and Man* (Boston: Little, Brown & Co., 1987), 117–18.

16. See n. 12 above.

17. Pliny *Natural History* 31.30.53; Pausanias, *Description of Greece,* trans. W. H. S. Jones, 5 vols., Loeb Classical Library (London: William Heinemann, 1935), 8.24.11.

18. J. L. Bintliff, "New Approaches to Human Geography, Prehistoric Greece: A Case Study," in *Historical Geography of the Balkans,* ed. F. Carter (London: Academic Press, 1977), 59–114, esp. 75.

19. C. Vita-Finzi, *The Mediterranean Valleys: Geological Changes in Historical Times* (Cambridge: Cambridge University Press, 1969), 107–15.

20. Brent D. Shaw, "Climate, Environment and History: The Case of North Africa," in *Climate and History: Studies in Past Climates and Their Impact on Man,* ed. T. M. L. Wrigley, M. J. Ingram, and G. Farmer (Cambridge: Cambridge University Press, 1981), 379–403, esp. 395.

21. H. C. Darby, "The Clearing of the Woodland in Europe," in *Man's Role in Changing the Face of the Earth,* ed. W. L. Thomas (Chicago: University of Chicago Press, 1956), 183–216, 186.

22. J. D. Hughes, "How the Ancients Viewed Deforestation," *Journal of Field Archaeology* 10 (1983): 437–45, esp. 437–38.

23. Marcus Tullius Cicero, *De natura deorum academica,* trans. H. Rackham, Loeb Classical Library (London: William Heinemann, 1933), 2.61.154.

24. Ibid., 2.60.151–52.

Chapter 5

1. C. Higounet, "Les forêts de L'Europe occidentale du Vᶜ au XIᶜ siècle," in *Agricultura e mondo rurale in Occidente nell'alto medioevo,* Settimane di studio del centro italiano de studi sull'alto medioevo, 13 (Spoleto: Presso la sede del Centro, 1966), 343–98, esp. 398.

2. Kenneth Clark, *Civilization: A Personal View* (New York: Harper & Row Publishers, 1969), 23.

3. E. Evans, "The Ecology of Peasant Life in Western Europe," in *Man's Role in Changing the Face of the Earth,* ed. William L. Thomas (Chicago: University of Chicago Press, 1956), 217.

4. C. Glacken , *Traces on the Rhodian Shore: Nature and Culture in Western Thought from Ancient Times to the End of the Eighteenth Century* (Berkeley and Los Angeles: University of California Press, 1967), 351.

5. A. R. Lewis, "The Closing of the Medieval Frontier, 1250–1350," *Speculum,* 33 (1958): 475–83.

6. W. G. Hoskins, *The Making of the English Landscape* (London: Hodder & Stoughton, 1951), 10.

7. Both quoted in Glacken, *Traces on the Rhodian Shore,* 304.

8. Quoted in J. W. Thompson, *An Economic and Social History of the Middle Ages (300–1300)* (New York: Century Co, 1928), 611.

9. H.-J. Nitz, "The Church as Colonist: The Benedictine Abbey of Lorsch and the Planned *Waldhufen* Colonization of the Oldenwald," *Journal of Historical Geography* 9 (1983): 105–23.

10. R. K.Gordon, ed., *Anglo-Saxon Poetry* (London: Dent & Sons, 1958), 295.

11. Quoted in H. C. Darby, "The Clearing of the Woodland in Europe," in *Man's Role in Changing the Face of the Earth,* ed. W. L. Thomas (Chicago: University of Chicago Press, 1956), 183–216, quote on 195.

12. R. Bechmann, *Trees and Man: The Forest in the Middle Ages,* trans. K. Dunham (New York: Paragon House, 1990), 295.

13. O. Schlüter, *Die Siedlungsräume Mittleuropas in frühgeschichtlicher Zeit,* pt. 1 *Erläuterungen zu einer Karte,* Forschungen zur Deutschen Landeskunde 63 (Hamburg: Atlantik Verlag Amtes für Landeskunde, 1952), 63.

14. V. O. Kluchevsky, *A History of Russia* (London: J. M. Dent & Sons, 1911–13) 5:244–45.

15. Glacken, *Traces on the Rhodian Shore,* 323.

16. D. Stenton, *English Society in the Early Middle Ages* (Harmondsworth: Penguin Books, 1952), 106.

17. Glacken, *Traces on the Rhodian Shore,* 339.

·18. *Mencius,* trans. D. C. Lau (Harmondsworth: Penguin Books, 1970), 164–65; R. Murphey, "Deforestation in Modern China," in *Global Deforestation and the Nineteenth-Century World Economy,* ed. R. P. Tucker and J. F. Richards (Durham, N.C.: Duke University Press, 1983), 111–28, quote on 111.

19. Shih Ching, *The Book of Songs: The Ancient Chinese Classic of Poetry,* trans. A. Waley (New York: Grove Press, 1960), 162, 212.

20. Quoted in F. Bray, "Agriculture," in *Science and Civilization in China,* ed. J. Needham, vol. 6 of *Biology and Biological Technology,* pt. 2, *Agriculture* (Cambridge: Cambridge University Press, 1984), 96–98.

21. Ennin, *Ennin's Diary: The Record of a Pilgrimage to China in Search of the Law (793–864),* trans. E. O. Reischauer (New York: Roland Press, 1955), 154.

Chapter 6

1. D. C. North and R. P. Thomas, *The Rise of the Western World: A New Economic History* (Cambridge: Cambridge University Press, 1973); E. L. Jones, *The European Miracle: Environments, Economies and Geopolitics in the History of Europe and Asia,* 2d ed. (Cambridge: Cambridge University Press, 1987); and W. Woodruff, *Impact of Western Man: A Study of Europe's Role in the World Economy, 1750–1960* (New York: St. Martin's Press, 1967).

2. J. Michelet, *Histoire de France* (Paris: Chamerot, Libraire-Editor, 1855), 7:ii–iii.

3. H. C. Darby, "The Face of Europe on the Eve of the Great Discoveries," in *The New Cambridge Modern History,* vol. 1, *The Renaissance, 1493–1520,* ed. G. R. Potter (Cambridge: Cambridge University Press, 1971) , 20–49, esp. 20.

4. Sir W. Ralegh, "The Art of Warre at Sea," British Museum , MSS Jones, B 60, fol. 323, transcribed in P. Lefranc, *Sir Walter Ralegh: Érivan: L'oeuvre et les idées* (Paris: Armand, 1980), app. D, p. 600.

5. The quote is from J. L. Abu-Lughod, *Before European Hegemony: The World System,* AD *1250–1350* (New York: Oxford University Press, 1989), 5.

6. L. White, Jr., "Cultural Climates and Technological Advances," *Viator: Medieval and Renaissance Studies* 2 (1971): 171–201, esp. 171–72.

7. F. Bacon, *Novum organum* (1620), in *The Physical and Metaphysical Works of Lord Bacon,* ed. J. Devey (London: Bell & Sons, 1911), bk. 1, cxxix.

8. D. Landes, *Revolution in Time: Clocks and the Making of the Modern World* (Cambridge, Mass.: Belknap Press of Harvard University, 1983), 89.

9. D. Sobel, *Longitude: The True Story of a Lone Genius Who Solved the Greatest Scientific Problem of His Time* (New York: Walker & Co, 1995).

10. L. White, Jr., "The Expansion of Technology, 500–1500," in *The Fontana Economic History of Europe,* ed. C. M. Cipolla, vol. 1, *The Middle Ages* (Brighton: Harvester Press, 1976), 143–74, quote on 143.

11. M. Berman, *All That Is Solid Melts into Air: The Experience of Modernity* (London: Verso, 1984), 15.

12. H. Van der Wee, "Money, Credit and Banking Systems," in *Cambridge Modern History of Europe,* vol. 5, *The Economic Organization of Early Modern Europe,* ed. E. E. Rich and C. H. Wilson (Cambridge: Cambridge University Press), 290–393, quote on 290.

13. I. Wallerstein, *The Modern World System,* vol. 2, *Mercantilism and Consolidation of the European World Economy, 1600–1750* (New York: Academic Press, 1980), 301–2.

14. M. Sahlins, "Cosmologies of Capitalism: The Trans-Pacific Sector of 'The World System,'" *Proceedings of the British Academy* 74 (1988): 1–51, quote on 43.

15. J. H. B. de Saint-Pierre, *Voyage to Isle de France, the Isle of Bourbon, the Cape of Good Hope, etc, With Observations on Nature and Mankind by an Officer of the King* (1771), 2 vols. (London: W. Griffin, 1775), 1:105.

16. C. Glacken, *Traces on the Rhodian Shore: Nature and Culture in Western Thought from Ancient Times to the End of the Eighteenth Century* (Berkeley and Los Angeles: University of California Press, 1967), 175.

17. J. Ray, *The Wisdom of God Manifest in the Works of Creation,* 12th ed. (London: John Ward and Joseph Rivington, 1691).

18. R. Descartes, *Discourse on Method* (1623), ed. F. E. Sutcliffe as *Discourse on Method and Meditations* (Harmondsworth: Penguin Books, 1968), discourse 4, 53–54.

19. F. Bacon, "Prometheus," in *De sapientia veterum* (Of the wisdom of the ancients) (1609), reprinted in *Essays,* ed. J. Pitcher. Harmondsworth: Penguin Books, 1985), 270–71.

20. Sir M. Hale, *The Primitive Origination of Mankind* (London: W. Godbid for W. Shrowsbery, 1677), 370.

21. K. Thomas, *Man and the Natural World: Changing Attitudes in England, 1500–1800* (London: Allan Lane, 1983), 192.

22. J. Locke, *Two Treatises on Government,* ed. P. Laslett (Cambridge: Cambridge University Press, 1960), 201.

23. The quote is from J. Winthrop, *Winthrop's Journal: "History of New England"* (1630–49), ed. J. H. Hosmer, 2 vols. (New York: Barnes & Noble, 1966), 2:83; and I. Mather *A Brief History of the War with the Indians in New England* (Boston: John Foster, 1676), 5.

24. A. Guyot, *The Earth and Man: Lectures on Comparative Physical Geography in Its Relation to the History of Mankind,* trans. C. Felton (Boston: Gould, Kendall, & Lincoln, 1849), 216–18.

25. J. H. St. John Crèvecoeur, *Letters from an American Farmer* (London: Thomas Davies, 1782), 55–57.

26. Thomas, *Man and the Natural World,* 196; and J. Houghton, *Husbandry and Trade Improv'd,* 4 vols. (London: Woodman & Lyon, 1681–83), 1:99, 4:258–82.

27. A. H. Smyth, ed., *The Writings of Benjamin Franklin,* 10 vols. (New York: Macmillan, 1905–7), 3:72–73; and W. Cooper, *A Guide to the Wilderness, or the History of the First Settlements in the Western Counties of New York* (1810) (Rochester, N.Y.: G. P. Humphrey, 1897), 5.

28. L. White, Jr., "The Historical Roots of Our Ecological Crisis," *Science* 156 (1967): 1203–7.

Chapter 7

1. G. Owen, *Description of Pembrokeshire* (1603), ed. H. Owen, Cymmrodorian Record Society Series 1, pt. 2 (London: Charles J. Clark, 1892, 1897), 1:86.

2. R. G. Albion, *Forests and Sea Power: The Timber Problem of the Royal Navy, 1652–1862* (Cambridge, Mass.: Harvard University Press, 1927), 57.

3. W. Sombart, *Der Moderne Kapitalismus* (1902), 4 vols., 2d ed. (Leipzig: Verlag von Duncker & Humblot, 1916–27), 2, ii, 1145–48.

4. J. Evelyn, *Sylva; or, A Discourse of Forest Trees, and the Propagation of Timber in His Majesty's Dominion* . . . (1664) (York: A. Ward, 1786), 1–2.

5. For Chomeley and others, see H. C. Darby, "The Clearing of the English Woodlands," *Geography* 36 (1951): 71–83.

6. W. Abel, *Agricultural Fluctuations in Europe from the Thirteenth to the Twentieth Centuries,* trans. O. Ordish (London: Methuen, 1980), 101.

7. F. Braudel, *The Mediterranean and the Mediterranean World in the Age of Philip II,* trans. S. Reynolds (New York: Harper Collins, 1972), 1:62.

8. W. Harrison, *The Description of England* (1587), ed. G. Edelen (Ithaca, N.Y.: Cornell University Press, 1968), 356; and F. Braudel, *Capitalism and Material Life: 1400–1800* (1967), trans. M. Kochan (New York: Harper & Row, 1973), 211.

9. Braudel, *Civilization and Capitalism,* vol. 1, *The Structures of Everyday Life: The Limits of the Possible,* trans. S. Reynolds (New York: Harper & Row, 1981), 366.

10. Ibid.

11. Braudel, *Capitalism and Material Life,* 216 ff.; and W. Minchinton, "Patterns and Structure of Demand, 1500–1750," in *The Sixteenth and Seventeenth Centuries,* ed. C. M. Cipolla, Fontana Economic History of Europe, vol. 2 (Brighton: Harvester Press, 1977), 83–176, quote on 138.

12. D. Defoe, *A Tour thro' the Whole Island of Great Britain,* 4 vols. (London: J. Osborn et al., 1742), 1:129.

13. E. L. Jones, *The European Miracle: Environments, Economies and Geopolitics in the History of Europe and Asia,* 2d ed. (Cambridge: Cambridge University Press, 1987), 84.

14. A. Standish, *The Commons Complaint* (London: W. Stansby, 1611), 2.

15. G. Hammersley, "The Charcoal Industry and Its Fuel, 1540–1750," *Economic History Review,* 2d ser., 26 (1973): 593–613.

16. H. Kellenbenz, "Technology in the Age of Scientific Revolution, 1500–1700," in *The Sixteenth and Seventeenth Centuries,* ed. Cipolla, 171–272.

17. Evelyn, *Sylva,* 209; and A. Yarranton, *England's Improvement by Sea and Land, to Out-do the Dutch without Fighting* (London: R. Everingham, 1677), 60–61.

18. Darby, "Clearing of the English Woodlands," 80.

19. G.-L Leclerc, comte de Buffon, "Mèmoiré sur la conservation et la rètablissement des forêts," in *A Treatise on the Manner of Raising Forest Trees, etc. to which is added Two Memoirs on Preserving and Repairing Forests and the Culture of Forests* (Edinburgh: G. Hamilton & J. Balfour, 1761), 83–105, 109–29, quote on 3.

20. Albion, *Forests and Sea Power,* 140.

21. Comte de Buffon, "Mèmoiré sur la conservation," 110.

22. K. Thomas, *Man and the Natural World: Changing Attitudes in England, 1500–1800* (London: Allan Lane, 1983), 209.

23. Ibid., 212.

Chapter 8

1. R. H. Tawney, *Land and Labour in China* (London: G. Allen & Unwin, Ltd., 1932), 13.

2. A. L. Crosby, *Ecological Imperialism: The Biological Expansion of Europe, 900–1900* (Cambridge: Cambridge University Press, 1976), 13.

3. Ibid., 199.

4. Ibid., 196.

5. J. Winthrop, *Winthrop Papers, 1631–1637*, 3 vols. (Boston: Massachusetts Historical Society, 1929–47), 3:167; Virginia settler quoted in H. Maxwell, "The Use and Abuse of the Forests by the Virginia Indians," *William and Mary Quarterly* 19 (1910): 81.

6. Crosby, *Ecological Imperialism*, 173–78.

7. J. M. Prest, *The Garden of Eden: The Botanic Garden and the Re-creation of Paradise* (New Haven, Conn.: Yale University Press, 1981), 30–56.

8. G. R. Crone, ed., *The Voyages of Cadamosto and Other Documents on Western Africa in the Second Half of the Fifteenth Century*, Hakluyt Society, ser. 2, vol. 80 (London: Hakluyt Society, 1937), 9.

9. R. Ligon, *A True and Exact History of the Island of Barbadoes* (1673) (London: Cass, 1970), 28, 24.

10. United Kingdom, *Calendar of State Papers, Colonial, 1675–76*, no. 973.

11. Sir H. Sloane, *A Voyage to the Islands of Madera, Barbadoes, Nieves, St Christopher and Jamaica* . . . (London: Printed for the author by B. M., circa 1707–25), 1:42.

12. C. F. Carroll, *The Timber Economy of Puritan New England* (Providence, R.I.: Brown University Press, 1973), 87.

13. T. Pownall, *A Topographical Description of the Dominions of the United States America* (1783), ed. L. Mulkearn (Pittsburgh: Pittsburgh University Press, 1949), 23; and F. J. marquis de Chastellux, *Travels in North America in the Years 1780, 1781, and 1782*, 2 vols. (New York: White, Gallacher, & White, 1789), 2:44.

14. R. Frame, "A Short Description of Pennsilvania by Richard Frame," in *Original Narratives of Early American History: Narratives of Early Pennsylvania, New Jersey, and Delaware, 1630–1709* (1692), ed. A. C. Myers (New York: C. Scribner & Sons, 1912), 303.

15. Jefferson quoted in A. O. Craven, *Soil Exhaustion as a Factor in the Agricultural History of Virginia and Maryland, 1606–1860* (Urbana: University of Illinois Press, 1926), 34; and E. Ruffin, *An Essay on Calcareous Manures*, 2d. ed. (Shellbanks, Va.: Farmers' Register, 1835), 12.

16. T. Anburey, *Travels through the Interior Parts of America in a Series of Letters by an Officer*, 2 vols. (London, 1791; reprint, Boston: Houghton Mifflin, 1923), 2:322.

17. Chastellux, *Travels in North America*, 1:49; and Latrobe, quoted in *The Pittsburgh Gazette*, 8 September, 1838.

18. B. Franklin, *An Account of the New-Invented Pennsylvania Fire-Place* . . . (Philadelphia: B. Franklin, 1744), 392.

19. A. M. Grant, *Memoirs of an American Lady: With Sketches of Manners and Scenes in America, as They Existed Previous to the Revolution* (1808), 2d. ed. (New York: D. Appleton, 1846), 2:258–59.

20. J. Schoepf, *Travels in the Confederation (1783–1784)*, reproduced as *Schoepf's Travels in the Confederation, 1783–84,* trans. and ed. A. J. Morrison (Philadelphia: W. J. Campbell, 1911), 5:36–37.

21. P. C. Perdue, *Exhausting the Earth: State and Peasant in Hunan, 1500–1850* (Cambridge, Mass.: Harvard University Press, 1987), 88.

22. Ch'ao-Ting Chi, *Key Economic Areas in Chinese History as Revealed in the Development of Public Works for Water Control* (1936), 2d ed. (London: Allen & Unwin Ltd., 1963), 22; and W. C. Lowdermilk and D. R. Wickes, *History of Soil Use in the Wu'T'ai Shan Area*, Monograph, Royal Asiatic Society, N. China Branch (London: Royal Asiatic Society, 1938), 4–5.

23. This and the following paragraphs are based on T. C. Smith, *The Agrarian Origins of Modern Japan* (Stanford, Calif.: Stanford University Press, 1959); and C. D. Totman, *The Green Archipelago: Forestry in Pre-Industrial Japan* (Berkeley and Los Angeles: University of California Press, 1989).

24. J. McMullen, *Idealism, Protest, and the "Tale of the Genji": The Confucianism of Kamazawa Banzan (1619–91)* (Oxford: Clarendon Press, 1999), 241.

25. Quoted in Totman, *The Green Archipelago,* 77.

Chapter 9

1. C. O. Sauer, "The Prospect for the Redistribution of Population," in *Limits of Land Settlement: A Report on Present-Day Possibilities,* ed. I. Bowman (New York: Council for Foreign Relations and the American Geographical Society, 1939), 7–24, quote on 8.

2. N. Briavoinne, *De l'industrie en belgique, causes de décadence et de prosperité, sa situation actuelle* (Brussels: Eugene Dubois, 1839), 1:185–86, quoted in I. Wallerstein, *The Modern World System,* vol. 3, *The Second Era of Great Expansion of the Capitalist World-Economy* (New York: Academic Press, 1989), 15.

3. "Report of the Committee on the Machinery of the United States," quoted in N. Rosenberg, ed., *The American System of Manufacturing: The Report of the Committee on the Machinery of the United States, 1855* (Edinburgh: Edinburgh University Press, 1969), 344.

4. D. Landes, *The Unbound Prometheus, Technological Change and Industrial Development in Western Europe from 1750 to the Present* (Cambridge: Cambridge University Press, 1969), 241.

5. D. R. Headrick, *The Tools of Empire: Technology and European Imperialism in the Nineteenth Century* (New York: Oxford University Press, 1981).

6. W. S. Churchill, *The River War: An Historical Account of the Reconquest of the Soudan,* ed. Col. Rhodes, 2 vols. (London: Longmans Green & Co., 1899), 2: 119, 124.

7. S. Olson, *The Depletion Myth: A History of the Railroad Use of Timber* (Cambridge Mass.: Harvard University Press, 1971), quoting H. Miller in *The Forester* 3 (January 1879): 6.

8. C. Glacken, *Traces on the Rhodian Shore: Nature and Culture in Western Thought from Ancient Times to the End of the Eighteenth Century* (Berkeley and Los Angeles: University of California Press, 1967), 501–3, 552 ff.

9. G.-L. Leclerc, comte de Buffon, *Histoire naturelle, générale et particuliére,* vol.
12, *De la nature, premiére vue* (Paris, 1749–1804.), xiii. Another edition: W. Wood, ed.,
*Comte de Buffon, Natural History, General and Particular: The History of Man and the
Quadrupeds,* 10 vols. (London: T. Cadell & W. Davis, 1812).

10. B. Keen, *The Life of the Admiral Christopher Columbus by His Son Ferdinand*
(New Brunswick, N.J.: Rutgers University Press, 1959), 142–43.

11. Glacken, *Traces,* 658–63, 668–71.

12. A. de Tocqueville, "A Fortnight in the Wilds," in *Journey to America,* ed.
J. P. Mayer (London: Faber & Faber, 1959), 325, and *Democracy in America,* 3d. ed.,
trans. H. Reeves, 4 vols. (London: Saundars & Otley, 1838), 2:74.

13. F. Parkman, "The Forest and the Census," *Atlantic Monthly* 55(1885): 835–39,
esp. 836; and F. J. Turner, *The Frontier in American History* (New York: Holt, 1920),
269–70.

14. A. Jackson, "Second Annual Message," in *A Compilation of Messages and
Papers of the Presidents,* comp. J. D. Richardson, 10 vols. (Washington, D.C.: Bureau of
National Literature, 1897), 3:1084.

15. Constantine, Count Volney, *A View of the Climate and Soil of the United States
of America* (London: L. Johnson, 1804), 213–16.

16. J. Lorain, *Nature and Reason Harmonized in the Practice of Husbandry* (Philadelphia: H. C. Carey & I. Lea, 1825), 25–27, and quotation on 335–36.

17. G. P. Marsh, *Address before the Agricultural Society of Rutland County, Sept
30th, 1847* (Rutland, Vt.: Rutland Herald, 1848).

18. G. P. Marsh, *Man and Nature; or, Physical Geography as Modified by Human
Action* (New York: Scribner's Sons, 1884). Another edition with an introduction by
D. Lowenthal, 2d ed. (Cambridge, Mass.: Harvard University Press, 2003).

19. J. Addison, *The Spectator,* 31 May 1712, 393; and W. Gilpin, *Remarks on Forest Scenery* (London: R. Blaine, 1794), 1:1.

20. Byron, *Child Harold's Pilgrimage,* canto 4, clxxvii; W. Wordsworth, "The
Tables Turned"; F. A. R., vicomte de Chateaubriand, *Recollections of Italy, England
and America on Various Subjects* (Philadelphia: M. Carey, 1816), 138–39; and
P. M. Marsh, ed., *The Prose of Philip Freneau* (New Brunswick, N.J.: Scarecrow Press,
1955), 196–202.

21. H. D. Thoreau, "Walking," in *The Writings of Henry David Thoreau,* ed.
E. Scudder, vol.9, *Excursions* (Boston: Houghton Mifflin & Co., 1866), 251–304, quote
on 672; and R. W. Emerson, "Nature," in *Nature, Addresses, and Lectures,* ed.
J. E. Cabot (Boston: Houghton Mifflin & Co., 1876), 1:15.

22. K. Thomas, *Man and the Natural World: Changing Attitudes in England,
1500–1800* (London: Allan Lane, 1983), 192.

23. Based on H. E. Lowood, "The Calculating Forester: Quantification, Cameral
Science and the Emergence of Scientific Forestry Management in Germany," in *The
Quantifying Spirit in the Eighteenth Century,* ed. T. Fränsmyr, J. H. Heilbron, and
R. C. Ryder (Berkeley and Los Angeles: University of California Press, 1990), 315–42;
and W. G. von Moser, *Grundsätze Forstöecomie* [Principles of forest economy] (Frank-
furt: H. L. Brönner, 1757), 1–93.

Chapter 10

1. H. Coleman, *The Agricultural and Rural Economy of France, Belgium, Holland
and Switzerland* (London: Petheram, 1848), 23.

2. H. J. Baudrillart, "Mémoiré sur la déboisement des montages," *Annals de l'agriculture français* 8 (1831): 65–78; and A. J. Blanqui, "Rapport sur la situation économique des départments de la frontiére des Alpes: Isè, Hautes-Alpes, Basse-Alpes et Var," *Académie des sciences morales et politiques, sèances et traveaux* 4 (1843): 353–64.

3. G. P. Marsh, *Man and Nature; or, Physical Geography as Modified by Human Action* (New York: Scribner's Sons, 1864), 201, 210.

4. C. Glacken, *Traces on the Rhodian Shore: Nature and Culture in Western Thought from Ancient Times to the End of the Eighteenth Century* (Berkeley and Los Angeles: University of California Press, 1967), 702.

5. M. A. Tsvetkov's calculations are in R. A. French, "Russians and the Forests," in *Studies in Russian Historical Geography,* ed. J. H. Bater and R. A. French (London: Academic Press, 1983), 1:23–44, esp. 40.

6. Quoted in French, "Russians and the Forest," 30, and "The Making of the Russian Landscape, "*Advancement of Science* 20 (1963): 44–56, esp. 51, for Golenishchev-Kutuzov.

7. French, "Russians and the Forest," 38.

8. V. O. Kluchevsky, *A History of Russia,* trans. C. J. Hogarth, 5 vols. (London: J. M. Dent & Sons, 1911–13), 5:244–45.

9. G. Hammersely, "Did It Fall or Was It Pushed? The Foleys and the End of the Charcoal Iron Industry in the Eighteenth Century," in *The Search for Wealth and Stability: Essays in Economic and Social History Presented to M.W. Flinn,* ed. C. T. Smout (London: Macmillan, 1979), 67–90, quote on 85–86.

10. A. R. M. Lower, *Great Britain's Woodyard: British America and the Timber Trade, 1763–1867* (Montreal: McGill-Queen's University Press, 1973), 18.

11. R. Johnston, *Travels through Part of the Russian Empire and the Country of Poland along the Southern Shores of the Baltic* (London: J. S. Stockdale, 1815), 75.

12. S.-E. Åström, "English Timber Imports from Northern Europe in the Eighteenth Century," *Scandinavian Economic History Review* 18 (1970): 12–32, esp. 30.

13. P. Fisher, *Sketches of New Brunswick* (St. John: Chubb & Sears, 1825), 72, reprinted as *History of New Brunswick* (St. John: Government of New Brunswick and William Shives Fisher, under the auspices of New Brunswick Historical Society, 1921).

14. A. Guyot, *The Earth and Man: Lectures on Comparative Physical Geography in Its Relation to the History of Mankind,* trans. C. Felton (Boston: Gould, Kendall, & Lincoln, 1849), 208.

15. J. Taylor, "Journal of Rev. John Taylor, Missionary on Tour through the Mohawk and Black River Counties, in 1801," in *History of the State of New York,* ed. E. B. O'Callaghan (Albany, N.Y.: Weed Parsons, 1854), 3:1107–50, quote on 1148.

16. J. Belknap, *The History of New Hampshire,* 3 vols. (Boston: Printed for the author, n.p., 1791–92), 3:95.

17. O. Turner, *Pioneer History of the Holland Purchase of Western New York* (Buffalo, N.Y.: Jewett Thomas, 1849), plates opposite 562, 564, 565, 566.

18. A. Hodgson, *Letters from North America Written during a Tour in the United States and Canada,* 2 vols. (New York: Samuel Whiting, 1823), 1:339–40, 2:318–19.

19. H. C. Darby, "The Clearing of the Woodland in Europe," in *Man's Role in Changing the Face of the Earth,* ed. W. L. Thomas (Chicago: University of Chicago Press, 1956), 183–216, 183.

20. B. Hall, *Travels in North America in the Years 1827 and 1828* (Edinburgh: Cadell, 1829), 2:135, and *Forty Etchings from Sketches Made with the Camera Lucida in 1827 and 1829*, 3 vols. (Philadelphia: Cary, Lea & Carey, 1829).

21. I. Weld, *Travels through the States of North America and Provinces of Upper and Lower Canada during the Years 1795, 1796, and 1797*, 2 vols. (London: John Stockdale, 1799), 1:232–33; A. Hodgson *Letters from North America Written during a Tour in the United States and Canada*, 2 vols. (New York: Samuel Whiting, 1823), 1:396–97.

22. L. Marx, *The Machine in the Garden: Technology and the Pastoral Ideal in America* (New York: Oxford University Press, 1964).

23. D. Millikin, "The Best Practical Means of Preserving and Restoring the Forests of Ohio," *Ohio Agricultural Report*, 2d ser. (1871): 319–33.

24. S. Olson, *The Depletion Myth: A History of the Railroad Use of Timber* (Cambridge Mass.: Harvard University Press, 1971), 10.

25. J. Hall, *Statistics of the West* (Cincinnati: J. A. James, 1836), 100–101.

26. R. L. Hartt, "Notes on a Michigan Lumber Town," *Atlantic Monthly* 85 (January 1900): 101–9, esp. 107.

27. R. D.Forbes, "The Passing of the Piney Woods," *American Forestry* 29 (March 1923): 131–36, 185, esp. 133.

28. Ibid., 136.

29. C. Totman, *The Green Archipelago: Forestry in Pre-Industrial Japan* (Berkeley and Los Angeles: University of California Press, 1989), 89.

30. E. S. Rawski, "Agricultural Development in the Han River Highlands," *Late Imperial China* 3, no. 4 (1975): 63–81, esp. 68.

31. R. T. Archer and P. J. Carol, "Dairy Farming," in *Victoria: The Yearbook of Agriculture for 1905* (Melbourne: Government Printer, 1905), 297–333, quote on 303.

32. W. E. Abbot, "Rinkbarking and Its Effects," *Journal of the Proceedings of the Royal Society of New South Wales* 14 (1880): 41–54, esp. 41.

Chapter 11

1. M. J. MacLoed, "Exploitation of Natural Resources in Colonial Central America: Indian and Spanish Approaches," in *Changing Tropical Forests: Historical Perspectives on To-Day's Challenges in Central and South America*, ed. H. K. Steen and R. P. Tucker (Durham, N.C.: Forest History Society, 1992), 31–39, quote on 31.

2. H. Low, *Sarawak: Its Inhabitants and Production, Being Notes during a Residence in that Country with His Excellency Mr. Brooke* (London: Richard Bentley, 1846), 225–26.

3. O. F. Cook, "Vegetation Affected by Agriculture in Central America," U.S. Department of Agriculture, Bureau of Plant Industry Bulletin no.145 (Washington, D.C.: Government Printing Office, 1909), 6; and Cook, "Milpa Agriculture, a Primitive Tropical System," *Annual Report of the Smithsonian Institution for 1919* (Washington, D.C.: GPO, 1921), 307–26, quote on 307.

4. W. Marsden, *The History of Sumatra, Containing an Account of the Government, Laws, Customs, Manners of the Native Inhabitants* . . . (London: Printed for the author, 1783), 62.

5. H. O. Forbes, *A Naturalist's Wanderings in the Eastern Archipelago: A Narrative of Travel and Exploration from 1878 to 1883* (London: Mason, Low, Marston, Searle & Rivington, 1885), 214, 132.

6. B. Heyne, *Tracts Historical and Statistical, on India. . . Tract XIX, Cuddapa to Hyderabad in the Year 1809* (London: Printed for Robert Baldwin and Black, Parry & Co., Booksellers to the East India Company, 1814), 302.

7. M. Rangarajan, "Production, Desiccation and Forest Management in the Central Provinces, 1850–1930," *Indian Economic and Social History Review* 31 (1994): 147–67.

8. A. Aubréville, "The Disappearance of the Tropical Forests of Africa," *Unasylva* 1 (1947): 5–11.

9. S. H. Olsen, "The Robe of the Ancestors: Forests in the History of Madagascar," *Journal of Forest History* 28 (1984): 174–81, quote on 174.

10. R. Grove, *Green Imperialism: Colonial Expansion, Tropical Edens, and the Origins of Environmentalism, 1600–1800* (Cambridge: Cambridge University Press, 1995), 168–263, 309–79.

11. B. Ribbentrop, *Forestry in British India* (Calcutta: Office of the Superintendent of Government Printing, India, 1900), 60.

12. H. Cleghorn, F. Royal, R. B. Smith and R. Strachey, "Report of the Committee Appointed by the British Association to Consider the Probable Effects in an Oeconomical and Physical Point of View of the Destruction of Tropical Forests," *Twenty-first Meeting of the British Association,* Ipswich, 1851 (London: British Association., 1852), 78–102, quotes on 80, 86, 82, and 85.

13. Sir T. Munro, "Timber Monopoly in Malabar and Canara," in *Major-General Sir Thomas Munro Bart: A Memoir,* ed. A. J. Arbuthnot, 2 vols. (London: C. Kegan Paul, 1881) 1:178–87, quote on 185.

14. Cleghorn et al., "Report of the Committee," 82, 83, 87, 88–89.

15. Documents printed in E. P. Stebbing, *The Forests of India,* 4 vols. (London: John Lane, 1922–26; reprint, Bodley Head, Ltd., 1962), 1:120–21.

16. S. Eardly-Wilmot, *Forest Life and Sport in India* (London: Edward Arnold, 1910), 9.

17. Quoted in D. R. Headrick, *The Tentacles of Progress: Technology Transfer in the Age of Imperialism* (New York: Oxford University Press, 1981), 64.

18. Ribbentrop, *Forestry in British India,* 61; and R. Wallace, *India in 1887 as Seen by Robert Wallace* (Edinburgh: Oliver & Boyd, 1888), 296.

19. Quoted in Stebbing, *Forests of India,* 2:99.

20. C. R. Markham, "On the Effects of the Destruction of the Forests in the Western Ghats of India on the Water Supply," *Proceedings of the Royal Geographical Society* 13 (1865): 266–69, esp. 266.

21. Quoted in V. Glendinning, *Trollope* (London: Hutchinson, 1992), 437.

22. J. Capper, *Old Ceylon—Sketches of Ceylon in Olden Times* (London: W. Whittingham, 1878), 32–34.

23. G. Bidie, "On the Effects of Forest Destruction in the Coorg," *Proceedings of the Royal Geographical Society* 16 (1869): 74–83.

24. Ribbentrop, *Forestry in British India,* 72 ff.

25. B. H. Baden-Powell, "The Political Value of Forest Conservancy," *Indian Forester* 2 (1876): 280–88, esp. 280, 285.

26. J. W. Grant, *The Rice Crops of Burma* (Rangoon: Superintendent, Government Printing and Stationery, 1932), 203–4.

27. The quote can be found in W. Dean, *With Broadax and Firebrand: The Destruction of the Brazilian Atlantic Forest* (Berkeley and Los Angeles: University of California Press, 1995), 138.

28. Ibid., 116.

29. Quoted in ibid., 138.

30. Ibid., 185.

31. A. Smith, *An Enquiry into the Nature and Causes of the Wealth of Nations* (1776), ed. E. Cannan (New York: Random House, 1937), 590.

Chapter 12

1. C. O. Sauer, "Prospect for Redistribution of Population," in *Limits of Land Settlement: A Report on Present-Day Possibilities,* ed. I. Bowman (New York: Council for Foreign Relations and the American Geographical Society, 1939), 8.

2. A. Woeikof, "De l'influence de l'homme sur la terre," *Annales de géographie* 10 (1901): 97–114, 193–215, esp. 97; E. Friedrich, "Wesen und Geographische Verbreitung der 'Raubwirtschaft,'" *Petermanns Meiteilungen* 50 (1904): 68–79, 92–95; and C. O. Sauer, "Destructive Exploitation in Modern Colonial Expansion," *Comptes Rendus du Congres International de Géographie, Amsterdam 1938,* 2 (sec 3c): 494–99.

3. C. O. Sauer, "The Agency of Man on Earth," in *Man's Role in Changing the Face of the Earth,* ed. W. L. Thomas (Chicago: Chicago University Press, 1956), 49–69, quote on 68.

4. A. Leopold, "The Land Ethic," in *The Sand County Almanac, and Sketches Here and There* (New York: Oxford University Press, 1949), 201–26, esp. 224–25.

5. A. Fuller, *The Forest Tree Culturist: A Treatise on the Cultivation of American Forest Trees* (New York: Geo. and F. W. Woodward, 1866), 5.

6. G. Pinchot, quoted in S. P. Hays, *Conservation and the Gospel of Efficiency: The Progressive Conservation Movement, 1890–1920,* Harvard Historical Monographs, no. 40 (Cambridge, Mass.: Harvard University Press, 1959), 1–4.

7. T. Roosevelt, "The Forest in the Life of the Nation," *Proceedings of the American Forest Congress* (Washington, D.C.: H. M. Suter, 1905), 3–12, quote on 8–9.

8. G. Pinchot, *The Fight for Conservation* (New York: Doubleday, Page, 1910), 14–15, 74.

9. G. Pinchot, "Forest Devastation: A National Danger and a Plan to Meet It," *Journal of Forestry* 17 (1919): 911–45, esp. 914, 922, 915; and Earle H. Clapp, U.S. Forest Service, *Timber Depletion, Lumber Prices, Lumber Exports, and Concentration of Timber Ownership: Report on Senate Resolution 311* (Capper Report) (Washington, D.C.: GPO, 1920).

10. W. B. Greeley, "The Relation of Geography to Timber Supply," *Economic Geography* 1 (1925): 1–11, fig. 1; and E. A. Zeigler, "Rate of Forest Growth," in U.S. Senate, *Report of the National Conservation Commission,* 60th Cong., 2d sess., 3 vols. S. Doc. 676, serial no. 5398 (Washington D.C.: GPO, 1909), 2:203–69, esp. 2:205.

11. R. Zon and W. N. Sparhawk, *Forest Resources of the World* (New York: McGraw-Hill, 1910).

12. G. Pinchot, foreword to ibid., viii.

13. Zon and Sparhawk, *Forest Resources,* 563, 594, 769, 692.

14. T. H. Gill, *The Tropical Forests of the Caribbean,* Tropical Plant Research Foundation: Charles Lawthrop Pack Forestry Trust (Baltimore: Read Taylor, 1931), 59, 60, 67, 66, 73.

15. Dean, *With Broadax and Firebrand: The Destruction of the Brazilian Atlantic Forest* (Berkeley and Los Angeles: University of California Press, 1995), 239–64, quotation on 255.

16. W. M. Hailey, Baron, *An African Survey: A Study of Problems Arising in Africa South of the Sahara,* rev. ed. (1938; reprint, London: Oxford University Press, 1957).

17. A. H. Unwin, *West African Forests and Forestry* (London: Fisher Unwin, 1920), 92.

18. P. B. Sears, *Deserts on the March* (Norman: University of Oklahoma Press, 1935).

19. J. Fairhead and M. Leach, *Misreading the African Landscape: Society and Ecology in a Forest-Savanna Mosaic* (Cambridge: Cambridge University Press, 1996), 2.

20. K. Boenten, "Commercial Agriculture in Asante," *Ghana Geographical Association Bulletin* 15 (1973): 40–49, esp. 46–47; and R. Galleti, K. D. S. Baldwin, and I. O. Dina, *Nigerian Cocoa Farmers: An Economic Survey of Yoruba Cocoa Farming Families* (London: Oxford University Press, 1956), 19.

21. J. E. Defebaugh, *History of the Lumber Industry in America,* 2 vols. (Chicago: American Lumberman, 1906–7), 1:272.

22. Zeigler, "Rate of Forest Growth," 2:203–69.

23. B. Kamarov, *The Destruction on Nature in the Soviet Union* (White Plains, N.Y.: M. E. Sharpe Inc., 1981), 217–18.

24. P. Stjernquist, *Laws in the Forest: A Study of Public Direction of Private Forestry,* Acta Societatis Humanorum Litterarum Lundensis, no. 69 (Lund: C. W. K. Gleerup, 1973), 69.

Chapter 13

1. P. W. Richards, "The Tropical Rain Forest," *Scientific American* 229 (1973): 58–67, quote on 59.

2. E. P. Hanson, *New Worlds Emerging* (London: Victor Gollancz, 1950), x–xi.

3. P. R. Ehrlich and A. H. Ehrlich, *The Population Bomb* (New York: Ballantine, 1968).

4. F. Osborn, *The Limits of the Earth* (Boston: Little, Brown, & Co., 1954), 153, 164.

5. E. Eckholm, *Losing Ground: Environmental Stress and Food Prospects* (New York: W. W. Norton & Co., 1976), 42.

6. World Resources Institute, *World Resources: An Assessment of the Resource Base That Supports the Global Economy,* World Resources Institute and International Institute for Environment and Development (New York: Basic Books and Oxford University Press, 1986–), 1986:70–75; 1988–9:71; 1994–5:27–28.

7. Alan Grainger, "Modelling Deforestation in the Humid Tropics," in *Deforestation or Development in the Third World?* ed. M. Palo and G. Mery, Bulletin no. 349 (Helsinki: Finnish Forest Research Institute, 1990), 3:51–67.

8. N. Guppy, "Tropical Deforestation: A Global View," *Foreign Affairs* 52 (1984): 928–65, esp. 932, 964.

9. Thomas Gill, "The Passing of the Great Mother Forest," Forest History Society, Gill MSS, Durham, N.C., box 10, 1931–36.

10. A. Chekov, *Uncle Vanya* (1900), in *Chekov's Plays*, ed. E. Fen (Harmondsworth: Penguin Classics, 1954), act 1.

11. B. Hibbard, *A History of Public Land Policies* (New York: Macmillan, 1924; reprint, Madison: University of Wisconsin Press, 1965), 421.

12. R. Zon, "Forests and Water in the Light of Scientific Investigations," app. 5 of *Final Report of the National Waterways Commission,* U.S. Cong., 62d Cong., 2d sess., 1927. S. Doc. 469 (1912; reprint, Washington, D.C.: U.S. Department of Agriculture Forest Service, 1927), 55.

13. W. W. Kellogg, "Mankind's Impact on Climate: The Evolution of Awareness," *Climatic Change* 10 (1987): 113–36, quote on 113.

14. J. Fairhead and M. Leach, *Reframing Deforestation: Global Analysis and Local Realities: Studies in West Africa* (London: Routledge, 1998), 180, 190.

15. M. Foucault, *The Archaeology of Knowledge,* trans. A. M. Sheridan (London: Tavistock Publications, 1972), 136–40, 189–95.

16. For the ideas of Darwin, Leopold, and Elton, see D. Takacs, *The Idea of Biodiversity: Philosophies of Paradise* (Baltimore: Johns Hopkins University Press, 1996), 9–40; and R. Carson, *The Silent Spring* (Harmondsworth: Penguin Books, 1962).

17. Y. Haila and J. Kouki, "The Phenomenon of Biodiversity in Conservation Biology," *Annales Zoologici Fennici* 31 (1994): 5–189, quote on 15.

18. E. J. H. Corner, "Suggestions for Botanical Progress," *New Phytologist* 45 (1946): 185–92, quote on 185–86.

19. P. W. Richards, *The Tropical Rain Forest: An Ecological Study* (1952), rev. ed. (Cambridge: Cambridge University Press, 1996), 404, 406–7.

20. F. H. Osborn, *Our Plundered Planet* (London: Faber & Faber, 1948); and W. Vogt, *Road to Survival* (London: Victor Gollancz, 1949).

21. A. Fedorov, "The Structure of the Tropical Rain Forest and Speciation in the Humid Tropics," *Journal of Ecology* 54 (1966): 1–11.

22. P. A. Stott, "Tropical Rainforest in Recent Ecological Thought: The Reassessment of a Non-Renewable Resource," *Progress in Physical Geography* 2(1979): 80–98, 84, and a summary of these ideas.

23. M. E. D. Poore, "The Values of Tropical Moist Forest Ecosystems," *Unasylva* 28 (1976): 127–43, 138.

24. P. W. Richards, *The Life of the Jungle,* Our Living World of Nature Series (New York: McGraw-Hill & Co., 1980), 194, 196, 199.

25. Richards, "The Tropical Rain Forest," 67.

26. A. Gómez -Pompa, C.Vázquaz-Yanes, and S.Guevara, "The Tropical Rainforest: A Non-Renewable Resource," *Science* 177 (1972): 762–65, 763.

27. W. M. Denevan, "Development and the Imminent Demise of the Amazon Rain Forest," *Professional Geographer* 25 (1973): 130–35, quote on 130.

28. A. Sommer, "Attempt at an Assessment of the World's Tropical Forests," *Unasylva* 28 (1976): 5–25, esp. 25.

29. U.S. Interagency Task Force on Tropical Forests, *The World's Tropical Forests: A Policy Strategy and Program for the United States,* Report to the President, Department of State Publication 9117 (Washington, D.C.: GPO, 1980), 7.

30. E. Linden, "Torching the Amazon: Playing with Fire," *Time,* 18 September 1989, 44–50, quote on 44.

31. N. Myers, *The Sinking Ark: A New Look at the Problem of Disappearing Species* (Oxford: Pergamon Press, 1979); and P. R. Ehrlich and A. H. Ehrlich, *Extinction: The Causes and Consequences of the Disappearance of Species* (New York: Random House, 1982).

32. P. R. Ehrlich, "The Loss of Diversity: Causes and Consequences," in *Biodiversity,* ed. E. O. Wilson (Washington, D.C.: National Academy Press, 1988), 21–27, quote on 25.

33. E. O. Wilson, *Biophilia* (Cambridge, Mass.: Harvard University Press), 121.

34. E. O. Wilson, ed., *Biodiversity* (Washington, D.C.: National Academy Press, 1988).

35. Definitions from World Resources Institute, *World Resources, 1992–93:* 292; and Food and Agriculture Organization, *Forest Resources Assessment, 1990: Guidelines for Assessment* (Rome: FAO, 1990), 5–9.

36. E. Matthews, "Global Vegetation and Land Use: New High-Resolution Data Bases for Climatic Studies," *Journal of Climate and Applied Meteorology* 22 (1983): 474–87.

37. A. Grainger, "Rates of Deforestation in the Humid Tropics, Estimates and Measurements," *Geographical Journal* 159 (1993): 33–44, esp. 34; and N. Myers, "Conversion Rates in Tropical Moist Forests," in *Tropical Rainforest Ecosystems: Structure and Function,* ed. F. Golley, Ecosystems of the World, no. 14A (Amsterdam: Elsevier Scientific Publishing, 1983), 289–300. esp. 292.

38. Sommer, "Attempt at an Assessment of the World's Tropical Forests," 5, 23.

39. G. O. Barney, "The Nature of the Deforestation Problem—Trends and Policy Implications," *Proceedings of the U.S. Strategy Conference on Tropical Deforestation,* 12–14 June, 1978 (Washington, D.C.: Department of State and U.S. Agency for International Development, 1978), 25–34, esp. 15. Later estimates are in J. Robinson and G. O. Barney, eds., "The Forestry Projections and the Environment," in *The Global 2000 Report to the President: Entering the Twenty-First Century,* pt. 1, *Environmental Projections,* Report Prepared by the Council for Environmental Quality and the Department of State (Washington, D.C.: GPO, 1980), 318–19; and N. Myers, *Conversion of Tropical Moist Forests,* Report Prepared for the National Council, Committee on Research Priorities on Tropical Biology (Washington, D.C.: National Academy of Sciences, 1980), 23–50, 175.

40. J.-P. Lanly, ed., *Tropical Forest Resources,* FAO Forestry Paper no. 30. Rome: FAO, 1982.

41. K. D. Singh, "The Tropical Forests Resources Assessment," *Unasylva* 44 (1993): 10–19.

42. *Tropical Forests: A Call for Action,* Report of an International Task Force Convened by the World Resources Institute, the World Bank, and the United Nations Development Programme, 3 vols. (Washington, D.C.: World Resources Institute, 1985); and Food and Agriculture Organization, *The Tropical Forestry Action Plan* (Rome: FAO, 1987).

43. R. A. Sedjo and M. Clawson, "How Serious Is Tropical Deforestation?" *Journal of Forestry* 83 (1983): 792–94.

Chapter 14

1. Thomas Gill, "The Passing of the Great Mother Forest," Forest History Society, Durham, N.C., Gill MSS, box 10, 1931–36.

2. W. M. Denevan, foreword to D. R. Shane, *Hoofprints on the Forest: Cattle, Ranching and the Destruction of Latin America's Tropical Forests* (Philadelphia: Institute for the Study of Human Relations, 1986), vii.

3. M. J. Dourojeanni, quoted in T. K. Rudel, *Tropical Deforestation: Small Farmers and Land Clearing in the Ecuadorian Amazon* (New York: Columbia University Press, 1993), 7.; and J. A. Tosi and R. Voertman, "Some Environmental Factors in the Economic Development of the Tropics," *Economic Geography* 40 (1964): 189–205, quote on 196.

4. R. E. Crist and C. M. Nissly, *East from the Andes: Pioneer Settlement in the South American Heartland* (Gainesville: University of Florida Press, 1973), i.

5. Ibid., iv, vi, and vii.

6. R. Nash, *The Conquest of Brazil* (London: Jonathon Cape, 1928), 287–88.

7. The quote is attributed to José Vieira Couto, a late eighteenth-century author, and to the title of W. Dean's *With Broadax and Firebrand: The Destruction of the Brazilian Atlantic Forest* (Berkeley and Los Angeles: University of California Press, 1995), 189.

8. Ibid., 266.

9. E. Moran, "Growth without Development: Past and Present Development Efforts in Amazonia," in *The Dilemma of Amazonian Development*, ed. E. F. Moran (Boulder, Colo.: Westview Press, 1983), 3–23.

10. S. B. Hecht and A. Cockburn, *The Fate of the Forest: Developers, Destroyers, and Defenders of the Amazon* (London: Verso, 1989), 102, 103.

11. M. Schmink and C. H. Woods, eds., *Contested Frontiers in Amazonia* (New York: Columbia University Press, 1992), 59 ff.

12. P. M Fearnside and E. Salati, "Explosive Deforestation in Rondônia, Brazil," *Environmental Conservation* 12 (1985): 355–56.

13. Hecht and Cockburn, *The Fate of the Forest*, 108.

14. J. Foweraker, *The Struggle for Land: A Political Economy of the Peasant Frontier in Brazil from 1930 to the Present Day* (New York: Cambridge University Press, 1981), 5.

15. Schmink and Wood, *Contested Frontiers*, 73, on the "Araguaia War"; and Tosi and Voertman, "Some Environmental Factors," 205.

16. The quotations that follow in the text are from Schmink and Woods, *Contested Frontiers*, 2–4, 348, 353–54.

17. Denevan, "Development and the Imminent Demise of the Amazon Rain Forest," *Professional Geographer* 25 (1973): 130–35; "Threat from Amazon Burn-Off," *Times* (London), 6 September, 1988; E. Linden, "Torching the Amazon," *Time,* 18 September 1989, 44–50, quotation on 44; A. Revkin, *The Burning Season: The Murder of Chico Mendes and the Fight for the Amazon Rainforest* (London: Collins, 1990); "The Month Amazonia Burns," *Economist,* 9 September 1989, 15.

18. P. M. Fearnside, "The Rate and Extent of Deforestation in Brazilian Amazonia," *Environmental Conservation* 17 (1990): 213–26.

19. The Legal Amazon is an administrative unit defined as "the Amazon" by the Brazilian government, which covers about 93 percent of the geographical forested area and consists of the whole states of Acre, Amàpá, Amazonas, Pará, Rondônia, and Roraima and approximately 50–60 percent of each of Matto Grosso, Goias and Maranhão.

20. E. Salati, M. J. Dourojeanni, et al., "Amazonia," in *The Earth as Transformed by Human Action: Global and Regional Changes in the Biosphere over the Past 300*

Years, ed. B. L. Turner II, W. C. Clark, R. W. Kates, J. F. Richards, J. T. Mathews, and W. B. Meyer (New York: Cambridge University Press, 1990), 479–93, esp. 486.

21. D. Skole and C. J. Tucker, "Tropical Deforestation and Habitat Fragmentation in the Amazon: Satellite Data from 1978 to 1988," *Science* 260 (1993): 1905–10.

22. W. F. Laurance, "Razing Amazonia," *New Scientist,* 15 October 2005, 34–39, quote on 35.

23. Shane, *Hoofprints on the Forest,* xii.

24. J. J. Parsons, "Forest to Pasture: Development or Destruction?" *Revista de Biologica Tropical* 24 (suppl.1, 1976): 121–38, quote on 126.

25. N. Myers, "The Hamburger Connection: How Central America's Forests Become North America's Hamburgers." *Ambio* 10 (1981): 3–8.

26. J. J. Parsons, "The Spread of African Pasture Grasses in the American Tropics," *Journal of Range Management* 25 (1972): 12–17, esp. 12.

27. Parsons, "Forest to Pasture," 132.

28. E. P. Eckholm, *The Other Energy Crisis: Firewood,* Worldwatch Paper no.1 (Washington, D.C.: Worldwatch Institute, 1975).

Epilogue

1. B. McKibben, *The End of Nature* (London: Viking Books, 1990); T. Banuri and F. A. Marglin, eds., *Who Will Save the Forests? Knowledge, Power and Environmental Destruction* (London: Zed Books, 1993); M. Colchester and L. Lohmann, eds., *The Struggle for Land and the Fate of the Forests* (Penang, Malaysia: World Rainforest Movement, 1993); N. Dudley, J.-P. Jeanrenaud, and F. Sullivan, *Bad Harvest? The Timber Trade and the Degradation of the World's Forests* (London: Earthscan, 1995); H. Beer and Z. Rizvi, *The Vanishing Forest: The Human Consequences of Deforestation,* Report of the Independent Commission on Human Rights (London: Zed Books, 1996); and P. M. Marchak, *Logging the Globe* (Montreal: McGill-Queen's University Press, 1996).

2. Tom Wicker, "The Forests Are Still Vanishing," *New York Times,* 24 March 1989, 21; "Amazon" *Chicago Tribune,* 12 March 1989, 1 and 29.

3. D. Bryant, D. Nielsen, and L. Tangley, *The Last Frontier Forests: Ecosystems and Economics on the Edge* (Washington, D.C.: World Resources Institute, 1997), 5 and table on 9.

4. R. P. Harrison's concept of an outside domain can be found in his *Forests: The Shadow of Civilization* (Chicago: University of Chicago Press, 1992), 247.

BIBLIOGRAPHIC ESSAY

THIS WORK covers and uses a wide range of geographical, historical, archaeological, anthropological, botanical, and paleobotanical literature. Quotations and works referred to in the text are in the endnotes, and as acknowledgements to tables and figures, but some of the main sources that would allow an entrée into the topics in the chapters are highlighted in this essay. But I am conscious of the omission of very many small but significant contributions in papers and chapters in a mass of publications that can only be accessed by going back to the original and larger version of this book.

In chapter 1, "The Return of the Forest," a good overview of the topic is in N. Roberts, *The Holocene: An Environmental History* (Oxford: Basil Blackwell, 1989). Essential material for the United States is in P. A. Delcourt and H. R. Delcourt, "Vegetation Maps for Eastern North America: 40,000 yrs BP to the Present," in *Geobotany*, edited by T. C. Roman (New York: Plenum Press, 1981), 2:123–66, and P. F. McDowell, T. Webb III, and P. J. Bartlein, "Long-Term Environmental Change," in *The Earth as Transformed by Human Action: Global and Regional Changes in the Biosphere over the Past 300 Years,* edited by B. L. Turner II, W. C. Clark, R.W. Kates, J. F. Richards, J. Mathews, and W. B. Meyer (New York: Cambridge University Press), 143–62. For Europe, B. J. Huntley and H. J. B. Birks, *An Atlas of Past and Present Pollen Maps for Europe: 0–13,000 Years Ago,* is indispensable. The tropics are well covered in A. S. Goudie, "The Ice Age in the Tropics," in *Environments and Historical Change*, edited by P. Slack (Oxford: Oxford University Press, 1999), 2–23.

Much of the material for "Fire and Foragers" (chap. 2) comes from a multitude of individual research papers. But fire in all its aspects is well covered in J. Goudsblom's thought-provoking *Fire and Civilization* (London: Penguin Books, 1999), and S. J. Pyne's *Vestal Fire: An Environmental History, Told through Fire, of Europe, and Europe's Encounter with the World* (Seattle: Washington University Press, 1997). The original thesis on "Pleistocene Overkill" comes in P. S. Martin and R. G. Klein, eds., *Quaternary Extinctions: A Prehistoric Revolution* (Tucson: University of Arizona Press, 1984). For demographic collapse in the Americas, see A. L. Crosby, *Ecological Imperialism: The Biological Expansion of Europe, 900–1900* (Cambridge: Cambridge University Press, 1986). Most of the evidence of early fire clearing in North America is elaborated in my *Americans and Their Forests* (New York: Cambridge University Press, 1989), and W. Denevan's "The Pristine Myth: The Landscape of the America's in 1492," *Annals, Association of American Geographers* 82 (1992): 369–85, contains new material. Evidence for Europe and the rest of the world is widely scattered, but P. I. Bogucki's *Forest Farmers and Stock-herders: Early Agriculture and Its Consequences in North-Central Europe* (Cambridge: Cambridge University Press, 1988) contains many leads.

All the works referred to above for chapter 2 are also relevant to chapter 3, "The First Farmers." The vast topics of plant domestication and the origins of agriculture are covered well in D. R. Harris and G. C. Hillman, eds., *Foraging and Farming: The Evolution of Plant Exploitation* (London: Allen & Unwin, 1988), with up-to-date information in Harris's later edited volume, *The Origins and Spread of Agriculture and Pastoralism in Eurasia* (London: UCL Press, 1966). R. S. MacNeish's *The Origins of Agriculture and Settled Life* (Norman: University of Oklahoma Press, 1992) provides a framework for understanding the many paths of change. Bogucki's *Forest Farmers and Stockherders* is essential reading for this chapter as are the exciting insights and leads that come in the many publications of A. G. Sherratt, for example, "The Secondary Exploitation of Animals in the Old World." *World Archaeology* 15 (1983): 90–104, "Plough and Pastoralism: Aspects of the Secondary Products Revolution," in *Patterns in the Past: Studies in Honour of David Clarke,* ed. I. Hodder, G. Issac, and N. Hammond (Cambridge: Cambridge University Press, 1981), 261–306, "Wool, Wheels, and Ploughmarks: Local Developments or Outside Introductions in Neolithic Europe?" *Bulletin of the Institute of Archaeology* (London) 23 (1986): 1–15, and *Economy and Society in Prehistoric Europe: Changing Perspectives* (Edinburgh: Edinburgh University Press, 1997).

"The Classical World" (chap. 4) has a rich literature of great antiquity. In this, as in many other chapters dealing with environment and culture before 1800, C. Glacken's magnificent *Traces on the Rhodian Shore: Nature and Culture in Western Thought from Ancient Times to the End of the Eighteenth Century* (Berkeley and Los Angeles: University of California Press, 1967) is a font of ideas, insights, and examples, as well as a beacon of scholarship beyond compare. Other than dipping into the many translations of classical authors in the Loeb Classical Library, excellent background into the classical world comes in M. Rostovzeff's two monumental works, *The Social and Economic History of the Hellenistic World,* 3 vols. (Oxford: Clarendon Press, 1941) and *The Economic and Social History of the Roman Empire,* 2d ed., 2 vols. (1924; reprint, Oxford: Clarendon Press, 1957), and in F. M. Heichelheim, "Effects of Classical Antiquity on the Land," in *Man's Role in Changing the Face of the Earth,* edited by W. L. Thomas (Chicago: University of Chicago Press, 1956), 165–82. *Trees and Timber in the Ancient Mediterranean World* by R. Meiggs (Oxford: Clarendon Press, 1982) is full of details of timber use, though little on deforestation, and D. J. Hughes's *Pan's Travail: Environmental Problems of the Ancient Greeks and Romans* (Baltimore: Johns Hopkins University Press, 1994) brings many contemporary insights to this distant past. The conflicting evidence and uncertainties of past climates and erosion is best summarized in J. Bintliff, "Erosion in Mediterranean Lands: A Reconsideration of Patterns, Processes, and Methodology," in *Past and Present Soil Erosion: Archaeological and Geographical Perspectives,* edited by M. Bell and J. Boardman, Oxbow Monographs 22 (Oxford: Oxbow Books, 1992), 125–32.

For "The Medieval World" (chap. 5), perhaps the best place to start with empirical evidence of clearing is H. C. Darby's unassuming but deeply penetrating essay "The Clearing of the Woodland in Europe," in *Man's Role in Changing the Face of the Earth,* edited by Thomas, 183–216, backed up, as ever with the wealth of detail and intellectual ideas in Glacken's *Traces on the Rhodian Shore* and R. Koebner's "The Settlement and Colonization of Europe," in *The Cambridge Economic History of Europe,* vol. 1, *Agrarian Life in the Middle Ages,* edited by J. H. Clapham and E. Power (Cambridge: Cambridge

University Press, 1941), 1–88. The many publications of the medievalist L. White Jr. bristle with new ideas and insights, particularly on technological innovations and attitudes to nature, and they are probably best summed up in his *Medieval Technology and Social Change* (Oxford: Clarendon Press, 1962). M. Cartmill, *A View to a Death in the Morning: Hunting and Nature through History* (Cambridge, Mass.: Harvard University Press, 1993), deals with the important topic of the role of hunting in forest awareness, and R. Murphey, "Deforestation in Modern China," in *Global Deforestation and the Nineteenth Century World Economy,* edited by R. P. Tucker and J. F. Richards (Durham. N.C.: Duke University Press, 1983), 11–28, is one of the first forays into the opaque topic of deforestation in China.

Chapter 6, "Driving Forces and Cultural Climates, 1500–1750," owes much to L. White's "Cultural Climates and Technological Advance in the Middle Ages," *Viator: Medieval and Renaissance Studies* 2 (1971): 171–201, and E. L. Jones's *The European Miracle: Environments, Economies, and Geopolitics in the History of Europe and Asia,* 2d ed. (Cambridge: Cambridge University Press, 1987). D. Landes, *Revolution in Time: Clocks and the Making of the Modern World* (Cambridge, Mass: Harvard University Press, 1983), is excellent on the implications of time keeping and its effect on modern life. The three volumes of I. Wallerstein's *The Modern World System* (London: Academic Press, 1974, 1980, 1989) are indispensable on core-periphery arrangements and global trade, and all of F. Braudel's works, particularly *Capitalism and Material Life, 1400–1800* (New York: Harper Row, 1973), which can be read with profit. A good historical atlas, like G. Barraclough, ed., *The Times Atlas of World History* (London: Times Publishing Co., 1978), makes many of the movements described in this chapter clear. Glacken's *Traces* and K. Thomas, *Man and the Natural World: A History of the Modern Sensibility* (New York: Pantheon Books, 1983) illuminate attitudes to the natural world.

The sources for chapter 7 ("Clearing in Europe, 1500–1750") are particularly varied and article-based. A good start on the timber crisis is J. Nef, *The Rise of the British Coal Industry,* 2 vols. (London: Routledge & Sons, 1932), which, though dated, is still relevant and covers a much wider ground than the title suggests. This should be read in conjunction with G. Hammersley's "The Charcoal Industry and Its Fuel, 1540–1750," *Economic History Review,* 2d ser., 26 (1973): 593–613, for its updated views. H. Kellenbenz, *The Rise of the European Economy: An Economic History of Continental Europe from the Fifteenth to the Eighteenth Century* (London: Weidenfeld & Nicholson, 1976), covers the continental-wide picture, as does C. T. Smith, *An Historical Geography of Western Europe before 1800* (London: Longmans, 1978). For woodland policy, J. Evelyn's *Sylva; or, A Discourse of Forest Trees, and the Propogation of Timber in His Majesty's Dominion* (London, 1664, and many modern editions since) is the key contemporary text on forest awareness and use, which taken together with Thomas, *Man and the Natural World,* give one a good idea of forest policy and attitudes. On naval needs, R. Albion's *Forests and Sea Power: The Timber Problem of the Royal Navy, 1652–1862* (Cambridge, Mass: Harvard University Press, 1926), like Nef's work on coal, is old but hard to beat.

"The Wider World, 1500–1750" (chap. 8) deals with many countries. The previously cited works by Crosby, *Ecological Imperialism,* and by Denevan, "The Pristine Myth," are essential for disease, animal, and plant invasions of the Americas. The central importance of sugar in the Atlantic system is comprehensively dealt with in J. H. Galloway, *The Sugar Industry: An Historical Geography from Its Origins to 1914* (Cambridge: Cambridge University Press, 1989) and Brazilian settlement and society in S. B. Schwartz, *Sugar Plantations in the Formation of Brazilian Society: Bahia, 1550–1835*

(Cambridge: Cambridge University Press, 1985). Early New England society and the timber trade are the theme of Charles Carroll's *The Timber Economy of Puritan New England* (Providence, R.I.: Brown University Press, 1973) and the detail of the backwoods economy of the early United States is summarized in my *Americans and Their Forests.* Cities and fuel use are the theme of C. Bridenbaugh, *Cities in the Wilderness: The First Century of Urban Life in America, 1625–1742* (New York: Rowland Press, 1938), and R. V. Reynolds and A. H. Pierson, *Fuel Wood Use in the United States, 1630–1930,* U.S. Department of Agriculture Circular 641 (Washington, D.C.: GPO, 1942). Murphey's "Deforestation in Modern China" can be supplemented by P. C. Perdue, *Exhausting the Earth: State and Peasant in Hunan, 1500–1850* (Cambridge, Mass.: Harvard University Press, 1987). The forests of Japan are very adequately covered in Conrad Totman *The Green Archipelago: Forestry in Pre-Industrial Japan* (Berkeley and Los Angeles: University of California Press, 1989), and his many articles cited therein.

Chapter 9, "Driving Forces and Cultural Climates, 1750–1900," covers perhaps the most complex era of interrelated forces and factors producing change in the world's forests. The outlines of the Industrial Revolution are in M. Kranzberg and C. W. Pursell Jr., eds., *Technology in Western Civilization,* vol. 1, *The Emergence of Modern Industrial Society—Earliest Times to 1900* (New York: Oxford University Press, 1967) and D. S. Landes, *The Unbounded Prometheus: Technological Change and Industrial Development in Western Europe from 1750 to the Present* (Cambridge: Cambridge University Press, 1969). World population shifts are in P. L. Demeney, "Population," in *The Earth as Transformed by Human Action,* edited by B. L. Turner II et al., 41–54. Advances in timber production and wood working are treated in depth in my *Americans and Their Forests.* The application of technology to overseas expansion is the subject of D. R. Headrick's two very readable little books, *The Tools of Empire: Technology in the Age of Imperialism, 1850–1940* and *The Tentacles of Progress: Technology Transfer in the Age of Imperialism, 1850–1940* (Oxford: Oxford University Press, 1981 and 1988, respectively). A. R. Lower deals with the Baltic as well as North America in *Great Britain's Woodyard: British America and the Timber Trade, 1763–1867* (Montreal: McGill-Queen's University Press, 1973). Attitudes to the forest once more owe much to Glacken, *Traces on the Rhodian Shore,* and Thomas, *Man and the Natural World,* while H. E. Lowood in "The Calculating Forester: Quantification, Cameral Science, and the Emergence of Scientific Forestry Management in Germany," in *The Quantifying Spirit in the Eighteenth Century,* edited by T. Fränsmyr, J. H. Heilbron, and R. C. Ryder (Berkeley and Los Angeles: University of California Press, 1990), 315–42, breaks new ground on forest management and attitudes.

Many of the above themes are picked up in "Clearing in the Temperate World, 1750–1920" (chap. 10). For French forests, see H. D. Clout, *Agriculture in France on the Eve of the Railway Age* (London: Croom Helm, 1980) and T. L. Whitehed, *Forests and Peasant Politics in Modern France* (New Haven, Conn.: Yale University Press, 2000). R. A. French, "Russians and the Forest," in *Studies in Russian Historical Geography,* edited by J. H. Bater and R. A. French (London: Academic Press, 1983), 1:23–44, is excellent on the Russian forests. The British experience takes us back to themes in chapter 7 on coal substitution dealt with in Hammersley, "The Charcoal Iron Industry and Its Fuel," and strategic naval supplies dealt with in Albion, *Forests and Sea Power.* The explosive expansion of deforestation in the United States is covered in my *Americans and Their Forests,* while Totman, *The Green Archipelago,* continues the story in Japan. The Australian experience is difficult to pin down, but a start can be made with my "Clearing the Woods," in *The Australian Experience,* edited by R. L. Heathcote (Melbourne: Longmans Cheshire, 1988), 115–26.

In a similar fashion, chapter 11, "Clearing in the Tropical World, 1750–1920," elaborates themes first picked out in chapter 9, particularly those in the two books by Daniel Headrick, *The Tools of Empire* and *The Tentacles of Progress.* H. H. Bartlett, "Fire, Primitive Agriculture and Grazing in the Tropics," in *Man's Role in Changing the Face of the Earth,* edited by Thomas, 652–720, is excellent on fire farming. Richard Grove, *Green Imperialism: Colonial Expansion, Tropical Island Edens, and the Origins of Environmentalism, 1600–1800* (Cambridge: Cambridge University Press, 1995), breaks new ground on the surgeon-environmentalists in India and is a good foil to E. P. Stebbing, *The Forests of India,* 4 vols. (London: John Lane, the Bodley Head Ltd., 1922–26), which is the more factual blow-by-blow account of Indian forestry and legislation. The many publications of J. F. Richards and associates (e.g., with M. B. McAlpin, "Cotton Cultivating and Land Clearing in the Bombay Deccan and Karnatak, 1818–1920," in *Global Deforestation and the Nineteenth Century World Economy,* edited by Tucker and Richards, 68–94) offer many revealing insights into the mechanics and outcomes of colonial rule and expanded peasant economies on the forest. W. Dean, *With Broadax and Firebrand: The Destruction of the Brazilian Atlantic Forest* (Berkeley and Los Angeles: University of California Press, 1995), is the essential introduction to the hitherto underresearched topic of Brazilian deforestation.

Chapter 12 ("Scares and Solutions, 1900–1944") is the introduction to the final part of the book, which is entitled "The Global Forest," a period when the interconnectedness of actions and events was beginning to be realized in the twentieth century. For the dawn of global awareness, see C. Glacken, "Changing Ideas of the Habitable World," in *Man's Role in Changing the Face of the Earth,* 81–88, and my "The End of Modern History," *Geographical Review* 88 (1998): 275–300. The American story and the career of Pinchot, Zon, Greeley, and others is well covered in my *Americans and Their Forests* and in S. P. Hays's seminal little book *Conservation and the Gospel of Efficiency: The Progressive Conservation Movement* (Cambridge, Mass.: Harvard University Press, 1959). *The Forest Resources of the World* (New York: McGraw-Hill Book Co., 1923) by R. Zon and W. N. Sparhawk is the first global survey and starting point for international comparisons. J. Fairhead and M. Leach's provocative analysis of West African deforestation in *Misreading the African Landscape: Society and Ecology in the Forest—Savanna Mosaic* (Cambridge: Cambridge University Press, 1996) is a good corrective to the conventional wisdom about indigenous clearing. The examples of the USSR and Sweden are covered in B. Barr, "Perspectives on Deforestation in the U.S.S.R.," in *World Deforestation in the Twentieth Century,* edited by J. F. Richards and R. P. Tucker (Durham, N.C.: Duke University Press, 1988), 230–61, and P. Stjernquist, *Laws in the Forests: A Study of Public Direction of Private Forestry,* Acta Societatis Humanorum Litterarum Lundensis, no.69 (Lund: C. W. K. Gleerup, 1973).

The controversy over the causes, rates, and remedies of global deforestation during the latter half of the twentieth century (chap. 13, "The Great Onslaught, 1945–95: Dimensions of Change") has generated a vast and ever-growing journal literature that is impossible to itemize. Overviews and summaries of arguments are in my "Forests," in *The Earth as Transformed by Human Action,* edited by B. L. Turner II et al., 179–201, and my "Forests and Tree Cover," in *Changes in Land Use and Land Cover: A Global Perspective,* edited by W. B. Meyer, and B. L. Turner II, 97–124 (Cambridge: Cambridge University Press, 1994), and W. B. Meyer and B. L. Turner II, "Human Population Growth and Global Land Use/Cover Change," *Annual Review of Ecological Systems* 23 (1992): 39–61. The biennial publication *World Resources: An Assessment of the Resource Base That Supports the Global Economy* (New York: Basic Books and Oxford University Press) is an invaluable source of up-to-date information. K. Brown and D. W. Pearce, eds., *The Causes of Tropical Deforestation* (London: UCL Press, 1994), and A. Grainger, *Controlling Tropical Deforestation* (London: Earthscan, 1990), contain much useful information. For biodiversity, D. Takacs, *The Idea of Biodiversity: Philosophies of Paradise* (Baltimore: Johns Hopkins University Press, 1996) and E. O. Wilson, ed., *Biodiversity* (Washington, D.C.: National Academy Press, 1988), are invaluable, however the discussion on the multiple and overlapping origins of the concept are entirely my own. Other sources of information are indicated in the acknowledgements to the tables and figures.

Chapter 14 ("The Great Onslaught, 1945–95: Patterns of Change") attempts to give geographical reality to the theories and ideas on why deforestation happens. Amazonia looms large, in terms of both area and literature as a focus of world deforestation. Early moves are contained in R. E. Crist and C. M. Nissly, *East from the Andes: Pioneer Settlement in the South American Heartland* (Gainesville: University of Florida Press, 1973), and Denevan's "Imminent Demise" (1973) and the update in "Swiddens and Cattle versus Forest: Development and the Imminent Demise of the Amazon Rain Forest Re-examined," in *Where Have All the Flowers Gone? Deforestation in the Third World,* edited by V. H. Sutlive Jr., Studies in Third World Societies, no 13 (Williamsburg, VA: William and Mary College, Department of Anthropology, 1981), 25–44, sketch in the broad view. Dean, in *With Broadax and Firebrand,* has admirable institutional and political material about deforestation. D. J. Mahar, *Government Policies and Deforestation in Brazil's Amazon Region* (Washington, D.C.: World Bank, 1989), E. F. Moran, ed., *The Dilemma of Amazonian Development* (Boulder, CO: Westview Press, 1983), S. B. Hecht and A. Cockburn, *The Fate of the Forest: Developers, Destroyers, and Defenders of the Amazon* (London: Verso, 1989) are rich in details. The many publication of P. M. Fearnside (e.g., "The Rate and Extent of Deforestation in Brazilian Amazonia," *Environmental Conservation* 17 [1990]: 213–26) repay careful reading. M. Schmink and C. H. Woods, eds., *Contested Frontiers in Amazonia* (New York: Columbia University Press, 1992), has excellent "grassroots" studies. Pastoral incursions are covered well in all the above and, especially, in D. R. Shane, *Hoofprints on the Forest: Cattle Ranching and the Destruction of Latin America's Tropical Forests* (Philadelphia: Philadelphia Institute for the study of Human Relations, 1986) and J. J. Parsons, "Forest or Pasture: Development or Destruction? *Revista de Biologica Tropical* 24, suppl. 1 (1976): 121–38. For the most recent and alarming assessment, see William F. Laurance, "Razing Amazonia," *New Scientist,* 15 October 2005, 34–39. For other areas, see H. C. Brookfield, F. J. Lian, K.-S. Low, and L. Potter, "Borneo and the Malaya Peninsula," in *The Earth Transformed,* edited by B. L. Turner II et al., 495–512, and J. Fairhead and M. Leach, *Reframing Deforestation: Global Analysis and Local Realities: Studies in West Africa* (London: Routledge, 1998). For the fuelwood crisis, see E. P. Eckholm, *The Other Energy Crisis: Firewood* Worldwatch Paper no. 1 (Washington, D.C.: Worldwatch Institute, 1973), which is a good introduction.

INDEX

Note: *Italicized page numbers indicate illustrations.*

abaca cultivation, 348
Abies (fir): early human impact and, 10;
  shipbuilding and, 73, 174; sources of,
  180, 280
Acacia arabica (Babhul), 337
acid rain, 474
Addison, Joseph, 258
Advanced Very High Resolution Radiometer. *See* AVHRR (Advanced Very
  High Resolution Radiometer)
adzes, 43
affluence, 140–42, 400
Africa: age of discovery and, 131; composition and range of forest in, 65,
  425, 429; core and periphery and,
  132; crops grown in, 320; disease in,
  239–40; extent and pace of deforestation in, 429; as "external area,"
  140; forced removal and exclusion
  of peasants in, 377–78; fuelwood
  shortage in, 465; global timber trade
  and, 469; grasslands of, 324; after Ice
  Age, 4, 9; imperialism and colonization in, 239–40, 321, 397; land-cover
  change in, 319, 373; migration to,
  237; motives for deforestation in,
  433; Muslim-Christian conflict in,
  111; palynological evidence in, 31;
  per capita timber consumption in, 77;
  "Pleistocene overkill" and, 18; population of, 237, 400; railroads in, 242,
  243; shifting agriculture in, 320; as

source of consumer and staple goods,
  140–141. *See also* East Africa; North
  Africa; southern Africa; West Africa;
  specific countries
African Survey, An (Hailey), 377
*âge des grands défrichements, le. See
  grands défrichements, les*
age of discovery, 127–49; attitudes about
  nature during, 226; cultural climate
  of, 128–29; discoveries during,
  129–34; human ascendancy over
  nature during, 142–49; land use
  during, *130;* modernity and, 137–42;
  technology and, 134–37; trade during, 130–31
agricultural clearing: in Africa, 377; in
  Asia, 380; Atlantic coastal forest and,
  376; as biggest cause of deforestation after World War II, 401, 460;
  in Brazil, 350, 377, 446; in China,
  310; for coffee cultivation, 353, *355;*
  for commercial crops, 340–42, 380;
  versus commercial logging, 213;
  in early twentieth century, 373; in
  Europe, 154–60, 266–67; forests
  as great reserve of unused land and,
  238; in the future, 472; magnitude
  of, in temperate world, 263–65; in
  Mediterranean region, 67–69, 71;
  permanent agriculture in tropical
  world and, 320–24; reforestation
  after, 425–26; in Southeast Asia, 347;
  for sugar cultivation, 350, 352; in
  United States, 387, 387–88; variable
  impact on forests of, 380; worldwide,

agricultural clearing: (*continued*)
338, 372. *See also* agriculture; *clearing entries;* shifting cultivation
agriculture: acreage-per-person calculations and, 59; adoption of Indian methods of, 201; agricultural revolution and, 36–37; in Amazon basin, 433–34; in ancient literature, 67–68; in Andean region, 434–37; animal power and, 43; bubonic plague and, 117; in classical world, 63, 80–81; climate and, 305–6; crop domestication and, 36–40; cropland in tropical world and, 373; crop rotation and, 94–95; crops from New World in China and, 219; crops of medieval Europe and, 95; defecation process and, 38; dust bowl and, 408; early spread of, *41;* ecological degradation and, 38; ecological imperialism and, 195; ecological symbiosis and, 37–38; erosion and siltation and, 311; establishment of, in United States, 290; expansion of, in temperate world, 263, 264, 265; for export in Southeast Asia, 346; fertilizer and, 208; grassland decline and, 325; land prices and, 154; land reform and, 439, 460; livestock interrunning with crops and, 69; naming of months and, 89; Neolithic European, 40–45; Neolithic Mesoamerican and South American, 45–52; in newly cleared land, 208; paradoxes of, in Brazil, 451–52; peasant cultivation in India and, 338–40; permanent, in tropical world, 322–24; plows and plow operators and, 94, 100, 286–87; in pre-Columbian Brazil, 198; "primary" and "consequent" phases and, 40; railroads and, 337; reasons for beginning of, 35, 37–38; revolution of Middle Ages, 89–90; stumps and, 292–93; for subsistence, 348; in temperate versus tropical world, 318–19; terracing and, 322; time needed to prepare ground for, 286. *See also* agricultural clearing; plantations; shifting cultivation; soil fertility and degradation; *specific crops*

Albion, Robert, 176
alder (*Alnus*). See *Alnus* (alder)
Aleppo pine. See *Pinus* (pine)
Alliance for Progress, 440
alluviation, 82
Alnus (alder), 6, 8
Amazon basin: agricultural development in, 433–34; motives for deforestation in, 432–33; pre-Columbian land use in, 31–32, 49. *See also* Andean region; Brazil
Ambrosia spp. (ragweed), 53
Americans and Their Forests (Williams), 471
Americas: crop exchanges and, 320; European imperialism and, 321; hearths of domestication in, 37; human ascendancy over nature in, 142; internal, 157, 178, 191; as periphery, 140, 239; as source of staple goods and bullion, 140, 141. *See also* Central America; Mesoamerica; New World expansion; North America; South America
Amerindians (of Mesoamerica and South America): extermination of, 376, 433; land use of, 50; myth of environmental harmony and, 49; population decline among, 49–51, *52,* 433–34; reservations for, 376; servitude of, 352, 433; shifting cultivation and, 321; temples of, *51;* trans-Andean migration and, 437; wood use of, 48. *See also* Native Americans (of North America)
Anburey, Thomas, 209
Andean region: agricultural development east of Andes in, 434–37, *438;* fuelwood shortage in, 464; grasslands in, 32–34; Ice Age in, 3; military conflict in, 435; population of, 435
Anderson, Rogers, 30
Angola, 397
Antigone (Sophocles), 67–68
Araguaia War, 451
Araucaria augustflora (Paraná pine), 376–77
Argentina: cropland in, 348; end of Ice Age in, 4; export trade and, 349;

extent of deforestation in, 377; as neo-European land, 238; railroads in, 243

aristocracy: Charlemagne's subdivision of forest and, *100;* deer parks and, 188; reforestation by, 182; reservation of forest areas by, 114, 116, 121, 151

Aristotle, 143

ascendancy. *See* human ascendancy over nature

ash. See *Fraxinus excelsior* (ash)

Ashton, Thomas, 415

Asia: colonization and, 239, 240; crop exchanges and, 320; early agriculture in, *41,* 60–61; end of Ice Age in, 3, 4; European imperialism and, 321; extent of deforestation in, 429; as "external area," 140; hearths of domestication in, 37; "Pleistocene overkill" in, 17–18; population of, 237, 380; railroads in, 242, 243; range of forest in, 429; as source of consumer goods, 140; state system in, 239; urbanization in, 61. *See also* South Asia; Southeast Asia

assarts, 99, 101, 104

astronomy, 143–44

Athens, 72, 74–75, 81

Atkins (governor of Barbados), 201

Atlantic islands, 196–98, 203, 213. *See also specific islands and island groups*

Atlantic Ocean, *193,* 203–4, 265–66

Attenborough, David, 80

attitudes about nature: during age of discovery, 226; in classical world, 85–86; during Enlightenment, 251–52; harmonies of nature and, 256–58; human consciousness of power over nature and, 64, 65, 68, 86; during Industrial Revolution, 226; in medieval world, 89; myths about nature and, 5; profit making and, 86; second versus first nature and, 86. *See also* attitudes about trees and forests

attitudes about trees and forests: in Australia, 316; in Brazil, 352; Christianity and, 146, 147, 148–49; in colonial North America, 147, 148, 208; deism and, 259; dust bowl

and, 408; efficiency versus aesthetics and, 366; during Enlightenment, 251–52; European imperialism and, 321; forests as wild and hostile and, 145–47; global versus local, 360, 371; in India, 343–44; in Japan, 309; love of trees and, 188–90; patriotism and, 259–60; pet-like status of trees and, 258; of pioneers in United States, 253–55, 293–94; rainfall and forest preservation and, 406–7; reforestation in France and, 270–71; religious associations and, 258–59; shifting cultivation and, 321; trees as tonics for civilization and, 258–60; U.S. timber famine and, 363; various uses for timber and, 167; worldwide, 262. *See also* attitudes about nature

Aubréville, André, 324

Augustine, 96

Australia: clearing and land cover modification in, 311–16, *312, 313, 314;* forest science in, 262; income levels in, 231; lumber business and, 317; as neo-European land, 238; railroads in, 243; reforestation in, 475; scrub clearing in, 316; as "settler empire," 263; shipping improvements and, 243; as source of timber, 279, 352; vegetation zones in, 311–12

Australopithecines, 17

Austria, 104

AVHRR (Advanced Very High Resolution Radiometer), 453

axes, 43, 49, 58, 198, 209

Azara, Felix, 196

Azores, 193, 197, 203. *See also* Atlantic islands

Aztec empire, *132*

Babcock milk-testing machine, 315

Babhul. See *Acacia arabica* (Babhul)

Backwoods Life in New England (anonymous), *206*

Bacon, Francis, 134, 144, 181

Baden-Powell, B. Henry, 344

Balée, William, 32

Balfour, Edward, 329, 333

Ballinger-Pinchot affair, 364

Baltic region: Atlantic/Baltic production and consumption system and, 265–66; cheapness of timber supplies from, 204; colonization of western Europe and, 105–6; duties on timber from, 283; geographical shifts in, *179;* geography of European timber trade and, *281,* 281–82, 301; as "internal America," 157, 178; peasant labor and, 301; political vagaries of, 282; as semi-colony of Britain, 281; shipping blockade and, 278, 279; as source of naval stores, 174; as source of raw materials for Britain, 278–81; timber in economy of, 283; timber processing in, 231, 232; timber trade of, 176–81, 266; topographical and climatic conditions in, 179–80
bamboo groves, 222
banana cultivation, 198, *449*
Bank of England, 138
Barbados, 200, 201, 202, *202,* 203
barley, little. See *Hordeum pusillum* (little barley)
Barney, Gerald, 428
Bartram, William, 58
baths, public, 76, 77
Baudillart, Henri, 270
beans. See *Phaseolus vulgaris* (beans)
Beaumont, Law of (1182), 112
Bechmann, Roland, 106
beech. See *Fagus* (beech)
Beginning, The (anonymous), *210*
Belknap, Jeremy, 285
Benedictines, 96, 97, 99, 101
Bengal tiger, 343
berries, favorable conditions for growth of, 30
Betula (birch), 6, 10, 23
Bible, 143
Bifänge, 99
Bintliff, John, 82
biodiversity: abundance and, 414–15; in Amazon basin, 32; "arrival" of, in mid-1980s, 421–22; in China, 120; climate change and, 411; coining of term, 421; cultural survival and, 420–21; endangerment of large wild animals and, 322, 323–24; during

Holocene epoch, 18; after Ice Age, 4–5, 10; in India, 342; and logging, 371; in Mediterranean region, 64–65; multiple meanings of, 412–13; origin of idea of, 412; pace and irreversibility of decline in, 417–18, 419; "Pleistocene overkill" and, 17–18, 21; publicizing and popularization of, 418–21; rhetoric versus reality and, 476–77; rising concern about, 411–13; special interests and, 478; speciation and genetic diversity and, 415–16; "standard trees" and, 261; tropical staple goods and, 141–42
birch. See *Betula* (birch)
Black Death, 91, 117
Black Legend, 49
Blane (collector of taxes in Canara), 331
Blanqui, Adolphe, 270
Bogucki, P. I., 45
Bolivia, 434–37, *438,* 439
Boniface (Saint), 97
Book of Hours, 155
Book of Odes (*Shih Ching*), 120
boosterism, 306
Boserupian thesis, 41
botanical gardens, 197, 328
bottle gourd. See *Lagenaria siceraria* (bottle gourd)
Boussingault, Jean Baptiste, 329
Brandis, Dietrich, 262, 344
Braudel, Fernand, 157
Brazil: acid rain in, 474; backwoods farmers in, 352, 356; *campo cerrado* of, 32, 325–26; clearing in Pará State of, *443;* coffee cultivation in, 351–53, *354, 374, 375,* 445–46; composition and range of forest in, 377; crops and cropland in, 320, 348, 351; before deforestation, 457; development schemes in, 448–50; exploitation by elites in, 349–50; export production in, 467; extent of deforestation after World War II in, 350–53, *355,* 355–56, 376–77, 452–57, *458;* extent of deforestation during colonial period in, 198–99; frontier life in, 450–52; Generals' plan in, 439–45, *441;* independence

of, 239, 352; mining in, 449–50; as neo-European land, 238; Operation Amazonia in, 440–41; paradoxes of agricultural development in, 451–52; planned settlement schemes in, 397; population of, 350, 355, 376, 442; prohibition of presses and libraries in, 351; ranching in, 200, 350, 442, 445, 447–48; reforestation in, 475; resistance to reforestation in, 476; road building in, 440–45, *441, 443, 454;* rubber cultivation in, 448; selective logging and, 468–69; settlers in Rondónia in, 445–48; as stepping stone to New World expansion, 198; sugar production in, 198–200; timber shortages in, 352; wood in industrialization of, 234

brazilwood, 204, 280

Brethren of the Sword, 105

Briavonne, Natalis, 228–29

Britain: access to timber and, 213–14; agricultural clearing in, 155; attitudes about trees and forests in, 145, 258; bubonic plague in, 117; building construction in, 178–79, 280–84; charcoal industry in, 172; clearing crusade in, 147; coal and coal industry in, 70–71, 76, 153, 164–66, *165,* 234; colonization and, 141, 213, 238, 328–29; consumption levels in, 231, 282; dairy products in, 317; early capitalism and, 137; European timber trade and, *281,* 282; extent of forest cover in, 150; failure to replant trees in, 176; foragers and fire in, 21; forests as refuge for criminals in, 146; forest science in, 262; fuelwood prices in, *153;* "ghost acreage" in, 166; global timber trade and, 276, 278; during *grands défrichements, les,* 106, *108,* 109; heating methods in, 164; homegrown lumber in, 176; after Ice Age, 7; as importer, 156–58, 181, 243; income levels in, 229; industrial potential of, 230; Industrial Revolution in, 228, 229; internal frontier of Europe and, 92; iron industry of, 170, 184, 215; land usage rights in,

113–14, 116; Mesolithic wooden artifacts in, 23; naval stores trade and, 213; Neolithic agriculture in, 43; new species of trees in, 258; population of, 151, 152, 278; protectionism and, 330; public baths in, 76; railroads in, 243; shipbuilding and, 174, 176, 178, 214, 330; shortages in, 151; soil fertility in, 81; sources of timber for, 266, 280–82; steel industry in, 122; substitution of fossil fuel in, 276; tea in, 340; timber shortages in, 152, 162–63, 166, 176; trade shifts of age of discovery and, 140, 141; types of fuel in, *165;* varieties of timber imported by, 373. *See also* Ireland; Scotland; Wales; *specific British colonies*

Broad Arrow Policy, 213

bronze, 78, 79

Bronze Age, 62

Bruegel, Pieter, 160

bubonic plague, 117

Buddhism, 121

Budowski, Gerardo, 31

buffalo, 29

Buffon, Georges-Louis Leclerc, comte de, 176, 181–82, 252, 253

building construction. *See* housing and building construction

burial-mound cultures, 53

Burma, 61, 330, 334, 346–48, 397

business and capitalism: birth of modernity and, 137–42; corporations and, 234; corrupt political alliances and, 467; critique of quest for profits in, 404; fuelwood trade and, 162–63; lumber industry and, 234, 301–4, 307, 381; penetration of India and, 326–34

Butea frondosa (Dhak) forests, 331

Byrd, William, 28

Byron, George Gordon (Lord), 259

Caeasarius of Prüm, 104

calendars, 89

calligraphy, pine soot for, 121

Cambodia, 61, 347, 468, 476

cameral science, 260–61

Cameroons, 131

Canada: acid rain in, 474; duties on Baltic timber and, 283; equilibrium in timber supply in, 467; income levels in, 231; as neo-European land, 238; railroads in, 242, 243, 336; reforestation in, 475; shipbuilding in, 279; as source of timber, 243, 265–66, 278–80, 282–83, 370

canals. *See specific canals*

Canary Islands, 193, 194, 197, 203. *See also* Atlantic islands

Candolle, Alphonse de, 37

capitalism. *See* business and capitalism

Capper, John, 318, 341–42, 356

Capper Report, 366

carbon emissions, 409–11

Caribbean: end of colonial rule in, 397; European occupation of, 197; forest destruction in, 374–76; fuelwood shortage in, 464; Great Clearing in, 201–2; as periphery, 239; as source of staple goods, 140; as stepping stone on passage to India, 326, 328; as stepping stone to New World expansion, 198; sugar production in, 200–203; timber trade and, 215

Carretera Marginal de la Selva, *436,* 436–37, 444

Carson, Rachel, 412

Cartesian dualism, 143–44

cartography. *See* mapping of forests

Catesby, Mark, 26, 29

Catlin, George, 24

cattle. *See* livestock and ranching

causes of deforestation: acid rain, 474; building construction, 223–24, 275, 317, 355–56; centralized planning apparatus, 391; charcoal production, 167–73; climatic stress, 474; commercial timber production, 213; consumer lifestyles and fast food and, 462; consumption patterns and, 140–42; corruption and, 152; crime prevention, 146; cultural climate and, 129, 134, 204–5, 475; dairying, 315–16, 317; demographic, 91–92, 398–400; early capitalism and, 136; economic efficiency, 166; elites' exploitation of forests, 475;

encouragement of grass growth, 316; in the future, 472–74; ideological, 91, 95–98; indiscriminate burning, 356; iron production, 167–73, 275; local hardship, 334; logging roads and, 469; manufacturing, 265; mining, 350; misconceptions about, 377–80; "multilayered cake" of, after World War II, 400–404; papermaking, 135; pasture development, 461–63; political and economic after World War II, 397–98; population growth, 235, 237–38; potash making, 275; railroads, 244–45, 299, 337–38, 353; refining of natural products, 265, 275; rhetoric versus reality and, 477; road building, 440–42, 469; "settler societies" in temperate lands and, 142; shipbuilding, 71–74, 265, 275, 280; smelting, 71, 75, 77–78, *79,* 80, 300–301, 380; steamboats, 337; sugar production, 197, 198–200; systems model of land use and, *403;* technological, 91, 92–95, 398–400; urbanization and, 67, 74–77; war, 157, 158, 176. *See also* agricultural clearing; fuelwood; livestock and ranching

cedar, 73

Central America: comparison of clearing practices and, 148–49; forest clearing in, 1940–82, *463;* forest destruction in, 374; motives for deforestation in, 433; pasture development in, 461; pre-Columbian land use in, 32; railroads in, 243; shifting cultivation in, 320–321; United States and, 397. *See also* Americas; Latin America; Mesoamerica; New World expansion

Ceylon. *See* Sri Lanka

Chain of Being. *See* Great Chain of Being

Chamaecyparis obtusa (hinoki), 309

charcoal: coal and, 122; coke and, 277; collection of, 122; and iron making, 167–73, 299, 299–301, 362; making of, *168–69;* for mining, 449; for Paris, 164; production of, after World War II, 464–66, *466;* for smelting, 78, 215

Charlemagne, 89, 98, 99

Charles II (England), 188
Chastellux, François-Jean, marquis de, 191, 206–7, 209
Chateaubriand, François-Auguste-Réné de, 259
chena, 320
Cheng Ho, 192
chenopod. See *Chenopodium berlandieri* (chenopod)
Chenopodium berlandieri (chenopod), 53
Chia Ssu-Hsieh, 121
Childe, Gordon, 23
Chile, 348–49
Ch'i Min Yao Shu (Chia Ssu-Hsieh), 121
China: acid rain in, 474; circa AD 1500, *132;* during age of discovery, 192, 216–20; agricultural expansion in, 264; coal use in, 166; comparison of clearing practices and, 148–49; core and periphery and, 131; devastated landscape of, 310–11; diversity of forests in, 120; early agriculture in, 60–61; end of Ice Age in, 4; energy crisis in, 218; European encroachment in, 240; extent of deforestation in, 264; form of government in, 217; fuelwood crisis in, 311; geography of, 218; Han-dynasty agriculture and, 61; as hearth of domestication, 37; hunting reserves in, 220; industrial potential of, 230; intensive land use in, 124; as land of "ponderous unknowns," 117, 119–20; lumber business and, 317; as major timber importer, 467; medieval, 89; during Ming dynasty, 119–21, 217–18, 219–20; population density in, 155; population of, 216, 218, 237–38, 263, 310; products of, 131; during Qing dynasty, 217–18; reforestation in, 475; rice cultivation in, 322; scarcity of information about, 216, 217; substitution of fossil fuel in, 276; during Sung dynasty, 122, *123,* 219; during T'ang dynasty, 121–22; technology of age of discovery and, 131, 134; urbanization and industry in, 122–24; wood in industrialization of, 234
Cholmeley, William, 155
Christianity: as anthropocentric, 148; at-

titudes toward forests and, 146, 147, 148–49; beliefs about God's judgment and, 195; ecclesiastical powers and forest clearing and, 95–98; and environment in medieval Europe, 89, 96; human ascendancy over nature and, 143. *See also* Crusades
chronology, tools for determining, 5–6
Church, Frederic Edwin, 24
Churchill, John, *189*
Churchill, Winston, 240
Cicero, 86, 96, 143
Cistercians, 97, 101
cities and urbanization: in age-of-discovery Europe, 160; agricultural surplus required for, 80; anthracite for heating in, 297; in Asia, 61, 124; as cause of deforestation, 67, 74–77; in classical world, 63, 74–77; fuelwood consumption and, 295–96; fuelwood supply for, 465; intensive land use and, 128; loss of human contact with surroundings and, 360; promenades in, 188; timber supply for, 301; water supply and disease in, 334
Civil War (United States), 280, 286, 336
Clapp, Earle, 366
Clark, Grahame, 34, 41
Clark, Kenneth, 88
Clark-McNary Act of 1924 (United States), 385
classical world (1100 BC–AD 565), 62–86; agriculture in, 63; attitudes toward nature in, 85–86; causes of deforestation during, 67–80; historical periodization and, 62; human ascendancy over nature and, 143; literate society in, 63–64; Mediterranean environment during, 64–67; "other classical world" and, 70–71; soil degradation in, 80–85
Clawson, Marion, 430
clearing in Europe: during age of discovery, 150–90; Baltic timber trade and, 176–81; by Benedictines, 97, 99, 101; for charcoal production, 167–73; Charlemagne and, 98, *100;* by Cistercians, 97, 101; depopulation resulting from, 270; iron making and, 167–73; plundering of trees and,

clearing in Europe: (*continued*)
181–82, *182–85;* preservation of
forests and, 183–86; recolonization
of abandoned lands and, 156; restrictions on, 152; in Russia, 271–72,
275–76; for shipbuilding, 174–81;
three stories of, 266; timber crisis
and, 151–54, 172. *See also specific
countries*
clearing in North America: broadcast
firing and, 26–28; commercial,
284–85; in early colonial times, 147,
148, 204; excessive logging and,
305; hired labor for, 285; landscape
of, 292–95; methods for, 54–55;
methods of, 207–9; newly cleared
land and, *293;* in New York, 289–90,
289–91; partial, 285; as plundering,
303; poem about, 208; process and
extent of, 284–92; rapidity of, 290;
by slaves, 209; stumps and, 305; time
required for, 286, 289; by U.S. state,
287–88; villages and, *56, 57, 58;*
waste and, 305, 307
clearing in United States. *See* clearing in
North America
clearing of forests: in Africa, 35, 36, 324,
377–80; agricultural routines and,
154–55; in ancient literature, 68–69;
annual burning and, 159; "baseline" vegetation and, 325; in Brazil,
443, 448, 449, 453, 454; in Central
America, *463;* in China, 60, 120–21,
122, 219, 310–11; in coastal deltas,
347; comparison of various societies',
148–49; definition of deforestation
and, 424–27; detecting location of,
431–33; disappearance of animals
and, 322, 323–24, 343; distribution
of wealth and, 90; downstream effects
of, 271; as evil, 344; exaggerations of,
270, 477; famines and, 331; financial
incentives for, 442, 444, 447–48;
geography of worldwide, 431–33;
herringbone pattern of, *448, 453,
454, 455, 455;* ignored by officials,
267; in India, 323–24, 328–34, 335,
343–46; industrial, 341–42; inventions to compensate for, 276; in Japan, 220–25, 308–9; labor required

for, *36;* as land improvement, 265;
in Latin America, 348–49; in less-
developed world, 371; making new
land and, 92–93; monasteries and,
97–98; motives for, 432–33; myths
about, 147, 325; Neolithics and,
40–45; pathways of deforestation
and, 424–27; in Philippines, 347–48;
pioneer mentality and, 283–84; as
problem, 405; as redemption, 254;
relative importance of reasons for,
77–78; Rousseau, Jean-Jacques, on,
35; severe consequences of, 475–76;
smoke of burning season and, *453;*
in South America, 462–63; in Sri
Lanka, 340–41, *341;* stumps and,
187, 208, 285, 292–93, 315; in
Thailand, *432;* time required for, 36;
underestimation of, 474; virtue and,
255; for war, 157. *See also* attitudes
about trees and forests; clearing in
Europe; clearing in North America;
documentary evidence; extent and
pace of deforestation
Cleghorn, Hugh, 329, 330, 334
Clements, Frederic, 408
Clementsian climax-equilibrium concept,
361
climate change: annual releases of carbon
and, *410;* deforestation and, 253,
256, 329; forest regrowth and, 379,
407; after Ice Age, 3–4, 6–10; Little
Ice Age and, 151, 160; in medieval
times, 92; Milankovitch hypothesis
and, 4; myths about, 325; rhetoric
versus reality and, 476–77; trace
gases and, 409–11
climax theory, 377–78
clock, invention of, 135–36
Clovis people, 18
coal and coal industry: in age-of-discovery
Europe, 164–66; Ballinger-Pinchot
affair and, 364; in Britain, 76, 153,
234; as charcoal substitute, 122, 277;
in China, 122; coke for smelting and,
277; extent of use of, 265; in France,
153, 234, 268, 269; in Germany,
154; heating value of, 166; Industrial
Revolution and, 166; production
volumes and, 165–66; proportion of

energy from, 235; quantity consumed, 234; for steam engines, 242; in United States, *236*; versus wood, 296–97

coffee and coffee trade: blight in, 340; in Brazil, 351–53, *354, 374, 375,* 445–46; as "green gold," 352; India and, 340; soil erosion and, 353; Southeast Asia and, 347; "virgin" forest and, 353, 376

coke, 277

Colbert, Jean Baptiste, 176, 185

cold war politics, 439, 440

Cole, Thomas, 24

Colman, Henry, 266, 267

Colombia: agricultural development east of Andes in, 434–37; Brazil and, 444; export trade and, 348–49; grasslands in, 33, 34; remaining forest of, 376

colonization: access to raw materials and, 239; in Amazon basin, 437, 440, 444, 445–48; arms gap and, 240; disease and, 239–40; during Industrial Revolution, 238–40; military control and, 240; types of territorial control and, 238–39; of western European forests, 97–101, 104–6, 116. *See also* imperialism

Columbus, Christopher, 129, 195, 253

Columella, 69

commerce. *See* trade

commons, the, 406

communication technology, 240–41

communism: cold war politics and, 440; Soviet lumber industry and, 381, 388, 390–91

composition and range of forest: in age-of-discovery Europe, 150, 151; in Australia, 311–12, 315; in Balkan region, 65; in Brazil, 198, 376–77; in Britain, 276; in Caribbean, 200; in China, 310; near cities, 465; in India, 331, *332, 333,* 339, *345;* Little Ice Age and, 151; in Mediterranean region, 64–65, 67; in North America, 30; in Russia, 272, 388; selective logging and, 468–69; soil quality and, 207; in Southeast Asia, 346–47; in Soviet Union, 391; in Sweden, 392–93; in tropical world, 371, 429; in United States, *367, 368,* 368–69, 382–83;

worldwide, 369–70, 381, 405, *419,* 423–24, 425

Condorcet, Marie-Jean-Antoine-Nicolas de Caritat, marquis de, 251

Confucianism, 121, 311

conservation movement: biodiversity and, 412; efficiency versus aesthetics and, 366; first stirrings of, 258; "five Ds" of deforestation and, 366; at turn of twentieth century, 360, 363–66; during World War I, 369

Constantinople, 131, 160

Constantinou, G., 78

consumption: during age of discovery, 140–42; iron industry and, 171; levels of, 231, 235, 473–74; patterns of, 140–42; production separated from, 133, 137; shipping improvements and, 243–44; sustainability and, 473–74; transportation and, 241–42. *See also* quantity of timber

Cook, James, 19

Cook, Orator Fuller, 320

Cooper, James Fenimore, 24

Cooper, William, 147

Copeland Report, 385, 387–88

Copernicus, 143

copper, 78, 79

coppicing, 170, 172–73, *173,* 184, 466

core and periphery: in 1900, 359; circa AD 1775, *133;* changing terminology for, 227; colonization and, 239; early European expansion and, 128, 131–34; "external areas" versus periphery, 140; post–World War II development aims and, 439. *See also* developed world; less developed world

Corner, Eldred J. H., 414

Corylus (hazel), 6, 8, 21, 23

Costa Rica, 463, *463*

Côte d'Ivoire, 323, 379, 469

cotton. *See* textiles and textile industry

creation, scientists' continued belief in, 251

cremation, 76

Crete, 65, 82, 112

Crèvecoeur, J. Hector St. John de, 147

Crist, Raymond, 434

Critias (Plato), 81

Crosby, Alfred, 194

Crusades, 112–13, 131, 134

Cryptomeria japonica (sugi), 309

Cuba, *327*, 349, 440

Cucurbita pepo (squash), 10, 53

cult of trees, 188, *189*

cut-and-get-out forest exploitation: American pioneers and, 283–84, 301, 305; in Sweden, 392

cutover areas, 306–8

Cyprus: Byzantine reconquest of, 112; forest clearing in, 68; forest composition in, 65; mining and smelting in, 78, *79;* Muslim expansion and, 111; shipbuilding and, 73; timber reserves in, 80

da Gama, Vasco, 131

dairying, 42, 315–16

Dalhousie (Lord), 336

Darby, Abraham, 277

Darby, Clifford, 85

Darwin, Charles, 412

Dean, Warren, 439

déboisement, 269–71

Declaration on the Human Environment, 416

Deere, John, 286

deer parks, 188

Defebaugh, James, 381

defecation process, 38

Defoe, Daniel, 166, 196, 259

deforestation. *See* clearing of forests

degradation, soil. *See* soil fertility and degradation

De historica plantarum (Theophrastus), 65

deism, attitudes toward forests and, 259

Demerara greenheart. See *Ocatea rodiaei*

Denevan, William M.: on imminent demise of Amazon rain forest, 418, 433; on pre-Columbian North American population, 59; on virgin forest myth, 12, 25, 34

Denmark, 41, 176, 178

deodar, 338

Descartes, René, 143–44

Des époques de la nature (Leclerc), 253

desertification, 378

De Soto, Hernando, expedition, 58

developed world, 230, 231. *See also* core and periphery; less developed world

Dhak (*Butea frondosa*) forests. See *Butea frondosa* (Dhak) forests

diamonds, 350

Dias, Bartholomew, 131

Dickinson, W. R., 35

Dionysus of Syracuse, 73

Discourse on Method (Descartes), 143

discovery, age of. *See* age of discovery

disease and health: bubonic plague and, 117; China's fuelwood crisis and, 311; cold weather and, 162–63; colonization and, 239; deforestation as cause of death and, 333–34; New World expansion and, 194; population growth and, 92; technological solutions and, 239–40; trans-Andean migration and, 437; water supply and, 334; Western medical technology and, 398

distribution of wealth. *See* wealth, distribution of

Dobyns, Henry, 59

documentary evidence: of Baltic timber trade, 281; of clearing in Africa, 377; of clearing in Australia, 312, 314; of clearing in early twentieth century, 372–73; of clearing in India, 328; of clearing in medieval world, 87–88; of clearing in North America, 205, 215; dark age in history and geography of deforestation and, 373; extent and pace of deforestation and, 285–86

Domesday Survey (1086), *102*

domestication: hearths of, 37, 416; multiple pathways of, 38–40

dominion, human. *See* human ascendancy over nature

Douglas fir. See *Pseudotsuga menziesii* (Douglas fir)

dredging of harbors, 82

droughts: deforestation as cause of, 333; dust bowl and, 361, 408; El Niño and, 469; in India, 331; reforestation efforts and, 407

dualism, Cartesian. *See* Cartesian dualism

dust bowl (United States), 361, 408

Dutch East India Company, 139

Dutch West India Company, 139

Dwight, Timothy, 29

dyewoods, 204

Eardley-Wilmott, Sainthill, 335
East Africa, 192, 353. *See also* Africa; *specific countries*
East India Company (EIC), 139, 328–31, 333–34, 336
eastern white pine. See *Pinus* (pine), *P. strobus* (eastern white pine)
ebony, 323
Eckholm, Erik, 464
ecofascism, 478
École des Eaux-et-Forêts, 270
ecology: Clementsian climax-equilibrium concept and, 361; early study of, 65; ecological imperialism and, 192–96, 197; equilibrium model of, 408–9
economic theory, deforestation after World War II and, 400–402
Ecuador, 317, 348–49, 434–37, 461
Egleston, Nathaniel, 299
Egypt, 73, 78, 81, 111, 240
Ehrlich, Anne, 399, 419
Ehrlich, Paul, 399, 419, 420
EIC (East India Company). *See* East India Company (EIC)
Eighth World Forestry Congress, 428
Elba, Isla, 78
Eliot, T. S., 420
Elizabeth I (England), 152
elm. See *Ulmus* (elm)
El Niño, 469
Elton, Charles, 412
emancipation: of the "common man," 96; of serfs, 275, 388; of slaves, 353
Emerson, Ralph Waldo, 260
Emile (Rousseau), 259
English Muscovy Company, 139
Enlightenment: attitudes toward forests and nature during, 251–54; forest regulation and, 260; preservation of forests during, 255–60; Scottish, 329
Enquiry into Plants, The (Theophrastus), 65
environmentalism: causes of deforestation under World War II and, 401–2; environmental crisis fatigue and, 478; growing concern after World War II and, 404; social benefits of forest preservation and, 405–6; special interests' exploitation of, 478
Epoch of Man, 252–55, 257

equilibrium model of ecology, 408–9
Eratosthenes, 68
erect knotweed. See *Polygonum erectum* (erect knotweed)
Erie Canal, 248, 296
erosion: in China, 219, 220, 311; in classical world, 65, 74, 81, 82, 84–85; coffee cultivation and, 353; in colonial Brazil, 199; floods and, 82; forest science on, 408; in France, 270; Great Clearing in Caribbean and, 201–2; in India, 337; Maya settlement and, *52;* rates of, 84; timber stripping and, 48; upland torrents and, 271; in Venice, *182–85*
Essay on Population (Malthus), 251
Estonia, 105
ethnography, 251
eucalypt forests, 311, 315, 316, 376
Europe: acreage-per-person calculations for, 59; circa AD 1500, *132;* circa AD 1775, *133;* agricultural expansion in, 264; agricultural revolution of Middle Ages and, 89–90; assimilation of technology by, 134–35; attitudes about forests in, 146; Christianity and environment in, 89; climatic stress to forests in, 474; colonization and, 238–40; destructiveness of global expansion of, 360–61; early agriculture in, *41;* early human impact in, 10; equilibrium in timber supply in, 467; "European Miracle" and, 127; extent of deforestation in, 264; extent of expansion of, 238; foragers and fire in, 21–23; forest cover of, *107,* 266; forests in folklore of, 146; geography of timber trade in, *281,* 281–82; grain trade in, 157; heating methods in, 164; human ascendancy over nature and, 144–45; after Ice Age, 3, 4, 6–8; internal and external frontiers of, 93, 95; iron industry in, 167–73, *171;* as major timber importer, 467; migration and, 237; Neolithic agriculture in, 43, 45; New World expansion of, 191–216; from periphery to core, 131–34; "Pleistocene overkill" in, 17, 18; population of, 151, 154, 237; railroads in, 242,

Europe: (*continued*)
243; reforestation in, 371; rise of state
system in, 137; sources of timber for,
265; standard of living in, 140; steam
power adoption in, 232–33; steel
industry in, 122; sustainable forestry
in, 471; timber crisis in, 172; use of
spices in, 140; vegetation cover of,
10,000–4,000 BP, 7

Evans, Estyn, 36

Evelyn, John: industry's effect on forest,
172; *Silva; or, A Discourse of Forest
Trees* by, 155, 185–187; on timber
shortage, 176; on "touchy humour"
of Yankees, 214

extent and pace of deforestation: in
Africa, 377; in age-of-discovery
Europe, 158, 160, 172–73; alarm
about, 150, 364, 366, 367, 380;
in Argentina, 377; in Asia, 380; in
Australia, 314, 316; in Brazil after
World War II, 350–53, *355,* 355–56,
376–77, 452–57, *458;* in Brazil of
colonial period, 198–99; in Britain,
216; in Canada, 284; in Caribbean,
201; in China, 217; in classical world,
84–85; in colonial North America,
208, 209, 216; documentary evidence
of, 285–86; in early medieval Europe,
98–101; forest balance sheet and,
382–85; forest fires and, 385; in
France, 266, 267; frontier versus
nonfrontier forests and, 477–78; for
fuelwood, 376, 466; future prospects
for, 471–78; during *grands défrichements, les,* 101–9; in Great Lakes
states (United States), 305; in India,
330–31, *333,* 335, 338–40; in Indonesia, 322, 459; in Latin America,
348, 376; in Madagascar, 325; in
Malaysia, 459, *460;* measurement of,
422–30, 452–53, 469; in Mediterranean world, *110,* 111–13; in New
Zealand, 317; in nineteenth-century
Europe, 266; in Paraguay, 458; in
Philippines, 347–48; population
levels and, 235; in Russia, 109, 111,
158, 272, *273, 274;* sawnwood versus
roundwood and, 466–67; in South
(United States), 307–8; in South Asia,

335; in Southeast Asia, 335, 347,
460–61; in Soviet Union, 388, 391;
in Sweden, 392, *393;* in temperate versus tropical world, 318–19,
372, 424; in temperate world, 263,
264, 265; in Thailand, 467–68; in
tropical world, 324, 373, 429, 469;
in United States, 284–92, *287–88,
289–91,* 294–95, 362, 366, 382; in
West Africa, 469; after World War
II, 395–96; worldwide in twentieth
century, 369–70, 395–96, *419, 427,*
427–428; worldwide throughout history, 356, 475

*Extinction: The Causes and Consequences
of the Disappearance of Species* (Ehrlich and Ehrlich), 419

extinction of animals, 18, 19, 21, 326

Fagus (beech), 5–6

famines: civil unrest and, 331; deforestation as cause of, 333; in India, 331,
343; in Ireland, 331; of timber, 359,
360, 362–71

FAO. *See* Food and Agricultural Organization (FAO)

farming. *See* agriculture

Fearnside, Philip M., 431, 454, 456

Federal Land Development Agency
(FELDA). *See* FELDA (Federal Land
Development Agency)

Federov, A., 415

FELDA (Federal Land Development
Agency), 459

fencing, in backwoods North America,
210–11

Fernow, Bernhard, 262

Fight for Conservation, The (Pinchot),
364

Fighting Temeraire, The (Turner), 279,
280

Fiji, 31

Finland, 158, 283, 371

fir (*Abies*). See *Abies* (fir)

fire: broadcast firing and, 26–28; to clear
vegetation, *16;* ecological adaptation
and, 13–14; as Faustian bargain,
13; foragers and, 12–34; before Ice
Age, 17–21; in Japan, 224; for North
American forest modification, 26–30;

in slash debris, 307; uses of by early hominids, 14–17, *15. See also* forest fires; shifting cultivation

firewood. *See* fuelwood

First Dutch War (1652), 176

First Punic War, 72

Fisher, Peter, 284

flint, 43, *44, 45*

flooding, 53, 82

folklore, attitudes about forests in, 146

Fomes fomentarius (tree fungus), 23

Food and Agricultural Organization (FAO): conservation of genetic resources and, 416; definition of forest by, 423, 424; estimate of worldwide deforestation rates by, 428, 430; five-yearly reports of, 472; on future demand for wood products, 473–74; inventory of forest resources and, 405, 418; questionable estimates in *Yearbooks* of, 424

food supply: foods conducive to gathering and, 30; in India, 336–37; rising population and, 416; systems of acquiring, *39*

foraging: concurrent with crop domestication, 55; fire and, 12–34; for fuel, 55; transition to agriculture and, 38–40

Forbes, Henry, 322, 405

Forbes, Reginald, 307

Forest Act of 1865 (India), 344

Forest Charter (1217), 116

forest fires: in Brazil, 350–51; ecosystem degradation and, 469; excessive logging and, 305; fire control programs and, 385; and reforestation in United States, 366; shifting cultivation and, 320–21, 323. *See also* fire; *specific forest fires*

forest management: cameral science and, 260–61; in coniferous forests, 371; coppicing and, 172–73, 184; education for, 186; forest manuals and, 186; in France, 270–71; fuelwood prices and, 268–69; in Germany, 266; growth versus consumption and, 370; in India, 330, 331–34, 344; iron industry and, 172; in Madagascar, 325; Mauritius as model for, 328; for maximum wood production, 260,

261–262; misconceptions of shifting cultivation and, 378; Ordinance of Waters and Forests (France, 1669) and, 185, 186; *Principles of Forest-Economy* (Moser) and, 261; rainfall and forests and, 407; in Soviet Union, 391; "standard trees" and, 261; state forests and, 183–84; sustainability and, 471; *The Tropical Forestry Action Plan,* and, 430; U.S. Division of Forestry and, 363–64; U.S. laws enabling, 363

Forest Management Act of 1897 (United States), 363

Forest Reserve Act of 1891 (United States), 363

Forest Resources of the World, The (Zon and Sparhawk), 367–69, 374

forestry. *See* forest management; forest science

Forestry Commission (Britain), 262

forests: in Benin, 379; biography of, 5–6; commercial uses of, 213–16; conflict and complexity in, 113–18; cult of trees and, 188, *189;* as defensive barriers, 122; definition of, 423; density of, in North America, 195, 204; documentary evidence of, 87–88; for emergency supplies for farmers, 335; in folklore, 146; four primary uses of, 464; as global resource, 371; grassland-forest edge and, 324, 350, 356; as haven for crime and criminals, 146; as haven of those willing to work, 437; human domination of, 252–55; human-made, 271; indigenous use of, in tropical world, 319–26; as land reserved for king, 87; literature of 1990s on, 472; managed versus nonmanaged, 394; as "mantle of the poor," 90, 450, 472; misconceptions about history of, 379–80; net change in worldwide, 372; open versus closed, 423, 424, 425; plundering of, *182–85;* reverence for, 91; rhetoric about deforestation and, 379–80; as safety valve for agricultural economies, 329; scrubland and, 316; state ownership of, 63; state protection of, 346; in temperate versus tropical

forests: (*continued*)
world, 394; theaters of deforestation and, 128; trees as crop and, 181, 184; as unitary and interdependent, 405; uses of, in backwoods North America, 209–12; as valued economically and culturally, 116; virgin forest myth and, 24–25, 31, 54, 195; weather protection and, 408; as wild and hostile, 145–46; woodlands versus, 423; yield of, 170, 269. *See also* attitudes about trees and forests; causes of deforestation; clearing of forests; composition and range of forest; extent and pace of deforestation; forest fires; forest management; forest science; mapping of forests; methods of clearing; preservation of forests; virgin forest

"Forests and Water in the Light of Scientific Investigation" (Zon), 407

forest science: climax theory and, 377–78; in Enlightenment-era Germany, 261–62; equilibrium model of ecology and, 408–9; misconceptions of shifting cultivation in, 378–79; rainfall and, 406–7; study of, 251–52; surveys and, 334; sustained yield and, 261; Theophrastus as father of, 69

fossil fuel, 276, *410*, 464–65. *See also specific fuels*

Foweraker, Joe, 450

France: agricultural clearing in, 266–67; band saw invention and, 232; bubonic plague in, 117; during classical era, 70; colonization and, 238; crop rotation in, 95; *déboisement* in uplands of, 269–71; descriptions of deforestation in, 270; energy crisis in, 269; estates of, 156; flint of, 43; food riots in, 267; forest cover of, 150, 266, 271; forest law of, 186; forest preservation efforts in, 116; French Revolution and, 251, 266; fuelwood prices in, *153*, 153, 269; during *grands défrichements, les,* 101, *103,* 104, 106; heating methods in, 164; homegrown lumber in, 176; Hundred Years War (1337–1453) and, 117; after Ice Age, 7; imperialist miscon-

ceptions of Africa and, 378; income levels in, 229; India and, 279; industrial potential of, 230; internal frontier of Europe and, 92; iron industry of, 267–69, *268;* land usage rights in, 112–13, 116; Little Ice Age famine in, 151; medieval,·89; Ordinance of Waters and Forests (1669) in, 176; plow's appearance in, 94; population of, 267, 269; railroads in, 243; during Second Empire (1852–70), 270–71; shipbuilding in, 176; smelting with coke in, 277; tension over forest destruction in, 266; timber crisis in, 151, 152–53; timber for shipbuilding and, 178; timber shortages in, 156, 163, 176; travelers and forests of, 146

Franciscans, 349

François I (France), 156

Franklin, Benjamin, 147, 212, 296

Fraxinus excelsior (ash), 8, 21

Freneau, Philip, 259

Friedrich, Ernst, 360

Frondist revolts, 156

fruit trees, 55

fuel, types of, in United States, *298. See also specific fuels*

fuelwood: in age-of-discovery Europe, 156, 160, 162–67; in backwoods North America, 212; in Brazil, 376; for brick making, 356; in China, 122, 218, 311; in classical world, 71, 74, 75, 76–77; coal versus, 296–97; collection of, *161;* as commercial product, 213; competition for, *268;* consumption levels of, 269, 272, 385; distribution of, 269; fossil fuels as substitute for, 464–65; future demand for, 472, 473; gathering of, 212, 221, 465; global deficits of, *464;* growing demand for, 465; in India, 342; for iron production, 267–69, 356; for mining, 449–50; motives for deforestation and, 433; population and, 373; prices for, 152–53, *153,* 163, 212, 268–69; production of, after World War II, 464–66, *466;* proportion of energy from, 235, 464, 465; proportion of income for, 160, 162, 465; proportion of wood used

as, 466–67; railroads and, 297, 338; retailing of, 465; in Russia, 272; shortages of, 163, 164, 212, 260; for smelting, 300–301; for steamboats, 295; for sugar production, 199–200; trade for, 162–63; in United States, 234–35, 295–97, 298
Fuller, Andrew, 362
Funnel Beaker Culture, 40, 43

Galileo, 143
genetic research, 416
Geographical Information Systems (GIS), 428
Gerald of Barri, 97
Germany: annual timber consumption in, 160; bubonic plague in, 117; during classical era, 70, 71; forest cover of, 266; forest destruction during World War II and, 388; forest management in, 266; forest science in, 260–62; during grands défrichements, les, 101, 104–5, 106; heating methods in, 164; horse-drawn spiked harrow in, 94; income levels in, 229; industry in, 229, 230; internal frontier of Europe and, 92–93; during Little Ice Age, 151; plow's appearance in, 94; preservation of forests in, 116, 186; railroads in, 243, 336; smelting with coke in, 277; as source of timber, 180; supply of masts and, 214; timber shortages in, 151, 152, 154, 156, 163
Ghana, 323, 379, 380
Gibbon, Edward, 80
Gibson, Alexander, 329, 331–33
Gibson-Blane report, 333
Gill, Thomas, 374–76, 405, 433, 454
Gilpin, William, 258
girdling. See methods of clearing
GIS. See Geographical Information Systems (GIS)
Glacken, Clarence, 87, 89, 114, 271
Global 2000, 428
globalization: communication and, 244; definition of modernity and, 137; Industrial Revolution and, 227; money and finance and, 138
Globular Amphora period (3400–2800 BC), 44

Gmelina arborea, 449
Godwin, William, 251
gold, 350
Golenishchev-Kutuzov (Russian landowner), 272
Golson, Jack, 18
Gómez-Pompa, Arturo, 417–18, 420
Goulart, João, 440
government, future forest preservation and, 475–76
Governors' Conference (United States, 1907), 364
Grainger, Alan, 425
Grand Canal, 122
Grande Carajás Project, 449–50
grands défrichements, les, 87, 88, 91, 101–9
Grant, Anne McVickar, 215
grass, European. See Poa pratensis (European grass)
grasslands: in Andean region, 32–34, 33; creation of, 28–30, 33, 324; forest edge and, 324, 350, 356; of Madagascar, 325; shifting cultivation and, 320; of Southeast Asia, 325; in temperate versus tropical world, 318, 319
Graves, Henry, 366
Gray, Asa, 29
grazing. See livestock and ranching
Great Chain of Being, 142–43
Great Fire of 1666 (London), 179
Great Lakes states (United States): abandonment of fields in, 387; clearing in, 286; cutover areas of, 306; forest encroachment in, 30; forest fires in, 305; frontier life in, 254; geographical shift of lumber production and, 303; iron industry in, 300; land acquisition in, 207; lumber production in, 233, 234, 303, 304–5; Native American land use in, 56; railroads in, 249, 299; as source of timber, 248, 294; timber plundering in, 303; transport of timber in, 247, 248; waste land in, 305
Great Plains states (United States), 249, 408
Great Reclamation, 104
Great Wall, 122

Greece: agriculture's arrival in, 40; attitudes about nature in, 85–86; comparison of clearing practices and, 148–49; forest composition in, 65; forests in folklore of, 146; harsh natural environment of, 82; human power over nature in, 64; imperial expansion of, 63; Neolithic age and, 62; river basins in, 82; sea power and, 72; smelting in, 78, 79; soil degradation in, 81, 82

Greeley, William: forest maps of, *367, 368, 382,* 478; Forest Service and, 366–67; revision of calculations by, 383, 385

greenhouse effect, 409–11

Greenland, 130

Green Legend, 49

Green Revolution, 416

Gregg, Susan, 45, *46*

Guadeloupe, 201

guaicum, 130

Guatemala, 32, 49

Guerre des Demoiselles, 271

Guinea, 131, *379*

Guppy, Nicholas, 403–4, 459

Gutenberg, Johannes, 135

Guyot, Arnold, 147, 263, 284

Haeckel, Ernst, 361

Hailey, A. M., 377

Hale, Matthew, 144

Hall, Basil, 292–93, 296

Hall, James, 301

Hammersley, George, 170, 171, 277

"Hansel and Gretel," 146

Harlan, Jack, 416

Harrison, R. P., 471

Harrison, Thomas, 136

Harrison, William, 162–63

harrow, spiked, 94

Hawaii, 18, 317

Hawkins, Benjamin, 58

hazel. See *Corylus* (hazel)

Headrick, Daniel, 239

health. See disease and health

heating, 76, 164, 296–97. See also fuelwood

Heidenreich, Conrad, 59

Helianthus annus (sunflower), 10, 53

Helena, Saint, 326, 328

Hellenistic period. See classical world (1100 BC–AD 565)

Henry III (England), 116

Henry the Navigator, 131

Heritiera fomes (kanazo), 342, 346–47

Heyne, Benjamin, 323–24

Hibbard, Benjamin, 407

hickory, 30

Hideyoshi, 222

Higginson, Francis, 28

Higounet, Charles, 87

hinoki. See *Chamaecyparis obtusa (hinoki)*

Histoire naturelle générale et particulière (Leclerc), 252–53

History of the Decline and Fall of the Roman Empire (Gibbon), 80

History of the Holland Purchase of Western New York (Turner), 289–90

Hodgson, Adam, 28, 263, 290, 294

Holland: at center of global timber trade, 276; as importer of timber, 157; population density in, 155; shipbuilding in, 174; soil fertility in, 81; trade shifts of age of discovery and, 141

Holocene epoch, 3, 18

Homer, 67

Homestead Act (United States), 444

Homo erectus, fire and, 17

Honduras, 51, 279, *327*

Hong Kong, 467

Hopkins, Stephen, 56

Hordeum pusillum (little barley), 53

horses, 43, 94

Houghton, John, 147

housing and building construction: in backwoods North America, 211; in Britain, 280–84; in classical world, 75; in the future, 473; in Japan, 221; Neolithic, 42; in pre-Columbian North America, 54; quantity of timber for, 167; in Russia, 160

Hudson River painters, 24

human ascendancy over nature, 142–49, 252–53, 257, 294

human rights, 116, 468, 478

Humboldt, Alexander von, 329

Hundred Years War (1337–1453), 117

Hungary, 104

hunting, 114, *115*, 116
Hussite Wars (1419–36), 117
Hyacum, 130
hydroelectricity, 233, *236*

IBP. *See* International Biological Programme (IBP)
Ice Age, 3, *3–5*, 6–10, 410. *See also* Little Ice Age
Iceland, 6, 129–30
Illinois-Michigan Canal, 294–95
imparkation, 156
imperialism: Andean region and, 434; colonial consolidation of India and, 334–46; ecological, 192–96; exchange of raw materials for manufactured goods and, 336; and knowledge of forest in Africa, 377; land use before, 324; military demands on forests and, 167; paradox of forest management and, 346; plantation monoculture and, 414; population collapse and, 194; resistance to, 194; resistance to reforestation and, 476, *477;* shifting agriculture and, 321; timber production and, 324; after World War II, 397
Inca empire, *132*
INCRA (National Institute for Colonization and Agrarian Reform), 445
India: acreage under cultivation in, 337; circa AD 1500, *132;* during age of discovery, 192; animals of, 323–24; capitalist penetration of, 1750–1850, 326–34; Cheng Ho's explorations and, 192; clearing, rainfall, famine, and health in, 330–34; colonial consolidation of, 1850–1920, 334–46; colonial-era elite of, 328–29; control of forests in, 323; core and periphery and, 131–32; drought in, 331; end of British rule in, 397; European imperialism and, 321; famines in, 331, 343; Forest Conservation Department in, 334; forest management in, 328, 343–46; Forestry Department in, 476; forest science in, 262; forests near cities in, 465; gunboats on rivers of, 240; hearths of domestication in, 37; industrial potential of, 230; land policy in, 323–24, 328–29, 333–35, 340, 342–46; motives for deforestation in, 433; Mutiny of 1857 in, 336; paradox of forest management in, 346; peasant cultivation in, 338–40; plantations and commercial farming in, 340–43; population of, 328, 335, 339; preservation efforts in, 329, 331–33, 343–44; railroads in, 242, 243, 336–38, 339; rainfall and forests in, 406; reforestation in, 475; reserved and leased forests in, *345;* restrictions on access to forest in, 406; shifting agriculture in, 320; as source of timber, 279; state control of forests in, 323; stepping stones on passage to, 326; sustainable forestry in, 471; wood in industrialization of, 234
indigenous use of tropical forest: appreciation of biodiversity and, 420; complexity of, 323; European misconceptions of, 319, 324–25, 377–78; forced removal and exclusion of peasants and, 376, 378; grazing and burning and, 324–26; noble savage myth and, 319; permanent agriculture and, 322–24; shifting agriculture and, 320–21; sustainability of, 420
indigo cultivation, 347
Indonesia: agricultural development programs in, 458–59; colonial land policy in, 347; early agriculture in, 61; elephants in, 322; end of Dutch rule in, 397; export production in, 380–81, 467; forest fires in, 469; motives for deforestation in, 433; overexploitation of forests in, 467, 468; planned settlement schemes in, 397, 459; reforestation in, 475; rice cultivation in, 322; shifting cultivation in, 320; spice cultivation in, 322
industrialization: in China, 122, *123;* colonization and, 239; industrial logging and, *248;* loss of human contact with surroundings and, 360; potential of various countries for, 230. *See also* Industrial Revolution

Industrial Revolution: attitudes about nature during, 226; colonization during, 238–40; decline of manufacturing in less developed world and, 229; as driving force of vegetation change, 227–35; income and consumption and, 229, 231; mechanization and motive power and, 231–35; pace and location of, 229; population and migration during, 235–38; reasons for beginning of, 228–29; technology and, 227; transition to coal and, 166; transportation and communication during, 240–51. *See also* industrialization

inequality. *See* wealth, distribution of

Innes (palynologist), 22

Intergovernmental Panel on Climate Change, 409–10

International Biological Programme (IBP), 416

International Board of Plant Genetic Resources, 416

International Council of the Union of Scientists, 416

Ireland, 23, 141, 331

iron and iron industry: in Brazil, 356; charcoal and, 299–301; in China, 119, *123;* in classical world, 78; closure of ironworks and, 171–72; coke for smelting and, 277; consumption levels and, 171; in Europe during age of discovery, 167–73, *171;* forest management and, 172, 184; in France, 163–64, 267–69, *268;* fuelwood and, 376; Industrial Revolution and, 229; in North America during colonial period, 215; prices of fuel products and, 277; replacement of copper and bronze by, 63; shipbuilding and, 279; smelting of, *79;* technology of production of, 169; types of furnaces and, 169; U.S. production volume and, 362; in West Africa, 380; wood consumption of, 277, 392

ironwood, 346

Ishikawa family, 221

Italy: during classical era, 71, 72, 73; early capitalism and, 137; forest composition in, 65; after Ice Age, 8; industrial

potential of, 230; internal frontier of Europe and, 92; railroads in, 243; smelting in, 78, *79;* timber shortages in, 163; tree crops of, 68

Iva annua (sumpweed or marshelder), 53

Iversen, Johannes, 21–22, 41

Jackson, Andrew, 255

Jamaica, 200, 201, 203

James I (England), 152

Janzen, Daniel, 415

Japan: during age of discovery, 192; building construction in, 221–23; as densely forested, 220–25; early agriculture in, 60–61; emigrants to Brazil from, 377; end of Ice Age in, 3; equilibrium in timber supply in, 467; erosion control in, 309–10; excessive clearing in, 308–9; forest destruction during World War II and, 388; forest exploitation in, *223;* as green archipelago, 309; industrial potential of, 230; Industrial Revolution in, 229; as major timber importer, 467; medieval, 89; population of, 221, 237, 310; preservation of forests in, 309–10; railroads in, 243; reforestation in, 475; urban fires in, 223–24; war in, 221–22; after World War II, 397

Jarman, H. N., 41

Jeejeebhoy, Jamsedjee, 279

Jefferson, Thomas, 208

Jerome, 96

Johnson, Edward, 28

Johnston, Robert, 282

Jones, Eric, 127, 166

Juglans (walnut), 10

Kalimantan fires, 469

Kamarov, Boris, 390

kanazo. See *Heritiera fomes (kanazo)*

Kellenbenz, Hermann, 170, 171

Kepler, Johannes, 143

Kern, M. G., 299

Khmer Rouge, 468

Kitts, Saint, 201

Korea, 61, 475

Kroeber, Alfred, 59

Kumazawa Banzan, 224

kumri: clearing practices and, 320, 323, 330, 333, 343–44; condemnation of, 334
Kyoto Treaty, 477

labor, 53, 96
Lagenaria siceraria (bottle gourd), 10
lalang (*Imperata* grass), 325
Lamberville, Jean de, 58
land bridges, 3
land cover: global transformation of, *228;* in tropical world, 373
Landes, David, 238
"Land Ethic," 361
landnam theory, 41, 42
land policy and land rights: in Benin, 380; in Brazil, 349–52, 356, 439–48, 450–51; in British India, 323–24, 328–29, 333–35, 340, 342–46, 380; of Charlemagne, 98–99; in China, 218; codification of usage rights and, 113–14, 116; corrupt political alliances and, 467; customary rights in India and, 344, 346; deforestation after World War II and, 401–2; evictions and, 114; exclusive land rights in Africa and, 380; *firebote* and, 113–14; forest regulation and, 260–62; freeholds and, 68; during *grands défrichements, les,* 101, 104; Hinduism and, 323; in Japan, 222, 309; land acquisition in colonial North America and, 207; log drives and, 246–47; in medieval world, 114; pasture development and, 461; population growth and, 114; reforestation and, 385, 407; resettlement schemes and, 397, 459–60, 461; sugar production and, 200; in Sweden, 392–93; trans-Andean migration and, 434–37; White Pine Act (Britain) and, 213–14. *See also* land use
land rights. *See* land policy and land rights
LANDSAT images, 312, 314, 453, 456
landscape change: from forested to "cultural" landscape, 99; siltation and, *83*
land use: changes of, in India, 337; complexity of, in tropical world, 323; crop rotation and, 94–95; extensive versus intensive, 124, 128, 343; land

improvement and, *265;* in Philippines, 347–48; rice cultivation and, 322; spice cultivation and, 322; sugar cultivation and, 199. *See also* land policy and land rights; shifting cultivation
Last Frontier Forests, The, 477–78
latifundia, 81, 86, 349–50
Latin America: crops grown in, 320; extent and pace of clearing in, 348; forest area and deforestation in, 1980 and 1990, 429; forested area of, 425; global timber trade and, 469; grasslands of, 324; after Ice Age, 4, 9–10; independence in, 239; land cover change in, 319, 373; migration to, 237; motives for deforestation in, 433; population of, 237, 400; railroads in, 242–43; United States and, 397. *See also* South America
Latrobe, Benjamin, 209
Laurentide Ice Sheet, 8
Law of Beaumont (1182), 112
Law of Lorris (1108–37), 113
Lebanon, 65
Leclerc, Georges-Louis (comte de Buffon). *See* Buffon, Georges-Louis Leclerc, comte de
Leopold, Aldo, 361, 412
less developed world, 230. *See also* core and periphery; developed world
Lewis, A. R., 92
Liberia, 323, 379
Library of Congress, 421
lignari, 77
Ligon, Richard, 201
lime. *See Tilia* (lime)
Linearbandkeramik. See Linear Pottery Culture
Linear Pottery Culture, 40
Lithuania, 178
little barley. *See Hordeum pusillum* (little barley)
Little Ice Age, 151, 160
"Little Red Riding Hood," 146
livestock and ranching: in Andean Amazon, 437; animal power for plowing and, 43; in backwoods North America, 209–10; in Brazil, 200, 350–51, 356, 442, 445, 447–48, *449;* in Central America, 461–63; in

livestock and ranching: (*continued*)
   classical world, 69, 71; during clearing, 290; clearing for pasture and,
   155, 158; creation of *campo cerrado*
   and, 326; in cutover areas, 275; ecological imperialism and, 195–96; erosion and, 48; grazing in woodlots by,
   294; grazing prohibitions and, 186;
   in India, 323; medieval agriculture
   and, 94; motives for deforestation
   and, 433; Neolithic agriculture and,
   42–43; New Zealand dairy farms
   and, 317; oxen on nearly cleared
   farms, 292–93; pasture development
   and, 461–63; soil fertility and, 69;
   swine feeding in forest, *113;* transhumance and, 69–70
Livy, 69
loblolly pine. See *Pinus* (pine), *P. taeda*
   (loblolly pine)
Locke, John, 146
loess, 42–43
log drives, 245–47, *247,* 249, 303, *304.*
   See also log jams; transport of timber
logging, commercial: American pioneers
   and, 284–85, 295, 301; as cause
   of deforestation, 213; motives for
   deforestation and, 433; selective, 425,
   468–69; in Southeast Asia, 380; in
   "third world," 398; in United States,
   301–8. *See also* log drives; log jams;
   lumber mills; timber and timber
   industry; transport of timber
log jams, *246*
Lombard, A. O., 249
London: coal use in, 166; as finance center, 138; Great Fire of 1666 in, 179;
   population of, 75, 160; shortages in,
   151, 163; timber business in, 283;
   timber consumption in, 167; timber
   imports in, 282
Longfellow, Henry Wadsworth, 24
longleaf pine. See *Pinus* (pine), *P. palustris*
   (longleaf pine)
Lorain, John, 256
Lorris, Law of (1108–37), 113
Louis XV (France), 152
Low Countries, 92, 94, 137, 140, 157. *See
   also specific countries*
Lowdermilk, Walter, 80
Lower, Arthur, 281

Lucretius, 68
Ludwig (king of Bavaria), 116
Ludwig, Daniel, 448–49
lumber industry. *See* timber and timber
   industry
lumber mills: company towns and, 234,
   307; finished products and, 250–51;
   hardwood and, 371; during Industrial
   Revolution, 231–32; motive power
   in, 232–33; multiframe mills and,
   180; productivity of, 232, 234; shifts
   in location of, 303; size of, 233–34;
   in South (United States), 306; technical innovations in, 231–34

Macedonia, 65, 73, 82, *83*
MacNeish, R. S., 38–40
Madagascar: elite control of forest in,
   323; myths and realities about
   deforestation of, 325; Polynesians'
   deforestation of, 18, 19, 21; as source
   of timber, 279
Madeira, 193, 197, 198, 203. *See also*
   Atlantic islands
mahogany, 204, 279, 280, *327, 349*
maize. See *Zea mays* (maize)
Malaysia: acid rain in, 474; agricultural
   development programs in, 458–59;
   export production in, 380–81, 467;
   extent and pace of deforestation in,
   460; motives for deforestation in, 433;
   overexploitation of forests in, 467;
   planned settlement schemes in, 397,
   459; shifting cultivation in, 320
Mali-Songhai, *132*
mallee scrub, 316
Malthus, Thomas, 251
Man and Nature (Marsh), 5, 257
mangroves, 342, 347
manorial system, 95–98
mapping of forests: in medieval Europe,
   88; of *Quercus* (oak), 183; of
   "virgin" U.S. forest, *367, 368,*
   368–69, 382
Marginal Forest Highway. *See* Carretera
   Marginal de la Selva
Markham, Clements, 340
Marsden, William, 321
Marsh, George Perkins, 5, 80, 257, 270
marshelder. See *Iva annua* (sumpweed or
   marshelder)

Martinique, 201
Marvell, Andrew, 196
Marxism-Leninism. *See* communism
Mather, Increase, 147
Matthews, Elaine, 423
Mauritius, 326, 328
Maxwell, Hu, 59
maygrass. See *Phalaris caroliniana* (may-grass)
McClelland, John, 329, 334
mechanization, Industrial Revolution and, 231–35
medieval world (c. AD 500–1300), 87–91, 142–43, 145
Mediterranean region: in classical era, 64–65, 66, 67; clearing in, *110,* 111–13; climate of, 84; fuelwood prices in, 269; grain-growing areas of, *66;* late Quaternary developments in, *85;* in Mesolithic period, 22; ship-building in, 71–74, 267; timber-growing areas of, *66. See also* classical world (1100 BC–AD 565)
Mencius, 119
Mendes, Chico, 452
Meseta, 158–59
Mesoamerica, 45–52
Mesolithic period, 17, 21–23
methods of clearing: broadcast firing, 26–28; burn-beating, 158, 272, 392; burning, 159, 197, 201, 207; in classical world, 69; clear-cutting, 201, 207–8, 285; in colonial Brazil, 198–99; coppicing, 170; girdling, 201, 207–8, 285, 292–93, 315; high-wire logging, 303; industrial logging and, 245–47, 272; logging bee and, 290; mass-production techniques, 178; in New England and Pennsylvania, 256; partial clearing, 201; selective logging and, 425, 468–69. *See also* shifting cultivation
Métraux, Alfred, 49
mettalurgy. *See* smelting
Mexico, 32, 47–49, 195, 348–49, 376
Michelet, Jules, 127
Middle Ages. *See* medieval world (c. AD 500–1300)
Middle Atlantic states (United States): abandonment of fields in, 387;

clearing in, 286, *289–91;* fuelwood consumption in, 296; geographical shift of lumber production and, 303; iron industry in, 215, 216, 300; land acquisition in, 207; log cabins in, 211; methods of clearing in, 207–8, 256; Native American land use in, 29, 56, 58; newly cleared land in, *293;* population of, 296; scarcity of timber in, 216; as source of timber, 212, 294, 296, 301; transport of timber in, 247, 303
Middle East, 40, 131, 319, 373
Middle Woodland times (0–AD 900), 53
Midwest (United States): agricultural clearing in, 387; extent of clearing in, 294; geographical shift of lumber production and, 303; Hinkeley fire in, 305; log jam in, *246;* Native American land use in, 29–30; sources of timber for, 248, 249; transport of timber in, 247, 248
Milankovitch hypothesis, 4
military: guns and gunboats and, 240; iron for armaments and, 168
Millikin, Daniel, 299
mining, 78, *118,* 215, 350, 449–50
Minnesota and Ontario Paper Company, 247
modernity, 137–42
monasteries, 97–98, 146
money and finance, 137–38
Mongolia, 310, 388
Montesquieu, Charles de Secondal, Baron de la Brède et de, 251
Montezuma II, 48
Morton, Thomas, 27–28
Moser, Wilhelm Gottfried von, 261
motive power, 231–35, 398, 399
mountain pine. See *Pinus* (pine), *P. laricio* (mountain pine); *Pinus* (pine), *P. nigra* (mountain pine)
mountains: bald, 119; as barriers to spread of agriculture, 47
Mozambique, 397
Mueller, Frederick, 262
Muir, John, 366
Mulan Weichang, 220
Mullens, Joseph, 316
Munro, Thomas, 330
Mutiny of 1857 (India), 336

Myers, J. G., 32
Myers, Norman, 419, 425, 428, 430, 462

Napoleonic Wars, 278, 282
Nash, Roy, 438
National Academy of Sciences, 421
national forests, in United States, 365
National Forum on BioDiversity, 421
National Institute for Colonization and
    Agrarian Reform. See INCRA (Na-
    tional Institute for Colonization and
    Agrarian Reform)
National Resources Inventory (United
    States), 364
Native Americans (of North America):
    abandoned fields of, 195, 204, 207;
    agricultural practices of, 208; beliefs
    about God's judgment on, 195;
    comparison of clearing practices and,
    148–49; crop domestication and,
    52–60; housing and, 54; as hunters,
    foragers, and farmers, 23–24, 26;
    land needs of, 59; methods of clearing
    of, 208; moving settlements of, 58; as
    "natural ecologists," 24–25; noble
    savage myth and, 319; population of,
    25, 195; pre-Columbian land use by,
    23–34, 52–60; terror of forest and,
    147; use of fire by, 26, 29; village life
    of, 56, 58; virtue of progress and,
    255; zonation of forest use by, 27. See
    also Amerindians (of Mesoamerica
    and South America)
natural gas, 236
natural history, study of, 251
naval stores, 174, 213
navigation tools, 131, 134–35, 136
neoclassical political economists,
    400–401
Neolithic period: acreage-per-person
    calculations and, 59; classical world
    and, 62; consequent (4400–3300
    BC), 43–45; continuity of technology
    and, 23; European agriculture and,
    40–45; after Ice Age, 10–11; late, 62;
    Mesoamerican and South American
    agriculture and, 45–52; pottery of,
    40; primary (5500–4400 BC), 40–43
neo-Malthusians, 400–401, 420
neo-Marxists, 400–401

Nepal, 464
Netherlands, 141, 150, 151, 282
nettles. See Urtica (nettles)
Nevis, 200, 201
New England: abandonment of fields in,
    387; Atlantic timber trade and, 203,
    214; biodiversity in, 414; geographi-
    cal shift of lumber production and,
    303; human impact on environment
    in, 257; iron industry in, 215, 300;
    methods of clearing in, 207–8, 256;
    migration to, 203; Native American
    land use in, 26, 28, 29, 56; "paper
    townships" in, 214; as source of tim-
    ber, 212, 248, 283, 296, 301; timber
    depletion in, 216; timber trade and,
    215; transport of timber in, 247, 303;
    "woodland rebellion" and, 214
New Guinea, 9, 31, 37
New Hampshire, 212
New Indian Forests Acts (India)
New World expansion: Atlantic islands
    and, 196–98; Brazil and Caribbean
    and, 198–203; disease and, 194;
    early voyages and, 192–93; ecologi-
    cal imperialism and, 194–96, 197;
    sea travel and, 193–94. See also
    Americas
New Zealand: clearing in, 311–16;
    equilibrium in timber supply in, 467;
    large fauna destruction in, 18–19;
    Maoris' deforestation of, 19–21; as
    neo-European land, 238; railroads in,
    243; reforestation in, 475; as "settler
    empire," 263; shipping improvements
    and, 243; as source of timber, 279;
    vegetation cover of, 20
Nicaragua, 32
Nigeria, 378, 380
Nissly, Charles, 434
nobility, Charlemagne's subdivision of
    forest and, 100
"noble savage," 319–20, 420
Nobumasa, 224–25
Normandy, 101–2, 104
North, Douglass, 127
North (United States): economic indepen-
    dence of, 213; forest alteration in, 30;
    timber depletion in, 216
North Africa: during classical era, 71;

core and periphery and, 131; land cover change in, 319, 373; soil fertility in, 81; as source of timber, 77. *See also* Africa; *specific countries*

North America: agricultural expansion in, 264; attitudes toward forests in, 145, 147, 253–55, 259; backwoods life in, 204–7, *206*, 209–12, *210;* climatic conditions in, 84; conservation movement in, 258; crop domestication in, 37, 52–60; early human impact in, 10–11; ecological imperialism in, 192–96; extent of deforestation in, 264; forested area of, 425; grasslands created in, 28–30; after Ice Age, 3–4, 8–9; Neolithic agriculture in, 47; patriotism and forests and, 259–60; per capita timber consumption in, 77; "Pleistocene overkill" in, 17; population of, 60, 204, 237; pre-Columbian land use in, 23–30, 31, 32, 52–60; preservation of forests in, 256–60; railroads in, 242, 243; rainfall and forests in, 406; as "settler empire," 263; silver from, 174; as source of naval stores, 213; as source of timber for shipbuilding, 178, 180–81; spread of settlement in, *205;* sustainable forestry in, 471; uniqueness of, 260; vegetation cover of, 18,000–500 BP, *9;* virgin forest myth of, 24–25. *See also* Americas; clearing in North America; Mesoamerica; New World expansion

Northwest Brazil Integrated Development Program. *See* Polonoreste

Norway: during Little Ice Age, 151; as source of timber, 152, 179, 180, 282, 371

"Notes on the Influence Exercised by Trees" (Balfour), 333

Nova Reperta (van de Straet), *130*

nut trees, 55

oak. See *Quercus* (oak)

Ocatea rodiaei (Demerara greenheart), 279

Oceania, 237

oil, 464–65

"old-field trees," 55

Older and Younger Fill, theory of, 84

Olea europaea (olive), 10

olive. See *Olea europaea* (olive)

OPEC (Organization of Petroleum Exporting Countries), 464

opium cultivation, 340

Opium Wars, 240

Ordinance of Waters and Forests (France, 1669), 176, 185, 186

Organization of Petroleum Exporting Countries (OPEC). *See* OPEC (Organization of Petroleum Exporting Countries)

Osborn, Fairfield, 80, 400

pace of deforestation. *See* extent and pace of deforestation

Pacific Islands, 18, 397

Pacific Northwest (United States): end of Ice Age in, 4; extent of clearing in, 289; lumber industry in, 303

Pakistan, 397

Paleolithic period, 17, 23

palynology. *See* pollen analysis

Pan, Lord of the Woods, 146

paper consumption, 473, 474

Paraguay, 458

Paraná pine. See *Araucaria augustflora* (Paraná pine)

Parkman, Francis, 24, 255

Parliamentary Committee of Inquiry (Britain), 233

Parsons, Jim, 461, 462

"Passing of the Great Mother Forest, The" (Gill), 433

Paul (Saint), 96

Paulini, Giuseppe, *182–85*

Pausanias, 82

peasants: blamed for deforestation, 377–78, 477, *477;* forced removal and exclusion of, 377–78; land use rights of, 114, 333

Peasants Revolt, 156

Penobscot boom, 247

Pepys, Samuel, 176

periphery and core. *See* core and periphery

Persia, 72, 131, *132*

Persian Gulf, 240

Persian War, 72

Peru, 32–34, 317, 348–49, 434–37, 440

Peter the Great, 158
Phalaris caroliniana (maygrass), 53
Phaseolus vulgaris (beans), 11, 43
Philippines, 347–48, 467
Philo, 96
Physiocratic school, 251
physiotheologians, 251
Picea (squash), 6, 8
Picea abies, 282
pigs. *See* livestock and ranching
PIN (Program for National Integration),
    444
Pinchot, Gifford, 262, 363–64, 366, 369,
    385
pine. See *Pinus* (pine)
Pinus (pine): fire regimes and, 32; forest
    alteration and, 30; for masts, 214;
    P. contorta, 393; *P. elliottii* (slash
    pine), 30, 306; *P. laricio* (mountain
    pine), 73; *P. nigra* (mountain pine),
    73; *P. palustris* (longleaf pine), 30,
    306; pollen production of, 6; *P. pon-
    derosa* (ponderosa pine), 30;
    P. resinosa (red pine), 30; *P. strobus*
    (eastern white pine), 30; *P. sylvestris*,
    393; *P. taeda* (loblolly pine), 30, 306;
    for railroad ties, 338; shipbuilding
    and, 73; uses of, 23; white pine, 304
pioneers: in Brazil, *447*; commercial clear-
    ing and, 284–85, 295, 301; "cut out
    and get out" mentality of, 283–84,
    305, 363; east of the Andes, 437;
    virgin forest and, 24
Pitt and Forester, 275
place-names, 100–101, 104, 106, 129
plague, 117, 194, 410
Plantago (plantain), 10
plantain. See *Plantago* (plantain)
plantations: coffee, *374, 375*; in India,
    340–43; invention of, 141; monocul-
    ture and, 414
Plato, 74, 81
Platter, Thomas, 163
Pleistocene epoch, 17–18, 21, 410
Pliny, 82
pneumonic plague, 194
poaching, 114
Poa pratensis (European grass), 29
Poe, Edgar Allan, 80
Poivre, Pierre, 326, 328

Poland, 43, *44*, 157, 178, *179*
political theory, 400–402
pollen analysis, 5–6, 22, 31
Polonoreste, 446
Polygonum erectum (erect knotweed), 53
ponderosa pine. See *Pinus* (pine), *P. pon-
    derosa* (ponderosa pine)
population: of Africa, 237; in Amazon
    basin, 433–34; of Amsterdam, 160;
    in Andean region, 435; of Asia, 237;
    of Baltimore, 212; of Boston, 212;
    of Brazil, 198, 350, 355, 376, 442;
    of Britain, 278; bubonic plague and,
    117; of Buenos Aires, 377; of Burma,
    347; of Caribbean, 203; of China,
    216, 218, 237, 310; in classical
    world, 74; collapse of, 49–51, *52*,
    194, 198; deforestation level and,
    235; density of, in Brazil, 350; density
    of, in Europe, 155, 158; density of,
    in Southeast Asia, 346, 380; of Edo,
    224; of England, 155; and environ-
    ment in China, 124; of Europe, 151,
    154, *162*, 237; European timber crisis
    and, 151, 152; explosion of, after
    World War II, 398–400; farming
    innovations and, 95; fertility and
    mortality and, 235, 237; firewood
    use and, 373; food supply and, 416;
    forest regrowth and, 379; of France,
    267, 269; in the future, 471–72;
    global growth in, 235, 237; global-
    ism and, 235; growth of as cause of
    deforestation, 92; of India, 328, 335,
    339; during Industrial Revolution,
    235–38; of Japan, 221, 237, 310;
    labor-cost-to-food-yield ratio and,
    53; of Latin America, 237; Malthus,
    Thomas, on, 251; of Mexico, 349;
    of New York City, 212; of North
    America, 194–95, 203, 204, 237;
    among North American Indians, 60;
    of Oceania, 237; of Paris, 160, 267,
    269; of Philadelphia, 212; pressure on
    forest resources and, 114; of Rio de
    Janeiro, 355; shifting cultivation and
    growth of, 378–79; slave raiding and,
    82; of South and Southeast Asia, 380;
    in temperate versus tropical world,
    318–19, 373; theories about effects

of increase in, 400–401; in "third world," 397; Thirty Years' War and, 156–57; transportation and growth in, 241; of United States, 284, 301; of USSR, 237; wars and, 117; of Western Hemisphere, 194; worldwide deforestation and, 371–72

Population Bomb (Ehrlich and Ehrlich), 399

Portugal: African explorations of, 131; Atlantic timber trade and, 203; Brazil and, 351; European expansion and, 132, 196; timber trade with New England and, 214

Posey, Darrell, 32

Post, Frans, *199*

"postsettlement," 25

potash, 211, 213

poverty, forests as "mantle of the poor" and, 90, 450, 472. *See also* wealth, distribution of

Pownall, Thomas, 205–6

"predation to production," 47

preservation of forests: as barriers to invasion, 219; in British India, 329, 331–33, 343; in Caribbean, 326, 328; in China, 121, 220; coppicing and, 172; ecology and order and, 408–9; from economic to environmental concern about, 257–58; during Enlightenment, 252, 255; in Europe, 116, 183–86; by France's three estates, 156; growth versus consumption and, 369–70; harmonies of nature and, 256–58; for hunting, 261; in India, 328, 329, 331–33; in Japan, 222, 224–25, 309–10; limits on iron production and, 171; opposition to, 183, 186; rainfall and, 406–8; rationale for, 185–86; reservation of U.S. forests and, 363, 364; scientific approach to, 185; social benefits of, 405–6; state forests and, 183–84; strong government institutions and, 475–76; in Sweden, 392–93; tree cropping and, 212; trees as tonics for civilization and, 258–60

"presettlement," 25

Principles of Forest-Economy (Moser), 261

printing press, 135

Program for National Integration. *See* PIN (Program for National Integration)

property, private, 86

Prussia, 105, 150, 176, 178, *179*

Pseudotsuga menziesii (Douglas fir), 30

Ptolemy, 143

Punic Wars, 72

Pyne, Stephen, 13, 16

pyrotechnology, 78. *See also* fire

quantity of timber: for breweries, 167; for building construction, 160, 167, 221, 222; consumed in age-of-discovery Europe, 160, 162, 163, 164; consumed in Britain, 176, 231, 282; consumed in United States, 231, 236, 301, *302*, 362; documentary evidence of, 281; exported by Brazil, 377; exported by India, 330; exported by Russia, 275, 276; for fuelwood, 212, 269, 272, 275, 295–96, 338; Great Lakes lumber production and, 304; for iron industry, 169–70, 171; measurement of, 261, 283; for mines, 392; per capita in classical era, 76–77; for railroads, 244–45, 297, 299, 300, 338–39; for Russian consumption, 275–76; for salt making, 167; for shipbuilding, 174, 278; for smelting, 78, *79*, 80, 215–16, 300–301, 392; for steamboats, 295; for sugar production, 199

Quaternary period, 3–5

quebracho, 377

Quercus (oak): Atlantic timber trade and, 203; forest alteration and, 30; after Ice Age, 8; in Mesolithic Britain, 21; pollen production of, 6; for railroad ties, 297, 299; scrub oak and, 308; for shipbuilding, 174, 176, 278, 282; sources of, 180; survey and mapping of, 183; as symbol of continuity, strength and patriotism, 258

quinine, 239–40

radiometric techniques, 6

rafts, 214–15, *248*, 248–49, 282

ragweed. *See Ambrosia* spp. (ragweed)

railroads: agriculture and, 337; in Australia, 315; in Brazil, 353; comparative
mileage of, 336; creosoting of ties
and, 338; deforestation and, 244–45,
299, 337; efficiency of, 242; food
supply and, 336; fuelwood distribution and, 269; global growth of,
242–43; impact of, 302; in India,
334, 336–38; as "juggernaut of the
vegetable world," 299; locomotive
invented and, 242; as "machine in the
garden," 299; movement of consumer
goods and, 336; rate of building of,
299; redwood ties and, 317; sleeper
cars and, 283; social disruption and,
336; in Southeast Asia, 347; stages of
lumber production and, 304; timber
consumption and, 297, 299; transport
of timber and, 249–50, 250, 303
rainfall and forest preservation, 406–8
raised fields, 50
Ralegh, Walter, 133, 191
ranching. See livestock and ranching
range of forest. See composition and range
of forest
Raubwirtschaft, 360
Ray, John, 143, 144
Reconquista, 129
recycling, 474
red pine. See Pinus (pine), P. resinosa (red
pine)
redwood, 317
reforestation: in arid regions, 64; in Brazil,
326, 350; bubonic plague and, 117;
in Caribbean, 202–3; in China, 475;
deer parks and, 188; in England, 188;
equilibrium between extraction and
regeneration and, 467; in Europe,
182, 186–90, 371; exaggeration of,
474–75; forest balance sheet and,
382; in France, 270; without human
interference, 51, 61; ignored in projects of deforestation, 382; livestock
raising and, 70; as mark of wealth,
188, 190; medieval land policy and,
116; as "moral awakening," 270; as
patriotic act, 189; peasants and, 270–
71; after population collapse, 51,
52, 60, 204, 325, 349; prevented by
stock grazing, 275; process of, 187;

proportion of cleared land returning
to forest and, 425–26; reasons for,
187–88; replanting and, 385; resistance to, 271, 476, 477; reversion of
abandoned farmland and, 372, 381,
385, 387–88; rhetoric versus reality
and, 476–77; second growth and,
385; Silva; or, A Discourse of Forest
Trees (Evelyn) and, 186–87; from
stumps, 351; in temperate versus
tropical world, 475; Timber Culture
Act of 1873 (United States) and, 407;
time required for, 380; transport of
timber and, 306–7; trees as tonics for
civilization and, 258; in United States,
371; volume of, 385; worldwide, 475
Reformation, 142
refrigeration, 315
religion, attitudes toward forests and, 145,
309. See also Christianity; theology
religious ceremonies, wood-burning in, 48
Renaissance, 134, 142, 143
resettlement schemes, 397, 459–60, 461
Ribbentrop, Berthold, 262, 329, 337
rice cultivation, 322, 340, 347
Richards, Paul, 31, 395, 414–15, 417
Rio International Convention, 422
Rival, Laura, 32
rivers: damming of, 246; deforestation's
effects on, 270; transport of timber
on, 73, 245–49; upstream deforestation and, 271
Robinson Crusoe (Defoe), 259
Roman world: attitudes toward nature in,
85–86; baths in, 76, 77, 188; boom
period in, 81; building construction in, 221; comparison of clearing
practices and, 148–49; decline of,
80–82; demand for timber in, 74–77;
freeholds in, 68; imperial expansion
and decline of, 63; Neolithic age and,
62; per capita timber consumption
in, 76–77; population of, 75; sea
power and, 72; smelting in, 78; state
ownership of forests in, 63; urbanization and, 67, 74–77. See also classical
world (1100 BC–AD 565)
Romantic movement, 258, 259
Rondski, A. F., 275
Roosevelt, Anna, 32

Roosevelt, Theodore, 359, 363–64
Rosen, Walter G., 421
rosewood, 280
Rousseau, Jean-Jacques, 35, 196, 259
Roxburgh, William, 329, 331
Royal Africa Company, 139
Royal Navy (Britain), 214
Royal Society, 176
rubber cultivation, 325, 448
Rudel, T. K., 431
Russia: agricultural expansion in, 264; ag-
    ricultural practices in, 157–58; clear-
    ing in, 271–72, 275–76; emancipa-
    tion of serfs in, 275, 353; extent and
    pace of deforestation in, 109, 111,
    264; forest cover of, 266, 273, 274;
    fuelwood consumption in, 167; gov-
    ernment responsiveness in, 475; after
    Ice Age, 7; icon and ax and, 109, 111;
    income levels in, 229; industrial po-
    tential of, 230; Industrial Revolution
    in, 229; migration and, 237; popula-
    tion of, 237; railroads in, 242, 243,
    336; rainfall and forests in, 406–7;
    Russian Federation's timber supply
    and, 467; as source of timber, 158,
    180, 265, 275, 370; steel industry in,
    122; timber for building construction
    in, 160; timber for shipbuilding and,
    178, 180, 214; underused and wasted
    forest of, 391; vegetation zones in,
    159; World War II and forest destruc-
    tion in, 388; Zon, Raphael, arrest in,
    369. See also Soviet Union

Sahel, 378
Sahlins, Marshall, 141
sal, 338
Salati, Eneas, 456
salt industry, 167
sandalwood, 323
São Tomé, 197, 198
Saouma, Edouard, 428
Sardinia, 266
Sauer, Carl, 31, 359–61
savannas, 32
sawmills. See lumber mills
Scandinavia: equilibrium in timber sup-
    ply in, 467; forest cover of, 266;
    hydroelectricity in, 233; after Ice Age,

7; immigration to U.S. from, 306;
    Neolithic agriculture in, 43; as source
    of timber, 178, 265, 266, 371; timber
    trade and geographical shifts in, 179
Schlict, William, 262
Schlüter, Otto, 106
Schmink, Marianne, 451, 452
Schoepf, Johann, 216
Schurz, Carl, 262, 362–63
Scientific American, 417
Scotland, 6, 70, 151
sea levels, 3
sea power, 71–73
Sears, Paul, 80
sea travel, 193
secondary products revolution, 42
second nature, 86
Sedjo, Roger, 430
sequoia, 30
sesmarias, 349–50, 353
Seven Years' War, 260
Shafranov, N. I., 275
Shane, Douglas, 461
sheep. See livestock and ranching
Shelter Belt project, 408
Sherratt, Andrew, 42
shifting cultivation: in Africa, 377; au-
    thoritarian conservation policies and,
    477; benefits of, for biodiversity, 418;
    in Brazil, 350, 438–39; in Caribbean,
    375; in China, 60, 310; definition
    of deforestation and, 425; forced
    removal and exclusion of peasants
    and, 376, 378; logging roads and,
    469; long-term effects of, 378–79,
    425–27, 431; Neolithic agriculture
    and, 40, 42; in Philippines, 347–48;
    in South America, 50; in tropical
    world, 320–21; Western misconcep-
    tions of, 319, 324–25, 376–79, 418,
    477, 477
Shih Ching, 119, 120
shipping and shipbuilding: abaca for rig-
    ging of, 348; during age of discovery,
    128, 131, 139, 151–52; Brazilian
    land policy and, 351; Britain as hub
    of timber trade for, 278–80; British
    timber consumption levels and, 282;
    changes in cargo and, 242–43; dur-
    ing classical era, 71–74; in colonial

shipping and shipbuilding: (*continued*)
North America, 214; construction
materials for, 242; in France, 267;
global improvements in, 242–43;
homegrown European timber and,
174, 176; iron replacing wood in,
279–80; in medieval Mediterranean
world, 111; propeller and, 242;
refrigeration and, 243, 316; shipyard
of eighteenth century and, *175;* teak
for, 330; timber shortages and, 267;
war to protect timber supplies for,
176; World War I and, 369. *See also*
steamboats
Sicily, 72, 73, 81, 111, 112, 151
Sierra Leone, 279, 379
siltation: in China, 121, 219, 311; chronology of, 84; in classical world, 82,
83, 84; forest science on, 408; in India, 337; of Venetian lagoon, *182–85*
Silva; or, A Discourse of Forest Trees
(Evelyn), 155, 185–87
silver, 79
silviculture, 309
Simmons, Ian, 21, 22
Sinking Ark, The (Myers), 419
Sketch of the Creek Country (Hawkins), 58
Skole, David, 456
slash-and-burn clearing. *See* shifting
cultivation
slash pine. *See Pinus* (pine), *P. elliottii*
(slash pine)
slaves and slavery: abolition of, 352;
in Atlantic islands, 197; attitudes
toward nature and, 86; in Brazil,
198–99, 349, 352, 353; in Caribbean, 201; clearing in North America
by, 209; coffee production and, 353;
colonization and, 239; in Cuba, 349;
emancipation and, 353; fuelwood
gathering by, 212; mortality among,
199; as replacements for European
farmers, 207; slave revolts and, 198;
slave trade and, 82, 204, 325; in
sugar production, *199;* tropical staple
goods and, 141–42
Slavic countries, 93, 97, 104–5
"Sleeping Beauty," 146
Sloane, Hans, 203
Slovakia, 170

smelting: in classical world, 71, 75,
77–78, *79,* 80; coke for, 277; in medieval world, 90; and timber supply
in France, 267–69; wood use and,
118
Smith, Adam, 226, *356*
Smith, J. B., 316
Smith, John, 28, 56
Smithsonian Institution, 421
"Snow White," 146
socialism, Swedish lumber industry and,
381, 391–94
Society of American Foresters, 366
"soft drug" culture, 141
soil. *See* erosion; soil fertility and degradation; soil science
soil degradation. *See* soil fertility and
degradation
soil fertility and degradation: in Africa,
81; in Atlantic islands, 198; in Brazil,
353; in British Isles, 81; in China,
121, 219; chronology of, 84; in classical world, 69, 80–82, *83–85;* cow
dung for fuel and, 343; deforestation after World War II and, 402;
in France, 270; in Holland, 81; in
Levant, 81–82; in Mesopotamia,
81–82; in North America, 208; spice
cultivation and, 322; in Sweden,
393–394; war and, 157
soil science, 69
Sombart, Werner, 154
Sommer, Adrian, 418, 427–28
Sophocles, 64, 67–68
South (United States): abandonment of
fields in, 387; agricultural clearing
in, 387; company towns in, 307;
Creek village life in, 58; cutover
areas of, 306–8; end of Ice Age in,
4; excessive logging in, 306–7; extent of clearing in, 289, 294; forest/
agricultural conversion in, *389;*
forest balance sheet of, 388; geographical shift of lumber production and, 303; hardwood forests of,
305; land acquisition in, 207, 208;
methods of clearing in, 208; Native
American land use in, 28, 29, 30, 56,
57; plantations of, 208–9; railroads
in, *250,* 303; timber plundering in,

303; timber trade and, 215; transport of timber in, 247
South Africa, 243, 467, 475
South America: agricultural development East of the Andes, 434–37, *438;* agricultural development in Amazonia, 433–34; clearing for pasturage in, 462–63; early agriculture in, 45–52; Neolithic agriculture in, 45, 47, 49; as "nuclear center" of crop domestication, 52; "orgy of clearing" east of Andes in, 437; "Pleistocene overkill" in, 17; pre-Columbian land use in, 31–32; shifting cultivation in, 320–21. *See also* Americas; Latin America; New World expansion
South Asia: forest destruction in, 380; fuelwood shortage in, 464; global timber trade and, 469; land cover change in, 319, 373; motives for deforestation in, 433; rice cultivation in, 322
southern Africa, as neo-European land, 238
Southeast Asia: biodiversity in, 414; British dominance in, 279; crops grown in, 320; extent and pace of deforestation in, 460–61; forest destruction in, 380–81; global timber trade and, 469; grasslands of, 324; land cover change in, 319, 373; motives for deforestation in, 433; population density in, 346; population growth rate in, 400; production for export in, 346; rice cultivation in, 322
Soviet Union, 230, 237, 243, 381, 388, 390–91. *See also* Russia
Spain: Atlantic timber trade and, 203; boom period in, 81; Byzantine reconquest of, 112; during classical era, 70, 71, 73; conquest of Canary Islands by, 194; after Ice Age, 7; iron industry of, 168–69; livestock raising in, 158–59; Muslim expansion and, 111; price of wood in, 163; shipbuilding in, 174; smelting in, 78, 79; timber crisis in, 151; timber exports from, 111; timber trade with New England and, 214
Sparhawk, William, 466–67

spices and spice trade, 322, 323
spruce, 393
SPVEA (Superintendency for the Economic Valorization of the Amazon), 442
squash (*Cucurbita pepo*). See *Cucurbita pepo* (squash)
squash (*Picea*). See *Picea* (squash)
"squaw wood," 55
Sri Lanka, 320, 340–41, *341*
Standish, Arthur, 150, 167
staple goods, tropical, 140–42
steamboats, 295
steam power, 232–34, 240–42, 249–51, 302, 306
steel and steel industry, 302
Stennis, J. L., 415
Stenton, Doris, 116
Stephenson, George, 242
Stewart, Omer, 13
stinkwood, 279
Stjernquest, Per, 391
Stocks, John, 329
Stott, Philip, 415
Strabo, 68, 70
Strachey, William, 56
stream flow, clearing and changes in, 256
Struggle for Land, The, 450
SUDAM (Superintendência de Desenvolvimento da Amazônia), 442, 444, 446, 448
Sudan, 240
Suez Canal, 242, 244, 326, 334
sugar and sugar trade: in Brazil and Caribbean, 198–203, 350, 352; creation of *campo cerrado* and, 326; in Cuba, 349; early European expansion and, 197; *engenhos* and, 198, *199,* 200; fuelwood for, 199–200, 352; in Philippines, 348; profligate land use and, 199; "soft drug" culture and, 141; Southeast Asia and, 347; yield and, 340
Suger, Abbot of St. Denis, 101
sugi. See *Cryptomeria japonica* (*sugi*)
Sumatra, 31, 321, 322, 325
sumpweed. See *Iva annua* (sumpweed or marshelder)
sunflower. See *Helianthus annus* (sunflower)

Superintendência de Desenvolvimento
da Amazônia. *See* SUDAM (Superintendência de Desenvolvimento da
Amazônia)
Superintendency for the Economic Valorization of the Amazon. *See* SPVEA
(Superintendency for the Economic
Valorization of the Amazon)
Surell, André, 270
Sweden: annual growth, clearing, and
wood use in, *393;* charcoal industry
in, 172; clearing for war by, 157;
cut-and-get-out exploitation in, 392;
emigration from, 392; iron industry
of, 169; shifting political boundaries of, *179;* socialism and lumber
industry in, 381, 391–94; as source
of timber, 158, 179, 371; timber for
shipbuilding and, 176, 178; timber in
economy of, 283
swiddening. *See* shifting cultivation
Switzerland, 266
symbiosis, ecological, 37–38
Syria, 65, 73, 112

Tacitus, 70
Taft, William Howard, 364
taxation, 334, 342–43, 442, 444, 461
Taylor, John, 285
tea and tea trade, 141, 340
teak. *See Tectona grandis* (teak)
technology: age of discovery and, *130,*
131, 134–37; continuity of, 23; dust
bowl lessons about, 408; horsepower
and, 93–94; Industrial Revolution
and, 229; "invention of invention"
and, 134; iron implements and, 63;
of medieval world, 90–91; Neolithic
developments in, 43, 49; plows and,
93–94; sawmills and, 231–32; trans-
mission of, 131
Tectona grandis (teak): in Burma, 334; in
India, 330; in Java, 347; for railroad
ties, 338; for shipbuilding, 279, 346;
state control of forests and, 323
telegraph, 244
temperate world, agricultural expansion
in, 263, 264, 265
Tempest, The (Shakespeare), 196
tepetate, 48

terracing, 50
Terry, Balaúde, 435–36
Tertullian, 96
textiles and textile industry, 229, 336,
337, 340, 342
Thailand: clearing in, 347, 380; early ag-
riculture in, 61; location of deforestation in, 431, *432;* overexploitation of
forests in, 467–68; population density
in, 380
theology: environmental movement and,
260; human ascendancy over nature
and, 143, 144
Theophrastus, 65, 69
"third world," 397, 398. *See also* less
developed world
Thirty Years' War, 156–57
Thomas, Keith, 145, 150, 188, 260
Thomas, Robert, 127
Thoreau, Henry David, 24, 80, 260
"Three Little Pigs, The," 146
Thucydides, 72
Tikal, 49–50, *51*
Tilia (lime), 6, 8, 21, 22
timber and timber industry: aggressive
acquisition of, in United States, 303;
alternative materials to, 224; annual
net growth of, in United States, *386;*
for building construction, 464; bulk
and value of, 283, 294–95; business of, 283; Chicago as hub for,
248, 250, 294; competition and, 73,
203–4; destructive practices of, 275;
documentation of trade and, 281;
equilibrium between extraction and
regeneration and, 467; excessive logging and, 305–6; felling process and,
177; forestry business and, 170, 178;
forest volume in United States and,
383, 384; gasoline-powered motors
and, 398, 399; global consumption
of wood products and, 469; global
trade and, 370–71, 468, 469; heating
value of wood and, 166; international
conflict over access to, 176, 213; from
luxury to necessity, 278; as major
commodity, 283; mechanization in
processing of, 231–35; Neolithic
use of, 42, 43; overexploitation of,
55; pre-Columbian North American

use of, *54–55;* prices for, 170, 224,
278; raiding enemy cargoes and,
279; replanting and, 385; for road
construction, 76; selective logging
and, 425, 468–69; shifts in U.S.
lumber production and, 303; shipbuilding and, 73, 174, 176, 464; size
of industry in North America, 214;
for smelting, 78, 79, 80; stripping
of, 48; in temperate versus tropical
world, 373; in "third world," 398;
timber extraction since World War
II and, 466–69; timber tribute and,
222; uses for inferior wood and, 398;
uses of, in United States, 1800–1975,
296; value of, 181; waste of, 292. *See
also* fuelwood; logging, commercial;
lumber mills; quantity of timber;
transport of timber
Timber Culture Act of 1873 (U.S.), 407
*Timber Depletion, Lumber Prices, Lum-
ber Exports, and Concentration of
Timber Ownership* (Congressional
report), 366
time, measurement of, 135–36
Tippoo Sahib, 279
tobacco cultivation, 325, 347, 348
Tocqueville, Alexis de, 226, 254
Togo, 323, 379
Tokugawa Ieyusa, 222–23
"Tom Thumb," 146
tools, Neolithic use of, 43
Tosi, Joseph, 434
Totman, Conrad, 309
towns: emerging from forest, 290; for
lumber workers and families, 303,
305, 307
trade: British trade policy and, 392; core
and periphery and, 130–34; exploitation and, 162–63; global, circa AD
1500, *132;* protectionism and, 279;
separation of areas of production and
consumption and, 133, 137; shift of
from Mediterranean to Atlantic, 174;
tropical staple goods and, 140–42.
See also specific products
transcendentalists, 260
transhumance, 69–70
transportation: core/periphery connected-
ness and, 241–45; during Industrial

Revolution, 240–51; political control
and, 241; speed of, 242, 244. *See also*
railroads; shipping and shipbuilding;
transport of timber
transport of timber: in Atlantic Ocean,
203–4; in Australia, 315; from
Baltic region, 179–80; bulkiness of
timber and, 181; in classical world,
73, 76; in colonial North America,
212, 214–15; continental system
of, 247–49; cost of, 245, 246, 247,
294–95; in Cuba, *327;* distances of,
181; elephants and, 330; environmental impact of, 306–7; free floats
versus supervised floats and, 224;
over ice roads, 303; industrial logging
and, *248;* during Industrial Revolution, 241; in Japan, 222, 224; log
drives and, 245–47, *247,* 249, 303,
304; log jams and, *246;* log marks
and, 246; mechanization of, 306–7;
in Ohio River valley, *248;* quantity of
timber moved, 249, 250; road haulage and, 303, *304;* in Russia, 282;
steam power and, 249–51; war and,
282; weather and, 249
travel, clearing of forests for, 146–47
Treaty of Paris (1763), 238
tree fungus. See *Fomes fomentarius* (tree
fungus)
Trichterrandbecher period (4000–3400
BC), 40, 43, *44*
Troels-Smith, Jorgen, 22
Trollope, Anthony, 341
Tropical Forestry Action Plan, The, 430
Tropical Rain Forest, The (Richards), 414
tropics: biodiversity in rain forest of,
414–15, 418; climate change in,
9–10; conference on deforestation
of, 418; early agriculture in, 37;
equilibrium between extraction and
regeneration and, 467; forest area and
deforestation in, 1980 and 1990, 429;
hearths of domestication in, 416; after
Ice Age, 31–34; pasture development
in, 461–63; pathways of conversion
in rain forest of, *426;* reforestation in,
475; responsiveness of governments
in, 475–76. *See also specific countries
and regions*

Troup, Robert, 262
Tsvetkov, M. A., 272, 275
Tucker, Compton J., 456
Turgenev, Ivan, 272
Turkey, 65
Turner, Frederick Jackson, 255, 359
Turner, J. M. W., 279, *280*
Turner, Orsamus, 289–90

Ukraine, 180
Ulmus (elm), 6, 8, 22, 23, 258
Unasylva, 405
Uncle Vanya (Chekov), 406–7
UNEP. *See* United Nations Environment
    Program (UNEP)
UNESCO. *See* United Nations Educa-
    tional, Scientific, and Cultural Orga-
    nization (UNESCO)
United East India Company, 347
United Kingdom. *See* Britain
United Nations Development Programme,
    401
United Nations Educational, Scien-
    tific, and Cultural Organization
    (UNESCO), 423
United Nations Environment Program
    (UNEP), 428, 430
United Nations, Food and Agricultural
    Organization (FAO) and, 405, 428,
    430. *See also* Food and Agricultural
    Organization (FAO)
United States: acid rain in, 474; aggressive
    acquisition of timber in, 303; annual
    forest growth and drain in, 384; an-
    nual net growth and use of timber in,
    386; as both importer and exporter
    of timber, 394; capitalism and lumber
    industry in, 381; cleared farmland in,
    387; closing of frontier in, 359, 362;
    consumption levels in, 231, 235, 282,
    385; energy source changes in, 235,
    236; equilibrium in timber supply in,
    467; expansion of, 284; forest bal-
    ance sheet in, 381–85, 387–88; forest
    science in, 262; Forest Service in,
    363–64, 366–69, 407; forest volume
    in, 383, 384; global timber resources
    and, 367–71; income levels in, 229,
    231; Industrial Revolution in, 229;
    lumber cut and consumed in, *302,*
    362; lumber industry innovation
    in, 233, 245, 301–8; migration to,
    237; national forests of, *365;* as
    neo-European land, 238; new forest
    growth in, 366; population of, 284,
    301; railroads in, 243, 336; rebirth
    of forest in, 385–88; reforestation
    in, 371, 475; shipbuilding in, 279;
    as source of timber, 265, 371; steam
    power adoption in, 232; timber
    famine in, 362–67; transcontinental
    railroad in, 242; transport of timber
    in, 248; virgin forest in, *367, 368;*
    as wooden country, 301; wood in
    industrialization of, 234–35. *See also*
    specific regions; U.S. entries
urbanization. *See* cities and urbanization
Urbarmachung. See Great Reclamation
Urtica (nettles), 21
Uruguay, 4, 348, 349
U.S. Congress, 364, 366
U.S. Forest Service, 299
U.S. National Academy of Sciences, 428
U.S. Patent Office, 233
USSR. *See* Soviet Union

Valckenborch, Lucas I. van, 160, *161*
Van der Wee, Herman, 137
van de Straet, Jan, *130*
Varro, Marcus Terentius, 68
Vavilov, Nikolai, 37, 416
Venezuela: agricultural development east
    of Andes in, 434–37; Brazil and,
    440, 444; export trade and, 349; pre-
    Columbian land use in, 31; remaining
    forest of, 376
Vereenigde Oostindische Campagnie, 347
Versailles, Palace of, 164
Victoria Gold Rush, 317
Vieira Couto, José, 352
villages, 45, *46,* 54–56, *57,* 58–59
Villicatio, 99
virgin forest: area of, in United States,
    367, 368; coffee cultivation in, 353,
    376; Greeley, William, on, 367, 478;
    myth of, 24–25, 31, 54, 195
Vita-Finzi, Claudio, 84
Voertman, Robert, 434
Volney, Constantin François Chasseboeuf,
    comte de, 256, 329

wainscot, 178, 180, 181
Waldhufendorf, 99, 101, 106
Waldsterben, 474, 476
Wales, 122
Wallace, Robert, 337
Wallerstein, Immanuel, 140, 191
Wall Street, crash of, 361
walnut. See *Juglans* (walnut)
war: access to timber and, 278, 279; age
    of discovery and, 131; colonial, 240;
    disruption of timber trade by, 180–
    81; New World population collapse
    and, 194; transition to modernity
    and, 137. *See also specific conflicts*
War of Independence (U.S.), 180–81
"waste" land, 92, 98
wealth, distribution of, 90, 140, 401–2,
    439, 450–51
Webster, Noah, 253
Weld, Isaac, 294
Wertime, Theodore, 78
West (U.S. region): end of Ice Age in, 4;
    forest alteration in, 30
West Africa: extent and pace of deforesta-
    tion in, 469; forest retreat in, 324;
    hearths of domestication in, 37; iron
    industry in, 380; landscape of, 323;
    motives for deforestation in, 433;
    rhetoric about deforestation and,
    379–80; Spanish and Portuguese
    explorations of, 193; sustainable
    forestry in, 471; time required for
    clearing in, 35, 36; vegetation zones
    in, 378. *See also* Africa; *specific
    countries*
Western culture, humans and nature
    and, 5
West Indies. *See* Caribbean
White, Andrew, 28
White, Lynn, 136–37, 148
white pine, eastern. See *Pinus* (pine),
    P. strobus (eastern white pine)
White Pine Act (Britain), 213
Whitmore, Tim, 415

Wicker, Tom, 476
William (king of England), 114
Williamson, Hugh, 253
Williamsport boom, 247
willow, 23
Wilson, Edward O., 395, 420, 421
wine production, 198, 203
Winslow, Edward, 56
Winter Landscape (Valckenborch), *161*
Winthrop, John, 147, 195
*Wisdom of God Manifest in the Works of
    Creation* (Ray), 143
Wisselbank, 138
Woeikof, Alexander, 360
women, "squaw wood" and, 55
Wood, Charles, 451, 452
woodcutting, *93*
wooden age, 160, 360
"woodland rebellion," 214
Wordsworth, William, 233, 259
World Bank, 401, 446
World Resources Institute (WRI), 401–2,
    430, 472
World War I, 307, 359, 369
World War II, 359, 388, 395
WRI. *See* World Resources Institute
    (WRI)
Wüstungen (village desertion), 145, 151

Yarranton, Andrew, 172
yellowwood, 279
yew, 23
Younger and Older Fill, theory of, 84

Zea mays (maize), 10, 43, 53
Ziegler, E. A., 367, 382–83
Zohary, Daniel, 416
Zon, Raphael: Capper Report and, 366;
    conservation efforts of, 367; forest
    balance sheet and, 382; forest studies
    of, 369–72, 407; on timber extrac-
    tion, 466–67
Zona de Mata, 351